Table of Contents

The Rural Municipality of Franklin 1

Agriculture 11

Business 28

Homes 39

Health Care 47

Organizations 49

Disasters 64

Sports 72

Entertainment 79

Education 88

Religion 100

Ethnic 107

Honor Roll 116

The Faces of Franklin 119

Acknowledgements

The Committee responsible for the compiling of *R.M. of Franklin Turns a Century,* consisting of:

Sandra Schultz
Drorthy Stewart
Claudia Eliuk
Eva Bially
Audrey Grier
Viara McVicar
Margaret Kathler
Carolynne Kathler
Helen Bially

Carol Wilkinson
Art Schulz
Jennie Mihaychuk
William Krashy
Georgina Taylor
Theresa Mulko
Garth Raw
Edith Thompson
Kathy Polischuk

Earl Simpson
Ted Schwark
Steve Stadnyk
Eileen Spence
Rose Fedorchuk
Wilma Poetker
Dorothy Shelby
Lorne Riach

wish to thank the many other people who helped with the production of this book. They are too numerous to mention, and the committee hopes the finished work will compensate for the countless hours spent gathering information, material and pictures. Special thanks are also due to Anthony Hudyma for the great deal of time and disruption the book involved, and Lynne Smith for the typing and the maps.

Apologies are given to the very many people who submitted material not included in this book. The response was so great that the limited space made selection extremely difficult. We hope the excellent and precious material gathered will be used to write further histories of the area.

Manitoba writer Susan Hiebert assisted the Book Committee in the production of this book, creating the outline and general shape of the story, as well as editing and writing.

Cover design by Ann Marie Cook, resident of Franklin Municipality.
Credits: Hardships and Progress of Ukrainian Pioneers, by Peter Huminiuk
        Arnaud Through the Years
        Dominion City Facts and Hyperbole — James Waddell
        Manitoba Archives
        Carillon News

Dedication

We possess great riches in Franklin Municipality — treasures not easily visible, but found in our hearts. Our wealth is in our rolling fields, our sturdy cattle and the peace of our homes. Our life is not to be found in thriving factories, huge businesses or great fame. Our life is our land and our families as it has been for generations.

We believe in, and strive to preserve, the legacy of our forefathers. This legacy contains a faith in God, an attempt at tolerance for all, and an obligation to help those in need. It is dedicated to public service, and hard work to provide for our families. It is based on unlocked doors, and hospitality and aid to friends and strangers alike. Our legacy has as its cornerstone, love and respect for our elderly, and great joy and pride in our children.

We dedicate this book to the future generations who will live in Franklin Municipality. May they continue to cherish and uphold this legacy into our second century.

Inside cover pictures:
    Front - Natural beauty in the Municipality of Franklin.
    Back - left top - Naturalization certificate
            - left bottom - Elaine Calder marries Bruce Smith in
                            Dominion City, 1972. Cliff Strange,
                            driver of the car.
        - right - 1983 Centennial Award Plaque
Inside front cover pouch:
    Maps of the RM of Franklin.

The Rural Municipality of Franklin

by Sandra Schultz

The Municipality of Franklin was formed in 1883 when the town of Emerson incorporated. This municipality stretched from the Red River in the west to a point 5 miles east of what is now Vita. It was bounded on the south by the United States, and the north by the municipality of de Salaberry.

Franklin contained land set aside for two Indian reserves. The west reserve beside the Red River contained 13,554 acres and the reserve at the rapids 800. In 1903 the Indian band sold 7680 acres of the west reserve to purchase two additional sections of land at the rapids.

A change in the municipal boundaries occured in 1902. Dissatisfied with the lack of schools necessary for the 400 children in their area, and unhappy with road and bridge construction, the eastern settlers led by Theodosy Wachna, and aided by Mathew Grier and L.G. Ramsey left Franklin and formed the new municipality of Stuartburn. Despite appeals to Winnipeg, Ottawa, and the Privy Council in London, the seceding area was required to assume an $11,500 share of the debts of Franklin Municipality.

Our municipality exists on what was once the eastern part of Lake Agassiz. The western end is a flat treeless plain of rich, heavy soil hampered by poor drainage. Running through the middle of the municipality is a distinct high ridge — the shore of the lake. This area has lighter soil, more stones and trees. The eastern end of Franklin is a heavily treed, rocky area of poorer soil, suited more to hay crops and containing many low wet areas.

Both animals and edible vegetation abounded throughout the municipality. Deer, moose, bobcats, foxes, squirrels, raccoons and wolves were to be found here. Flocks of ducks, geese, prairie chickens, grouse and passenger pigeons provided food for the early settlers. The woods and meadows contained mushrooms, wild grapes, saskatoons, pin and choke cherries, raspberries, strawberries and black currants. Quantities of seneca root dug and dried often provided the only cash income for many pioneers.

Drainage, road building, and inadequate funds have plagued our municipality since its formation. In 1884 the municipality instituted a policy of statute labor. Each person assessed $500 or under was to provide 1 day free labor on public works, for each additional $500 of assessment, another day was required. Everyone between 21 and 60, not otherwise assesed, was to provide 1 day's labor. Statute labor was computed separately for each land parcel, and there was a $1.50 per day fine for not performed labor. People could have their labor computed with a reduction of 25¢ per day if they paid within one month of the tax rolls final revision.

The start of the Jordan Ditch, c. 1910.

Building roads in Franklin. c. 1918.

The municipality was divided into small areas, with pathmasters to assign and oversee the labor, collect fines for labor unperformed, and collect computations.

Pathmasters for 1884:

W. Grant	T. McRae
I. Moffat	N. Dure
A. Bell	A. Young
R. Vicars	Wm. Barber
T. Sharmon	R. Scott
W. Darling	W. Robertson
T. Coulter	A. Kirkpatrick
S. Barber	W. Craig
A. Collins	J. Craig
D. Harlow	J. Gunn
F. Carver	D. Timlick Jr.
W. Bland	I. Dickson
A. Gurd	D. McKercher
I. Anderson	C. McKellop
C. Ross	T. Batten
W. Hosick	L.G. Ramsey
T. Varey	W. Webster
R. Hurd	O. Hamel
R. Miller	I. Goff
I. Chamberlain	W. Leask
J. Lang	G. Devitt
T. Haddon	A. McBean
W. Fields	F. Adams
R. McMillan	
I. Smith	

Ferry at Dominion City. 1940's.

Bridge over Roseau at Dominion City.

The municipality is bisected or bounded by the Red, Rat, Joe, Roseau and Jordan Rivers.

In 1880 the bridge at Dominion City was constructed, in 1882 another at the cemetery was built. In 1895 a bridge was built at Langside. Individual farmers constructed many smaller bridges to gain access to their property and the municipality reimbursed them.

In 1883, the council paid the following:

N. Stewart	1 bridge	$24
R. McWillam	1 bridge	$10
L. G. Ramsey	1 bridge	$8
J. O'Donnell	6 bridges	$90
P. Coutts	4 bridges	$60
Jos Hunter	1 bridge	$25
I. Carrier	1 bridge	$10
R. D. Smith	1 bridge	$20
D. Timlick	on bridge account	$225
J. Eyres	2 bridges	$35
P. Coutts	12 culverts	$60
J. Baskerville	grading	$114.20

In 1886 Franklin entered an agreement with the Rural Municipality of Montcalm to pay $100 and $25 per year for a ferry across the Red. In 1888 they built a bridge across Mosquito Creek with the Rural Municipality of de Salaberry, their cost share being $62.50.

Bridge being moved from Dominion City to Roseau River in 1938. Shows bridge moving along Highway No. 201.

Ferry over Red River at Letellier. 1949. Crossing are Blanche Von Dracek's parents, Mr. and Mrs. Minarz, Julia Minarz, and friends.

Hand powered cable crossing over Roseau River at Senkiw. Donald and Tom Spence are crossing with their luggage.

Swinging bridge at Senkiw over the Roseau River. This is the oldest swinging bridge in Manitoba.

Early transportation was along the Red River or overland by the two main trails. The St. Paul trail from Fort Garry, followed an older Indian trail called the Crow Wing, and led to St. Paul, Minnesota. On the west side of the Red River was the Pembina Trail which led from Fort Garry to the source of the Minnesota River. The east route was more widely used as there was less danger of Sioux attack, it was more sheltered and the many streams which crossed it provided fresh water. Ruts worn into these trails by Red River carts can still be seen in isolated spots of our municipality.

By 1883, there appear to be only isolated parcels of land still belonging to the Metis. Between 1873 and 1883, the title of these lands, signified by Metis scrip, had been sold to the incoming settlers, often at a very low price. The few areas of land not sold seem to have been abandoned, in many cases, and purchased by others at tax sales.

By the Convention of London, 1818, the 49th parallel was declared the boundary between Canada and the United States. From 1872 to 1875 surveyors appointed by the Boundary Commission, marked the border in our area. Led by Captain Cameron and assisted by the U.S. Cavalry, they headquartered at Fort Dufferin, but established several camps at different points along the border.

The first official customs was established at West Lynne in 1873, and F. T. Bradley was the first customs officer. In 1879 he moved his office into the post office at Emerson, but lack of space necessitated the building of an official port of entry in 1882.

The first customs office at Tolstoi was in that town in 1947. Victor Moore and Dan Kreitz were first officers. Lloyd Foy was the first customs officer when the new building opened at the border in 1954.

From its inception, the Municipality of Franklin was determined to provide extensive services to its inhabitants.

In 1883 they commissioned James Duncan to build a town hall for $1840. The main floor was to be used for social activities, the second floor as council chambers.

In 1884, the second Tuesday of every month was set as the date of council meetings and salaries for councillors were $2 per day and 10¢ per mile.

Labor districts and pathmasters were organized to complete public works.

Ads were purchased in various publications to attract new settlers.

Businesses were encouraged and tax incentives offered. The grist and flour mill of James Spence was exempted from taxes for 10 years, in 1885.

A bylaw governing public morals in the municipality was passed in 1890. Anyone who was drunk, disorderly, indulged in any vice, used profane language or violated the Sabbath, or anyone involved in any indecent exhibition could be fined $25 or given 25 days at hard labor.

The lack of fencing made necessary the appointment of poundkeepers.

Poundkeepers 1887

Wm. Morrison	W. Morkill
R. Hempton	S. Barber
G. Parks	N. Varey
J. Young	J. Spence
M. Annable	E. Mortlock
R. Curran	W. Webster
J. Robinson	R. Smith
W. Hosick	J. Long
D. Timlick	F. Carrier

Owners of impounded animals were subjected to the following daily rates:

Stallions — $2	Calves — 20¢
Horses and mules — 50¢	Sheep — 20¢
Bulls — $1.50	Swine — 30¢
Cows and oxen — 25¢	

Businesses were licensed. Hotels were required to pay $50 per year, auctioneers $25, and anyone having 2 pool tables $25. In order to encourage local businesses, and discourage transients, hawkers and peddlars were charged $10 per man and $40 per horse or mule. Transient traders were charged a license fee of $50.

The municipality bore a responsiblity for its citizens when they were ill. In 1884 council granted $50 to Malcom Angus owing to sickness. In 1886 they paid the E. Bayles family $2 weekly for four months due to sickness.

Municipal doctors were reimbused for sick calls and for vaccinating school children.

Law enforcement was also considered a municipal matter. In 1885 W. Findlay and A. Scott were paid $1 each for watching "suspicious characters". By 1894 Alex Waddell was appointed special constable and sanitary inspector.

In 1887 the council assumed some responsiblity for cemeteries, appointing T. Coulter, R. Scott, J. Duncan, to look after Dominion City cemetery, H. Preston for Greenridge, and councillors Lindsay and McBean for Ridgeville.

Control and extinction of wolves (coyotes) was achieved by the Wolf Bounty — $2, for every wolf killed. In 1897 the municipality paid bounty on 60 wolves, in 1898, 87 and 1899, 83.

Council established a system for registering births, deaths, and marriages and compiled a voters list in 1886.

Donations were sent to hospitals, orphanages, agricultural societies, Children's Aid and the patriotic fund.

Finally, the municipality attempted to encourage residents to begin weed control. In 1885 they paid J. King and W. Hosick $3 each, for 2 days pulling thistles. In 1910 they paid $1141 to residents, for cutting weeds.

1885 Budget

Revenue	
Taxes collected	$27,452.94
Interest and tax penalties	3,740.39
Partial Expense List	
Borrowed by debentures	$95,000.00
Interest on debentures	5,687.00
Other interest	105.00
Lawyers fees	500.00
Public works	1,696.27
Running expenses	2,313.98
Election expenses	70.00
Salaries	1,252.80
Schools	2,363.69
Legal expenses	1,154.93
Advertising	17.25
Stationery and Printing	187.63
Hall fuel and lights	37.35

The combined problems of road building, drainage control and lack of municipal funds are perhaps best illustrated by the case of:

Lucy M. Curran versus the R.M. of Franklin 1885

May 6, 1884.

Lawyer F. Burham submits a letter to council regarding damages to the property of R. Curran, due to the incompletion of the two mile road and its drains to the Joe River.

Council replies it will look into the matter and attend to the petition as soon as possible.

November 24, 1884

F. Burham submits a letter regarding the claim of R. Curran for damages by overflow of two mile road ditches into his land, and threatens immediate legal action.

Council replies it regrets it can do nothing, as it had no money.'

February 9, 1885

Council's lawyers, Hagel and Davis request a $200 advance regarding the Curran case. They also request that Lucy M. Curran, the plaintiff be examined.

February 10, 1885

At a special council meeting Reeve Allen and Councillor Duncan are required to look up evidence and prepare to go to court.

February 11, 1885

In the Court of Queen's Bench, County of Selkirk, Lucy M. Curran alleges:

a) "that the defendents so negligibly and unskillfully built and constructed a public drain . . . that large quantities of water were carried through the plaintiff's land . . . and rendered said lands unfit for cultivation or crop."

b) "that it was the duty of the defendents to build and construct said drain in a careful and proper manner without causing any unnecessary or avoidable damage or injury."

c) "that the defendents . . . without continuing the drain, negligently, carelessly, and improperly left the same unfinished and without any outlet.

March 17, 1885

The R.M. of Franklin pleads:

a) not guilty to the first count

b) as a second plea they state the said land is not the plaintiff's as alleged.

c) The defendents say that they did what is complained of, by the plaintiff's leave.

May 15, 1885

The Honorable Mr. Justice Taylor finds all issues for the plaintiff and awards Lucy M. Curran $500 for assessed damages and $294.37 costs of suit.

May 23, 1885

Council is billed $18 costs for completion of Curran ditch survey.

July, 1886

Council passes a bylaw to raise taxes 1 ⅛ mills across the municipality to satisfy the Lucy M. Curran judgement, total costs of which are over $2,000.

Our municipality today has a population of 2,033 and contains the following villages or post offices:

Carlowrie - from Carlowrie Castle, Scotland

Roseau River - after river

Rosa - abundance of wild roses

Senkiw - from a village near Zalitztsi in Halychyna

Tolstoi - from Count Leo Tolstoi

Overstoneville - German upper stoneville

Woodmore - parts of two farms Woodlands and Moore

Greenridge - descriptive

Ridgeville - after the ridge

Fredensthal - German peaceful valley

Arnaud - misspelled from Father Aulneau, La Verendrye missionary

Dominion City - changed from Roseau Crossing

Stuartburn - after early farmer Stuart Miller

First snowplow in municipality, on a road near Greenridge.

Maintainer, used for road building and maintenance by Franklin Municipality. c. 1940. Driver, Alton Johnston.

The Dominion City Volunteer Fire Brigade was tentatively formed in 1951, when several concerned citizens met to discuss the possibility of working towards forming a fire brigade to serve the Municipality.

The village at this time was protected by a small chemical unit pushed on a two wheeled cart with a water unit which was pumped by hand. It was housed in the Maynes Bros. garage which is where the Credit Union building now stands. The last time it was utilized was when the Frank Curran residence was destroyed by fire in 1947. The United Church bell was usually rung alerting the people in the village of such emergencies.

In early 1951, Mr. Lloyd Baskerville and Mr. Hugh Kelly, who were instrumental figures in forming the brigade, held discussions with several interested citizens of the community, at the L. O. Baskerville and Son garage and the Bank of Commerce respectively. It was realized there was a great need for adequate fire-fighting equipment for the town and surrounding districts.

A truck purchased from L. O. Baskerville at a minimal fee which outfitted with a pump and tank designed by Min Namba and W. E. (Bud) French, both mechanics. In the following two years, the volunteers operated without formal organization.

In March 1951 the fire truck and several men were summoned to the Ogilvie elevator fire and again in January 1952 when the Arnaud Mennonite Brethren Church was destroyed by fire.

To help with operating costs, funds were raised by sponsoring Sports' Days, dances, bake sales and teas. The volunteers donated a lot of their time in keeping the equipment in running order.

On January 9, 1953, a meeting was held at Baskerville's garage to formally organize the Dominion City Volunteer Fire Brigade. Mr. Cliffort Baskerville was nominated chairman. Lorne Ramsey was elected as the Fire Chief of the newly formed brigade. The first deputy Chief was Matt Borodenko, second deputy was W. E. (Bud) French. Truck drivers were Rod McKenzie, Maurine Paley and Ken French.

In the ensuing years, the meetings were being held in the Great West Motors garage, which also housed all the equipment. The fire department served the R.M. of Franklin and for several years the town of Vita and Roseau River Indian Reserve.

An Auxiliary one ton truck was purchased from L. O. Baskerville and Son for the sum of $650.00 in the year of 1956. The original fire truck was replaced in 1962 when a new unit, Mercury 700 was purchased from Great West Motors for the sum of $3,258.00 To keep up with the increasing

demand for fire protection a one ton truck, equipped with pumping unit, was purchased in 1968, replacing the fire auxiliary truck.

As firefighting costs were steadily on the increase, negotiations were made with the council of the R.M. of Franklin to assist financially by allocating a yearly grant.

The municipality built a new fire hall in 1970 which houses all the fire trucks and all other equipment. One of the biggest assets to the brigade was when a new pumper unit G.M.C. Thibault was ordered by municipality and delivered to Dominion City in 1977. The latest acquisition made the Dominion City Volunteer Fire Brigade one of the best equipped for its size in the province.

A more elaborate and efficient alarm system has been installed complete with fire siren phones and 20 on the conference line. All trucks are equipped with C.B. radios, and the pumper unit with a mobile phone, assuring instantaneous response to emergencies that may occur. Twenty-six members are affiliated with the department. The only member of the brigade since its origin and still active today is Ken French who has served for 31 years. Kimberley and Patrick, his two sons, are now members as well.

In a period of over three decades all past and present members have played an important role in fire protection in the community and surrounding district. They are to be commended for their outstanding service and devotion to the department.

Volunteer Fire Brigade
Membership Roll 1951-1982

Honorary Members: Hugh Kelly; Lloyd Baskerville

Chiefs: Lorne Ramsey; Matt Borodenko; Glenn Ginn; Bryan Nichols; Barry Gushuliak

Deputy Chiefs: Matt Borodenko; W. E. French; Bryan Nichols; Ken French; Patrick French

Secretary Treasurer: Colin Granger; Glenn Ginn; Harold Ostberg

Members: Jim Anstett; Armand Ballast; Herman Ballast; Clifford Baskerville; Cam Baskerville; Bev Berrington; Herb Bobrowski; Matt Borodenko; Charlie Boutet; Barry Boutet; Harold Bultz; Gordon Brad; Dale Brad; Allen Brown; Bob Cherewayko; Henry Casper; Ben Comeault; Keith Empey; Fred Dalmage; W. E. (Bud) French; Ken French; Pat French; Kim French; Laurent Fortin; Colin Granger; Glenn Ginn; Barry Gushuliak; Lorne Hancox; Pete Hiebert; Archie Hunter; Gordon Jamieson; L. R. "Skip"

Keeley; Bruce Keller; Terry Kizuik; Wally Korpan; Hugh Lamont; Lorne Lamont; Rod McKenzie; Gus Mol; Min Namba; Ed Murray; Bryan Nichols; Nick Osachuk; Harold Ostberg; Dale Palmer; Maurice Paley; Stan Pearse; Terry Pearse; Hub Peterson; John Peterson; Lorne Ramsey; Ron Ramsey; Abbie Raw; Jacob Rubinfield; Alf Sawatsky; Bert Simpson; Len Schultz; Irving Scott; Keith Scott; Jim Scott; Chester Skene; Cec Smoley; Taras Sokolyk; Ray Sawchuk; Ed Stefiuk; Norman Solnes; Frank Stevenson; Kasper Szmigelski; Bill Taylor; Ed Thom; Paul Walters; Alan Wood; Nick Woronchuk; and Allan Weedmark

Bryan Nichols, Fire Chief, John C. Hunter, Reeve, Anthony Hudyma, Secretary-treasurer in front of modern fire truck. 1982.

Dominion City Volunteer Fire Bridgade's fleet of trucks, 1982.

Members of the Dominion City Volunteer Fire Brigade, 1982.

Police services are provided by the R.C.M.P. detachment im Emerson. Medical, hospital and care home facilities are administered by the Morris hospital district.

Huge road graders and snow plows, assisted by modern scrapers accomplish in a day what once took weeks for the statute laborers. Drainage ditches are constructed with monstrous culverts, and the paving of main roads is done by the provincial government. In 1957, the ferry over the Red River was replaced by a bridge.

1982 Estimated Budget

Revenue	$1,411,179.60
Interest	20,000.00
Other Revenue	92,400.00

Partial Expense List	
Borrowed by debentures	100,176.13
Interest on debentures	10,246.44
Legal Expenses	2,000.00
Public Works	364,500.00
Running Expenses	53,000.00
Election Expenses	1,500.00
Salaries	154,500.00
Schools	732,099.00

Continuing to meet on the second Tuesday of each month, the 1983 council of the Rural Municipality of Franklin must face the problems of drainage, road improvement, rising costs, and a balanced budget. They must attempt to provide requested services to their population without raising taxes.

Their problems are as complex and difficult as those of their predecessors 100 years ago — their solutions are as limited.

The more things change, the more they remain the same.

Reeves and Councillors of the R.M. of Franklin

1883 and 1884
Reeve - D. G. Dick
Councillors:
W. Lindsay   R. Taylor
W. Linklater   M. Whitley
A. W. Foulds   S. Sullivan
Clerk - W.   Morkill
Treasurer - A. Waddell

1885
Reeve - G. G. Allen
Councillors:
M. Whitley   S. Sullivan
W. Lindsay   I. Casson
H. Preston   J. Duncan

1886
Reeve - Wm. Lindsay
Councillors:
A. McBean   J. Lang
J. Bullis   P. McBean
R. Scott   J. Duncan
Sec. Treasurer - T. Coulter

1887
Reeve - Wm. Lindsay
Councillors:
R. Scott   P. McBean
J. Lang   J. Duncan
H. Preston   W. H. Baldwin
Sec. Treasurer - T. Coulter

1888
Reeve - James A. Lang
Councillors:
W .H. Baldwin   P. McBean
R. Scott   H. Preston
J. Duncan   H. Lawson
Sec. Treasurer - T. Coulter

1889
Reeve - James A. Lang
Councillors:
P. McBean   W. H. Baldwin
H. Lawson   J. Duncan
R. Scott   H. Preston
Sec. Treasurer - T. Coulter

1890
Reeve - Samuel Sullivan
Councillors:
P. McBean   C. McKillop
W. H. Baldwin   J. Baskerville
R. Scott   J. Duncan
Sec. Treasurer - T. Coulter

1891
Reeve - Samuel Sullivan
Councillors:
J. Baskerville   C. McKillop
R. Scott   J. Duncan
L. Peto   C. Baldwin
Sec. Treasurer - T. Coulter

1892
Reeve - Samuel Sullivan
Councillors:
G. Baldwin   J. Duncan
C. Baldwin   J. B. Smith
R. Scott   H. Preston
Sec. Treasurer - T. Coulter

1893
Reeve - Samuel Sullivan
Councillors:
C. Baldwin   J. Duncan
R. Scott   H. Preston
J. Smith   A. McBean
Sec. Treasurer - T. Coulter

1894
Reeve - Samuel Sullivan
Councillors:
H. Preston   C. Baldwin
J. Duncan   R. Scott
A. McBean   J. Carleton
Sec. Treasurer - T. Coulter

1895
Reeve - W. Lindsay
Councillors:
A. McBean   R. Scott
H. Baldwin   W. Gunn
H. Preston   J. Carleton
Sec. Treasurer - T. Coulter

1896
Reeve - James A. Lang
Councillors:
H. Baldwin   M. Bland
A. McBean   J. E. King
R. Scott   H. Preston
Sec. Treasurer - T. Coulter

1897
Reeve - James A. Lang
Councillors:
H. Baldwin   J. E. King
R. Scott   A. McBean
M. Bland   H. Preston
Sec. Treasurer - T. Coulter

1898
Reeve - Wm. Lindsay
Councillors:
J. E. King   J. Bland
R. Scott   E. Post
A. McBean   L. H. Peto
Sec. Treasurer - T. Coulter

1899
Reeve - Wm. Lindsay
Councillors:
R. Scott   J. King
E. Post   J. Bland
C. Baldwin   G. Parkes
Sec. Treasurer - T. Coulter

1900
Reeve - Wm. Lindsay
Councillors:
R. Scott   J. Carleton
E. Post   C. Baldwin
J. King   W. L. Ross
Sec. Treasurer - T. Coulter

1901
Reeve - Wm. Lindsay
Councillors:
H. Stewart   J. King
J. Carleton   R. Scott
E. Post   J. McCartney
Sec. Treasurer - T. Coulter

1902
Reeve - Wm. Lindsay
Councillors:
W McCartney   O'Brien
R. Scott   E. Smith
J. Carleton   H. Stewart
Sec. Treasurer - T. Coulter

1903
Reeve - James A. Lang
Councillors:
E. Smith   J.McCartney
R. Scott   H. Nicely
H. Stewart   M. Grier
Sec.Treasurer - T. Coulter

1904
Reeve - J. McCartney
Councillors:
R. Scott   H. Stewart
H. Nicely   C. Burnell
M. Grier   J. McRae
Sec. Treasurer - T. Coulter

1905
Reeve - J. McCartney
Councillors:
J. McRae   A. Ferguson
H. Stewart   M. Grier
H. Nicely   R. Scott
Sec. Treasurer - T. Coulter

1906
Reeve - J. McCartney
Councillors:
R. Scott   H. Stewart
M. Grier   Smith
J. McRae   H. Nicely
Sec. Treasurer - T. Coulter

1907
Reeve - J. McCartney
Councillors:
E. Smith   J. Hunter
F. S. Bell   A. Ferguson
H. Stewart   G. Bowser
Sec.   Treasurer - T.   Coulter

1908
Reeve - J. McCartney
Councillors:
E. Smith	A. Ferguson
J. Hunter	W. Gunn
G. Bowser	J. Empey

Sec. Treasurer - T. Coulter

1909
Reeve - J. McCartney
Councillors:
H. Stewart	J. King
W. Gunn	E. Smith
J. Hunter	G. Bowser

Sec. Treasurer - T. Coulter

1910
Reeve - J. McCartney
Councillors:
W. Gunn	J. King
G. Bowser	F. Coates
E. Smith	J. Hunter

Sec. Treasurer - T. Coulter

1911
Reeve - J. McCartney
Councillors:
E. Smith	J. King
J. Hunter	F. Coates
W. Gunn	G. Bowser

Sec. Treasurer - T. Coulter

1912
Reeve - J. McCartney
Councillors:
E. Smith	S. Gibson
E. Scott	J. King
J. Hunter	F. Coates

Sec. Treasurer - J. Witty

1913
Reeve - J. McCartney
Councillors:
S. Gibson	E. Smith
W. Casson	E. Scott
J. King	F. Coates

Sec. Treasurer - J. Witty

1914
Reeve - J. McCartney
Councillors:
S. Gibson	E. Scott
W. Casson	J.D. Baskerville
J. King	F. Coates

Sec. Treasurer - J. Witty

1915
Reeve - J. McCartney
Councillors:
W. Casson	E. Scott
S. Gibson	F. Coates
D. Timlick	J.D. Baskerville

Sec. Treasurer - J. Witty

1916
Reeve - J. McCartney
Councillors:
W. Casson	E. Scott
S. Gibson	H. Stewart
D. Timlick	J.D. Baskerville

Sec. Treasurer - J. Witty

1917
Reeve - J. McCartney
Councillors:
W. Casson	H. Stewart
S. Gibson	D. Timlick
E. Scott	J.D. Baskerville

Sec. Treasurer - J. Witty

1918
Reeve - J. McCartney
Councillors:
S. Gibson	D. Timlick
E. Scott	W. Casson
J.D. Baskerville	G. Turner

Sec.　　　Treasurer - J.　　　Witty

1919
Reeve - Hamilton Stewart
Councillors:
S. Gibson	E. Scott
W. Casson	J. Baskerville
D. Timlick	G. Turner

Sec. Treasurer - J. Witty

1920
Reeve - Hamilton Stewart
Councillors:
S. Gibson	E. Scott
W. Casson	J. Baskerville
D. Timlick	J. Dowswell

Sec. Treasurer - J. Witty

1921
Reeve - James Hunter
Councillors:
E. Scott	D. Timlick
S. Gibson	H. Batten
S. Johnston	J. Dowswell

Sec. Treasurer - J. Witty

1922
Reeve - James Hunter
Councillors:
S. Johnston	H. Batten
E. Scott	T. Collins
D. Timlick	S. Gibson

Sec. Treasurer - J. Witty

1923
Reeve - James Hunter
Councillors:
S. Johnston	H. Batten
E. Scott	T. Collins
D. Timlick	S. Gibson

Sec. Treasurer - J. Witty

1924
Reeve - James Hunter
Councillors:
S. Johnston	H. Batten
E. Scott	S. Gibson
D. Timlick	T. Collins

Sec. Treasurer - J. Witty

1925
Reeve - James Hunter
Councillors:
T. Collins	D. Timlick
H. Batten	S. Johnston
E. Scott	R. Weiss

Sec. Treasurer - J. Witty

1926
Reeve - James Hunter
Councillors:
T. Collins	R. Weiss
D. Timlick	W.R. Johnston
H. Batten	D. Lamont

Sec. Treasurer - J. Witty

1927
Reeve - James Hunter
Councillors:
W. Johnston	T. Collins
D. Timlick	D. Lamont
H. Batten	S. Gibson

Sec. Treasurer - J. Witty

1928
Reeve - James Hunter
Councillors:
H. Batten	W. Johnston
S. Gibson	D. Lamont
D. Timlick	T. Collins

Sec. Treasurer - J. Witty

1929
Reeve - James Hunter
Councillors:
D. Lamont	S. Gibson
T. Collins	W. Johnston
D. Timlick	J. Casson

Sec. Treasurer - J. Witty

1930
Reeve - James Hunter
Councillors:
D. Lamont	T. Collins
D. Timlick	S. Gibson
W. Johnston	J. Casson

Sec. Treasurer - J. Witty

1931
Reeve - James Hunter
Councillors:
D. Lamont	S. Gibson
T. Collins	J. Casson
W. Johnston	S. Tophen

Sec. Treasurer - J. Witty

1932 - 1933 - 1934 - 1935
Reeve - James Hunter
Councillors:
S. Gibson   D. Lamont
T. Collins   W. Johnston
J. Cassen   S. Tophen
Sec. Teasurer - J. Witty

1936 - 1937 - 1938
Reeve - James Hunter
Councillors:
J. Casson   W. Johnston
D. Lamont   S. Gibson
S. Tophen   J. Morrison
Sec. Treasurer - J. Witty

1939
Reeve - James Hunter
Councillors:
S. Tophen   J. Morrison
M. Brad   R. Weiss
J. Casson   W. Johnston
Sec. Treasurer - J. Witty

1940 - 1941
Reeve James Hunter
Councillors:
S. Tophen   J. Morrison
M. Brad   R. Weiss
J. Casson   W. Johnston
Sec. Treasurer - R. Witty

1942 - 1943
Reeve - Thomas A. Collins
Councillors:
M. Brad   J. Morrison
S. Tophen   R. Weiss
W. Johnston   B. Davison
Sec. Treasurer - R. W. Witty

1944
Reeve - Thomas A. Collins
Councillors:
J. Morrison   W. Johnston
R. Weiss   B. Davison
S. Tophen   W. Scott
Sec. Treasurer - R. W. Witty

1945
Reeve - Thomas A. Collins
Councillors:
W. Johnston   R. Weiss
W. Scott   J. Morrison
N. Paley   S. Tophen
Sec. Treasurer - R. Witty

1946 - 1947 - 1948
Reeve - Thomas Collins
Councillors:
N. Paley   W. Scott
N. Baskerville   R. Weiss
B. Davison   W. Mayner
Sec. Treasurer - R. Witty

1949
Reeve - Wm. Johnston
Councillors:
N. Baskerville   W. Schwark
B. Davison   W. Schultz
N. Paley   W. Scott
Sec. Treasurer - R. Witty

1950 - 1951 - 1952
Reeve - Wm. Johnston
Councillors:
N. Baskerville   W. Schwark
W. Schultz   B. Davison
N. Paley   W. Scott
Sec. Treasurer - R. Witty

1953
Reeve - Wm. Johnston
Councillors:
W. Schwark   W. Scott
N. Baskerville   G. Kirkpatrick
W. Schultz   N. Paley
Sec. Treasurer - R. Witty

1954
Reeve - L. O. Baskerville
Councillors:
W. Scott   W. Schwark
W. Kyle   N. Paley
W. Schultz   G. Kirkpatrick
Sec. Treasurer - R. Witty

1955
Reeve - L. O. Baskerville
Councillors:
W. Scott   G. Kirkpatrick
W. Schultz   W. Kyle
W. Schwark   J. Ostrowsky
Sec. Treasurer - R. Witty

1956
Reeve - L. O. Baskerville
Councillors:
W. Schwark   W. Kyle
W. Schultz   W. Scott
G. Kirkpatrick   W. Melosky
Sec. Treasurer - R. Witty

1957
Reeve - John Hunter
Councillors:
A. Runke   W. Kyle
T. Pott   S. Walters
W. Melosky   W. Scott
Sec. Treasurer - R. Witty

1958 - 1959
Reeve - John Hunter
Councillors:
T. Pott   W. Kyle
M. Borodenko   A. Runke
S. Walters   W. Melosky
Sec. Treasurer - R. Witty

1960 - 1961 - 1962
Reeve - John Hunter
Councillors:
W. Melosky   M. Brad
T. Pott   S. Walters
J. Hoplock   W. Kyle
Sec. Treasurer - R. Witty

1963 - 1964
                   Reeve - John Hunter
Councillors:
J. Hoplock   M. Brad
W. Kyle   T. Pott
W. Melosky   A. Schultz
Sec. Treasurer - R. Witty

1965
Reeve - John Hunter
Councillors:
W. Kyle   T. Pott
S. Budey   M. Brad
J. Hoplock   A. Schultz
Sec. Treasurer - H. Foxworthy

1966
Reeve - John Hunter
Councillors:
W. Becker   J. Hoplock
B. Comeault   W. Kyle
T. Pott   S. Budey
Sec. Treasurer - A. Hudyma

1967
Reeve - John Hunter
Councillors:
W. Becker   W. Kyle
J. Hoplock   S. Zaretski
B. Comeault   T. Pott
Sec. Treasurer - A. Hudyma

1968 - 1969
Reeve - John Hunter
Councillors:
M. Brad   J. Hoplock
T. Pott   S. Zaretski
W. Kyle   W. Becker
Sec. Treasurer

1970 - 1971 - 1972   1973 - 1974
Reeve John Hunter
Councillors:
J. Hoplock   W. Becker
G. Kyle   S. Zaretski
W. Kyle   T. Pott
Sec. Treasurer - A. Hudyma

1975 - 1976
Reeve - John Hunter
Councillors:
S. Zaretski   G. Kyle
W. Janzen   W. Grier
J. Hoplock   L. R. Schultz
Sec. Treasurer - A. Hudyma

1977 - 1978 - 1979
Reeve Henry Enns
Councillors:
J. Hoplock   W. Janzen
L. R. Schultz   S. Zaretski
G. Kyle   W. Grier
Sec. Treasurer - A. Hudyma

1980
Reeve - Archibald Hunter
Councillors:
R. Tetrault   W. Grier
J. Hoplock   W. Janzen
B. Nichols   S. Zaretski
Sec. Treasurer - A. Hudyma

1981 - 1982
Reeve - Archibald Hunter
Councillors:
S. Zaretski   B. Nichols
W. Janzen   R. Tetrault
G. Pott   W. Grier
Sec. Treasurer - A. Hudyma

Agriculture

by Art Schultz and Ted Schwark

The Municipality of Franklin consists of two distinct geographical terrains, a flat treeless, heavy soiled area west of the "ridge" and a lighter soiled, treed area east of the "ridge".

Settlers moved into the ridge area in the 1870's, most coming from eastern Canada. They came as individuals, rather than a block of settlers organized to open a new settlement. W. L. Morton indicates in his history of Manitoba that merchants at Emerson encouraged settlement of the first two townships east of the Red River, along the Border. The years following were very wet, and the crops drowned.

That accounts for the fact the records show the farmers who located on the flats did not stay. Successful farming here was not possible until after the drainage systems had been implemented.

With the arrival of the railway to Emerson from the United States in 1878, it became possible for people to come from Ontario by rail. This induced homesteaders to come west, and the eastern portion gained increasing numbers of settlers, until all available land on first the ridge, and then west of the ridge was taken up.

With few tools and less machinery, these pioneers began their struggle for survival. Those who had hand plows and tools, shared them with those who did not.

As soon as the first furrow was turned, the seed was broadcast by hand. Some farmers could scatter the seed either hand, and were often hired to seed a crop for their neighbours.

The scattered grain was then covered with a wooden harrow pulled by whatever power was available. The first farm energy were a horse and an ox.

There were few sources for cash income in these early days. Gerald V. Fitzgerald, an old country Englishman, located on the SW¼ of 34-1-4E (present owner Rich Weiss), was one who had more money at his disposal than the average settler. He acquired considerable land, and kept livestock, and therefore employed several men. The temporary railway built from Dominion City to the gravel pit located close to Ridgeville in 1879, for the purpose of hauling gravel to ballast the rail line from Emerson to St. Boniface, provided local men with employment and cash income.

Some farmers were able to obtain employment with the railway and construction work going on at Emerson, which was in the middle of a building boom.

However, when it became known that Emerson would not be the "gateway to the west", this building boom came to an abrupt stop in 1882.

Even though there was little cash available, these early settlers lived well and independently. The virgin soil grew fine samples of grain, which was ground into flour at the Gretna Mill, and later at either the Hudson Bay or Pocock Grist Mills at Emerson, or the Hutterite Mill at Dominion City. Gardens provided them with nourishing vegetables. Wild fruit and game added variety to their menus. Fresh meat in the fall of the year was no problem, as the stubble fields were full of prairie chickens, wild ducks and geese. Most of the farmers carried a shot gun with them while they ploughed. One of the early settlers said wild geese were so thick and so large, they chased him off the field before he could get his muzzle loaded ready to shoot. The resourceful homemakers made their own soap, candles, yeast cakes and cheese. They sewed clothes for the entire family, and knitted all the necessary apparel, such as socks, mitts, and other woolen garments. Some made leather mitts and moccasins from hides the Indians tanned.

There was a year, one of the first ones, when their crop of wheat, small as it was, froze. This wheat made very poor bread. When ground into flour at the grist mills it looked all right, but when baked it turned out dark, sticky and unpalatable. It was "bread that would not rise".

But the hardships were of minor significance compared to the drought of 1890. No rain fell from Spring until fall. What little crop that grew, was cut with a mower. It was known as the "winter of no butter". Some feed for the livestock was obtained from the United States and seed for next spring was imported by the Government.

Fortunately the bountiful crop of 1891 compensated for the previous year's losses.

The nearest town was the only market for surplus farm products. The prices for these were very low. The price of eggs varied from 8-12¢ a dozen. Hogs were dressed at home and sold for

Grid 1 (Sections 35, 36 / 26, 25 / 23, 24 / 14, 13):

J+W GINN	F. McGEE	F. McGEE	J. McLENNAN
J+W GINN	H. LAIDLOW	A. CROSS	J PRICHARD
H.B.Co.	J. CRAWFORD	G.W STRANGE	I. CASSON
H.B.Co.	H.B.Co.	P. CAMPBELL	W. KNOX
M. KENNEDY	J ADAMS	G.G. ALLEN	W LINKLATER
W.R. BURRAGE	J. ADAMS	J.D. HAM	W LINKLATER
F. LANNOTLE	F. GREEN	J. LANG	J. CROWTHER
P/G. CLOSE	F. GREEN	P. McGREGOR	P. McGREGOR

Grid 2:

H 1878 ANN TAYLOR	S 1882 JOSEPH WILLIAMS		H 1879 JAMES McLENNAN
ANN TAYLOR	NWMP 1880 ALONZO GEORGE WASHINGTON		
H.B.Co.	S 1880 ALONZO GEORGE WASHINGTON	S 1878 RICHARD TERROT	H 1874 ISAAC CASSON
H.B.Co.	H.B.Co.		
H 1878 MICHAEL KENNEDY	CPR 1880 ROBERT CAMPBELL	MBG 1874 DUNCAN CAMPBELL	H 1878 WM. LINKLATER
NWMP 1881 MICHAEL KENNEDY	ROBERT CAMPBELL	MBG 1874 HENRIETTA ANELIA HOOPER	H 1878 WM. LINKLATER
		MBG 1878 JAMES ALEX LANG	MBG 1875 WM. CROSBY MAHAFFY
MBG 1874 PATRICK GEO. CLOSE		NWMP 1881 PETER S. McGREGOR	H 1877 PETER S. McGREGOR

Grid 3:

EDWARD THIESSEN	JOHN ENNS		
EDWARD THIESSEN	EDWARD THIESSEN	JOHANN LEHENBAUER	
JOHANN LEHENBAUER		F.H. SHELBY	F.H. SHELBY
		HILDA PENNER	HILDA PENNER
ALGONKIN FARMS	JOHN KING	HAROLD PENNER	JOHANN LEHENBAUER
ALGONKIN FARMS	HAROLD PENNER	HAROLD PENNER	HILDA PENNER
HAROLD PENNER	JOHN STEPANIUK	HAROLD PENNER	ALGONKIN FARMS
GERHARD FRIESEN	HILDA PENNER	BILL KING	BILL KING

Survey showing land ownership covering Sections 35, 36, 26, 25, 23, 24, 14, 13, 3-3 El, 1873, 1883, 1882.

Abbreviations:
H. - Homestead
M.G.B. - Military Bounty Grant
C.P.R. - Canadian Pacific Railway
S.L. - School Land
S. - Sale (Government)
N.W.M.P. - North West Mounted Police

List showing changes in land ownership 1885 to 1982, covering the NW ¼ and NE ¼ of 13-3-3 El; the SW ¼ and SE ¼ of 14-3-3 El; NW ¼ and SW ¼ of 25-3-3 El; NW ¼ and SW ¼ of 35-3-3 El.

► indicates where research left off and took up again in 1933.

NW ¼ 13 -
James Lang — 1885
►
Adam Graydon — 1933
J. W. Graydon — 1937
R. J. Graydon — 1947
Cornie Penner — 1967
Harold Penner — 1975

NE ¼ 13 -
Archibald Howell-Hough & Campbell — 1885
Frank Lamothe — 1886
Rev. Calvin Mackay — 1887
►
George Graydon — 1933
Mathew Graydon — 1975
Algonkin Farms — 1977

SW ¼ 14 -
Frank Lamothe — 1885
P. G. Close — 1886
►
N. Booth — 1933
N. H. Voth — 1934
Katherina Voth — 1950
G. B. Friesen — 1968

SE ¼ 14 -
Frank Lamothe — 1885
P. G. Close — 1886
Rev. C. Mackay — 1888
►
Gabriel Wasylician — 1934
Gerhard Friesen — 1940
G. Friesen - N½) — 1941
A. A. Janzen - S½) — 1941

NW ¼ 25 -
Isaac Casson — 1885
►
F. O. Shelby — 1933
F. H. Shelby — 1945

SW ¼ 25 -
Isaac Casson — 1885
►
S. S. Board — 1933
S. & A. Dearborn — 1935
Issac Goertz — 1941
H. C. Penner — 1965
Hilda Penner — 1977

SW ¼ 35 -
Alex Riddell — 1885
W. H. Stevenson — 1886
Manitoba Loan Co. — 1887
►
Great West Life — 1933
Louis Kreitz — 1935
A. Dearborn — 1945
Leonard Smidt — 1951
Wm. Smidt — 1962
Ed Thiessen — 1974

SW ¼ 35 -
W. H. Stevenson — 1885
W. J. Gill — 1888
►
Jacob Braun — 1933
Frank Thiessen — 1951
E. G. Thiessen — 1964

6¢ a pound. Those who had cows set the milk in flat pans so that the cream would rise. They skimmed the cream by hand and made butter in either crock or wooden dash churns. During the winter the butter was colored with strained carrot or goldenrod juice for a better appearance. Butter for sale was packed in 15 to 50 pound tubs and considered well sold at 12¢ a pound. Wheat averaged from 39-45¢ a bushel.

In the late nineties life became less wearisome as new conveniences were added both indoors and out. Housewives were overjoyed at the installation of such luxuries as the cream separator and revolving churn. The men folk welcomed the introduction of more modern machinery, which greatly assisted them in the cultivation of more land. The gatling gun and broadcast seeder were replaced by drills. The portable steam thresher soon supplanted the old horse-power threshing machines. Doubtless the first wire, followed by the twine binder, created a great sensation in the district but no less so than the arrival of the first large steam traction engine and thresher. When threshing from the stook began the cage wagon racks were introduced. The year 1895 was acclaimed as a bumper crop of wheat. Those farmers with more land under cultivation spent many long hours on the road from fall until spring hauling their bountiful crop to the nearest elevator. It was sold at 33 cents a bushel. This period became known as the "horse and buggy" days. There was as much status attached to the acquisition of a brand new buggy as there is in the present day to the purchase of a new car.

The ridge was a distinct rise of land which marked a decided change in terrain, soil and vegetation. It is the edge of Lake Agassiz. West of the Ridgeville road the land is composed of heavier, sticky soil and is part of that which is referred to as the "flats". The flats was an area east of the Red River which was low land, flat, devoid of trees, with little natural drainage and characterized by heavy soil called gumbo. This land was difficult to plough as the moldboards of plows seldom cleaned and it required much more horsepower to pull tilling implements such as plows, cultivators, etc. but it was free of stones. The land east of the ridge was higher land, lighter soil, tended to be treed mostly by poplars, had many stones less fertility for wheat or barley but better suited to pasture and hay crops. Farmers of the western region could break up nearly all their acreage but usually left some for pasture for the cattle and horses they needed. The lack of drainage at first and the mud in wet weather made it difficult to find a good site for building. Many hauled in gravel or lighter soil to try to improve

their yards. Most farmers planted some trees for shelter or windbreak. The great plague of the summer months if a wet year were the swarms of mosquitoes. Good drinking water could not be found and later dugouts were made near these homes to supply water for domestic use and for their animals. The first crops to be produced here were mainly wheat, oats or barley. Later such crops as rye and sweet clover were added. Today there is much more diversity of crops but in the early days wheat was king. In drier years such as the early thirties more frequent summerfallowing was found necessary to hold moisture for next year's crop often second and third crops were found to be very light. Today's methods of farming have changed greatly with less summerfallowing, more fertilizers used and more and more weed killers are used.

The eastern half of the district is quite a contrast. Most of the land there is much higher and less suited to growing cereal crops. Some of the land is extremely stoney and there are areas of gravel. Over the years nearly all the gravel of this area has been removed for various purposes probably the main one for surfacing roads. The best known pit was the Zass pit. There are other lesser areas still farmed over. Much of the land was never broken because of the difficulty of plowing it up. Besides the necessity of clearing trees and shrubs, it was in some cases so full of stones that it was useless to attempt breaking it. Wells could be dug in this area and good drinking water was usually plentiful. There often was the problem of quicksand accumulation in the wells and they had to be cleaned out regularly to lower the well below the water table. On Section 3 of the Angus McBean-Turner farm there was a wet area commonly called a bog. When the Turners took over the farm they found several barrels sunk into this bog. Upon enquiring of the neighbor, he was informed that each of the barrels belonged to a separate neighbor and they often obtained water from there. Although there are many large stones throughout the area probably no farm had a larger piece of granite than the one found on the Morrison farm on the north west quarter of Section 9. Some geologists from the University have visited this rock and are amazed at its size and its location so far from ones of similar size. No one knows how much of it is below ground but the part above ground is quite a size. Nearly every farm in the eastern area had a large stone pile or piles which are added to each year. Those stones contributed greatly to the wearing out of machinery, especially plough shears, cultivator teeth and discs. Many a doubletree was broken when an implement hit one of these solidly. No matter how many were dug out and picked off the field there is still an endless supply waiting to surface. There are easier ways of dislodging them with modern machinery, but they are a continuing problem. Some farmers resort to burying the larger ones and work over the top of them.

The eastern part of the district produced more livestock as stones did not interfere with the production of good grasses and the trees provided them with shade and some protection from insects.

Also in the eastern district some of the farmers discovered a soil condition known as alkali. It showed up much more on very dry years when the crop seemed to burn out or it grew only pigweed. Farmers learned that it produced better oats than wheat so it was planted more to oats. Today's farming methods have almost eliminated the effects of alkali. It has been learned that summerfallowing is not good for alkali and that growing of alfalfa on it improves its productivity.

The western part of the Municipality was not settled successfully as early as the eastern. Many of the western sections changed hands more often, since the first settlers there had little success before drainage came in and soon gave up.

The great problem of the flats was the lack of drainage. Most fields contained large pot holes which did not drain and could not be seeded, or, if seeded, were drowned out by heavy rains. Eventually there were efforts on the part of the municipality and provincial government to provide drainage for the area. The natural direction of drainage was in a north-westerly direction. Near Emerson two natural watercourses drained into the Red River, the Bradley and Jo Rivers. Because of the steeper slopes of the ridge, the run-off water from the east flowed quickly westward into the flats and added to their problem.

Because such waterways were flooding the nearby flats each spring, in 1926 a ditch was completed to the American Border across the flats just below the ridge between the ditch and the dike the run-off water steered northward and no longer deluged the flats.

The farmers who benefited from the building of this drainage ditch were assessed a drainage tax for a number of years to help pay for its construction. Later the government took over the system and its maintenance and the special tax was dropped. The ditches have been greatly improved to handle run-off, and in 1982, with improved equipment, farmers have made their own systems to drain these pot holes. The land of the flats is now very highly assessed as a result of its increased potential of production.

The turkey industry in Franklin by Jack

Gilchrist, with 1,000 poults in 1947. By 1957 there were 30 producers turning out 89,000 turkeys. John Tanchak, the largest grower in the area reached maximum production of 28,000 birds in 1963. The turkey industry enabled local farmers to sell grain without waiting for open quotas. After 1960, the easing of grain surpluses, improved cattle prices, decrease in turkey prices and increas in feed prices, caused the turkey industry in Franklin to decline.

After World War I, there was quite an influx of veterans. The government had a plan under the Soldier's Settlement Board which helped people interested in farming to buy land. Most of the land was bought in April of 1919 for approximately 40 to 45 dollars an acre. The veterans found they could not make a living, and some sold their land at five dollars an acre and quit their claim. They were given assistance for their livestock and machinery but most of them did not have a farming background. Farming was impossible under wet conditions.

Another American who had a large land-holding in the Arnaud-St. Elizabeth area was H. L. Emmert. He owned 20-25 sectins of land. He became ill in 1922 and, having no immediate family to leave his holdings to, he willed his real estate to Cornell College in Iowa. The director of the College needed cash and he decided to convert all these holdings into cash in 1925.

At this time the Mennonite Board of Colonization, headquarters in Rosthern, Saskatchewan, was was looking for opportunities to settle newly-arrived immigrants. Roy Loving was an engineer and farm supervisor for the Emmert Foundation and Emmert Land Agency from 1919-1929.

Foreign investment and ownership are not something new to the Municipality of Franklin. Around 1911, an American entrepreneur by the name of Henry H. Lyman purchased many acres of prime farmland around Arnaud. By 1920 he had acquired and developed about 12,000 acres which 6,000 were seeded to grain, primarily wheat. The land was divided into five ranches: Ranch No. 1, NE ¼ 9-9-3E; Ranch No. 2, NE ¼ 18-3-3E completed by 1917; Ranch No. 3, NE ¼ 28-3-3E was built in 1919, Ranch No. 4, SW ¼ 27-2-3E probably in 1911; Ranch No. 5, NW ¼ 14-2-3E in 1923. With a foreman in charge, each ranch operated as a separate unit with its own complex buildings including a large 8-10 room house for the foreman with running water, a coal furnace and other modern conveniences, bunk houses for the hired men, horses, cattle and hog barns. Some ranches even had silos and each had ample storage bins for grain with No. 3 boasting a regular grain elevator with grain pit and mechanical rig for unloading. Each ranch also had a machine shop, repair and blacksmith shops. Farming equipment consisted of 27 tractors, four threshing machines (separators), 35 binders and drills and other equipment in proportion. The "Big Four" gasoline engines were a common sight on the ranches. They were great for breaking land and later pulling 12-furrow plows.

Mr. Lyman operated a hog-raising business and to some extent a cattle feed-lot choosing only high-quality animals.

The farm was eventually left to Mr. Lyman's son, Wm. H. Lyman. When he died, it went to his wife who in turn left it to a brother and sister. The ranches were eventually sold to Mennonite immigrants coming to Canada after the Russian Revolution. The Mennonite Board of Land Settlement, with offices in Altona, assisted in finding land for them. Forty-four families were assisted to buy the land belonging to Lyman Farms at $63 per acre.

Managers of Lyman Farms were: John H. Baetke, R. J. Hamilton, Colin McMillan and Neil Baskerville.

In the late 1890's most of the farms were self sufficient. Everyone grew large gardens and all had livestock poultry and swine. The barter system was then incorporated. Farmers would skim the cream off milk, set the milk to cool in pans, and then use the skimmed cream to make home made butter. This butter was sold to a local stores or given to peddlars sent from the merchants in Emerson in exchange for the many staples that the farmers needed. Other items used for trade in the barter system were eggs and home made products which were in turn traded for sugar, coffee, tea, salt, livestock was shipped to stock yards in Winnipeg for ready needed cash.

During the 30's there were creameries at Dominion City and Tolstoi. These creameries sent trucks to pick up cream right from the farms and upon returning to the creamery, it was made into butter. The biggest problem of the day was trying to keep cream sweet. This problem was solved when each farm constructed an ice house and packed large blocks of ice into these ice houses in the winter months, packing it well with sawdust, and the ice kept the cream fresh and sweet. In the late 1920's there was also a market for cream in the U.S.A. People were able to haul their cream to Pembina, North Dakota and realize a much higher price than they could in Canada.

During the 1930's there were also may beef rings operating. This beef ring consisted of 20 to 25 farmers joining together. Each farmer was required to supply one beef at a certain time during the summer months. This group hired a butcher who killed a beef every Friday and dressed it. One twentieth, or one twenty-fifth, which ever the case may be, was delivered to each of the participating farmers.

The early settlers were also very dependent upon their neighbours in times when there were shortages of labour. The farmers banded together and gave one another a hand. This was especially used when a barn was being raised or helping out in time of sickness. It was not uncommon to see 12 or 14 neighbours working together on one farm when the need arose. This problem was also pertinent at harvest time, therefore threshing rings were formed where labour and equipment from several farms was combined and the extra help did away with extra help that would have had to be hired.

The early methods of harvesting crops were very crude. They were cut with a cradle, hand bound, stooked, placed in stacks and later thrashed with a flail. But as the years wore on, after World War I and the first labour shortage, steam engines came onto the scene. Just prior to the steam engines, horse-powered separators were used. They were hand fed and did not have blowers or feeders. The twine on the stooks had to be cut by hand and the grain was also bagged by hand. Once the steam engines took over, a crew of 20 to 25 men which toiled from dawn to dusk bringing in the harvest could now be replaced by a farmer and his wife. In the 1920's, the machines were somewhat smaller and more portable with the larger oil pulls and Rumeleys providing the power.

During World War II, because of the shortage of labour, the pull-type combines came into the picture. Some were as small as six foot models while others were 15 to 18 foot models. The average on the flats at this time was the 12 foot model which made quite a change in the way of harvest.

The eastern portion of the Municipality differed significantly in vegetation and soil type. Consequently the development of agricultural land differed from that in the western region. There is a definite demarcation between the west and the east. The west is mostly "flats" as already explained, while the east is predominantly a forested region with poplar, oak and maple the common trees. This region contained a lot of low lying swampy land. The higher areas contained a lot of rocks. Development of this area proved to be a slow and difficult task. But through hard work, perseverance and determination land was cleared and roads were built. This process was aided and speeded up by the introduction of tractors, bulldozers, backhoes and stone pickers. Much of the low lying land was drained by a system of drainage ditches. What used to be swamp and stone is now in crops and hayland. The land underwent a remarkable transformation and became most productive.

Currently the eastern part of the district produces livestock and grain. It is excellent for forage crops such as timothy, brome grass and alfalfa; cereal crops such as wheat, oats, barley, rye, buckwheat, flax and corn; oil crops such as sunflowers and rapeseed; as well as alfalfa seed and sweet clover seed. Mixed farming remains a predominant agricultural activity. Raising cattle, both beef and dairy; hogs, sheep and poultry contributes substantially to the income of the area.

It is both interesting and significant to look historically at the difficulties and problems that the first settlers experienced in opening up the eastern region. The homes were usually small but were gladly shared with others. Building homes was not an easy task as supplies and money were not as easy to come.

Digging wells by hand was another task not easily accomplished. Many times digging would produce a well, but no water. Clearing land and breaking it up, so gardens could be planted, was an important duty. Crops of wheat, oats and buckwheat were sown, so a bountiful harvest would produce grain which was ground into flour at a neighbouring flour mill in Stuartburn. Bread was baked in clay bake ovens. Homesteads were made up on virgin land. Berries, hazel nuts and mushrooms were plentiful. These were picked and dried for winter use.

During the spring and summer seneca roots were plentiful. Women would take their small spades, knap sacks on back, and head for the woods where they would dig the roots. When their bags were full, they would return home, dry the roots and sell or trade them for groceries.

The first variety of wheat grown by the early settlers was a Russian variety, Turkey Red. It was brought over by the Mennonites in 1874 and found its way into the Municipality. The next variety grown was Red Fife. This variety was grown several years, but had very limited rust resistance. The next variety to appear on the market was Marquis which was of very good milling quality but also had very limited rust resistance. After this came some of the well known varieties such as Thatcher, Ceries, Redman, Coronation, Selkirk, Neepawa and the present day variety of Benito, which is one that is largely grown because of its resistance to disease and rust.

Hans Lillijord, a farmer in the Arnaud area introduced the first variety of rust resistant wheat, Thatcher 2303, to the Canadian Prairies.

Lillijord was a native of Minnesota and a graduate of the University of Minnesota in 1913. He took up farming near Arnaud, S½ 1-4-3E. He spent the winters in Minnesota, frequently spending some time at the agronomy Department of the University. He became involved in the development of Thatcher wheat. In 1934 Lillijord brought 15 bushels to Manitoba. In spite of severe drought and grasshopper problems, his new wheat produced 20 bushels to the acre. The next year he seeded 220 acres and in spite of a severe rust infestation that year, Thatcher wheat yielded 40 bushels per acre. At this point Minnesota Authorities insisted that every bushel harvested by Lillijord belonged to Minnesota. The Canadian Government stepped in and entered the business of buying and selling certified seed.

Lillijord's persistance and interest in advancement of farming methods and new varieties of seed grain brought great strides to the growing of wheat on the prairies.

In the Durum, they started with Mindum Durum, which was followed by Amber. Amber was grown very successfully until the mid 1950's when a new strain of rust called 15-B attacked the entire crop and the crop for that year was a total loss. Then there was a period of years when there was very little Durum grown because there were no rust resistant Durum on the market. In the late 1950's, a variety called Coulter came on the market which was grown successfully for several years, and now has been replaced by Wacomah.

In 1937 farmers were farming considerably larger acreages of land. The average farmer worked a half section and possibly three quarters of a section, with the odd few working the entire section. With the coming of the horse disease, sleeping sickness, in the fall of 1937, most of the farmers found themselves with no power to work their acreage. As a result, tractors began appearing. It was the three plow model on steel wheels, not anywhere near the modern tractors of today. It did supply enough power to do the work previously done by horses.

In 1949 to 1952, the entire Municipality was electrified. This made quite a change in the farm life. Old battery operated radios fell by the wayside, the coal oil lamps, and all other appliances thought to be so essential were now replaced by new and electrified gadgets. This brought life on the farm for the housewife much in line with her city counterpart, giving them freezers, television, electric stoves, vacuums, and what have you.

Some of the young people who took part in World War II, whether navy, army, or air force, did not return to their farms. They stayed in the cities and took some of the more lucrative jobs thereby causing a labor shortage.

In the early 1960's some of the farmers found that they could no longer run a viable operation on their present acreage, so they sold their land. Some sold to their neighbours and moved into the city. The vast majority of land in the Municipality was sold to foreign interests. These foreign people did not have any interest in farming as such, but were looking for a way to invest their dollar. This created very large farms but at the same time depopulated the Municipality. The part of the Municipality that was well settled with someone on every quarter section of land, now had hardly any building sites left. What was considered an excellent building site created by one family over a lifetime, was being entirely destroyed by bull dozers as soon as the foreign interest took over. By the 1970's however families from France and Germany began to immigrate and settle on these large farms.

The first elevator in Dominion City was built by Alexander Waddell before 1900. By 1915 Grain Growers Grain Co., Lake of the Woods, Ogilvies and Randall and Gee and Mitchell all had elevators in Dominion City. The United Grain Growers purchased the government elevator in 1926. In 1950 a new annex was built and in 1957 it was enlarged. Some of the elevator managers were James Waddell, H. Birsbin, D. McDonald, Alex Calder, M. Cruichshank, D. Sutherland, W. Bigger and in 1982 James Anstett.

At Ridgeville in 1901, George Pocock erected an elevator which was purchased in 1919 by N. M. Paterson & Sons. It was rebuilt in 1934 and the second elevator added in 1947. The managers were A. McKinnon, E. Post, D. Pickell, Roy Wyche, C. Turner, R. Brown and M. Braun. The elevator was closed in 1981 when the C.N.R. tracks were removed.

At Fredensthal an early elevator was built by the Northern Elevator Company, it was destroyed by fire. In 1951 the farmers of the area formed a co-operative elevator under the name Fredensthal Co-operative Association, collected $20,000 as a guarantee fund and paid Manitoba Pool Elevators, who built an elevator in 1952, in 1955 an annex was added. Due to the rail abandonment, the elevator was relocated to the main C.P.R. line near Emerson. Original Board Members of Fredensthal Pool Elevator were: Frank Casper, Ted Schwark, William Schwark, Wilbert Seward, Ted Steg, Gordon Kirkpatrick and Wallace Morrison. The present board of directors are Ross Collins, president, Allan Peto, Arthur Schultz, Secretary-Treasurer, Wilf Felsch, Tim Schultz, Dennis Schultz, Robert Felsch, vice-president.

In 1918 the farmers in the Tolstoi area pooled their resources and built the Ruthenian Elevator on a co-operative basis. The manager was W. Kolodzinski. It was closed in 1930.

Mr. Joe Sullivan ran the Ogilvie Milling Company in Arnaud. He was followed by J. McVicar Sr. and Wm. Campbell. The Canadian Grain Elevator was operated by Jerry Beech, Mr. Stevenson, Mr. Ferris. Upon amalgamation with the Canadian consolidated Grain Company, this letter was run by D'Arcy Reynolds, Jim Bingham, and Fred Kathler. In 1959 the United Grain Growers bought the Canadian Consolidated and later the Ogilvie elevator. Agents for U.G.G. have been Brian Lang, Roy Phillips and Joe Irvine.

The C.N.R. rail line from Emerson to Sprague has now been abandoned. When it was built in 1902, there were daily trains from Emerson to Sprague and at one time there was even a daily passenger service from Emerson to Sprague. This continued on until in the 1920's when they cut back to three trains a week. In 1967 they decided to abandon the line from Ridgeville east, leaving a spur of 10.4 miles that provided service to the elevators when they deemed it necessary.

This service continued from 1967 to 1980, when the C.N.R. applied to the Rail Transport Commission to abandon this line completely. In 1980 it was decided to relocate the elevator at Fredensthal onto the C.P.R. main line west. As a result of this, the railway made application to the C.T.R.C. to have the rail line abandoned. The rail was lifted in the summer of 1981. This rail line abandonment has caused a hardship to some of the farmers. At one time it was possible to haul your grain with horses and be within a six mile radius of an elevator. Later, small trucks were used, and it was still possible to haul your grain with a half ton or one ton truck. But as it is now, the farmers at the eastern end of the Municipality have roughly 25 miles to haul their grain. This no longer makes it a viable operation. As a result, it is necessary to buy larger trucks, regardless of the size of a farm.

During the mid 1930's, the Canadian Wheat Board was established. This was created by the farmers to take the risk out of selling grain. The huge fluctuations in prices that were evident during the 1920's, were eliminated. It did not matter whether a farmer delivered in January or September, he received the same price for the grain. This also created a quota for the principal grains, namely wheat, oats, barley, rye and flax. This quota is based on the farm's acreage, and a farmer cannot deliver in excess of his quota. When there is no market or demand for the grain, he has no money, even though he may have had an excellent crop. As a result, farmers switched to cash crops, mainly oil seeds (sunflowers, soya beans, buckwheat and canola), peas, lentils, faba beans, corn and sugar beets. These cash crops are non quota crops, allowing the farmer to sell them immediately and providing immediate cash. Since much of the produce from cash crops is exported by Canada, the farmer has to guarantee to deliver his crop to market the year it is grown.

During the late 1960's and 1970's, much of the livestock disappeared from the grain farms, and these farmers turned to cash crops. Others began to specialize in dairy or beef cattle, hogs or poultry. The small, completely self sufficient, mixed farm, family owned and operated, had disappeared.

THE PARADE OF FARM MACHINERY IN THE LAST 100 YEARS

It was to the traditional walking plow that the virgin soils of this country first yielded to. It was all that the first homesteaders had. The prairie was plowed, left for a while for the vegetation to decay, then turned back. This was called 'back setting' before their seed was broadcast by hand.

At the turn of the century small disks to be used to cut up the sods in better preparation for a seed bed appeared on the market. The harrow was used to level the land and to cover the seed after planting.

The first drills to be used were shoe drills which never were too satisfactory because they did not work too well in trash nor did they place the seed deep enough in the soil. It was for this reason that the machine companies built a new type of drill prior to the twenties. This new type of drill had disks that rotated for furrow openers, allowing for deeper seed placement and ease of draft. Today, many farmers use what is called a discer-seeder, particularily in the heavier land. These diskers prepare the land and seed the crop in one operation thus saving time and energy. After a number of years of tilling the soil and much of the fiber in the soil had disappeared, the disk was not used too satisfactorily for the killing of weeds of for the preparation of a seed bed.

About 1912 the first cultivators came on the scene. They proved satisfactory for weed killing, especially once it became necessary to start the practice of summerfallowing the land. The cultivator is still a very popular machine with farmers today.

How many changes have we seen in the harvesting of crops? First used was the scythe, laying out the grain then gathered and tied by hand, then the cradle, a device that was attached to the scythe and gathered the grain together in proper sized bundles for tying and with each sweep of the scythe. From there they advanced to the reaper, a machine that was drawn by two horses, cutting the grain and again depositing it in proper sized bundles to be tied by hand. From the reaper to the binder proved to be a great time and labour saving device. The first binders used wire for tieing but this was later replaced with twine. With the coming of the tractors came the 10 foot binder which was driven with the tractor power take off. This proved much more adaptable in wet or soft ground because it did not depend upon traction to run the mechanism. Following the binders came the swathers to be used with the combines. this led to a great change in the harvesting of crops. What a change we have witnessed in the harvesting methods in the last century.

From the scythe to the cradle, to the reaper then the binder to the first small combine which was drawn by a tractor to the large self-propelled units that we see in the fields today. Yes, and what a difference in price too! At about $1000 for the first small unit to $100,000 to $115,000 for the largest models today.

When we talk of harvesting, we must not forget about the threshing outfits. In the beginning, the pioneers used the same methods they were accustomed to in the 'Old Country', namely to flail to separate the grain from the straw of their small crops. When more grain was grown, small threshing separators were bought that were powered by horses. The horses were driven round and round and in this way power was delivered to the machine. These first machines had neither a feeder nor a straw blower. The sheaves were placed on a platform then the twine was cut and fed into the machine by hand. The straw came out on a carrier which dropped in on a pile a short distance from the machine. It then required a man with a team and 'bucking pole' to move the straw a distance away and leave it in long rows for the farmers use as required.

Next came the stationary steam engine that was used for power for operating the threshing machines. To move these units from place to place they were hauled around by teams of horses. The small stationary engines were replaced by larger and more powerful steamers that propelled themselves with their own power. Many of these powerful steamers were also used to break the virgin prairie soils, pulling large plows of six to eight and 10 bottom size. To operate these steamers, one man was required as a fireman and another man and team with a water tank to supply the water for the steam. In the early days when water supplies were scarce on the prairies, this often created a problem to find enough water. To operate a threshing machine required a very large amount of men, sometimes as many as 20. Eventually the steamer gave way to the gas engine because they proved more efficient were less combersome and did not require so much man power for their operations.

Perhaps the greatest change of all came in the use of power for the operation of the farm. The first power was provided by oxen, sometimes one ox and one horse, then all horses. Horses proved their value for many years, for power for farm machinery, for freight transportation, for travel, for riding on the ranches as well as for sport. Horses were replaced to a certain extent with a few farm tractors such as the 'Happy farmer', the 'Waterloo', 'Boy', the 'Titan', and some others make about 1910, but these never were too successful, so that the horse was still the old reliable.

Then in the late twenties and early thirties, the machine manufacturers started to build a much more efficient and reliable machine and some farmers began to buy tractors again.

In 1936 and 1937, many horses contracted encephalitis, a disease carried by mosquitoes, destroying many horses, leaving the farmers no choice but to convert to tractor farming. By 1950 ti was very rare to see any horses on a farm.

From then on there has been a continuous change in farm tractors. In the 1930's came the rubber tired tractor. In the 1940's came the diesel tractors with their great savings in fuel plus a cheaper grade of fuel. For a while some farmers on the heavy land tried the cats or caterpillars, but they were too slow, and too rough and dirty to drive proving not to be successful.

Then in the seventies came the four wheel drive tractors which prove very popular today. What a change from the first 25 horsepower to today's 350 horsepower machine. What about the change in cost? Anywhere from $500 to today's price of $100,000 and more.

With the improvement of the roads and the building of more highways, trucks began to make an appearance. They would go right into the farmers' yard, and load the stock and take it to market. So before long, the local stockyards disappeared. Because of the convenience, more and more trucks were used for long distance hauling of all products leaving the railroad with the hauling only of grain. Because the line was left with the hauling of grain and fertilizer, the line from Ridgeville east was abandoned in approx-

imately 1970 and later tenders were called and private contractors removed the rails and ties for reuse in other countries such as Mexico. Then on March 5th, 1981, the last train was run from Emerson to Ridgeville thus ending an 80 year history of service to the Municipality.

At the present time, the last part of the railway is being removed and farmers will remove the top layer of sand and gravel for their own use and all the quarter sections that were at one time divided by the line will again be farmed as one unit.

In 1878 the CPR constructed a line from Emerson to St. Boniface and in December of 1878 the first regular train arrived at Winnipeg with 20 passengers aboard. It travelled at the unbelievable speed of 26 miles per hour. Because of the lack of passengers, the 'passenger' ceased running about 1968.

With the end of the passenger and baggage service came the delivery of all mail by truck on a daily basis.

Because this line connects with the Soo Line in the U.S. it enjoys much International trade hauling potash, newsprint, butane, propane and other chemicals, and hauling back farm machinery, automobiles, trucks, and piggy-back trailers. It is quite common to see trains that are over a mile in length. Over the years, many changes have taken place, such as the gradual conversion from steam to the diesel-electric locomotive. No longer do we see a train chugging along pouring out long, black clouds of smoke.

Huge tank cars are used for all liquid materials, and many of the box cars once used for grain are being replaced by hopper cars. The hopper cars, many of which are built of aluminum are lighter in weight, allowing for more freight to be carried in them. They are much more convenient for the elevator agent to load, and also easier to unload at the terminals with their slide openers at the bottom.

Because of the International trade this line will continue to run indefinitly.

Yes, if only our forefathers could see the change. How grain was handled in bags, then the use of the 'scoop' shovel, until today the grain augers, some up to 70 feet in length which reach to some of the tallest steel bins of today. Yes, even the Vac-vator to suck the grain bin clean and load it into the truck. Most every farm today has a front end loader, a modern day convenience for lifting and carrying loads, a must on a cattle farm. These are some of the changes that have taken place. What changes will the next 100 years bring?

John and Bob Oatway with their teams, c. 1899.

David Badgely hauling grain to load on box car at Overstoneville.

Threshing on the Nisely farm. c. 1900.

Tom Ostberg seeding in 1935.

Jacob Hutt plowing. 1916.

John Hunter, age 16, and Archie Hunter stacking sheaves for threshing into oblong stacks. c. 1917.

Water tank for steam engine on Grier farm.

Peter Chubey hauling heating supplies. 1963.

Unloading grain from Lyman Ranch into box cars at Arnaud, 1918. Franklin farmers feeding the world.

Murray Lendrum's A. R. John Deere - 1937 - Case separator.

L to R - Bessie Minarz, Julian (Minarz) Elias, Blanche Von Dracek, stooking oats, 1948.

One of early combines in Franklin Municipality. Sold to Lendrums by Herb Post. Combine was known as a "clipper" or "potato bug".

Ted Schwark and son-in-law Alfred Wagner getting ready to seed SW¼ 3-1-3 E1, 1950.

Lunch time for threshing gang on Timlick farm, 1942.

Landry Construction clearing land on Stadnyk farm at Carlowrie. 1947.

Christopher Schnell with team of horses and gang plow. 1950.

The spirit of Franklin - when farmer Mike Brodoway was ill, a bee of 11 farmers did his field work.
L to R: standing, Henry Danyleyko, John Pamula, Peter Olynyk, John Hoplock, Roy Mayner, Bill Fedorchuk, Clarence Grobowski.
Front: Bill Bilan, Jack Bially, Melton Zaporzan, David Runky, Henry Hoplock, Mike Brodoway.

Getting hay in for winter on W. P. Kathler farm.

John Paley harrowing with his four horse team of Percherons at Rosa. 1923.

Ron Spence pitching sheaves. 1957.

John Kozak's threshing outfit. 1929. Bill Kozak, John Kozak, John Wnuk, Paul Kozak.

Harold Morrison and 1929 John Deere.

Threshing on Harry Hancox Sr. farm c. 1936. 25-2-2 E1. The grain hopper was a portable wooden structure on wheels which held the grain while the truck was unloading.

Henry Steg hauling sugar beets to Fredensthal. 1942.

Sawing wood are Tom Pott, Ed Pott, Fred Post and Jim Griffin. Backs turned not named.

Barbara Gilchrist feeding the pigs at her grandmother's farm.

Pigs on the W. P. Kathler farm.

Turkeys on Stewart Froom farm. 1954.

Geese on Timlick farm. Newbridge.

Holstein cows on Hancox farm.

Gerrard Hurd, butchering hog, 1936.

Anton Mihaychuk raking hay. 1941.

23

Lloyd and John Lindsay combining in early 1940's. top, Wally Lenton, Lloyd Lindsay. Centre, Laverne Lindsay, John Lindsay bottom.

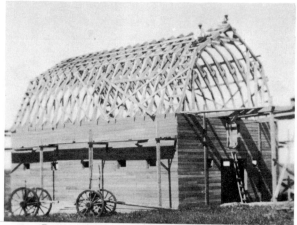

Barn going up on Gateson farm. 1933.

Round straw bales on Vernon Wilkinson farm, 1975. Lassie and Rick Wilkinson.

Sheep and straw roof barn at Tom Chubey's place.

Sugar beet load at loader in Arnaud.

Feliz Geiler and Peter McClaren sawing logs at Woodridge. 1914.

Cream truck stuck on road. August Steinert, Bob and Don Mayne helping Murray Lockhead get back on road.

Gardens were very important to the mixed farmer. Here Mike Timchuk and Gene Dawydiuk cultivate the Timchuk garden. 1945.

Violet Ann Parkes, later married Wm. Stowe, milking cow. c. 1900.

Rodney Klapka milking cow, c. 1982.
Part of modern pipe line milk system. Jar receives the milk from the pipe line, and when it reaches a certain quantity pumps it into a cooling tank. Wilkinson farm, Ridgeville.

Cattle on Peter Timchuk farm. 1929.

Shirley Kingstone tending bee hives on SW ¼ 18-1-5 E1.

Sharpening fence poles with circular saw on Clarence Yahnke farm. Clarence, with father-in-law Garnet Gunn.

Steve Tanchak cutting grain with binder and oxen.

Mrs. Homer Nisely feeding chickens. 1925.

Chicken run on farm of Ludwig Schultz. NW ¼ 2-1-3 E1. 1946.

Sam Waldner's chicken barn at Tolstoi. Sam raises 4,000 birds every three months. 1982.

Roy and Ross Grier hauling hay.

Field of cultivated hemp. Used to make cloth, seed was processed for cooking oil. Mary Paley, c. 1910.

Cutting sunflowers for silage, 1945. Hancox farm.

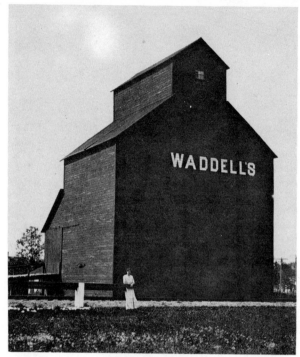

Waddell's Elevator.

N. M. Paterson elevator, 1943. D. G. Pickell's car in picture.

Harold Ostberg seeding, 1982.

D. H. Loeppky combining. 1981.

Art Schultz with 2705 M. F. tractor with cultivator, getting ready to incorporate Treflon. 1980. NW ¼ 7-1-4 E1.

Bert Davison and his IHC Mogul Traction engine.

Cows and calves cooling off in pond on SW ¼ 3-1-4 E1. 1951. Art Schultz farm.

Spring calves, on Art Schultz farm. 1959.

Sheep on the Kingstone Overstone Sheep Ranch, SW ¼ 18-1-5 E1. 1981.

Lesley, Candace, Kenten, Morris, Audrey with (cow) Trudie at the Morris Stampede, 1972.

Business

by Steve Stadnyk, Dorothy Stewart,
Georgina Taylor

The role of business in the early days of colonization in Manitoba was to supply the needs of settlers. As the farming methods changed, so did business. At first horses needed to be shod, and one of the most important people in the community was the blacksmith. Many of the early settlers were themselves blacksmiths and did the work on their own horses. A talented man soon found himself busy looking after many horses in the community. With stability and affluence come the need to establish blacksmith shops or smithies. Franklin municipality was well looked after in this respect.

Many blacksmiths moved gracefully from the needs of serving the farmer when he used horsepower, to serving him when he changed to gas powered machinery, and became first welders, and then garage men.

Blacksmiths were Andrew Davison at Green Ridge, Joseph Muzyka in Rosa (1939), and in Ridgeville, Rudolph Laufersweiler (1910-1930), Alexander Ingram (1930-1941), John Dzioba who began in Overstoneville (1941-1968), and Ronald Spence (1969-present), Arnaud, R. Scowcraft, Mr. Robin, Adolph Smidt. In Tolstoi the first blacksmith shop was built by Frank Majewski in 1912. He operated the shop for 37 years, retiring in 1949. In Fredensthal Ed Laufersweiler had a blacksmith shop in 1924. Joseph Muzyka in Rosa, 1939 was a blacksmith.

When people began to travel long distances with horses, communities needed livery barns.

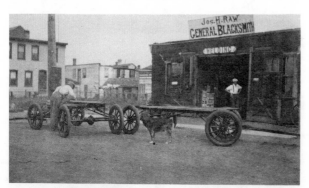

W. H. Parker, General Blacksmith. Bought shop from Robert Hempton c. 1900, sold to Dave Spence c. 1928 Dominion City.

Jos. H. Raw, blacksmith, building school vans. c. 1936. Purchased shop from Charlie Taylor, sold to L. O. Baskerville in 1930's in Dominion City.

W. H. Parker, in front of his shop at Dominion City.

Bob Gillespie, working in Parker's shop in Dominion City.

Herman Sipma working in his shop in Dominion City.

Taxi service provided by Robert Francis Millar, Stuartburn, shown here with his roan drivers and Bill McPhail of Manitoba Provincial Police, early 1930's. Sleigh was double seater equipped with foot warmers and bearskin and sheepskin robes.

Ridgeville Livery and Feed Stables.

Irving Simpson Livery Barn, Dominion City. 1900. Mr. Simpson in white shirt. Just east of Queen's Hotel.

First big twin city tractor Franklin Municipality bought, in 1918, from Jack McVicar, Arnaud. Tractor was operated by Clarence Gunn.

GARAGES

By the late 1930's horses were replaced by cars, trucks and tractors and garages were needed.

Herb Post had an international warehouse in Ridgeville which burned in 1922. In 1923, Mr. Post, who sold Grey Dort cars, built a cement garage. His business included John Deere and J. I. Case dealerships.

Ted Walters began business in Albert Wilkinson's garage in 1937. In 1946 he purchased the Post garage and continued the business until 1960, when he moved to Emerson. Henry Lenton began business in the Wilkinson garage in 1947, selling Cockshutt and Massey Harris machinery and Ford cars and trucks. From 1960-62, Min Namba of Dominion City rented this garage and in 1962 it was purchased by Norman Grier.

At Rosa, John S. Paley operated an International Harvester machinery dealership and Imperial Oil Fuel.

In Tolstoi Eugene Oryschak sold his Massey Harris dealership to George Choboter in 1953. George's Garage and Service is the only garage now operating there. Dan Tanchak and Sidney Machnec had a garage and welding shop in Tolstoi in 1939. Steve Tkachuk has a welding shop in 1982.

Paul Samborski had the last garage in Roseau

River. The community is now served by Cec's Esso and Auto Supply located at the corner of Highway #201 and 59.

John McVicar Sr. took over the Imperial Oil Agency at Arnaud in 1918. Together with his sons Donald and John Jr. he also had international Harvester and Cockshutt agencies. Donald gave up the machinery agency in the 1940's. John Jr. retired as an Imperial Oil agent in 1981, following 50 years of service. His son Bill and wife Jo Ann continue to run the agency.

In 1948 Ben Comeault became the McColl Frontenac oil business in Dominion City. This changed to Texaco and was joined by his son-in-law Barry Gushuliak in 1971.

Lorne Ramsey had the North Star oil agency, later Shell, in Dominion City. This business was taken over by his son Ron in 1981.

J. P. Isaac built a garage in Arnaud in 1945 and sold it to J. H. Poetker and sons in 1950. In 1967 it was purchased by Aron Isaac and named Arnaud Motors. In 1982 it is owned by Henry Enns, who has built a new garage.

Mike and Jack Bially established their British American Oil agency in Tolstoi in 1946. They sold International Harvester machinery for 25 years. In 1949 they built a garage on highway #59 and began to sell Ford cars and trucks in 1950. They had been Gulf oil agents for 30 years.

Around 1896 the Coulter Bros. (Maitland and Wilbur) operated a garage and implement dealership in Dominion City. This was a large building located west of today's Credit Union. At this same time the Morkill's had a furniture store in the upper part of the garage. In 1918 Bill and Sam Maynes purchased the business. The upper story was used for a wedding place, for dances, chautau-quas, etc. The Maynes Bros. also acted as Bankers for many years, cashing grain cheques and carrying many people financially. They had various machinery dealerships, the Imperial Oil agency and Ford car dealership. The business was sold in 1950. The various owners afterwards were Dan Danylechuk, George Bieber, Friesens and Herman Ballast. The building was destroyed by fire in November 20, 1971 (and Ballast's moved their business to formerly occupied Hiebert's garage).

Bert Whitherspoon took over the building (about where today's post office is and at that time next to the Schimunek blacksmith shop), from Adolph Schwark and started an International agency. Ballasts rented this building for a time and later Matt Borodenko rented this building and opened a Massey Harris dealership. In 1966, Matt moved his dealership south of town. In 1975 he sold the business to Ed Milne.

Great West Motors, Dominion City, began as a Massey-Harris garage. The first owners, William Gunn and Johnson Pick, sold to Bert and Ted Lange. George Bieber bought it in 1943, sold to John Paley in 1944. John Paley built the present building. Since then John and Pete Paley, Maurice Paley and Emil Cherewayko have been owners.

L. O. Baskerville built his garage in 1939. He had a Case and Cockshutt dealerships and sold Dodge cars and trucks. His son, Cliff later took over. Boundary School Division, after its formation in 1967, rented office space in this garage and finally bought the whole garage.

Putting the horses out of work, Jim Timlick and his Model T Ford. 1926. - New Bridge.

Massey Harris Garage, Dominion City, owned by Mr. Bieber.

L. O. Baskerville garage, built 1939. Now site of Boundary School Division office.

Rosa Transfer and driver Wm. Yasinski.

Ridgeville and Woodmore Transfer, 1959, hauling culverts.

Scott-Aitkin Transfer. 1946. - Dominion City.

TRANSFERS

When the settlement of Stuartburn, St. Malo and Sarto, and the ones between the Rat River and the Roseau River came into being, something more in the way of roads was required than the network of trails that had served the municipality until then. One of the reasons for agitation in the 1940's for better roads was the birth of transfers and the truck system. Franklin was also in need of bridges, and in 1953 the government approved a bill to spend $75,000. towards the construction of a bridge at Letellier because the ferry could not be used during the spring thaw. This bridge was in Montcalm Municipality, but served Franklin.

In 1926 R. Laufersweiler started trucking cream

to Noyes, Minnesota, with a model T. Ford. The enterprise grew to a fleet of seven modern cream trucks. In 1966 Mr. Laufensweiler sold to Fred Nickel.

Les Ramsey of Ridgeville started the first transfer service in Franklin around 1930. In 1933 Walter Kirkpatrick began to serve the locality. He sold to Fred Felsch, who sold to Jerry Krymal in 1948. In 1950 W. Wachna prospered when the big turkey farms began to locate in the municipality, requiring feed to be trucked in, and the birds trucked to market.

Gawronsky brothers started a transfer business in Rosa in 1937, before there were any decent roads. He sold to Nick Kohut in 1939, who in turn sold to Metro Martinuik, who sold to Mr. Thorvaldson from whom Oscar Wiens bought. Rosa Transfer is no longer in business. The area is served by Morin's Transfer, St. Malo.

The Ridgeville and Woodmore Transfer hauled culverts for the highway and drainage projects in Franklin, as well as cattle, turkeys and feed. Some of the staples it has carried through the years are beer, oil, groceries, chemicals and fertilizers.

The Dominion City Transfer was begun by Lloyd Baskerville and Bill Ball, sold to Les Ramsey, Rheinhold Bohn and its present owner is Roger Cadieux.

BANKING

The first financial institutions within the municipality were the local merchants. They cashed grain checks and even provided loans to their customers. Before the Mortlock bank was built in Dominion city, Maynes Bros. provided much of these services for the town. In 1919 the Merchants Bank of Canada was built, but it burned in 1923. A building was moved from Arnaud and became the Bank of Montreal, Bruce Allan was the first manager.

The bank closed in 1932. The town was without a bank until 1950, after the depression lifted. In 1950 the Canadian Bank of Commerce opened in a small shack on Waddell Avenue, Hugh Kelly was the manager. This bank relocated very shortly, to a two story building east of the Queen's Hotel, where the second floor became the manager's living quarters. In 1959 Wally Korpan became the bank manager and the Bank of Commerce amalgamated with the Imperial Bank. In 1963 they moved to their present building. In 1967 Hub Peterson became manager, during his tenure there were no staff changes for 10 years. Harvey Sawchuk became manager in 1979. The present bank manager is John L. Davis.

32

Banque d'Hochelaga, Ridgeville

Canadian Imperial Bank of Commerce, Dominion City, 1975 staff.
L to R: Eileen Gunn, Diane Lamont, Bernice Weninger, Hub Peterson, Joanne Wolanski.

Mortlock Private Bank, c. 1900. On road, Neill Baskerville driving his dog.

The Valley Credit Union was established in 1964, with the first ten shareholders being Albert Pomrenke, James Seward Arnold Schewe, Henry Wiebe, Clifford Baskerville, Lucien Bouchard, Leon Vandeviere, Abe Hildenrand, James Waddell and John Walters. It began as the Dominion City Credit Union and the first year end statement showed assets of $9,198.00. In 1980 the name was changed to Valley Credit Union, Morris is the head office, Dominion City a branch office. In 1981 a new building was constructed and the assets were $2,141,009. Managers have been Aria Nielson, Raymond Ginn, Dale Palmer, Fred Wall, Georgina Taylor. Present Manager is Elsie McLennan.

Arnaud had an early bank manager, W. J. Phillips.

HOTELS AND RESTAURANTS

Arnaud had an early bank manager, W. J. Phillips.

The needs of early travellers were met in the homes. It is a proud memory of the early settlers of Franklin that no one was ever turned away from the door, even if the meal shared was only potatoes.

Walter and Elsie Kolodzinski have a famous hotel in Tolstoi, well known internationally for its home cooking, warm hospitality and its small male only beer parlor, and kitchen which doubles as dining room.

Arnaud hotels were The Travellers Home Boarding House, managed by Mrs. A. Plante, Arnaud House, managed by S. Graydon, and the Arnaud Hotel, run by the Arnaud Trading Co.

Ridgeville had early hotels but for 32 years was without one, until Stan and Mike Fosty built one in 1946. E. Gretschman opened the first beverage room in 1962. This hotel was badly damaged by fire in 1964, and was rebuilt and moved to the corner of Highways #201 and 59. It is now The Corner Inn, operated by Fran and Willie Laniuk, who bought it in 1974.

The Ridgeville Co-op Community Club operates a beverage room and restaurant on the site of the L.O.L Hall. Herman Ratchinsky opened a cafe in Ridgeville in 1937. Albert Wilkinson also operated it as a restaurant. Lauferswielers ran a restaurant upstairs over their cream truck depot for many years.

In Dominion City the Queen's Hotel was built by Martin and Balfour in 1879. Its early proprietors were George Brad, Wm. Little, Herb Gandy and Mrs Sarah Brad. In 1928 it was purchased by Jim Waddell, who re-built in 1948. Owners through the years were Sylvester and Rudy, Gus and Vera Mol, Kasper and Jean

Gunn's Cafe. Had first television in Dominion City.

Matt Boradenko's Restaurant. Former bank building in Arnaud, and in Dominion City. Brought to Dominion City by Joe Casson with horses, in winter, via the river hill.

Queen's Hotel, Dominion City, built 1948. Very modern with twenty rooms, hot and cold water. Built by Dick Weninger and men, plumbing by W. Hicks and Son, wiring by Neil Sullivan.

Szmeyelski, Ray Sawchuk, Jack Hollinsworth and Rae Joyal, Jack Rubinfield and Allan Wood, Ken McDonald, Gerry and Lois Lyons, and in 1982, Geraldine Shell and Mark Lawrence.

In 1945 Mabel and Louis Solnes purchased a cafe in Dominion City from Charlie Chung. They ran this business until 1979, when it was sold to Karl and Carol Syndal.

Matt and Rae Bordenko began a restaurant in Dominion City in 1946. They sold to Pete Kandia and his sister Eva Pawliw in 1959. Matt also had a movie theatre in Dominion City from 1949 to 1962.

STORES

Ridgeville's first store was opened in 1903 by Roy Whitman. Then followed the McGirr and Hinton Store, and the I. Rosenstock Store in 1914. Whitman's store went through a series of changes in ownership, some of the names being Heath, Clifford, G. Seward, J. Rosenstock and Stoffman, and J. Lolynchuk in 1943. The following year the store burned. A new building was erected, and in 1946 John Tanchak took over the operation of the store. In 1975 he sold it to Andy Grier who in turn sold it in 1977 to Eileen, Mrs Ron Spence, the present owner. J. Rosenstock's store was sold to Mike Fostey in 1916. Fostey sold his business in 1948 to a man named Onysko, who shortly sold to G. Kautz. Kautz continued in business until 1957. The store was demolished in 1960.

In Carlowrie John Chubaty built the Carlowrie General Store in 1934. It was more a trading post than a store in the modern sense, and people brought eggs, seneca roots, horsehair, and fur pelts for barter. In 1945 Chubaty sold to John and Mary Baron, who sold to Oswald Earl, with P. Danylchuk being the last owner. It is now closed.

Nick Dolynchuk and his son Alex were in the store business in Tolstoi for 37 years. They bought the store from P. Jureu in 1918, and Alex and his wife Claudia ran it after Nick's retirement, until 1975. It is now owned by John and Helen Stasiuk.

One of the early stores in the Fredenstal area was Ginsburg and Moir, 1914, sold to Wm. Pomrenke in 1919.

C. Ward started the C. Ward General Merchant Store in Woodmore in 1936. That year four loaves of bread cost 25 cents, eggs 12 cents a dozen, bars 5 cents each, and cigarettes 10 cents a package. In 1960 Ray and Ina Mae Pott took over the store, who sold to Yellands in 1977, who sold to George and Linda Hildebrandt in 1979. The Hildebrandt's run it as a convenience store and post office.

Browns had a store on the St. Paul Trail before roads were built in Franklin. Pococks from Emerson had a travelling store, delivering goods from farm to farm by wagon. Pitch was a merchant in 1940 to 1950, who bartered fresh fruit for butter and eggs.

In Green Ridge Andrew Davidson left a record of having sold flour for $1.00 bag, tobacco 25 cents, port 40 cents, butter 20 cents, and 1 pair of boots cost $2.25 in 1880. In 1907 a water closet cost $8.40. In 1888 binder twine sold for $3.50, and in 1894 two bags of flour cost $3.50. The

Casson family had a store in Green Ridge for 25 years, beginning in the late 1920's.

In Rosa the store and post office were combined in a building owned and operated by Peter Tanchuk. A new building was erected by Bill Romanuik, which is owned by W. Walford in 1982. Another store opened in John Paley's home in 1925, but operated a short time only. In 1927 his brother Samuel took over the store. In 1941 the business was passed on to John S. Paley. Another Rosa merchant was Dan Kohut, who established a general store in 1940, operating it until his death in 1969.

The first store in Roseau River was started on April 4, 1938, by Thomas Pott, Jr. It was sold to Mr. and Mrs. Mokrynski in 1944. In 1945 a new structure was erected. The first gas pump in this area was set up by M. Mokrynski. They continued in the store until their retirement in 1973, when their daughter and husband, Lillian and Taras Pohrebniuk continued the business. In December, 1975, the store closed its doors. Presently the building is used for living quarters by Mrs. Mokrynski, and since March 1, 1981, part of it has been a post office. John Kohut also had a store in Roseau River.

There is no store at Senkiw in 1982, but some of the names of former storekeepers are J. Salamandyke, Steve Rybuck, Machaisky, Dmytro Kolton, Alex Salemandyk and Vern Kyes.

The first business in Arnaud seems to have been a store, run by the Smith Brothers out of a boxcar on the railway siding. The boxcar later became Arnaud's first railway station. The Smith Bros. built the first small store building in 1900. They then built a new and larger store, and opened a lumberyard in 1902. The store was later sold to Rufus Collins, who eventually went out of business. Abe Janzen bought the vacant building and moved it to his farm, converting it into a barn. A man named Ledeaux also had a store in 1902. A succession of store owners in Arnaud are Carter, G. M. Hollingsworth, Arnaud Trading Co., W. A. Wilson, Friesen, A. C. Penner, and in 1982, Mr. and Mrs. Cam Nichols.

In Overstoneville Bill Mykytuik operated a store in the 1920's. Paul Wasylishen started a small grocery store which he operated until 1938. In 1938 Mike and Mary Stadnyk bought his business, and the next year got the post office. In 1956 the store was sold to Ewen and Ethel MacDougall, who operated it until 1962, and the post office transferred to the Bially home.

M. Ditlovitch had a store in Dominion City. Other owners of this store through the years were Werry Bros., Herb A. Gibson, Henry Ramsey, E. G. Ladd, Mike and Anne Sokolyk and son

Taras. In July, 1974, the Sokolyk's opened a new building.

Another store in Dominion City was north of the hotel. It is first remembered as being operated by a man named Little, then Anderson Bros., Charles Stimpson, Mushaluk. It became a church for a short time.

A new store with a modern idea went up in 1947. It was the locker plant, where people could rent lockers and store frozen goods. It was built by Dick Weninger, with the help of Ken Peters and Ed Solnes. Ken Peters ran it for a couple of years, then sold to Maurice and Gene Kelly. Maurice continued in the store until the mid 1970's, when home freezers took over.

In 1982 Dominion City is served by a modern Co-op store. A MacLeods Store was opened in 1954 by Ben Kruger and Jake Hoeppner. In 1959 two extensions had been added, and in 1954 it contained $15,000. worth of hardware stock. In 1958 Hoeppner left Dominion City, and Ben Kruger sold the store to Pete Kruger in 1965. Bryan and Gwen Nichol bought the store in 1974, and operated it until 1981.

The pedlar wagon was a familiar sight in Franklin Municipality before the arrival of the railroad, and even after. Some came from Winnipeg or Emerson, and occasionally local merchants would take to the road. A barter system usually existed, with the women on the farm exchanging farm produce for hardware, groceries, dry goods, fancy goods and women's garments. Barter was butter, eggs, horsehair, cow hides, garden vegetables in season, and seneca roots.

G. Kautz, Raleigh Dealer, winter rig. 1934. Ridgeville.

C. Ward Store, Woodmore. 1955.

Mrs. Ballast serving Stanley Ginn, customer, Herman H. Ballast Garage, Dominion City. 1962.

H. B. Clifford Store, Ridgeville, 1910 to 1920.

Carlowrie Store and Hall.

Willet Simpson, Rena Wilson and Mrs. Wilson at Wilson's Store, Arnaud. c. 1919.

Rosa Store, 1982.

Dolynchuk's Store, Tolstoi. Family operation. Alex and Claudia, in front children Orest, Teresa and Ted.

Sokolyk's Solo Store, opened 1974 in Dominion City. Note Norman Solnes home back left.

No meat arrived wrapped in plastic in 1916. Here Ray Loving and Tom Stadnyk butcher hogs for men on Rohrer and Sheppard Ranch, Arnaud. They butchered every second day.

LUMBER

There were many saw mills along the Roseau and Rat rivers until the turn of the century. Wood was cut east in the winter, dumped on the ice, and floated down in spring. Local men were hired to break up log jams. Sawmills were located at 19-3-6 E1, 24-3-5 E1, and John Paley had a steam powered mill on NW ¼ of 8-3-4 E1. Mr. Sprague was one of the most prominent lumber men working in the eastern area. Many of his logs, branded with the letter S, were "lost" during the long log drives and can be "found" in the early homes constructed on the ridge.

The Canadian Elevator Co., affiliated with the Monarch Lumber Co., started a lumber yard in Ridgeville in 1931. In 1933 the yard was sold to W. E. Riach, who had been yard manager for 16 years. In 1938 he increased the business by adding a North Star fuel agency. When he retired in 1947, his sons Lorne, Alvin and Stewart took over. In 1968 Lorne's son, Duaine, bought the business.

The first lumber yard in Dominion City was operated by Frank Turner, then by Sandy Calder. North American managers were Jim Fetterley, Lorne Wood, Fred Delmage, Jim Hainstock, Happy (A. G.) Froom, Norris Ginn, Frank Stevenson.

Main street of Ridgeville. Hauling lumber in 1920.

THE MAIL AND POST OFFICES

The mail was vital to the early settlers. They walked miles in all kinds of weather to get a letter. Organized mail service arrived in stages.

The Dominion City Post Office was established in the Duncan McKercher residence, now the home of W. A. Taylor. The mail was sent to Dominion City by railroad and distributed by courier to Woodmore and Green Ridge. The Post Office was located in the Turner home, Andersons store, Mortlock Bank and Locker Plant. It was moved from a site east of Syndals Cafe into the new building opened in May, 1960.

Postmasters were: Duncan McKercher 1876-1883, Robert Taylor 1883-1910, Miss M. J. Taylor 1910-1915, Mrs. W. S. Turner 1915-1928, Hjalte S. Anderson 1928-1945, John Grant Murchinson 1945-1951, William A. Taylor 1951-1981, Georgina Ginn 1981-.

Carlowrie received its post office in April, 1894, located on 34-3-4 E1, Colin Campbell postmaster, Augustin Carriere of St. Malo carrier. His pay was $65.00 a year. It is interesting to note that the application for a post office contains an official request for a description of the "character of population" to be served. These are described as "Irish and Scotch origin". Carlowrie postmasters were Colin Campbell, 1-4-94; Paul Lipischak 1-12-23; Wasyl Pupeza 1-2-27; John Baron 31-5-47; Pearl Stadnyk, 9-12-53; Osborne Earle 17-8-54; Peter Danylchuk 4-2-59; Pearl Danylchuk 12-9-61; Pearl Stadnyk 7-7-65.

Rosa Post Office was opened 1-12-1907. Postmasters were Peter Tanchuk 1-12-1907, Maria Tanchuk 20-1-36; Nick Kuryk 23-9-41; Mary Muzyka 10-7-45; Natalie Romaniuk 22-11-46; Wm. Bodnarchuk 15-12-47; Dianne Walford 17-10-75.

Overstone (Tolstoi from 1911) was opened in 1898, with the first master being Alex Yarmey, Nykola Kudryk from April 4, 1911, to 1913, Joseph Rosenstock 1913-1917, Peter Manzie 1918 to 1949; Eugenia Manzie 1949 to 1962. Dan Ewacha.

Woodmore Post Office began in 1902. Before 1902 mail had been handed out of a mail bag. With the establishment of the post office, mail came three days a week, from Dominion City by horse and buggy. Postmasters were Cliff and Frances Ward, Roy and Ina Pott, Lou and Sylvia Yelland, George and Linda Hildebrand.

In the early days settlers obtained their mail at Emerson. The first post office at Ridgeville was established at the Bidlake home, later known as Weineke farm, north and west of Bill Wilkinson's, near the "five mile road". It was then transferred to the McMillan home, now the Rzepks farm, from where it went to the Wm. Wilkinson residence. When the railroad arrived and the village developed, the post office was transferred to the McGirr and Hinton Store. It then moved to the Whitman Store, Fostey's Ice-Cream Parlor, and to the Stringer residence. Mrs. Stringer served as postmistress for 33 years. It was then moved to the Brown home in 1962, and to Andy Grier's Store in 1975. In 1977, Eileen Spence, granddaughter of William Wilkinson, and third generation to act as postmaster, took over the position and still holds it in 1982.

Ridgeville Post Office, opened 01-11-1879. Postmasters, John Bidlake, Gerald Vessey, Fitzgerald, Robert McMillan, Wm. Wilkinson, George W. Hinton, Roy Whitman, A. W. Heath, H. B. Clifford, George Seward, Thomas McComb, Mrs. Beatrice Stringer, Walter J. Brown, Andrew F. Grier, Eileen Spence.

Overstoneville post office was opened in 1939. Postmasters have been Mike and Steve Stadnyk, 1939 to 1956; Ethel MacDougall 1956 to 1962; Nancy Bially.

Arnaud post office opened 1-9-1879. First postmaster was John Ginn, 1-9-79; J. M. Martineau, 1-7-87; Edmondston Smith 1-4-01; Alexander Jones 14-9-29; Christopher Omer Seed 15-3-56; Susan Enns 7-1-64.

Green Ridge opened 1-10-1879, Wm. Foulds, 01-10-79; Mary Casson, 01-01-02; James Casson (01-11-21); Joseph Casson 23-09-31; James Casson 01-09-36; Henry H. Casson 04-10-56; James C. Casson 15-06-62.

Roseau River opened 28-8-1950. First postmaster was Paul Samborski, 28-8-50; Nettie Samborski 16-5-78; Paul Samborski 25-11-80; Mrs. L. Pohrebniuk 28-02-81.

Roseau had a post office which opened 1-12-1895, the postmaster was John E. King, and

McLaren's log drive, 1906.

it closed 31-1-1903. Location was 18-3-4 E1.

Senkiw post office opened 1-1-1913, closed 14-8-1968. First postmaster was Tanaska Tofan, 15-3-1914, who died; Wasyl S. Smook, 13-10-24; John Lobur 14-3-44; Demetre Kolton, acting, 15-9-46, who died; Sophia Nolton acting; Steve Rybuck 3-4-50; Alex John Salemandyk 12-5-64; Margaret F. Kyes acting; Margaret F. Keyes 14-8-68.

Tolstoi post office building, c. 1912. Mary Kudryk, George, Steven and Nastia Kudryk.

Frank Jones hauling mail from Dominion City to Greenridge and Woodmore. 1940.

Post Office, Dominion City, 1946.

Wm. Barber and his mail wagon, pulling mail from train to post office in Dominion City.

Sawmill owned and operated by William Zaporzan at Rosa.
L to R: Larry Zaporzan, Robert Balaniuk, Steve Budey, Leonard Balaniuk and William Zaporzan.

Sawmill owned by John Paley of Dominion City, NE corner 8-3-4 E1, now Walter Melosky farm.

Homes

Home of Mr. and Mrs. Alex Tkachyk, Tolstoi, built 1907. Shown are family and friends, July 12, 1930.

Log house built by John Wilson Dickson, 1895, located in centre of 25-2-4 E1. Logs were cut and hauled from evergreen forests to the east, and put up by a local "bee". Occupied by grandson Bruce Dickson and family until fall 1967.

Robert Scott house, built 1878.
L to R: Cuthbert Scott, Howard Scott, Ed Scott, William Scott. Father Robert in centre back with beard. Scott daughters not named.

Wm. and Martha Fields, 27-1-4 E1. Lily and Martha Wilkinson in door, taken in 1884. Log cabin built in 1879. Eleven of William and Rose Wilkinson's 14 children were born in this cabin.

Sullivan home, 1874.

House on NE¼ 13-1-4 E1, photographed c. 1960. Logs under siding, thought to be built by Stephan Kraynyk c. 1896. Lived by Kraynyk, Cherneski, Leach, Sam Bredin, Gabriel Gaetz, Ernie Gaetz, and finally Vernon Wilkinson families.

William Wilkinson frame house, built 1904. Ridgeville.

Home built by James Auld, 1906, 28-1-4 E1. Cement blocks. Bought by Herb Wilkinson in 1918. Taken over by son William in 1959.

Sam Stringer homestead on the flats, NW¼ 7-2-4 E1. This was a soldier's settlement home. 1919-1927.

Built by Bill Stewart for H. D. Lenton, a cinder block house with attached car garage, not shown. Taken March 4, 1966. Now Norman Grier home.

M. Timchuk home. 26-1-4 E1. Built 1952.

Don Stewart home, built by Don, in Dominion City, 1974.

Ray Pott home. Greenridge, 1980. First wooden basement in area, constructed from pressure treated lumber.

Musician Heather Bishop home on SE ¼ 8-2-5 E1. Solar home, built with help of Heather's father, Ned Bishop. Has passive solar heat, 13 inch thick double stud walls, 18 inch insulation in ceiling, shutters on windows to prevent heat loss, post and beam style construction, is octagonal in shape and has dome skylight.

Dr. J P. McLean home, Senkiw. Built 1981. Modern log and stone.

Steve Tanchak's first home, and oxen he used for labour on farm. c. 1900.

Wakaruk's thatched house.

Peter Timchuk homestead, SE ¼ 36-1-4 E1, in 1930, height of mixed farming in Canada.

Ted Schwark home on farm NE¼ 7-1-4 E1, taken 1955. Note summer kitchen and lean to over ice well. House built 1915.

Home of Beatrice Stringer, Ridgeville. Post office from 1929 to 1962.

Peter Makoweski House, 1929. Tolstoi.

William Morrison home, NW¼ 9-1-4 E1. Built by William and Aleck Morrison, brothers, c. 1880. Addition to left came later.

Fred Felsch Sr. farm buildings, SW¼ 18-1-4 E1.

McKerchar home, built 1874. Wa. A. Morkill bought it in 1901, and W. Taylor in 1951. Dominion City. Credit Manitoba Archives.

Residence of manager, Lyman Farms. c. 1930.

James Hunter house, NE¼ 32-2-4 E1, and son Clark Hunter's home built 1934.

Home of Samuel and Amy Devitt, Carlowrie. Note style of windows and door, and top of chimneys. c. 1946.

Philip Mayner homestead, NE ¼ 16-1-5 E1. c. 1915.

House built in 1910 by Tomko Fedorchuk. Clay walls covered with board in 1940's. Torn down in 1977. 4-2-5 E1.

Log house built by Harry Spence, with help from neighbours, 1932. 26-2-4 E1, on banks of Jordan River. Johny Spence shown in picture. Ron Spence lived here 1949 to 1965.

Home of J. A. McVicar Sr. built c. 1937, Arnaud. Carpenter was Nels Moen (now located on Smith Farm at Newbridge.

August Casper farmstead, barn built 1925, house 1939. Taken 1942.

North side of ice house built by Dymtro Kozak in 1924, still standing in 1982. Walls six feet high, all cement, used in summer to store cream, milk, sauerkraut and dills, before hydro came to Franklin.

Dr. O'Brien house, in Dominion City. Owners 1903 to 1911, O'Brien, then Wenniger, then Japs, 1974 to 1980 Winston Herr, 1980 - Alfred Hormann.

Tolstoi post office and living quarters, owned by Mr. and Mrs. Peter Menzies. 1982.

This barn was the first home of Mr. and Mrs. David Marshall, on NE ¼ 10-1-4 E1.

The Marshall home on NE ¼ 10-1-4 E1, built by Mrs. Marshall and her sons.

Second Marshall home, showing family on verandah.

Lloyd Lindsay home, built c. 1906. In 1940, renovated house, now lived in by Terry Lindsay.

Harry Hancox house, built in 1904, with wood hauled from Vassar. Ted and Edna Hancox home, replacing 1904 model, built in 1963 on same site.

Brian and Gwenn Nichols, Dominion City.

Barn on Shelby farm, built 1917, by W.A.F. Wilson. Grand opening was a dance with music provided by Mr. Wilson the Pepper Brothers on fiddles. Pie social included. A man had to pay 1 cent a pound for the woman who baked the pie he got by auction, and she was his supper partner.

The Val Scholte farm home, built 1902.

Albert Neumann home. Brick house, with lumber addition for summer use only. NW ¼ 4-1-3 E1. Built turn of century, photographed 1919.

John A. Palmer home, built 1906.

Log shelter for cattle on V. Wilkinson farm.

Wasyl S. Smook house, built 1901.

Friesen Farm, taken 1948. 33-3-3 E1.

Be it ever so humble, any house can be a home with the right kind of people in it. This scene fairly pulsates with the spirit of the people who weathered the hardships of pioneer life in Franklin Municipality. Believed to be the home of Fred and Lena Snead at Green Ridge, c. 1930.

Health Care

by Carol Wilkinson

As there were no doctors until 1897 nor a hospital in Franklin, the role of the midwife was a very important one. There was a doctor in Emerson in 1880 but by the time someone would travel miles by ox and cart or by horse, the baby, which had a habit of waiting for no one, would have made his appearance.

The midwives seemed to work in certain areas. This, too, was due to the fact that they couldn't get very far very fast — at least by today's standards — and when they were needed they were needed in a hurry.

These ladies were well respected by the women whom they assisted. Grandma (Mrs. William) Jack of Ridgeville was one of these midwives. She carried with her a little black bag and was once asked what was in it. The inquirer was informed that she would know when she was old enough. Other midwives were: Mrs. Alexander Taylor, Dominion City. Later Mrs. Sadie Bradley; Mrs. George Devitt, 1882 in the Arnaud-Carlowrie area; Mrs. Dan McKinnon, 1890, in the Arnaud-Carlowrie area; Mrs. Lew Carpenter, 1900's, in the Arnaud-Carlowrie area; Mrs. Carleton, 1900-10, in the Arnaud-Carlowrie area; Mrs. Minnie Miller, 1899, in the Tolstoi area; Mrs. J. Schwartz in the Tolstoi area; Mrs. Felsky in the Tolstoi area; Mrs. Anastasia Drewniak, Mrs. Kwiatkoski were later in the Tolstoi area; Mr. Romaniuk, 1900, in the Tolstoi area; Mrs. Isaac Casson and Mrs. Theodore Strange (Davison) in the Greenridge area; Mrs. Goyman in the Woodmore area; Mrs. William Fields and Mrs. William Jack, 1878-1880's in the Ridgeville area; Mrs. Thomas Collins, 1890, in the Ridgeville area; Mrs. Abe Beckstead, 1900, in the Ridgeville area; Mrs. Cherneski was still delivering babies in the Ridgeville areas in the 1940's; Mrs. Paskarek in the Rosa area; Mrs. A. Nowalsky in the Rosa area; Mrs. K. Chubey in the Rosa area; Mrs. Paskarek, 1915, in the Stuartburn area.

Mrs. M. Nedohin was a chiropractor in the Overstoneville area helping many people over the years and practicing until she was over 80.

There was no doctor in the Dominion City or area until 1897. For three years (1879-80-81), when a C.P.R. spur line ran to the Greenridge district and a thousand workers were in the area, a doctor, employed by the C.P.R., was available most of the time and he also served the town on the side.

When home remedies didn't work and the people were desperate, a doctor was summoned from Emerson by telegraph.

In 1880 Dr. James Bedford came from the United States to Emerson.

The Municipality of Franklin has never had a hospital of its own other than a private one operated by Dr. O'Brien in Dominion City. Midwives, for many years, took care of the arrival of babies. The first doctors people of the Municipality had were in Emerson. Franklin's first doctors, Dr. Murrough O'Brien, arrived in 1897. He was assisted in 1898 by Dr. Maxwell Wallace who later set up a practice in Emerson and who also served the Municipality as a Medical Officer. Other doctors were Drs. Houston, C. V. McClelland, Robertson. There then was a period of eight years when there was no doctor in the Municipality. Dr. H. V. Waldon, of Vita, was a highly respected doctor who served many of Franklin's residents over many years. Following public meetings, it was decided to hire a Municipal doctor. These doctors were Drs. Dyck, Beaton, Friesen, Riddell and Artes. After Dr. Artes left about 1968, the Municipality has again been without a doctor.

Home remedies were the standard medical practice for most pioneer families. Young oak trees or branches were stripped of their bark. The bark was boiled until the water was dark brown. When cool, it was used mainly to heal open ulcers, wounds, wire cuts, or any other cuts and it sure healed. The bark of plum trees is good for the same thing.

Puff balls — when they are ripe (dark brown) break them open and the powder inside is good to stop heavy bleeding such as bit cuts or when de-horning cattle. Take a handful of the powder and hold it against the wound until the bleeding stops.

Rub leaves of the hare bell between hands to cure a headache.

Indians planted leafy spurge, used for medicinal purposes, on the Russell Mayne farm.

Resin weed (sticky type) which grows on alkali, was boiled down to a jelly-like substance, and used to cure prairie itch.

Pincherry was boiled and used for colds. Willow bark was boiled to obtain aspirin.

Camomile tea was a sure cure for anything that ailed you. These bitter herbs grew in the backyards and the little pods were dried and made into a tea. This tea was used to cure everything from an ulcer to ordinary depression. It was also supposed to be good for menstrual pain.

To open a blister or relieve bruises, a fresh, young plantain leaf was picked and laid over the wound with a hot compress. This usually healed the festering wound.

A medicine made by cooking herbs called "Alpenkraüter" was used even in Canada for relief of upset stomach.

People used to grow Semnia or Hemp. From the green seed they used to make (Crooplie) ether and used it as a liquid pain killer.

Some of the other remedies people used probably seem extremely unsanitary by today's standards but their effectiveness cannot be denied. When Nellie (Daneleyko) Dzioba fell into a smudge and burned herself, her grandfather plastered her with cow manure. It is said that burns plastered with cow manure left no scars. Cow manure poultices were used for chest colds, soiled flannel socks wrapped around the neck were supposed to be good for sore throats and cow urine was supposed to bring relief to sore breasts and was used for washing sore eyes.

Organizations

by Rose Fedorchuk

The first organizations in Franklin Municipality were brought from wherever the early settlers came, and transplanted very much in the image of the original. As time went on, many were eliminated, others modified to fit the society which evolved, and yet others were born here.

A large number of the anglo saxon pioneers belonged to the Orange Lodge, already established in Winnipeg among the Lord Selkirk settlers. An invitation issued to members of the Orange Lodge in Franklin Municipality for a banquet in Winnipeg for April 24, 1919, reads, in part "A reunion, Camp Fire and Old Timers' Talk and Banquet of the Red River Valley Settlers to company with the Veterans of the Fenian Raids and the congenial spirits of the Red River Expedition of 1870 and the Veterans of the Riel Rebellion will be held . . ."

The Masonic Lodge was given Dispensation to institute a lodge in Dominion City by the Grand Lodge of Manitoba on March 23, 1911, and Penza Lodge No. 120 A. F. and A. M. of Dominion City, Manitoba, was formed. The name was taken from the Canadian Pacific Railway placard placed at the driving of the last spike.

The first officers of Penza Lodge were appointed by the Grand Master; Wor. Master Gilbert E. Cambell, Senior Warden Charles L. Maynes, Jun. Warden Lawrence D. Smith. These officers and the following appointed officers were installed by R. W. Bro. D. McLean D.D.G.M. of District #1 Winnipeg. Treas. Alexander S. Calder, Sec. Alexander S. Little. Inner Guard. Robert W. Dunlop. Tyler, Thomas Coulter. Several members of Emerson No. 6 were present. The first death of a Charter Member occurred in 1916, when Bro. Thomas Coulter was buried with Full Masonic Rites in Dominion City in October of that year.

In 1921 they obtained their National Flag, that same year attended an international meeting at the Pembina Lodge No. 2 where they were presented with an American Flag. Our first meeting place was a room above A. S. Little store. In 1926 they purchased the old Methodist Church and converted it into a Lodge room. The first meeting was held May 26. The Lodge continued to meet in this building until 1956, when the present building was erected.

Donations were made to the Peace Gardens Project, Eye Scanner which is installed in the Health Science Centre, Masonic Temple Winnipeg and numerous charities. We are proud of our history, and most of all the good Fellowship which has taken place among the 177 members we have received into the Craft.

The following are Past Masters of Penza Lodge No. 120: G. E. Campbell —1911-12; C. L. Maynes - 1913-21; A. S. Little - 1914-20; A. S. Calder - 1915-22; F. E. Graham - 1916; H. Lawson - 1917; Jno. R. Witty - 1918; V. Shoulte - 1919; C. V. McLelland - 1923-24; K. A. McDonald - 1925; G. D. Robertson - 1926; W. W. Casson - 1927-46-74; W. T. McLelland - 1928; J. A. McVicar; Sr. - 1929; C. E. F. Fry - 1930; C. D. Gaynor - 1931; A. G. Froom - 1932; H. W. Davison - 1933-36-48; D. Ditlovich - 1934; N. G. Baskerville - 1935; Don McVicar - 1937-38; H. Spence - 1939-49-47; Len Andrews - 1941-1942; E. Snead - 1943-44; E. Collins - 1945; R. W. Witty - 1949; W. J. Smart - 1950; B. W. Witherspoon - 1951; M. H. Smith - 1952-65; W. L. Lindsay - 1953-68; F. Casper - 1954; J. P. Bingham - 1955; R. C. Oatway - 1956-69; D. B. Sutherland - 1957; T. Steg - 1958-70-75; H. T. Kelly - 1959; C. A. Cameron - 1960-68-69; M. Lochhead - 1961-67; L. Ramsey - 1962-66; R. B. Dickson - 1963-64; W. Bonkowski - 1971; J. C. Casson - 1972-77; C. C. Hunter - 1973-81-82; Wm. Schreuder - 1976; W. Schnell - 1980.

INDEPENDENT ORDER OF FORESTERS

On August 1st, 1894 a meeting was held in the school at Green Ridge for the purpose of starting the Independent Order of Foresters. W. F. Waddell was Chairman and Dr. Bedford examined those present and instructed them in the Order. Present were Fred Post, Dr. Bedford, Wm. Oatway, John Knox, W. J. Spence, J. Oatway, Isaac Casson, Charles Burrell, Robert Gunn, James Hunter and John F. Gunn. Every meeting brought in new members until every man in Green Ridge was a member, Wm. Gunn at the second meeting and George Ball, James Brown and Andrew Davison on August 15. By the third meeting they had need of a scribbling book and three lamps and coal oil. By December they decided to have a "Poverty Social" January 1st, 1895. At the next meeting they decided to hold it at the Town Hall in Dominion City and to buy 10 pounds of sugar and two pounds of tea. After all the work and planning they rented the hall for $3.50, a curtain for twenty-five cents, sugar thirty cents, tape ten cents, and a medal for thirty-five cents. They took in $39.78.

The following are excerpts from the first minute book, which tell a great deal about the Foresters and the community:

A concert with Reverand McHaffie delivering a lecture was held in the church, and netted $30.00.

Dr. Bedford died, and the Order contacted Dr. Patterson in Winnipeg to help them secure another doctor.

Nails were secured for the hall, to shingle the roof. Two kegs of four inch cut, two kegs of three inch cut, one keg two and a half inch cut, and one keg of five inch wire spikes were bought. At a meeting on May 30 it was decided to erect the hall on June 18. By June 15 they had decided against a picnic and to build the hall on June 24 and 25. They did hold the picnic, and took in $59.85 at tables, and $96.61 at the lemonade stand, but paid out $73.85 for expenses, ending with $32.00 clear.

By September 21 the frame and the rough siding on the hall was completed, and the members posed for their picture. They ordered a door, windows, paper, siding and flooring from W. Morkill, and paid Carlton for his lumber.

On November 14, 1896 they were planning a December concert, at which the Jackson Harby troop from Winnipeg played. The Foresters cleared $11.85 after paying $1.00 for church rent and fuel.

The Methodist Church asked for the hall to serve their first Thanksgiving dinner.

On October 14, 1897 Mr. J. R. Clark was asked to come and give a lecture. He was paid $15.00 and they made $7.65. On November 29, 1897 they were planning a "Bee" and were hiring a carpenter. They were also planning a Ball for New Years and charge $1.00 a couple. Their bank was changed from Molsons to the Bank of Ottawa. In December they reported receiving $100.00 from picnic. In January they planned a public installation of officers and each member was to bring a basket. January 31, 1898 they bought wood for

$2.00 and the hall was officially received from the building committee. A fee of $2.00 was to be rent and all damages to be paid by renter. They planned a stable, with each member bringing two posts, but the idea was squashed. A gramophone was mentioned from R. Oatway for a dollar. April 25, 1898 condolences were given to R. McLelland (Death of Wife). The final report of building committee was given by J. Dickson and a church parade was planned for June.

They decided to paint the hall, using first coat of yellow ochre and second white lead. A porch the size of a platform was planned (kitchen). Painting "bee" to be Monday July 4. The Presbyterians asked for the hall for a picnic. The paint for the hall cost $8.75, bought from George Agnew. They had not yet got the "bee" going on July 9th, so planned for July 18 and also to get lumber for door frames. By July 25 they decided to hire T. Varey to paint the hall. He charged $8.00. Another bill from Agnew for oil and lead for $2.15 and from Presbyterian church for oil and shingles $6.00. Morkill was paid $16.75 for lumber and insurance was $1.80.

A concert for December 30 was planned and December 31st they reported $25.25 from concert and donated $3.00 to finish church stable.

They bought $1.85 lumber and coal oil and pen and ink as well as a frame and glass costing $3.00 for their charter.

On March 27, 1899 the deed to the Hall was reported in bad shape.

In May, 1897, a picnic was being planned, and the Foresters were busy getting workers for the lemonade stand and to help with sports. Adults were charged 25 cents and children fifteen cents admission. Emerson, St. Vincent and Dominion City were invited. The ham for the picnic cost $4.84 on July 3rd. The building fund paid Morkill $190.00. Three brass lamps and three bracket lamps were bought for the hall, and 12 common chairs and two arm chairs were also proposed, but the idea was turned down. Another $125.00 was paid on the hall debt, and the hall was insured at two-thirds its value. (In 1982 this hall stands with chairs and stove as was).

Dr. O'Brien had come to Dominion City by August 16, 1897, and the Foresters asked him to be their examining doctor.

On April 11, 1899, the topic of the meeting was the fact that William Leak had been shot, and his funeral. The Foresters were to have charge of the funeral. They purchased crepe for the Foresters and Mrs. Leak, and made 40 crepe bows and seven sashes. By May they were paying Mrs Leak $50.00 mortuary benefit.

Dr. O'Brien charged $14.00 for services and

joined the lodge in May, 1899. At this meeting another picnic was being planned and on June 19, John Knox was paid $4.50 for stove wood. On June 25 they reported making $86.81 at the picnic, to be applied to the hall debt. On July 31, the final bill for the hall, of $17.20 was paid. Money raised by a special collection was sent to the Winnipeg General Hospital.

In October the Foresters had a "bee" to plow for Charles Foulds.

Dr. O'Brien asked for a special meeting on November 13, 1899, and proposed forming an entertainment club to hold monthly concerts during the winter months. Nothing was decided, except to have another special meeting, this one open to the public.

On March 26, 1900, a communication was read from the Supreme Court of Foresters asking for funds for soldiers in the Boer War in Africa. By June the following had joined the Foresters - George Strange, R. Post, Ridley Post, Sam Foulks and Joe Casson.

At this meeting money was designated to the victims of the Hull and Ottawa fires.

William Walter Weedmark joined the Foresters in December, 1900.

C. Woolard had gone to fight in the Boer War in Africa, and was wounded. He claimed sick benefits from the Foresters. Condolences were offered to the Royal family, and this meeting closed with "God Save The King".

A reception was planned for C. Woolard on March 25, 1901, but was put off until May, when he would be able to attend and tell of his participation in the African War.

There was no picnic in 1901, but a church parade was planned. The first minute book closes with a note that a window was put into the antiroom, a lock on the door, and latches on the windows, the stove pipes were moved down by means of rods, and the hall foundation was banked.

The Foresters continued until October 5, 1953, when attendance was down to eight members. These were Ross Oatway, Wallace Casson, Elsworth Post, James Casson, Clark Hunter, Theo Strange, Henry Casson and Nelson Casson. These members moved a motion to transfer the hall to the community club, and a meeting was set for October 15, 1953, for the purpose of officially transferring the hall and establishing the community club.

PATRONS OF INDUSTRY

A local farmers' organization, The Patrons of Industry was formed in the Woodmore district in 1892. The original members were: J. Dickson,

Wm. Kirkpatrick, Wilbur Hurd, Ellery Post, Wm. Dickson, Henry Young, Orlin Post, Peter McLaren, J. Spence, Duncan McLaren, Albert Hamblin, Francis Pott, J. Kirkpatrick, T. H. Scott and Isaac Casson.

The organization was formed to promote better farming methods and social welfare of the community. A meeting on November 20, 1894 discussed the need for a hall a size of 20 feet by 30 feet. Wilbur Hurd and Isaac Casson volunteered to cut tamarack logs. Other members agreed to haul them home, a distance of 30 miles.

The hall still stands today, neglected, weatherbeaten and worn, a reminder of a pioneer past. For 63 years it served its community well as a meeting house, a centre for socials, dances and a church. Two schools beside it have gone and now a newer community centre stands across the road. The old hall looks on, as rugged as the forefathers that built it.

THE UKRAINIAN WOMEN'S ASSOCIATION OF ST. OLGA OF TOLSTOI

The U.W.A. of Tolstoi is a branch of the U.W.A. of Canada. It took the name "St. Olga". She was the Princess of Kiev of Ukraine. The Tolstoi Ukrainian Women's Club is affiliated with the U.W.A. of Canada. At the present time, the National Executives and offices are in Edmonton, Alberta and the Provincial Executives are in Winnipeg. The branch adopted the constitution and the by-laws of the said Association of Canada. This Association was the first independent Ukrainian Women's organization in Canada. It was a remarkable achievement unfolded amid a multitude of hardships, but grew to an organization of national importance and recognition, contributing to the growth of each community.

The National Group was formed in 1926 and in 1928 a group of Tolstoi Ukrainian Orthodox women became interested in the organization, held meetings and in October of 1928 held a meeting in the Ukrainian National Home (a hall) to elect their first committee. The minister's wife, Maria Hrycyna was the first president. Others in the committee were Pearl Kosowan (Arseny); Theresa Melenick (Nazarevitch); Mary Woroniuk; Olga Dolynchuk (Popiel). Members who joined the first few years were Katherine Kostyniuk, Sophia Tkach, Domka Podolsky, Anna Tesarsky, Natalie Shydlowsky, Mary Nazarevitch, Anna Kozlowsky, Annie Sereda, Katherine Kowalchuk, Mary Peleshok, S. Kaluska, A. Kosowan, A. Lozowy, A. Kranyk, D. Yarmie, A. Zuliak, I. Dolynchuk, A. Fostey, D. Kosowan, B. Kalushka, A. Fetor, A. Slobodian, Justine Olinyk, A. Weleshun, H. Nazarevitch, D.

Romaniuk, A. Yarmie, M. Romaniuk, M. Skorochid, Mary Tkach, M. Drewniak, I. Dykun, M. Tofan, M. Yaremie, N. Podolsky, M. Dutka, J. Zulkowsky, T. Kucian, A.Kassian, M. Horbul, N. Dolynchuk, L. Antonishka, M. Kwasnitski. Past Presidents were M. Hrycyna, K. Kostyniuk, M. Nazarevitch, A. Majowska, I. Melenick, D. Apaniuk, O. Dolynchuk, M. Berizetsky, A. Shydlowsky, M. Ulyian, M. Woroniuk, A. Tetor, C. Dolynchuk, D. Olinyk, P. Kosowan, T. Kwasnitski, J. Stepanenko and now N. Bially.

Members act as teachers of religion, as well as the Ukrainian language, held theatrical productions, honouring renowned authors and poets, and commemorating events such as Christmas and Mothers Day with concerts.

The birth of a united approach to the problem of creating valid cultural patterns in a new land brought out the rural women, who toiled in the fields with their husbands, separated by long distance from their neighbors and from centres of cultural activity, isolated, groping for individuality, for understanding of their role in making the vast prairie their home gave them the incentive to work in their organization and attain their identity. This brought them out of their homes, gave them a feeling that they were part of a greater purpose and assimilate with other nationalities and be a part in the building of Canada. By learning, working, co-operating, this was achieved. They began to sense that their dress, their customs and traditions, their religion and their language, all that set them apart from their neighbours was an integral part of a beautiful, unique, cultural heritage. Feelings of insecurity and inferiority were gradually supplanted by confidence in themselves. The organization beckoned them to preserve and embellish their ancestral achievements and to transmit them to their children. Through the U.W.A. of Canada, these wives and mothers found themselves by giving their services to a cause that endorsed them with a feeling of belonging to a nation and an enduring sense of mission.

In 1975, another 13 members received life memberships, namely, Claudia (Dolynchuk) Eliuk, Annie Shydlowsky, Mary Arseny, Anastasia Tanchak, Mary Nazarevitch, Pauline Donaleyko, Mary Bachynsky, Teenie Fostey, Effie Matichuk, E. Kolodzinsky, M. Stefiuk, Anne Solomon, Nettie Holodryga. The committee today is: Past-President - Teenie Kwasnitski; President - Nancy Bially; Vice-President - Claudia Eliuk; Secretary - Mary Matichuk; Financial Secretary - Kay Arseny; Treasurer - Joyce Stepanenko.

The Rosa branch was found in April 1928. The first committee were: President - Mrs. Mary Tanchak; Vice-President - Mrs. K. Chubey, Treasurer - Mrs. Lena Kohut; Recording Secretary - Miss Pauline Braschuk; Financial Secretary - Mrs. Barbara Tanchak; Controllers - Mrs. Sophia Holodryga and Miss Mary Ewanchuk. There were fifteen members listed. Past Presidents are: Mary Tanchak - 10 years; Anne Baron - 25 years; Mary Paley - 7 years; Mary Chubey - 5 years; Susie Chubey - 7 years.

The 1982 executive is: President - Mrs. Susie Chubey; Vice-President - Mrs. Mary Chubey; Recording Secretary - Mrs. Gloria Smoliak; Corresponding Secretary - Mrs. Anne Baron; Treasurer - Mrs. Marilyn Chubey; Controllers - Mrs. Lily Canek and Mrs. Shirley Chubey.

The Holy Rosary Society was formed in Tolstoi in 1915 by Mrs. Pauline Kwiatkowski. The present executive are Mrs. John Wnuk and Mrs. Metro Manzie.

Former group leaders were Mrs. Anna Majewski, Mrs. Helen Goletski, Mrs. Helen Grabowski and Mrs. Frances Grabowiecki.

THE TOLSTOI UKRAINIAN CATHOLIC WOMEN'S LEAGUE

The Tolstoi Ukrainian Catholic Women's League was organized on November 25, 1964. The organizational meeting was held at the home of Mr. and Mrs. Jack Bially at Tolstoi.

Fr. M. Dawydko, the parish priest, was influential in this league's formation. The first slate of officers were: President - Mrs. Lily Kozak; Vice-President - Mrs. Helen Bially, Secretary - Mrs. Hazel Hoplock; Treasurer - Mrs. Margaret Hanischuk; Social Committee - Mrs. Helen Bially, Mrs. Mary Kozak, Mrs. Margaret Kasian; Auditors - Mrs. Eva Bially, Mrs. Elsie Kolodzinski.

The league's aim is to develop and enrich the religious and spiritual life of each member and the parish.

UKRAINIAN CATHOLIC WOMEN'S LEAGUE OF CANADA (U.C.W.L.C.)

The Ukrainian Catholic Women's League of Canada Rosa Branch, was formed on March 13, 1963 with the helpful guidance of parish priest Rev. Ewhen Olinek and two organizational members from Winnipeg namely Mrs. P. Darewych and Mrs. Juba (mother of former Winnipeg mayor Stephen Juba).

As only seven ladies were present at this first meeting only a partial committee was named. First president was Elsie Budey, vice-president was Jennie Mihaychuk, secretary was Pauline Ewonchuk, treasurer was Anna Paley, convenors were Anne

Salamacha, Anne Chubaty and Doris Tkachuk. On February 4, 1964, two auditors, Margaret Paley and Theresa Zaporozan completed the committee. Holding office as Presidents were: Elsie Budey - 1963-65, 1969-71, 1973-74; Anne Chubaty - 1966-68, 1979-82, Pauline Ewonchuk - 1972, Jennie Mihaychuk - 1975-78. The spiritual leader of the organization is the parish priest. The league presently consists of 29 members.

The Ukrainian Catholic Women's League of Canada (U.C.W.L.C.) established in Winnipeg in 1944 by uniting different regional and local women's organizations, is affiliated with the Women's council of the Ukrainian Canadian Committee since 1944, the World Federation of the Ukrainian Women's Organization since 1952, the World Union of Catholic Women's Organization since 1957, the World Congress of Free Ukrainians since 1975. Their fundamental aims are:

1) To develop and enrich religious and spiritual life of each member and each parish, thereby strengthening the Ukrainian Catholic Church in Canada.

2) To preserve and develop Ukrainian culture in Canada.

3) To become fully aware to the needs of family, community, and country. To strengthen the spiritual dimensions and moral values of Canadian life. To initiate and support social development programs to exemplify Christian ideals of social justice and love, particularly those related to the dignity of human beings and the sacredness of the

4) To initiate and support programs of charitable actions.

The local branch is supportive of the objectives of the National U.C.W.L.C. and in addition assist financially the Ukrainian National Home, the Catholic Church, youth clubs, catechism classes, Ukrainian Dance Clubs and other religious and cultural needs.

THE INDEPENDENT ORDER OF ODD FELLOWS

The Independent order of Odd Fellows is a benevolent organization, and was organized in Dominion City c. 1921. A gentleman by the name of Treleaven was the original organizer. Meetings were held in the upstairs of the old municipal hall.

The main object of Odd Fellows is to help their fellow man. Before medicare, members in need of assistance during illness would receive help, and there exists an impressive funeral rite which is used when a lodge member is buried. A senior care home in Winnipeg is supported by all Odd Fellows.

The Dominion City Lodge dissolved somewhere in the 1950's, due to the lack of membership. Some members joined the neighbouring lodge communities, and others pay their dues to the head lodge in Winnipeg.

GREENRIDGE INDEPENDENT ORDER OF GOOD TEMPLERS LODGE NO. 69

On March 28, 1893, Mr. and Mrs. J. W. Vaughan conducted a series of Gospel temperance meetings in the Presbyterian Church and 150 people signed the pledge of total abstinence. The Lodge was begun with 49 charter members, with meetings every Friday evening. The trustees were Isaac Casson, George Addison and James Hunter. This was an organization taking in the young people as well as women. The church received $2.00 an evening rent, and members were charged 25 cents men, 15 cents women, for attending.

A literary program was planned for each meeting. Nettie Oatway, Maggie Dickson, D. Black and Thomas Spence were among the early planners.

The first big project for the Green Ridge Templers was when the Dominion City Templers asked them to help close down the liquor licence in the Dominion City Hotel. They succeeded in closing the hotel for four years.

It appears that the meetings were held with the purpose of furthering intellectual debate among members, and essays, dialogue, speeches, recitations, songs, readings, instrumentals and lectures were the order of the day. On November 8, 1894, Reverend Elliot had married, and the debate was "resolved that the life of an old maid is happier than that of an old bachelor."

The community was torn in two by the Templers, with the drinkers on one side and the non drinkers on the other. There is an undated meeting, probably December 2, 1896, when the property of the Templers was disposed of and the organization folded. Isaac Casson, James Dickson, Fred Post, A. C. Hunter, G. Addison, Mrs. T. Spence, Rod McLennan and W. Hurd are mentioned in these minutes.

THE ORDER OF THE EASTERN STAR

Late in 1950 Mrs. Myrtle Witherspoon and Mrs. Sally Bingham began to make plans to form a chapter of Order of the Eastern Star. January 29, 1951 an organization meeting was held in the Masonic Temple, with some Grand Chapter Officers from Winnipeg, to explain the fundamentals of the Order. March 3, 1951 Dominion City Chapter #50 was instituted, with 34 charter members by Selkirk Chapter #35.

There are 19 surviving charter members at present.

The Order is a benevolent organization, which contributes to Cancer Research, Heart Fund, Arthritis and Rheumatism, Diabetic Society and Estarl, which is an Eastern Star training Awards for Religious Learning. A church service is an annual event. Meetings are held the 2nd Thursday of each month, except in July and August, in the Masonic Temple.

THE GREEN RIDGE PIONEER COMMUNITY CLUB

A meeting was held in the Independent Order of Foresters' hall November 5, 1953 for the purpose of transferring the hall over to a community club. The three trustees of the Independent Order of Foresters' hall were retained as trustees, being Elsworth Post, Ross Oatway and Nelson Casson. Mac Smith and John Palmer were trustees added, with Theo Strange as Secretary and Mac Smith as Chairman. The by-laws of the Foresters were to be followed in the running of the hall. The fees were set at $8.00 for residents and $12.00 for non-residents.

In September of 1954 the title was transferred.

In March of 1954 they found they had to have more directors to comply with The Companies Act, so Henry Alstadt, Alfie Spence, Jean Hunter, Elmer Kirkpatrick and Mathew Graydon were added. There were now twenty-one members, paying $1.00 annual dues.

In 1955 they were getting wood for heating the hall from Mac Smith and Elesworth Post. The members began worrying about the condition of the hall, mainly the plaster, and in 1958 when Nelson Casson was president, they decided to line the hall with Buffalo Board and check the wiring in the kitchen.

In 1959 John Palmer was President and other improvements were made. The foundation was extended to accommodate toilet facilities and wood storage.

Dances and concerts were held to pay for the repairs, as well as collections throughout the community. The kitchen was modernized but the old wood stove still heats the hall.

The hall is now used for 4-H parties, Women's Institute meetings, elections, special meetings, card parties, family and church affairs, as well as a place to serve lunches after funerals. President - 1954-1980 - Elesworth Post; 1980-present - Reinhold Steinke. Secretary - 1953-1980 - Theo Strange; 1980-present - Doug Gunn.

THE CANADIAN RED CROSS

The Canadian Red Cross has been a presence in the Municipality of Franklin for many years. During the first world war a group of women got together to pack boxes of food and knitted scarves, socks, and so on to send to veterans, through the Red Cross. This was repeated during the second world war.

A volunteer door to door campaign to collect money for the Red Cross used to be held, before the United Way came in, and the funds were used to supply blood to hospitals, buy sickroom equipment such as wheelchairs, crutches, public health services, water safety and swimming lessons, Tracing and Reunion services for war refugees. These funds also supplied arts and crafts to veterans in hospitals, and helped in times of floods, tornadoes and other disasters, both at home and abroad.

From 1951 to 1955 the Red Cross, in cooperation with the Women's Institute, organized swimming lessons for adults and children in the Roseau River. The Canadian Legion built an outdoor swimming pool in Dominion City in 1956, and the Legion Auxiliary took over the responsibility of organizing the Red Cross swimming program from 1956 to 1978. In 1978 the Elks took over the swimming pool, and the Mom's Club now supervises the swimming lessons.

The Red Cross has also been responsible for blood donor clinics in the municipality.

DOMINION CITY COMMUNITY CLUB

A meeting was held in the town hall on January 31, 1944, for the purpose of forming a Community Club. The first executive was L. O. Baskerville as president, Herb Gibson as vice-president and Joseph McCracken as secretary-treasurer. Their aim was to provide community activities and to work towards the building of a community hall.

In 1946, the first community hall was the old, renovated, municipal hall. Building plans for the new hall began in 1949 and by July 21, 1950, K. Peters officially opened the hall at the ribbon cutting ceremony.

Over the years the club operated the rink and hall, and sponsored carnivals, quiz teams, telephone whists, dances, field days, sport days, fairs, fowl suppers, horse-shoe tournaments, bingos and much more. The club is presently working towards an addition for the Community Hall.

THE TOLSTOI DISTRICT
COMMUNITY CENTRE

The Tolstoi District Community Centre was begun as a Centennial Committee in 1967. Mike Bially served as president for 1967 and 1968 and Elsie Kolodzinski as secretary for both years.

In June a Centennial parade was held in town, and a pioneer dinner. Over 2,000 people attended.

In 1968 the Centennial Centre purchased the Tolstoi School and property.

George Chobotar became president in 1969 and Elsie Kolodzinski remained secretary for 1969 and 1970. George Chobotar held office in 1970 also. For the 1982 term, John Drewniak is president with Janet Tkachuk as secretary.

The centre has provided the district with an Annual Beer Garden since it first organized. The day begins with soft ball games in the morning. Perogies are served at noon, and a barbeque and confectionary stand is available all day.

The community centre is used for small parties and family gatherings.

DOMINION CITY AND DISTRICT
HORTICULTURAL SOCIETY

The Society was formed December 4, 1956 when Mrs. M. Shelby asked our local Agricultural Representative, Mr. John Negrych, to call a meeting of interested persons. We became a committee of 53 members under the local Agricultural Society and so remained until 1958 when we became a Society. Our membership has continued to grow through the years. The local Agricultural Society and local businesses donated $250.00 with which we were able to carry on for the first three years. Mr. Thom, our local school Inspector, was the first President with Mrs. Garnet Kyle as Secretary-Treasurer and a slate of directors from St. Elizabeth, Letellier, Dominion City, Arnaud, Green Ridge, Carlowrie, Ridgeville, Friedensthal and Emerson. We had three different telephone exchanges, winter roads and muddy spring roads to compound our problems. Our first group of directors established the format we still follow. We try to have directors' meetings quite often to thrash out business to be presented at regular meetings. Each director is responsible for certain jobs, such as raising money, setting up shows, collections of money, prize lists, displays, publicity, show entries, group projects and procuring and distributing plant material. Members who have held offices through the years include: Mr. Don Thom, Mrs. Cec. Kyle, Miss Edith Thompson, Mrs. Eleanor Palmer, Mrs. Evelyn Hopkins, Mrs. Lil Kreitz, Mrs. Iona Schultz, Mrs. Jean Pow, Mrs. Lorraine Seward, Mrs. Beatrice Schewe, Mrs. Bertha Walters, Mrs. Martha Schwark and Mr. Walter Remus.

A project to beautify our towns was begun and many donated trees which have been planted throughout our district in the past few years. Our society has taken trips to various places to gain knowledge, admire the work of other people and to obtain material. Some members have taken in exhibition school and judges school and we now have Mrs. Shelby, Mrs. Kreitz, Mrs. Schwark, Mrs. Hopkins and Mrs. Gunn who can act as judges at other shows. We hold Slide Competitions and Home Ground Competitions each year as well as Scrap Book and Essay Competitions for the younger set. We have donated to the International Peace Garden, Skinner Memorial Fund, Stevenson Memorial Fund, Harp Retirement Fund and a Horticulture Bursary Fund. Our landscaping of Franklin Manor and Emerson South Haven still goes on. Tolstoi has also joined us with 5 members. For our Manitoba Centennial year, we planned a new project of an Arts and Craft Exhibition. We have also been honored by having our founder, Mrs. M. Shelby, become a M.H.A. Director. Many fine orchards and gardens can be found in the area which members usually find time during the summer to visit. Mrs. M. Shelby, Arnaud, Mrs. F. Kreitz, Letellier, Mrs. C. Penner, Carlowrie, and Mrs. Rose Fedorchuk, Tolstoi, have especially fine rural home grounds. Mrs. Lewthwaite, Emerson, Mrs. R. Ginn, Dominion City, Mr. Thom, Dominion City, Mrs. Wm. Schultz, Ridgeville and Mr. W. Remus, Emerson, have lovely urban home grounds.

Ceramics was taught so members could make their own plant containers.

Trips were made to secure driftwood after the members became interested in dried arrangements. We also go blueberry picking when they are available.

In 1982 Edith Thompson is President, Anne Penner is Secretary and Bertha Walters is Treasurer.

WOMEN'S INSTITUTES

The person responsible for the origin of the Arnaud Women's Institute was Mrs. George Hollingsworth, formerly of Indiana, who came to the elevator town of Arnaud in 1907. Mrs. Hollingsworth didn't have a chance to meet many of the Women so she decided to try to get them together.

On Monday, May 31, 1915 the Extension Service invited the ladies of Arnaud vicinity to meet Mrs. Crawford at a meeting to be held in the Arnaud Church for the purpose of seeing a demonstration. Miss Crawford gave a talk on "Home Economics Society". She asked the ladies what they thought about organizing such a society at Arnaud and meeting once a month. Twelve ladies gave their names and Mrs. Hollingsworth was elected president, Miss Annie Lang vice-president, and Mrs. Jim Treleaven secretary-treasurer. They planned to hold a meeting on June 8, 1915.

There was no meeting on June 8, owing to bad roads, but a week later the ladies met in Hollingsworth's store and made plans to hold their first regular meeting on July 8, 1915.

Miss Rose Comber was appointed as convenor of social affairs and Mrs. Wm. Wilson as program convenor.

Thus, in July 1915, the Arnaud Home Economics Society was organized with the following charter members — Miss Annie Lang, Mrs. Wm. Wilson, Mrs. Jas. Treleaven, Mrs. Geo. Hollingsworth, Mrs. A. Linklater, Miss Rose Comber (Mrs. Earl Thompson), Mrs. A. Rollin, Mrs. Chas. Thompson, Mrs. Roy Erb, Mrs. Eva Noble, Mrs. J. T. Noble, Mrs. R. F. Erb, Mrs. A. Thompson, Mrs. M. Graydon, Miss Ella Rourke, Miss Katie McKennon (Mrs. Ed. Stuart), Miss Minnie Stewart (Mrs. Lamb), Mrs. John King, Miss Sarah Calder. Our charter is Number 25.

Mrs. Hollingsworth was their president for five years and at the end of that time had 74 members.

At this time, the First World War (1914-1918) was on, and the ladies turned their attention to ways and means of raising money for war work. One idea was doing baking and selling it to bachelors. Boxes were sent to the boys overseas regularly.

Topics on the program in the early years included such subjects as Winter Management of Laying Hens, Settlers of the Early Days, Propagating Plants, Taking the Drudgery out of Housecleaning and Lotions to Enhance your Beauty. Demonstrations included Crochet Stitches, Homemade Candy, Simple Dishes Prepared with a Fireless Cooker, Making Patchwork Quilts, Butter Making and Refooting Stockings.

Presidents to 1926 included Mrs. Hollingsworth, Mrs. McCrystal, Mrs. Hamilton, Mrs. Wilson and Mrs. Andrews.

On the Twenty-fifth anniversary of the Arnaud Women's Institute, Mrs. Sarah (McDougall) Wilson was presented with a life membership by the Institute she had served so well.

During the war years, 1937-1945, War Saving Certificates were purchased regularly, boxes were packed for overseas, wool was purchased for knitting socks to include in the boxes and Red Cross

sewing was done.

Welfare work has always been a highlight of all Women's Institutes. During the war years it was Bundles for Britain and British Children's War Service Fund, also the Blind Institute, Children's Aid, Retarded Children's Fund, Peace Garden support, March of Dimes and local hospitals. When the extreme northerly Women's Institutes were first organized, monetary aid was given.

Names of those entered in the Book of Remembrance are as follows: Mrs. Kathleen Andrews, Mrs. Rene Wilson, Mrs. Elizabeth McVicar, Mrs. Annie McCelland, Mrs. Jane Shelby, Mrs. Violet Shelby, Mrs. Barbra Calder, Mrs. Mary Boutet and Mrs. Josephine King.

Life memberships given since 1965 include Mrs. Mabel Dearborn, Mrs. Lillian Gainer, Mrs. Dorothy Shelby, Mrs. Irene Calder, Mrs. Effie Calder and Mrs. Christine Nichols.

The Arnaud Women's Institute now consists of eighteen members, with Mrs. Helen Dyck as President and Mrs. Eleanor Bergen as Secretary.

In the words of Mrs. Christine Nichols, "The Women's Institutes in general have given our rural women a progressive outlook, a sense of their responsibility, a better interest in their province, and a realization that on them, the homemakers on the nation depend. The Women's Institute has been a great spiritual force for making not only better homes, but a brighter and happier world".

In Woodmore the first ladies' organization was called the "LOLILA'S", meaning love, live and laugh. It was started in 1934 by Mrs. F. Snead and Miss Ellen Francis. Their first meeting was held at the home of Mrs. F. Batten. The members of the newly formed club were Millie and Clara Badgley, Gladys Snead, Marguerite Mayne, Maggie and Emma Smith, Annie Batten, Lily Froom, Lena Snead and Ellen Francis. Some of their activities included making quilts, packing boxes to send overseas and Red Cross sewing. They held several raffles with prizes donated by local residents. They also sponsored picnics and dances; with proceeds they built a kitchen onto the old hall.

The LOLILA'S lasted for eleven years but when the membership began to fail and interest waned two of the members namely Mrs. G. Snead and Mrs. E. Post turned to the Green Ridge Womens' Institute which had previously been organized. They attended several of their meetings and were greatly interested in the work done there. They asked Mrs. Hector Spence to come to Woodmore and give them a general idea of the workings of the W.I. Mrs. Spence graciously accepted and on November 22, 1945 she attended a meeting here and helped organize the first Women's Institute in the Woodmore Area.

The meeting was held at the home of Mrs. E. Johnston and by a ballot vote the following officers were elected: Mrs. C. Ward - president, Mrs. E. Snead - first vice-president, Mrs. G. Post - second vice-president, Mrs. R. Mayne - secretary, Mrs. E. Johnston - treasurer and Mrs. W. Palmer and Mrs. Tom Pott were auditors.

The Dominion City Women's Institute began as a Home Economics group in June, 1915, and were named Women's Institute in October, 1922. When first formed they belonged to the Morris district.

In 1941 the Southern District was formed at Vita. Mrs. Waldon was the first president, Mrs. Roy Whitman of Ridgeville was secretary-treasurer. The first convention was held in the United Church at Dominion City in 1942.

The W.I. helped organize the Roseau Music and Arts Festival in 1940, and carried this for many years. They have been active and supportive in many areas of community life benefitting the entire municipality, with members carrying out the directive of the Institute motto to be of service to mankind.

Tolstoi Women's Institute also had an Institute organized in May of 1961 with over 30 members. In 1967 they planted shrubs at churches, community centre and customs. They have donated to charitable organizations and sponsored courses on drivers safety, home nursing, hairdressing, wok cooking, interior design and tailoring.

Presidents have been Bernice Chobotar, Doris Olynyk, Jean Germain, Judy Tinkess and Rose Fedorchuk. Secretaries have been Rose Fedorchuk, Ruth Kozak, Pauline Goetz, Pauline Hartig, Frances Pamula and Bernice Chobotar.

Dated September 21, 1935, the minutes of the first meeting of the Green Ridge Women's Institute read "Nineteen ladies met in the Green Ridge school with the object of organizing a Women's Institute in our district". Mrs. Dave Spence called the meeting to order.

Mrs. Root, from Emerson, the district president at the time, was present. The officers elected that day were: Mrs. Gordon Kirkpatrick - President, Mrs. Dave Spence - first Vice-President; Mrs. Clarke Hunter - second Vice-President; Miss Alice Hunter - Secretary and Miss Mary Casson - Treasurer.

Members dues were 25 cents and 10 cents for lunch money each meeting. Meetings were held in the school the second Saturday of each month, and there were 35 members.

Programs varied, for example - they planned a whist drive and dance, donated $1.00 for prizes for whist and $3.00 for music for the dance.

A talk on some aspect of health was given at each meeting. Hot chocolate was served to school children every noon during the winter months.

Handicrafts and home and family oriented courses were held for the members. In the early days it was understood that the hostess must insure there was a pail of water and a supply of wood ready for the stove for each meeting. It was a major decision when a large pot to heat water in and a dipper was bought.

In the early years the responsibility for caring for the local cemetery was taken on. A Caretaker was hired for $25.00 a year.

A dental clinic was organized in the Green Ridge school with help from the board. Each child was asked to bring 25 cents towards the cost.

The Women's Institute sponsored the Music and Speech Arts festival work with the help of the teachers. It was felt it was important for each child to take part and an elimination contest was held in the district, with winners going to the nearest festival.

On October 18, 1939, 23 women from Ridgeville and surrounding district met to organize Ridgeville's first Women's Institute. Mrs. S. R. Root of Emerson presided.

The first president was Mrs. Ray Empey, first vice-president was Mrs. Roy Post, second vice - president was Miss Annie Collins, secretary - Mrs. Roy Whitman and treasurer Mrs. Ezra Post.

Meetings were held the second Wednesday of each month. At the present, they are still held at that time. Most meetings were held at the home of Mrs. E. Eichman. She was given 35 cents for the use of her home. Later, meetings took place at the Ridgeville Curling Club Room and now are held at members' homes.

In the early 1940's our W.I. concerned itself with projects related to war work. Much sewing, knitting and quilting was done regularly for the Red Cross. Used clothing was collected and sent to Britain. Boxes of homebaking, socks etc. were sent to our local boys overseas.

Whist drives were a popular way of raising money during the first years, also pie socials, rummage sales, hobo teas, variety programs and shadow socials. Today means of raising money are catering to banquets, sales and business meetings.

Our present membership is 17. The following are the executive for 1982: President - Iris Wachna; Vice-President - Lee Chubaty; Secretary - Louise Lenton; Treasurer - Mildred Weiss; Board member - Louise Lenton.

We work, learn, laugh together, care and share

always working for the main objective Home and Country.

DOMINION CITY MOM'S CLUB

On April 17, 1979 a group of Dominion City area women met to form the Dominion City Mom's Club. Their purpose was to organize activities and offer opportunities for the children in the area. In the following three years they organized the following projects - Summer '79 Park Crafts and Recreation Program, bus trip to Rainbow Stage (Winnipeg), disco dancing lessons, Manitoba Puppet Theatre presentation, two Actors' Showcase presentations, movies, Red Cross Babysitting course, bus trip to a Raffi concert (Winnipeg), a Diet and Nutrition Course and a Wok Cooking Course for women and in 1980 participated in the Dominion City Centennial.

Since its conception, the Mom's Club has organized the Red Cross swimming lessons for pre-schoolers. Prior to this the lessons were run by the Legion Auxiliary. The Mom's Club raised funds by sponsoring bake sales, clothing parties and Fun Fair in June, 1981. Money raised was used for Dominion City Park Improvements. Purchases made were new swing seats, two metal climbers, a tether ball game, a volleyball game and a merry-go-round.

DOMINION CITY AGRICULTURAL SOCIETY

The first people in Franklin who actively promoted the growing of vegetables and fruits, and in doing handicraft work, were the schools. In the fall the children would show their articles at the various schools at small fairs sponsored by the Extension Department. Dominion City, a consolidated school, was the center of a large school area, and had a large Fall Fair. Many of the smaller schools had gardens.

With this beginning it was natural for 4-H groups to be formed. Then it became important for an Agricultural Society to be formed in the Municipality, so that everyone who had something that he felt was good enough to exhibit, would have a place to show it.

Agricultural Fairs became larger and were promoted and supported by the Extension Branch of the Department of Agriculture. They provided unbiased competent judges, and things were arranged so they did not know who the exhibitors were.

In 1946, the Agricultural Society was reactivated after the war. The treasury had seven dollars in it. It had no buildings, and no property of their own large enough to build on. The small exhibits, canned fruit, vegetables, preserves, handicrafts etc. were shown in the Community Hall. Meals were served there. However the Board had a member, Jim Waddell, who donated land to the Agricultural Society for the erection of some buildings and a ball diamond. The Society had been given three lots some years earlier from the Waddell property.

The Society applied for a charter in 1926 but there was a time during the World War 2 when no fairs were held.

Loading chutes had to be borrowed, and to make it easier to load cattle and horses, an earth ramp was built at the south side of the property. There were also two large portable structures on skids, with wire cages to hold poultry. One of the farmers living nearby stored these on his farm during the rest of the year, to save them in good shape.

All sizes of cattle and horses had to be registered. There were five classes of heavy horses. Class 6 was roadster or carriage horses. Class seven was harness horses, big and small. Class 8 was a quick hitch contest. Class 9 was a saddle class, and class 10 saddle ponies. Class 11 was horse jumping, barrel racing and musical chairs.

As for cattle, the exotic breeds had not come into the area, so the three beef breeds, Shorthorn, Hereford and Angus were shown. In the dairy classes the Holsteins predominated, with Jerseys shown some years. There were no Brown Swiss entries in those days.

The 4-H exhibits were a very important part of the Agricultural Fair, and helped in many ways. The Fair provided a place for all the Clubs to come together to show their products. These were grain, calves, hogs or crafts. Each 4-H member had parents who contributed at the gate. Exhibitors got in free.

For a number of years there were three Beef Calf Clubs in Franklin Municipality, Ridgeville, Green Ridge and Woodmore, and a Club from Arbakka also came to compete. Each Club had its own placings and all competed for Grand Champion, Reserve Champion, etc. The top calves always brought a premium price. There was even an auction right on the grounds one year.

The four horse hitch and saddle horse events like relay races and barrel racing always drew a crowd at the Fairs. Judging the 4-H entries was popular too. Prize money was small in those days, and the Dominion City people and those from surrounding areas were very generous in providing special prizes, which helped greatly to attract exhibits.

Long before the Agricultural Society was organized, there was a race track on the Waddell property. It was about half a mile long, and properly contoured at the ends, which made it a pretty good race track. Harness racing was the thing then, and people can remember Wally Arthurs and Joe Baskerville racing their pacers around the track, with Wally's beard divided down the middle, and flowing out over his shoulders.

Wallace Casson was president from about 1936 to 1940. Then there was the war. Then from 1936 to 1953 Gordon Kirkpatrick was president. John Hunter was president from 1953 until 1966. At that time the Fair was dropped, and the organization broke up. The Dominion City Fair was considered a "C" class Fair, and many of the "C" class Fairs ended then, and the "B" class Fairs like Morris, got bigger. The 4-H Clubs from Franklin now go to Morris.

Raymond Ginn and Colin Granger both put in several years as Secretary-Treasurers. This was a big job at Fair time when all the livestock and small exhibits had to be classified and registered. Those two men managed the finances of our Fair Board so well that we always had a dollar or two left over at the end of each year.

The Fair was always in the first two weeks of July, and was called a two day Fair. The exact dates were always arranged with the Extension Department, so the judges could go from fair to fair. The hall exhibits had to be entered the first day, so the judging could begin early the second day. Entries could not be seen until the judging was all over. Livestock, poultry etc. had to be on the grounds early on the second day and be entered in the proper class.

The Fair opened with a parade of 4-H leaders and their Clubs, headed by the band. One year we had the Winnipeg Police Pipe Band. Dominion City always had a band with Jim Waddell as leader.

Neil Sullivan was the local T.V. and radio man at the time, and was generous with his time and equipment. He set up a P.A. system on the Fair Grounds.

A baseball tournament was a regular part of the Fair Day, and there were races for the children. The Casey Shows came to Dominion City Fair for several years. Some of the Implement Companies displayed their machinery on the grounds, but space limited their displays.

The climax of each Summer Fair was the dance held in the Community Hall at night. The music was supplied by the Raymond Ginn orchestra. Raymie played the drums, Bernice Weninger was at the piano. Bill Becksted played the violin, and Mr. Dunn from Pembina played the banjo.

Dominion City Summer Fair was a credit to the Agricultural Society and the district. Through the hard work of everyone it was one of the best in the province, and a big event at that time, which drew exhibits over a radius of 50 miles. Fairs now are bigger and farther apart, and lack the neighborly interest they once had.

4-H CLUBS

In 1951-1952 a 4-H Club called the Flying Saucepans was organized at Tolstoi. President - William Hanischuk, Vice-President - Bernice Grabowski, Secretary - Jean Donaleyko, Leader - Mrs. Lena Skolny.

The lessons and meetings were held at Mrs. Lena Skolny's home once a week.

In 1954 a 4-H Potato Club was formed. Fifteen members joined this club, and the varieties of potatoes were: Columbia and Russet. The meetings were held at the school, with the following officers: Leader - Mr. N. J. Topolinicky (local teacher), Assistant Leader - Doris Olynyk, President - Jarvis Ewacha, Vice-President - Jean Olynyk, Secretary - Ruth Donaleyko

In 1955 ten members joined with the following officers: Leader - Mr. J. M. Skokotenly (local teacher), Assistant leader - Doris Olynyk, President - Jarvis Ewacha, Vice-President - Betty Ewacha, Secretary - Boris Nazarewich.

In 1958 and 1959 twelve members joined the Potato Club with the following officers: President: Adele Kolodzinski, Vice-President - Adele Kolodzinski, Secretary - Bonnie German, Local Leader - Mrs. E. Bially, Assistant leader - Mrs. M. Onysko.

There also were sewing clubs instituted in the early 1950's. The leader of this club was Mrs. Helen Grabowski.

In the 1970's a new club called the Tolstoi Skillful Workers was organized and the projects were, sewing, handicrafts, photography, etc. This club carried on a few years. The head leaders were: Mary Timchuk, Elaine Bzowy and Pauline Gaetz. Assistant Leaders: - Rose Fedorchuk, Jean Germain, Helen Bially, Bernice Chobotar, John Drewniak, Joyce Drewniak and Nancy Bially.

A Senkiw 4-H Potato Club was organized in 1954 by J. A. Negrech with thirteen members joining. The Potato variety was the Russet, and the meetings were held at the Senkiw School with the following officers: Leader - Mr. Maurice Kohut, President - Johnny Rybuck, Vice-President - Iris Rybuck, Secretary - Peter Rybuck.

In 1955 another variety of potato was added which was the Columbia. This year there were 16 members and they met at the Community Hall with the following officers: Leader - Harry Andrushko, Assistant - Maurice Kohut, President - Maurice Rybuck, Vice-President - Stanley Rybuck, Secretary - Peter Rybuck.

The Overstone 4-H Potato Club was formed

in 1958 with Mr. J. A. Negrech of Vita supervising. Five members joined and the meetings were held at the members' homes every third week of the month, with the following officers elected: President - David Runke, Vice-President - Shirley Mayner, Secretary - Fred Olynyk, Local Leader - Doris Olynyk, Assistant Leader - Mrs. Lena Runke.

The variety of potatoes the "Netted Gem". The same club continued into 1959 with six members joining.

Bradley area had their first club called Bradley Stitches in the year 1946, with supervisor Doris Baskerville. The following officers were elected: Local Director - Mrs. A. Huculiak (local teacher), President - Eleanor Grabowski, Vice-President - Olga Labaty, Secretary - Jean Wnuk. Date of joining - September 27, 1946, date of exhibition - June 4, 1947.

The next few years there were garden clubs formed. In 1958 a club called "Bradley Busy Workers" was organized, and the joint projects were: Potato, Garden and Swine. There were 19 members enrolled, with the following officers: President - Elsie Solomon, Vice-President - Eva Zahara, Secretary - Marian Wnuk, Local Leader - Mr. Maurice Yarmie, Assistant Leaders - Mr. Paul Kozak, Ernest Kozak and Peter Kozak.

In 1959 a Bradley Potato Club carried on, and the variety of potatoes was "Netted Gems" with seven members enrolling. Their leader was Paul Kozak.

In November 1934 the Green Ridge Junior Grain Club was organized under the leadership of Mr. Wallace Casson. In 1935 samples of Durham Wheat won 2nd and 3rd prizes at the Toronto Royal, and 1st and 2nd and 4th placings in a Winnipeg Seed Show.

In 1948 Mr. Ed Manness was leader of the Woodmore Calf and Swine Club. Later in 1957 the Woodmore Merry Makers - a sewing club lead by Mrs. Louise Dickson and Mrs. Joyce Grier was successful.

The Franklin 4-H Tractor Club was formed in 1952 by Ag. Rep. John Negrych. Leaders in this group were Russell Mayne and Norman Grier.

Green Ridge Calf and Seed Clubs were also active in the early 1950's and 1960's. Leaders were Wallace Casson, John Hunter, Theo Strange and Doug Gunn.

The Green Ridge Sunshine Sewing was organized in 1951 and continued for 10 years as an active group. In 1964 the group reorganized as the Silver Thimbles under direction of Mrs. Alice Timlick.

In 1966 their name changed to Golden Nuggets under leadership of Mrs. Bernice Graydon.

In 1966 the Calf and Seed Club was functioning under the leader Sandy McLennon followed in 1967 by Cliff Hunter.

In 1970 the Green Ridge Combined Club formed under the direction of Mrs. Irene Hunter. There was a membership of 25 from both our districts, projects tackled that year were clothing, handicraft, photography, woodworking, seed and welding.

In 1971 the name changed to Woodmore Combined Club, had 20 members under direction of Mrs. Eileen Spence.

In 1973, Mrs. Marget Badgley became head leader of our club and has served that position to date. With her, doing their part were Louise Dickson, Violet Spence, Hazel Carrier and Carilynn Badgley. Rod Badgley completed the leaders for this year.

In 1981-1982, Leader - Marget Badgley, Assistant Leaders - Louise Dickson, Margaret Pott, Linda Hildebrandt, Maryann Hildebrandt, Lorne Pott and Donald Mayne. President - Kent Grier, Vice-President - Lorne Pott, Secretary - Laurel Carriere, Treasurer - Barbara Rettaler, Club Reporter - Tammy Pott, Scrapbook - Rachel Smith.

In March 1953, a meeting in the the Arnaud School was called to order by Mr. Stevenson, the district Agricultural representative. It was decided to form a Garden Club. The Club was called the Carlowrie 4-H Garden Club. A discussion of details regarding garden club operations took place. Ten members joined at this first meeting. Lorraine Calder, Colin Calder, Robert Shelby, Frances Shelby, Robert Shelby, Hazel Calder, Cameron Calder, Shirley Shymco, Gordon Shelby and Ruth Dearborn. Joining for Achievement Day only were Sharon Neimor and Myrna Shelby.

Election of Officers resulted as follows: President - Lorraine Calder; Vice-President - Hazel Calder; Secretary-Treasurer - Bob Shelby; Club Reporter - Frances Shelby. Mrs. Violet Shelby was chosen club leader. The secretary treasurer collected the money from each member for the seeds, 10 varieties of vegetables were to be planted. Total cost for seeds per member amounted to 40 cents each. Plans were made to meet again every second Friday, alternating in Carlowrie and North Star School.

The Arnaud 4-H Garden Club was organized by Mr. D. Stevenson, agricultural representative from Morris, with Christine Nichols as leader. In conjunction with their garden plots, the club members carried on various projects to raise money, mainly by putting on concerts and sale of work. The proceeds of these were shared jointly with the Crippled Children's Fund, a worthy project and one they were keen on supporting. This club was rated first in the province one year and another year rated third, which was quite an honor. In a contest open to leaders of 4-H in the three prairie provinces, relating to activities, etc. carried out by any particular club, Christine Nichols had the honor of winning first prize for her entry, which was a beautiful leather briefcase.

In 1954, a Beef Club was formed by John Calder as club leader. The first Achievement Day was held at the home of Ralph Calder.

In November, 1957, a meeting under the guidance of the local Ag. Rep. Mr. John Negrych of Vita, was held to discuss various clubs and obtain information on each one. It was decided to form a combined beef, grain and garden club.

The Officers elected the first year for the combined club were: President - Lorraine Calder, Vice-President - Ruth Dearborn, Secretary - Hazel Calder, Treasurer - Colin Calder. Leaders chosen were: Beef - John Calder with Ralph Calder assistant. Grain - Mr. Floyd Shelby with Robert Shelby assistant. Garden - Mrs. Violet Shelby with Mrs. R. Calder as assistant.

The Rosa Happy Homemakers 4-H Club first organized under the head leadership of Alice Ostrowsky. A total of 30 members completed projects in the year. Foods and Clothing were the outstanding projects. Home Design was added to the list of projects in 1969. Mrs. Agnes Hildebrandt took over head leadership this year and the club continued until 1970. During the span of this time the club had been named Reserve Champion at Morris Rally along with numerous other project awards. Over the three years that the Homemakers existed the following served as leaders - Alice Ostrowsky, Agnes Hildebrandt, Mary Zacharias, Elsie Budey, Tina Penner, May Sawatzky, Agatha Unrau, May Grabowski, Maryann Hildebrandt and Joyce Schurko.

In 1973 the Roseau River Busy Beavers 4-H Club was formed under the head leadership of Maryann Hildebrandt. Other leaders over the next four years included, Alice Ostrowsky, Mavis Koop, Kathy Polischuk, Cathy St. Godard, Hilda Peters, Joyce Schurko, Cathy Penner, Tinna Dreger, Elizabeth Penner, Linda Hildebrandt. Projects taken were clothing, foods, crafts, gardening, conservation, dog training, hunter safety, home nursing and self determined and junior leader.

In 1977 Cathy Wood became head leader and the club continued until 1979 with leaders being Joyce Schurko, Alice Ostrowsky, Hilda Peters, Cathy St. Godard. Unusual projects for this period were mechanics, cake decorating, slide and tape and photography.

In Ridgeville in the fall of 1949, the first 4-H Seed Club was organized under the leadership of Mr. Frank Casper and Mr. Ted Steg. The executive for the first year was President - Raymond Steg, Vice-President - Joe Rzepka, Secretary - Clarence Lange. By 1952 they had 18 members which included two girls, Lorraine Schwark and Mary Anne Pow (nee Steg).

In 1952 the Beef Club and Garden Club began. Leaders were Mr. Web Seward and Mr. Wm. Schwark. There were 14 members. Officers were, President - Dennis Seward, Vice-President - Wayne Schwark, Secretary - Lorraine Schwark, Treasurer - Mary Ann Steg, Club Reporter - Danny Seward.

In 1954 the Clothing club began on September 24, 1954, with a membership of 15. Officers were: President - Lois Spence (nee Zass), Vice-President - Shirley Lane (nee Laufersweiler), Secretary-Treasurer - Joyce Drajeski. The leaders were Elsie Bodnarchuk and Mary Paley, teachers at that time. The 4-H program was implemented into the school system and each Friday from 3-4 o'clock we worked on our 4-H project. Other members for the first year were Joan Walters, Darlene Klapka, Donna, Lenore and Audrey Laufersweiler, Louella Harder, Kathy Drajeski and Delores Wilkinson. At that meeting the first name was chosen "Ridgeville 4-H Busy Finger". Home Ec. was Miss Lula MacLeod.

The name Ridgeville 4-H Combined Club replaced the original Ridgeville 4-H Busy Fingers sometime during the late 60's early 70's.

Membership in 1982 was 10 members with 5 leaders and a social convenor. Members were President - Shenda Grier, Vice-President - Audra Froom, Treasurer - Josephine Wieler, Secretary - Barbara Steg, Club Reporter - John Pow. Other members were Suzy Wieler, John Stephens, Wendy Lazaruk, Kori Kerda and assoc. member - Jeffrey Froom. Club leader and crafts leader, Mary Ann Pow, Cooking leader Dianne Lazaruk, Clothing leader Ruth Kerda, Special projects leader Edie Grier and Social Convenor Jo Anne Froom. Vita Ag. Rep. is Wally Happychuk, Home Economist of Wendy Epp, Program Assistant is Marlene Drewniak.

The Lorraine Sharon Schwark public speaking trophy is presented every year since 1966 to the top public speaker of Ridgeville Club. 1966 - Lyne Schultz; 1967 - Audrey Gushuliak, 1968 - Myrna Chubaty, 1969 - Elaine Wachna, 1970 - Elaine Wachna; 1972 - Peggy Lenton, 1972-73-74 - Elaine Wachna; 1974 - Colleen Chubaty, 1976 - Evelyn Pott, 1977 - Carol Nicholson, 1978 - Wendy Steg, 1979 - Wendy Steg, 1980 - Kathy Wachna, 1981 - Shenda Grier, 1982 - Audra Froom.

The Lorraine Sharon Schwark Junior Demonstration trophy is presented every year to the top Junior Demonstration team in the Vita Area. 1968 - Tanya Petrah - Sherry Wilkinson , 1969 - Theresa Fedorchuk - Sandra Drewniak, 1974 - Cindy Grier - Colleen Chubaty, 1975 - Carol Nicholson - Cindy Grier, 1977 - Patricia Riach - Tracy Brown, 1978 - Carol Kohut - Kathy Wachna, 1979, Doreen Steg - Shenda Grier.

In Dominion City the 4-H organized in 1948. Mrs. Ken Peters started the sewing club in the Dominion City school, with the help of principal H. Sharpe. There were no Home Economics classes in school, and 4-H sewing was taught in classrooms, alternate Fridays, from grade 7 up. Mrs. Harry Sharpe taught knitting, and the girls were split into two groups. In 1951 the group left the school, and met in private homes. August Huff instructed the boys in woodworking at this time. During the years the 4-H expanded to include beef clubs, seed clubs, an auto club, public speaking, a fashion club, which changed to a banners club and uniform club, among others.

RAFT

In 1979 it was decided by the town businessmen that Ridgeville needed an organization along the lines of a Chamber of Commerce to look after specific problems relating to the town and surrounding farms. Some of the things felt to be of importance were poor service from Manitoba Telephone System, a possible water supply and sewage system, and a lack of a tree shelter belt around the town. After calling a public meeting, a committee was formed consisting of Don Cook, Edie Grier, Norm Grier, Iris Wachna, Eileen Spence, and the name of the RAFT (Ridgeville Area Future Thinking) was coined. There are now private phones in town, and an assurance that farm homes are scheduled to receive similar service. The water supply has ot been resolved, but engineers have assessed the feasibility of a new system. In 1979 Ron Spence was nominated as chairman of the Tree Planting. Spring of 1980 saw 4,000 trees arrive from Indian Head. The Ridgeville 4-H undertook to plant 200 trees in 1982 as part of a group project.

B.P.O. ELKS 1967-1982

The Dominion City Elks Lodge #516 was organized on November 30th, 1967. The Lodge was instituted on December 13th, 1967 with the following officers being installed: Exalted Ruler - F. Stevenson, Leading Knight - Ed Murray, Loyal Knight - Ray Sawchuk, Lecturing Knight - Amie Cadieux, Secretary - Glen Ginn, Treasurer - Harry Smart, Inner Guard - Clayton Gray,

Trustees - Ben Comeault, Mike Sokolyk and Garnet Kyle, Publicity Director - James Anstett, Esquire - D. Kirkpatrick, Organist - G. Mulko. Other members were L. R. Keeley, T. Hancox, L. Hancox, H. Lamont, W. Schnell, A. Gallant, A. Casper, G. Calder and Stan Nelson.

The membership of the lodge has grown from 23 in 1967 to 59 in 1982. This steady growth has enabled the lodge to become one of the most successful organizations in the area.

Over the years, the Dominion City Elks have supported a number of organizations, which are enjoyed by the people of the R.M. of Franklin. Although financial support has been a great part of many projects, the Elks have worked with others in the community to simply organize other projects.

In the past 16 years the Elks have supported the Franklin Manor, Dominion City swimming pool and park, Dominion City Curling Club, Dominion City Community Club, Golden Age Centre, Skating Rink, Minor Hockey, Family Disaster Funds and Low Rental Housing.

ROSEAU VALLEY BRANCH #160, ROYAL CANADIAN LEGION

In early 1945 veterans of the recent war were trickling back to the Franklin area. They wanted to continue the associations which had begun in the various units of the Armed Forces, and have a forum where their memories could be talked over and kept alive.

In April that year they had a meeting in the local school in Dominion City and decided to organize a branch of the Royal Canadian Legion. Wilf Schnell and Tom Pott, intended to call the organization the "Franklin and Roseau Valley Branch". The annual dues were set at $3 per member.

Their efforts were successful, and on July 9th they were presented with their charter "for the newly formed Branch called Roseau Valley Branch #160" . . . so somewhere along the line 'Franklin' had been dropped from the title.

Meetings were held in the school, later in the hall at the Oddfellows Building. The Legion was active in sponsoring Sports Days and other events.

DIn June, 1956, after many fund-raising efforts, and the expenditure of pounds of elbow-grease, the Legion opened their swimming pool on the bank of the Roseau River on Taylor Avenue. The first Pool Committee was made up of Bill Taylor, 'Buddy' French and Bert Witty.

In the fall of '56, the Branch decided to do something about getting their own hall, and after some negotiations with Ed Manness they bought his shop, east of the MacLeods store for the grand sum of $825. The fact that they didn't have any spare money after opening the swimming pool didn't stop them. Joe Boutet suggested that the Legion borrow $500 from the bank, and then he and Frank Casper offered to lend the Branch $200 each to purchase the property and carry out some renovations. Needless to say, the boys jumped at the offer, the deal actually completed and possession taken in February of 1957.

There have been a number of renovations since that time, but the building is still in the same place, and is still the home of the Roseau Valley Branch of the Legion.

Girl Guides were formed in Dominion City c. 1939, under the leadership of Mrs. Brisbin. The 1940 members were Louise Hancox, Eileen Houston, Margaret Houston, Shirley Curran, Bernice Ramsey, Betty Lou Ginn, Lucille Scholte, Eleanor Ginn, Bernice French, Donna Bradley, Betty Ramsey, Dorothy Johnson.

Boy Scouts were formed in Dominion City in 1939, under the leadership of Alex Wilson. Some of the early members were Garth Raw, George McAdam, Wally Taylor, Cliff Baskerville, Ken Muchinson, Roy Solnes, Carl Christiansen, Leonard Anderson, Walter Pearse, George Opocensky, Ralph Weedmark, Matt Borodenko, Tom French, Gerald Pearse and Frank McCormick.

A Ladies Orange Benevolent Association was active in Ridgeville in the early part of this century. Members included Dora Woods, Mrs. Ed. Jack, Lily Woods, Mrs. Woods, Beatrice Wilkinson Stringer, Rose Wilkinson, Mrs. Abe Seward, Martha Wilkinson, Mrs. Hess Irvine and Bertha Wilkinson.

THE EASTERN GRASSLAND SOCIETY

An organization, the Border Beef Producers, was searching for ways to increase their Net Farm Income by identifying and demonstrating ways of reducing cost of production of their forage-livestock operations. Its directors visited the Teulon project under the direction of the Manitoba Department of Agriculture with Grassland Specialist, Peter Jones. So impressed were the directors, that they immediately approached the Minister of Agriculture, Sam Uskiw with their request for the establishment of an Eastern Grassland Society for the Eastern Region. Mr. Uskiw approved the program.

In June, 1972 the Eastern Grassland Society was established as a joint venture between cattlemen of the Eastern Region of Manitoba and the Manitoba Department of Agriculture. The executive consisted of: President - William Ostrowsky, Rosa, Vice-President - Norm Picklyk, Caliento, Secretary - Judy Dodds, Ste. Anne, Treasurer - P. D. F. Wiebe - Grunthal, Directors - René Lambert, St. Malo, Paul Bartel, Kleefeld, Grassland Specialists - Frank Pitura, Gil Lahoy, Livestock Specialist - Ray Solomon, Agricultural Representative - Andy Sirski, Project Manager - Roger Berard.

The project site was located at Rosa, Manitoba, 47 miles south of Winnipeg on PTH 59. One hundred fifty acres were leased for a period of five years from William Ostrowsky. One hundred twenty acres were in pasture with the balance in corrals, winter facilities, access roads, and native bush. The soil was Pine Ridge fine sandy loam.

The pasture area was separated into six separate paddocks ranging in size from 12 to 52 acres each. Easy access was available to all paddocks by a connecting lane and to the corrals and handling facilities. The perimeter fence was a five wire, single strand, barbed wire fence. Cross fencing between paddocks was with suspension fencing posts eighty feet apart. Spruce and tamarack posts and rails were used in the construction of the facilities. Water was supplied from a central well and supplied to each paddock by means of below surface plastic piping.

Throughout the five year project, fall rye, orchard - timothy grass mixture, crested wheat - intermediate wheat, oats and corn were seeded. Cattle were grazed on these fields from May to October. Rotational grazing was used. Surplus hay was cut and baled for use in the latter part of the grazing season. An average of seventy head were maintained in the project each year. The local farmers of the Eastern Region provided the cattle for the project.

Disasters and Stories

by Edith Thompson

In 1914, on the 22nd of June, Nykola Zaporzan, age 14 died instantly on the farm of his parents, Mr. and Mrs. Ivan Zaporzan, while driving a team of horses.

He slipped at the heels of a hitched team, and was kicked in the head by the horse, killing him.

That same day his brother Sam Zaporzan, was at La-Verne, Saskatchewan. He was thrown off a bronco, which he tried to ride. He was unconscious, but survived. Word of the accident at La Verne was exchanged with the more tragic news of the death of Sam's brother Nykola.

* * * * *

Tornadoes always develop on a hot day with high humidity. The wind seems to come from the south west against clouds which begin to turn dark and threatening. There is usually a striking sky effect with light and dark clouds swirling and moving fast. They seem to churn and work till a funnel forms and the clouds begin streaming upwards. By then the funnel is moving and may be down to the ground. This has been happening more and more often in this area. We look to the south west and listen for warnings on Altona radio as they would have wind of it first. The Vita disaster in 1955 started back at the ridge and gained strength till it clobbered Vita with disastrous results. The hospital to which many from Eastern Franklin go, was hit hard and lost its roof so that the third story was removed. Many homes and business were wrecked. In July, 1973 a severe tornado struck the W. Seward farm.

The tornado that hit Aubigny was another which went further north. High winds have often done damage and at the Davison farm about 13 big 60 year old trees were uprooted in one of these storms. It was impossible to cross over the lawn for fallen trees.

In 1979 the twister struck again at Smiths at Woodmore wrecking the barn and buildings.

In 1977 Carlowrie was struck. It began as a wind at Arnaud and followed the highway down 217 east till it came down and sheered off the hydro and telephone poles on both sides of the road. Directly in line was Corney Penners where it struck the house. Ann and Corney were upstairs and Ann immediately started for the basement but Corney was worried about the barn and was going there but returned when Ann called. They sheltered in the vegetable room leaning against the door to keep it closed.

The house shook about them. When it seemed it was over they came up to a sight unbelievable and it was nearly an hour before they saw anyone or anyone came to see how they were. Trees were stripped of branches down to the bare trunk. They lay like match sticks showing how the wind swirled from Carlowrie to Rosa. The one wall of the living room was gone and the furniture with it. The fridge was turned around in the kitchen, shingles were gone from the roof and the wall board throughout the house was loosened. Their lovely plantation of siberian elm were broken and spruce were leaning. Machinery, like a swather was wrecked, the greenhouse was wrecked, as was the garage made of cement block, and barns and metal bins. The storm swept on towards Rosa.

It hit the home of the Klems, taking the house and contents into the bush in a big circle. The little car belonging to the daughter was put in the basement. Mr. and Mrs. Mike Klem were killed, but the daughter, Mrs. Joann Grenier, who was pregnant at the time, was alive, but she lost twins. She and daughter Terra were rushed to St. Pierre and St. Boniface Hospitals. Terra died, but Mrs. Grenier lived to be in another tornado two years later.

The wind then crossed the 59 Highway removing about 12 feet of black top right out of the road, a shovel was driven into a tree. It hit the camp of the road gang working on the Grunthal highway and put their machinery and trailers into the ditch. The lovely elms near Chubeys were wrecked. Trees now were showing a different swirl pattern to those back in Carlowrie. The wind and swirling tornado lifted and left the area.

At Carlowrie other homes were damaged, Calders' new home was damaged slightly. The Mel Schlorffs lost their house, possessions and the garden was blown out. Even the potatoes were gone, yet a robin in her nest by the house was not touched. The lovely valley was made into a war devastated landscape. Big beautiful trees were twisted. Bins and furniture were hanging from the trees.

The tornado struck after supper and it was dark before folks got word of the twister and came to help. Next day the Mennonite Disaster and neighboring men and women arrived to clean up and mend what they could. By summer's end Penners had the house repaired, garage and barn and bins replaced and Schlorffs who had all their buildings lost, had a new house.

It will be years before nature can replace the trees.

* * * * *

Early in Franklin's history a Thunder storm came up. Mr. and Mrs. Tanchuk were making grain stacks, using oxen to haul the bundles. Both were killed by lightning along with the oxen. They left five children.

Indians claim at one time there was a flood that stretched from the ridge as far as Morden and that they had canoed the distance on creeks that drained into the Roseau.

Davisons were making hay in June, 1938, near the correction line to the north of their place when a storm developed very quickly. Ab Foulds took his team to his home but the others ran to Dick Posts farm and put their horses in the barn there. The men were standing about in the barn talking and waiting for the storm to pass when light-ing struck. Bert Davison was leaning on the rump of his team and went down behind them as they fell dead. In their death throes they struck him repeatedly in the face. Theo Strange was beside his team and they fell, taking him down with them. A hen in the manger was O.K. but the horses were dead, their shoes blue. Dick Post was struck as well. Bert Smith had started for the house but ran back with the help of Wallace Post. They lifted the big horse from Theo and dragged him out.

The men were taken to the house in great pain. They tried to reach a local doctor but all were out. They called Hallock and that doctor came. There was little he could do but said it was a miracle they lived. It was six months before the pain left and they could wear shoes. Evidently nerves were badly damaged and had to regrow.

* * * * *

Archie and Walter Ochremchuk who lived on a farm where the nuisance grounds are located, were burning grass around the yard. They had some shrubs or brush that would not burn readi-ly so Archie got some gasoline and threw it on the brush. The resulting explosion burned him badly. Walter came to his aid and was burned also. They were rushed to Winnipeg, having to cross the Ferry. The older one, Archie, died on May 12, 20 years old, and was buried from Arnaud church with internment at Dominion City. Walter, died May 17, 18 years old. He was buried from the Dominion City United Church.

* * * * *

May 2nd, 1896, with ice still on the river, it rose nine feet in 24 hours. By May 4th, it was spreading overland. By May 5th, anyone living along the Red had to leave with their cattle and few possessions. The ice began to move and wrecked homes, barns and possessions of anyone living along the Red to the north.

In 1852 another flood lasted from May 12 to June 12.

1882 was another flood year with towns like Emerson and Dominion City in the path of destruction.

In 1893 the Red flooded again, Emerson had a population of 4,000, but this final insult from the river caused Emerson's boom to burst.

1948 was a preview for the 1950 flood. The R.C.M.P. patrolled the river in power boats and visited farms to see if people were in need of help.

Cattle and animals of all kinds were moved out of the flood area. With the river rising rapidly at Grand Forks, farmers and town dwellers had time to prepare. They had special quotas to enable them to moved grain out, and furniture and animals were taken out or put up in the barn loft or second floor in houses.

The Roseau River flooded due to the Red being higher and holding the Roseau back. Over half of Dominion City was flooded, and it spread across country north to Arnaud. The traffic bridge was under water and the railway bridge had two feet to go. $60,000 damage was done to roads and bridges.

Families had to double up. Indians were moved to a tent encampment on the Ridge and in 1950 they went to Rivers. The Red Cross was helping where it could. Water had to be boiled or chlorinated. Warnings came out on how to clean and sterilize basements after the flood. People were told to let the water fill the basement otherwise it might collapse from outside pressure.

Peter Goertzen, S.W. of Arnaud, built his cattle stalls three feet higher and kept them dry even though they were inches from the ceiling. Some folks had chickens in the loft. One farmer saved his place as he had built his own dyke. Reeve W. R. Johnston asked for two boats for Arnaud to get the people out of flooded areas. These were donated by Winnipeg citizens.

In 1950 snow fell and added to the misery around April 15th. This flood was 20 inches higher than in 1948. It flooded 60,000 acres. By April 27 farmers were again moving livestock and drinking water was brought in by train. Work trains were busy keeping the track from washing out. School children were let out and helped with sand bagging. Police delivered mail and groceries to those who remained on the farms. It was soon over and crops were planted in most fields after debris was removed. Seeding was late but the crops turned out fair in the fall.

There have been two more flood threats to Dominion City when the children were asked to help sand bag the newly made dykes that now protect homes along the river and the towns and reserve. With grain bins up on high pads and the circle dykes around the towns there is not the fear of another devastating flood. The dykes can be made higher by adding sand bags and plastic which makes a good temporary dyke.

Now the talk is to put in more dams on the tributaries and so hold back water for irrigation and stock and thus prevent so much water on stream all at once.

Residents of the valley will always listen for the forecasts in April to tell them if floods are expected but we hope the terror that went with early floods will not occur again.

* * * * *

On August 4, 1981 a Borgers truck collided with the C.P.R. train at the intersection of 201 in Dominion City. Seventeen cars were derailed three of them containing propane, one of these, began to leak. Plans were made for the evacuation of the town if necessary. Members of the Dominion City Volunteer Fire Brigade and equipment monitored the site, 24 hours a day, for six days until the wreckage was cleared. The truck driver was unhurt.

* * * * *

Sometime before 1939 the U.G.G. elevator at Dominion City was struck by lightning and burned to the ground. It was rebuilt in the same spot. Sure enough it was hit again and burned and again rebuilt. It still stands. Sandy Calder was the elevator agent at the time.

* * * * *

Danny Reese, who was a school teacher at Carlowrie before becoming a customs agent at Emerson, tells the story of being caught by a prairie fire raging through the farm yard where he lived with an uncle. His only means of escape was the well. He got into it and was saved.

* * * * *

In 1911 fire destroyed the hotel in Ridgeville and another one was built slightly north of the original. Fire struck again in 1914, destroying three adjacent business quarters, the W. H. Post International Implement warehouse, Rosenstock Store and the Hotel. The store was rebuilt, the implement business was re-established across the street, but it was many years before Ridgeville could boast another Hotel.

STORIES

There seem to be quite a contrast in the lives of some of the pioneers. 1875 William and Martha Fields took up a homestead southeast of Dominion City, long before the days of drainage ditches on the 'flats'. They lived in a sod house that leaked so badly whenever it rained. Mrs. Fields would stretch her hand to the floor to see how deep the water was before arising from her bed in the morning. On one occasion they had to feed the straw from the roof of their sod house to their cattle until they could raft in some hay.

On the other hand, 'Veezie' Fitzgerald was a well-to-do Englishman who came to Canada in 1880. He built an eight-bedroom home near Ridgeville (on the Rich Weiss farm). He had his own private bath room heated with a box stove, and also an outdoor toilet with a velvet covered seat heated with a box stove. Hired help built the fire in these private rooms before the honorable gentleman used same. His cellar was always amply supplied with beer and whiskey. Whenever he needed more money, all he had to do was write home to England. Even in 1902 the pioneers in the eastern end of the municipality faced hardships. Mrs. C. Slobodian (Annie Kochman) relates a few memories from the past. "To get the title for his homestead, mostly bush and muskeg, (Mr. Kochman) had to walk to Winnipeg 65 miles on foot around muskegs and sloughs as there were no roads then, just bush and prairie. So they bunched together, four or five men, and went to Winnipeg - Dad for the title, the others on business. They would buy the most important items, pack them in socks, and start for home again. Then Dad got a job on the railroad, and weekends he would come home to do a little brushing and clearing land. Mother told us at harvest time she would strap me on her back, and put my older brother Bill under a stook and tell him to stay there, then she would go and lead the oxen while my uncle worked the binder. Later my uncle had a little grocery store. Bill and I would snitch an egg from the chicken barn and go and buy a sucker. But Mother soon got wise to that, and no more suckers. How well I remember, to make a few cents, Mother and I and a few other ladies would take our spades and go miles to dig Seneca root. We'd get thirsty, we would dig a little hole in the slough to get a drink. It took a lot of digging for one pound of roots.

In these times of highly technical farming and cultivation it's difficult to envision the abundance of fruit and wildlife in the days of the pioneers.

As told by Mary Casson of Green Ridge, "Wild strawberries were so abundant that if a white cow lay down, when she got up again she was red where she had touched the ground. The air was so full of the sounds of wildlife - the owls and coyotes made such noises, we could not always sleep. Once when I opened my door, my hens came in. There was a fox after them".

Fresh meat in the fall of the year was no problem as the stubble fields were full of prairie chickens, ducks and geese. One early settler claimed the wild geese so thick and large, they chased him off the field before he could have his muzzle loaded ready to shoot.

Wolves were also plentiful and bold. Pioneer mother, Mrs. Stewart of Ridgeville took a blazing stick of wood from the stove and threw it among the savage animals which had driven their farm dog right to the door of their home.

* * * * *

Mrs. Thomas Woods, born Ida Agnes Hanson to Norwegian parents, made her arrival into the world on board a ship destined for the United States. The ship's captain claimed the right to name her, and named her 'Ida Agnes' after his ship.

* * * * *

David Phillips was the first editor of the Dominion City Advertiser, and wrote many articles under the name of 'Little Johnny'. The following excerpts are taken from Little Johnny's Prayer.

"At the Blue Ribbon Lodge, at Dominion City, before the Godly few assembled Friday, August 1, 1884.

Dear Lord: As this is my first attempt to pray before the public, please do hear me through. Fill my chuck full of Thy knowledge and help me pray for the lost sheep of our field. Please Lord do help our Blue Ribbon Lodge with five or six dollars to buy papers and good books to help the temperance cause. And now Good Lord, I hope I don't ask too much but if Thou would be so

kind as to pour out some blessings on the following needy few.

Dear Lord, look down on James Ramsey, fill his mouth with ivory that he may grind his conscience down to patent process and help him to bare light on the quill that is so often in his hands that his accounts on earth will compare with those in heaven.

Good Lord, bless the shoemaker James, help him to pray. He means good for he and the pastor are the whole prayer meeting. The church members must have jumped the fold and gone into the thicket.

Good Lord, look down on our Warden and Council, make them explain what sundry accounts means and extra expenses.

Bless poor Bob Taylor, touch the hem of his garment, that he may be made whole, help his lopsidedness that he may walk erect. Soften his heart on the 50 dollars that he is reaching out his hand for. Give him warning, stay their hands from dipping too deep in the people's pockets.

Lord, look into the heart of Big William, the Clerk of Council. Teach him to curtail his expenses, teach him to know that there are poor in our land. Stay his hands that when he grabs for dollars he will only get cents.

Bless poor Sullivan, bless his uncles and his aunts, bless the bridge money to the whole family, and remember he is young in the Council work. But temptation is strong and he is likely to go astray. Hold him also by the hands that he may dig no deeper into the empty safe of our poor people.

Now Lord, peep into the heart case of Mark Whitely, he is old and full of years, he needs Thy precious eye on him every moment, have compassion on him, pay him just dues if he does look for more.

Lord, teach the whole shebang to withdraw from the Council board for we cannot say with the Good Book 'Well done thou good and faithful servants'.

And Good Lord, look down on the Queen's Hotel. Bless the Lord at the bar. Teach him the evils of selling whiskey. He knows it is wrong to sell tangleleg to his neighbors. Teach him to sell pure wine and not make his neighbors drunken. Put his customers on short allowance at his bar.

Good Lord, please accept Little Johnny's Prayers. Good Night".

* * * * *

Just before the turn of the century, Dominion City was policed by Warden Dyck. Others to follow in his footsteps were Irvine Simpson, Harry Ball, Sam Johnston, Bill Barber, Stafford Pearse,

George Robertson, Matt Borodenko, Bryan Nichols, Art Backman, L. R. (Skip) Keeley.

One who had a police badge for years in the eastern part of the municipality was Joe Casson, and Mr. Treleaven was town constable for Arnaud.

Earle Simpson writes, "I don't know the wages which all of these good cops got, but it was a very small amount. Something in the region of $10 or $20 per year. However, by the time it got up as far as Matt and Bryan, it had graduated to $80 and $90 per month. Later Art Backman received $250 per month. We wonder why? When the old jail was in use in Dominion City my father, who also ran the livery barn at the time, used to have to lock up a few from west of town who seemed to get too much vanilla or kikapoo juice. He would stable their horse, and both would be released in the morning. We used to have in our possession a large turnkey about six inches long which was used for the old jail".

* * * * *

Prior to 1900 Sam and John Graham came from Coleraine, Ireland to live with their mother and sister on the farm now occupied by Don and Dorothy Mayne. When Mrs. Graham returned to Ireland, Sam took over the farm, and John worked as a blacksmith in Alberta.

Len Leach was from Cornwall, England, and homesteaded near Sundown. In the thirties, these three bachelors retired to a lot across from the Woodmore store, which became known as Bachelors' Corner. Len Leach and John Graham shared one cabin, and Sam Graham lived in a separate house. The corner became a popular spot for the young men of the district to meet for a game of checkers, and to hear stories of the past.

The three men enjoyed arguing, especially Len and John. These two planted their own variety of potatoes. One day Len hurried into the house as smoke was pouring out of the windows, to find John relaxing on the couch. Potatoes were burning in a pot on the stove. "Why don't you shut the heat off!!!" Len said. John replied, "You turned it on, didn't you?"

An electrical extension cord ran from John and Len's house to Sam's which operated his only light bulb. If John was annoyed with Sam, he would pull the plug and leave Sam in darkness for the remainder of the night.

* * * * *

It seems that Irvine Simpson had a very good chum who was courting a girl a few miles east along the Roseau River. As is still often the case today, some parents disagree with daughters as to their mate. The parents wanted their daughter to have nothing to do with this nice young gentleman.

Everyone used horses in the winter, and people east of town towards Green Ridge used the "bush road". This road went down past where Ronnie Pearse lives, along the river for a ways and directly towards the river, crossing where Leslie Brad lived. This road was very narrow and it was hard to pass in certain places.

One day the girl's parents met the boy's parents on this road, and the young maiden jumped from her parents' long sleighbox into the cutter driven by her boyfriend's father. Before the team with the sleigh and box could turn around, the couple were long gone. When the parents finally caught up to them, they were married and visiting at the home of Mr. and Mrs. Robert Scott, three and a half miles south of Dominion City.

Although the names of the couple will not be mentioned, the family accepted the young man who turned out to be one of the town's outstanding citizens.

* * * * *

"One of the pleasant features that has disappeared from our present age, which lent charm and variety to a former day, is the sound of sleighbells. These were open or closed bells, as well as Victoria bells, Swedish, or Norwegian chimes. The Boundary road was a much travelled thoroughfare, and we could pick out the distinctive bell sound of the different teams. Dad had rather large bells that came from Ontario. We knew them as soon as the sleigh topped the hill at the Beckstead farm. Then it was time for us boys to light the lantern, ready to put the team away".

* * * * *

One evening was rather unusual, when Mrs. Dupchak (from the Carlowrie area) went to close up her chickens for the night, she noticed a big black cat with a white stripe on it's back.

Since skunks are a North American animal, she'd never met any such animal while in Poland.

To her dismay, she found out that the big black cat sprayed her with a rather strong perfume when Mrs. Dupchak tried to shoe it outside. She ran for the house, only to be told to go back outside in the night by her husband, and strip down to her birthday suit and wash with hot water and home-made soap. This weakened the perfume somewhat, but she spent the night alone on the bed. Her whole attire was buried in the ground. One is not too far from wrong, saying Mrs. Dupchak has been initiated.

According to Bill Lindsay, Ridgeville, the best fun of all was the custom of chivareeing newlyweds.

"One evening after the wedding of Bill McBean and Nellie Marshall, 12 young fellows gathered up some gun powder and were going to make a heck of a big noise. It was quite breezy out and the matches kept going out. Determined to have their fun, one of the lads volunteered to squat over the powder to top the draft and yes, you guessed right, the powder went POOF! He got burned badly and no one saw his face for a couple of months".

* * * * *

The Soldier Settlers on the 'flats' were well known for their zest for living, especially the bachelors. One evening a few of them decided that things were just a bit too quiet, and that a nice home-cooked turkey supper might just fit the bill. As it happened, one of their unsuspecting neighbors happened to be raising a few turkeys so they quietly, and with a bit of difficulty, caught the biggest of the batch and got it ready for the oven. They then went in to visit the neighbor, and talked his wife into cooking up a first class meal with turkey being the star on the menu. A most pleasant evening was reported had by all, including the host who especially enjoyed their generosity in sharing their turkey with them. It wasn't until quite some time later that the boys thought to let their neighbor know 'from whence came the bird'.

* * * * *

In the twenties when liquor was an open affair in Manitoba, Prohibition was in full force in United States. Rum runners were certainly a busy lot all along the border south of Franklin Municipality. Roads east of our municipality were almost non existant. For traffic coming from north to south, the three main bridges across the Roseau River were at Dominion City, Langside and Green Ridge. So it was natural that the rum running routes would be concentrated in this area, and also that some of our prominent business men would become Rum Runners. The following is an excerpt from a story told by Earle Simpson, Dominion City.

"It was the night of the famous 'Long Count' fight between Jack Dempsey and Gene Tunney (1927). I was working for Bob Ramsey at his farm two miles east of Dominion City. Ben Ramsey (his son) was there at the time and they decided they would like to hear the boxing match on the radio. Being only about two radios in town, they decided to drive to the home of Les Ramsey near Ridgeville. We started out in an old Model T truck, driving along the old prairie trail which is now 201 highway, til we came to the corner where the road now turns to Ridgeville.

A few yards from this corner was always a real bad mud hole, and as history shows, this was one of the wettest years. Stuck in the middle of this bog was a large touring Cadillac. We tried everything to help the driver get it out. Then Ben decided to get his team, but the horses couldn't budge the car. As the back seat was all closed in with side curtains, Ben asked the driver if he had a load on. 'Yes, he did', 2500 pounds all in nice square cases. So he had to unload all these cartons and stack them on the side of the road. Just as he got everything piled neatly, a little 1927 Ford Coupe pulled up and tried to drive around us. Now, the Mounties drove a Coupe like this at that time and when the driver stepped out wearing a cowboy-type hat, our driver exclaimed 'Oh My God, I've had it'. However it wasn't a policeman. We gave him a little pull, he handed over a dollar bill, and went on his way. After a lot of trouble we succeeded in pulling out the Cadillac. Then there was the job of loading it again. It was whiskey in the boxes, it was worth $25 a pint. However, it was none of our business.

The driver said he was on his way to meet a certain prominent man living near the border. But when we told him the man had been knocked off the day before, he exclaimed 'You'll get paid good for this'.

He gave Ben $35 for himself and his team, Bob $20, and me being a kid 15 years old he gave me $10 for 'keeping your mouth shut'. This whole episode took about four hours, so needless to say we didn't hear the Dempsey-Tunney fight which Tunney won".

* * * * *

Another story tells about the prominent man from Ridgeville hauling his wares across the border in barrels. He would always include a couple of barrels of gas with the shipment. On one particular occasion, he was apprehended. As luck had it, when the mounties checked, they opened the barrels containing gas. And so the gentleman was able to go on his way with his contraband.

Mrs. Alf Solnes and Bill Barber boating out from Annie Scott's house after taking Betty home from work at telephone office. 1950.

Clarence Gunn and Mildred Brad on Roseau Reserve, 1950 flood.

Olie Larson in boat, near railway bridge, May 6, 1950.

Clifford Neuman's farm in distance. Joe River near Emerson, May 6, 1950.
L to R: Bert Davison, Nelson Casson, Henry Casson.

New Bridge, 1950.

Ridgeville to Emerson railroad track, 1950.

1956 spring flood at Alfred Schultz farm, 24-1-3 E1, in 1956.

The tornado in 1977 left farmers frustrated and helpless. Courtesy Carillon News.

Three lives were lost during the 1977 tornado at Rosa, when the Michael Klein home was completely destroyed. Remains of basement, including the car which was carried from the yard into the basement, seen here.

Lightning does strike twice. Gordon Kirkpatrick repairing his house after being struck for second time. Came in from gable peak, through metal bed, out the south wall to roof pipe and cistern. Neighbours with bucket brigade put out attic fire. No one was hurt.

United Grain Growers elevator burning in Dominion City. c. 1939.

Train derailment at Dominion City, (year). Courtesy Carillon News.

Sports

by Margaret Kathler

Ridgeville - Dominion City Baseball Team 1905
Back: Dick Craig, George Lockhead, Jim Jack, Bill Craig, Jack Varey, Jake Kirvell, John Heck, Bob Lockhead, Les Ramsey, George Gunn, Ike Adams.
Front: Joe Raw, Lloyd Hempton, Bert Scott, Harry Barber, Jim Waddell, Bob Scott, Henry Larsen, Mr. Winegardener, Wally Taylor.

Picture taken in 1943 of Ida Jane Simpson holding the curling trophy she won at age 73.

1950 Ridgeville Ladies Curling Club.

Swiming lessons at New Bridge.

Ridgeville Ball Team, c. 1910.

Senkiw Ball team. 1956.

Curling, 1974 - Lloyd Hempton, Ray Scott, Ken French, Earle Simpson, Art Heck, Bert Simpson, Mike Stefiuk, and Don Scott. Dominion City.

Woodmore Men's baseball, 1952.

Curling, c. 1920, Dominion City. Mildred Hempton, Lizzie Taylor, Agnes Jones, Katie (Hempton) Weninger in front of D.C. Curling Rink.

Ridgeville Hockey team, 1939.

Wolf hunting near Ridgeville, 1928. Harry Wilkinson and Herb Wilkinson.

Hunting birds, 1910, Bill Maynes, E. Mortlock, Jessie Ostberg, at Bow Park farm.

Figure skating, Jewel Heinrichs, Tracey Hunter, Stacey Ramsey, Tammy Pott 1979.

Roseau Valley All-Stars 1977, 12 and under.
Back row (l-r): Ron Ramsey, coach (Dominion City), Mark Lambert (St. Malo), Tim Bell (Morris), Rick Hildebrandt (Morris), Omer Seed (Arnaud) Representative of the Royal Canadian Legion, Perry Wnuk, (Dominion City), Larry Derksen (Dominion City), Murray Pott (Ridgeville), Barry Fraser (Morris), Rick Wilkinson, (Ridgeville), Gordon Jack (Ridgeville), Mike Wiebe (Morris), Gordon Pott (Ridgeville) manager.
Front row: Denis Trudel (St. Malo), Harvey Gunn (Greenridge), Harvey Colette (St. Malo), Mike Anstett (Dominion City).

Ridgeville Hockey team, 1937.
Front Row (left to right): Lorne Riach, George Alexander, Calvin Turner, John Stowe, and Allan Fostey.
Second Row: Stanley Fostey, Andy Gilchrist and Dunk Pickell (coach).
Back row: Henry Lenton, Clayton Morrison, George Lenton.

1949 ball team, Dominion City.
Back (l-r): Vincent Ratchinsky, Gordon Solnes, Irving Scott, Ben Comeault, Matt Bordenko, Norman Solnes, Bob Boutet.
Front: Min Namba, Bill Turner (coach), Boyd Solnes (waterboy), Doug Rattie.

Greenridge Softball Team, 1935.
L to R: standing ?; Beatrice Oatway; Winnie Hamblin, Doris Kirkpatrick, Hannah Lange, Sarah Casson.
Sitting: Ruth Alstadt, Gertie Barnes, Verna Kirkpatrick, and Iona Kirkpatrick.

Roseau Valley Little League team in Winnipeg playoffs c. 1965. Coach Fred Kathler.

Tolstoi Baseball Club
Bottom: John Mykytiuk, Bill Nedohin, Paul Kulyk, Mike Arseny, Onufrey (Snootch) Probinzansky. Top, Bill Olynuk, Felix Kulick, Walter Wachna, Mike Chesko.

Greenridge Baseball Team, 1921 to 1923. Hector Spence, John Hunter, Wallace Casson, Bert Casson, Donald Gunn, Charlie Gagnon, Fred Casson, Walter Kirkpatrick, Elmer Kirkpatrick.

The Man-Sota League Cup won by Rosa in 1951
Front: William Pupeza, Steve Budey, William Shydlowski (league president), J. R. Solomon, Peter Paley, Wilfred Palmer, Victor Yasinski.
Back: Bert Chubey, Bert Palmer, Larry Kohut, Peter Ewonchuk, George Palmer, Maurice Lakusta, Andrew Kasian.

Ridgeville Girls Baseball Team
Back: Beatrice Stringer, ?, Dora Woods, Alice Wilkinson.
Front: Lily Wilkinson, Jean Smith, Bertha Wilkinson, Annie Collins. Arthur Woods sitting in background.

Winners of States-Dominion League 1953
Back: Lorne Ramsey (coach), Ben Comeault, Irving Scott, Gordon Solnes, Norman Solnes, Rod McKenzie, Lloyd Stewart.
Front: Hugh Kelly (manager), Johnny Ayatte, Roger Boutet, Bob Boutet, Jimmy Baskerville, Chester Stewart, Don Ramsey (bat boy).

Dominion City Oldtimers

This photo was taken in 1932 at Morris during the South-East League semi-finals, Dominion City vs. Morris. Back, Gordon Sullivan (deceased), Jimmy Taylor, Winnipeg, Kenny Hampton, Edmonton, Donc Murchison (deceased), Charlie Unsworth (deceased), Abbie Raw, Piney; front, Stan Ginn (Dominion City), Bill Turner (deceased), Tommy Speer, (whereabouts unknown), Walter Wedmark, Portage.

The Dominion City Flyers

Dominion City Flyers were the Morris Tournament Champions. Team members in random order were Brian Solnes, Vern Wiebe, Randy Ostberg, Rick Pohl, Ron Ramsay, Ron Stewart, Mel Boutet, Arch Hunter, Dave Boutet, Jim Scott, Pat Murray, Bruce Lamont, Barry Gushuliak and Taras Solkolyk.

Dominion City Hockey 1932, coach Albert Raw.

Dominion City, 16 and under, team 1962
Top (l-r): J. Arcand, H. Post, G. Ballantyne, A. Hunter, B. Boutet, D. Namba, B. Carver, B. Scott.
Bottom: B. French, M. Boutet, R. Namba, K. Pott, R. Weedmark, R. Goosen, H. Hancox.

Arnaud Hockey
Back: Oscar Wiens, Bill Dearborn, Lothar Schroeder Peter Dyck, Fred Kathler, Werner Pauls, Aron Isaac, Ed Thiessen, Art Kathler.
Front: Waldo Thiessen, Robert Braun, Johnnie Janzen, Werner Schmidt, Elvin Kathler.

Dominion City Original/Flyer Hockey Team formed 1963, Provencher Hockey League.
Back: J. Arcand, L. Ramsey, C. Gray, G. Ginn, C. Ramsey, D. Gruenke, C. Gray, C. Sabo, B. McQuay, B. Solnes, front, T. Minchuk, D. Namba, K. Gruenke, A. Hunter, R. Huff, E. Thom.

Dominion City skating rink. 1957-1958. Rink was financed and built by voluntary help from people in the Rural Municipality of Franklin.

L to R: Mrs. Ed Jones, Mrs. Gordon Kennedy, Mrs. Doctor McClelland, Mrs. Duncan Gillespie. 1918. Dominion City Curling rink wall.

Two rinks from Ridgeville, March 13, 1936 winners of Beaubien Cup.
Front: Ethel Lindsay, Agnes Ingram.
Second row: Beatrice Stringer, Lillie Riach, Mrs. Roy Post.
Third row: Rose Laufersweiler, Alice Lindsay, Annie Collins.

Bert Simpson and John Peterson with four large Canadian geese shot at Roseau River in 1981, largest 11 lbs. 3 oz.

Taken in front of Dominion City Curling rink c. 1928. Dave Ditlovitch, Miss Haldorson, Kenneth Hempton, Louis Taylor.

Swimming at Bow Park, 1912.

1931 Woodmore Ball Team. Lloyd Stewart, Wilbur Hurd, Russell Mayne with Ted's dog Nick, Bert and Henry Smith, Ted Snead, Mr. Goodwin (teacher), Gerrard Hurd, Ellery Post, and Cliff Ward. Taken in Bob Dickson's field.

Dominion City swimming pool, officially opened in 1956.

Bill and Morris Donaleyko, with pelts of rabbits, skunks and squirrels.

Carnival in outdoor skating rink in Dominion City.

Entertainment

by Wilma Poetker

IN THE HOMES

In spite of the hardships of pioneer life, a delightful social life developed. Visiting was considered a social duty, and it was not unusual to bundle the entire family into a sleigh or wagon and drive miles to pay an unexpected call on friends or relatives. Callers were not permitted to leave before they were well fed on delicious but simple home-made food.

Houseparties were an important social event. Hand written messages were sent out by personal messengers and 40 or 50 people would arrive by team and wagon for an evening of dancing to volunteer music, usually harp and a mouth organ. In Ridgeville, Dora Lenton or Annie Collins and Abe Beckstead supplied music on a piano or organ and violin.

Some of the dances enjoyed were the Heel and Toe, Golden Slipper, Rush Polka, The Sally Water and Square Dances. At the turn of the century when the Waltz and Two-Step were introduced, they were called round dances.

Baby sitters were unheard of, so children came too, babies sleeping on piles of coats and older children sitting quietly on benches or chairs.

A reading club "Chytalnya Prosuta Vechernia Zoria", (Evening Star Reading Club), began in 1907, in private homes with Eudokia Andrushko as first librarian. Books were donated and later a special fund was set up so that new books could be purchased. A library still exists with the Women's League in charge.

Neighbors often got together in homes where they held stripping feather, teasing wool, quilting bees, pigeon shoots and hockey for the men. They celebrated birthdays, anniversary, christening or housewarming.

Young people would gather regularly in groups to sing to the accompaniment of guitars, mandolins and violins. By 1904 there were teachers in Franklin who would give instruction in piano and organ. They would travel to an area by train or buggy and stay a day or two at one home and give lessons. Advanced students went to St. Mary's Academy or St. Jean Convent or Mrs. Anderson in Dominion City.

PICNICS

Picnics were a prominent form of entertainment in days gone by. People travelled suprising distances in summer to attend picnics. A 12th of July Orange Man's picnic was held annually. At Ridgeville the Schiebe Farm, and later the Kiel Grove, at Green Ridge the O'Donnell farm, and later the Knox farm across from the school, were popular picnic spots.

The ladies prepared food for days ahead, donating pies and salads.

The Foresters and Templars ran the picnics in the 90's. The men organized the picnics and sold lemonade. This was their way of making money. Sometimes none was made, and a loss was recorded. Fifteen dollars would be a big take. Food was served on long tables outdoors, featuring cold meats, salads and pies. Ice-cream was a highlight and a big hand powered freezer was kept going all day.

Wild Tiger Lilies and Pink Lady Slippers were picked to decorate the tables. Water was heated for dishes, sometimes in a boiler, or in the cooker used for heating barley for pigs.

On the May 24th picnic there were often fresh radishes and onions in the picnic salads.

Picnics were also held on July 1st at Woodmore, Green Ridge, Dominion City, Emerson and across the line at Orleans and Lancaster, Minnesota. Baseball was an important feature with teams from Ridgeville, Woodmore, Green Ridge and Orleans, Minnesota playing in a tournament. Races of all kinds were participated in by everyone, prizes were small.

Concerts were put on frequently by various groups. Churches and schools had Christmas concerts. Drama groups were organized and catalogues poured over to find suitable plays. These were usually three acts, and were put on in spring and fall or every two or three weeks.

The Templars put on concerts at every meeting

with guests from other clubs.

The Loyal Orangemen's Lodge met once a month. The ladies group was affiliated. A hall was built in 1912 and was the centre of social life at Ridgeville for years.

CONCERTS

All the schools held Christmas concerts. Santa was always a citizen of the area and kept everyone guessing as to his identity until he arrived at the end of the concert put on by the teacher and pupils.

As they grew larger the local schools could not contain crowds so the local halls were used for the event.

Various acts for presentation were practiced over and over again, the end result being that each act was presented as near to perfection as possible. It was a great deal of work, especially for the teacher. Nevertheless, everyone enjoyed the ritual.

During practice sessions at the hall a few older boys were chosen to make fires each day. This got them away from classes for a couple of hours. Some halls had two heaters, one in the front near the stage which was removed before performances.

The hall or school was decorated and a piano moved in. Sometimes the local orchestra helped with the concert.

In 1920 the Chautaiqua toured the country and before it arrived local people paid in money to be sure the performers would receive their royalties. If it was a success, monies were returned. A huge tent was erected, or a local hall might be used. The finest orchestrations, instruments, singing and recitations were put on. A ticket for a week's performances was $7.50. The whole country side purchased tickets.

Drama clubs performed in most areas and put on one or two plays a year. At Arnaud these were often in German, while groups at Tolstoi performed Ukrainian plays.

ORCHESTRAS

The "Skreech Owls" was an orchestra started in Woodmore in 1949, original members were Ronald Spence - violin, John Spence - guitar, Cliff Grier - accordian, Morris Grier - violin. Mrs. Ethel Spence allowed them to practice in their home. Theodore and Edward Ganske replaced the Spence Brothers in 1955. They played in talent shows, house parties, socials and weddings.

Dominion City had a dance band supplying music for weddings, dances and socials for miles around the country. In 1912 Raymond Ginn on

drums, Roland Fry on piano grew to an eight piece orchestra by the 40's known as the "Hoodlums" and later as "The Bandits". Raymie played for 60 years while Bernice Weninger played the piano for 30 years.

With the event of Rock music dominated by guitars the band phased out in 1976 as the trend to taped music came in.

The March 17th dance in the Arnaud Hall is still an annual event. Now Orchestras from a distance come to play to a full hall.

The Chubey Brothers played at many weddings in the eastern end of the municipality, the "Family Love" group is particulary popular now.

CHOIRS

Petro Salamancha of Rosa was a talented man with a good voice and knowledge of music. He conducted the first choir, which with time achieved a remarkable level of performance. They presented variety concerts and sang Sunday mass. Invitations from other churches were accepted during special occasions.

The Arnaud Girls Choir was organized in 1960 by Mrs. Wilma (Harder) Poetker. Their aim was to learn to sing and enjoy good music, and pass this enjoyment on to its listeners. They performed at social functions, banquets, weddings, senior citizen homes, hospitals and festivals. In 1975 Handbells were added.

The community choir of Dominion City was formed to sing Good Friday services in the community hall. Marlene Gruenke is leader in 1982. They sing for Remembrance Day Services, and Carol Services in December.

EXCURSIONS

In early times enjoyable outings to Winnipeg Beach or Lake of the Woods were taken by special train which picked up people along the "Soo Line", or at Ridgeville. Boating and swimming was indulged in as well as steamer excursions out on the lake. The train left at 8 a.m. and arrived back late in the evening. The band often went along to provide music.

Fowl suppers are still big events in Franklin with the districts vying with one another to have the best menus. Ridgeville, Woodmore, Arnaud, Tolstoi and Rosa still carry on this tradition.

Social events within the municipality remain centered on family and community. Children working in the city come home for weekends bringing friends with them. Grandchildren who live away return to spend summer vacations and take swimming lessons. Everyone attends community suppers, funerals, memorial services, weddings and anniversary parties. Children come back for Christmas, house parties and unexpected company for supper are commonplace. Visiting continues at the slower pace of the country.

Opera House, Dominion City, later Maynes Hall.

"Family Love", musicians from Tolstoi
Back L to R: Gayle Neduzuk, Nestor Shydlowski, Linda Shydlowski.
Front: Bradley Neduzuk.

Song festival of combined Arnaud Choirs 1940's

Square dancers at Friedensthal 1958
L to R: Marg Pomrenke, Emil Pomrenke, Art Ganske, Myrtle Ganske, Art Schwark, Ruth Schwark, Harry Hopkins, Evelyn Hopkins.

Band-Its 1970
L to R: Bill Beckstead, Raymond Ginn, Al Bauer, Bernice Weninger.

Tolstoi Drama Group presented plays in Ukrainian 1949 picture.
Front row: Orest Kosowan, Orest Dolynchuk, Jean Fostey, Mrs. Topolnitski, Mr. Topolnitski, Mrs. M. Arseny, Olivia Kolodzinski.
Back row: Wm. Shydlowsky, A. Zulkowsky, Mr. Hryhor, Orest Shydlowsky, John Kosowan.

Tolstoi Ukrainian Dance Group 1967
L to R: Audrey Hoplock, Carol Bially, Sylvia Panisiak, Nestor Shydlowski, Sharon Hoplock, Debbie Kolodzinski, Nancy Kozak.

Chubey Brothers orchestra at John Ewonchuk wedding.
L to R: Peter Chubey, Paul Chubey, Harry Chubey.

Rosa Ukrainian dancers, 1981
Back row: Johnny Stepaniuk, Tammy Stepaniuk, Allan Chubaty, Elizabeth Christiuk, Taras Derbowka, Leanne Matichuk, Vincent Stepaniuk, Instructors Ronald and Jarvis Yasinski.
Second row: Jason Matichuk, Shane Chubaty, Robert Boyechko, Evelyn Wood, Kenny Walford, Rachel Chubaty, Robert Stepaniuk, Beverly Stepaniuk.
Third row: Walter Stepaniuk, Gail Chubaty, Wallace Wood, Tracy Boyechko, Paul Stepaniuk, Laurie Chubaty, Robbie Walford, Jeffery Chubaty.
Front row: Tammy Chubaty, Ryan Chubaty, Kim Tkachuk, Jeffrey Chubaty, Cindy Wood, Mark Stepaniuk, Tanya Germain, Patricia Pohrebnuik.

Arnaud V for victory drill 1939 at school Christmas concert. Teacher, Mr. P. R. Harder.

Hallowe'en dance Dominion City Community Hall 1980.

Senkiw school Christmas concert 1959
L to R: Anne Ostrowsky, Rose Ostrowsky, Sophie Tkachyk.

Musical evening at the Bill Stewart home.
L to R: Ken Saunders, Miss Moore, Minnie Seword, Bill Stewart, Mrs. Bill Stewart, Walter Ross, Mae Hermiston.

Trophy winners Dominion City Music and Arts Festival.
Top row L to R: Loise Clair Weninger, D.C. Solomon Trophy for spoken poetry; Judy Janzen, Arnaud, Rene Jutras Trophy for piano; Lonna Weninger and Frieda Kruger, D. C. tied for the Poetker Trophy in piano; Rosemary Manchal of Arnaud and Billy Dickson of Morris who tied for the D.C. Legion Trophy for vocal solos; Heather Ann Cameron of D.C. who tied for the Dr. Artes trophy for piano; Tanys Taylor.
Front row: Miss Peters, Arnaud, Emerson W.I., Trophy for choir; Mrs. McVicar D.C. grade 8 teacher; choral reading Dr. Dick Trophy; Edith Schmidt, Verna Enns, Arnaud, McLeod Shield for vocal duet; Shiela Rettaler, Ridgeville, John Hunter Trophy for public speaking; Edgar Toews and Lillian Schmidt of Arnaud tied for Hudson Bay trophy for vocal solos; Laurel Froom, D.C.J. Waddell Trophy, A. G. Regier Trophy, and tied with Heather Ann Cameron for Dr. Artes Trophy, all piano, Mrs. Wilma Poetker, Arnaud music teacher. Courtesy Carillon News.

Plane at Dominion City 1930. Kenneth Hempton, Maxine Curran. This plane took people for rides. It crashed and burned the next week.

Interior of Ridgeville Hall decorated for Christmas concert c. 1911.

Curtain on wall of Dominion City Community Hall, originally in Coulter Bros. Hall and Maynes Bros. Hall.

Greenridge I.O.F. Hall decorated for Forresters dance before 1900.

Compliments of Mr. Geo Brad,
Of the Queen's Hotel, Dominion City.
With respect for the company of

Mr. & Taylor and Ladies

WEDDING PARTY,
To be given in the Town Hall,
Dominion City, on
Wednesday Evening, November 3rd, 1886.
DANCING AT 8 O'CLOCK.

Mr.

The wedding Ceremony will take place at 4 o'clock P.M. in All Saints Church And the Supper at 7 P.M. at the Hotel at which Your presence is requested

Invitation of Mr. George Brad to "his" wedding 1886.

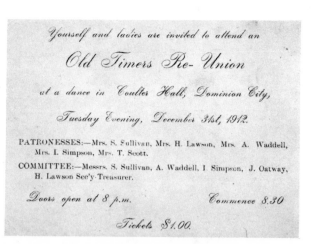

Yourself and ladies are invited to attend an

Old Timers Re-Union

at a dance in Coulter Hall, Dominion City,

Tuesday Evening, December 31st, 1912.

PATRONESSES:—Mrs. S. Sullivan, Mrs. H. Lawson, Mrs. A. Waddell, Mrs. I. Simpson, Mrs. T. Scott.

COMMITTEE:—Messrs. S. Sullivan, A. Waddell, I. Simpson, J. Oatway, H. Lawson Sec'y-Treasurer.

Doors open at 8 p.m. Commence 8.30

Tickets $1.00.

Rosa Town Hall 1982.

Senkiw Community Hall.

★ PROGRAM ★

1 O, Canada
2 Blessing Rev. M. Nixon
3 Welcoming Our Guests W. R. Houston (Chairman)

BANQUET

4 Toast "The King" A. S. Calder
5 Address A. S. Calder
6 Entertainment Fred Wray
7 Toast "Department of Education"
   Proposed by C. Moore reply from Dr. Fletcher
8 Entertainment Fred Wray
9 Toast "The Trustees" Proposed by
   Mr. Stanbridge, reply from Dr. McClelland
10 Len Vintus Entertainment McMullen

★ PROGRAM ★

11 Toast "The Ladies" Proposed by
    R. F. Curran, reply from Mrs. Jos. Casson
12 "Our Municipal Council" Proposed by
    Mr. Werry, reply from S. Gibson, W. Johnston
13 Entertainment Fred Wray
14 "The Staff and Van Drivers" Proposed by
    W. S. Scott, reply from Wm. Skidmore
15 Len Vintus McMullen
16 Thanks to Women's Institute J. A. Scholte
17 A Few Words for the Visitors L. P. Bancroft
18 Entertainment Fred Wray
19 Old Timers Alexander Waddell

"Auld Lang Syne."

Program of complimentary Banquet by school trustees 1936.

Group at Greenridge School preparing food for I.O.F. men building hall.

Back row L to R: Mrs. John R. Post, John Knox, Margaret Oatway McEwen, James Hunter, Jim Nixon, Fred Post, Emma Post, Mr. John Smith.

Middle row: Mrs. Fred Post, Mrs. Jim Dickson, Mrs. Andrew Davison.

Front row L to R: Mrs. Froom Sr., Mrs. Jim Dickson, Jessie Oatway, Rithy Post (Mrs. Steve Post), Annie Dickson, (Mrs. Jim Aikens), Sara McLennan (Mrs. Tom Spence).

Front Row: Alex Kirkpatrick, Dunc. McLaren, Jim Kirkpatrick, Jack Bland, Jim Froom, Jack Thoms, Charlie Chamberland, Robert Ramsey, Archie Hunter, John Carlton.

2nd Row, Kneeling: Fred Post, Charlie Foulds, Jack Knox, John Gunn, Jim Dickson, Wm. Casson, Jack Oatway, Andrew Davison, Robert Gunn, Jim Hunter, Jack Spence, Henry Casson.

Standing: John Adams, Wm. Gunn, Tom Scott, J. D. Baskerville, Tom Mason, Tom Witty, Isaac Casson, Charlie Burrel, Wm. Dickson, John Froom, Homer Nisely Ben Brewster, Hans Shultz, Harry Ball, Wm. Gunn, John R. Post, Geo. Addison, Joe Baskerville, Dan Kirkpatrick, Robert Oatway, Charlie Wollard, Wm. Liske, Walter Stockdale.

Some of these men arrived in the Green Ridge area as early as 1870 and most were here by 1878. This being nearly 20 years later some of their sons are in the picture. It was taken on the occasion of the building of Green Ridge Forresters Hall. This building is still in use as a community hall.

85

Muskeg Limited picks up passengers at Ridgeville for a days excursion to Lake of the Woods, Warroad, Minnesota, about 1918.

Arnaud Girls Choir 1973

Back row L to R: Joan Sukkau, Sandra Isaac, Monica Kathler, Cindy Namba, Judy Baskerville, Patricia Sukkau, Elvina Poetker, Wilma Poetker.

Second row from back: Barbara Friesen, Jacqueline Kathler, Marilyn Kathler, Brenda Bergen, Marcia Wachna, Holly Palmer, Kim Dyck, Lois Thiessen, Mary Ann Enns, Sharon Friesen.

Third row: Elaine Wachna, Arlene Enns, Ruth Wiens, Millie Friesen, Arlene Isaac.

Kneeling: Joyce Isaac, Monica King, Sharlyne Poetker.

Front row: Jennifer Palmer, Darlene Kathler, Kathy Penner, Teresa Wiens.

In 1948 the Dominion City Band was the pride of the community, well organized, and in constant demand to play at various fairs and field days. Its members ranged from 12 to 66 years of age. From left to right they are: Front row: Jim Waddell, Raymond Ginn, Eleanor Ginn, Fay Boutet. Second row: Mamie Gunn, Elmer Boggs, Louis Kein, Wallace Kein, Bill Barber, John Schroeder, Eddie Clupp, Norris Ginn, Stan Ginn, Gracie Ratchinsky, Iris Ginn, Roland Jones, Lenore Raw. Back row: Phyllis Ramsey, Gayle Lamont, Ruby Anderson, Nena Maynes, Lorne Woods, Johnny Gunn, Cliff Gunn, Doreen Barber, Audrey Smart, Charlie Marks, Clarence Henry, Beverly Gainer, Harvey Ratchinsky, Bert Grant, Matt Raw, Dr. Skinner, Vic Bobrowski.

87

Education

by Audrey Grier

By 1875 much of southeastern Manitoba had been surveyed south of the Roseau River, bordered by the Red on the west. The influx of settlers soon led to school districts being formed. Some of these first districts were quite large, but as settlers stayed and families enlarged more schools sprang forth. There were 20 schools established between 1880 and 1900.

Children walked to school. Your size usually determined when you started school, especially if the distance was many miles. You finished school when work demanded your labor on the farm. Classes were held during late spring and summer months. Many mothers carried some teaching in their respective homes during the long winters. Parents ploughed furrows for children to follow.

Slates were used for many years. The school boards were responsible for texts in the three R's and these precious books were well looked after and often served family after family. 1915 to 1920 scribblers began to make their appearance in schools. During the early 1940's workbooks were used.

The early one-room schools were heated by a pot bellied stove or an iron box heater. Either stove would cook the children next to it while other less fortunates would be shivering in their woollens. Water was often carried from a pioneer's well sometimes a mile away.

Once a school was well established then the settlers would build a barn to house the horses. Children then would drive a horse and buggy (or cutter in wintertime) and the horses would be sheltered. Often families took turns transporting the children to school. But there were those who still walked. Quite often children would stop at a neighbor's house to rest and warm themselves before going the rest of the distance home.

Nearing 1913 consolidation started. School vans were introduced in some areas. These were democrats or covered vans pulled by horses. These vehicles were forerunners of our big orange school buses.

During the 1920's and thru 1930's and into the 1940's transportation to most country schools did not change. Occasionally now a more fortunate child would be driven to school in a car or pick up. Lunches were carried in lunch boxes instead of a jam pail or three cornered piece of cloth. The thermos made its appearance.

The curriculum now included "social studies", a combination of history and geography, French or German took the place of Latin; Mathematics turned into Algebra and Geometry. Workbooks flared up in almost every subject and the schoolboards rebelled against the cost often forcing the teacher into consultation with the parents to purchase needed aids.

During the years 1945 to 1955 there was a teacher shortage. In order to keep many of the outlying small schools open, the Department of Education allowed prospective teachers upon completing their Grade XII to "Permit Teach" for a year before taking their training. And very often these young people finished their training and became excellent teachers. Many ended up married to the most eligible bachelor in the district.

During the 1960 to present time the introduction of modern equipment has lessened the need for manual labor on the farms. Children grew up and left for the city. The population grew less. Small schools closed and the remaining students were driven to consolidated schools.

Now today children often travel a distance of 40 miles between home and school. They have modern sports equipment, large airy gyms, highly qualified teachers and a wide choice of studies, cafeterias, air conditioned rooms, often carpeted for quietness and well stocked libraries.

Oh, little Red School House, you've come a long — long — way . . .

ROLL CALL

The school bell rings in September
The teachers answer its call
And come again to their places
The teachers — God bless them all.

From mountains and plain and valley

They rally again to the ranks
To solve a thousand problems
To cope with a thousand pranks.

As again to the black board army
They come from far and wide
We will find answered the last roll call
And crossed to the other side.

And now to all the teachers
To old and young and short and tall
The thick and the thin and the gay and the grim
The teachers — God **bless them all.**

FRANKLIN SCHOOLS

	School	Closed	Pioneer Teacher
1880	Dominion City #45	Still functioning	Miss Maggie Smith
1972-82	Roseau Valley Collegiate	Still functioning	
1880	Springbank #104	1958	Sarah McLennan
1880-84	Ridgeville #102	June 1972	Effie Post
1882-85	Woodmore #310 (Fairview)	1965	Matilda Baskerville
1882	Greenridge #75 (Parry)	1967	Miss Yoemanns
1883	Manchester #251	1946	Miss Jennie Gunn
1884	Bow Park	1913	Miss Heale
1884	Langside #230	1963	Elizabeth Greene
1884	Middleview	Phased into Stockport	
1884	Stockport	Burnt down 1943	
1884-86	Rosetta-Carlowrie #421	1965	Peter McArthur
1885	Bradley #369	1967	W. Kolodzinsky 1910
1885	Erin #385	1913	
1885	Stuartburn #536	1902 formed Municipality of Stuartburn	M. Shore 1890 G. A. Curran
1890	Overstone #1106	1961	Lou Jacobs
1891	Purple Bank	1902 into Municipality of Stuartburn	
1896	Newbridge #877	1913	Gertie Calder Sarah McLennan
1896	Jordan		
1899	Timlick #1013	1955	J. T. Gamy
1900	Pleasant View		
1901	North Star #1103	1966	Annie Calder 1903
1902	Arnaud #1175	1972	Mr. Burham
1903	Czerwona S.D. #1224 changed to Tolstoi (1918)	1967	Theodore Kochan 1906
1904	Emerado #1237	1958	Pastor Henry Becker
1906	Senkiw #1387 once called Rosa	1967	Theo Sankey
1907	Melrose #1421 (Whitley)	1913	
1901	Plankey Plains #1083	1970	Minnie Kelly
1913	River Ranch #1161	1967	Ellen Breadner
1914	Zelota #1746	1965	Basil Smook
1916	Baskerville #1819 (at Rosa)	1967	Elie Jenkins
1926	Lyman Centre #2145	1953	Mr. Alexander Dirks
1974	Greenbank Mennonite School	Still functioning	Jacob Martens
1966	Hutterite Glenway Colony School	Still functioning	Henry Enns Lorna Lamont

DOMINION CITY #45

A search of municipal school records states that Roseau School district was mentioned in the minutes of May 3, 1880, which stated that "the place formerly occupied by council is now rented as a schoolroom". It is mentioned that the location of the first school building was the Fry House directly south and west of Dr. O'Brien's home. In 1901 a four-room school was built in the area still used as a school yard for the primary school.

Consolidation came into effect in 1913 when Whitley, Erin, and part of Bow Park joined Roseau school district.

In 1914 the school was considered unsafe. In 1916 a new sixroom building was built just east of it. The tender of $18,456 of Halldor Sigurdson was accepted, the old building was sold for $840. Four teachers were accepted on staff. The west side ground floor was rented out for public meetings, band practices and entertainment evenings with proceeds to be given to a piano fund.

Due to shifting soil, cracks appeared in the walls during the summer of 1919. The repairs totalled $3,251.86. During the early 50's a part of the roof was damaged by a severe windstorm.

Enrollment increased, in 1946 a sixth room was opened. In 1947 Mrs. Merrill taught 34 beginners in the old municipal hall (now site of Lutheran Church). In 1948 a two-room annex built from a van shed was placed at the southwest part of the main school. Later a third room was added known as the "chicken coop".

For many years following consolidation, pupils were conveyed by horse driven vans mounted on wheels or sleighs as seasons demanded. First vans were purchased in June 1913, John Scott drove to Whitley area, Erv Simpson to Erin — wages were $3 a day. Frank Gray drove for many years and during wartime handled three van routes. There was seven vans during 1919 - a van cost $325.

Thru the years a good drinking water supply for the school was a main concern. Ice was melted in a galvanized tank. Hot summer days created a problem when demand exhausted supply.

Electricity was installed in December 1935. The February light bill for 1936 totalled $1.15.

In 1940-49, teaching staff numbered eight teachers with Grade XII being taught first time by Harry Sharpe, well-known area teacher. 1956 saw the new Primary School built and the annex removed.

The old brick school closed its doors December 1965. Students continued their studies in the basement of the United Church till June 1966. Boundary Division was formed. High school students were bussed to Emerson for six years.

Roseau Valley Collegiate opened in 1972. At present most of the pupils in the west part of the division attend R.V.C. exceptions are Grades I - VIII at Emerson, Glenway Colony school and Roseau Reserve (1963-1980).

As well as offering academic courses, University Entrance, and General Business Education, R.V.C. holds courses in Home Economics, Industrial Arts, Computer Science, Power Mechanics and Cosmetology. Students are bussed to Altona for food service and carpentry, and to St. Jean for welding.

The collegiate has a total staff of 23 teachers from Kindergarten to Collegiate. Peter Yarmie, Douglas Gruenke, Ray LeNeal and Bev Berrington are the four principals to staff the Collegiate since 1972.

It is an interesting fact to note that this Collegiate remains as the only school to withstand the shifting population throughout the Franklin Municipality in the one hundred years.

Erin school was situated in Twsp. 1, Rge. 3E Sec. 22, 25-28, 32-36. Later was added 31-1-3E to W ½ of 5-2-3E.

Melrose or **Whitley** formed in 1907 from lots in the St. Agathe Parish, Lots 88, 90, 92, 94, 96, 98, 100-112, 12-14, Lots A, B, C, 1-2-2E and W ½ 6-2-3E.

Bow Park was situated in Twsp. 2, Rge. 1, Sec. 24, 25 and 26.

On April 8, 1890, Sec. 22, 27, 34, Twsp. 2, Rge. 3E was added to Roseau School district. This school was located on the west side of Roseau River across from the Maynes and Huff farms. At one time the Brad children, Clarence, Jessie, Laura and Leslie were the only students. German settlers in the area increased the enrollment only for a short time.

ARNAUD #1175

The first settlement was made in the Arnaud district about 1877. No record of formal school districts in that era are available. In 1902 a one-room school was established and was formerly called Arnaud. It had four students in attendance. In 1925-26 a teacher, Mr. Whitley, taught night school to the new Canadians. In 1938 a new two-room school house was built - Peter Harder and Ethel Reynolds were first teachers. This continuation school was built through the efforts of J. P. Isaac, Henry Sukkau and Alex Jones who spared no time and effort to see the project through. Seventy-two pupils were enrolled from Grades I to IX. In 1955 Lyman Centre school annexed to Arnaud to make it a three-room school.

In 1972 Arnaud school closed its doors and children were bussed to Dominion City to attend Roseau Valley Collegiate.

LANGSIDE

Langside was a small one-room school built on a two acre lot on the NE ¼ of section 12-3-3E. The lot was donated by a settler James Lang for use of a school yard as long as necessary. In 1905 a second school replaced the original school. This building still stands as a landmark and reminder of passed era. Garnet Coulter, mayor of Winnipeg, once taught at this school. An interesting fact of this district that in the 79 year history only four Secretary-Treasurers served the board. These were James Lang, Anne McLelland (Lang), Garnet Lang and Florence Boutet (King). In 1958 the school closed and in 1963 the district was dissolved with students attending Dominion City, Green Ridge and Arnaud.

TIMLICK #1013

The Timlick S. D. was located in the north western part of the R. M. of Franklin comprising of 12 ½ sections of land in Twsp. 3, Rge. 2E. This school was formed by by-law 209, May 9, 1899. It was named after the Timlick families who settled the area in the 1880's. The Pearse families arrived in 1886 and throughout the following years both families contributed greatly to the functioning of this school. The settling of Lyman ranches increased the enrollment in 1924. During the 1950 flood the water washed thru the school. The outhouse and barn were swept away. The school was moved to higher ground. It was closed in 1955.

NORTH STAR #1103

This school was known as the "school on wheels". In 1901 to 1923 it sat in the middle of a section. Mr. Hay was Secretary-Treasurer and D. Sullivan a trustee.

In 1913 it closed and pupils attended Arnaud. In 1922 the school opened again and was moved to NE corner of section 31-3-4E. First teacher here was Marion L. Williams at a wage of $84 a month. In 1937 the school moved to SW corner of Sec. 31; in 1938 moved back to present site. In 1950 building was sold and a new school built. In 1966, low enrollment caused the school to close. John Krueger bought the building and has turned it into a beautiful home.

LYMAN CENTRE

In the fall of 1924 and spring of 1925 a large group of Mennonite families came to the Arnaud district from Russia where the Revolution had caused them to lose their land and much of their personal possessions. Mr. H. H. Lyman was willing to sell. A sale contract was established and 44 families promised to pay $63 per acre. A school was needed and Lyman Centre sprung into existence. English lessons were very necessary and for a short time many parents attended evening classes to learn the language.

The school continued for 27 years and in 1953 it closed its door ending a memorable era for many students.

ROSETTA — CARLOWRIE #421

In 1884, May 6, application was made to Council for Rosetta S. D. including, Twsp. 3, Rge. 4E, Sec. 8-29, 32-36, Twsp. 3, Rge. 5E, Sec. 7-8, 17-19, 29-32.

On December 10, 1884, necessary proofs were not forwarded so school district was cancelled. June 9, 1885, motion to council, "Whereas Henry Timlick and thus have petitioned to have the following lands included in a Protestant School District, N½ of Section 8, Section 9, 10, 13, 14-17, 20, 21-28, 32-36. Twsp. 3, Rge. 4E and Sec. 18, 19, 30, 31 in Twsp. 3, Rge. 5E. The pupils attended Rosetta school till 1913 when the school closed for one year. The pupils attended Arnaud. In 1914 the school opened again under the name of Carlowrie.

In 1924 a new, larger and modern school was erected. This unit served as a classroom and community centre till 1965. It was then closed and moved to Vita to serve as a classroom till the new Vita school was built in 1969.

GREEN RIDGE

In the early 1880's Green Ridge school was known as Parry chosen because the site was in Parry Township, later in 1913 changed to Perry.

This school was frame, built of sided logs, lined with lath and plaster all wainscotted three and a half feet high from the floor. In March 1882, the first teacher's salary was $400 a year and a month's holiday in August. In 1903 a stable was completed costing $150.

In 1914 Perry changed to Green Ridge Consolidated No. 1704 with the addition of Newbridge and part of Bow Park. On October 1, 1920 a new modern two-room school was built with 16 students in high school and 23 in lower grades.

There were seven van routes in 1966 when Woodmore school was moved to the Green Ridge site to house students. Two years later the school closed. Students were bussed to Dominion City, Ridgeville and some attended St. Pierre. This was quite a trying time with indecision and many ratepayers fighting the change.

NEWBRIDGE

Newbridge originated in 1896. It was a school 18 × 26 with an inside metallic roof. Annie Scott (Hunter) attended this school and at age 86 recalls when she was 16, she and four other students studied shorthand from Mr. Doublday. In 1913 Newbridge consolidated with Green Ridge.

WOODMORE SCHOOL #310

In 1882, August 15, in Council a by-law was passed to establish a school district of Fairview. Motion moved by J. Casson and seconded by R. Coates. On February 12, 1884, the name was changed to Woodmore by superintendent of Education.

The first school was a frame structure built by Joseph J. Moore with volunteer help. It had a shingled roof and the walls were later covered with tin siding painted red. The name Woodmore apparently is an abbreviated combination of Frank Woodhead and J. J. Moore — two settlers of the district. At first the school district covered almost a whole township but as other surrounding schools became organized the district was reduced to 16 square miles.

The first school was opened in 1885 with the first teacher being Matilda Baskerville. (Mrs. William Fraser of Emerson).

The little red tin school house was about 32 feet by 22 feet. It had three windows on each side facing the north and south and a small porch attached. Enrollment at the school was 16 to 24 students for many years. Children walked to school and fortunate indeed was the youngster who would "get a ride to school".

In autumn of 1927 a new larger school building was opened. It was equipped with a basement, furnace and indoor toilets. This school served the district until 1965 when at a ratepayers' meeting the vote was 40 to 23 that the school close and join Green Ridge in consolidation, September, 1966.

The school moved to Green Ridge and served as a classroom. Further consolidation forced the school to be sold. It is now resting in Vita.

JORDAN

In 1896, April 14, by-law 190 provided for the alternation of the boundaries of the public school district of Parry #75, Woodmore #310, Rosetta #421 for the formation of the new public school district of Jordan all in the R. M. of Franklin. Twsp. 2, Rge. 4E, Sec. 34; Twsp. 3, Rge. 4E, Sec. 3-5; Twsp. 3, Rge. 4E, Sec. 1, 2, 11, 12; Twsp. 3, Rge. 4E, Sec. 8, 9, 10, S½ 13-17.

RIDGEVILLE #102

The Ridgeville school district was organized in 1880, but it seems classes were conducted only in the summer months. Apparently, teachers salaries and other expenses must have been paid by local funds, for it was not until 1885, that the first Provincial Grant of $10 was made to the Ridgeville School. The school was located on the hill north of Ridgeville, across the road from the Timchuk residence with the assumption that this would become the future townsite. In 1914 this building was moved to the present school site. As the enrollment increased, reaching a high of 52 in 1926, it was deemed necessary to enlarge the school by adding a new section to the north end of the classroom in that year. The trustees, staunch supporters of better educational opportunities for the children, worked unceasingly until in 1928, they were able to add another classroom, which was the beginning of the Ridgeville High School. Four students in Grade IX were enrolled as the first high school class that year. The first Grade XI graduating class in 1933 consisted of three girls. In 1958 Springbank and Emerado School Districts consolidated with Ridgeville which accounted for the erection of the present building. Ridgeville now boasted a two-room high school, Grade XII inclusive. School vans were introduced to transport children to and from school.

With the consolidation of Overstone S. D. in 1961, the Overstone school was moved to the Ridgeville school site to serve as a classroom for Grades 1 - 3. The record high enrollment of 130 pupils in the school was reached in 1963. In 1966 the Zelota S. D. consolidated with Ridgeville S. D. With the vote finally accepting the Boundary Division in 1966, the Ridgeville High School ceased to exist, and the high school students were transported to the Emerson High School. In the March referendum, 1967, the Boundary Division accepted the single board system.

SPRINGBANK #104

The district was formed in 1880, November 10. The first building, erected in 1882, served as a church and also served the Overstone district as well. Pioneer teachers were Sarah McLennan, Lottie Agnew from Dominion City who taught for $7 a month and her board. Others were Libby Christie, J. Stewart, Effie Post and Edith Hurd.

The old school was sold, moved north of Ridgeville then moved again and remodelled to become a home for Mr. and Mrs. Rod McLennan. It is now owned by Ken and Cindy Toll.

The second school was built in 1935, closed in 1958 when consolidation with Ridgeville, and is now the home of Earl and Ethel Lamont in Dominion City.

OVERSTONE #1106

In 1890 the eastern district was well populated. A school was built but was abandoned as the settlers left. Charles Burbidge, one of the first to come, remained and prospered. Jack Goetz farmed this homestead - now owned by Shirley Kingston.

In the late 1890's the immigration of European settlers again settled in the eastern districts. The abandoned Bradley School was moved to the Overstone site and became the first school.

In 1914 a new school was built. There were 72 pupils attending that year under the direction of Lou Jacobs of Emerson who received a monthly wage of $35.

In the spring of 1953 the school burnt down - classes carried on in an empty house for completion of term. A new school was ready for the fall term.

In 1961 Overstone consolidated with Ridgeville - pupils and school both moved to Ridgeville and in 1972 this school closed. The little Overstone school in 1974 moved back to the eastern district and now serves the Greenbank Mennonite school near Tolstoi.

ZELOTA

In 1914, Mr. Roy Toews accepted a contract for $100 to build a 20 × 34 × 12 school house in the Overstoneville district. Basil Smook, the first teacher, was paid $10 a month. Chairman for the first Zelota school was John Nedohin (Anko), trustees were Thomas Yabolinski and John Seward, secretary was Ezra Post.

In 1955 a modern school was built situated east of Bert Nedohin's farm. In 1965 the school closed with consolidation with Ridgeville.

Zelota pupils were an enthusiastic group, especially keen on sports and did well in field day competitions.

CZERWONA S. D. - TOLSTOI

In 1903, March 10, by-law 241 provides information of Czerwona. Twsp. 1, Rge. 5E, Sec. 25-29, 32-36. Twsp. 11, Rge. 5E, Sec. 1-5, 8-12.

The school was built in 1904. The name Czerwona means "Red School". It opened in 1906 for spring and fall term. School was opened for 124 days with 26 boys and 15 girls in attendance. Government grant was $76.50. In 1918 the name changed to Tolstoi. In 1935 the school burnt down. The teacherage was moved onto a location on the seven mile road called Tolstoi No. 11.

In 1949-50 a three-room school was approved in Tolstoi. Boundary School No. 16 had taken over the school locally in 1967. The school is now the Tolstoi and District Community Centre.

BRADLEY

In 1885, May 12, "Whereas certain of the ratepayers have petitioned this Council in the form required by law to establish a school district to be known as Bradley. Therefore School Council of R. M. of Franklin enacts as follows. That the following lands be formed into a Protestant School District, Twsp. 1, Rge. 5E, Sec. 15-30, Twsp. 1, Rge. 4E, Sec. 13, 14, 23, 24 and 25, (later March 13, 1901 Section 13, 14, 23, 24 broke away to be part of Overstone."

Bradley school was named after a settler, Mr. Bradley, who settled in the area in the 1880's. Many of the English settlers moved from the area. The school was closed. Later it was moved to the Overstone S. D. and became its first school. In the late 1890's an immigration of European people to this eastern region soon required a new school to be built in 1904. In 1916 another room was added and high school was taught till 1959. With consolidation the Bradley pupils were bussed to Vita Collegiate.

MANCHESTER

In 1883, January 16, a by-law was passed to form a school in the Red River settlement Twsp. 1, Rge. 3E and river lots 26-84 inclusive. This school was called Manchester No. 251.

MIDDLEVIEW

In 1884, April 18, by-law 84 formed the school district of Middleview (formerly part of Manchester) located in Twsp. 1, Rge. 3E, Sec. 1-4, 9-16, 21-28, 33-36.

STOCKPORT

In 1884, December 10, by-law 99 amending by-law 84 was passed by Council establishing Middleview School District to form Stockport on site NE¼ of Section 9. Unfortunately in 1943 the school burnt. Pupils transferred to Emerson and Emerado.

EMERADO

The Emerado school district consisted of Twsp. 1, Rge. 3E, Sec. 10, 11-14, 23-26, 35, 36.

The early school was called "Fredensthal". The average distance for pupils from school was one and a half miles. In 1917 the teacherage was built. Pastor Henry Becker instructed 70 pupils in German and English languages. After the last recess religion was taught. Teachers' salary in 1920's was $850 but dropped to $450 during depression years. In 1928 a new school was built. Farms grew larger, enrollment decreased, and finally Emerado closed its doors in 1958. The school was purchased by the Fredensthal congregation and the pupils attended Ridgeville school.

SENKIW

From the year 1900 to 1906, the area of Senkiw was well settled with families. A school was built with a two-room teacherage. It was of board construction only for the inside walls that were clay plastered and nicely white-washed. The school was named Rosa School District after the Roseau River that flowed through the district. (Later in 1928 the name changed to Senkiw).

The first 16 pupils were all beginners. Usually a caretaker was hired to start the morning fire. Other chores, carrying firewood, and filling water fountains were done by older students.

No report cards were used before the late 30's. Some slates were used but these were breakable. Scribblers and pencils were supplied by the school, readers came later and these were bilingual. Opposite each English word was the Ukrainian translation. These were replaced by Manitoba Readers till about 1922 when Canadian Readers made their debut.

Most students carried their lunch to school - jars of cocoa or soup were placed near the box stove to warm in winter months. In 1927 an addition to house library books, an entrance lobby, and a cloakroom was added to the school house.

In 1947, growing population demanded a larger modern school. In 1965 a referendum was defeated in the Senkiw, Carlowrie and Plankey Plains districts to join the new school division system. Finally in 1967 Boundary Division No. 16 was formed and Senkiw school closed.

PLANKEY PLAINS was built in 1901 and enlarged in 1910. Windows were changed and a porch added in 1940. This school rests as a barn on the David Runke farm.

A new school was built in 1958 by John Didychuk a local lumber dealer. When consolidation closed the other small schools in the area, this school housed the Grade I and II students for three years. Older grades attended Ridgeville or Vita. In 1970 Plankey Plains closed its doors but still served as a community meeting place. In 1978 it was moved to Roseau River Park and now serves as a community centre.

RIVER RANCH

The Carleton family were cattle ranchers near Rat River and were instrumental in starting the first school appropriately named River Ranch School. The Carleton six children were the first and only students. Later in 1924 night classes offered information to 17 adult students. This class was so popular that another teacher was hired. In 1935 the school was administered by Official Trustee from Winnipeg. In 1951 local trustees were elected again. Initially River Ranch School was built near the Rat River. In 1930 it was moved west closer to the community where it remained until 1967. It was moved to Vita, used as a classroom and then as a book repository till the new school was built.

BASKERVILLE school opened with a class of 29 students belonging to 11 families. By 1918 the school enrollment had grown to 42 pupils. This school when first built also served as a community centre and a place of worship until a hall and church were built. In 1967 with consolidation the school was sold to a local resident. It has since been demolished.

STUARTBURN began in 1880 when W. S. Miller and the ratepayers petitioned the council to have the following lands into a Protestant School District.

Twsp. 2, Rge. 5E, Sec. 10-15, 22-27. Twsp. 2, Rge. 6E, Sec. 7-9, 16-21, 28-30.

In 1888 Leonard Ramsey donated land and built a one room school which was used till 1916.

In 1902 Stuartburn separated from Franklin and formed their own municipality.

Purple Bank, first called Purple Hills because of the abundance of crocuses, was formed in 1891. This district also opted out of Franklin in 1902.

GLENWAY COLONY SCHOOL five miles east of Dominion City began with 11 children, taught at the beginning by Lena Waldner, a colony resident. Henry Enns taught the 1966-67 term; Lorna Lamont from 1967 to 1982, enrollment now is 22 children. The school is under the superintendentship of Boundary Division #16.

Grades I - VIII are taught and high school grades are taken by correspondence. Due to the absence of television and radio on the colony, Language Arts is the subject that gets priority. These skills are important to acquire information and follow directions. Mathematics is stressed as the metric system and complex farming methods demand a thorough knowledge. Science, Social Studies, Art and Physical Education are part of the curriculum. Outdoor sports are enjoyed in school hours and on the colony in the evening. Children age five to 15 receive German language instruction from Sam Kleinsasser, a colony resident. Tyrolean is the spoken language on the colony. At the age of 15 the boys begin apprenticing in different trades, assisting in all phases of the farm work. The girls begin home economic courses in the colony kitchen and at home. They become very proficient in sewing and useful crafts.

Through the combination of English and German school and the practical knowledge obtained on the colony the student is prepared for the future.

GREENBANK MENNONITE SCHOOL is situated two miles south and one mile east of Tolstoi and began with two families with a pupil enrollment of 10. In the next two years there were 19 students. The parents of these children wished for a close teacher - student and teacher - parent relationship that is not always possible in larger schools. They felt the active family involvement in the school was very positive. The Christmas and Easter programs and the family picnics are real highlights every year.

Also the children have good sense of responsibility regarding school property. They feel such attitudes are very beneficial to develop.

The parents hire qualified teachers who follow the school curriculum with emphasis on religion.

1922 class Senkiw, teacher John Tanchak
L to R: Peter Andrushko, John Salamandyk (back) Stephen Smook (front with book) Stephen Shewchuk, Peter
J. Salamandyk, Peter W. Smook, Peter W. Salamandyk, John Pupeza, William Andrushko, Annie Smook (Sidor), Lena
Smook, Dora Smook (Sidor), Annie Lobur (back), Mary Shewchuk, Mary J. Ewonchuk, Lena Shypak.

Water fountain and wash basins used in Dominion
City School until it closed in 1965.

Woodmore school van driven by Jim Dickson.

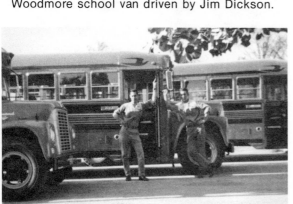

1966 first school busses Boundary school division
- H. Ballast, A. Ballast.

Stockport school

DOMINION CITY SCHOOL
DISTRICT NO. 45
Franklin, Manitoba

ANNIE CALDER, Teacher

PUPILS

Lizzie Hay	Stanley Gunn
Annie Witty	Garton Hutchinson
Herbert Arthur	August Schmitke
Willie Johnson	Isabel Wyness
Eva Hempton	Katie Barber
Keith Witty	Ian Robertson
Willie Hutchinson	Theron Patterson
Hardy Baskerville	Roy Heck
Lizzie Hancox	Eddie Graydon
Raymond Gunn	Grace Hassett
Tom Morkill	Bert Simpson
Laura Brad	Dorothy Fry
Wallace Spear	Gilbert Lovering
Elspeth Moffatt	Mary Hutchinson
May Heck	Nellie Hancox
Alfred Hancox	Mary Witty
Wilby Preston	Fritts Fry
George Palmer	Willie Little
Herbert Roff	Ernest Hay
Alice Graydon	

SCHOOL BOARD

James Scott	Alexander Waddell
John R. Witty	

1908 Class, Dominion City, Christmas card presented to teacher.

Manitoba school readers used 1914-1923.

Bow Park School
L to R: Clarence Brad, Miss Heale, the teacher, Jessie Brad, Laura Brad, Leslie Brad.

These were the only pupils at the time the picture was taken. At one time German settlers in the area filled the school - for a short time only. School located West side of Roseau River across from the Maynes-Hoff farms. Samuel H. Maynes was secretary treasurer of the school.

Woodmore school at field day 1938, teacher Frances Batten, Ralph Batten, Lenora Grier holding banner.

Playing ball Emerado School 1940's.

Ridgeville School 1940, preparing for field day.

Two Green Ridge schools, 1920 and 1948.

96

River Ranch School, Rosa.

Tolstoi II 1936

Zelota School

Two Woodmore schools 1885, new one 1927.

North Star School

Overstone School

Langside School

Springbank school 1923.

Baskerville school and Teacherage.

Lyman Centre school 1926.

1924-25 class Czervona School

L to R (kneeling) 1st row: Tony Kulyk, Paul Kulyk, Bill Kraynyk, Felix Kulyk, —, Nellie Majewski, Walter Kolodzinski, Alex Dolynchuk, Nestor Kostyniuk.

L to R, 2nd row: (white dress) Teklia Drewniak, Mary Wolawka, Mike Kshyna, John Dolynchuk, Harry Domytrak, Helen Kostynuik, Mike Dutka, —, Metro Mandzie, (on back part face showing) Bill German, Jack Mandzie, Helen Oryschak, Mary Majewski.

L to R, 3rd row: John Kulyk, Bill Olynyk, —, Mary Domytrak, Alexander Yarmie, Olga Yarmie, Mike Oryschak, Annie and Rose Dutkewich, Helen Hardibura, Kathy Dutkewich, Pawlina Rutlowski, Christy Oryschak.

Standing below: Pawlina Rutkowski, Annie Zulak, and Olga Mandzie.

Plankey Plains 1901.

Arnaud School 1926.

Greenridge graduation class about 1900 - Andy Spence, Llewie Davison, Calvin Knox, Eddie Oatway, Tassy Knox, Nellie Devitt.

Arnaud School 1938.

Dominion City Schools; a) first school b) 1916 school c) Roseau Valley Collegiate 1972 d) Dominion City Primary School 1982.

Carlowrie School.

Boundary School Division office, Dominion City.

Dominion City School Concert

Friday, February 6th, 1931

Choruses - By School

O Canada! .... Winter is Coming.

Chairman's Address

Address of Welcome	Susie Weedmark
Dance	Irene Bradly
Recitation, "Mouse and the Cake"	Kathleen McCormick
Folk Dance	Primary Girls
Danny Boy .... Song	Seniors
Recitation, "Buddy's Courtship"	Susie Weedmark
Folk Dances *Bernice & Betty*	Junior Boys and Girls
Hoe and Rake Drill	Seniors
Recitation, "The Watermellon"	Adeline Brooks
Fairy Drills	Girls, Room III.
Minstrel Show	Boys, Room IV.

Play, "WHEN KITTY ELOPED"

Characters

Hattie—The Vansant Maid	Ethel Coates
Payson—The Family Lawyer	Allwyn McClelland
Miss Tompkins—Secretary of Mrs. Vansant	Mildred Coates
Mrs. Vansant—A Wealthy Widow, known as the Duchess	Maxine Curran
Jerome—The Vansant Butler	Fred Maxfield
Kitty Vansant—Daughter of the Duchess	Florence Jones
Hal McAllister—An Adventurer	Donald Gillespie
Molly McAllister—McAllister's Second Wife	Lillian Weninger
Hal, Jnr.—McAllisters's Son	Fred Treleaven
Bill Grimes—Circus Manager	Willie Taylor
Kitty Vansant—(The Second)-Grand Niece of the Duchess	Ruth Calder

ACT I.

Scene in Mrs. Vansant's home. Her Daughter, Kitty, Elopes with her Riding Teacher, Hal McAllister

ACT II.

Twenty Years Later

Scene: The home of Hal McAllister's—the Circus Rider— and Molly, his Second Wife

ACT III.

Home of Mrs. Vansant. Same year as Act II. Kitty, the Niece, whom Mrs. Vansant has adopted, falls in love with the younger Hal McAllister

Dominion City school concert 1931.

Religion

by Eva Bially

As soon as the settlers had acquired a makeshift shelter and enough food to sustain their physical needs, they began to attempt to provide for their spiritual ones. Despite the variety of creeds, the differences in language and basic beliefs, all followed the same path toward the establishment of churches. Services were held in various homes by travelling ministers or priests and baptisms, marriages, confirmations and confessions were performed en mass when clergy were available.

Precious cash was readily donated toward a building fund, as was land for church sites, material for construction and labor for the actual building. Bells and candlesticks were purchased, altars and pews carved by hand.

The men of the church were its builders, deacons and preachers, the women were its heart. They were the ones who provided meals for the travelling clergy, who embroidered the altar cloths, who staffed the Sunday Schools, who organized concerts, who prepared food for the church picnics, suppers and feast days. They starched the garments for baptisms, confirmations and weddings, they arranged the flowers on church altars, they polished the pews and windows in the houses of God and they washed and dressed the dead.

These were the women of each church in the municipality, striving to preserve their heritage, studying the faith in their auxiliaries, leagues, and sisterhoods and conscious of the need for spiritual maintenance in changing conditions throughout 100 years.

Many churches were constructed throughout the municipality in the days of dense settlement and limited transportation. As settlement patterns changed so did the churches. Some amalgamated, others closed. Many stand abandoned, but their builders are not forgotten. Throughout the municipality memorial cairns honor the pioneers who transplanted their faith to a new land.

Woodmore Sunday School Group of 1899.

Back row L to R: Guy Post, Alexander Kirkpatrick, Richard Batten Jr., Daniel Kirkpatrick, James Grier, Frank Batten, George Grier, Fred Badams, Elizabeth Kelly, Mrs. Richard Batten Sr., Mrs. Ellery Post, Edith Post, Edith Hurd, Dr. M. C. O'Brien in doorway, Annie Dickson, Olive Grier, Mary Batten, Bertha Hurd, Ida Post, Emma Post, Lillian Hamblin, Adeline Kelly, Alice Hamblin, Mabel Post.

In front row: John Badgley, LeRoy Post, Ezra Post, Fred Hamblin, George Kelly, Charles Batten, two small children, Edward Post and Melville Badgley.

All Saints Anglican Church, Domninion City. Moved to present location 1908, consecrated 1912.

Interior of St. Marys Anglican Church Ridgeville, consecrated in 1906.

Mortgage burning, 1963 at Dominion City United Church built on land donated by James Waddell.
L to R: Wallace Spear, Raymond Ginn, Bernice Weninger, Rev. Edward Blezzard, Don Thom, Lorne Ramsey, Rev. Carl Ridd, Hugo Unruh and Mrs. Wallace Spear. (from Carillon)

Greenridge United Church built 1881 on land donated by Andrew Davison with the Ridgeville United Church added as a Sunday School room in 1976.

Arnaud United Presbyterian Church built 1904 with memorial cairn erected 1981.

Interior of Zion Lutheran Church, Fredensthal, original built 1900. Rebuilt after 1930 tornado. Joined by Overstone Trinity in late 1950's. Courtesy Manitoba Archives.

Interior of St. Pauls Lutheran Church Dominion City, 1882, purchased by congregation in 1954.

Hope Lutheran Church moved onto land donated by Alstadt family at Greenridge in 1903.

Overstone Baptist Church built in 1900 on land donated by Carl Zilke moved in 1931. Horse drawn, stove heated cabooses in front.

Roseau River Ukrainian Baptist Church built 1954, joined by Overstone Ukrainian Baptists in 1965.

Tolstoi Ukrainian Catholic Church rebuilt after first one burned in 1927.

Interior of Holy Eucharist Ukrainian Catholic Church at Rosa built in 1924.

Plankey Plains Ukrainian Catholic in Roseau River built in 1939. (from Carillon)

102

Interior of Holy Trinity Polish Roman Catholic Church at Tolstoi built in 1929, on the occasion of Rev. Father Kwiatkowskis 40th anniversary.

St. Michael's Ukrainian Orthodox Church, the first Ukrainian Church built in Canada, near Gardenton in 1899.

Holy Ghost Ukrainian Orthodox Church at Tolstoi built in 1927. (from Carillon)

Rosa Ukrainian Orthodox Church built in 1928. (from Carillon)

Mennonite Brethern Church, built at Arnaud, burned in 1952.

Ukrainian Orthodox Church at Senkiw built in 1921 on land donated by Stephen Goyman.

Mennonite General Conference built at Arnaud in 1944.

Rhinelander Mennonite Church at Roseau River.

Sommerfeld Mennonite Church, Tolstoi, first church built in 1930's, replaced in 1968.

First Kingdom Hall, built at Dominion City, 1963.

Ridgeville Anglican Church Ladies 1930.
Back row L to R: Dora Lenton, Beatrice Stringer, Ida Woods, Jessie Stewart, Mrs. A. Gilchrist, Martha Clifford, Alice Lindsay, Mrs. Abe Seward, Mrs. Bill Coombs.
Second row L to R: Mrs. Tom Collins, Mrs. Montgomery, Mrs. Wm. Wilkinson.
Front row L to R: Annie Collins, Rose Wilkinson.

Zion Lutheran Church Women 1967
Back row L to R: Rena Zass, Bertha Walters, Jane Schiebe.
Second row L to R: Lorraine Riach, Lil Schultz, Geraldine Becker, Erna Geiler, Myrtle Ganske. Front row L to R: Annie Wagner, Mabel Collins, Elsie Schultz, Alma Hartig, Emma Marks.

Tolstoi Ukrainian Catholic Women League members at American Bicentennial parade in Lancaster, Minnesota 1967.
Back row L to R: Jean Germain, Elsie Kolodzinski, Mrs. H. Podolsky, W. Kolodzinski.
Front row L to R: Rose Fedorchuk, Eva Bially, Sandra Dolynchuk, Helen Bially.

Rev. John Scott, minister at Greenridge 1880-81.

Visitation of His Excellence Archbishop Maxim Hermaniuk to Sacred Heart Ukrainian Catholic Church at Tolstoi in 1976.

L to R: Rev. M. Dawydko, Sherry Kozak, Theresa Fedorchuk, Archbishop Hermaniuk, Sandra Dolynchuk, Gwen Kozak, Rev. T. Krawchuk.

As well, a Ukrainian Catholic Church was built at Plankey Plains in 1939, and a Ukrainian Baptist Church at Dominion City occupied the present Lutheran Church until 1954, this Baptist Church joined Roseau River. A mission church which served both the Roseau River Indian Reserve and the town of Dominion City was in operation from 1954 to 1976.

THE CEMETERIES OF FRANKLIN

The faith of the pioneers was tested often in times of sickness and death. The gravestones of the cemeteries of Franklin tell their own tale of sorrow and loss.

Greenridge — Established on land donated by Theodore Strange - earliest grave - George Gunn 1877.

Dominion City — A municipal cemetery - Sarah Brad 1850 - 1884.

Ridgeville — On land donated by Robert Coates family - John Madill 1834 - 1885.

Fredensthal — A church cemetery - William Jahnke - 1899. Private Plot on 31-2-5E - Stephen Post 1810 - 1879.

Plankey Plains Ukrainian Catholic Cemetery — On land donated by J. Pawloski - Amelia Polischuk 1889 - 1897, Annie Polischuk 1898 (infant).

Overstone Lutheran Cemetery — on 9-1-5E - Mrs. L. Schnell and twins 1915.

Tolstoi Holy Trinity — Nick and Amelia Lipischuk infants 1913.

Ukrainian Independent Cemetery — Peter Arseny 1904 age 1 year. Wasylena Arseny 1905 age 1 year.

Rev. W. Kudryk, Tolstoi, one of the first Ukrainian Orthodox priests ordained in Canada.

Ukrainian blessing of graves and food offering in memory of the deceased.

Headstone at Ridgeville Cemetery; Mary Edna Hermiston - 1886 - age 15 years. James Clayton Hermiston - 1889 - age 3 years.

Ethnic

by Claudia Eliuk

The Rural Municipality of Franklin has been settled by succeeding waves of immigrants. Ethnic groups emigrated in numbers, each settling in a separate part of the municipality, each providing its own language, culture, churches and schools. They have now overlapped and our municipality is truly a Canadian mosaic in miniature. Babies of the 1970's and 1980's often possess an oma, a grandperé, a baba and a grandpa.

It is possible within the boundaries of our municipality to attend a church picnic or a graveyard service held in the same location for nearly a hundred years, to observe a pow wow near the river, to partake of faspa and to eat holopchi at a wedding — often in the course of a single weekend.

The names of the original settlers in each group are too numerous to mention. They can be seen in the changing land maps of our municipality and are documented in the family histories.

The original settlers of this area were the Ojibway Indians who were driven west by the intrusion of white trappers and settlers into the lake regions of Ontario. They settled Reserve 2A in 1913 with a population of 186, and Reserve 2 in 1917 with a population of 200. Today the majority of the Ojibway Indians are on Roseau River Reserve #2 which has a population of about 960, 500 of whom reside on the reserve.

The earliest white settlers were English, Scottish, Irish and Welsh, and came from the British Isles, Ontario and the United States. They travelled by way of the Great Lakes to Fishers Landing, by boat to Emerson and then by ox cart. Some travelled the Dawson Trail to Winnipeg and walked to their land claims, often leaving families to follow later. With the coming of the railways and the spur gravel line, after 1879, many settlers arrived with tents, lumber and animals by train. The lack of drainage in the flats where they originally settled prompted most to move to the higher ground of the ridge by the 1890's.

Already at Carlowrie were the French families of Laferme and Gabriel and Napoleon Lafournaise.

During the 1890's a large group of German people left their homes in the southern Ukraine to emigrate to Canada. Under Russian law they could not acquire ownership of the land they had by now farmed for 40 or 50 years, and they had not taken out Russian citizenship. They arrived in Winnipeg and many moved to Gretna area where they worked for Mennonite families until they learned the language and ways of the new land. By 1896, they moved into the flats homesteads abandoned by the original settlers, and began farming.

In 1896, 27 families of Ukrainians, oppressed by the taxation, fearful of war, and discouraged by the lack of land in Austria came to Franklin. They were encouraged by the Canadian governments' campaign for new settlers and its promise of provisions for the first year. They settled in a colony in the eastern end of the municipality and by 1900 their number had grown to 337 families.

These were joined by a group of Polish families who had sailed from Hamburg, Germany in 1896 and 1897.

In 1898, fearing conscription, a group of Hutterites from South Dakota formed a small colony near Dominion City. In 1905, the war over, they returned to the United States. It was not until 1966 that a nine family colony was again established in the municipality.

Conditions prompted a large number of Mennonites to leave Russia in 1924 and settle in the Arnaud, St. Elizabeth and Dominion City areas. Sponsored by the Mennonite Board of Colonization, 100 families purchased land from the Lyman Ranch, Gainer farms and the Emmert Foundation.

The civil unrest and the aftermaths of the world war resulted in some 20 Czech families coming to the municipality between 1924-1929.

Scandinavian immigrants from the northern United States settled in the Dominion City, Caliento and Arbakka regions. Others came from Holland after World War II.

Recent immigrants to our municipality are farmers from both France and Germany. These people have sold their acreages in Europe and purchased large farms here to begin again the cycle of settlement in a new land.

The route from Lake Superior to Fort Garry, explored in 1857 to 1858, cost $5 from Toronto to the Lakehead, and $25 to the Forks of the Red and Assiniboine. This consisted of 96 miles by railroad from Toronto to Collingwood, 532 miles by steamer from Collingwood to Fort William, 45 miles by wagon from Fort William to Shebandowan Lake, 310 miles broken navigation in open boats from Shebandowan Lake to north west angle of the Lake of the Woods, 95 miles by cart or wagon from north west angle, Lake of the Woods to Fort Garry.

The American route, more popular, was via the Lakes to Duluth, by train to the Red River, and from there by boat or stage to Fort Garry. Alternately, they could bypass the Lakes and travel all the way by rail, via Chicago and St. Paul, to Fisher's Landing, near Crookston, Minnesota, in less than three days. It cost $42.50 first class, and $21 immigrant class in 1878.

After 1878 and the completion of the line from St. Vincent (opposite Emerson) to St. Boniface, a person could travel from Quebec to Winnipeg in four days, $51.85 first class, $34 in an immigrant car.

— taken from ''by section, township and range'' by John Langton Tyman, Assiniboine Historical Society. 1972. Permission to be requested.

ANGLO SAXONS

The first settlers to the ridge were mainly English and Scottish, with a few Irish and Welsh. They came directly from the old country, or from Ontario, Quebec, and the States. One family came out, and word went back til other families followed.

The very early settlers came by way of the Great Lakes to Fisher's Landing and by boat to Winnipeg, then by ox cart to Emerson and the ridge. Others came from the States via Chicago and by boat. A few came in the Canadian way by the Dawson Trail to Winnipeg in the years 1884-78.

Quite a few walked out to the ridge to claim their land, leaving families to follow later. The Foulds were drivers on the ox trains and must have liked the land in the area as they later homesteaded on the St. Paul Trail. This Trail was the route for many from Winnipeg. With the coming of the train and the spur gravel line, some settlers arrived with tents, lumber, and animals by train, being landed right at the ridge (after 1879).

The first homesteads were built of local logs,

likely from Menisino to the east, to be replaced with frame homes from boards purchased after local lumber yards started up. In an attempt to keep the life style to which they were accustomed in the old country, some brought pianos, violins, and organs. They were then able to organize musical evenings in their homes. Perhaps the highlight of an evening might have been French Minuet, Waltz Qaudrille, Heel - Toe Polka, or Reels. Many of the women had been taught to play piano. Fine embroidery work was a favorite pastime of the women also, and it was not long before they decorated their homes with shelf hangings, curtains, and bedspreads.

They brought with them books of poetry and stories, and small Bibles. Later a large family Bible was brought from the east along with more books and magazines were glued on the log walls and white washed over to make presentable wall paper.

Most homes had jugs and bottles in which they brought out preserves, and into which they put sweet, rich preserves which would keep with little or no seal. However, sealers were not too long in coming, and the wild fruit preserved for winter. There was an abundance of edible fruit to be found such as Saskatoons, Chokecherries, Pincherries, Raspberries, Strawberries, Cranberries, Currants, also Asparagus and Mushrooms. The early settlers had a few cows, chickens, and pigs to supply them with meat, eggs, butter. Some even kept sheep for its meat and wool for spinning. Each homestead would have a small vegetable garden. This produce would be stored in a cellar dug under the house, while the meat would be smoked, put in a brine, or frozen in the winter. For greater variety in meat there were the wild prairie chicken, partridge, ducks, and geese. It was a common practice to hang these on a nail on the side of the barn until the bird fell to the ground, when it would be considered ready for cooking. A typical English type meal would have been Yorkshire pudding, mashed turnip, roast beef, roasted potatoes and gravy. Sometimes the Yorkshire pudding would be changed to dessert by adding currants and served with chokecherry syrup. Homemade ice cream was a real treat. Crushed ice from the ice-house would be placed in a bucket with salt. A covered pail of pure cream would then be set in the ice and agitated til it thickened.

The settlers had little new clothing besides what they had brought with them. The pioneer women would buy bolts of material, usually from Emerson, then sew their clothing by hand which meant thousands of tiny stitches. Imagine the luxury when they were finally able to purchase a treadle sewing machine. Their husbands would take butter, pork, and other surplus produce to Winnipeg and return after four or five days with supplies of flour, raisins, sugar, salt, maybe a Hudson Bay blanket, and lastly if there was money, the family might get a choice in the way of clothes.

Hard work and sacrifice seemed to be the guiding light for these settlers. There were a few days free of work, so picnics and gathering at the river or local hall were great events. The men enjoyed baseball from early days and walked many miles for a pick-up game. Later, even the women had a team. Hockey was played on the river. In early 1900's a Scotsman introduced curling which soon became a favorite of many.

Religion was always of great importance, and no one worked on Sunday. Only those chores which couldn't be put off, such as milking cows, would be performed. On Saturday the wife would prepare meats and pies which could be served cold the next day. Church played a big part in the life of the settlers and until the building was erected, they met at the homes for their services which included weddings, christenings, and funerals.

Weddings were usually small affairs. Most young couples would be married at the bride's home by a travelling preacher. The ceremony would be followed by a supper for relatives and neighbours. One of the customs seemed to be chivareeing the newlyweds. This usually took place after dark when a group of neighbours would congregate outside the couple's home. As soon as the last lantern was extinguished, the crowd would start a commotion of bells jingling, and pans clanging in hopes the couple would invite them in for refreshments.

When there was a death in the family, a casket would be prepared by a local carpenter, while close friends would help to prepare the remains, and sit with the family overnight. Usually the next day the preacher would perform the service at the home with neighbours present. After following the casket to the cemetery, everyone would return to share a meal with the bereaved family.

Other customs seem to have followed through from the pioneers, such as family gatherings for Christmas dinner which used to consist of a meal featuring goose. Boxing Day was set aside for visiting friends and neighbours. Easter was celebrated by attending church, and followed by a ham dinner. Thanksgiving Sunday the church would be decorated with garden produce and grains, then the family would return home for a turkey supper with Cranberry sauce, and pumpkin pie for dessert.

One custom that had a definite link with the old country, but which has since faded away was the presenting of cards to neighbours stating that "Miss Jane Doe" would be 'at home' on a certain day.

At dances, they had cards which were hopefully filled with the signatures of dance partners for the evening. Gone also are the Box Socials where the women would make up elaborately decorated boxes of lunch to be bid on by the men, and later shared at lunch time, with the buyer.

GERMANS

The people of the flats were primarily of German culture. Few of these new settlers had the privilege of obtaining homesteads, due to the fact that this area had been settled by Anglo Saxons during the period 1875 to 1890.

Most of the quarter sections, were improved enough to warrant immediate building of homes. These new settlers were thrifty, soon became prosperous, and the first new homes came on the scene about 1905 to 1915.

Building materials were hauled many miles by horses and sleighs. Some of the materials were hauled from as far east as Piney. It would take one week to complete a trip, with stop overs at a various camps to feed their horses, and bed themselves.

Their houses were all of frame construction, and most had two full stories. The walls were studded at 14 feet with a gable roof giving ample space for ten foot ceilings and very good ventilation, although requiring extra heat during the winter.

Garden produce grew very well and provided them with food for the winter. Every family would put up a 45 gallon barrel of cucumbers and of cabbage.

Beef and pork raised on their farms were dressed and the meat cured at home. Wheat for flour was gristed at Pocock's Mill at Emerson and later at Stuartburn and Gardenton.

The only supplies they purchased were sugar, coffee, tea, salt and pepper. The rest of their diet consisted of produce, grown on their own farms.

The customs that these people had acquired in Russia were brought to this new land. Their church was their main interest and social life was limited to walking distance. They observed all their church holidays with great feeling.

Christmas was celebrated for three days, Christmas day and the day after were observed with church services, and the third day after Christmas for family visits. Sundays were strictly observed and a bare minimum of their daily chores were carried out. Easter was also a high point in their lives, as this was one of the days

109

they celebrated with communion at church. Maundy Thursday, Good Friday, Ascension Day, all had the proper place in their hearts and these holidays were strictly observed.

The highlights of their lives was their marriages, and the wedding celebration that followed. Most of the celebration lasted for three days, with most of the community taking part. The preparations for these celebrations, were accomplished with a minimum of expense to the people involved. There were no handwritten invitations to the guests, but were invited in person, by a friend appointed by the bride's parents to do so. The first and second days were spent eating, drinking and dancing. The third day, (or after wedding) was put on to recuperate from the first two, but usually was no different than the first two days.

Their clothing were mostly homemade and were styled on the lines of the European country they came from. Wool was homespun, from that socks, mitts, sweaters, underskirts etc. were made.

A bare minimum of clothing were purchased from some of the travelling peddlers through barter.

THE UKRAINIANS

In 1896 the first group of Ukrainian settlers came by train to Dominion City and then by wagons or walking to their destination. Starting from scratch they formed a large colony of Ukrainian places now known as Tolstoi (formerly Oleskiw), Shevchenko (now Vita), Rosa, Senkiw, Gardenton, Arbakka, Caliento, Sundown and Sirko. The land was sub marginal, stony and swampy. Pine, spruce tamarack, poplar trees and shrubs and some hay meadows covered the soil here. The Roseau River flows diagonally across the territory to the northwest. The first settlers came in August, too late to plant gardens or to find work. They were poor and had to build homes to provide for their families.

The first winter was harsh and they required food. The government provided flour, cornmeal and potatoes, at the cost of $341.55. The following years the men went to earn money working on railway crews, bush camps, harvesting, and so on. Wages were poor. A man earned $50 for a season. Girls went to do house work at $20 to $30 a season.

They brought with them from their home land some clothes, sheets and blankets. Some other supplies brought were tools, hatchet, spade, hammer, chisel, scythe, hoes, garden seeds, onion, garlic, horse radish, dried corn cobs and dried herbs. Holy pictures were packed between pillows, other articles brought were a small bottle of Ho-

ly Water, a prayer book, Bible, Ukrainian School primer, few utensils, some dress clothes and food in a cloth bundle.

By 1898 there were 150 Ukrainian families in Franklin and by 1900, 337 families.

On the basis of "Dominion Land's Act", the homestead could be acquired when the owner lived on it a year, cultivated 30 acres. This procedure had to be repeated three years.

Their first task was to build some shelter for the coming winter. Usually a dug-out, which was framed with rafters and covered with sod. Ledges of sod were cut inside for seats, shelves etc. Hay or swamp reeds were used for beds. The floors were mud. Often from rain soaked earth it turned into a mud hole. The second home was a two-room house with a porch. It was built of logs or slabs, the empty spaces between logs were filled with a brown clay, mixed with hay and then whitewashed with white lime stone. The roofs were covered with thatch. Men had to get employment to buy a stove, beds, etc. So the women were left at home and worked hard getting wood, stones to be picked for foundations, and farm chores, garden, hay, etc. They also went digging seneca root for which they traded in stores for flour, sugar, shoes, clothes, etc. Trees were cut for cord wood and sold for 40 cents a cord.

Hunting was done as a necessity, wild ducks were killed for food, feathers were used for pillows, rabbits were used for meat and skins for clothing. Neighbors helped each other and shared the plow, tools, outdoor bake oven and oven, often they had a community garden. The Ukrainian settler had to depend entirely on his own brain and brow, and hard work.

They built a millstone for grinding wheat and buckwheat used by all neighbors, it served as a small flour mill. Another machine was called an olijnia - an oil pressing machine for squeezing oil out of flax and hemp seed. This oil was used for cooking. Weaving looms were common and they made their own cloth for shawls, scarves, aprons, and articles of clothing. But they had to buy supplies like sugar, matches, coal oil, salt, shoes, windows, doors, etc.

Later when sheep were raised which provided wool, and the women made home spun sweaters, socks, mitts from the yarn. They also made comforters when wool and cloth was available. Usually the neighbors held "Bees" to help each other make quilts, the men to help one another in the building of homes, barns, etc., and even for the harvesting of crops. After a year when the garden was planted and vegetables in supply, barrels of sauerkraut and dill pickles were made. Potatoes, beets, beans, etc., made the food supply as well as a hog was butchered and they cured salt pork, chickens were raised and that provided them with eggs and meat. One of the first priorities was for a settler to buy a cow so that they could have milk for the children.

The Ukrainian Christmas Eve supper and Carols are based on ancient customs. January 6th is Christmas Eve, observed by the Julian Calendar. The supper consists of 12 lenten dishes. When the star appears the celebration begins. Small handfuls of fine hay in memory of the Christ Child, who lay in a manger is strewn under the table or table cloth. The Kolach, a braided bread, with a candle is set in the middle of the table - it symbolizes prosperity. The meal is blessed with the traditional Christmas greeting ''Christos Rodyosia;'' Christ is Born and the family replies ''Slaveem Yaho'', Let us Glorify Him. Forty days before the Christmas Eve is Advent, a season of fasting. So on Christmas Eve the absence of meat in the 12 dishes served on Holy supper represent the 12 apostles and are food products of the field, garden, orchard and stream. Wheat is a symbol of continuous life and is served first. It is cooked and flavored with poppy and honey. It is followed by appetizers of pickled herring and pickled mushrooms. Then is served a soup called ''Borsch'', made of beets, beans and cabbage. The fourth course is holubsti (cabbage rolls), pyrohy - dumplings, several kinds with potatoes, sauerkraut and fruit, followed by several kinds of fish, jellied, baked or fried, mashed dry beans, mushrooms and gravy, for dessert stewed dried fruit and pastry. The evening continues with the singing of carols. After midnight or early morning church services are attended and after dinner members of the various churches go out carolling house to house. The donations collected go to the churches.

The date of Easter is set similar to that of the Passover. During this period the women are busy making ''Easter Egg'', baking special traditional food such as the Paska, an ornately decorated round loaf of bread, and the ''Babka'', a sweet leavened bread often decorated with a cross. Forty days of lent is again observed. The Easter Basket with food are taken to church to be blessed by the priest. The food placed in these baskets are the ''Paska'', ''Baba'', boiled eggs, cottage cheese, butter, horse radish relish, meat such as ham and sausage and pysanka - Easter Eggs. A candle is placed in the middle of the basket and is neatly covered with a beautiful embroidered cloth. After the church services at which all sing the traditional hymn ''Khrystos Voskres'', the food is blessed and the family goes home for a special Easter breakfast.

The wedding feast also plays an important part in the ceremony of marriage. The eve before the wedding a gathering of all attendants, parents and relatives gather around the table and braid a wreath of myrtle and ivy for the bride with appropriate songs. Before the wedding ceremony the couple is greeted by the parents at the entrance of home or hall with three loaves of Kolachi (bread and salt) and give their blessings to the young couple before they go to church. In church during the ceremony an embroidered scarf is placed on the floor for them to stand on. Also the priest places crowns on their heads. Wine or Communion is given to them and attendants hold candles. After the ceremony the wedding party and guests enter the banquet hall to the music of the Wedding March. On the table is a ''Koravai'', a very large sweet bread decorated with dough ornaments such as doves and greenery, symbols of peace, love and happiness. Presentation of money is a common custom.

The districts of Senkiw, Tolstoi, Rosa, Plankey Plains today have beautiful churches built by pioneers. The ''onion'' domed edifices Byzantine design are most outstanding, transplanted from the old country.

THE MENNONITES WHO CAME IN THE 1920'S AND 30'S

The Mennonites who came from Russia after 1920 had adopted the German culture. Their practical heritage allowed them to make their homes and farms comfortable.

From the door of the house, a path of rough boards or a constructed wooden walkway led to the ''summer-kitchen''. An empty grain bin might double for this purpose from spring to fall. Inside you would see the indispensable ''Meeahgropi'' (cauldron), an invaluable source of hot water on washdays and at butchering time, when it was used for rendering lard as well. The cookstove also found its way into this building in hot weather, to keep the house cooler in summer. Ideally the summer-kitchen would have a concrete floor. Most often God's good earth served under foot. It was a good place to house a batch of young chickens in early spring, it was also used for quick meals from spring to fall. This saved some cleaning in the house proper, at the same time avoiding unnecessary changing of clothing and footwear at mealtimes in busy seasons. Came butchering, the sausage (beef, pork or mixed) could be stuffed here. It was suitable for plucking and drawing chickens as well. Later when prosperity and electricity came upon the scene, machine sheds with concrete floors made the summer-kitchen obsolete.

A cherished institution of the community was the weekly "Kranzchen" (little circle). Thursday afternoons were the "sunny" spots to look forward to. Monday to Wednesday may have been cloudy. When Thursday dawned the sun came out, or so it seemed. A time for the workworn, homemaker wife to relax and enjoy the fellowship of her church sisters. Together they could plan and achieve a few meaningful projects: their mission outreach. With flying fingers they knit socks for the family (or for the mission sale), or stitched some pretty colors into a pillow-case or tea towel. It was a day to enjoy and revive the soul. A short meditation was presented by the leader of the loosely organized group. A good book, read aloud in instalments, was a treat to those who saw little else than milk pail, dishes and diapers the rest of the work week. Then it was time for coffee and some homemade "goodies". (Hostesses rotated). This was the time to unload and share. It brought the needed opportunity for caring. Meantime the husbands would visit in an upstairs room, exchanging news and new ideas. Their excuse for an afternoon off was quite legitimate: with horses and sleighs, even with the first cars, women needed a driver.

Music has been very closely associated with the religious life of the Mennonite church. They have enjoyed a tradition of hymn singing motivated by the need to worship. At first choirs performed at "Jugendverein" and later also sang in the regular worship service. Later pianos, guitars, violins and other musical instruments became part of household furniture. Gradually trained choir leaders emerged and many young people began taking music lessons. Pianos were installed in churches and homes. Anthems and cantatas were attempted by many choirs and saengerfests became annual events.

Kinship ties are strong. At Christmas, Easter and Pentecost, the high holidays of the year, three days each are accorded the status of a Sunday. The first two days are devoted to family reunions, with the third day given over to visiting friends. Other, more general occasions for meeting were all engagement celebrations, weddings and funerals. For an engagement or a wedding the entire company was served a sumptuous banquet and in good weather tables would be set up outside at the bride's house. Wedding receptions were often held in the shed above the barn. Funerals were simple and solemn occasions held from the church or the home. Following the burial the mourners would have a simple repast of Zwiebach and coffee.

Young people worked with their parents. Girls helped in the home, cleaning, sewing and baking. Frequently they helped with chores, milking and gathering eggs. When necessary they were able to assist the young mother of toddlers. Saturdays were set aside to prepare the house for Sunday. The floors must be scrubbed and the home in readiness for company. The aroma of freshly baked bread and buns set a festive mood, and drifted out into the yard to father and sons. The young men and boys were employed along side their dads in all phases of farm labour. Harvestime which could drag on into winter brought the communal threshing crew to the crop owner's table. Daughters and daughter-in-law were appreciated then. As farm machinery and finances improved, the neighbor's help was no longer required. The son and daughter were free to go to work or to high school. Progress brought many changes and an easier, not necessarily happier, life.

The Road to Franklin

The route from Lake Superior to Fort Garry, explored in 1857 to 1858, cost $5.00 from Toronto to the Lakehead, and $25.00 to the Forks of the Red and Assiniboine. This consisted of 96 miles by railroad from Toronto to Collingwood, 532 miles by steamer from Collingwood to Fort William, 45 miles by wagon from Fort William to Shebandowan Lake, 310 miles broken navigation in open boats from Shebandowan Lake to the north-west angle of the Lake of the Woods, 95 miles by cart or wagon from the north-west angle, Lake of the Woods, to Fort Garry.

The American route, more popular, was via the Lakes to Duluth, by train to the Red River, and from there by boat or stage to Fort Garry. Alternatively, they could bypass the Lakes and travel all the way by rail, via Chicago and St. Paul, to Fisher's Landing, near Crookston, Manitoba in less than 3 days. It cost $42.50 first class, and $21.00 immigrant class in 1878.

After 1878 and the completion of the line from St. Vincent (opposite Emerson) to St. Boniface, a person could travel from Quebec to Winnipeg in four days, $51.85 first class, $34.00 in an immigrant car.

Taken from "by section, township and range" by John Langton Tyman, Assiniboine Historical Society, 1972, used by permission.

Wilkinson Family Bible. c. 1886.

Ukrainian wedding cake.

Wedding cake of Mr. and Mrs. Harry Wilkinson.

Mrs. T. Mulko and Dorothy with Czech dolls. in costume.

Present owner of this precious head scarf or shawl is Mrs. Leona Tetrault. It is a beige color with pink flowers and green leaves. This shawl belonged to Leona's Great Grandmother. Mrs. Henry Hartwig Sr. and is 85 years old.

Log cabin quilt made by Mrs. Macdonald, more than 100 years old. Made of silk and velvet pieces.

Ukrainian Easter eggs.

Katie Stepaniuk in Ukrainian costume.

Present owner of this dress is Mrs. Leona Tetrault. This dress belonged to Leona's Grandmother Mrs. Mathilda Schwark. It was bought in 1910 and is made of a fine white cotton, some eyelit cotton and insets of lace. There are fine tucks all around the dress. It buttons down the back and is ankle-length.

Clock owned by Dr. McClelland, lamp of Mr. and Mrs. F. O. Shelby, brought from United States.

Nick Arseny in Ukrainian costume.

Arnaud Mennonite Frauenverein and quilt.
Left, Tina Loewen, son Clifford, right Mrs. John Poetker, son Jake.

Representing Franklin Manitoba Canadian culture. Priceless items, once everyday utensils. Steve Stadnyk displays a Peerless 2 roller mangle, used for ironing, a milk bottle, milk strainer, 3 gallon cream can, enamelled coffee pot, a pound butter print and butter ladle.

Rosa Dance Club 1964
L to R: Patricia Sapack, Ronald Mehaychuk, Marianne Meconse, Ronald Hrynenko, Elsie Chubey, Larry Salamacha, Alice Chubaty, Jerry Kuryk, instructors - Petro Salamacha, Jennie Mehaychuk.

Honor Roll

**FOR KING AND COUNTRY
MEMBERS OF FRANKLIN MUNICIPALITY
WHO HAVE VOLUNTEERED
FOR ACTIVE SERVICE
WITH
CANADA'S FIGHTING FORCES**

BOER WAR

Ball, Harry
Woolard, Dr. Charles

**NORTHWEST
REBELLION**

Froom, Edgar
Froom, Jim

**PHILLIPEAN—
AMERICAN WAR**

Mason, Tom

**AMERICAN
CIVIL WAR**

Strange, Theodore

FIRST WORLD WAR 1914 — 1918

* Killed

Anderson, A
Arthur, A. M.
Brown, Sanford
Brown, Charles
Black, Leslie*
Branston, H.
Benedicktson, B.
Badgley, John
Carlson, M.
Chase, George*
Collins, H.*
Collins, Edward
Collins, Rufus
Craig, William
Davis, H.
Davison, Herbert
Denyer, A.
Drebitts, Peter
Drebitts, John
Drebitts, Dmytro
Empey, B.
Fauconnier, P
Feely, J.
Fertash, Harry
Francis, H.

Froom, Roy*
Gainer, William
Gainer, Nelson
Gainer, Charles
Gunn, Clarence
Gunn, Hector
Hamblin, W. H.
Hanna, Thomas
Hurd, Gerard*
Hodges, A.
Hofer, C.
Hofer, O.
Holgate, I. M.
Holgate, Maurice
Horton, Thomas
Jack, M.
Johnson, J. H.
Johnson, F.
Johnson, C.
Jolly, Alex
Jones, Wm.
Kirkpatrick, Everett
King, Joseph
Krasky, Dmetro
Lenton, H.

Liddle, George
Linklater, Ernest
Marshall, A.*
Marshall, W.*
Mason, Wilf
McLennan, Samuel
McRae, William
Miller, Floyd
Miller, Robert*
Nelson, William
Nisely, William
Parkes, L.
Pawlischak, Anthony
Peto, Edgar
Pott, Thomas E.
Pott, Edmund
Pott, Charles
Pott, Horace
Rourke, M.
Seely, John
Scholte, Edwin
Schultz, Ted
Schwark, Adolph
Shone, A.
Smith, Stewart

Smith, T.
Smith, H. E.
Smith, C.
Snead, Fred
Smith, Guy
Stewart, John
Stewart, R.
Stewart, James
Stewart, W.
Stokes, Hugh*
Stowe,
Summer, C. C.
Shymansky, Steve
Summer, R. J.
Summer, G. A.
Taylor, A.
Taylor, Arthur
Treleaven, T.
Turner, Frank
Ward, J.
Wakefield, Charles
Weiss, A.
Weiss, T.
Wilkinson, H.
Woods, A.

SECOND WORLD WAR

Accobe, Pete
Anderson, Leonard W.
Andrushko, Harry
Arseny, Sam
Arseny, Metro
Auld, J. C.
Auriat, Louis Charles
Badgley, Audrey
Badgley, Bryce
Badgley, Milton
Barber, Allan T.*
Barnes, H. J.
Barnes, T. C.
Bachynski, Bill
Bachynski, Mike
Batten, Kenneth N.
Baskerville, Dawson
Bially, Jack
Bially, Milton
Boese, D.
Borodenko, Mathew
Borodenko, Theodore
Boutet, J. C.
Boutet, P. J. C.
Bohn, Reynold
Braun, H. J.
Brown, Walter
Brodoway, Mike
Broszeit, Ed.
Burrell, George E.
Bzowy, Walter
Casper, Frank
Casper, Harry E.
Casson, Ian M.
Casson, H. H.
Casson, Amy E.
Casson, Bruce H.
Casson, R. L.
Christianson, Pete
Chubey, Jack
Chubey, Bill
Chubey, Mike
Chubey, Harry
Chubey, Paul
Clifford, Doug
Clifford, Lawrence
Colley, B.
Collins, H. W.
Cox, H.
Cox, George
Craig, Lawrence
Curran, John M.
Dawson, James
Donaleyko, Maxim
Dolynchuk, Steve

Drebitts, John
Drebitts, Walter
Drebitts, Dave
Drebitts, Peter
Drewniak, Mike S.
Durksen, D.
Dupchak, Richard
Dyck, John
Dyck, Peter
Dzioba, Donald
Eliuk, John
Empey, Keith
Empey, Bruce
French, Thomas G.
French, Wallace E.
Fostey, Allan
Fostey, Stan
Froom, Herbert
Froom, Douglas
Foy, Lloyd
Gainer, Nielson
Gaynor, Charles D.
German, Bill
Gilchrist, Cecil
Gilchrist, Jack
Gilchrist, A. B.
Gilchrist, William
Gilchrist, Alex
Gilchrist, Bennie V.
Graydon, Glynn
Graydon, R. J.
Grabowoecki, A.
Graboski, Victor
Greenaway, George J.
Green, W.
Grier, Earl
Grier, Roy E.
Griffin, Benjamin
Griffin, Daniel
Gunn, Don
Hall, Ian E.
Hanischuk, Metro
Hanischuk, Harry
Henry, Albert
Henry, Clifford
Henry, Joe N.
Hiebert, J.
Hicks, Keith
Houston, Eileen M.
Houston, John O.
Houston, Rae E.
Hopalock, Joe
Hopalock, Mike
Hopalock, Bill
Hrynenko, Mike

Hunter, John C.
Hurd, Aylmer W.
Hurd, Wilbur D.
Hurd, Douglas
Hurd, Jeanne
Hurd, Edna
Ingram, George
Jack, Ruth
Jaculak, M.
James, John
Johnston, L. J.
Jones, W. L.
Jones, Garnet M.
Jones, R. A.
Kehler, John
Kiyan, Jack
Kiyan, Marlin
Kiyan, John
Kohut, Alex
Korotash, John
Krahn, K.
Krahn, G.*
Kreitz, Dan
Kreitz, Fred
Lasuta, Bill
Lasuta, Mary
Laufersweiler,
Lauryniuk, Fred
Lenton, Tom
Lenick, Mike
Lenick, George
Lenton, Henry H.
Lendrum, George
Lindsay, Laverne
Lindsay, Donald
Lipischuk, J.
Lipischuk, L.
Lochhead, H.*
Lochhead, E. G.
Lochhead, M.
Maksymchuk, William
Maksymchuk, Steve
Maksymchuk, John
Marshall, Alan
Matichuk, Bill
Matichuk, John
McLennan, K. R.
McClellend, Wm. S.
Miller, John
Miller, Floyd
Morrison, Clayton
Morischuk, John
Moore, Henry
Murchison, Duncan G.
Murchison, Thomas G.

Murchison, Edward A.
Nedohin, Henry
Nedohin, Milton
Nedohin, Bert
Nedohin, Harold
Nelson, Louis
Nelson, Tony
Oatway, D. R.
O'Hara, Charles A.
O'Hara, W. George
Olden, G. R.
Olden, M. E.
Ostrowsky, Jack
Paciorka, John
Paley, Wasyl
Palmer, J.
Pamula, John
Pamula, Mike
Pappel, Lew
Parker, Robert Arnold
Pawlischak, Wm.
Pearse, Ernest W. G.
Pearse, Gerald
Pomrenki, William T.
Podolsky, Peter
Post, Archie
Post, Leonard
Post, Wallace
Post, Garnet E.
Pott, Elison
Pott, Harold W. E.
Pott, Horace E.
Pott, Harry W.
Pruski, Steve
Pupeza, William
Ramsey, Lorne L.
Ramsey, R. Lloyd
Riach, Eleanor
Riach, Lorne
Roberts, Harry
Russell, Jack
Schellenberg, William
Schnell, Donald L.
Schnell, Wilfred
Scholte, M. Lucille
Scholte, Willis M.
Schwabe, Henry
Schwark, Arthur
Seed, C. O.
Sennie, Ed
Sennie, Stephen
Shewchuk, John
Skene, Chester
Smidt, W.
Smith, Arthur W.

Snead, Norman
Snowball, E.
Solnes, Edward G.
Solnes, Bernice L.
Solnes, T. Elnora
Somerville, James G.*
Spence, Beverley E.
Spence, D. W. E.
Spence, Keith
Spence, Hayne
Steinert, Albert
Steinke, Arthur
Steinke, F.
Stewart, Gordon
Stewart, Winnifred
Stewart, Claire
Stewart, Stan
Stewart, Harvey
Stimpson, Herbert

Stimpson, Sydney J.
Stowe, Charles
Stowe, John
Stranske, Dan
Stadnick, A.
Sullivan, Neil
Suppes, Fred
Sereda, Bill
Shdlowski, Bill
Slobodian, Mike
Smook, Harry*
Smook, William
Steinert, David
Stewart, Lloyd
Tanchuck, Anna
Tanchuk, Maurice
Tanchuk, Steve
Taylor, Mary Jane
Taylor, James

Taylor, Wallace
Taylor, Wm. A
Thiessen, J.
Timlick, G. R.
Timlick, H. M.
Timlick, Jas.
Timlick, K. C.
Timlick, T. H.
Timlick, Elwood
Todoruk, Mike
Tofan, Mike
Toews, G.
Turner, Edwin
Turner, Ross
Turner, Stewart
Urbonoski, Joe
Varcoe, Stella
Varey, Wm.
Vannato, Robert

Wakefield, Charles
Weedmark, F. R.
Weedmark, J. N.
Weedmark, R. S.

Weedmark, W. W.
Weldon, E.
Weldon, L.*
Whitman, Allan
Whitman, George
Wiebe, Dick (Sr.)
Wiebe, J.
Weiss, Alvin
Weiss, W.
Wilkinson, Ray F.
Zilkie, Dan
Zilkie, Harold

Memorial to Henry Smook, died 1945. Kneeling is his uncle, Peter Smook - Rosa Cemetery.

THE FACES OF FRANKLIN

edited by Susan Hiebert
compiled by Historical Committee

The following is a collection of pictures showing the people of Franklin, the best assets of any community. Included are families who have lived in this municipality for more than a century, and others who have come recently. Many came and went, their stay in this corner of the world short and uneventful. All, however, made a contribution to the lifestyle of the community. They used their talents, their strengths and their abilities to create a standard of living which the present citizens have inherited. It is to their memory, and for our enjoyment and enlightenment, that we present their faces:

A

MICHAEL ANDRUSYK

Michael, son of Steven and Mary Andrusyk, married Mary, daughter of Michael and Ustina Gawronsky (nee Didychuk) in 1936. They lived at Senkiw SW ¼ 5-3-5. Michael's death in 1950 left Mary with three children.

Helen married Dennis Smith, son of Tom and Fern Smith in 1953.

Iris married William Wachna, son of Dmytro and Anna Wachna in 1955.

John married Carol Lindsay, daughter of John and Rita Lindsay in 1964.

Mary Andrusyk now lives at Ridgeville.

Michael and Mary Andrusyk, 1936.

Mrs. Mary Andrusyk, with children, l to r; Helen Smith, Iris Wachna, John Andrusyk. 1980

WALLACE ARTHUR

Wallace Arthur was born in Charlottetown, P.E.I., May 4, 1851. His parents moved to Goderich, Ontario, where he married Mary Ann Million on January 15, 1877. Edwin, Mona, Nina, Roy and Fred were born here. They came west via Hansel, North Dakota, where he operated a bakery. Alice, Joe, Jane and Herb were born here. In 1897 he came to Franklin Municipality and farmed Section 6-2-3E. He built a huge barn in 1905. The farm is now owned by Ken Gruenke.

Mary Ann Wallace died March 12, 1918. Edwin, Joe and Herb farmed along the Red River. Later their farm was sold and Herb bought a half section from Walter Anderson, south of Dominion city. Herb lived with wife Rosa (Warrask) in Dominion City. His children, Trudy, Noel, Pat, Jessie, May, Edwin, Bruce and Jimmy all are married and live outside the municipality.

L to r; Ed, May, Alice, Nina, Jane Herb.

Grandad, Wallace Arthur, with Giner and Riley on way to Morris fair.

EMIL ALSTADT

Emil Alstadt came to Manitoba, Canada from Wolhynien, Russia with his wife Emilige (nee Pahl) and eleven month old son Erich in 1898.

They came to Dominion City and settled along the Roseau River on land which is now part of "The Glenway Colony Farms".

Emil worked for farmers wherever jobs were available for several years. His first job was with Samuel Maynes (Sr.) cutting wood.

In 1900 they bought SW ¼ 27-2-4E on the ridge from a land company. This quarter was all bush and had to be cleared by hand.

Later on they also bought SE ¼ 28-2-4E.

They raised a family of four sons and three daughters. Three sons were farmers in Green Ridge. Erich, Daniel, and Henry. Gustave went to Chicago, U.S.A. and worked in a machine shop. He is retired and lives in Dominion City. Ida married Henry Krebs (a Lithographer) and lived in Winnipeg (both deceased). Emma married Emil Boggs (deceased), who had a shoe and paint shop in Dominion City. Emma lives in Dominion City.

Elsa married Alec Fels (a jeweller) and lives in Roland, Manitoba.

Emil Alstadt died in 1941. Emilige passed away in 1968.

Both were laid to rest in Friedensthal Cemetery.

Erich Alstadt was born in Wolhynien, Russia 1897. He came to Canada at the age of eleven months. With the exception of a few years when his parents lived in Roseau, near Dominion City, he lived a greater part of his life at Green Ridge.

Erich bought the SW ¼ 34-2-4E from a land company in 1918. He dug a well, still in use, supplying the water for stock and household in 1892.

In 1920 he married Amanda Knut of Friedensthal.

Amanda was born in Friedensthal in 1900, daughter of August and Julianna (Rachinsky) Knut.

They had a daughter Ruth and a son Bernhard, born in Green Ridge.

Erich later bought and farmed NW ¼ 24-3-3E, which he sold to C. Penner. He farmed SW ¼ 4-3-4E in Green Ridge, known as Richard Post farm, also the SE ¼ 34-2-4E until his death in 1962.

Amanda died in 1964. They were laid to rest in the Friedensthal Cemetery.

Mr. and Mrs. Emil Alstadt

Their son Bernhard took over the family farm. His sister Ruth has made her home with him.

Henry Alstadt was born June 16, 1915. He farmed with his father on the home place from the time he left school.

In 1941 he rented the home farm and began farming on his own.

In 1943 he married Mary Johnstone from Woodmore. Their daughter Sharon was born in 1945.

In 1948 Henry and Mary bought N ½ 30-2-4E from Wm. Hartwig and a part of NE ¼ 21-2-4E from Herbert Davison as a building site.

In the 1960's they bought the NW ¼ 27-2-4E from Ewald Bohn.

In 1968 Henry was employed by Boundary School Division as Transportation Supervisor, a position he held until his retirement in 1980.

Henry and Mary still live on the farm in Green Ridge.

Daughter Sharon graduated as an R.N. Nurse from Winnipeg General Hospital in 1965.

In 1967, she married John Enns, a school teacher. They live in Winnipeg, where John teaches school.

They have four children, Jason, Justin, Noel and Tessa.

JACOB ARSENY

One of the first pioneers in the Tolstoi area was Jacob Arseny. He was the son of Michael and Irene Arseny of the Ukraine. He came to Canada in 1897 and settled on the NW 33-1-5 E at Tolstoi. That same year he married Maria Pidherny. Here they farmed until they passed away and the sons continued to farm. They were active in church and community affairs, and had 11 children.

John married and moved to the U.S.A., is now deceased.

Nick married and moved to the U.S.A., is now deceased.

Ann married and moved to the U.S.A., is now deceased.

Wasyl married Mary Tymchuk of Stuartburn. They farmed in this area and Wasyl was a Watkins dealer for many years. He held positions as school trustee, secretary of church and hall.

They had two girls:

Sonya is married to Bud Horasym and now living in Thunder Bay. They have three children.

Patricia is married to D. Oliver. They live in the U.S.A., and have two boys.

Pearl married John Kosowan. Both were great workers in the church, hall and the community of Tolstoi. Many drama plays were staged under

121

John's direction. He often acted as Master of Ceremonies at anniversaries and weddings.

They had four children:

Orest married Florence Dziedic. Both teach in Winnipeg. They have two children.

Boris is a mechanic living in Winnipeg.

Zane is a plumber living in Winnipeg.

Adele, deceased at the age of eight.

John has died and Pearl resides in the village of Tolstoi.

Michael married Mary Antonishika. Mike was school trustee, church president and hall president for many years. He died in 1977. They farmed at Tolstoi, and had three daughters:

Elaine married Gerry Caspar. They have one son and live in Calgary.

Sonya married Walter Wasylyshn. They have one son and live in St. Andrews.

Ruth Ann married Wm. Boucher. They have a daughter and a son, and reside in Winnipeg.

Steve married Marian Toffan. They live in Thunder Bay. They are deceased.

Metro, a war veteran, lived in B.C. now deceased.

Katherine married P. Peterson. They live in Toronto and have three children.

Sam, a war veteran, lived in Winnipeg. He had a jewellery and watch repair shop. Sam died in 1974.

Paul married Kay Prokipchuk. They are still farming in Tolstoi on the homestead. They have two children.

Audrey, married to Ralph Burgess, lives in Lloydminster, Alta.

Wayne married Louise Seniuk and lives in Emerson where Wayne is Customs officer. They have one daughter, Cara.

Jacob Arseny's first home, 1898.

Jacob Arseny's second home, 1918.

Present house on Arseny farm.

Family of Mary and Mike Arseny, l to r; back, Sonya and Walter Wasylyshun, son Peter, and Wm. Bouchard; front, Ruth Bouchard and daughter, Mary Arseny, Elaine and son.

Left: Dokia Pidhirny, 1924, mother of Mrs. J. Arseny. *Right:* Wedding, William and Mary Arseny, November 6, 1926.

Children of J. Arseny, l to r; Sam, Bill, Pearl, Katherine, Mike, Paul, 1960.

Metro Arseny. July 21, 1945; Sam Arseny, 1940

Jacob Arseny and Anna, second wife, married 1929. C. 1930

Left: Four generations, l to r; back, Cara, Wayne and Paul Arseny; sitting, Anna Arseny.
Right: Paul and Kay Arseny.

Left: Audrey and Ralph Burgess.
Right: Louise, Cara and Wayne Arseny.

John and Pearl (Arseny) Kosowan, 1960.

Children of John and Pearl Kosowan, l to r; back, sons Zane and Orest, Florence, wife of Orest, and Boris; front, Pearl Kosowan with two grandchildren. 1980.

GEORGE ADDISON

George Addison married Delilah Post in 1865, at Madoc, Ontario. They came to Manitoba in the 1870's, farming the NW ¼ of 17, with their buildings located on the NE ¼ of 17.

George was born in 1845, died in 1925. Delilah was born in 1844 and died in 1914. Their children were Hattie, born 1868, Alice, born 1880, and George Jr. 1867-1936.

123

JIM ANSTETT

L to r; standing, Michael, Terrence, RoJean, Margaret (nee Brooks); seated, Jim Anstett. 25th anniversary picture, October 31, 1978. Jim was the United Grain Growers manager at Cordova, then Dominion City from January, 1964 and is still manager at Dominion City elevator.

JOHN ADAMS

John Adams came from Cornwall, Ontario, with his brother Edwin in 1875 to homestead. John returned to Cornwall to marry Mary Rombaugh.

John was a good carpenter as well as farmer. He belonged to the Forester's Lodge, and helped to build the Forester's Hall at Green Ridge which is still in use today. He was a member of the Presbyterian church at Green Ridge, and helped to build the Church and Manse. For many years he was an elder in the church, and clerk of the session.

John and Mary's first home burned down in 1897. The house he built then is still being used.

There were five children. Two daughters, Katherine and Alice, died at an early age.

Margaret married (Muir) and went to live in Chicago.

Ike Adams at Franklin, Mich., July 4, 1929.

124

Ike Adams and Fred Snead

William worked on the railroad, married, and he and Minnie lived in Winnipeg. They had five children.

Isaiah farmed with his father then married and moved to western Manitoba. He and Lottie had two children.

John retired to live with William in Winnipeg, died at 85 years of age. Mary died in 1916. Both are buried in Green Ridge cemetery.

B JOSEPH BASKERVILLE

Joseph Baskerville was 19 years of age when he left Ireland for Canada in 1846. He was born at Castle Otway, Tipperary County, Ireland. He and his parents, one sister and four brothers spent six weeks crossing the Atlantic.

In 1853 Joseph married Catherine Johnston, and the couple acquired land at Bytown (Ottawa), and farmed there until 1878 when he and his wife and four sons and four of their five daughters moved to Dominion City. They arrived here by train through the United States. Joseph and Catherine homesteaded section 20-2-4 E1, and later moved to the Langside area.

Joseph was born in 1827, and died July 26, 1981. Catherine died Februry 7, 1903. Buried in Green Ridge. They were married in the Township of Gloucter, Ontario, on October 27, 1853, by Rev. Wm. Lochead.

Margaret Jane was born July 23, 1854. She had two husbands, Edward Duncan, whom she married February 4, 1879, and Paul Langille, August 28, 1883. She died July 27, 1931.

Elizabeth was born October 2, 1855, married John Waterworth September 18, 1882, and died January 31, 1926.

John David, born, April 10, 1857, married Sarah Jane Oatway December 26, 1888, and died January 31, 1926.

James Johnston, born March 23, 1860 married (Unknown) January 1, 1900, died September 7, 1922.

Joseph Hardy, born March 24, 1862, married

Family of Joseph and Catherine Baskerville, l to r; back, Edward Duncan, son of Margaret Duncan, Robert, James, John David, and Joseph; front, Eleanor, Margaret, Louise, Mrs. Joseph Baskerville, Elizabeth, Matilda.

Elizabeth Linklater January 12, 1892, died August 15, 1943.

Annie Matilda, born January 16, 1864, married William W. Fraser January 12, 1892, died August 27, 1949.

Sarah Louise, born October 18, 1866, married John C. Ginn, October 11, 1893, died December 14, 1939.

Eleanor Gertrude, born October 3, 1869, married Lee Nelson July 7, 1897, died September 17, 1929.

Robert Groves, born May 26, 1871, married Maude Alice Haynes December 21, 1898, died June 15, 1948.

JOHN DAVID BASKERVILLE

John David Baskerville farmed in the Langside area until 1924. He and his sons did custom threshing for many years. Mr. Baskerville was a public figure and used to chair meetings in the district, and was often called upon to act as master of ceremonies at public affairs. He was responsible for much of the drainage work in the Green Ridge area, and represented the Emerson constituency as M.L.A. during World War I.

He had seven children:

Clifford Waterworth, 1890 to 1917, did not marry, attended agricultural college in Winnipeg before enlisting in 222 Battalion, W and was killed in action, November 14, 1917.

Milton Grove, 1893 to 1973, married, name unknown, had no family, was a captain in World War I, and a Squadron Leader in World War II. Later he was a real estate agent in Vancouver.

Lloyd Oatway, 1895 to 1973, married Laura Brad, had two children, Clifford, Margaret.

Wallace Roy, 1896 to 1981, married Marjorie Lawson, had three children, Doris, John and Gor-

don. Was a pilot in World War I, then worked for C.P.R. and later until retirement with Department of Immigration.

Wilmer Wylie, 1896 to 1898.

Warren Wylie, 1879 to 1976, married Emma Paulson, had no family, moved to United States.

Cynthia Lyle, born, 1904, married Donald Robertson, has one son, Jack, was educated at Dominion City and took teacher training at Manitou, Manitoba. Now resides in Vernon, British Columbia.

J. D. Baskerville's original house in Dominion City. Now owned by Wm. Bultz.

NEILL GROVES BASKERVILLE

Neill Groves Baskerville was born in Dominion City on August 17, 1900, only child of Robert Groves Baskerville and Maude Alice Maynes. Neill received his education in Dominion City, and in 1916 took a business course in Winnipeg. After graduating he took a position as bookkeeper for John Strutt of England who owned large tracts of land at Meadows, Manitoba, and Kindersley, Saskatchewan.

In 1920 Neill and his father bought land at

Mr. and Mrs. Bert Baskerville and Neill.

Dominion City which they operated until 1934. This farm is now owned by Mrs. William R. Kyle.

In 1934 Neill became farm manager for the Lyman Farms at Arnaud, holding this position until the Lyman land was sold.

In 1935 he married Mary Isabella Ostberg, only daughter of William and Isabella Ostberg of Dominion City. In 1936 they took up residence in the Lyman Farm home at Arnaud, residing there until 1953.

From 1942 to 1953 Neill was councillor in Ward five, Franklin Municipality, a period which saw many improvements made to roads, bridges, and drainage.

In 1953 they moved to Winnipeg, and resided there until Neill's death in 1972.

Neill and Mary had one son, Robert William Baskerville, born in 1939.

Robert married Jane Sellwood in 1961, they had three children, Neill Bruce, Brian Leslie, and Shannon Leigh.

Robert passed away suddenly in 1972 after undergoing heart surgery.

In 1982 Mary Baskerville makes her home in Winnipeg.

Neill and Mary Baskerville, and son Robert.

Bill and Irene Kyle, Mary and Neill Baskerville, 1948.

Lyman Farm house, built 1921.

Neill Baskerville threshing, 1920's.

Neill and Mary Baskerville wedding, 1935.

Left: L to r; Robert Baskerville, son Neill Bruce, father Neill Baskerville.
Right: L to r; Neill Baskerville, Robert Baskerville; front, Bruce, Brian and Shannon Baskerville, children of Robert.

Mr. and Mrs. Dawson Baskerville. Dawson was the son of Joseph Baskerville, pioneer. Mrs. Dawson was Josephine Taylor, daughter of Mr. and Mrs. Alex Taylor, also pioneers. They were married May 7, 1929, and had 10 children.

Dawson Baskerville family, l to r; back, Eileen, Cam, Lillian, Doug, Josie (mother) and Warren; middle, Janie, Jim; front, Valerie, Dawn.

DAWSON BASKERVILLE

Dawson Ross, born Jan. 26,1903, died Jan. 28, 1963 and Josephine Marie (Taylor), born Aug. 31, 1907, died Jan. 13, 1974, were married in Winnipeg on May 7, 1929.
Lived in house where Franklin Manor is now situated. They had 10 children:
Douglas married Eldean (Raw). Children, Reba Lee and Ryan.
Cameron married Jo-Ann (Jamieson). Children, Kelly and De-Ann.
Muriel Elizabeth, deceased, Lillian and Fred Banscombe.
James married Maida (Lent). Children, Dawn, Dean and Barry.
Eileen married Keith (Cyr). Children, Brent, Curtis and Craig.
Velma.
Warren married Carol (Sorgenfrie). Children, Babette and Leesa.
Dawn married Murray (Tallant). Children, Melanie, Spring and Zane.
Valerie married Cecil (Smoley). Children, Stuart, Kent and Kyle.

Lloyd and Laure E. Baskerville.

Jayne, Scott and Chantelle.
Valerie and Cec Smoley and their three sons are the only members of the family still living in Dominion City.

LLOYD BASKERVILLE

Lloyd Baskerville, 4th generation in Franklin, farmed at Langside until 1928, when he sold the farm to M. Penner. He then worked for Harry Ball, and formed a trucking business known as "Ball and Baskerville". In 1930 Lloyd started a farm equipment dealership out of a rented office in the North American Lumber building. In 1939 he built the structure now occupied by the Boundary School Division, and sold farm machinery, automobiles, electrical appliances, and even wood burning stoves were sold from this store. General Insurance formed an important part of the business. In 1968 his son Clifford took over, and Lloyd and Laura moved to the west coast, where

L to r; seated, Kathy, Laure E., Cliff, Gordon, Judith and L. O. Baskerville.

127

L. O. Baskerville Garage, Dominion City.

Lloyd died in 1973. Laura moved back to Dominion City in 1974, and now resides in Franklin Manor.

There were two children:

Clifford married Margaret Jean Renton in 1955, and has three children, Judith, Kathleen, and Gordon.

Margaret married Jim Fiddler, and has two children, Geraldine and Valerie.

RUDOLPH BULTZ

Rudolph Bultz was born Feb. 24, 1892, in Lutz, Poland. He immigrated to Detroit, Michigan, where he was employed by the Ford Motor Co. He met and married Wilhelmina Huff, also from Poland, in Detroit in 1917.

In 1921, with their small daughter Ruth, they came to Canada to farm. They tried various places before moving to section 12-3-3 E1 on the Roseau River in 1935.

Mr Bultz lost his leg in a farm accident in 1937 and on June 11, 1939 Mrs. Bultz passed away after a lengthy illness.

Mr. Bultz continued to farm with his sons, Bill and Harold until 1949 when he moved into Dominion City. However he really loved the farm and continued to come to the farm almost every day. He liked nothing better than to get on his old John Deere and go out into the field. He passed away on July 11, 1973 at the age of 81 and is resting beside his wife in the Dominion City cemetery.

The Rudolph Bultz's had four children:

Ruth born Feb. 1, 1920 in Detroit, Michigan. She married Lorne Ramsey and they had five children.

Donald, wife Donna and children Kelly, Lisa and Mark. They reside in Edmonton, Alberta.

Calvin, wife Mary Jane and children Jennifer, Tim and Jamie. They reside in Steinbach, Man.

Valorie, husband Ed Thom and three girls Pat, Carla and Krista. They live in Russell, Man.

Ronald, wife Linda and sons Tyson and Tyler.

They live in Dominion City.

Kathy, the youngest daughter is presently nursing in Saskatoon, Sask.

Edna, born Feb. 4, 1923 Baldur, Man. She married Morris Kelly and they had one son, Alan, who is continuing his education at Red River College in Winnipeg.

Bill, born Sept. 27, 1924, Sperling, Man. He married Mildred Solnes and they had four daughters.

Judy, husband Archie Hunter and children, Michael, Tracey and Jordy.

Carolyn, presently employed in St. Boniface Hospital in Cardiology Unit.

Susan, employed as a nurse to a surgeon in the Boyd Building in Winnipeg.

Lori, employed in St. Boniface Hospital. She is a secretary in Anaesthesia.

Harold, born May 1, 1928 at Starbuck. He has not married and presently farms in partnership with his brother Bill on the home farm.

Rudolph and Wilhelmina Bultz on their wedding, 1917.

Rudolph Bultz and his grandchildren, 1957, l to r; Carolyn Bultz, Judy Bultz, Kathy Ramsey, Don Ramsey, Susan Bultz, Ron Ramsey, Valerie Ramsey.

Left: Bill Bultz, Ruth Bultz, Edna Bultz.
Right: Bill Bultz with his horses.

Bill and Mildred Bultz on their 25th wedding anniversary, L.-R.: Bill Bultz, daughters Carolyn, Lori, Judy, Susan, and Mildred Bultz.

Left: Rudolph Bultz on his John Deere.
Right: Bill and Harold Bultz, plucking ducks. 1945.

GEORGE BRAD

George Brad emigrated from England to Manitoba in 1880, and Sarah M. Pearse emigrated with her family from Devonshire, England in 1884. They were married in All Saints Anglican Church November 3, 1886. Mr. and Mrs. Brad owned and operated the Queens Hotel from 1886 to 1887, later moving to a private home on Brad street west. Mr. Brad passed away in 1904 at the early age of 54 years, leaving his wife to raise a large family. Children of this marriage, all born in Dominion City: Ethel, Arthur, Wilfred, Alva, Florence, Eliza, Laura, Clarence, Leslie, Jessie.

Leslie was born January 14, 1903. He received his education at Bow Park School, Green Ridge and Dominion City. In 1924 he married Mildred Easterby, who was born June 1906 in Dominion City. He farmed the SE ¼ of Section 35-2-3 E. In 1943 they moved to the Roseau River Reserve, where he was Indian Agent until 1958. Then they moved to Dominion City. Leslie also served on the council of the RM of Franklin for 18 years. Leslie passed away January 23, 1982. Children of the marriage were Gordon, Wallace, Douglas.

Gordon was born in Dominion City, 1926 and was educated at Green Ridge School. In 1953 he married Mary Boaler from Otterburne, Man. They farm Section 1-3-2 E and take an active part in community affairs, he also has the Wawanesa Agency. They have two sons, Dale and Calvin.

Dale was born in 1956, attended Dominion City school, employed as weed inspector in RM of Franklin. He married Sharon Sawka from Vita in 1977.

Dustin Brad, born to Dale and Sharon June 16, 1982.

Wallace was born in Dominion City in 1927. He attended Green Ridge and Dominion City schools. Employed as a clerk in the RM of Franklin from 1946-49, also with the North American Lumber. In 1951 he married Edna Casper of Dominion City, moved to Aneroid, Sask. in 1952 and was employed with the Citizens Lumber Co. In 1958 they moved to Russell, Man. where he is Secretary-Treasurer for the town. They have two children, Terence and Catherine.

Douglas, deceased in 1955.

Sarah M. Brad, 1956, with her four youngest children, born between 1898 and 1905, in Brad-Pearse home on Brad Street west, south of the Anglican church, l to r; Laura Brad Baskerville, Jessie Brad Maynes, Leslie Brad, Clarence Brad.

Wallace and Edna Brad and family, l to r; Catherine, Edna, Wallace, Terence.

Family of Sarah Mudge (Pearse) Brad, and George Brad. Taken with their six children who were born in Queen's Hotel, Dominion City. Hotel was owned and operated by George Brad, l to r; back, Alva, George Brad, Sarah Brad; middle, Ethel, Florence, Eliza, Wilfred; front, Arthur. All born between 1888 and 1896.

Leslie and Mildred Brad, 50th wedding anniversary.

Children of Leslie Brad, l to r; Douglas, Wallace, Gordon Brad.

Mr. and Mrs. Gordon Brad, 1953.

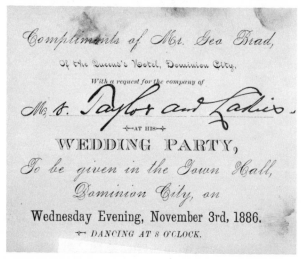

Invitation to Wedding Party, Pearse - Brad wedding. Note compliments of groom, bride not mentioned.

Dale and Sharon Brad, 1977.

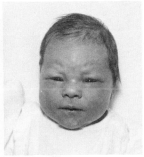

Left: Calvin Brad, son of Gordon Brad.
Right: Dustin Leslie Brad, son of Dale and Sharon Brad.

JOE BOUTET

Joe Boutet was born in St. Savour, Quebec and spent his early years there. In 1910 he came west to the Arnaud district at the age of 16, not knowing a word of English, and worked as a stooker for Gorden Ironside. From there he worked for Ted Lang for two summers. In 1912 he ran a barber shop and pool room on Arnaud Main Street. In winters he worked in bush camps and railway camps all the way from Kenora, Ontario to Tete Juane, Alberta.

In 1916 Joe joined the army and later transferred to the Air Force. Upon discharge he married Mary Ross of Peterborough Ontario, and they came west as bride and groom in 1918 and again he worked on the farm of Arthur Erb. In 1920 he and his wife moved to their own farm home in the North Star district. In 1931 they moved into the Langside district where Joe farmed and ran a trucking business. In 1939 the family moved into the town of Arnaud.

The following year Joe and his eldest son Charles, joined the Cameron Highlanders and served overseas for the duration of the war. In 1942 his eldest daughter, Doreen joined the CWAC and his son Bob also joined the Army. In 1944 all four returned home following discharge. In 1946 Joe and Mary resumed farming in the Langside district. In 1951 they moved to Dominion City to retire in a home Joe built himself. Joe moved to Franklin Manor in 1982. His wife Mary passed away April 12, 1981.

Garnet started school in Arnaud. About 1955 he joined the RCAF as an accountant and has been posted all across Canada. In 1956 he married Carol Milan and they have two children Farley and Lindsey. At the present time he is stationed in Winnipeg.

Roger started school at Langside and in 1957 married Dorothy Botham. He and his wife have four children, Keith, Susan, Karen and Lynn and they live in Winnipeg. Roger worked as a mechanic at Century Motors until it closed and is presently working at Southwood Motors.

Faye started school in Langside. In 1949 she married George Opochensky. They farmed close to Dominion City and had 5 children, Bobby, Janet, Julie, Joan and Angela. Faye passed away in 1972. She was predeceased by her son Bobby.

Doreen, eldest daughter of Joe and Mary started school in North Star district and following her discharge from the Army married Leslie Pool. They had two children, Bryan and Brenda. In 1953 she married again and she and her husband Ty Markham, an engineer have two children, Marilyn and Dale and live in Beeton, Ontario.

Charles started school in North Star School. He joined the army in 1940 and during the war he met and married Barbara Storvald in England. In 1946 he brought his bride home to England. In 1951 they moved to D.C. where they still reside. Charles works on the grader for the RM of Franklin. Barb is a custodian at the school. They have five children, Barry, Shirley, Melvin, Diane and David.

Beverly, like Garnet, started school in Arnaud and finished her schooling in Dominion City. In 1958, she married Donald Froom of Dominion City. Don is a teacher in high school and they are presently living at Westbank, B.C. They have four children, Kimberly, Colleen, Grophan and Christopher.

L to r; back, Charles Boutet, Bev Froom, Garnet Boutet, Roger Boutet, Faye Opocensky, Bob Boutet, Doreen Markham, Ted Boutet; front, Mary and Joe Boutet.

L to r; back, Mel Boutet, Shirley Berington, Dave Boutet, wife Sandra, Diane Boutet, Barry Boutet; front, Barb Boutet, Mary Boutet, Joe Boutet, Charles Boutet.

L to r; Larry Boutet, wife Iren (Kahlain), Lynda (Kein), Dennis Boutet; front, James and Iona (Casper) Boutet. James lived in Arnaud and was employed by the CPR until 1946, when he married Iona Casper, and in 1947 moved to Emerson where he was dray man for 15 years. From 1961 to 1978 he worked for the Department of Public Works. They have two sons, Dennis and Larry. Inset: Chad (4) and Janine (2), children of Dennis Boutet.

Robert Boutet family, l to r; back, Gregory, Richard, Norman, Elaine, Claudia, Laurel, Florence, Tony, Bob. Robert married Florence King in 1951. They farmed at Langside until 1966, when they moved to Letellier. Robert works for the Rural Municipality of Montcalm. They have seven children. Norman married Lucie Boulanger of Hartney in 1976, and lives in St. Norbert with daughters Faith and Nicole. Richard married Leah Dick of Fort Frances in 1977, lives in Rosenfeld with sons Mathew and Stephen. Claudia nurses in Victoria, B.C., Gregory is a carpenter in Victoria. Laurel is attending University of Manitoba, and Anthony is in high school in Dominion City.

Norman and Lucie Boutet and Joshua Robert.

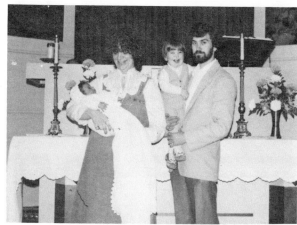

Stephen, Leah, Mathew and Richard Boutet.

Left: Dorothy Ann (Hancox) and Barry Joseph Boutet. *Right:* Dave and Sandra Boutet, married September 20, 1980.

Melanee Jay Boutet and Sherry Boutet, daughters of Barry Boutet; Kim Boutet.

L to r; Farley, Garnet and Carol Boutet, Lindsay. Garnet started school in Arnaud. About 1955 he joined the R.C.A.F. as an accountant, and has been posted all across Canada. In 1956 he married Carol Milan, and they have two children, Farley and Lindsay. At present he is stationed in Winnipeg.

Mel and Louise Boutet; Carey (4), Kevin (2½).

JACOB BOEHLER

Jacob Boehler was a blacksmith in Warsaw, Poland, and was employed in a pumping station before coming to Canada in 1891. He worked on the railway coming west, and was joined by his wife Katharine and the four oldest children in 1892. She was unable to locate her husband upon arrival on the prairie, and found employment with a Mennonite family at Gretna until the RCMP had found Jacob in Saskatchewan. In 1900 they bought land at Ridgeville, adding to it until they owned the entire Section 31-1-4 E1. Jacob hauled lumber from 65 miles away to build his first barn in 1903. Five more children were born to the Boehlers while living at Ridgeville.

Jacob and Katherine Boehler. Their children were Emma, Albert, Jacob, Gustev, Leopold, Adolf, Otto, John, William, Emeneul, Reinhold, and Henry.

Mr. and Mrs. Jacob Boehler going for a drive.

PHILIP BRODOWAY

Mr. and Mrs. Philip Brodoway farmed at Overstoneville until their passing, Philip in 1963, and Anna (Gylywoychuk) in 1966. They were married at Tolstoi in 1914, and had six children; Tennie, Nettie, Johnny, Ollie, Ruth, and Mike, who died in 1964.

LUKIAN BIALLY

In 1897, Lukian Bially at the age of 4½, and his sister Mary, 10, came to Canada from Western Ukraine with their parents Ivan and Anna Bially. The family homestead was the NE¼ 30-1-5 E1 in the Overstoneville area.

Mr. Bially remembers his ocean voyage to the new land and his experience of losing his hat which the wind blew off his head. If it wasn't for a protective person aboard, he would have jumped ship to retrieve his hat. His recollections of early days of oxen, horses, steam engine, threshing and working the new land is vivid and interesting now at the age of 92.

On February 13, 1913, Lukian married Anna Stadnyk. In 1916 Mr. Bially became the first entrepreneur in the Agricultural community of Overstoneville. He had acquired a substantial amount of machinery which included a steam engine which was used to break new land for himself and others, a threshing machine, saw mill, grain crusher and a Happy Farmer tractor. Mr. Bially also purchased a Model T Ford car in 1916 for $800, which was a community first.

Lukian would saw lumber for people in the district and crush grain which was brought by bag on the people's backs. Mr. Bially also remembers threshing until freeze-up and milling flour which

60th Anniversary of Mr. and Mrs. Lukian Bially and family, Tolstoi Manitoba, 1973. L to r: front, seated, Robert Williams Jr., Carol Kreitz, Linda Frederick, Pat Bially, Edward J. Bially; middle, Eva Bially, Effie Williams, Mr. Lukian Bially, holding great-grandson, Christopher Bially, Mrs. Lukian Bially, Mrs. Olga Fredrick, Mrs. Ruby Bially; back, Milton Bially, Mike Bially, Robert Williams, Michael Bially, Daniel Fredrick, Helen and Jack (John) Bially, James Bially, and Allan Fredrick.

took a bit of know how before a proper texture of flour was made.

Mr. Bially made his work much easier in 1930 when he purchased a John Deere model "D" tractor. His last tractor for his farming endeavors was an International Harvestor "W4".

Farming his land as well as renting acreages carried on to 1959 when the couple retired and moved to Tolstoi. In 1976 Mr. and Mrs. Bially became residents of the Vita Personal Care Home where they will celebrate their 70th anniversary in 1983.

Mr. and Mrs. Bially had four sons and two daughters.

Their eldest son, Bill, married Ruby Pepper at Windsor, Ont., they had two sons, James and Kenneth. Bill passed away October 30, 1970 and son Kenneth's accidental death was on July 22, 1977, which left a young widow with two young children, Bradley, age two and Nicolle Cynthia, six months. James and Pat live in Belle River, Ontario, they have two young hockey players, Christopher and Andrew.

Mike married Eva Wachna, they reside at Tolstoi. Their only daughter, Carol, married Kenneth Kreitz, Emerson. They have two daughters Jeri-Lyn and Jill and a son Michael who married Kathy Derewianchuk, and lives in Norway House.

John (Jack), married Helen Dolynchuk, they reside at Tolstoi, their only son Edward John, resides in Winnipeg.

Olga married Daniel Fredrick, they live in Dunedin, Florida and Montreal. Their only son Allan and wife Jane live in Edmonton, with daughter Allyson.

Effie married Robert Sydney Williams, Dor-

val, Quebec. Their only son Robert Jr. and his wife Cindy live in Toronto. They have two sons, Nicholas and Matthew.

Milton, at the age of 50, passed away in 1950.

25th Wedding Anniversary of John and Helen Bially, son Edward John.

Michael Bially, and wife Kathy (nee Derewianchuk), married 1977.

134

Mike and Eva (nee Wachna) Bially

Henry and Helen Bially, children James and Cheryl.

Bernice Bially and husband Lorne Goy.

Carol Bially and husband Keneth Kreitz, daughters Jeri-Lynn (6) and Jill (1). Married 1974.

L to r; Donny, Nancy and Nestor Bially, Jarvis. 25th wedding anniversary, 1978.

Peter Bially, youngest son of Ivan Bially, and wife Margaret. Overstoneville 1962.

L to r; Bill Bially, Molly Bially, Steve Stack, Ruby Bially, 1945.

135

Mary (Bially) and Steve Prusky, 1972.

Elsie, Travere (back), Dale, and Frank Bially.

FRANK BATTEN

In 1878 Richard Batten and his half brother Thomas received their homestead claims in Emerson. The two men's families emigrated from Erie county in Pennsylvania. Originally the Battens were from Cornwall in England. The farms were located in the Woodmore area on Section 20-2-5 E. The brothers built a log house with a thatched roof and the families shared this home for a few years. Richard Batten died in 1884 from typhoid fever. His wife Barbara Batten managed her farm with help from her neighbors and her four children: Frank, Richard M., Charles and Mary. Barbara Batten had a Sunday School class in her home and in 1900 she opened the first post office in the Woodmore area. She was postmistress until 1913 when W. T. Ward purchased her farm and the post office duties were taken over by him and his wife Lillian. Their son Clifford established a store across the Morden Sprague highway from the original home. In 1940 his wife Frances took over the duties in the post office which had been established by her grandmother 50 years before.

Mrs. Barbara Batten's daughter, Mary, lived with her mother in Woodmore, and later on in Winnipeg. Barbara Batten died in 1942 so Mary returned to live in the Woodmore area. Her house was located on her brother Frank's farm. Charles

Batten married Cora Sloss and he was a United Church minister in Canada and the United States.

Frank Batten farmed in the Woodmore area until he retired to Emerson. Graham Batten purchased the farm he now operates from his father on Section SE 19-2-5 E.

Thomas Batten and his wife Ellen had two sons: Henry and Fred. Henry married Charlotte Froom and their daughter Lois Matthews now lives in Winnipeg. Fred and his wife nee Annie Pott had two children.

Ralph died in his teens and Daisy Nagaele lives in the United States.

In 1976 Richard Lorne Batten bought a few acres on the NW corner of 8-2-5 E from Clifford Ward. It was nearly a century before, that his grandparents, the Richard Battens started a homestead on section 20-2-5 E. Lorne and his wife nee Elaine Hunter Robinson moved to Woodmore in 1976 from St. Vital. Previous to his retirement, Lorne served as a pilot in the R.C.A.F. for five years during the second World War. Latterly he was employed as a salesman for Fiberglass Canada Ltd. Lorne and Elaine have two daughters, Rae and Clare.

Rae married Joseph Brooks of St. Paul, Minnesota and has three sons. Paul, Brent and Chad.

Clare married Ronald Bratenstein of St. Vital. They reside in North Delta, B.C. with their daughters Tammy and Tracy.

Lorne's father was Richard M. Batten who was a partner in the Real Estate Co. of Gunn and Batten. His wife was Christine Armstrong of Fergus, Ontario. Their daughters are Lillian Ballard, Lorraine McEwan, and Betty Clarke. A daughter Elenor Noble died in 1937.

THE FRANK BATTEN FAMILY

J. Frank Batten purchased the E ½ of 19-2-5 E at Woodmore. In 1909 he married Maggie Graham from Green Ridge, where she lived with her mother and two brothers Sam and John. Maggie Graham was born in Coleraine, Ireland. Mr. and Mrs. Frank Batten were good community and church workers. Their four children were named Frances, Graham, Kenneth, Nevin and Margaret. Frances was a teacher at Stuartburn, Fredensthal and Woodmore schools. In 1940 she married Clifford Ward and was responsible for the post office work as well as helping in the store. Frances and Cliff's son, Larry, now resides in Port Perry, Ontario and works at the University of Toronto. Frances passed away in 1967. Graham married Alice Johnston in 1950 and bought the farm from his parents. They have three chidren. Kenneth Nevin served in the armed forces overseas for five years after which he farmed in the Marais district. He now resides in Victoria, B.C. Margaret married Bill Coombs of the R.C.M.P. Their four sons are Bob, John, Tom and Ted. A fifth son, David, died as a young child while they were residents of Whitehorse in the Yukon. Margaret and Bill and family live in Victoria, B.C. with the exception of their oldest son Bob, who is a doctor and lives in Halifax with his wife Ernestine.

Mr. and Mrs. Frank Batten retired to the Emerson area, where Mrs. Batten passed away in 1960 and Mr. Batten in 1963.

GRAHAM BATTEN

Graham Batten bought his father's farm and he and his wife, the former Alice Johnston, still operate the farm. Graham and Alice were married in 1950, the flood year, at Westminster Church in Winnipeg. From this marriage there are three children.

Sandra married Bill Hawryluk and lives in Winnipeg. She is a member of the ladies ball club and still participates whenever possible.

Allan married Gleness Johnston, lives in Calgary and has two children, David and Karen. Kevin also lives in Calgary.

Mr. and Mrs. Frank Batten, 50th wedding anniversary, 1959.

Wedding picture of Graham and Alice (nee Johnston) Batten, April 22, 1950, l to r; Henry Alstadt, Nevin Batten, Graham Batten, Alice Batten, Jean Zilkie, Mary Alstadt.

Mr. and Mrs. Tom Batten, who homesteaded SE ¼ 20-2-5 E1, Woodmore.

Left: Allan Batten, wife Gleness, baby Karen and David. 1982.
Right: Kelvin Batten.

Frank Batten home, Woodmore, built 1908.

Sandra Batten, Bill Hawryluk, wedding October 1978.

ALEXANDER BORODENKO

Alexander and Olga Borodenko with children Ada, Walter, Theo, Matt and Alex Jr. immigrated from Bakivce, Ukraine, crossing over on the Ship Oscar II and docking in Halifax. They arrived in Dominion City July 3, 1928 where they farmed until Alexander and Olga retired and moved to Winnipeg in 1952.

Children born in the Dominion City area were Nick, Helen, Peter, Ruth, Vera and Henry. Now residing in the Toronto area are Ada, Walter, Helen, Vera and Henry while Alex Jr. and Peter are in Winnipeg, Ruth in California and Matt and Nick in Dominion City.

Walter, Theo and Matt served overseas in World War II and Nick in the Korean War.

On their return from World War II in 1946, Matt and Theo started a restaurant business on the main corner in Dominion City and called it Montreal Cafe. Theo remained until his marriage to Joyce Lepischuk of Stuartburn in November, 1947. He then moved to Winnipeg and worked for the Coca-Cola Co. until his retirement to Strathclair in 1981.

Matt and Rae, (married June 30, 1947) continued in the restaurant business. In January, 1949, during a big snow storm, their first daughter Karen was born at home. The same year Matt bought the Dominion City Theatre which he operated until 1962 when he tore it down and sold the property to the Canadian Imperial Bank of Commerce. In 1953 a second daughter, Debbie was born. Both girls grew up and graduated school in Dominion City, later moving to Winnipeg.

In August, 1975 Karen married Melvin Siemens of Altona, and Debbie married George Giesbrecht of St. Laurent. Their children are Tennille Siemens (1981), Tanya (1978) and Tiffany Giesbrecht (1981).

In July, 1959, the Montreal Cafe was sold to Eva Pawliw and her brother, the late Peter Kandia.

In 1962 Matt started a Massey Ferguson dealership in the old Schwark building under the firm name of Matt's Implement Sales Ltd. and in 1966 constructed a new garage building on Highway 201. He acted as Town Police for several years and the local Auctioneer.

Nick, Irene and family moved to Dominion City from Winnipeg in June, 1974, and Nick worked with Matt in the dealership. Due to poor health, Matt sold the Massey Ferguson franchise in December, 1975 and is retiring in Dominion City. He still does auctioneering and turns into Dominion City's Santa Claus at Christmas.

Alexander, daughter Vera, wife Olga Borodenko.

Henry and Hazel Borodenko, 1979.

Walter Borodenko and wife Lydia, 1944; twins Jimmy and Carol, 1947.

Carol (Borodenko) and husband Jim Culbert, Toronto. Gareth and Erin Lia

138

Jimmy Borodenko and wife Heather. 1977; Carrie Amanda Borodenko.

Nick and Irene Borodenko, 1979; Darcy Borodenko.

Matt and Rae Borodenko, married Blaine Lake, Saskatchewan, June 30, 1947; Karen and Debbie.

Debbie (Borodenko) and George Giesbrecht, daughters Tanya and Tiffany. 1981.

Bruce Borodenko and wife Jill, 1981.

Karen (Borodenko) and Melvin Siemens, daughter Tennille, 1978.

Rick Borodenko, wife Pat, son Cully, 1979.

139

Peter Borodenko, wife Anne, son Darren and daughter Lisa, 1979.

Byron, Ruth (Borodenko) and Fred Boggs, 1976.

L to r; Margaret Borodenko, wife of Alex Jr., Alex Jr., their daughter Helen, Helen's husband Ken Holmes. 1959. There are two children, Gary and Sharon, not shown. Helen and Ken Holmes have two daughters Kathy and Elaine.

Family of Theo Borodenko, 1977, l to r; Joyce Borodenko, wife of Theo, son Wayne, his wife Sharon, Linda (Borodenko) and husband Murray Rapley, Theo (with back to viewer), son Larry. Children, of Linda and Murray Rapley, Janine, Jeffrey and Marsha.

Vera (Boredenko) and husband Dave Radford, sons Randy and Darryl, 1964.

L to r; Henry, Peter, Nick, Alex, Theo and Matt Borodenko, mother Borodenko.

Evelyn Suchoboky, daughter of Ada (Borodenko) and Nick Suchoboky, 1963.

Matt Borodenko as Town Cop, 1960.

Matt Borodenko as local Santa Clause, Dominion City Skating Rink, 1980.

REINHOLD BOHN

Reinhold and Verna Bohn were married June 23, 1950. They farmed at Greenridge for seven years.

They have six children Shirley, Dianne, Ronald, Richard and their twin daughters Barbara and Deborah. Verna and Reinhold sold their farm in 1956 and moved to Dominion City where they purchased the Dominion City Transfer. Reinhold operated the transfer until he sold it to Roger Cadieux in 1973. Reinhold then retired and suddenly passed away a year later on March 29, 1974.

Their daughter Shirley married Walter Smadella of Winnipeg and they have two daughters Michelle and Jennifer.

Dianne married Ken McClelland of Emerson and they have two children Brian and Chelsea.

Ronald married Cheryl Ann Taylor (nee Eisner) of Winnipeg.

Richard and Barbara and Deborah reside at home.

Reinhold and Verna Bohn

Reinhold Bohn and his transfer, with Barbie and Debbie sitting on truck, 1969.

Shirley, Dianne, Ronald, Richard, Barbara and Deborah Bohn, 1966.

RUDOLPH BOHN

Rudolf Bohn was born in Gustapo, Russia, October 18, 1885. In 1903 he immigrated to Canada with his parents, Gottlieb and Wilhelmina Bohn and four brothers and one sister. They came in the Greenridge area, and bought a farm from Mr. Christie.

In 1910 Rudolph married Ottilie Keehn. She was born in Russia March 8, 1891. In 1908 Mrs. Bohn's family, Rudolf and Agusta (nee Biederman) Keehn and three sisters and three brothers immigrated to Canada and settled in the Emerson area. Ottilie and brother Ted Keehn didn't come to to Canada until a year later because of eye problems.

Rudolf and Ottilie Bohn took over the farm in 1910 until 1946 when they retired to Emerson. There were six children born and raised on that farm.

Emily (Mrs. Joe Ellek), Olga (Mrs. Julius Schmidt), (Reinhold deceased, 1974), Hilda (Mrs. Albert Walters), Ewald and Emil. A son predeceased the parents in infancy.

In 1946, their son Ewald, took over the farm until 1954 when he sold the farm to Henry Alstadt.

Ottilie Bohn passed away August 1972, Rudolf Bohn passed away May 1969.

Rudolph and Ottilie (Kuhn) Bohn

L to r; back, Reinhold Bohn, Ewald Bohn, Emil Bohn; front, Emily Ellek, Olga Schmidt, Hilda Walters.

Left: Mae and William G. Barker, and grandson Richard Bohn. 1966.
Right: Verna, Allan and Doreen Bohn, 1971.

Left: Mae Ginn, daughter Verna Bohn, Shirley Smadella (granddaughter), Michelle and Jennifer Smadella (great-grandchildren), 1980.
Right: Mae Ginn, daughter Verna Bohn, granddaughter Dianne McClelland, great-grandchildren Bryan and Chelsea, 1981.

WILLIAM G. BARKER

Mr. and Mrs. William G. Barber were married on February 11, 1918. Bill worked as a labourer for many years and also carried the mail from the train to the post office until he retired and suddenly took ill and passed away on July 21, 1971. He was 83 years old. They have three children, Allan, Verna and Doreen.

Allan married Phylis Javes of Greenridge and has three children; Cheryl, Betty and Judy.

Verna married Reinhold Bohn of Green Ridge and has six children, Shirley, Dianne, Ronald, Richard and twin daughters Barbara and Deborah.

Doreen married John Everall of Neepawa, they have three children Jean, Donald and Lynda.

Mrs. Barber later married Stanley Ginn and lived in Dominion City until Stan's death in 1981.

Mrs. Ginn has 12 grandchildren and 12 great-grandchildren.

Mrs. Stan Ginn is presently living in the Franklin Manor in Dominion City. She is 85 years old.

JACOB G. BRAUN

Jacob G. and Agnes (Enns) Braun arrived in Canada August 8, 1924, from Russia via the Empress of France. They came to Arnaud in October, 1925, where Jacob had purchased land. Upon arrival in Arnaud they shared a seven room house, west of the railway tracks with Mrs. Braun's widowed sister and her six children, their daughter Elizabeth and her husband John H. Poetker, J. Janzen Patchler, and nine members of the Abe Harder family. The Braun family had nine members to start with, and it was a very full house. Slowly people moved leaving the Brauns and the Poetkers in possession until the 1940's, when the house was torn down.

Jacob G. Braun died in 1951, at age 78; Maria Braun in 1966, age 87; Mrs. Abe Harder in 1937, age 27; George Braun in 1950, age 44; Jacob Braun in 1966, age 62; Henry Braun in 1978, age 59; Elizabeth Poetker in 1973, age 71.

L to r; back, Peter, George; middle, Mary, Elizabeth, Mrs. Maria Braun, Mr. Jacob Braun, Jacob, Cornelius; front, Agnes, Henry. 1924.

PETER BRAUN

Peter and Mary Braun (Bergen) were married in Arnaud in 1926. They had six children, Elsie, Henry, John, Edward, Frank, Jake and Mary.

Coming from Russia in 1923, Peter Braun, along with his brothers Dietrich, David, Frank and sister Margareta came to live in Arnaud in 1925. Along with William Kathler and Heinrich Bergen, they worked the Lyman Farms, Ranch No. 5. Mary Bergen, daughter of Heinrich and Maria Bergen, also came to Arnaud in 1925, immigrating from Russia in 1923. Her brothers Jake and Henry Bergen and her sister Agatha grew up and were married in the Arnaud area. Her youngest brother, Heinrich, died at age 16 and was buried at the United Church in Arnaud.

L to r; Albert Braun, Peter and Mary Braun, Martha Braun, Elsie Braun.

L to r; back, Peter Braun, Mary (Enns) Braun, son Henry; front, seated on knee, Edward, John and Elsie.

BEV BERRINGTON

Bev and Shirley Berrington. Bev Berrington came to Dominion City in 1964 to teach school and play hockey. He married Shirley Boutet in September, 1965. He is presently the principal at Roseau Valley Collegiate. They have three children, Darcy, Damon and Deidre.

Damon Berrington, (14), Darcy Berrington (16), Deidre Berrington (8).

Elijah Boyles, his daughter Mrs. Wm. Parker, son Melville Parker, daughter Mary Parker, in front of Boyles home c. 1914. Elijah Boyles was an early pioneer in Franklin.

ERNIE BUSS

L to r; Ernie Buss, Delma Buss, Robbie Buss, Laurie Buss, Calvin Buss. Ernie and Delma (Weiss) Buss moved to Friedensthal in 1975, and one year later bought W. Brown's house in Ridgeville. Although retired, Ernie did carpentry, and Delma worked part time at the Co-op Community Club. In 1979 they moved to British Columbia. Robbie is married to Laurie Spink, and they own the NW¼ of 30-1-5 E1, where they keep bees.

LUCIEN BOUCHARD

L to r; front, Andre, Therese and Lucien Bouchard; middle, Marie, Helene and Yvonne; back, Michel, Gilles. Helene, the oldest of the Bouchard children, is an accountant living in Winnipeg. Andre, his wife Mary-Ann and daughters Paula and Lisa, live on the farm. Yvonne and husband Gerry McNabb and son Brent live in Winnipeg where Gerry works for a messenger service. Marie is a registered nurse in northern Manitoba. Michel and his wife Tracy live in St. Pierre, where they own and operate a service station. Gilles lives in Dominion City. Mr. Bouchard was involved in 4H, The National Farmers Union, the Co-operative movement, and was president of the local credit union for many years.

Left: Therese and Lucien Bouchard. They married in 1947 and came to live in Dominion City. With half a section of land purchased from Mrs. Monseau, the couple engaged in mixed farming.
Right: Lucien Bouchard, 1945.

WASYL BZOWY

Wasyl Bzowy, born 1853 in Synkiw district Zalishchyky, Galicia, Austria (Western Ukraine), son of Ivan Bzowy and Dokia Kohut of Synkiw, died May 17, 1917 in Stuartburn. Wife Maria, born 1857 in Synkiw, daughter of Andry and Hofia Koshman of Synkiw died February 10, 1913 in Stuartburn.

Children on landing: Petro eight years, Ivan four years, Wasylyna two years.

They arrived in Canada on S.S. Arabia, landing at Quebec May 26, 1897.

Daughter Wasylyna married John Paley of Stuartburn, resided in Dominion City.

Son Ivan and wife Maria resided at Vita.

Son Peter married Gorpina Lennick and farmed the SE ¼ 9-2-5 E1 at Tolstoi. They had 11 children:

John and wife Annie, Stonewall.
Mary, husband John Mihychuk, Winnipeg.
Doris, husband Peter Andrusko, Winnipeg.
Olga, husband Peter Pchey, Stonewall.
Walter, wife Anna, Winnipeg.
Nick of Toronto.
Bill and wife, Scoltand.
Verna and Ed Klem, Selkirk.
Paul and Elaine, Tolstoi.
Jennie and Peter Thissen, Winnipeg.
Annie and Peter Mychen, Winnipeg.

THOMAS HENRY BRADLEY

Ed was born in Dominion City in 1895, and his wife Sadie was born in Bridgewater, South Dakota in 1894.

She came to Manitoba in 1910 with her parents, Jim and Isabelle French, also two brothers, who settled on 10-2-3 NE.

Ed and Sadie were married in Winnipeg in 1918.

They had a family of two daughters, Mrs. Irene Raw of Dominion City, Mrs George Cox of Vancouver and son Eugene of Edmonton.

Ed worked for many years as a mechanic for Coulter and Maynes Bros.

Later he spent a few years in Copper Mountain Mines in British Columbia.

On returning to Dominion City, he ran the Filter Plant until he retired. He passed away November, 1966.

Sadie was a nurse and always ready to give a helping hand.

She also worked for Mr. and Mrs. Matt. Borodenko in their cafe from 1950-1959, then spent a few years in Macleods store working for Mr. and Mrs. Ben Krugar. Sadie passed away in November 1980.

Irene married Albert Raw in 1935.

They had a family of three, Eldean Baskerville of Edmonton, Albert Lee (deceased) and Terry of Edmonton.

Albert was an operator of the ferry on the Red River from 1940-1948. They had a small store on the bank of the Red River up from the ferry which Irene looked after. When the ferry closed, Albert worked for the Department of Highways until he retired in 1970.

Irene meanwhile worked in Gibson's and Anderson's store and later was a hairdresser.

Left: Thomas Henry Bradley was born in South Wakefield, Ottawa County, Ontario, November 17, 1861. In 1890 he married Sarah Jane Wright, at Dominion City. They had two sons, Ed and Charlie, and one daughter, Annie.
Right: Four generations of Thomas Bradley family, l to r; Ed Bradley, his father Thomas Bradley, holding great-granddaughter Eldean Raw on his lap, Irene (Bradley) Raw.

LEON BACHYMSKI

Leon Bachynski came to Canada in 1928 from Bedrykiwic, Zalishchyky, Tornopal. He worked for Michael Dzobia and married Mary Dzobia in 1929.

In 1938 he bought the SE 1-2-4 E1. They had five children, Ollie, Donald, Nettie, Myron and Alexander.

Ollie and Ben Presibella live in Minneapolis, U.S.A. They have two daughters, Kimberely and Chris Donald and Mary Bachynski live in Toronto. They have five children, Marie, Dianne, Lester, Michael and Kevin.

Leon and Mary Bachynski, on their 50th wedding anniversary, l to r; back, John Kornopel, Kimberly Presibella, Mary and Leon; front, Christina Presibella, Cassie Bachynski, Toros Kornopel, Alex Kornopel, Stephan Bachynski, Greg Bachynski.

Nettie (Bachynski) Koronpel, Alexander Bachynski; front, Toros, Alexander and John Kornopel.

Nettie and Vladimier Kornopel live in Minneapolis. They have three sons Johnny, Alexander, Foros.

Myron and Lois Bachynski live in Minneapolis. They have three children, Cassie, Stephan, Greg.

MILTON PAUL BRAUN

Milton Paul Braun came to Ridgeville from Kane in 1977, and served as the elevator agent for N. M. Paterson. When the elevator was closed in February, 1982, he was transferred to Morris. In 1978 he married Cindy Diane Spence, and they have two sons, Michael Blaine and Darcy Paul.

DIEDRICH BOSCHMANN

Diedrich and Rosale Boschmann; The Boschmanns came from south of Morden in the autumn of 1920. They bought the SE ¼ 12-2-5 E1 from Wm. Kasowan for $2,400. The Boschmann's had two sons. Bernhard was born in 1922 and Diedrich in 1924. They spent their life on this farm until Diedrich's death in 1978, and Rosale's in 1970. Diedrich Jr. moved across the road from the home farm, and out of the municipality of Franklin, but owns 80 acres of the original quarter.

ABRAHAM MAURICE BECKSTEAD

Abraham Maurice Beckstead, born September 26, 1874 in Morrisburg, Ontario, was the son of Abraham Volkman Beckstead, born April 3, 1832.

Abraham came by boat to Emerson in 1881, where he lived till 1892, when he took up farming east of Emerson along the international boundary.

He was married to Katherine Depew, born November 22, 1869 in Stony Creek, Ontario, in 1899 at St. Lukes Anglican Church, Emerson. There were four children:

Kathleen Mae, born May 1901, married Dr. R. Bechtel, 1935. They had two daughters, Lana and Yvonne. Both Mr. and Mrs. Bechtel are deceased.

William, born September 1904, married Helen Gilchrist, 1931. There were no children.

Donald Keith, born December, 1906, married

Elsie Weiss, 1931. William is deceased. They had three sons:

Gary and Betty and their three children Blake, Scott, Barbara, 2 grandsons (one deceased).

Garfield and Sanse, two children Mike and Donald.

Dean and Diane, two children, Laurie and Adam.

Laurier, born October 1910, married Selma Sunberg in 1934. They had one son, Larry.

Mr. and Mrs. M. Beckstead retired to Emerson in 1931 after farming 39 years. Abraham died May 1954, Katherine died December 1960.

A. M. Beckstead 50th wedding anniversary, l to r; back, Don, Elsie, Mae, Doc, Helen, Bill, Grandma; front, Lana, Grandpa.

Laurier and Selma Beckstead

Grandma and Grandpa Beckstead; Helen and Bill Beckstead.

Mae, Bill, Don, Laurie, 1951.

Children of Don Beckstead, l to r; front, Betty, Elsie, Diane and Laurie; back, Sanse, Garfield, Dean, Gary. 1977.

Abe Beckstead hunting.

Bill Beckstead c. 1908.

148

JOHN BIALKOWSKI

Mr. and Mrs. Stanley Bialkowski immigrated from Mielnica, Ukraine with their children Mike, John, Peter, Christina and Anna and bought the SE ¼ 22-2-5E from Frank Miller of Woodmore. The children attended Plankey Plains School and also Holy Ghost School in Winnipeg. When Mr. and Mrs. Stanley Bialkowski Sr. passed away they left the homestead to their son, John J. Bialkowski.

John married Rose Wolfe and had two children, Olga and Stan. By working hard on the farm they soon purchased more land, the SW ¼ 22-2-5 from Guy Post, and the NW ¼ 22-2-5 E from Paul Klem. Their first car was a 1930 Model A which was purchased from Paul Wasylyshen for $400. They purchased a John Deere A R from Herb Post dealership in Ridgeville in 1945 for about $1200.

Both John and Rose are active in community affairs and have faithfully served the Polish Catholic Church in Tolstoi. Their daughter Olga is married to Don Erko, has four children and lives in Minneapolis.

Son Stan is married to Elsie Polischuk, has two children and lives in Winnipeg.

Barn on J. J. Bialkowski farm.

Left: Mr. and Mrs. Stanley Bialkowski, who farmed SE ¼ 22-2-5 E1, and left homestead to their son John upon their death.
Right: John and Rose Bialkowski, 1957.

John and Rose Bialkowski, Stan and Olga.

ISIAH BADGLEY

Isiah Badgley came from Hastings County near Tweed, Ontario to Woodmore in the late 1870's. In 1889 he married Jessie Kelly (nee Mayne). First they lived on the NW 13-2-4 later moving onto the old Allan place NW 30-2-5. They had two children John and Melville. In later years Melville moved to B.C. where he resided until his death. John served in World War I from 1914-1918. On November 5, 1919, he married Susan Toews of Stuartburn. They moved into their new home on SE ¼ 14-2-4. They had seven children.

Milton of Burlington, Ontario.
Audrey Fast of Penticton, B.C.
Bryce on the home farm.
Keith of Winnipeg (deceased).
Lyall of Winnipeg.
Allan of Brandon.
Alma Pries (deceased).

John served as school trustee for many years, also on the Hall board. He was a member of the Canadian Legion. They moved to Dominion City in 1953, later to Steinbach where they resided until his death in 1967. Susan, a victim of Multiple Schlerosis, has been in a wheelchair since the early 1950's and lives in a personal care home in Winnipeg.

Bryce took over the home farm in 1953. He married Marget Pott of Woodmore. He was in the army in World War II and was wounded overseas. He is a member of the Canadian Legion also the B.O.P. Elks. Marget is a member of Canadian Legion Auxiliary. She is a chartered member of Woodmore W.I and a leader of the local 4-H Club, and interested in most sports, having played softball for years.

They have four children:
Robert of Morris.
Elaine Bennett of Hinton, Alberta.
Rodney of Winnipeg.
Bruce at home.

In 1970 they built a new home on the NE ¼ 14-2-4 but the old home still stands where it was built in 1919.

Isiah and Jessie Badgley, son Melville.

John Badgley and wife Susan (Toews), with grandson Robert Badgley.

L to r; front, Bruce Badgley, Clara Badgley on his knee; back, Karolynn Badgley (nee Baldwin), Robert Badgley, Linda (Kehler) Badgley, Rodney, Marget (Pott) Badgley, Douglas Bennett, Bryce, Elaine (Badgley) Bennet. Inset, Angie Bennett, daughter of Douglas and Elaine Bennett.

LEO BEAUPRE

Laurette, holding Nicole, born 1976, Richard, born 1967, Irene, born 1969, Marie, born 1968, Roger, born 1965, Paul, born 1966, and Leo Beaupre. Leo and Laurette were married at St. Malo August 18, 1962. In 1977 they moved to Woodmore and managed a dairy farm on SW ¼ 24-2-4 E1. In 1979 they bought the farm and dairy herd, and in December 1981 suffered the loss of their farm buildings and cattle in a fire. A new barn now stands, and in 1982 the Beaupre's are again milking cows.

HARM BALLAST

On April 8, 1953 Harm Ballast and wife Lyntje (Klok), with sons Herman and Armand, left the Netherlands and emigrated to Canada. Arriving at Halifax on April 17, 1953 they boarded the train and came to Winnipeg, stayed at the Immigration Hall for about a week and on April 21, 1953, came to Dominion City where Harm was employed by Bert Witherspoon.

They lived in the house now owned by Charles Boutet. Herman and Armand attended school in Dominion City and started without any knowledge of the English language.

On October 31, 1953, Sytje Klok, Lyntje's mother, emigrated to Canada and Dominion City. She lived with the Harm Ballasts until her health failed. Lyntje was in the Otterburne Nursing Home for a few years until she passed away on May 11, 1968 at the age of 82, and is buried in the Dominion City Cemetery.

Harm Ballast ran a successful implement business, the Ballast Garage, in Dominion City.

On December 15, 1975 while on a trip to Texas, Lyntje was killed in an automobile accident. She is buried beside her mother in the Dominion City Cemetery.

Harm survived the accident which put him in hospital for five months. He lived with son Herman and family for another six months, and remarried in 1979 to Johanna Van Vliet.

Herman Hendrik Ballast came to Canada at the age of nine. He attended Dominion City school. Starting again in grade one to learn the English language he continued on until he completed grade 11. In 1962 he attended the Manitoba Institute of Technology and completed the Diesel Mechanic course. He worked for his father to get his apprenticeship. On April 27, 1968 he married Arlene Isabel Duncan of Hilton, Manitoba. Arlene was employed at the Manitoba Telephone Office in Dominion City at the time. They purchased the old Louis Schuminik house. On June 15, 1970 their first son David Bruce Ballast was born. Daniel John Ballast was born May 9, 1973 and a daughter Jennifer Elaine born on December 15, 1976. Nancy Nicole Ballast was born February 14, 1980.

Herman has been employed in the family business all his life and at the present time is president of Ballast's Garage Ltd. and runs an independent parts and service centre. Herman is a volunteer fire fighter on the Dominion City Fire Department and is at present the president of the Dominion City Community Club.

Armand Arthur Ballast came to Canada at the age of eight. He attended Dominion City School. After leaving school he worked for local farmers, gravel contractors and spent a few years in the north. He married Wendy Vince from Ashern in 1967. She was employed in Dominion City telephone office. Living in Dominion City for many years they raised a family of four: Andrew, born December 9, 1968, Gregory, November 2, 1969, Vincent, October 10, 1976 and daughter Carissa born March 7, 1973.

Armand was on the U.V.D. of Dominion City for many years, a volunteer fire fighter and a curler. He was employed in the family business from 1972 until he went to Southman Agri Sales in Morden in March 1981. The family moved to Morden in June, 1981.

Herman, Lyntje, and Armand Ballast, 1953.

Arlene Ballast, Nancy, Daniel, David, Jennifer, and Herman Ballast, 1981.

Sytje Klok, and Lyntje Ballast.

Mr. and Mrs. Harm Ballast, arriving in Halifax, 1953.

Wendy and Armand Ballast, children, Greg, holding Vince, Carissa and Andy.

SAMUEL P. BARBER

Samuel P. and Margaret (Gordon) Barber came to Dominion City on May 10, 1878, from Straton, Ontario.

Their family were: Orilla Fitchett (adopted), Polly Barber (Goff), Sarah Barber (Brock), Wilbur Henry Barber (adopted), Anna Bessie Barber (Sullivan), Robert Gordon Barber, Florence Annie Barber (Cannem), Edna Mae Barber (Dawes), Elsie Catherine Barber (Armstrong), Leonard John Barber.

Elsie Armstrong is still living in Calgary.

Wilbur Henry Barber (1855-1901) married Ellen Bland (1858-1915). Their children were:

Samuel Edward Barber, 1880-1922, married Katie Lee Bratton. They had no family.

Charles Henry (Harry) Barber, 1881-1922, never married.

Margaret Eleanor Barber, 1883-1958, married Dr. Charles Murrough O'Brien. Their children were:

Marwell, 1903-1904.

Muriel married Hamilton McKee and still living in Saskatoon, Saskatchewan.

Joseph Bertrand (Bert) Barber, 1885-1974, married May Delay. Their daughter was:

Laurie, 1913-1981, married Ross Empey.

Robert Hanley Barber, 1887-1963, married Jane Arthur. Their daughter was:

Audrey, married Ted Blanchett and is living in Edmonton, Alberta.

John Sylvester Barber, 1890-1901.

Wilbur Fredrick (Fred) Barber, 1891-1973, married Mary Turner. They had no family.

Frances Annie Barber, 1894, still living in Windsor, married Hiram Robert Johnson. Their three sons were:

L to r; back, . .?, Charlie Dunn, Bessie Dunn, Jerry Lupul, Ethel Calder, Margaret Blanchet, Audrey Blanchet, Edna McDonald, Ted Blanchet, Barbara Blanchet, Nell Winchester, Neil McDonald; front, Hammie McKie, Mavis, Tommy, Katie, Muriel McKee, Bill Winchester.

John Chalmers Thom and Katie (Barber) Thom, with daughter Mavis.

Delbert (Del).
John (Jack).
William (Bill).
Katie Eileen Barber 1898-1981, married John Chalmers Tham. They have one daughter:
Mavis, living in Edmonton.

FRANCIS BRISNAHAM

Mrs. Jane Brisnaham (maiden name unknown), was born in the township of Fitzroy, Ontario on December 5, 1833 and married Francis Brisnaham in 1851. They had three children:

Mary married Joshua Craig, Ridgeville.

Annie married David Storie, Emerson.

Cornelius did not marry.

Francis came to Franklin in 1877, with his son-in-law Joshua Craig. He chose SW ¼ 7-2-4 E for his homestead and the NE ¼ of SE 7-2-4 E for his preemption. He built a sod house and barn that summer. In 1878 his family came out. Mr Brisnaham died in 1884 and Jane moved to Emerson where she resided till the time of her death on February 23, 1924. They are both buried in Greenridge cemetery. Joshua and Mary Craig, Ridgeville, farmed and he plastered several houses aroung. David and Annie Storie operated a bakery and boarding house in Emerson. Mrs. Storie helped out as midwife in time of need as her mother had done, as long as her health allowed. Mrs. Storie had two sons, Ernie and Tom and a daughter, Mae. Cornelius acquired the SE ¼ Section 36-1-4 E P.M. in 1883. In fall of 1888, he helped to build the local church and walked back and forth from his farm every day. One night he did not return home and after a few days hunting through the bush, he was found dead. His death remained a mystery. He was 35 years old. His land was later bought by Pete Timchuk in 1906.

Left: l to r, Jane Brisnaham, granddaughter Margaret Patch, holding great-granddaughter Eva Patch, Mary Craig, Jane's daughter at right.

Right: Annie (Brisnaham) Storie, who acted as mid-wife to many women after her mother was no longer able to work.

HENRY KLASSEN

In the year 1924 in August, Henry and Katrina Klassen (nee Bergen) came to Canada from Russia. Their son Henry, who had come to Canada one year earlier, met them in Winnipeg and took them to a farm at Prairie Rose, near Landmark, Manitoba, where they worked on a farm till December of that year. They then purchased a farm located ½ mile west and one mile north of Arnaud. Here they lived till their deaths. Katrina passed away in 1931. Henry passed away in 1934. They had a family of 11 children of which two passed away in Russia. The children were:

Jake, married Helen Dyck, deceased in 1952.

Henry, wife Katherine Dyck, deceased 1961.

Isaac, wife Helen Kathler, second wife Margaret Loewen, third wife Aganeta Enns, deceased 1970.

Peter married to Susan Loewen, retired in the Lac du Bonnet area.

Henry and Kathrina (Bergen) Klassen

Mary, husband Korny Krahn, came to Canada as a widow and presently resides in Cottonwood Manor, Kelowna, B.C.

Margareta, married Henry Bergen, deceased in 1976.

Anna, married Abe Bergen, presently living in Donwood Manor, Winnipeg.

Susan, married Andrew Sawatsky, retired in Neubergtal, Manitoba.

Elizabeth, married John Klippenstein, widowed in 1936, presently retired in village of Neubergtal near Altona, Manitoba.

BERNHARD BERGEN

Bernhard and Maria Bergen (nee Doerksen) came to Canada in 1924 from Russia. After spending a year working for farmers at Reinfeld, a village close to Winkler, they moved to Arnaud in the fall of 1925 and settled on a farm two miles east and 3¾ miles south of Arnaud. From a family of 10 children only three came to Canada. These were Abe, Kathrina and Henry. Kathrina and her husband Peter Dyck and family stayed at Winkler. Bernhard and Maria Bergen made Arnaud their home until their deaths. Maria passed away in March of 1931 and Bernhard passed away in December of 1941.

Abe and Anna Bergen (nee Klassen) farmed together with Abe's parents and his brother Henry till the fall of 1933 and then moved to a farm five miles west and three miles south of Arnaud. In 1938 they moved to Fannystelle. Abe passed away in Spring of 1962. Anna at present resides in Donwood Manor in Winnipeg. Their children,

Abe and Mary live at Starbuck.

Tena, husband Victor Schmidt in Portage la Prairie.

John and Anne at Morden.

Jake and Mary at Homewood.

Bertha and husband Henry Neudorf in Winnipeg.

Pete and Freda in Carman.

Henry came to Canada in January of 1924. Margareta, with her parents Henry and Katrina Klassen came to Canada in August of 1924. They were united in marriage June 11, 1932. At first, together with Henry's parents and his brother Abe, they farmed two miles east and 3¾ miles south of Arnaud. In 1934 they purchased a farm five miles west of Arnaud. In the fall of 1966 they moved to Arnaud where they retired. In June of 1974 they moved to Winnipeg and resided in Dorwood Manor till their deaths. Henry passed away on March 29, 1976 and Margareta passed away May 5, 1976. They had been blessed with four children:

Henry married Tena Kathler November 1, 1958. They farmed four miles east, one mile south of Arnaud. Due to Henry's failing health, they moved to the town of Arnaud in 1973. Henry passed away September 28, 1981. Tena is presently living in Arnaud. Their children are:

Brenda, working in Winnipeg at Federated Insurance.

Warren in Winnipeg.

Keith attending Roseau Valley Collegiate.

Harry is married to Eleanor Warkentin.

Margaret is married to John N. Janzen.

Henry and Margareta Bergen

Henry and Tina Bergen, Warren, Brenda, Keith.

Bernhard and Maria (Doerksen) Bergen

John Bergen lives in Morris and is employed with Andres Wines as winery supervisor.

L to r; Corinne, Valerie, Johnnie, Margaret, (seated) Cheryl. Margaret Bergen married John N. Janzen in 1964. They farm five miles south and ½ mile east of Arnaud. The Janzens have three girls, Cheryl, Corinne and Valerie, all attending the Roseau Valley Collegiate in Dominion City.

L to r; standing, Terence, Darren, Bradley, Randall, sitting, Eleanor and Harry J. Bergen. Harry, the second born son of the late Mr. and Mrs. Henry B. Bergen lived his childhood years on the family farm, 24-3-2E. In 1962 Harry married Eleanor Warkentin of Pigeon Lake. In 1966 they took over the family farm, when the Senior Bergens retired to Arnaud. In 1975 they bought and moved into the former John Sawatzky house in Arnaud; where they still reside.

At present Harry is an assistant manager at the Manitoba Pool Elevator at Fredenstahl West. Eleanor is a homemaker, helping out wherever necessary. The four boys; Bradley, Darren, Terence, and Randall are attending Roseau Valley Collegiate and Dominion City Elementary School.

BEN BREWSTER

Ben Brewster was born in Lincolnshire, England, in 1857. While working in a dry goods store he met Alice de Weldycz (born 1860) and married her in 1880.

Ben went into the hotel business first in the Isle of Wight, and later in London. The Brewsters read about the land available for farming in Manitoba, and arrived in Winnipeg in April, 1887. They purchased the Metis Script to 240 acres, being the NW ¼ and the N ½ of the SW ¼ of 3-3-4 E1.

Alice Brewster died of typhoid fever in 1908, and Ben passed away in 1928. He had retired to Dominion City in 1925 after selling his farm to his son-in-law, Hector Gunn. His widowed daughter Polly and her two daughters lived with him. During his life he worked for a grain growers organization, a consolidated school at Green Ridge, and for prohibition. He envisaged a generation of young people growing up and knowing the taste of liquor, and not wanting it.

Catherine, born December 26, 1889, took teacher's training, and taught in the area for a few years. In June, 1912, she married W. F. Yeo. She made her home in Winnipeg until her death in October, 1980.

Frances (Polly), born August 29, 1891, took her mother's place in the home after her mother died. She was 17 years old, caring for a family of nine, and she did it very well. In 1915 she married Edwin Scott. They farmed near Dominion City until his death, when she moved to Dominion City with her father. She later moved to Winnipeg. Polly had two daughters, Ruth and Doris. She died in July, 1965.

Elsie, born January 18, 1893, was never very strong. She was a good student, and also taught school. She married Harry Matheson in July, 1917, and lived in Winnipeg until her death on Christmas day, 1924. She and Henry had two children, Alice and Jack.

Grace, born October 15, 1894, lived only till February of the following year.

Ada, born September 6, 1896, took her turn at keeping house for her father. In 1918 she took her nurse's training in St. Boniface Hospital. After graduation she went to the Mayo Clinic in Rochester, Minnesota. Returning to Winnipeg she and her sister, Catherine, who was then a widow, opened the Brewster Nursing Home on Sherbrooke Street in Winnipeg. She retired in Winnipeg and died April 3, 1976.

Ruth, born April 23, 1899, taught school for several years, then married Thomas Ostberg. They farmed near Dominion City, Manitoba until her

155

death in January, 1955. Ruth and Tom had one son, Harold, who farms near Dominion City and is married with a family.

Gertrude, born January 11, 1901, kept house for her father for six years. She married Hector Gunn in 1924. They bought the Brewster farm where they made their home and raised their five children.

Laura, born June 25, 1904, never really recovered from the scarlet fever which she had when she was 10 years old. She married Patrick Flannery in 1939 and lived in Winnipeg until her death in 1942.

L to r; back, Polly, Katie; front, Ada, Arthur, Elsie Brewster.

An Indian grave on the Ben Brewster farm at the time of its' purchase. When this picture was taken the structure was collapsing, missing the peaked roof.

Ben Brewster; Arthur Brewster

Green Ridge-Newbridge quilting group, in front of log house built by neighbouring bee after the first Brewster house burned. Alice Brewster is third from left, Laura Brewster is child on left.

ANDREW BARON

Andrew Baron was born in Western Ukraine in 1860. He came to Franklin in 1898, homesteaded 35-5-1 E1, receiving title to same in 1903. Wasylena (Koshman) Fertash came from Western Ukraine, in 1898, a widow with two children, Harry and Annie Fertash. Andrew and Wasylena were married in 1899. They had six children, William, 1900; Michael, 1903; Peter, 1904; Mary, 1906; Steve, 1908 and John, 1913.

Harry Fertash served in the war from 1914 to 1918. Andrew and Wasylena moved to British Columbia in 1920, where Andrew died in 1924, Wasylena in 1936.

John came back to Franklin and married Mary Chubaty in 1934. They had two children, Ronald

Walter, 1935; Leonard William, 1936. John and Mary moved to British Columbia in 1937, came to Carlowrie to buy Chubaty's Store in 1945, and moved to Winnipeg in 1953.

Harry Fertash - half brother to Baron's on mother Baron side. England in 1918.

Andrew and Wasyline Baron with children, l to r; John, born 1913, Steve, born 1908, Mary, born 1906, Peter, born 1904, Michael, born 1903, William, born 1900.

LUDGAR BRUNEAU

Ludgar Bruneau, son of Oscar and Lydia (Breault) Bruneau was born April 20, 1895, in St. Jean Baptiste. His grandparents, Theophile and Philomene (Marion) Bruneau came from St. Gabriel de Brandon, Quebec, c. 1879. Theophile's children were Melvina, married Charles St. Godard; Oscar, married Lydia Breault; Philippe, married Ida Dionne; Napoleon, married Candide Fillion; Exilda, married Mathias Fillion; Rose Anna, married Dominique Morissette; and Lia, married L'Abbè.

Oscar and Lydia were married in 1889, and then moved back to Quebec. Ludger came out to Franklin in 1916, to river lot 197. He served in the war, and came back to marry Angelina Marion, a teacher, in 1919. In 1923 Ludgar sold river lot 195 to Adelard Dupuis and moved to 35-3-2 E1. In 1954 he moved to St. Jean Baptiste, where he died March 20, 1982, age 86 years. Lydia still lives there. Their children are:

George, married Celima Gregoire, is a mixed farmer on St. Mary's Road, and has three children, Marc Gaston, Georgette Pauline and David.

Yvette, married Armand St. Godard.

Lorraine, married Harvey Foss.

Rose-Marie, married Roger Bremeault.

Anne-Marie, Rose-Marie's twin sister, married Richard Roy of St. Pierre Jolys. In 1982 the Bruneau family has six generations in Manitoba, many of whom have lived and were born in Franklin.

Back; George Laurraine, Rose Marie, Ephrem, Anne Marie, Yvette, Aimé; front, Léo, Ludger and Lydia (Breault), Jeanine.

GEORGE BURRELL SR.

George Burrell, Sr. immigrated to Canada with his wife, Agnes, and children, from Lincolnshire, England, in the early 1880's. He went to Ontario, where he operated a store at Hamilton, until 1879 when they came to Franklin to homestead the NE ¼ of 1-2-4 E1. In later years they lived on the NE ¼ of 26-2-4 E1, owned by Robert E. Millar, their son-in-law.

Their children were George, Agnes, Margaret, Peter and Charles. Agnes married Robert K. Millar, Margaret married Charles Brown, Charles married Sarah Grier, George, a teacher, married Margaret Wincup. Peter farmed the SE ¼ of 1-2-4 E1 for a time.

CHARLES AND JAMES E. BROWN

Charles and James E. Brown came from Vermont. They worked for the Hudson's Bay Company c. 1868. They had a store on 34-2-4 E1, along the St. Paul Trail. In 1982 wild plum and currant bushes still mark the spot where they had their garden.

Charles married Margaret Burrell, and their children were Jim, Charles, William, Sanford, Lawrence, Helen and Flora.

ALEXANDER H. BLACK

Alexander H. Black came from Ontario in the 1870's. He homesteaded the NW ¼ of 24-2-4 E1 in 1878, on which he had squated for several years. There were five children, James, Mary, John, May and Esther.

C ISAAC CASSON

Isaac Casson, born February 14, 1842, died November 15, 1911.

Mary Steele, born March 25, 1845, died December 6, 1940.

Isaac and Mary married in Scotland on November 15, 1865. They came to Dominion City in 1874, homesteaded NW ¼ 25-3-3 E1. Their children are:

Henry Casson, born October 17, 1866, died April 17, 1914.

William Casson, born June 21, 1872, died April 20, 1945. William married Maroah Post, born January 15, 1878, died August 20, 1975. They were married on October 25, 1898. They had a family of nine boys and two girls.

Mary Casson, born May 13, 1874, died February 12, 1889 of diptherea.

Joseph Casson, born February 7, 1876, died January 27, 1943. Joseph married Flora McLennan who died in 1953. They were married on December 23, 1902. They had a family of two boys:

Angus Casson, died July 1936. He had one son, Ian McLennan, born August 24, 1919, died November, 1979.

Murial.

Archabald Calhun Casson, born February 20, 1878, died 1953, married Lela Bell Watson, born October 24, 1884, died March 28, 1957. They were married September 27, 1911. They had a family of one boy and three girls.

Isaac Casson, Jr., born November 3, 1879, died April 17, 1961, married Susan Gainer, who died in 1913. They married December 25, 1912. There are no survivors from this branch.

James Casson, born October 29, 1883, died October 26, 1956, married Elizabeth Pott, born July 11, 1892, died July 17, 1975. They were married December 28, 1916.

James Carlisle Casson, born July 11, 1919, married Dorothy Margaret Skoglund, born September 16, 1925, died October 8, 1981.

James Alfred Grant Casson, born October 11, 1947, married Juliette Gosselin, February 26, 1971.

Leanne Elizabeth Marie, born January 26, 1974.

Ryan James, born May 5, 1977.

David Carlisle Casson, born March 19, 1949, married Wendy Rolston.

Raymond James Aurele, born January 7, 1975.

Barbara, born May 5, 1977.

Linda Darlene Casson, born January 17, 1952.

Jean-Pierre Joseph George Parenty.

Christine Michelle, born January 16, 1980.

Chantal Dorothy, born September 3, 1981.

Thomas Boyd Casson, born July 15, 1953, married Diane Ida Marie Dumaine on October 18, 1980.

Garnet Charles, born December 14, 1956.

Leslie Lionel Ronald, born March 28, 1962.

Amy Eleanor Steel Casson, married John Armand Palmer, January, 1947.

John Myles Howard.

Alana Holly Faith, married Stephen Wieting.

Jennifer Elizabeth Joyce, married Robert Stefanchuk.

The original Isaac Casson home, with a porch and balcony added in 1918, and the store addition built in early 1930's.

Centennial Post Office Celebrations at Green Ridge, l to r; Henry Casson, former postmaster, Dorothy Casson, postal assistant, Carlisle Casson, postmaster, Per Holting, Public Affairs, Manitoba Postal District. Inset, Mary Casson, first postmistress at Green Ridge, 1902.

Isaac Casson family, l to r; back, William, Isaac Jr., Joseph, Henry; front, Mary Casson, Eleanor, Isaac Casson Sr., James, Archie. c. 1900.

William Casson family, front, Sidney, Bob, Stan, Mrs. Casson, Sarah, Mary, Bert, Henry, Bruce, Nelson, Wallace, Fred, Mr. Casson.

Fred Casson standing, son William, and wife Florence.

Henry H. Casson family, l to r; Dwight, Joyce (Mrs. Dwight Casson), Eleanor (Mrs. Henry Casson), Henry Casson, Kristy Lou.

L to r; back, Lela Casson, Archie Casson, Grace (Casson) Stewart, George Stewart. Maroah Casson in foreground.

Left: Ian Casson and wife Murial, last member of Joseph Casson family. Died 1979.
Right: James Casson, postmaster, 2nd generation on pioneer farm, and his wife Elizabeth, storekeeper. c. 1937.

L to r; back, Edward Warmus, holding Kristen, Karen Warmus, Tony Warmus, Fern (Casson) Warmus, daughter Bonnie Josephs; front, Eric Warmus, Carl Josephs.

John Palmer and Eleanor Casson, married January 7, 1947. Raised three children, John Myles Howard, Alana Holly Faith, Jennifer Elizabeth Joyce.

Jean Pierre Parenty and wife Linda Casson, married June, 1974. Christine and Chantel Parenty.

J. C. Casson family, l to r; back, Carliste, Juliette (Chantel), Diane and Dave Casson; front, Alma Wheeler, Leslie, Raymond, Tom, Alice Gibson, Leanne (on knee), Garnet, Dorothy, James, Ryan (on knee), Garnet, Dorothy, James, Ryan (on knee), Christine (on floor). Missing are Linda Parenty, Jean Pierre Parenty, Wendy Casson, Barbara Casson. Inset, Diane, wife of Thomas Casson.

James Carlisle and Margaret Casson, third generation on original Casson homestead.

Fourth and fifth generation Cassons, Wendy, wife of David Casson, and children Raymond and Barbara, 1980.

Mrs. Wm. Casson and grandchildren, l to r; back, Dwight, Blaine; front, Kristy Lou, Grandma Casson, Randy.

Grace Casson, sons Lewis, Kenneth, Ronald (in front) and Wallace Casson.

EDWIN WHITAKER CREMER

Edwin was born in the county of Essex on December 4, 1882 to Edwin and Delia Cremer. He came to Canada as a young man, working in the North Battleford area, where he homesteaded. He then moved into the Green Ridge area, and worked for many different families as a farm hand. He was caretaker for the Green Ridge school for many years. He married Bella Houlde and retired to a log cabin on the high banks of the Roseau River on the Collin's place. He lived there until the water had washed the bank away and his cabin was in danger of going into the river. The last two years of his life were spent in the Menno Home for the aged in Grunthal. He died April 10, 1965 at the age of 83 and was buried in the Green Ridge cemetery.

Ted Cramer and his horses, c. 1929. Man on cultivator unknown.

WILLIAM COOMBS

William Coombs was one of three sons and six daughters born to Emily and Charles Coombs, a farm laborer in England in 1886.

He married Edith Ann Poulton, one of four daughters and two sons born to William Poulton, a glasscutter in England in 1887.

They were married in Wordsley Church, Stafford, on February 26, 1910 and came to Canada later that same year. They resided in Winnipeg where four children were born. Two boys died in infancy and another later in 1926 in Ridgeville.

In 1919 they moved to Ridgeville and purchased the E½ of 27 from Bert Bennet, where they resided until retiring to the former Ernie Pearce home in Dominion City in 1950.

The Coombs sold the south ¼ to Roy Wilkinson the present owner, and the north ¼ was given to their daughter Hilda, Mrs. Wm. Gilchrist, in 1945. The Gilchrists had two children, Shirley May and Sheldon Dale. After William's death the land was sold to D. Harder and Hilda moved to Dominion City. She remarried in 1958 to Earle Stowe and returned to farm until 1969. The Stowes now live in Winnipeg.

Earle Stowe was employed with Esso service before acquiring his present job at Wyatt Rentals.

Hilda worked eight years for Sears Polo Park store before retiring.

Shirley took a business course and worked for an insurance company until her marriage to Chris Thordarson in December, 1972. They, along with daughter Shannon, moved to Ear Falls, Ontario about 1½ years later, where Chris is employed with Griffith mines.

Sheldon took his grade 12 at Gordon Bell and a two year course at Red River Community College. He married the former Marilyn Kein in 1972 and is now employed with R.M. Hardy Associates as a Civil Engineering Technologist.

Marilyn is employed with Campbell Lane Associates as Insurance Manager.

L to r; Hilda Coombs, Louise and Elsie Lauferswieler, in front of Wm. Coomb house.

Earle and Hilda Stowe, 1979.

Left: Sheldon and Marilyn Gilchrist, 1973.
Right: Chris, Shirley and Shannon Thordarson, 1981.

CAMPBELL-CALDER FAMILIES

The Campbells were one of the first settlers at Carlowrie. They came from Scotland to Ontario in 1869. Colin Campbell, the youngest brother preceded the families to Manitoba in 1873. He bought land at Mosquito Creek, the NW ¼ 34-3-4 E1 and NE ¼ Section 33-3-4 E1, from Genevieve Allard on the 10th of December, 1878.

The Calders arrived in October, 1879. They all came by train to Emerson via the United States and from there by wagon. William and Annie (Campbell) Calder and two daughters Mary and

William and Edith Coombs, 1910.

Annie settled in the Green Ridge area in the NE ¼ 35-2-4 E1. While living there two more children arrived, George and Sarah. Following the death of William Calder in 1886, his widow Annie and family moved in with her brothers and sisters at Mosquito Creek.

In December 1915 George Calder purchased the farm and equipment from Colin Campbell. On April 5, 1916 George married Hazel Nisely. They had two sons, Ralph and John. In January 1922 an epidemic of measles went through the community and Mrs. Calder fell ill and died on February 2. George continued farming until the early 1950's when he returned and his sons took over. With keen interest in farming he continued to live on the farm in the summer months with his son Ralph and family, and in Winnipeg with his sister Annie during the winter months until the time of his death, November 20, 1963.

RALPH CALDER FAMILY

Ralph Calder married Irene Hamblin April 3, 1940. They have two children, Lorraine, who married William King October 20, 1962, and has two children, Monica and Caroline and Colin who married Barbara Dietz April 3, 1976 and they had two children, George and Brenda.

More land was purchased and Colin and his father continued to operate a mixed farm.

On May 17, 1980 Barbara became seriously ill. She passed away on July 11, 1980 and was laid to rest in the Green Ridge Cemetery.

Left: l to r; George Calder, Colin Campbell, Mrs. Wm. Calder, Sarah Layton (Calder), Annie Calder.
Right: George and Hazel (Nisely) Calder, married April 5, 1916.

George Calder in centre, his sons Ralph (left) John (right).

L to r; Colin Calder, Ralph Calder, Lorraine (Calder) King, Irene Calder.

Barbara, holding Brenda, and Colin Calder, holding George. 1980. Married April, 1976.

ALFRED HENRY CHEALES

Alfred Henry Cheales completed one year of Medicine at Edinburgh, Scotland before emigrating to Canada to learn about farming. Because of his training, Alf was often referred to as Doc Cheales. He married Jane Spence (1873-1957). They settled on the NE ¼ 13-2-4 E1. Jane was often called on to act as midwife, or nurse, during epidemics. From 1913-1923 they lived in Dominion City, then moved to Winnipeg where Jane joined the Victorian Order of Nurses.

Six children were born of this union. Two sons died in infancy. Edith, born on a visit to England, Harry, Mary (died age 12) and Allan.

Edith, a school teacher, married Heward Skillen

and had three children Bob, Wallace and Agnes.

Harry married his cousin Ella Spence and had one son, Clifford.

Allan taught school 12 years before becoming ordained. He married Edweana Bucknell and has two children, Noreen and Louise and six grandsons.

Removing annex of Paterson Elevator 1981. Donald cook purchased the elevator after it was closed.

DONALD I. COOK

Donald I. Cook and family purchased the SE ¼ of 35-1-4 E1, formerly the Busotski farm, in 1968

Edith, Jane Cheales, and Mary.

Ridgeville from the air.

from D. D. Harder. The family consists of Don, his wife Muriel (nee Smith), Bruce, Malcolm and Hugh. Bruce lives in Edmonton and the rest of the family is involved in farming in the Ridgeville area. Their major crop is corn. The Cooks also operate a fertilizer and chemical business, Boundary Agro, in the village of Ridgeville, and purchased the Patterson elevators in 1981. The Cook family originated in the Dugald area where the farm settled by A. B. Cook in 1878 is a centennial farm. Muriel's family, the Smiths, farmed in the Bergen area west of Winnipeg in 1879.

GEORGE CHOBOTER

George and Bernice Goletski were married in the Holy Trinity Roman Catholic Church in Tolstoi, on August 2, 1947. Prior to living in Tolstoi, they made their home in Haywood, for three years where George was employed as an apprentice mechanic for Tougas and Rouire, International Harvester dealers. He completed his apprenticeship there and became a fully licensed mechanic in 1950.

Mr. and Mrs. Choboter then moved to St. Jean Baptiste, where George was temporarily employed by Tessier Brothers prior to relocating in Vancouver in the year 1951. They returned to Manitoba in 1953 and George purchased the property in Tolstoi from Eugene Oryschak and went into business for himself.

A garage and service station was built in 1953, and in 1954 George became a fully franchised dealer for the John Deere Company and remained with them for 20 years.

Mr. and Mrs. Choboter had three children, Brian, Dennis, and Valerie. George has been a director, president and vice-president of the Tolstoi Community Centre. He also served on the

Roman Catholic church committee and Parish Hall Committee.

Mrs. Choboter organized the Tolstoi Women's Institute in the year 1961 and became their first president, later taking on secretarial work for the group, as well as being the first secretary of the Tolstoi District Community Centre.

Bernice Choboter was appointed postmaster of Tolstoi on September 21, 1974 and holds this office in 1982.

BEN COMEAULT

Ben Comeault came to Dominion City in April, 1948, to take over the McColl Frontenac bulk station, now known as Texaco Canada. Ben travelled back and fourth from Letelliar to Dominion City for a couple of years.

In 1949, he married Gisele Bouchard, daughter of Mégilde and Léa Bouchard of Letellier. They decided to move their house from Letellier across the Red River in the winter of 1950 and live in Dominion City.

They raised a family of seven children, five girls and two boys.

Paulette is a nurse living in Hawaii.

Jeanne married Doug Hooper of Winnipeg and is now residing in Ste. Adolphe with their three children, Dawne Louise, Keith and Dana. Jeanne works part time at Victoria Hospital.

Louise married Mel Boutet of Dominion City and they live in Transcona with their two sons, Carey and Kevin. Louise works part time at the Bethania Mennonite Personal Care Home in Winnipeg.

Carole married Barry Gushuliak from Emerson and they live in Dominion City with their two daughters Keela and Jaydee.

Barry has been Ben's helper for the past 10 years and Carole is employed part time at the Emerson Personal Care Home.

Denise married Rick Pahl from Emerson and resides in Dominion City. She is employed full time at the Emerson Hospital.

L to r; Dennis, George Choboter, Valerie, Brian, Bernice Choboter seated.

Ben and Gisele Comeault. Married April, 1949.

Marc attended cooking school in Altona and is at present working at "Chicken Delight" in Morris during summer months and is the caretaker of the skating rink in Dominion City in winter.

René is attending the University of Maine on a scholarship and playing hockey for the Maine Black Bears.

Ben and his family have been involved in sports such as hockey, baseball, figure skating, swimming and water skiing.

L to r; Rene, Louise, Paulette, Marc, Carole, Denise, Gisele, Ben and Jeanne, 1978.

L to r; back, Rick Pohl, Doug Hooper, Mel Boutet, Barry Gushuliak, Rene Comeault; front, Denise, Marc, Louise, Ben, Jeanne, Carole.

Left: Downe Louise, Keith and Dana Hooper.
Centre: Keela Raye and Jaydee Gushuliak.
Right: Carey and Kevin Boutet.

JOSHUA CRAIG

Joshua Craig came to Franklin from Carleton County, Ontario, in 1877, to homestead the SW ¼ 7-2-4 E1, and pre-empted the NW ¼ of 7-2-4 E1. His wife was Mary Brisnaham of Arnprior, Ontario, whose family also came to Franklin, as did Joshua'a brother William and sister Margaret.

Joshua and Mary had seven children:

Francis, 1875 to 1976.

Richard, 1877-1967, lived on his Uncle William's homestead until moving to Rest Haven Home, Steinbach. He married Elizabeth Kelly, who died 1915. They had four children, Marvin, Lawrence, Muriel, who married Ellwood Hughson, Pilot Mound, and Garnet who lived on the home farm. After Elizabeth's death, Richard married Violet Mason, and they had one son, Russell.

Annie, 1882, married Robert Lockhead. They had two sons, Murray and John.

Margaret, born 1880. She married Herbert Petch, a Salvation Army Officer. They had three children, Eva, who married Oliver Douglas of Middedosa, died 1980; Mae, who married Fred Freeman, Whiterock; Herbert, of Trail, B.C.

John, 1887-1975. He married Georgia (?) and had three children, Jack, James and Barbara.

Archibald, 1890-1972. He married Violet Hamblin, Woodmore. They had four children, Annie married Reinhold Steinke, Green Ridge; Effie, who married John Calder, Carlowrie; Earl and Clarence on home farm. Archie is buried in Green Ridge Cemetery, and Violet lives in the Red River Lodge, Morris.

William, 1884-1972. Married Gladys Baker, Waskada, had one son, Alvin. Gladys died 1930's, William remarried Lilly Leaman, 1939. In 1941 they moved to Emerson where William took a position with the Customs. Lilly died 1976, Duncan, British Columbia.

William Craig; Archie Craig, Minnie Craig.

Left: Garnet Craig and Faye Timchuk, married 1939.
Right: Margaret Jane Craig, who married William McDonald.

Richard Craig and his school van.

Minnie 1893-1972. Married Thomas Hamblin of Woodmore. They had five children. Gertrude, married Winston Eyres; Hazel, married Jack Trickey; Wallace; Hector; Phyllis, who married Tony Koslock.

Joshua's brother William homesteaded the NW ¼ of 4-2-4. He married Salka Slusarchuk of Roseau River, and died childless in 1915.

Margaret Jane Craig, sister of Joshua and William Craig, married William McDonald and they lived on the SW ¼ of 4-2-4 now owned by Dennis Seward. A grass fire burnt their buildings, and they lived with her brother William on the NW ¼ 4-2-4 E until Margaret's death, July 1890, age 38 years. Her son James lived in Oregon, U.S.A. William McDonald died in 1904 at the age of 62 years and both are buried in Green Ridge Cemetery.

THOMAS COLLINS

Thomas Collins, born 1847, emigrated to Canada when he was 16 and worked as a farm laborer near Kingston, Ontario. In October 1871 he married Mary Ellen Mink. In the spring of 1892 he came to Manitoba to work on the Morrison farm near Ridgeville. Mary and their nine children joined him that fall to homestead SW ¼ of 16-1-4E.

The children were Joseph, Mary Jane (Min), Will, Johnny, Alicia, Jim, Thomas George, Annie, Charles Henry. Dora, Henry and Charlie were later born on this Springbank Farm. In time Thomas and his sons farmed seven quarters of land with horses.

Mary died in 1929, Thomas in 1939.

Joseph Collins (Joe Collins) born 1872, married Jennie Dellabough and settled on SE ¼ 18-1-4E. Joe and Jennie had five children.

Tom who died as a teenager of spinal meningitis.

Merton moved west in 1931 and homesteaded in the Whelon district. He married Janet Thomas. They have five daughters - Phyllis, Edith, Shirley, Myrtle and Gladys. Myrtle, an R.N., died in 1975.

Mary, Joe's last child, died while in Letellier convent attending high school.

Mary Jane (Min) born 1874, married Harry Franks in 1893 at Ridgeville. They had 10 children, Clara, Edna, Arthur, Alice, Mabel, Laura, Walter, Hazel, Clarence, Jean. Min died in 1968.

William Collins, born 1877, left for Saskatchewan in 1902 to farm in the Goodwater area. He died in 1920.

John Collins, born 1879, married Alice Kurtz in 1913. After farming in Saskatchewan he operated a blacksmith shop at McCreary until his death in 1958. John and Alice had seven children - Dorothy, Orville, Jean, Lois, Muriel, Alice and Mildred.

Alicia, born 1881, married James Alexander in 1903 and homesteaded near Weyburn, Saskatchewan. They had 12 children, Ellen, Edith, Gladys, Alice, Fred, Evelyn, Hugh, George, Donald, Gerald, Norma, Verna. Alicia died in 1973, two months after their 70th wedding anniversary.

Jim Collins, born 1884, married Phoebe Buxter in 1904 and homesteaded in the Goodwater, Saskatchewan area. In 1914 they moved to Montana. Their eight children are Bill, Vera, Robert, Roy, Donald, Ellen, Charles and Archie.

Thomas Collins, born 1887, married Mary Hutt in 1926. Until his passing in 1955 Tom was very active in community affairs serving as reeve for six years, councillor for 14, and as church warden at St. Mary's Anglican Church. Tom and Marys' children were Hazel, Florence, Evelyn and Neil. Hazel is married to Donald Nedohin and has two sons, Dale and Douglas. Florence married Alfred McDonald. Evelyn married Gerald Schoffer and they have three children, Wendi, Larry and Linda. Neil married Joan Geske, they have two children, Keith, and Irene and until 1964 they farmed the Collins' family farm.

Annie, born 1888, never married and lived at home caring for her parents. She also looked after Tom's family when his wife died. Annie died in 1946.

Charles Henry Collins, born 1890, died at three years of age.

Dora, born 1893, married Harry Lenton in 1915. They had five children, Henry, Edith, Tom, Rita and Laura.

Henry, 1896, enlisted in the army and was killed in action in 1918.

Charles Collins, born 1898, married Marth Steg in 1923. In 1926 they moved to SE¼ 19-1-4E and farmed there until 1947. They had two children, Ross and Eileen. Ross married Mabel Kein and continued to farm the home farm. They had three children, Faye, Douglas and Bruce.

Faye married John Homer and resides in Vancouver. Doug resides in the Ridgeville district as does Bruce.

Eileen married John Chubaty in 1945. They moved to the SE¼ 10-1-4E, and have five children, Bryce, Brent, Myrna, Colleen, and Timothy. Another son, Lorne, died in 1958.

In 1970 Bryce married Lee McMillan. They have two children, Gail and Wayne and reside on the SW¼ of 15-1-4E.

Brent also farms and lives on the NE¼ of 3-1-4E. Myrna married Brian Maxwell in 1975, they have one son Barry. Colleen is a nurse at the Morris Hospital, and Tim is completing his grade 12.

William and Alicia Collins, children of Thomas Collins.

Thomas and Mary Collins, Sr

Thomas Collins home on 16-1-4 E1, 1893.

Dora and Annie Collins with their new hats, 1912.

L to r; James, Alicia (Alexander), Johnny, Thomas Jr., children of Thomas and Mary Collins.

Left: Henry Collins, killed in action September 29, 1918, 222nd Battalion.
Right: Tom Collins, 1914.

James Neil Collins and wife Phoebe. c. 1940.

Mary Jane Collins and husband Harry Franks, c. 1940.

Charles and Martha Collins, 1980.

L to r; James Neil Collins, Roderick John McElroy Collins. c. 1900.

Ross Collins family, l to r; Bruce, Ross, Mabel, Faye and John Homer, Doug.

L to r; back: Bruce Collins, Doug Collins, Ross Collins, Charlie Collins, John Chubaty, Wayne Chubaty, Bryce Chubaty, Brent Chubaty, Tim Chubaty; middle, Colleen Chubaty, Faye Homer holding Laura, Martha Collins, Eileen Chubaty, Lee Chubaty, Myrna Maxwell holding Barry, Brian Maxwell; front, Mabel Collins, Gail Chubaty, 1980.

ROBERT FRANKLIN CURRAN

In 1880, Robert Curran, his wife Lucy, daughter of Henry Robinson, and two children, came west from Ontario, looking for farmland. While living in Kingston Frederick was born in 1873, and Gertrude in 1875.

The family first settled at Morris. Then they moved to Emerson, before the first flood of 1882, where they located north of town on a farm near the "Joe" bridge.

The Currans were prominent members of the Presbyterian Church and when plans were laid to have an agricultural fair in Emerson in 1879, Robert became a director for his area.

Robert Franklin was born on February 10, 1883. He passed away in 1924, in Texas.

Gertrude married Archibald Vickers and they moved to Saskatoon, Saskatchewan, where they lived with their three children, Gerald, Vera, and Glen.

Fred married Nellie Grant and they located three miles west of Dominion City where they farmed for about 10 years before moving to Texas, in 1919. They had one son, Grant, who lives with his family of three in Tyler, Texas.

Frank and Rosanne Copeland were married in 1907. Rosanne was born 1886, daughter of Alexander Copeland and his wife Sarah Thompson.

The Currans settled on a little farm north of the Joe River Bridge, and there Clifford was born in 1909. He died at the age of one and a half years. The Currans moved to a farm on the edge of Dominion City where Maxine was born in 1911. Glen was born in 1913 and died at the age of nine. Edna May was born in 1914.

In 1922, Frank moved his family into town and with the help of a hired man, farmed the quarter section west of town.

John Maxwell was born in 1925, Shirley in 1928, and Beverly Jean in 1930.

Rosanne passed away in 1954, and at the age of 75, Frank passed away, October 17, 1958.

Maxine and Edna became school teachers, Shirley and Jean graduated nurses, and Jack, after serving with the R.C.A.F., 1942-1945, returned to farming in Dominion City.

Maxine lives in Grand Forks, N. Dakota. Her husband, Clarence Meissner, passed away in 1977. Their children are Judith and Donald.

Edna married Hugh Francis and they lived in Gypsumville. Hugh passed away in 1977. Their children are John, Maxine, Alix, Norma, Harold, Rosanne and Shirley. In 1980 Edna married James Pugh, and they reside in Winnipeg.

John married Ethel Stringer and lives in Dominion City. He has a son, Jay.

Shirley and her husband, Dave Boese, live in Emerson. Their children are Blythe, Brian, Robyn, Jeri-Lyn, Darcy, Beverly, and Tracy.

Jean married Barry Hawking, and lives in Edmonton, Alberta with daughters Dawn and Judith.

L to r; back, Nellie Curran, Robert Curran, Louise (Baskerville) Ginn; front, Fred Curran, John Ginn.

169

Rosanne (Copeland) Curran, wearing silver and gold medals won for elocution; Robert Franklin Curran.

L to r; back, Barry, Dawn, Jean (Curran) Hawkins; front, Judith.

Dave and Shirley (Curran) Boese, l to r; back, Brian, Garry Goossen, friend, Dave, Blyth, Robyn, Jeri-Lyn, Darcy, Shirley, Phil (Dave's brother); front, Beverley, Tracy.

Ethel (Stringer) and John Curran, 1980.

Jay Franklin Curran (son of John and Ethel Curran), and cousin Laura Anne McMurray.

Annie Curran (skip), Ida Simpson, Edith Scott, May Barber, 1937.

Judy (Meissner) granddaughter of Frank and Rosanne Curran, and Steve Gabar, 1980. Wedding in New York.

170

Left: Clarence and Maxine (Curran) Meissner, and daughter Judy.
Right: Don Meissner, and his father Clarence Meissner.

TOM CHUBEY

Tom Chubey and his brother Mikita came from Europe in 1896. They settled near the present site of Roseau River village, and in 1907 moved Northwest of Rosa.

In 1908 Tom married Anne Ewonchuk and in 1920 they moved to Dufrost until 1923 when they returned to Rosa, and the following year moved to Carlowrie.

Tom and Anne had 14 children, two of which died in infancy.

Andrew, who died in 1975, married Lena Prokipchuk, died 1976. Their children are Vincent, Ivan, Chris (Tepley).

Peter married Anne Drebit.

Nellie married John Ostrowsky, who died 1963. Their children are Bill, Peter, Florence (Nielson), Harry, Rose (Smook), Anne, Maurice, Bobby.

Bill.

Mike.

Mary married Don Rostosky. Their children are Ruth, Nick, Elizabeth.

Tom and Anne Chubey

Steve.

Nick married Jean Burkowski. He has a son, Jeffrey.

Paul.

Harry married Mary Dishnick, sons Taras, Tommy.

Effie married Krist Christuik, children are Orest Raymond, Patricia, Elizabeth.

Violet married Victor Zinyk and children are Steven, Billy, Anne.

Tom Chubey died in 1954, and Anne in 1962.

Michael Chubey   Jack Chubey   William Chubey

Harry and Paul Chubey

Terry Chubey, sons Glen and Gordon, and wife Shirley.

171

Wedding of Peter Chubey and Annie Drebit. L to r; Lena Ballan, Violet Chubey, bride Annie, groom Peter, Mike Chubey, Steve Slobodzian. Taken in front of Carlowrie store and hall.

Tom Chubey Jr., his wife Susan, daughter Tara, and baby Michael.

L to r; back, Harry Chubey, wife Mary (Dishnick), sons Thomas and Taras; front, Lawrence and Fekla Dishnick, Mary's parents. Fekla (Redka) Dishnick was born in Poland in 1900, and Lawrence was born in the same village, Gradoslawice, in 1897. They were married in 1922, and came to Franklin Municipality in 1929. The first summer Lawrence worked for David Japs, and in the fall he, with John Dupchaks, rented a farm from Ted Lang. The depression made this a failure, and they worked as labourers in the Arnaud district until 1935, when they bought a farm on which they lived until 1973. Mrs. Dishnick died in July, 1973, and Lawrence resides in the Vita Personal Care Home.

L to r; back, Andrew, Peter, Nellie; middle, Tom Chubey Sr. holding Harry, Anne holding baby Effie; front, Mike, Paul, Nick, Steve, Mary, Bill.

JOHN CALDER

John Calder and his wife Effie Craig of Ridgeville live on the SE ¼ 34-3-4 E1. They have four children.

The oldest daughter Hazel is married to William Bochinski. They reside in Winnipeg and have two sons, Randi and Brian. After several years of teaching and running her own nursery school, Hazel is now training horses at Assiniboia Downs.

The youngest daughter, Elaine, chose teaching as her career. She married Bruce Smith of Winnipeg. They have two sons Cory and Shane.

Cameron, the elder son, married Betty Lou Weir of Ste Agathe. They have one daughter, Lynne. Cameron, along with his dad and brother

L to r; back, Hazel, Bill, Elaine, Bruce, Brian, Betty Lou, Cameron, Glen; front, Randi, Cory, John, holding Kristy, Lynne, Effie holding Shane, Darcy, Mary Anne. Inset, Jeremy, born 1981.

Glen operate "Calder Farms", a grain and hog operation.

Glen married Mary Anne Neufeld of Horndean. They have two sons Darcy and Jeremy and one daughter Kristy.

RUDOLPH CASPER

Rudolph Casper was born in Russia on December 24, 1882. On January 7, 1912, he married Augusta Leuck who was born December 25, 1895. They immigrated to Canada in 1913.

They stayed with his brother Fred who was living in the Green Ridge district.

They bought a farm south of Dominion City in 1930.

Due to Rudolph's illness they were forced to sell their farm and move to Dominion City, where Rudolph passed away on July 3, 1954. Augusta remained living in Dominion City for the rest of her life. She died September 1, 1976.

They had nine children. They are Fred, Walter, Flora, Hilda, Alma, Henry, Mabel, Edna and Adeline.

Fred Casper was born December 13, 1913 in Green Ridge where he got his education. At age 17 he moved to Dominion City with his family and worked on the family farm till 1939 when he married Alma Woltman of Dominion City. At that time they bought their own farm, one mile north of his parent's farm. They continued farming for 23 years. In 1968 they sold their farm and bought a home in Dominion City. In 1978 they retired after working in Thompson and Dominion City. They are the parents of two children.

Gerald was born May 17, 1942, took his education in Dominion City. Before moving to Thompson in 1967 he worked on the family farm, also that year he married Elaine Arseny of Tolstoi. In 1973 they moved to Brandon and then on to Calgary, Alberta in 1975. He is now working on construction. They have one son: Judd Owen born May 5, 1975.

Darlene was born June 29, 1945 and married Dan Lewis Jr. of Emerson and is presently living in Edmonton, Alberta. They have one daughter Tanya Gillian born July 19, 1970.

Walter Casper was born December 31, 1914 in Green Ridge where he got his education. At age 16 he moved with his family to Dominion City. He worked on the family farm until marrying Esther Clupp of Dominion City in 1943. They moved to a farm five miles south of his parents' farm.

In 1948 he bought the Dominion City Dray from his brother Henry. He continued with this work, hauling freight, ice and coal until 1951 at which time he sold his business to Charlie Hartig. He then started working for the Province of Manitoba Department of Public Works, continuing with them for 29 years until his retirement in 1979.

They are the parents of five children:

Brian Calvin, born September 8, 1948 took his education in Dominion City, married Sheila Andres, originally from Roblin, Manitoba on June 26, 1976 and are presently residing in Winnipeg.

Brian is employed by the Bank of Nova Scotia and has two children Jacqueline, born March 7, 1980 and Brett born October 10, 1981.

Douglas Glenn, born August 13, 1949, got his education in Dominion City. He joined the Royal Canadian Mounted Police in 1969. He married Lyn Schultz from Ridgeville in 1971. They have lived in Vancouver and Prince George, British Columbia, Esterhazy, Saskatchewan and now reside in North Battleford, Saskatchewan.

They have two children, Tanya Lyn, born September 5, 1974 and Troy Douglas, born December 22, 1975.

Valerie Lois was born May 13, 1951 and is married to Robert Johnston from St. Catherines, Ontario August 12, 1972 and now reside in Winnipeg.

They have one son, Chad William born April 2, 1979.

Janice Marlene was born October 26, 1954 and married Taras Sokolyk of Dominion City October 6, 1979 and now resides in Dominion City.

Wayne Harvey was born April 5, 1961 and took his education in Dominion City. He is now working at Fraser Art Supply in Winnipeg.

Flora was born February 23, 1916 and married Eric Flagel from Emerson in 1937, now living in Flin Flon, Manitoba.

Hilda was born December 11, 1917 and married Henry Ratchinsky of Ridgeville in 1938, now living in Dominion City.

Alma was born December 31, 1919 and married Ted Walters of Emerson in 1939, now living in Morris, Manitoba.

Henry was born June 2, 1922, got his education in Green Ridge and Dominion City schools. He worked on the family farm until 1946 when he married Evangeline Boiteau of Letellier, Manitoba.

Mabel was born May 4, 1925 and married Paul Walters of Emerson in 1946, now living in Dominion City.

Edna was born August 1, 1929 and married Wallace Brad of Dominion City in 1949, now living in Russell, Manitoba.

Adeline was born August 6, 1951 and married Wallace Kein of Dominion City in 1956, now living in Pine Falls, Manitoba.

Rudolph and Augusta Casper

Left: Evangeline and Henry Casper.
Right: Flora (Casper) Hazel, husband Erick Hazel.

INGWER CHRISTIANSON

Ingwer and Christine Christianson immigrated to Canada in April 1925, accompanied by their two sons Carl, age four, and Peter, age three.

They settled near Ridgeville where Ingwer worked as a farm laborer until 1926 when they made their home on the SE ¼ 4-2-3 E1. Ingwer continued working for a nearby farmer until the fall of 1929, when he began farming on his own. He rented the quarter they live on plus 90 acres, NE 33-1-3, from the G. F. Christie estate. In 1938 they also rented the SW ¼ 3-2-3 from B. A. Funk of Selkirk. The home quarter was bought in 1941. In 1954 they retired and took up residence in Dominion City. Ingwer passed away in 1968, Christine in March of 1970. Their home was purchased by Mike Stefiuk.

Carl was married in October, 1944, to Olga Geske of Emerson. They made their home in Winnipeg for 12 years where Carl was employed by C.N.R.

Fred Casper family, l to r; Tanya Lewis, Alma, Gerald Casper, holding son Judd, Elaine, Mrs. Gerald Casper, Fred, Don Lewis, Darlene (Casper) Lewis.

They had two children, Lorne (deceased 1982), and Judy. Carl and his family moved to Sacramento, California in April of 1956 where they presently reside. Judy married Jeff Karstadt in 1966, and they live in the United States with their two daughters.

Peter served in the R.C.A.M.C. from December 1942, until March 1946. In July 1946, through the V.L.A., he purchased SW 3-2-3 from B. A. Funk of Selkirk. In October 1954, Peter married Solrun Bjornson who had come from Arborg to teach in Dominion City. They lived on SE ¼ 4-2-3. In 1960 Peter bought the farm from his parents and in 1962 they built a new home. In 1962 Peter and Soli expanded their farm operation by purchasing the E ½ 33-1-3 from L. M. Brad of Dominion City. In 1976 they sold their land to Powatin Farms of Germany and in 1978 moved to a new house in Emerson where they now reside.

Peter and Soli had three children, Donna, Valdine and Calvin.

In 1978 Donna married Ron Sawatzky of Emer-

Walter Casper family, l to r; back, Walter and Esther Casper, Brian and Sheila Casper, Douglas and Lyn Casper, Wayne Casper; front, Bob and Valerie (Casper) Johnston, Taras and Janice (Casper) Sokolyk, Tanya and Troy Casper on floor. Insets, Jacqueline and Brett Casper; Chad William Johnston.

son. They live in Winnipeg.

In 1979, Valdine married Grant Rodewald, an Emerson area farmer and they live in Emerson. Calvin is presently attending the University of Manitoba and lives at home with his parents.

Peter, Valdine, Calvin, Donna and Soli Christiansen.

Christine and Ingwer Christiansen

Judy and Lorne Christiansen, Olga (Geske) Christiansen; Carl Christiansen.

LEOPOLD KASPER

Leopold Kasper and family came from Dereshna, in Wolien, Russia.

In 1901 he immigrated to Canada with his wife, eight children, and two nephews, Friedrich and Rudolf. They arrived in Ellis Island, New York and proceeded to Emerson where they lived for one winter.

From Emerson Leopold and family moved to North Dakota, where they farmed five miles west of Pembina until 1909. Natalie, August, Friedrich and Rudolf remained in Manitoba. In 1909 Leopold and family decided to move to Prelate, Saskatchewan, where homesteads were available.

They packed their belongings and moved into a boxcar at Emerson for the trip west. In the meantime the youngest son Henry became ill with measles and they were quarantined in the boxcar for one month. Finally however they arrived at their homestead where they farmed until 1919.

In 1919 Leopold retired and he and his family moved to Portland, Oregon except for William and his family who remained in the Prelate district. There they resided for the rest of their lives.

Meanwhile Friedrich and Rudolf got married and farmed at Dominion City where they later retired and died.

August Casper married Carolina Drajeske (nee Kein) a widow with three children. He farmed in the Emerson district, where he later retired and died.

In Manitoba when applying for Canadian citizenship, August, Friedrich and Rudolf spelled their name with a "C" (Casper), which was the spelling used in Germany from where their ancestors came. However Leopold and family in Prelate kept the Russian version "Kasper". In the Russian language a "C" is pronounced as an "S".

Leopold Kasper (1851-1924) married Karolina Kehnke. Their children were:

Natalia, 1883-1931, married Wm. Rothenberger.

Ida 1885-1951, married Rudolf Felsch.
August 1887-1946, married Carolina Drajeske.
Othelia 1888-1951, married Manuel Sept.
William 1892-1976, married Adolina Wenzel.
Henry 1898-1960, married Beatrice Kennedy.
Adolf 1894- .
Hilda 1900- , married Roy Phaneuf.
Wanda 1903- , married John Day.
Martha 1905- , married John Patrick Day.

AUGUST CASPER FAMILY

Theodor William (Drajeske) 1900-1943, married Olga Reichert, was educated as a Lutheran minister and served his church in northern Saskatchewan (Runciman) until his death. They had two daughters.

Elsie (Drajeske) 1902, married Louis Sauder. They farmed and retired at Emerson. They have one daughter and two sons.

Mabel (Drajeske) 1906, married Thorvaldur Peterson and lived in Winnipeg, Manitoba until Thorvaldur retired from I.H.C. They now live in Kelowna.

Frank 1910, married Elsie Steg, and farmed in the Ridgeville district until World War II when he enlisted and served as an Armament Officer in the R.C.A.F. for four years. After the war he farmed for several years. Then he worked for the Manitoba Power Commission and the city of Saskatoon as an electrical engineer until his retirement. They now live in Winnipeg, and have two sons.

Arthur 1912-1978, married Anna Weiss. He farmed in the Fredensthal area until his retirement. He then moved to Dominion City. He has one son.

Lilia 1914, married William Theodor Schultz. They farmed near Fredensthal, and then worked in Winnipeg for several years and now live in Emerson. They had two daughters.

Henry 1920-1982, served in the Canadian Army in Canada and overseas, was severely wounded i n Belgium. After the war he obtained a Diploma in Agriculture and farmed east of Emerson until 1963. Because of wounds received in the war he spent the rest of his life in hospitals and care homes, and with his sister Mabel and her husband Thorvaldur in Winnipeg and Kelowna.

Leopold Kasper family, l to r; back, Adolph, Henry, Martha, Hilda, Matilda, Ida; front, August, Leopold Kasper and wife Karolina (Kehnke), Natalia.

August Casper's stepchildren, l to r; Elsie Theodor William, Mabel.

Sandra and Ernie Casper, 1965. Ernie married Sandra Backman, of Melville, Saskatchewan, in 1965. Sandra was born in England, and they have two boys. Keven, born 1966, Curtis, born 1970; Kevin Casper and Curtis Casper.

176

Dennis A. Casper, born April 4, 1946, in Vita. He graduated from North Dakota State University in 1970 with a B.Sc.E.E. in Electrical and Electronics Engineering. Dennis was employed with Saskatchewan Telephone in 1970, and presently is Section Manager in Systems Development. He married Bernice Elaine Nickel in 1972 and they have one son and one daughter.

Robbi Darin Casper was born March 28, 1978.

Dana Marie was born May 10, 1981.

Dennis' brother Howard H. Casper was born April 9, 1939 in Vita. He graduated from North Dakota State Universtiy with a B.Sc. in May 1966. He earned his Masters in May, 1968 and Ph.D in December 1971 in Agriculture. He is employed at North Dakota State University as assistant professor in Toxicology.

Howard is married to Sandra Peto, 1963. They have two sons. David Howard Casper, born May 8, 1968, and Lorne Andrew Casper, born February 22, 1972.

Howard and Dennis are the sons of Frank Casper.

L to r; Bernice Casper, holding Dana-Marie, Dennis A. Casper, holding Robbi-Darin.

L to r; Wm. T. Schultz, his wife Lilia, Frank Casper, his wife Elsie, Anna, her husband Arthur Casper, Henry Casper.

August and Carolina Casper

Howard H. Casper, Lorne Andrew, Sandra Casper, holding David Howard.

HERBERT CLIFFORD

Herbert Bruce Claude Augustus Clifford was born in Kent, England May 12, 1883. He arrived in the Ridgeville area in 1906. For the next four years he worked at the Pulp Mills at Mafeking. July 29, 1910 he married Martha Ann Wilkinson, the first wedding to be performed in the St. Mary's Anglican Church, Ridgeville. They bought Roy Whitman's store. In October, 1919, he was killed in an accident while starting up a lighting plant in the store. The next year Martha sold the store back to R. Whitman. They had three sons, Lawrence, Harold, Douglas.

Harry and Martha Clifford, 1910.

Lawrence and Mary Clifford. Lawrence Bruce is a graduate of Aeronautical Engineering and was a flying officer in World War II. After discharge he joined Canadair in Montreal, and is with their missile section. June, 1943, he married Mary Reid in Ottawa. They have two daughters, Anne and Mary.

Anne married Jean Gagne, 1970, and has one daughter, Genevieve.

Mary married Richard Cabell, in 1970, and they have three children, Rebecca Ariel, born 1975, Miriam Alanna, born 1981, Nathan Ezekiel, born 1978.

Harold, Phyllis, Carol and Greg Clifford. Wm. Harold George Clifford married Phyllis McIntosh in 1943 at Dauphin, where they live. Harold works as a parts and maintenance man, and Phyllis is an accountant. They have two children, Carol and Gregory.

F. Scott, Phyllis, Ian Scott, Carol Clifford, Mrs. H. Francis, Harold. Carol and Ian Scott have three children, Jody, Julie, Tracy.

Jody, Tracy, Julie Scott.

Gregory married Carla Gagen in 1981, at Clearbrook, British Columbia.

Douglas and Mary (Smye). Clifford married in 1941. They have five children, Gilbert, Kenneth, Jo-Anne, Bonnie, and Duncan.

Gilbert Clifford, his wife Karen Jonasson, married 1978. They have one son, Kevin.

L to r; Mark, born 1977, Graham, born 1979, Shawn, born 1975, Geoffrey, born 1973, children of Kenneth Clifford. Kenneth married Christine Pinchbik 1968 and has four children, Geoffrey, Shawn, Mark, Graham.

Bryan Moore, husband of Jo-Anne Clifford, married 1972. They have three children, Kelly Moore, born 1974, Katherine born 1980, and Leah Moore, born 1977.

Bonnie and husband Frank Borgford, married 1976. They have one son, Gilbert, (on his second birthday).

Clarence and Olga Cameron, Chinchilla awards, CCT 52 A Show Champion, CCT 51 A Reserve Show Champion, Winnipeg.

CLARENCE CAMERON

Clarence Cameron and his father J. Allan Cameron moved to Dominion City in 1937 from the dried out area of Saskatchewan. Clarence was born at Tyvan, 45 miles southeast of Regina. When they arrived in Manitoba they bought the 160 acre Farm 5½ miles northwest of Dominion City from John Schmidki, which Clarence farmed until 1979.

In 1939 Clarence married Olga Larson; together they raised two sons and a daughter.

Donald, now of Ottawa, where he is Director of Tarriff Policy and Program Development with the Federal Government. He married Dianne Carruthers of Virden in 1963. They have three children Kevin, Janice and Allan.

Neil married Judy Cook of Brandon in 1966. They also have three children, Laura, Douglas and Susan. Together they own and operate a Resort Business on the Georgian Bay at Pointe au Baril, Ontario.

Heather Ann married Barry Carver of Dominion City in 1971. They have one daughter Regan and live in Neepawa where Butch is employed with the Provincial Water Resources.

Tom Reidstra and Sons of Norval, Ontario bought out the Cameron Chinchilla herd of over 200 animals following the 1980 National Show in Winnipeg.

Clarence and Olga moved their house into the village of Dominion City in the summer of 1980, after selling their farm of 240 acres to Mr. and

Mrs. Wayne Hildebrand of Emerson, Manitoba.

Clarence's father J. Allan Cameron was born and raised near Owen Sound, Ontario, and spent the latter part of his years with Clarence and his family. His mother, the former Laura Lemon, died in 1916, when Clarence was only 19 months old.

Clarence and Olga Cameron.

Heather Ann (Cameron) Carver, Regan and Barry Carver live at Neepawa where Barry works for the provincial government.

The Donald Cameron family reside in Ottawa, where he is with the Federal Customs.
L to r: Dianne, Janice, Kevin, Donald, Allan.

The Neil Cameron Family own and operate a resort on Georgian Bay.
Back, l to r: Judy, Susan, Neil.
Front: Laura, Douglas.

ALFRED COLLINS

Alfred Collins was born in Ontario. He and his brother Edmund came to Manitoba in 1879. Alfred farmed East of Dominion City. Edmund had a blacksmith shop in Dominion City which he sold to Wm. Parker in 1904 before moving to Russell. Edmund had three boys, George, Charlie and Ralph and one girl Eva.

Alfred married in Ontario, and both his wife and infant daughter passed away there. He then married a Miss Ross and had one daughter, Olive. His second wife passed away in 1889. He married Elizabeth Aldrich in 1890. He took up homestead on the Roseau River at Green Ridge in 1896. He cut logs and made a house and barn. The house remained until the late 1970's and the barn still remains. They had three boys, Rufus, Edward and Arthur. Alfred and Elizabeth remained on the farm until 1927, then moved to Winnipeg. Mr Collins passed away in 1921 and Mrs. Collins in 1939.

Rufus received his education in the Newbridge school. He married Ann Blinkinsop in 1929 and had a store in Arnaud. They had two children Grace and Olive. In 1943, he moved to Winnipeg where he worked for 17 years for Bristol Aircraft and then Silverwoods Dairy. He retired in 1965. Anne passed away April 12, 1982. Rufus is 93 years old and still bowls and looks after himself.

Arthur received his education in the Newbridge school. He worked for the Kiwanis Ranch in Arnaud and then spent six years in the Ninette Sanitorium. He moved to Wiseton, Saskatchewan and married Bessie Dickson in 1929. He resided in Saskatchewan until his death in 1930.

Edward received his education in the Newbridge

and Green Ridge schools. In 1940 he came back to the family farm until 1967 when he moved to Dominion City Manor. He moved to the Morris Valley Lodge in 1977 where he passed away April 8, 1978, age 80. He was buried in Green Ridge.

Alfred and Elizabeth Collins

OTTO CLUPP

Otto and Caroline Clupp moved from Letellier to a farm three miles south of Dominion City in 1925 where they farmed until 1961 when they retired to Winnipeg. Two sons, Edward, his wife Dorothy, Lorne, his wife Hazel, three daughters, Florence (Mrs. Anderson), Evelyn (Mrs. Ron Jones), and Elaine (Mrs. Greg Schwenneker) all live in Winnipeg. Two daughters, Esther (Mrs. Walter Casper) and Theresa, (Mrs. Osborne Scott), live in Dominion City, one daughter, Violet, died in 1952. Otto Clupp died July 1973.

L to r; back, Elaine, Lorne, Evelyn, Theresa, Esther, Edward, Florence; sitting, Caroline and Otto Clupp.

Finn and Florence (Clupp) Anderson, Diane, Marilyn, Brad.

L to r; Lorne Clupp, his wife Hazel, Pam and Jeff.

L to r; back, Ronald Jones, Evelyn (Clupp) Jones; front, Brent, Christine and Dianna Jones.

Gregory Schwenneker and Elaine Clupp.

Left: Ed and Dorothy Clupp.
Right: Steven Chiffins, grandson of Ed Clupp.

L to r; Kenneth, Calvin, Sheldon and Andrea Clupp, children of Ed and Dorothy.

MICHAEL CIRKA

Michael Cirka came to Canada from the West Ukraine in 1926. He stayed with his cousins the Halosis for a few years, then worked for farmers. In 1927 his wife Maria (Gabryk) and daughter Anna came. He bought property, but kept on working out, until 1934 when a loaded wagon passed over him and killed him. Anna and Maria went to Winnipeg, where both worked in sewing factories, after selling the farm.

Anna married Tommy Buick, a musician. They have three children.

Michael, Anna and Maria Cirka.

JAMES CALDER

James Calder was born on the Island of Islay, Scotland. He married a woman named Walton, and lived on Section 35-2-4 E1.

Their children were George and Elizabeth. George was born in 1881 and died a bachelor at age 44 in 1942. George left his estate to the Winnipeg Foundation and his name is listed each year in their accounts.

Elizabeth was born in 1884, and died in a home in 1947.

It is of interest that three weddings were performed by a travelling preacher in the fall of 1879, when James Calder was united in marriage to Miss Walton, Robert Kennedy Miller married Agnes Burrell, and Mary Ann Strange married Andrew Davison.

 D   MOSES DITLOVITCH

In front of Ditlovitch Store, Moses Ditlovitch, Alma Spence, Gladys Ditlovitch.

Mr. and Mrs. Moses Ditlovitch, on their 60th wedding anniversary, 1969. Mrs. Ditlovitch was born in Austria, and Moses Ditlovitch came from Russia. They married in Austria in 1905, and came to Dominion City in 1907. They lived here for 35 years, where they owned and operated a General Store. In 1942 they moved to Winnipeg. Their children were Dave, deceased, Fanny, Mrs. A. Makin, Calgary, Nellie, Gladys, Mrs. L. Jampolsky, Vancouver, Harry, deceased.

Fanny Ditlovitch in front of her father's store.

Dave Ditlovitch, getting a good look at Dominion City.

GUSTAV DRAJESKE

Gustav and Telene Drajeske. Gustav was born in Poland on February 2, 1868, and came to the U.S. in 1892. He worked for Frank Morris, farmer, at Neche, for two years. Here he met Telene Sperling, from Dresden, North Dakota, and married her January 5, 1894. They had nine children: Augusta died at age two due to burns received when falling into a kettle of scalding water, and Gustav Jr. at age 20 years in the 1919 flu epidemic. In 1915, Telene, 39 years of age, died when the farm dugout from which she was dipping water caved in, causing her to fall to her tragic death. The Drajeskes bought the NW¼ 12-1-3 E1 in Franklin in 1896, and farmed this until 1940. Their son Henry took over the farm until 1972, when he sold the land to Pete Kohut of Ridgeville.

JAMES DUNCAN

James Duncan of Greenridge, and his granchildren, l to r; Walter, Edna, George, and Reginald Wood.

L to r; back, Henry and Herman; centre, Mrs. Reinhold Lange, Mrs. Fred Poffel, Mrs. Wm. Krietc; front, Emil. 1926.

JAMES DICKSON

James Dickson, born in Scotland, married Margaret Wilson and came to Canada in 1841. The family settled in the Ottawa Valley in the County of Renfrew, Ontario. In May 1879 they came to Manitoba to homestead in the district of Arnaud. This parcel of land is located 2½ miles west and ½ mile south of the present village of Arnaud and is on the west side of the road which they used going from Dominion City to St. Jean.

In 1889 the family moved East to the Woodmore district to NE ¼ Sec. 25, Township 2, Range 4.

Not all of the nine children came to Manitoba. Some remained in Renfrew and their decendents are still living in the area.

Those who came were Agnes, married to John Ronald - buried in Green Ridge Cemetery. Margaret, married David Carswilt and lived in the Manitou district.

John Wilson Dickson remained on the farm, married Ann Carswell from Ontario in 1865 and it is the descendents of these two who maintain the old farm today. John and Ann are buried in the family plot in Green Ridge cemetery. Their children:

Janet who married Tom Scott of Dominion City, has four children.

James married Cordelia Post, farmed in the Green Ridge area for some time, later homesteaded in Wiseton, Saskatchewan. They had four children.

Margaret married John Oatway, Green Ridge and had two children, Wilfred and Annie. Margaret and John died at a relatively early age and the children went to live with their grandparents. In 1910 they moved to Dominion City.

David lived most of his life in Saskatchewan homesteading in the Wiseton area. He married Margaret Mailtand Wemyss and they had four children.

William spent part of his life on the farm and did carpentry. Later he moved to Calgary. He married Margaret Hempton of Dominion City and had one son, Claude.

John Dickson married Margaret Spence of Green Ridge. Most of their lives were spent in Winnipeg where John owned and operated a taxi business. They had seven children.

Robert Alexander remained on the farm where he lived with his mother and sister Annie. His father was absent from home a great deal as he was a competent carpenter and bridge builder and work was plentiful. Annie married Jim Acres of Dominion City. There were no children.

A log house was built in 1895 on Section 25.

Robert married Ella Post in March 1910 and lived in this house till they retired to Dominion City in 1950. This couple is buried in family plot in Green Ridge cemetery.

Bob and Ella had three children.

Ivy married William Greenlay, and lives in Winnipeg.

Lorna married Hugh Garven of Saskatchewan. Hugh is now deceased, and Lorna makes her home in North Vancouver. They had three children. Janice (Mrs. Raymond), Halifax; Arlene (Mrs. Bryan Parker), Calgary; and David, wife Jennifer and small daughter Pamela, live in North Vancouver.

Bruce remained on the farm to carry on. He married Louise Johnson, Woodmore. Later they bought their present home in Green Ridge district but continue to farm the old place. They had three children, Linda, teacher, living at home. Patricia married Bob Piche, Willow Bunch, Saskatchewan and son James living at home, now 18.

It is interesting to note that the last man in line at this time is named James, as was the first young man who came with his wife and family to Canada from Scotland in 1841.

Left: Anne Carswell Dickson, wife of John Wilson Dickson.
Right: James Dickson with his first grandchild, Eloise Madill.

Jim, Louise and Bruce Dickson, 1980.

Mr and Mrs. James Dickson. James was born January 29, 1868 at Arnprior, Ontario, and came to Franklin with his parents at the age of 12. He married Cordelia Mabel Post of Greenridge in 1898, and they had four children, Raymond Wilson, born April 20, 1901, who moved to Saskatchewan; Anna Elizabeth, born October 20, 1904, married Arthur Collins, 1930; Allan James, born July 1, 1906, schoolteacher; Vera Eleanor, born April 14, 1908, married Charlie Madill 1930. James died 1942, and Cordelia in 1970. Both are buried in Saskatchewan, where they went to live with their son Raymond upon their retirement.

Pat, 1961; Linda Dickson

Robert Dickson family, 1954, l to r; Ivy Greenlay, Bruce Dickson, Ella Dickson, Robert Dickson, Lorna Garven.

Robert and Ella (Post) Dickson, 1915.

NYKOLA DOLYNCHUK

Nykola (Nick) and Irene Dolynchuk were one of the first business people in Tolstoi in 1918. Nykola Dolynchuk came to Canada in 1906 and Irene arrived in 1896. They were married in 1909. Then they both went to work for a farmer in St. Vincent, U.S.A. and lived there for five years. During this time they learned the English language. They saved some money, and came to Tolstoi and bought a farm. They farmed for a few years and in 1918 Mr. Dolynchuk opened a General Store in Tolstoi.

They had four children, John, Alex, Nestor and Mary.

John married Olga Popiel. Their children are, Helen and Ronald.

Helen married Dr. I. Mayba. She has two sons and lives in Winnipeg.

Ronald married A. Malonchuk, has three children and lives in Ontario.

Alex married Claudia Wachna. Their children are Orest, Ted and Teresa.

Orest married Sylvia Zurkowsky. They had twins, Jamie and Jodi, who live in Winnipeg.

Ted is single and works in the North.

Teresa married Larry Bell. She has two daughters Tanya, Tiffany and one son, Chad. They live in Lethbridge, Alberta.

Nestor married M. Bachynsky. They have three sons, Dr. Ken Dolynchuk, Mark and Michael.

Mary married Nick Hrynick. She has two children, Patsy and Dennis and lives in Winnipeg.

Mr. and Mrs. Nick Dolynchuk moved to Dominion City farms in 1943. In 1946 they moved to Winnipeg and went into business with sons John and Nestor.

Alex and his wife Claudia remained in Tolstoi and continued the general store, trucking and im-

185

plement business. They ran the business for 38 years and retired in Tolstoi in 1975. Alex Dolynchuk died in 1977.

Nykola Dolynchuk died in 1967 and Irene died in 1974.

Nykola and Irene Dolynchuk, on their 50th wedding anniversary in 1958.

L to r; Alex Dolynchuk Orest, Claudia, Ted, Teresa. On the occasion of their 25th wedding anniversary.

Jodi and Jamie, twins of Orest Dolynchuk, Claudia (Dolynchuk) Eliuk, and Orest Dolynchuk.

L to r; back, Tanya and Tiffany Bell, Claudia (Dolynchuk) Eliuk, daughter Teresa Bell; front, Chad Bell.

186

EMIL DRAJESKE

L to r; back, Joyce, Ken, Cathy, Teena (Timchuk) Drajeske, Emil Drajeske; front, Robert, Linda; insert, Karen. Emil Drajeske and Teena Timchuk were married in 1939. They owned the Pool Room and Barber Shop in Ridgeville from 1947 to 1956. Emil was also a carpenter, and Teena was a hairdresser and seamstress. They had six children.

Lynda Drajeske married Keith Downer in 1974. They have two children, Brian and David.

L to r; Deanna, Joyce (Drajeske) Shallock, Fritz Shallock, Cheri; standing, Randy; insert, Susan, born 1974. Joyce and Fritz were married in 1960.

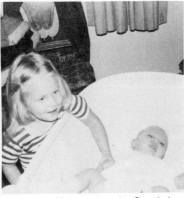

Robert Drajeske, whose wife's name is Gerri, has two children; Rebecca Drajeske, born 1975, Angela Drajeske, born 1973.

Left: Ken Drajeske, whose wife's name is Mary, and his son Stevie.
Right: Cathy (Drajeske) Menow, whose husband is Jerry Menow, and her son, Tommy.

RUDOLF DOERN

Rudolf Doern was born in the village of Dalky, Austria on June 23rd, 1877. His mother died when he was very young. He was 14 years old when he and his brother Ed, came to Canada and settled in the Gretna area, working out to make a living. In 1902 he was wed to Theresa Purpur. They were blessed with two daughters, Caroline and Edith but in 1905 his wife passed away.

In 1908 he married Augusta (Gussie) Weiss. She was born in Drashna, Russia on December 18, 1890, and had come to Canada with her parents in 1895. Rudolf and Augusta farmed in the Letellier district for sometime, then moved to Morris where they farmed for several years. In 1919 they bought land in the Friedensthal area, and lived on section 23, township 1, range 3E. They farmed here until 1947 when they retired to Dominion City. This marriage was blessed with four boys, William, Fredrick, Edward and Walter

and six girls, Emma, Violet, Theresa, Sophie, Lillian and Dorothy.

Carrie married Otto Clupp, Edith married Gus Weiss, Emma married Ernie Bochinski, Violet married Arnold Smithe, Theresa married Fred Knutt, Sophie married Gordon Kein, Lillian married Herb Schultz, Dorothy married Gus Schorein, Walter married Geraldine Huff, Edward married Elsie Gluck, William married Bella Thom.

Rudolf passed away August 19, 1953 and Augusta Doern November 23, 1964. William passed away December 20, 1974, Frederick in 1934 and sister Emma, September 16, 1966.

In 1982 Edward, Walter, Caroline, Edith and Dorothy reside in Winnipeg, Violet in Vulcan, Alberta, Theresa and Sophie in Morris and Lillian in the Friedensthal area.

Rudolf and Augusta Doern.

L to r; Rudolf Doern, son Walter, brother Leo, son Edward, son William 1946.

The daughters of Rudolf and Augusta Doern, standing according to age, Carrie, Edith, Emma, Violet, Theresa, Sophie, Lillian, Dorothy.

L to r; back, Ernest Bochinsky, Geraldine and Walter Doern, Gus Scharein, wife Dorothy, Violet and Arnold Smithe; middle, Fred and Theresa Knutt, Herb and Lillian Schultz, Sophie and Gordon Kein, Bella Doern; front, Carrie Clupp, Edward and Elsie Doern, Edith Weiss. Missing from this family picture are the parents Rudolf and Augusta Doern, Emma, Otto Clupp, and Gus Weiss, deceased.

MARC DUBOIS

Marc and Lauran (Spence) Dubois, and daughter Janine. Marc Joseph Louis Dubois came to Green Ridge district from St. Malo. He bought the NW corner of 27-2-4E from Henry Alstadt. In April, 1981, he married Lauran Francis Spence. Marc works for the Water Control Division, and Lori is a clerk at the Ridgeville Store. They have one child, Janine Martha Anne.

JOHN DAVIS

John Davis arrived in Dominion City on March 9, 1981. He was transferred from Elkhorn, Manitoba by the Canadian Imperial Bank of Commerce to become the new Bank manager at Dominion City. He was followed by his wife Pegi and two children, Janice and Warren in April, 1981.

JACOB DREWNIAK

Jacob Drewniak married Maria Bednar, daughter of Paul and Maria Bednar, in the Village of Postolowka, Holichina, Austria. They came to Canada on June 10, 1910 on the ship Oskar.

There were no homesteads left so they bought 160 acres for $1,200 from Metro Tkachuk, on Section 13-5-1-E1.

They arrived with six children, Katherina, six years, from Jacob's previous marriage and five daughters of Jacob and Maria's. Three more daughters were born in Canada.

Nellie, born in 1898, Annie, born in 1900, Maggie, born in 1904, Tennie, born in 1906, Julia, born in 1908, Sally, born in 1912, passed away at three years of age, Sophie, born in 1914, Frances born in 1916, passed away in 1919.

Jacob and his wife Maria found life very hard in Canada. In 1916, September 7, Jacob suffered a heartattack while doing field work and died. Maria with her small children farmed till all her daughters married. She left the farm at 80 years of age to live with her daughter Julia and husband John Kozak. She passed away in 1963 at the age of 83 years.

Her daughter Nellie married Peter Todoruk, Tolstoi. Annie married Sam Polynchuk, Leader, Saskatchewan, Maggie married Peter Bially, Overstoneville, Tennie married Stan Kulyk, Tolstoi, Julia married John Kozak, Tolstoi, Sophie married Walter Otto, Orleans, Minnesota.

Left: Maria K. Drewniak.
Right: Nellie (Todoruk), daughter of Maria Drewniak.

Left: Peter Tesarski and bride, with flower girl Margret Tesarski, and Peter's mother Katherina Tesarski, step daughter of Maria Drewniak.
Right: Annie Drewniak and husband Sam (Palynchuk), 1917.

L to r; Maggie Bially, Tennie Kulyk, Julia Kozak, Sophie Otto, daughters of Jacob and Maria Drewniak.

NELLIE (DANELEYKO) DZIOBA

Nellie Daneleyko came to Canada in 1892 at the age of one year. Her family settled in the Overstoneville area, just east of Ridgeville. Nellie married John Dzioba and they had four children,

Nellie (Daneleyko) Dzioba

Edward, Donald, Lawrence, and Irene. Mr. Dzioba ran the blacksmith shop in Ridgeville for many years, having take over from "Scotty" Ingram. When Mr. Dzioba retired, he sold his shop to Ronald Spence. After Mr. Dzioba died, Mrs. Dzioba became a resident of the personal care home in Vita. Both were known for their devotion to the church. Mrs. Dzioba loved her flower garden and was a caring, concerned person.

JOHN DERKSEN

John and Eva Derksen. The Derksens bought the NW ¼ 14-1-4 E1 from Arnold and Beryl Keyes in 1980. They have two children, Valerie and Larry at home.

ANDREW DREWNIAK

Andrew (Andruch) and Maryna Drewniak immigrated to Tolstoi from the village of Postaliwka, West Ukraine in 1910, and farmed section 12-1-5 E1.

Martin and Walter Drewniak, and Walter's grandchild.

189

L to r; back, Sophie Solinis, Caroline Drewniak, holding daughter Victoria, John Makoweski, holding his daughter Jean, (Teenie) Makoweski, Walter Drewniak, Eddie Politzer; middle, Maryna Drewniak, holding grandson Eddie Politzer, Andrew Drewniak; front, grandson Albert Solinis and Nellie (Drewniak) Politzer. 1938.

They had six daughters, Annie Porozuik, Katie Shyposh, Sophie Solinis, Nettie Ostofichuk, Nellie Politzer and (Teenie) Makoweski, and two sons, Walter and Martin.

Both Mr. and Mrs. Drewniak passed away in 1956. They had 14 grandchildren and 11 great-grandchildren.

MAXIUM DONALEYKO (DANYLEJKO)

Maxium Donaleyko (Danylejko) was the son of the late Mr. and Mrs. Andrew Danylejko (Andrij) who homesteaded the SW 21-1-15 in 1899, coming from the Western Ukraine.

In 1919, Maxium married Annie Melynchuk. They farmed on this land until their death. This land is now owned by the third generation of the family (Andrij) Henry Donaleyko.

Maxium and Anne were a hard working couple. Besides all the regular farm work, he was also employed for 22 years on the railway. They had a keen interest in beekeeping, experimenting in many variety of fruit trees as well. Mr. Donaleyko enjoyed photography, and many scenes in the early days were photographed by him.

Their children are: Henry, Maurice, Daniel, two daughters - Mrs. Helen Gerula and Mrs. Pauline Gerula. There are six grandchildren and three great-grandchildren.

Form No. 39 A.
10,000-4-07.

Vol No. 20   No. 128   Ref. 377818

Department of the Interior,

Ottawa SEP 16 1908 190

Sir.

I enclose herewith Letters Patent for SW ¼

Section 21 in Township 1 Range 5 East West of the Principal Meridian, in the Province of Manitoba

Please sign and return to this Department the accompanying form of receipt.

I am, Sir,

Your obedient servant,

PERLEY G. KEYES,
Secretary.

Andrij Danylejko, Esq.
Oteskiw,
Man.

A document from the Department of the Interior dated September 16, 1908 made to Andrij Danylejko, Oleskiw, now Tolstoi, Manitoba.

Mr. and Mrs. Maxium Donaleyko, 1921.

OLESKA (ALEX) DOMYTRAK

Originaly from Galicia, in the Ukraine, Oleska (Alex) Domytrak arrived in Halifax in 1902. He was married to Katherine Antonyczuk whose family arrived at the same time.

In 1903, he bought a farm two miles west of the present site of Tolstoi, from Steven Post.

Their children were John, William, Mike, Harry, Mary, Jacob.

Jacob died as an infant.

Mary was married to Andrew Krashewski and still resides in the district.

Mike and Harry died in their teens.

William taught school in Zelota, Lord Roberts, later at Sidney, then MacGregor. He died in 1978.

John left for Detroit, Michigan in 1926, where he attended the Ford Technical School, and later worked at Ford Motor Company for a few years. As the depression caused lay-offs, he returned to Tolstoi where he farmed, did blacksmith work, and had the local P.S.V. license.

In 1936 he married Olga Yarmie and moved into a farm one mile west of Overstoneville post office, where he farmed and did blacksmith and machine work. Here he had an engine driven metal-working lathe, one of the first in the district. In 1940, they bought the Joe Tesarski farm ½ mile south of Tolstoi. John died here in 1966 and Olga in 1968.

Their children were: Alex, Joan, Walter, Sonia, and Bohdan.

Alex attended University at Kingston, Ontario and Winnipeg, and taught high school in various places in Manitoba as well as Ghana and Australia. He married the former Ann Harland from Rivers, Manitoba and now reside in Pinawa. They have two children, Dianne, and Carolyn.

Joan attended the University of Manitoba and taught school in Sprague, Roblin and Winnipeg. She is married to Richard Manty of Winnipeg, where they now live. They have one son, William.

Walter took machinest training at the Manitoba technical Institute (now Red River Community College) and worked in Winnipeg. He married the former Helen Chumak of Winnipeg. They live in Edmonton, Alberta where Walter is a machinist. They have three children, Irene, Larissa, and Tonia.

Sonia took R.N. training and was a Registered Nurse with the Canadian Armed Forces for two terms, and was stationed in parts of Europe. She married Walter Kamel of Montreal and now live in Toronto, Ontario.

Bohdan or Budd, attended University of Manitoba then worked in Winnipeg for a few years. He returned to the family farm in 1972.

In 1980 he moved to St. Pierre where he farms. He married the former Esther Hofer of Winnipeg.

Left: Oleksa and Katherine Domytrak.
Right: John and Olga Domytrak, 1963.

SAMUEL DEVITT

Samuel and Amy Devitt

Mr. and Mrs. George Devitt, on George's 74th birthday, 1928. He died December 4, 1935.

Mr. and Mrs. Carl Carlson, parents of Amy Devitt.

BILL DREBIT

Left: Bill and Nastia Drebit, parents of Peter, John, Walter, Dmytro, Lena (Mrs. Stanley Andrusyk), Annie (Mrs. Peter Chubey).
Right: Dmytro Drebit, served in France, Belgium, Holland and Germany.

Left: Peter Drebit, left, was prisoner of war in Hong Kong for four years, 10 months. John Drevit, right, was stationed in Soffield, Alberta, for two and a half years, in an experimental station.
Right: Walter Drebit, army, served in Korea and Egypt for 10 years.

E

JOHN P. ENNS

L to r; back, Henry, Peter, Agatha and Henry P., John; front, Elizabeth, Peter J. Enns, Helen, Agatha Enns, Agnes, holding Eleanor. c. 1941. Peter J. Enns and his wife left Russia in 1926, and because of an eye disease was not able to enter Canada. He went to Mexico until he was healed, and arrived in Arnaud in 1933. Their farm was three miles south of Arnaud. John Enns and his wife Agnes were married in 1939. In 1951 they bought the J. Poetker farm, and in spring, 1980, their daughter Eleanor and husband John Kathler took over the farm. The Kathlers have three children, Jacqueline, Tim and Mark. Madeleine Enns teaches in Winnipeg, John and his wife Sharon have three boys and one daughter. Len and his wife Sue live in Waterloo, Helmut and wife Janet have two boys and live at Brighton, Ontario. Lottie and husband Rudy Braun live in Winnipeg.

John K., John E., Agnes, Lottie, Rudy, Sharon, John, Madeleine, Helmut, Len, Eleanor, Mark, Jacqueline, Tim, Justin, Jason, Noel. John P. Enns family at Rudy and Lottie's wedding, 1977.

JOHN EASTERBY

John Easterby and his wife, Hannah (Redshaw) emigrated to Canada in 1880 from Yorkshire, England. They settled at North Ridge (Woodmore) later moving to a farm north of Dominion City.

Fred Easterby was born at North Ridge on

March 27, 1884. On April 11, 1904, he married Anna M. Crampton. He received his early education in Rosseau School, first school in Dominion City. Fred was a carpenter by trade also held an Engineer's Diploma and did considerable cement work. He built many sidewalks in Dominion City and was overseer on the construction of several steel and cement bridges during 1915-20 one still remains over the Jordan.

Their children are Annie Timlick (nee Easterby) and Mildred who married Leslie Brad. Mildred and Leslie have three children, Gordon, Wallace and Douglas.

John and Hannah Easterby

L to r; Anna M., Mildred, Annie, Fred Easterby. c. 1912.

Geese on John Easterby farm, c. 1914.

L to r; standing, Anna M. Easterby; Mildred, Hannah Easterby (Mrs. John) and Annie. c. 1912.

L to r; Gordon Brad, Leslie Brad, Mildred (Easterby) Brad, Douglas Brad, Wallace Brad, 1945.

Bridge built by Fred Easterby over Joe River near Emerson in 1920.

Maria Elyk; Harry Elyk

HARRY ELYK

It is with pride and thankful feelings that Wasyle Elyk pays tribute to his mother, Maria Elyk, for her courage and foresight in coming to Canada alone to make a new home for her family. Her brother in the Ukraine was an agent for a steamship company, with his help she secured passage in 1911. She came from the village of Senkiw. In 1912, her husband Harry and their children, John, Anna, Mike, Bill (translation of Wasyl) and Katie left Antwerp on the S.S. Carpathia. They were not able to prove up a homestead in Franklin Municipality, but rented different farms, cutting hay on shares, fixing up the mud plastered log houses and thatching old roofs. Gradually they became farmers, with the usual chickens, cows and pigs.

Anna married Jake Lozowy in 1912. Their children are Mitch of Thunderbay, Bill of Toronto, and Mary of Winnipeg.

John left home soon after they came to Manitoba, and is now deceased. Katie married Martin Horen, lived in Ontario, and they are both deceased, leaving no family. Mike lived in Idaho, his wife Violet is deceased and they had no family. Bill left Manitoba about 1927 for Saskatchewan. He and his wife, Opal, have three daughters.

JACOB EATON EMPEY

Jacob Eaton Empey was born in 1862, Napanee, Ontario and became a carriage maker. He came to Bathgate, North Dakota, where he married Odoriah A. Eastman, born in Ottawa, Ontario. Later the Empey's homesteaded in the R.M. of Franklin and at one time Jake had a Farm Implement Business in Dominion City.

Jake and Odie had five children. Two daughters

predeceased them - (Effie 1881-1914), (Veda 1888-1901). Their third daughter (Ethel) married Morton Peto. There were also two sons, Raymond Minor, who married Marjorie Dupuis, and Horace Bernard (Bernie) 1887-1962 who married Myrtle Bell Fraser (1900-1978) in 1921. Bernie and Myrtle farmed near Ridgeville at what later became known as the Turkey Farm, and raised four sons. They were:

Donald Keith (Keith) 1922-1976 married Lorraine Turner (1926-1972) in 1946. They adopted two children, Leonard Keith (Len) born in 1951 who married Judith Elaine Danielson in 1972. Their son Donovan Lea was born in 1977.

Their daughter Lorraine Joy (Joy) was born in 1956. After Lorraine's passing, Keith remarried in 1972 to Mable Jean Shiells of Sault Ste Marie. They returned to Emerson in 1974, where their son Jacob William was born in 1975.

Bruce Edwin, (1925) married Mary Louise Fritch of Winnipeg. They had three daughters, Bonnie (1948), married to Bruce Baier, Peggy (1952), and Barbara (1958). Peggy married Greg Indrysuk and her children are, Jamie (1975), Christina (1979) and Michael (1981).

After Mary Louise's passing in 1968, Bruce remarried to Gerri Pike and is presently living in Michigan.

Fraser Eaton (1928), married Irene Schultz. They moved to California with their three children, Lloyd (1950), Dwayne (1960), and Loreen (1956).

Howard Raymond (1931) married Myrtle Hassett of Dominion City. Their four children are: James (1953), Colleen (1956) married to Al Gibson, Brian, (1959), married Judy Reimer, and Allan (1962). Howard and Myrtle are presently living in Thunder Bay.

Jake (1862-1946) and Odie (1863-1939) along with their two daughters Effie and Veda are interred in Ridgeville Cemetery, as well as Jake's mother Sarah Norton Empey (1833-1890). Bernie and Myrtle, Ray, Keith and Lorraine are interred in Emerson Cemetery.

Jake's sister Althear was married to Robert Lindsay. Their daughter Shaddi married Ray Long and they are living in Emerson.

RAYMOND MINOR EMPEY

Raymond Minor Empey, the younger son of Jacob Eaton, was born in 1889, near Bathgate, North Dakota.

Raymond lived in Ridgeville all his life with the exception of a short time in California. He and his brother Bernard worked the family farm until 1926 when he purchased the Charlie Madill farm NW ¼ of 4-1-4E. He also owned 80 acres across the road from this quarter.

In 1930 Raymond married Marjory Eleanor Dupuis who was born near Emerson, 1899, and whose parents were John Franklin Dupuis and Margaret Jane Fraser. The maternal grandparents, Donald and Marjory Fraser came to Canada from Inverness, Scotland in a sailboat in 1854 and to Emerson in 1881. On the paternal side great grandfather Dupuis was born in Quebec. As a very young boy he was drafted in to the Army of Defence. After the battle of Chryslers farm in 1813 he was discharged near Kingston at the age of 16 when he received a scrip to purchase land there. Great grandmother Eleanor Baker was an only child whose grandparents came to Halifax in the 1700's with the United Empire Loyalists. They later moved to Ontario. Grandmother Sabra Lucinda Hochebaum was Holland Dutch - a name used to distinguish them from Pennsylvania Dutch who were German.

In 1934, Raymond bought the SW ¼ of 4-1-4E from W. Becstead and in 1954 the NE ¼ from G. Streick. The farm was sold in 1966 when Raymond was forced to give up farming.

He never had the chance to enjoy late retirement as he was in and out of hospital after the sale of the farm until he passed away in 1968.

After Raymond's death Marjory remained in Emerson until 1980, at which time she moved to a senior citizen apartment in Winnipeg.

L to r; back, Bruce, Keith; front, Myrtle Empey, Jacob Empey Sr., Bernie Empey.

Empey Farm, on Turkey Farm, Ridgeville.

Left: Odoriah and Jacob Empey, 1929.
Right: Raymond and Marnory Empey, 1929.

L to r; Lloyd, Irene Empey, Fraser Empey, Dwayne, Loreen, 1973.

Bernie and Myrtle Empey

Leonard Empey, son Donovan Lea (six months), wife Judy, 1977.

L to r; Allan, Brian, Myrtle, Howard, Colleen, Jim Empey, 1976.

Bruce Empey, Gerri, Barb, Peg, Bonnie and Bruce Baier, 1969.

Keith Empey, Jake and Mable, 1976.

Keith Empey, Len, Joy, Lorraine, 1956.

L to r; back, Bruce, Barb, Mary Louise, Myrtle, Bernie, Irene, Howard; front, Keith, Lorraine, Len, Myrtle, Jim, Lloyd, Fraser, Bonnie, 1954.

F BENJAMIN, JOHN AND STEWART FROOM

Benjamine Froom came from Edwardsbourgh, Ontario, in 1975. His son Edgar came ahead of the family and filed a claim on the SE ¼ of 17-2-4 E1. Later Edgar took a pre-emption on the SW ¼ 17-2-4 E1. Benjamin had stayed in Old Kildonan, and moved his family to Green Ridge in 1979. He had four sons and two daughters. His youngest son was John, who was 10 years old when he came to Franklin. The rest of the family married and got places of their own, but John stayed with his father until Benjamin's death in 1893, when he took over the land.

John married Alice Addison in 1900. John's mother lived with them until her death in 1916.

John and Alice had one son, Stewart, and two daughters, Lenora and Mae. Lenora married William McLennan in 1920, Mae married John M. Robinson in 1932.

Stewart left the farm when his father retired in 1929. He went to Saskatchewan and married Sarah Jane McCormick in 1931. He came back to Green Ridge, after moving around a bit, to farm the NW ¼ 9-2-4 E1. His son Ronald, who married Lorraine Rettaler, bought the home farm.

Stewart's daughter Mary Alice married Stanley Lindsay in 1955. They farm the SW ¼ of 21-1-4 E1 and the NW ¼ of 20-1-4 E1 and the SW ¼ of 19-1-4 E1. They have one son, Vance Charles, born 1956, and two daughters, Rhonda Mae, and Shelley Anne.

Benjamin Froom married Nancy Rombough. Their children were Edgar Jacob, who married Charotte Ramsey, Willis Elijah who married Hattie Addison, James Benjamin, who married Mary Pott, Margaret Edith who married Robert Ramsey, Armina Agnes, who married William Gunn and John Wilford who married Alice A. Addison.

James Benjamin Froom, the third oldest son of Benjamin Froom, married Mary Pott in 1897. They farmed at Green Ridge, and had seven children. Margaret Mariak, born in 1898, William Stanley, 1902, John Benjamin Theodore 1904, James Thomas 1909, Clarence Melville 1911, Herbert Horace 1916, and Douglas Lloyd 1919.

Herbert Froom married Annie Moore in 1942. They had three girls, Annie, Bernice, who married Jim Palmer in 1945, and had one son, and Margaret, who married James Cowan in 1922.

William married Ruth Lie in 1947, Benjamin married Lillian Ward in 1931, Jim married Edith Wrolsted and had six children. Douglas married Grace Helderson in 1941, and had one son. Melville married Alice Moore in 1935. Their children are Donald Charles, born 1935, Maxwell Clarence, 1937, Lorne Cameron 1931, Russell Henry, 1942, Glen Allan, 1947.

Donald married Roberta Jackson, 1957. They had two children, Fay Alice and Darryl Robert. Maxwell married Dorothy Rellaler in 1959. Their children are Pamela Ann, 1960, Bonnie Lou 1961, Randolph Paul, 1964, John Charles 1968, Karen Joy 1971. Pamela is married to Jacob Giesbrecht, and has two children, Joseph Gail, 1978, Jeremiah Daniel, 1980. Glen married Jo-Ann Kerda in 1969. Their children are Claudia, 1970, Jeffrey Glenn, 1973, Michelle Ann, 1976. Lorne married Anne Peplinski in 1977. They have one son, Michael Benedict. Russell lives with his parents.

Edgar Froom, oldest son of Stewart Froom was born 1856, and married Charlotte Ramsey in 1880. She was from Point Levy, Quebec. He participated in the Riel Rebellion in 1885.

His family are: George, who married Claire Schoeler and lived in Rainy River. He was born in 1882, at Green Ridge, died 1954. Edith, married James Miller, and lived in Stuartburn where their daughter Ethel still keeps a store. She was born in 1884, and died 1969. Annie, born 1886, married George Strange, and died in 1976 at the age of 94. Willis Edgar, was born in 1887 and died in 1970. Leonard, born 1889, married a Wilson and lived in Swan River, dying in 1982. Allison, was born in 1894, died in 1974, married Mildred Graham, and lived in Dominion City. They had four children, Garry, Don, Carol, and Laurel. Mildred lives in the Red River Valley Lodge in Morris. Charlotte, born in 1896, died in 1976, married Henry Batten. Bessie was born in 1892, and died in 1914. Roy, was born in 1891, and died in 1972. He married Stella Watson and lived in Florida. Edward was born in 1901, and lives in British Columbia. Eleanor was born in 1904, married Alfred Williams, had nine children and lives in Winnipeg.

Stewart Froom, 1916.

Left: Mary and Stanley Lindsay, children, l to r; Shelley, Vance, Rhonda.
Right: Sadie and Stewart Froom, Mary (7), and Ronald (9). 1942.

John and Alice Froom, children Lenora, Stewart, May. c. 1908.

Children of Edgar and Charlotte Froom, taken when their mother died, l to r; George, Willis, Annie, Edie, Eleanor, Charlotte, Alison, Leonard.

197

Lottie (Mrs. Henry Batten) holding baby Ethel Millar, who runs store at Stuartburn in 1982. Married Sam Pawloski. Man in picture is Morris Holgate.

L to r; George Froom, Jack Ramsay, Chalotte Ramsay Froom, Gary Froom.

Four generations; Lily Moore, Annie Froom, Dorothy Mayne, Gwen Mayne.

Edgar and Charlotte Froom, with son George. c. 1883.

Willis Edgar Froom. Railway mail clerk seated in front of case where he was given speed and efficiency test once a year. His lowest mark was 99 percent. c. 1915.

Left, Annie (Froom) Strange, George Strange, right, Edith (Froom) Millar, Jim Millar.

The Ramsey Family, Mrs. Ramsey, left, Mr. Ramsey, right, l to r; boys, George, Jim, Bob, Jack on floor; girls, Charlotte (Mrs. Edgar Froom), Minnie, Nell, Annie, Grace on floor.

Left: Herbert and Annie Froom, married 1942. They have three daughters, Dorothy Louise, married Donald Mayne, and have a son and daughter; Doreen married to Harry Ostrowsky and have a son and a daughter; Donna Anne married Allan Walters, and have two daughters. The Frooms farmed at Woodmore until they moved to Grunthal for a few years, then retired to Woodmore where Annie died in 1982.
Right: Jack and Lily Moore, parents of Annie Froom.

Left: Harry and Doreen Ostrowsky, Wanda and John.
Right: Allan and Donna Walters, Tara and Kimberly.

Donald, Dorothy, Gwen and Allan Mayne.

John and Alice Froom

L to r; back, Dennis, Dianne and Allan; front, Ron and Lorraine Froom, 1980.

Lorne and Anne Froom and Michael.

199

L to r; back, Randy Froom, Jake Giesbrecht, Maxwell and Dorothy Froom, Pam Giesbrecht, Bonnie Froom; middle, Melville and Alice Froom, Joseph Giesbrecht; front, John and Karen Froom.

Don Froom, holding Joy, Roberta Froom, holding Darryl.

L to r; back, Audra, Glenn Froom, wife Jo-Ann (Kerda); front, Jeffrey, Shelly.

Left: Mary (Pott) and James Benjamin Froom, 1924. *Right:* Margaret (Froom) and Jim Cowan.

Alice and Melville Froom, 1979; Russell Froom.

Lily (Ward) and Benjamin Froom Jr., 50th anniversary, 1981. Ben and Lily were married 1931. They purchased the former Ezra Post homestead and still reside at Woodmore, renting their farm land.

BERNHARD FRIESEN

L to r; top, Victor Friesen, Peter Friesen, Linda (Mrs. Frank) Friesen, Frank Friesen, Jake Sawatzky, George Friesen; bottom, Betty (Mrs. Vic) Friesen, Joyce (Mrs. P. B.), Mrs. Ben Friesen, Ben Friesen, Mary Sawatsky, Nitha (Mrs. George) Friesen. The Friesens moved to the fomer Nick Voth farm, 15-3-3 E1 at Arnaud in 1952. They lived on this farm until 1961, when they retired to Winnipeg. George Friesen, his wife Nitha and sons Bradley and Michael now run the farm. Their daughter Sharon lives in Winnipeg with husband Lorne Klassen. Peter, his wife Joyce and their four children, Barbara, Gordon, Donna and David farm at Arnaud. Mary and husband Jake Sawatzky and their two children, as well as Frank, wife Linda and two children live in Winnipeg. Victor, wife Betty and daughter live in British Columbia.

Geroge B. Friesen, l to r; back, Bradley, Sharon; front, Michael, Nitha, George.

PETE FRIESEN

Pete and Dinah (nee Schwab) Friesen came to the Ridgeville district in 1947. Their children attended Overstone, Ridgeville, Emerson, and Dominion City schools.

Boyd married Marge Poschner in 1959 and they have three children, Gail who is married to Lane Wirsh. They have a daughter, Kylie. Boyd's other two children are Rae-Anne and Daryl.

Yvonne married Reg Laufersweiler in 1963 and

L to r; back, Boyd, Yvonne, Dennis; front, Brian, Peter, Dinah, Marilyn Friesen.

they have three daughters, Maureen, Sherry and Cora.

Dennis is not married.

Marilyn married Ken Walters in 1965. They have three boys, Greg, Todd, and Trevor.

Brian and his wife, Heidi, were married in 1972. They have two children, Darcy, and Casandra.

The Friesens farmed on the SW 6-1-5E until 1967. They presently live in Carman.

WILLIAM FOSTEY

L to r; back, Ernest, husband of Ruth Fostey, Ruth, Jean, Ronald Baron (Jean's husband), Mrs. Johnny Fostey, Johnny Fosty, Audrey Fostey and husband Jerry; front, William and Tennie Fostey. William Fostey and Tennie Brodoway were married in Tolstoi in 1935. They lived at Overstoneville until moving to Emerson in 1967. William was a carpenter, who died in 1979. They have four children, Jean, Ruth, Johnny and Audrey.

HERBERT STEPHEN FRANCIS

Herbert Stephen Francis was born May 3, 1894 at Leeds, England. In 1912 he came to Canada and joined the Army in Canada in 1914. On his discharge he purchased the NE ¼ 2-1-3E through the Soldier Settlement Board. Crop losses due to constant flooding forced him to quit the claim in 1923.

On November 12, 1924 he married Martha (Wilkinson) Clifford, a widow with three sons. He then took over the Massey Harris agency in Ridgeville until 1930, when he was transferred to Dauphin. In 1939 he became investigator for D.N.A. in Winnipeg, until retirement in 1959. In 1977 they moved back to Franklin until Martha's death in 1979. Herb now lives in the St. Adolphe Nursing Home.

They have one daughter Eileen, who is married to R. Spence.

Herbert Stephen Francis; Eileen Francis, 1935.

Martha (Clifford) Francis, holding Doug, Harold and Lawrence. 1919.

TOMKO FEDORCHUK
(formerly Federczuk)

Tomko Fedorchuk, formerly Federczuk, and Helen Federczuk arrived in Canada on May 22, 1897 with three children. Tomko was born in 1850 in Bilche Zoloti, district Borshchiv, Galiciv Austria, Western Ukraine. He died August 23, 1924 at Tolstoi.

Helen was born in 1874 in Micholkiw, district Borshchiv, and died January 14, 1951 at Tolstoi.

Their children were Okasana, 11, Ivan, 10, Harry one year.

They bought their homestead for $10, the SE ¼ 4-2-5. children born here are Mary, Annie, Katherine and Alex.

Harry Fedorchuk born February 12, 1896, married Anna Andrusyk in 1927. They had three children Mary, Bill and Sonia.

Mary married John Grabowiecki June 3, 1947. They have three children, Casmier, Brian, Carol.

Bill married Rose (Kozak) October 22, 1955. They have two children, Theresa and Kenneth.

Sonia married Maurice Romaniuk, November 1954. They have six children, Barbara, Marcia, Greg, Nick, Elena and Patrick. They live in Winnipeg.

L to r; back: Mary (Nyznyk), Helen Fedorchuk holding grandchild Sonia Fedorchuk, Annie Nyznyk; front, Nettie Nyznyk, Bill Fedorchuk, Mary Fedorchuk. 1934.

Harry and Anne Fedorchuk, 1952. L to r; standing, Sonia, Bill, Mary. 25th wedding anniversary.

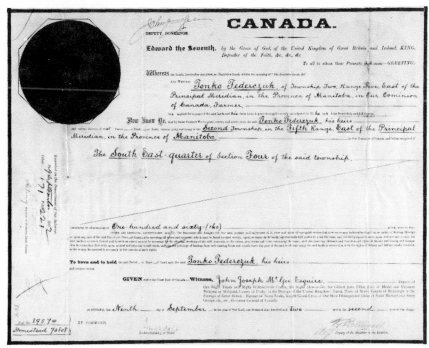

Dominion Lands Grant title to Tomko Federczuk, 1902.

Bill and Rose Fedorchuk, 25th wedding anniversary, 1980. L to r; Rose, Kenneth, Theresa; sitting, Bill.

JACOB P. FRIESEN

Jacob P. Friesen, son of Peter I. and Agatha (Rogalsky) Friesen was born in Marjewka, South Russia. The family arrived in Canada in 1925, and settled on the farm 33-3-3 near Arnaud. He married Margaretha Penner November 15, 1928. Their family consisted of seven children, Peter, Katherine, Margaret, Mary, Agatha, Nitha and Sally.

Mr. and Mrs. Friesen retired to North Kildonan, Winnipeg, in 1971. Mrs. Friesen died March 31, 1978 of cancer. Their son Peter and his family took over the home farm.

Margaretha (Penner) Friesen, Jacob P. Friesen.

L to r; back, Ed and Katherine (Friesen) Giesbrecht, John Janzen, George Friesen, Mary (Friesen) Bergen, John Bergen, Agatha (Friesen) Bergen, Jake Bergen, Wally Harder, Peter Friesen; front, Margaret (Friesen) Janzen, Nitha (Friesen) Friesen, Jacob and Margaret Friesen, Sally (Friesen) Harder, Nettie (Enns) Friesen. 1978.

Nettie, Peter, Wendy and Glenn Friesen, 1977.

JAMES P. FRENCH

James P. French was born in Ardley, Quebec, February 1857. He left home at an early age and went to the United States. In 1895 he married Isabel Reed, who was born in Bristol, Quebec in 1867. They were married in Bridgewater, South Dakota. They had three children, Sarah born 1896, James born 1898 and Robert born 1905.

In 1908 they came back to Canada, settled on a farm west of Dominion City, until they retired in Dominion City.

Sarah, married Edward Bradley, Robert never married, and James Jr. married Eva Hempton June 18, 1919, and had a family of 12 children. Two died in infancy. The 10 children were all raised and educated in Dominion City.

Wallace was born in 1920, married Maude Radford in 1944. They raised eight children, William Patricia, James, Ronald, Roxanne, Keith, Kathy and Terry.

Dorothy was born in 1921, married Edward Solnes in 1938. They had four children, Delores, Velma, Sandra and Darryl.

Jean was born in 1922, married Albert Kuhn in 1943, and raised three children, Robert, Wayne and Brenda.

Bernice was born in 1924, married Matthew Graydon in 1945, raised five children, Clifford, John, Marjorie, Donald and Gordon.

Thomas was born in 1925, married Wanda Desrosiers in 1962 raised three children, Charlotte, Nicole, and Amber.

Kenneth was born in 1928, married Madeline Henning in 1951, raised five children, Kimberly, Patrick, Maxine, Sherri-Lynn and Blair.

Norma was born in 1930, married Roderick Forbes in 1962. They raised two children, Mark and Naomi.

Vaughan was born in 1932, married Pat McKinnemy in 1962. They had one child Norrie Joan was born in 1935. She married Joseph Noonan in 1955. They had five children, Dale Thomas, Daniel, Lorrie, and Michael.

Gweneth was born in 1941 and married Bryan Nichols in 1962, they had two children, Todd and Dean.

Mrs. James French Sr. passed away in 1934 at the age of 66 and James Sr. died at the age of 93 in 1950. James Jr. passed away in 1970. Mrs. James French Jr. died in the house he was born in, in 1967.

James Sr. kept busy with his buck saw, and scythe until he was 92 years of age. He looked after the cemetery for many years after a hard days work in the bush or on the land. He also cared for his invalid wife.

Wallace French, Thomas French, Edward Solner, Albert Kuhn, Maude French, all served in the second world war. Wallace was wounded in action and spent many months in the hospital in England.

Jim and Isabel French

L to r; James Albert, James Percival French, Sarah (French) Bradley.

Jean (French) Kuhn and Albert Kuhn; Thomas French.

Left: Dorothy (French) Solnes, and husband Edward Solnes, 1942.
Right: Maude, Radford, Wallace French, wedding May 6, 1945, England.

L to r; back, Wallace, Vaughan, Ken, Tom French; front, Jean Kuhn, Joan Noonan, Dorothy Solnes, Norma Forbes, Gwen Nichole, Bernice Graydon, all nee French.

FREDERICK FELSCH

Frederick Felsch Sr. and wife Pauline (Drews) came to Gretna, in 1892 from Wolingan, Russia. In 1896 they moved with seven children to Friedensthal and settled on SW 18-1-4E where two more children were born. In 1898 his brother Louis and his wife came to live with them before moving to Emerson. Although the farm was in Springbank, South Dakota, their children attended Emerado School to take advantage of lessons being taught in German.

Augusta (1882) married Charles Sundberg; Rudolph; Minnie (1891) married Ted Kein; Julia married Paul Jeske and had two girls, Thelma and Martha; Bertha; Helen and Mathilda died in their teens; Rudolph married Ida Casper and had three children, Lydia, Irene and Esther; William; Frederick Jr.

Frederick Jr. (1899), the youngest child, was the only one to remain in the municipality where he farmed the land his father settled on. In 1925 he married Amanda Mueller and they now reside in Emerson. They have two children, Margaret, married Emil Pomrenke, Wilfred, married Evelyn

Berg of Menisino in 1954 and continues to farm his grandfather's land with the help of his three sons.

Robert married Carol Adcock in 1978 and has one daughter, Jennifer.

Charles married June Marcynuik in 1979; and has one daughter, Leslie.

Frederick Felsch Jr. and Amanda Mueller, 1925.

Frederick Felsch, Sr.; Pauline (Drews) Felsch, c. 1944.

Rudolph Felsch and Ida Casper

Back, Paul Jeske; front, Thelma, Julie (Felsch) Jeske, holding Martha.

L to r; Augusta (Felsch) Sundberg, Minnie (Felsch) Kein, Bertha Felsch, Fred Felsch. Jr.

Wilfred Felsch; William Felsch

L to r; Robert Felsch, Carol Felsch, June Felsch holding Jennifer, Charles Felsch.

Wilf, Evelyn (Berg) and Leslie Felsch.

WILLIAM FIELDS

In 1872 William and Martha Fields, both originally from England, and their only child, Rose, moved to Winnipeg from Montreal. William was employed by the governor, and his occupation as listed on an old Insurance Policy was engineer.

In May 1873, he moved to 2-1-3 E1. Flooding conditons existed on the flats so he was forced to re-locate on a new homestead SW ¼ 27-1-4E in 1879. He also purchased lots 108, 111 in Roseau Crossing, now Dominion City, from Alex Waddell. In 1884 he purchased the SW ¼ 27-1-4E, and farmed until his death 1888. Martha was one of the earliest mid-wives in the area, and she remained on the farm with her daughter until her death in 1906.

They had one daughter, Rose Martha, who married William Wilkinson.

Fred Jr., Amanda and Margaret.

206

L to r; back, unidentified; front, William Fields, Martha Fields, Rose Martha.

PETER I. FRIESEN

Peter I. and Agatha Friesen came to Arnaud from Russia in 1925. Mr. Friesen bought the 33-3-3 E1 from the Emmert Foundation. In 1935 they moved into a house on Gerhard's farm, where they lived until Peter died in 1953 and Agatha in 1957. The four youngest Friesen children farmed in Franklin - John on 36-3-2 E1, Gerhard 31-3-3 E1, Peter P. 32-3-3 E1, and Jacob P. remained on the home farm.

L to r; back, Dan, Peter M.; front, Jennifer, Esther, Lynette. Peter is the oldest son of Gerhard Friesen, and got his education at Empress School and the Mennonite Collegiate Institute, Gretna. In 1962 his uncle Peter P. Friesen died, and Peter M. took over the farm on 32-3-3 E1. He married Esther Kuhl from Morden in 1965. They had a broiler breeder poultry operation for 10 years, and in 1982 are grain farmers.

Left: Gerhard and Neta Friesen. Both were born in Russia. They are mixed farmers, and their children are Peter, married Esther Kuhl, Gerhard, married Kathy Braun, Katherine, married Ed Cornelsen, Neta, married Jacob Loewen, Jacob, married Emily Dueck.
Right: Jacob G. Friesen and Emily (Dueck) Friesen. Farmers at Arnaud, on the former G. P. Friesen farm.

L to r; back, Gerry, Gerhard; front, Richard, Kathy (Braun) Friesen. Mixed farmers on the NE ¼ 31-3-3 E1, formerly the George Toews farm.

TELESPHORE FILLION

Telesphore Fillion, son of Louis Fillion, was born January 5, 1888, at St. Jean Baptiste. In 1911, he married Anna Baril, and farmed on the north boundary of Franklin Municipality, just west of St. Jean Baptiste, until 1929. In 1929 they moved east of town, and in 1945 they retired to St. Jean Baptiste. Anna died in 1961, Telesphore in 1966.

They had 13 children, Emile, born in 1912, married Annette Granger in 1935; David, born in 1914, married Florence Marion in 1938; Josephine, born 1915, married Armand Dumontier in 1935; Marie, born 1917, married Wilfred Dupuis in 1933; Ida, born 1919, married Maurice Berard in 1944, was widowed, married Henri Peterson in 1960; Solange, born in 1920, married

Albert Bérard on June 15, 1943; Gérard, born in 1922, married Thérèse Sabourin in 1953; Albert, born in 1924, married Jeannine Bruneau on September 25, 1946; Antoinette, born in 1925, married Lionel Marion on June 20, 1943; Irene, born in 1927, remained single; Denise, born in 1929, married Georges S. Marion on October 27, 1949; Lucien, born in 1931, married Elizabeth Desrosiers on July 31, 1954; Ulysse, born in 1936, married Emma Sabourin on May 9, 1959, died in 1970.

Albert Fillion took over the family farm in 1945, moved to river lot 240 but kept on farming the land. He and Jeannine (Bruneau) have a family of seven. Yvette, married Tim Robina, and has two children, Jocely, married Ron Sinclair and has one child; Claude lives at Stonewall, has a wife and two children, Ginette married Jeffery Johnson, has one son; Colette works in Winnipeg; Estelle works in Winnipeg; and Danielle is at home. In 1979 Albert and Jeannine retired to St. Jean Baptiste.

The Telesphore Fillion family

Front, Estelle, Danielle, Colette; back, Claude, Yvette, Jeannine, Albert, Ginette, Jocelyne.

Front, Jeanette; back, Emile, Leo, Lorraine, Raymond, Marcel, Annette, Paul, Armand.

WILLIAM FOULDS

William Foulds came from Northern England. He married a woman named Daniels, and settled on the NE ¼ of 28-3-4 E1, and took up the NW ¼ of 27-3-4 E1. He was the first mail man in the district, and would walk to Emerson and bring the mail on his back.

Their family were John, Sam, Charlie, Albert, Robert, and Bella, who married Ted Creamer. Sam had tuberculosis and was bed ridden for years, and repaired watches. Charlie was caretaker of the Green Ridge school. Albert was a horse trainer, Robert a teacher, who was studying to be a druggist at the time of his death from influenza.

David Fillion family

Mrs. Foulds, Charlie Foulds, Bob Foulds.

G MATTHEW GRIER

Matthew Grier and Sarah Whyte were married in 1862 in Brantford, Ontario. Matthew was born in Scotland in 1842 and came to Canada as a child. The family arrived in Manitoba in 1885 and settled at Woodmore. There were 11 children:

John 1863-1949.
Sarah 1866-1949.
Mary Jane 1868-?
Andy 1870-1921.
Earnest 1872-1958.
Edward 1874-?
Ralph 1876-1949.
Herbert 1878-1955.
Olive 1881-1966.
James 1883-1962.
George 1885-1963.

Matthew held a commission as a Police Magistrate, and his knowledge of horse medicine won him respect in the municipality. First Herbert and George, and then Herbert's son Roy carried on this medicinal care of livestock until veterinarians were established in Franklin. Matthew Grier died in 1924 and Sarah, his wife, predeceased him in 1923.

A few years after the death of James in 1962 the homestead half section was purchased by Morris, grandson of Matthew Grier, and is still a productive farm.

The W. D. Grier farm is the SE¼ of 18-2-5E. Ownership is dated back to 1886 when Sarah Grier, wife of Matthew, purchased the land. These pioneers planted a row of maple trees along the east side which still stand today, a familiar landmark.

In 1945, Bill and Joyce settled on this farm. They operate a mixed farming unit, Bill also is serving as a Councillor for Ward 4. They have raised six children.

Cheryl and Earl Robinson live in Winnipeg, Manitoba. Terry and Marlene (Lendrum) live in Edmonton. Patricia and Wilbur Bilachuk live in Arbakka, Manitoba. Christopher and Daphne (Olafson) live in Riverton, Manitoba. Gregory in Edmonton and Russell in Winnipeg.

David E. Badgley was born February 15, 1874, in Hollowell, Ontario. His parents were David Badgley and Elizabeth Yomans. He married Henrietta Kleinsteuber of Hastings County in 1888, and in 1899 settled on the SW¼ of 21-2-5 E1. Lena Ica was born August 19, 1901. Edith Christina was born September 29, 1903. In 1908 Carl Melton was born, in 1911 Clara Dorothy, in 1914 Tomas Albert, and in 1916 Mildred Rose was born. Edith Christina married Herbert Grier and had 10 children. Herbert died March 24, 1955.

Mabel Edith, born 1922, married Cecil Kleinsteauber, and had one girl, Gale. Roy Ernest married Edna Gill, and had two sons and one daughter. Willie Donald married Joyce McClenna, had six children. Ross Ralph married Audrey Hoar, had four children, divorced, and married Gertie Danylchuk. Lewis Herbert, born October 10, 1930, and Lori married Fern Belnap, and has one daughter. Morris David, born October 10, 1932, married Audrey Jack, and has two daughters and one son. Clifford Allen, born August 24, 1936, married Sonya Bozyk, and lives on the old homestead. They have three daughters. Shirley Hazel Louise, born September 8, 1938, married Art Phlip and has two sons, Tyler and Brett. Ada Pearl, born March 24, 1945, married Bill Tinkess, and has two sons, John and Jesse.

JAMES GRIER

James Grier (1883-1962) married Lena Badgley (1901-1947) on November 13, 1919.
They had 13 children:
Ethel and Harold Gilchrist live in Vancouver, B.C.
Earl and Kay (Roberts) live in Rennie, Man.
Lenora and William Maryshak live in Penticton, B.C.
Norman and Edith (Goll) live in Ridgeville, Man.
Murray and Mary live in Fort Smith, N.W.T.
Vera and R. Webster, G. Goyot live in Penticton, B.C.
Alvin and Beatrice live in Medicine Hat, Alta.
Neal and Lorraine (Lesperance) live in Brandon, Man.
Lillian and William Jack live in Ridgeville, Man.
Allen and Marion (Malley) live in Spruce Grove, Alta.
Andrew (twin of Allen) and Betty (Bogseth) live in Stoney Mountain, Man.
Brian and Carol (Warketine) live in Winnipeg, Man.
Joyce (Gilchrist) lives in Vancouver, B.C.
Two children passed away in infancy.

HERBERT GRIER

Herbert Grier (1878-1955) married Edith Badgley on April 6, 1921.
They had nine children:
Mabel, Roy, Willie, Ross, Lewis, Morris, Clifford, Shirley and Ada.
Roy, Willie, Morris and Clifford reside in Woodmore, Manitoba.

Olive Grier (1881-1966) married Tom Stewart. They had three children:

Lyla, Hazel, Lewellyn, and one step-daughter Vinie.

CLIFFORD GRIER

Clifford Allen Grier, youngest son of Herbert and Edith Grier, married Sonya Bozyk of Vita on March 7, 1959. They took up residence on the Herb Grier farm 16-2-5 E1.

They have three daughters:

Donna is a civil servant with the Provincial Government, Beverley, a graduate nurse from the Brandon Mental Health Centre, and Lisa is completing her education at Roeau Valley Collegiate in Dominion City.

Cliff and Sonya have a mixed dairy, beef and grain farm.

ROY GRIER

Roy Grier and Edna Gill were married in Windsor, England on March 14, 1946 while both were serving with the R.C.A.F. at Lincolshire base, England.

Edna was born in Woodgreen, North London.

In 1946 Roy returned to his farm in Woodmore. Edna followed in 1947. They operated a mixed farm until the mid 70's, and now operate a grain farm.

They have three married children:

Bradley, Richard and Trudy.

MORRIS GRIER

Morris and Audrey Grier were married June 29, 1957. They purchased the former Guy Post farm SW 17-2-5E and operate a dairy business. In 1969 they purchased the Matthew Grier homestead and now farm a section of land.

The Griers started their Brown Swiss herd in 1961 with the purchase of 14 animals from an American breeder in Warren, Minnesota. They have been showing purebred Brown Swiss cattle since 1964.

Today the Griers keep a herd of 90 head with 40 cows milking. The high butterfat productivity of the breed and its quiet, friendly nature attracted the Griers to this breed of cattle.

They have three children:

Lesley is attending University of Winnipeg completing her degree in Education.

Candace is a legal secretary in Winnipeg.

Kenten is completing his Grade XII.

NORMAN JAMES GRIER

Norman Grier began his apprenticeship in mechanics under Ted Walters in 1946. He worked for various firms and in various places until 1962 when he purchased the Ridgeville Service Garage and took up residence in the George Gushiliak home. In 1957 he married Edith Ethel Gall, and their children are:

Len.

Glen Dale, who attended Red River Community College and is a mechanic. He married Marianne Enns.

Cindy Hope.

Sandra Lyn.

Leonard Brian is married to Kimberley McCallum and lives in Winnipeg with son Jackson Gabriel.

Cindy Home married Kenneth Toll and lives in the former Beverley Spence home.

James and Lena Grier

Matthew and Sarah Grier

L to r; back, Agnes Lilian, Charles Burrell; front, Sarah Margaret, Charles Edward (in dark dress), Ruth Viola (in chair), Sarah (Grier) Burrell, Mary Jane.

Edith Badgley, Herbert Grier, Olive Grier.

Back, Edith (Grier) Badgley, David, Henrietta, Clara; front, Millie Badgley and Mabel Grier,(daughter of Edith) 1926.

Ralph, John, Andrew and Ernest Grier.

Tom Badgley, well-known carpenter of the Woodmore area.

George Grier and Mary Jane Grier.

Cliff, Lisa, Bev, Donna and Sonya Grier.

Left: Kathy and Richard, Danielle and baby Nicole (not shown) Grier. They live in North Battleford, Saskatchewan.
Right: Trudy and Brent Mitchell, married March 1979, they reside in Surrey, B.C. Inset, Derek Mitchell.

L to r; back, Willie, Roy, Ross, Lewis, Clifford Morris; front, Ada (Tinkess), Edith, Mabel (Kleinsteuber), Shirley (Phlip).

Trudy, Edna, Bradley, Carol, Roy, Edith, Richard Grier.

Kelsey and Joey, sons of Bradley and Carol Grier.

Edith, Kenten, Audrey, Candace, Morris and Lesley.

Front row, l to r; Willie and Joyce Grier, Teresa Grier, Darrin, Robinson, Nyle Robinson, Crystal Grier, Gregory Grier, Russell Grier, Marlene Grier.

Back row, Earl Robinson, Cheryl Robinson, Wilmer Bilachuk, Jason Bilachuk, Karen Bilachuk, Patricia Bilachuk, Daphne Grier (hidden), Christopher Grier, Terrence Grier.

Children: Cheryl, Terrence, Patricia, Chris, Greg, Russell.

Trevor, Carol (Warkentine), Brian, Terri Grier.

Paul, Lorraine, Neale, David Grier of Brandon. Inset, Christopher - son of David and Debbie (Ribbit).

212

L to r; back, Brian, Andy, Allen, Neale Alvin, Murray, Norman; front, Joyce, Lillian, Vera, Lenora, Ethel, Earl (1962).

Back, Glen, Norm, Shenda, Len; front, Mariane, Edie, Kim; kneeling, Ken and Cindy (Grier) Toll.

WILLIAM GEILER

Otto Geiler came to Canada from Hohenleuben, Germany, in 1902. In 1897 he had married Christine Walfrun. They came to Ridgeville in 1904, to the Burrbidge place. In 1905 they purchased the NE ¼ of 6-1-5 E1. They had ten children. One of them was William, born September 1, 1911. He bought the family farm when he married Erna Broszeit in 1943.

They had five children:

Margaret married Dennis Schwark in 1964. They have two children, Michael and Kristen.

Linda married George Hildebrand in 1965. They have two children, Raymond and Tannis.

David married Marie Unrau in 1972. They have three children, Jeffrey, Jennifer and JoAnna. They live in Winnipeg.

Sharron married Jack Zacharias in 1970. They have three children, Sandra, Leanne and Sheldon. Jack passed away in 1980 following a tragic air accident. Sharron lives in Altona.

Adeline married Frank Weedmark in 1974. They have one daughter Shannon, and live in Winnipeg.

William and Erna farmed until 1974, when they sold to R. Tait, and retired to Emerson. Linda and Margaret also live in Franklin municipality.

Christine's parents, Heinrich and Anna Walfrum, came to Canada in 1914, lived in Franklin for a short time, then moved to Brandon. Anna died in 1930, and Heinrich came back to Franklin to die in 1937.

Erna (Broszeit) Geiler came to Canada with her parents in 1924. Her grandfather and other family members arrived the same year. Erna's father was Alfred Broszeit, and five children were born to him and his wife Natalie, in Ridgeville, being: Gertrude, Agnes, Helmut, Edward, Harold.

The Broszeit's moved to Emerson in 1956, after the accidental death of their youngest son Harold.

Alfred died November 10, 1966, and Natalie lives in the Altona Personal Care Home.

Gertrude Broszeit remained single, Agnes married Irvin Hoffman, has a son, Glen; Helmut married Marion Friese, has five children: Douglas, Richard, Brian, Wesley and Debbie; Edward married Helen Dyschuk and they have one son Darryl.

George and Linda (Geiler) Hildebrand were married in 1965. In 1976 they came to the NW ¼ of 16-2-5 E1, and purchased the Woodmore Store, renaming it the G ¿ L Convenience Store. Linda is also postmistress, and George commutes to Winnipeg where he works for Versatile Manufacturing.

Otto and Christine Geiler, 1956.

William and Erna Geiler

Sitting, Otto and Christine Geiler; l to r; Wanda, Clara, Lily, Herman, William, Felise; missing, Alma, three other children deceased in early childhood.

Alfred and Natalie Broszeit

Broszeit family, l to r; back, Natalie, Alfred; middle, Gertrude, Agnes, Erna; front, Harold, Halmut, and Edward.

Raymond, Linda, George Hildebrand; front, Tannis.

214

L to r; standing, Dennis Schwark, George Hildebrandt, Marie (Unrau) Geiler, David Geiler, Jack Zacharias, Frank Weedmark, Michael Schwark, Raymond Hildebrandt.

Sitting, Margaret (Geiler) Schwark, Linda (Geiler) Hildebrandt, Erna Geiler, Wiliena Geiler, Sharron (Geiler) Zacharias holding Sheldon, Adeline (Geiler) Weedmark holding Shannon.

Sitting front, Tannis Hildebrandt, Kristen Schwark, Leanne Zacharias, Jennifer Geiler, Jeffrey Geiler, Sandra Zacharias, missing, JoAnna Geiler.

IWAN GERMAN

On July 7, 1897 the family of Iwan and Oksana German arrived in Canada from the Ukraine. Iwan, son of Danylo German and Maria Andrusyk, was born in 1838, wife Oksana in 1844. They arrived with Elia and wife Katherine, Fred, Maria, Matey (whose wife and five children were left in the Ukraine) and Gaberal.

Iwan and Oksana German homesteaded the N.W. ¼ 12-2-5 in 1899. Iwan died April 29, 1925, Oksana died March 9, 1937, in Tolstoi. Elia German and his wife Katherine lived six miles east of Stuartburn for the first six months in 1897 till the fires burnt their log cabin. They moved back

Murray, Terry, Donavan, Lois (Kowaliuk), Kenneth, Glenn, Jeanne and William.

to the section of 15-2-25 to file the homestead S.E. 3-2-5 on August 20, 1898.

Their first family was a set of twins which died in infancy. They had a family of three daughters and two sons: Mary, Lena, Ann, John, William.

They lived on the same homestead till Katherine died on June 1, 1948 and Elia died on January 14, 1949.

For two years William German served in the Royal Canadian Artillery and was stationed in P.E.I. and Vancouver where he met his wife, Jeanne.

William and Jeanne German are living on the S.E. ¼ 3-2-5 in the Franklin Municipality. Their family consists of:

Kenneth and his wife Margie, their children Kevin and Tanya.

Donavan.

Glenn and wife Joan.

Terry and wife Diane.

Murray and wife Betty.

Lois and husband Steve Kowaliuk, their children Rebecca and Stephanie.

ADAM GRAYDON

Adam Graydon and his wife came from Beaverton, Ontario in 1872 with his family: Adam, Robert, Samuel, Thomas, Jack, Alice (Mrs. Joe Sullivan), and one daughter remained in Ontario.

Adam Graydon Jr. married Jane Blinkensop in 1886 and came to farm S. 13-3-3 E1 in 1900.

Adam and Jane raised two boys:

George, born in 1887.

John, born in 1889.

John remained on the family farm until 1945. He moved to B.C. in 1947 where he resided until his death in 1960.

George married Ferron Devitt in 1917 and farmed S. 13-3-3 E1 until 1947 when they retired to B.C. They remained there until their death, George in 1961 and Ferron in 1972.

George raised four children:

Agnes, born in 1918. She married Alfred Coffman in 1945 and had one daughter Zenna.

Robert, born in 1919. He married Ealliene Elliott in 1946 and had three boys, Thomas, Allan and Robert. Robert farmed his grandfather's farm until 1967.

Matthew, born in 1921, married Bernice French in 1945. They had five children, Clifford (1946), John (1947), Marjorie (1949), Donald (1952) and Gordon (1953). Matthew and Bernice have lived and farmed in Franklin municipality all their lives.

Clifford married Rose Ellen Smith of Colorado

and has one son, Warren. They live on the old Bill Hosick farm.

John married Debbra Lewis of Vernon, B.C. and has three children, Jay, Jamie and Chyanne. They live in the Woodmore district. John farms and works as a boiler maker.

Marjorie married Michael Stepaniuk of Rosa and has four children, Tammy, Vincent, Robert and Walter. They farm in the Rosa area.

Donald married Peggy Lou Lenton and has two children, Kimberley and Shawn.

Gordon married Laura Bingham and has two children, Crystal and Shane. They live in Dominion City. Gordon lives in British Columbia.

Glynn Graydon married Hazel Forbes in 1949 and lives in B.C. They had two children, Jean (deceased) and Patricia.

L to r; back, Clifford, John, Marjorie, Gordon, Donald; front, Bernice and Matthew.

Titan Tractor and plow used on Graydon farm.

LEO GRABOWSKI

Leo, born in 1864 in Poland, and Mary, born in 1866 were married in Winnipeg. They lived in North Dakota for three years, then bought a homestead in Canada (SW ¼-4-1-5 E1).

They had seven sons and four daughters. Five sons, all deceased, farmed in the Franklin municipality.

Since 1982 two grandsons, Ambrose and Joe Grabowski with their mother, Mary, wife of the late Lawrence Grabowski, have been farming the original homestead.

John was born in 1895 in North Dakota and came to Canada with his parents. He was raised on the homestead of Leo Grabowski. He went to the Bradley School, and worked on different farms.

In 1925, he married Helen Petrowski. They farmed on S.E. 9-1-5 for 30 years.

They had one daughter and one son who died in infancy.

They then retired to Tolstoi. Helen was active in community affairs. They are both now deceased.

Leo and Mary Grabowski

John and Helen Grabowski

COLIN GRANGER

Colin Granger arrived in Dominion City in 1951. He was a grain buyer employed by Lake of the Woods Milling Company. Colin was born in North Battleford, Saskatchewan.

In 1952 Colin married Helen Matheson of Tilston, Manitoba. They resided in the old Baskerville House on Ginn Avenue for 20 years.

Their children are:

Judy Ann, born in August, 1952.

Deborah Lee, born in February, 1954.

Edward Grant, born in December, 1956.

Raymond Gerald, born in September, 1961.

Lake of the Woods Milling Company was bought out by Ogilvie Flour Mills and later sold to Manitoba Pool, which it still remains.

In 1971 Debbie married Larry Rettaler. They have one son, Jackie Norman.

In 1972 Judy married Gilles Graveline of Letellier. They have three children, Chad, Jason and Candice.

In the winter of 1972, Colin transferred to the Pool elevator at Centennial Siding in West St. Paul, and the family moved to Winnipeg.

Grant married Karen Ballegear in 1978. They have two children, Carla and Bradley.

Raymond is finishing his education and living in Winnipeg.

Colin left the Manitoba Pool Company in 1975 and now is employed with Grain Insurance and Guarantee.

Colin Granger family, 1981.

MICHAEL GAWRONSKY

Michael Gawronsky arrived in Franklin in 1898. They had a friend Alex Tkachyk who had arrived a year earlier, who took them in. His wife was Justina Didychuk, and they were both born in the Ukraine. They had three children: John, Mary, Alice.

Michael died in 1946, and Justina Gawronsky died in 1982. They are buried at Plankey Plains Cemetery.

Alice (Gawronsky) (Zgoralski). Harrowing on the farm in Woodmore.

John Gawronsky haying.

Harvesting in 1939. Alice Zgoralski (nee Gawronsky) on the tractor.

JIM GILBERT

Jim Gilbert came to Manitoba from Lochlin, Ontario in 1898. He settled in Woodmore, buying the N.E. ¼ 14-2-4 E1 where he built a shack on the hill, still known as the Gilbert Hill. He heard that if a man moved to Texas and bought land he could make a fortune, so Mr. Gilbert sold

Jim Gilbert

his farm and got land in Texas. Things didn't work out, and he returned to Woodmore. He worked at various jobs, here and in Arnaud. He was a horse man for a number of years, and was known as a kind friend and neighbour.

JACOB GUENTHER

Mr. and Mrs. Jacob J. Guenther, parents of 11, who had suffered heavy financial losses during the depression, heard of available land in Franklin municipality. Checking it out, they bought a quarter section minus two acres of NW ¼ 26-2-5E from Hudson's Bay Company in 1935. This was totally open, uncultivated land with no buildings on it. Because there were no fences around the acreage, roaming herds of cattle grazed it in summer.

Jacob was in the group responsible for the first Mennonite church in the community. He was also a member of the local school board in the late 40's.

The Guenthers retired to Gretna in 1959. Both died in 1976: Mrs. Guenther on July 12 and Mr. Guenther on October 21. Both were 89 years of age.

Mr. and Mrs. Guenther beside just recently planted evergreens.

Rose, Susan, Mrs. Jacob Guenther, Mr. Jacob Guenther and Elizabeth, gathered on a Sunday forenoon for a devotional and sing-a-long under the cottonwoods at the south end of the house.

ABRAHAM GATESON

Abraham Gateson came to Neche, North Dakota, from Poland about 1904. Here he met Alvina Hentz, who had arrived the same year. They married, and came to farm the NE ¼ of 19-1-5 E1.

They had eight daughters: Hilda (Strege), Emma (Carlson), Esther (Kachman), Edythe (Nelson), Violet (Strege), Tillie (McBride), Sarah (Nicholson), Evelyn (Gaetz).

Abraham died in 1940, and Alvina lived with her daughter Evelyn, Mrs. Philip Gaetz. In 1945 she and Violet moved to Morris, where she married J. Kran. Alvina died in 1974.

Abraham and Alvina (Guertzen) Gateson.

L-r; Hilda, Violet, Emma, Tillie, Esther, Sarah, Edythe and Evelyn.

JACOB GOLETSKI

Jacob Goletski and Helen Malicki emigrated to Canada with their parents from Austria in 1897. Jacob was 17 years old, Helen age 12. They were married January 12, 1900, by Father Groetchel, a visiting missionary priest of the Oblate Order of Mary Immaculate. They made their home on Jacob's homestead in Gardenton. In 1917, Jacob purchased SW ¼ section 10, three and a half miles north of Tolstoi, from Ferdinand Reid.

Mr. and Mrs. Goletski had 10 children; two died in infancy and Nellie at the age of 13, John, Joe, Stanley, Frank, Walter, Mary, and Bernice.

They commuted to the land in Tolstoi until 1933. In 1932 Mr. Goletski purchased the SW ¼ section 15 from Blackered and Funk, who had taken it over for taxes. He farmed these two quarters jointly with his son Frank until 1950 when he retired to live in Tolstoi, purchasing a home from Steve Slobodian. In 1960, Mr. and Mrs. Goletski purchased a small residence next to their daughter, Mrs. George Choboter, where Mrs. Goletski died in 1965 and Mr. Goletski in 1967.

Frank and Antoinette (Hacault) Goletski were married in the Holy Trinity Church in Tolstoi June 14, 1942. Antoinette was a former resident of Bruxelles. In 1950, when Frank's parents, Mr. and Mrs. Jacob Goletski, retired to live in the village of Tolstoi, he took over the family farm.

They had five children: Edward, Veronica, Lawrence, Rosemarie, Richard.

Frank and Antoinette farmed until 1967 when they sold to Ron Griffin. They now make their home in Kelowna, B.C.

Mr. and Mrs. Jacob Golestki with their youngest daughter Bernice Choboter in 1943.

Four generations. Stanley, Jacob, Bert, and Christopher Golestki.

Mr. and Mrs. Frank Golestki with their grandchildren, Cindy Charlene, Shelley, Randy and Dana.

40th Wedding Anniversary. Larry, Richard, Edward, Mr. and Mrs. Frank Golestski, Rosemarie and Veronica.

JACOB GOETZ

Jacob Goetz (1860-1928) and wife Elsbitha (1866-1938) immigrated to Canada in April 1898 with four children: Gabriel age 12, Susana age seven, Christina age four and Josef age three. They settled at Gretna, where John was born in

1899 and Jacob Jr. in 1900. In 1901 they moved to Tolstoi. Margaret was born in 1902.

Later they moved to Overstoneville area by the one mile road and farmed there for the remainder of their years. William was born in 1908 and remained on the home place until his retirement to Rideville in 1971. Three children had died in infancy.

Jacob died on April 28, 1928, and Elsbitha died on June 2, 1938.

Gabriel married Anna Edinger.

Susana married Leopold Schnell.

Christina married Harry Krietz.

Jacob married Annie Keil.

Margaret married Jim Cutt.

William married Elsie Schnell.

Gabriel Goetz, born in Manasten, West Galicia on October 20, 1886, and his wife Anna Edinger farmed until 1954 when they retired to Emerson. Gabriel died on June 21, 1975 and Anna on July 18, 1977.

They had eight children:

Edward married Julia Nedohin and farmed in the Overstoneville area, then moved to Winnipeg. They have two children: Marlene, who married Tom (Allan) McDougall and they have two sons, Tom Jr. and Jim (their daughter Sharon died in 1972); and Clarence, who married Esther Ward.

Eva, died in 1946, married Walter Fast of Overstoneville, they had one son, Bobby, who is married and has four children; Bobby resides in Winnipeg.

Hilda married Walter Davidson. They have two daughters, June and Beverley. June with husband Gary Saunders and their two daughters live in B.C. Beverley, and her husband Don Skog, live in Flin Flon.

Margaret married Jake Suppes of Overstoneville. They have two sons, Grant and Blaine. Grant with wife, Joan, and two children live in Calgary; Blaine with wife, Louise, and their two children farm at Plumas.

Phillip married Evelyn Gateson of Overstoneville and farmed at Glenboro. They have two sons, Collin and Gerald. Collin has two daughters and lives in Bedford, Nova Scotia, and Gerald is in Ottawa.

Elizabeth married August Epler. They have two sons, Gary and Dennis. Gary with wife, Rosemary, and three children farm at Brunkild and Dennis with wife, Marilyn, and two children live in Strathmore, Alberta.

Ernie married Elona Rentel and farmed in Franklin from 1949-1965. Due to ill health and three major operations he had to give up farming and lives in Emerson. They have two children, Wayne and Donna Lynne. Wayne with wife, Annette, and two sons live in Pilot Mound, and Donna Lynne with husband, Brian Knutt, and son Cory live in Emerson.

Russell, died in 1969, married Evelyn Geske. They have one son, Bruce, who lives in Winnipeg.

Jacob Goetz Jr. married Anna Elizabeth Keil in 1924 and farmed the SW ¼ 18-1-5E. They had two children, Gordon and Lorraine. Anna died in 1947 at the age of 44. In 1951, he married Olga (Kusmaul) Latschislaw. She had three young sons, Theodore, Herman and Karl from her previous marriage. They retired from farming in 1967 and moved to Emerson. Jacob died in December 1981. Olga is presently living in Emerson.

Gordon married Laura Lenton in September, 1949. They rented the NE 7-1-5E until 1954 when they moved to Ridgeville. Gordon was a caterpillar operator for W. T. Schultz from 1950-55, loading gravel. In 1956 they purchased and moved to the NW ¼ 22-1-4E, where they still reside. Gordon was a turkey rancher from 1955 to 1967, and a Registered Hereford breeder. He sold his beef herd and went to work for the Department of Public Works, Emerson, in 1978.

Laura began clerking at J. P. Tanchak's General Store, Ridgeville, in 1954 and continued working in the store until 1976.

She is presently employed as Clerk-Receptionist with Agriculture Canada, Food Production and Inspection Branch at Emerson.

Lorraine married Stewart Riach.

Step-sons (Olga (Kusmaul) Latschislaw's children):

Theodore and wife, Dorothy, reside in Portage la Prairie. They have three sons.

Karl resides in Winnipeg.

Herman was accidentally killed in 1968, leaving a wife and two sons.

WILLIAM GOETZ

William Goetz married Elsie Schnell in 1939 and they worked the family farm SW 8-1-5E. In 1971 they sold the farm to Larry Retaller and moved into Ridgeville.

They have four children: Harold, Elizabeth, Calvin, and Audrey.

Harold married Margaret Fehr in 1967. They have three children, Jason, and twins Keith and Kevin.

Elizabeth married Vladmir Kozak in 1967. They have two children, Laurie and Glen.

Calvin married Sharon Boyd in 1972 and they have two children, Trevor and Shannon.

Audrey married Bill Hermon in 1980 and their two children are Donavan and Christie.

220

Jacob and Elsbitha (Schoffer) Goetz

Gabriel and Anna Goetz with Edward, Hilda, Beth, Ernie, Phil, Margaret and Russell, 1958.

Gordon, Jacob and Anna Goetz, Lorraine, 1938.

Harold, Calvin and Betty Goetz.

Left: Gordon and Laura Goetz, 1949.
Right: Calvin, holding Shannon, Sharon and Trevor Goetz.

Harold, Margaret, twins Keith and Kevin and Jason Goetz.

Front, William and Elsie Goetz; back, Audrey, Harold, Calvin and Betty.

Laurie, Betty and Glen Kozak.

Margaret and William Goetz

Audrey holding Donavan and Christie Herman.

221

ISAAC GOERTZ

Isaac Goertz arrived in Arnaud from Russia in 1930. In 1938 he bought 320 acres of land in Franklin, with a barn. This farm was sold to Martin Penner in 1964, and the Goertz's retired to Winnipeg.

They have five children:

Isaac Jr. and his wife, Frieda, live in Ontario and have five children.

Mary and her husband, Henry Wiebe, and six children live in Manitou.

Nitha and Martha live in Winnipeg.

Olga and her husband, Henry Wiebe, have three children and live in Winnipeg.

Four generations, Isaac, Isaac I., Peter I., Kami M. Goertz.

Four generations, Isaac, Isaac I., Bernhard W.J., Andrea Goertz.

JOHN GOERTZEN

After leaving the home place near St. Jean in 1947, John and Frank Goertzen bought 11-3-3E from Mr. J. Steiben. There were only about 60 acres under cultivation at the time, the rest being bush.

Their mother, Helen Goertzen, lived with them.

Frank and John Goertzens farm, 1960.

Back, Kristine, Geneva, Tracy; front, Norma, Zane, John, 1980.

In August, 1962, John married Norma Fay Poole from Butte Falls, Oregon. They lived on the farm until October, 1965, when they bought the former Mary Schmitke house in Dominion City. In 1973, they sold both the farm and home and bought the Wiebe house at 150 Baskerville Ave. where they presently reside.

They have four children: Sara Kristine, Geneva Gaye, Tracy Dawn and Jared Zane.

FRANK GAETZ

Frank Edward Gaetz, son of Adam and Mary (Wnuk) Gaetz, was born at Vita. Adam and Mary Gaetz farmed on section 5-1-5 where they raised 10 children, of which Frank was second youngest.

Frank attended Overstone School, and was baptised and confirmed in Tolstoi Roman Catholic Church. For many years Frank farmed with his father and worked in Winnipeg.

Frank is now a member and on the board of Green Ridge United Church. In 1981, was elected trustee for Boundary School Division, Ward seven.

In 1968, Frank married Patricia Ann Pearse and in 1969, bought the farm previously owned by Joseph and Rose Graboski, section 16-1-5.

Back, Frank and Pat Gaetz; front, Lyle and Jacqueline.

Patricia is the daughter of Archie and Laura (Pott) Pearse of Dominion City. She attended school in Dominion city and St. Jean and was a member of Dominion City 4-H Club for five years. In 1966, she took L.P.N. training at Manitoba Red River College and Steinbach Hospital. Patricia nursed at Misericordia and St. Pierre hospitals, and is presently employed at Vita Health Care Centre. Patricia is a member of Green Ridge United Church.

Frank and Patricia have two children:

Lyle James attends Dominion City Elementary School.

Jacqueline Dawn is still at home.

Both children were baptised and attend Sunday School at Green Ridge United Church.

MICHAEL GANSKE

Michael Ganske purchased the SW ¼ 25-1-4E and NW ¼ 24-1-4E from Nick Kassian in 1947. He was married to Julianna Frank.

They had two children:

Emma (Mrs. Peter Enns) of Bagot.

Reinhold.

Reinhold bought the home farm after his father's death in 1950. He is married to Martha Steinke and they have three children:

Gloria lives in Winnipeg.

Sharon married Randy Brown.

Randy.

Reinhold and Martha Ganske.

Gloria, Sharon, and Randy Ganske.

VICTOR GRABOWIECKI

Victor Grabowiecki arrived at Ridgeville in March, 1913 from Chicago, Illinois.

Victor married Frances Graboski, daughter of Leon and Mary Graboski on April 13, 1915 at the Holy Trinity Church at Tolstoi by Rev. Bronislaw Heinz.

In 1919 they sold their land to Jacob Basaski and moved to Arnaud where they purchased a quarter section from Henry (Timlik). They lived on this farm till March, 1924 when they moved to N.W. 23-3-4. In 1937 Victor purchased SW ¼ of section 26-3-4 E1.

Victor and Frances had four children:

Johnny was born on May 16, 1924. He married Mary Fedorchuk, daughter of George and Anna Fedorchuk in June, 1947. They lived on the family farm with their three children: Casmir resides in Edmonton, Brian and wife Pat (nee Woronuik) live in Vancouver, and Carol Lynn lives in Winnipeg.

Rose Mary was born May 6, 1927 and died in 1936.

Their daughter, Victoria, married Samuel Johnston in 1945. Samuel died in 1978. They had two daughters, and lived in Hamilton, Ontario.

Their son, Anthony, married Jean Mary Cook, daughter of Maude and Abraham Cook of Sheffield, England in October, 1945. They live in Winnipeg and have four children.

In 1957 Victor and Frances left the farm and moved to Tolstoi. Frances passed away in April, 1973, at the age of 76. Victor passed away in March, 1975, at the age of 81.

Johnny and Mary lived on the family farm till October, 1978, when they sold their property to Paul Friesen and moved to Winnipeg.

Victor and Frances Grabewiecki.

Casimer, John and Mary Grabowiecki, Brian and Carol Lynne.

Eveleyn, Victoria (Grabowiecki) Johnston, Samuel Johnston and Valerie.

224

Anthony and Mary Grabowiecki (nee Cook) and their four children.

Patricia, James, Theresa, Laurence.

SARAH GILCHRIST

Sarah Gilchrist came to Franklin from Scarborough, Ontario with her four sons: Robert, Andrew, Jack and Jim.

They landed in Emerson on April 3, 1893 and took up a homestead on the north-west quarter of 12-1-4. This land is now owned by her granddaughter, Barbara Gilchrist, who also owns SE ¼ 14-1-4 E1.

Robert Gilchrist purchased NE ¼ 2-1-4 E1, around 1895. This land is now owned by his daughter Sarah Gilchrist, who still lives in the old frame house with her son Ken and brother Alex. This house was built about 1900. Robert married

Harriet Stewart. He died in 1960, and Harriet in 1980.

They raised nine children: Alex, Barbara, Andrew, Jimmie, William, Cecil, Sarah, Ben and Ruby.

Cecil married Lucy Hooker in Hove, England in 1943. They have four children and live in Winnipeg.

Ben also moved to Winnipeg in 1947, where he married Willa Turner in 1949. They raised three children. Both brothers worked for the City of Winnipeg, where Ben is still employed.

Ruby married Rudolph Kusmal in 1947, and they have four children. Ruby now lives in the United States.

William married Hilda Coombs in 1946. They had two children, and lived on a farm near Ridgeville until William's death in 1955.

Jimmie died in 1952. He suffered with asthma most of his life.

Alex purchased SE ¼ of 11-1-4 E1.

Cecil and his wife Lucy bought 10 acres from Alex, where they have a cottage and grow a garden.

ANDREW GILCHRIST

Andrew Gilchrist was born on October 10, 1876 in Scarborough, Ontario.

Andrew died in 1971, from army wounds.

Ella Smith was born on December 12, 1874 in Barrie, Ontario.

Andrew came to Ridgeville in 1892 with his mother and brothers. They took up a homestead on SW ¼ 13-1-4 E1.

In 1903, Andrew and Ella were married, and they had four children:

Helen (Gilchrist) Bechstead was born on February 21, 1905.

Jack Leslie was born on August 10, 1907.

Harold Smith was born on October 21, 1908.

Nelson Andrew was born on October 1, 1911.

Left: Andrew and Ella Smith.
Right: Sarah Gilchrist in her garden, 1930.

Mrs. Sarah Gilchrist, her daughters Barbara, Sarah, Ruby and her son Ben.

Robert Gilchrist and his six sons, Alex, Andrew, Jim, Bill, Cecil, Ben.

Centre, Mrs. Sarah Gilchrist; and three of her sons Robert Jack and Jim and Mr. and Mrs. Otto Fidler and baby.

Ken Gilchrist baling straw on Alex Gilchrist farm.

Barry and Lynda Gilchrist, Judy and Ron Smith; front, Jacquelyne, Nelson and Emma Gilchrist. They lived on the Gilchrist homestead of SW 13-1-4E.

Left: Andrew and Ella Gilchrist on their 50th wedding anniversary, February 5, 1953.
Right: Dick Gilchrist (grandson of Andrew and son of Harold). Born July 9, 1944.

Back, Bill Beckstead, Mr. and Mrs. Andy Gilchrist, Harold Gilchrist; front, Helen Beckstead, Carol Gilchrist, Ethel Gilchrist.

Left: Jack Leslie Gilchrist (son of Andrew) born August 10, 1907. Married Mildred (Tillie) Zass, January 24, 1942.
Right: Helen (daughter of Andrew) born February 21, 1905. Married November 5, 1931 to William Beckstead, born September 12, 1904.

Andy Gilchrist and Tim Wilkinson raising the centennial flag, 1966. Mr. Gilchrist, Ridgeville's oldest citizen and Tim, youngest registered student in school.

Left: Barry, Lynda and James Gilchrist, 1979.
Right: Judy and Ron Smith with children, Shannon and Byron.

MARGARET ROSS GRAY

Margaret Ross Gray came west in 1901 with her four sons and one daughter, leaving the eldest son in St. Thomas, Ontario to carry on his practice as a doctor. Margaret's husband, a Baptist minister, had passed away suddenly of a heart attack a short time before.

Their children were: Dr. Thomas Gray, Ontario, Jack, James, Frank, George, Norman, and Lillian.

They have all passed away.

She lived and farmed in the Erin School District for about six years.

Norman went through to be a druggist, and owned and operated the Ultra Drug Store, at the corner of Higgins and Main in Winnipeg, for about 35 years. Norman then retired in Vancouver.

Lillian became a registered nurse and was employed in Winnipeg for many years.

Jack and George took up farming in Saskatchewan.

James became collector of Customs at Sprague until his retirement.

Mrs. Gray died at the age of 83 years.

FRANK V. GRAY

Frank married Leila E. Spackman in 1902. They had five daughters and one son:

Arla Gruenke of Dominion City.

Lloyd of Winnipeg.

Alice Iola Ginn of Winnipeg.

Frances Kapitan of Winnipeg.

Madeliene Lang of Winnipeg.

Thelma Tanning of Vancouver.

Frank and Leila farmed in Franklin until 1918. They sold out and bought a farm at Riordon Siding. About 1920, Frank became bailiff of the County Court of Emerson. In 1932, he bought the Wallace Arthur farm and his son, Lloyd, took over the home place. Mr. Gray continued as bailiff until 1943 when he resigned after almost 35 years of service. He sold his farm to his son-in-law and daughter, Albert and Arla Gruenke, and he and Mrs. Gray moved to Winnipeg.

Frank Gray died on January 13, 1964 and Leila Gray on August 2, 1965.

About 1932, Lloyd R. F. Gray, bought the farm from his father. In 1935, Lloyd married Lillian Rust, and they had a family of four:

Carmen lives in Winnipeg.

Lila McCreadie lives in Courtney, B.C.

Clayton lives in Louisiana.

Marilyn McNamara lives in Trenton, Ontario.

While farming, Lloyd was busy raising cattle and horses, and took an interest in sports. He and the boys became interested in horse racing. After selling the farm, they went into racing at Assiniboia Downs, in Winnipeg, where he and Carman are still active.

Back, Arla, Thelma, Alice, Lloyd, Francis, Madelaine; front, Liela and Frank on their 60th wedding anniversary.

Margaret Ross Gray

Lloyd and Lillian Gray and family; Dan, Lila, Marilyn and Clayton.

ALBERT GRUENKE

Albert was the fourth child of a family of 12, born to Mr. and Mrs. Emil Gruenke at Plum Coulee, who came to Franklin municipality.

Albert later farmed independently at Morris. He married Arla L. Gray in 1940 and they lived at Morris for three years. In 1943 they bought the Gray farm.

Their family includes two boys:

Douglas, who died on January 29, 1977.

Kenneth.

Albert farmed from 1943 until 1970, when his son, Ken and his wife Gladys, took over.

Kenneth Orval Gruenke married Gladys Kroeker on June 13, 1970 at Morris, Manitoba. They now farm at Dominion City.

Their children are;

Vincent Blake, born on October 5, 1971.

Dixie Michelle, born on January 28, 1974.

Douglas, older brother to Kenneth, attended Manitoba Teacher's College after completing his high school education in Dominion City. After teaching one year at Middlebro, he returned to

Dominion City to become principal of the elementary school. In 1963, he purchased the Floyd Hassett farm, south of Dominion City, in section 20. In 1964, he married Marlene Goodman from Melita, also a teacher. They had three children: Lynda, Trent, and Krista.

Douglas, Ken, Albert and Arla Gruenke.

Ken, Gladys, Dixie and Vincent Grienke.

Douglas, Marlene, Lynda, Trent and Krista Grienke.
228

SAMUEL GIBSON

Samuel was born in 1875 at Listowel, Ontario. He was the son of the late Mr. and Mrs. Thomas Gibson, of Scottish ancestry. Samuel Gibson came to Emerson at the age of 20 years.

Rachel Etta, eldest daughter of Henry and Margaret Baldwin, was born in 1879, and came with her parents to Emerson in the 1880's.

Samuel and Rachel were married in Emerson in 1899, and settled in the Stockport district where four of their children were born.

In 1912, they moved to the Manchester district, where they purchased River Lot 46 from the late Charlie Root. Another four children were born to them in this district.

Samuel and Rachel had eight children: Morley, Wallace, Hazel, Gladys, Margaret, Ross, Elwood, and Garnet.

Hazel married Charles Alex Fraser. They are retired and live in Emerson. They have a son, Wilton and a daughter Earlene.

Gladys married Gabriel Schnell, and they are also retired in Emerson. Gladys passed away in 1980.

Margaret married Lorne E. Peto, and they live in Emerson. They have three children, Allen, Sandra and Elaine.

Elwood and Doreen (nee Ross) were married and took over the home farm. They have a son, Dwight and a daughter, Susan. Dwight married

Samuel, Rachel and Etta Gibson.

Wendy Rodewald, and they live in Winnipeg with their two daughters Kyla and Jill. Susan married Bruce Milne and they live in Lethbridge, Alberta.

Garnett, who joined the staff of Customs in Emerson, married Lillian Oakden, and they have two daughters, Greta and Lisa.

Morley farmed nearby, and was predeceased by his first wife, Alda Bain, only daughter of Mr. and Mrs Robert Bain of the Manchester district, leaving an infant son, Howard, who grew up with his grandparents. Howard and his wife, Louisa, reside in Halifax. They have a son, Ian and a daughter, Carolyne. Morley married Pauline Timchuk of the Ridgeville district, who became his second wife. They eventually gave up farming and moved to Don Mills, Ontario, where Morley served with the American Embassy for over 30 years. Morley passed away in 1978.

Wallace worked for the Manitoba Telephone System until his retirement, when he and his wife, Edith, moved to Victoria.

Ross, who died suddenly in 1976 at the age of 62 years, was assistant postmaster in Emerson. He was married to Alice Skaglund of Morris and they had one daughter, Candace.

Samuel Gibson died in 1938 at the age of 62 years.

In 1946, Rachel moved to Emerson. Rachel maintained her own suite in Southgate Haven until she died in 1973, at the age of 93 years.

JAMES GRIFFIN

James was born in Dominion City in 1880. His mother, Mary Timlick and father, James Sr., moved here from Ontario in 1878 with one daughter, Annie. They stayed at the Queen's Hotel in Dominion City. James Sr. drove freight for the government from St. Paul to Winnipeg. He disappeared in 1879.

James Jr. got his schooling in St. Agathe, but returned to Dominion City to drive horses for Mr. Simpson. He drove the first mail to Woodmore in 1902.

He married Annie Schwartz in 1911. She was born in Plum Coulee in 1890, and at the age of 13 years, worked as a cook in the first hotel in Emerson.

Annie died in 1933 with diptheria. James died September 30, 1953.

They had 11 children, one died in infancy: Fern Smith, Mary Fear, Grace Leslie, Dan, Ben.

Harry, Margaret Olden, Earl, Jim, and Lloyd.

Harry Griffin purchased the farm on which he resides E ½ 13-2-4E in Woodmore in 1942 from the Manitoba Farm Loan Company.

In 1921, his father and mother had lived here and this was where Harry was born.

He married Irene (Smith) in 1943. They had two children: Ronald Dale and Allen Blair.

Ronald married Karen McLennan in 1964 and they had one daughter. They lived in the Tolstoi area until Ronald passed away in 1980. Karen and Kimberley now live in Emerson where she is employed.

Allen lives on the home farm.

In 1967, Harry purchased the farm of the late Mr. and Mrs. William Palmer.

Ronald Dale Griffin and Karen Dianne McLennan purchased the W ½ 10-2-5 E1 in the Tolstoi area in 1967. Former owner was Frank Goletski whose father Jacob Goletski homesteaded the land.

In May of 1971, a daughter Kimberley Dahn was born to Ron and Karen. Ronald purchased SE ¼ 21-2-5 E1 from Ben Froom in 1976.

Ronald enjoyed his life of farming up until his demise in 1980, due to a chronic kidney disease and his brother Allen now resides there and rents both farms.

Earl and Gwen Griffin live in Winnipeg. They have one daughter:

Shiela.

Earl is employed at C. P. Railroads. They have land and a home at Green Ridge.

Lloyd and Grace Griffin live in Victoria. They have four children: Robin, Jennifer, Heather and Rosemary.

They also have one granddaughter. Lloyd spent 20 years in the Navy.

James and Annie Griffin, 1911.

Fern, Mary, Grace, Margaret, Dan, Ben, Harry, Earl, Jim and Lloyd Griffin.

Earl, Gwen and Sheila Griffin.

Grace and Robert Leslie

Jim and Eileen Griffin family, l to r; Jim, Leslie, Maureen, Brian, Francis, Robert, Elizabeth, Linda, Eileen and Ken, grandchildren, Michael and Andrew. They all live in Winnipeg. Jim is employed at Manitoba Hydro.

230

Mary (Griffin) and Clifford Fear have two daughters Carol and Gail. Carol is married to Dave Jarvis and they have two daughters Heather and Suzanne. Clifford is retired from C.N. as draftsman.

Mr. and Mrs. Rod Griffin, Dan, Cheryl, Robert, Eleanor, Keith, Jeff Griffin; front, Eliza Griffin.

Harry, Irene, Allen, Ronald, Karen and Kimberly Griffin.

Robin Griffin, Rose Mary Griffin, Jennifer Griffin,

Lloyd and Grace Griffin, Heather and husband Scott.

Left: Benjamin and Margaret Griffin.
Right: Jerold, Glenn and Tommy.

Ben died December 4th, 1972. He worked for Manitoba Telephone. Glenn maried Loraine Jones and they have two children David and Rachel. All reside in Winnipeg.

GEORGE GREINER

George Greiner came to Manitoba with his parents and Eda, John, Paul and Joe in 1905. They farmed at Ogilvie until 1921, when a man named Beecher traded his farm at Arnaud with Mr. Greiner. He wanted light soil, and the Greiner's wanted heavy soil. They farmed this land until 1925, when Mennonite refugees from the Russian revolution came into the Arnaud area and purchased the farm, being E ½ of 2-4-3 E1, 34-3-3 E1 and N ¼ 35-3-3 E1. The Greiners moved to Iowa, from where they had come. While at Ogilvie, six children were born to them:

Leona, Lawrence, Katherine, Dorothy, Raymond, and Leonard.

George Greiner Sr. died in 1942, Mrs. Greiner in 1944 and John in 1954.

JOHN GINN

In 1874 John Ginn Sr. and two of his sons, from Cartwright, Ontario, arrived to homestead the NE ¼ 27-3-3 E1 on which, in part, the town of Arnaud is now situated.

Mrs. Ginn, the former Eleanor Jane Kerr, and the rest of their children arrived the following year.

William Ginn acquired the E ½ 5-4-3 E1.

John Ginn Sr. died in 1882, and was buried in the Arnaud cemetery. The following year, the family with the exception of William, moved to North Dakota.

Mrs. Ginn passed away in the late 1890's, and was buried at Crystal, North Dakota. Mr. Ginn's remains were then moved to Crystal, N.D.

William moved to Dominion City in 1883, and died in 1894.

John and Eleanor Ginn had eight children: John C. Jr, William, James, Robert, Thomas, Minnie, Annie, and Lottie.

John C. Jr. moved to Dominion City, and in 1893 he married Louisa Baskerville. John died in 1939, and Louisa in 1941. They had four children: Stanley, Kathleen, Raymond, and Norris.

Stanley was married to Mae Barber who resides in Franklin Manor. He died in 1981.

Kathleen married Jack Empson, and died in 1924.

Raymond married Margaret Skene in 1925. They have four children: Eleanor, Betty-Lou, Iris, and Glenn.

Eleanor is employed by Canada Post Corporation. She married Henry Casson who is retired from Canada Customs, and they live in Emerson. They have two children: Dwight and Kristy-Lou.

Dwight married Joyce Pohl. They live in Winnipeg with two children: Rachel and Ryan.

Kristy-Lou is a registered nurse, and lives in Houston.

Betty-Lou married Jerry Lewis, who was the post-master at Morris. They had three children: Kim, Brock, and Lori. Jerry passed away in 1973. Betty-Lou is now married to Joc. March.

Kim is married to Joanne Clubb, lives in Edmonton, and they have one son, Michael.

Brock married Lori Loewen and lives in Winnipeg.

Lori Lewis has her bachelor of registered nursing and lives in Winnipeg.

Iris and husband, Gordon Solnes, live in Vancouver. They have three children: Michael, Carla, and Andrea.

Glenn is employed by Manitoba Highways as a grader - snowplow operator. He is married to Georgina Hiebert, who is post-mistress in Dominion City. Georgina and Glenn live in the Ginn family home in Dominion City. They have three children: Richard (Dale), Geoffrey, and Deanna.

Raymie Ginn is a resident of the Personal Care Home in Emerson. His wife, Margaret, lives in Franklin Manor.

Norris Ginn married Alice Gray. Norrie farmed and had various jobs in the Dominion City area. He then retired to Winnipeg. Norris passed away in 1980, and his wife, Alice, lives in Winnipeg. They have two children: Clifford and Bonnie-Lou.

Clifford lives in Medicine Hat with his three children: Beverly, Darcy, and Craig.

Bonnie-Lou is married to Pastor Danny Gales and they live in Medicine Hat. They have three children: Shannon, Kevin, and Andrea.

Raymie and Marjorie Ginn

Left: Eleanor (Ginn) and Henry Casson.
Right: Dwight and Joyce (Pohl) Casson.

Kristy-Lou, Ryan and Rachel Casson.

John C. Ginn, l to r; back, Stanley, Kathleen, Louisa (Baskerville); on knee, Norris J. Ginn; sitting, Raymond B. Ginn.

William Ginn; Stanley D. Ginn

Back, Dave and Geoffrey; front, Glenn, Diana, and Georgina.

232

Mike, Carla, Iris, Gordon and Andrea Solnes.

Left: Jos March and Betty-Lou Gihn-Lewis.
Right: Kim and Joanne (Clubb) Lewis. Inset, Michael.

Left: Brock and Lori (Loewen) Lewis.
Right: Bruce and Lori (Lewis) Lamont.

Norrie and Alice Ginn

Cliff, Craig, Bev and Darcy Ginn.

L to r; back, Danny Gales, Shannon; front, Kevin, Bonnie (Ginn) Gales; on knee, Andrea.

GEORGE GUNN

In 1875 George and Annie (Riley) Gunn and family came from Carlton Place, Ontario. George froze to death in 1878.

Their children were: John, Bill, Jim, Robert, Norman, Ed, George, Annie, and Maggie.

Jim was in the Klondike at the time of the Gold Rush.

Bill lived where Reinhold Steinke now lives.

Norman lived where the Daniel Alstadt farm used to be.

Robert stayed on his dad's farm.

John, born in 1858, took up a homestead in 1880 along the Roseau River, on Hudson Bay Company land. He married Estelle McGunnion. They had six boys: Clarence, Hector, Howard, Garnet, Gordon, and Donald, and Estelle who died in 1936.

In 1934 Garnet married Laura Spence, daughter of Thomas and Sarah Spence. Their children were: Gary and Sylvia.

Gary married Myrna Wilson of Emerson in 1967. They live in Brandon, Manitoba.

Sylvia married Clarence Yahnke of Dominion City in 1963.

When Laura died in 1957, Garnet sold his farm

233

to Merton Olden and moved to Winnipeg. Garnet remarried in 1958 to Lorna Loring. Lorna died in 1969. Garnet remained in Winnipeg until 1981, when he returned to Dominion City.

Clarence Gunn married Emma Kroeker, daughter of Pete Kroeker of Stuartburn in 1930. They rented the Kim Dickson farm until 1936, when they moved to Dominion City and rented Billy Mykichuk's store and operted a lunch counter. Clarence operated the Franklin Municipal caterpillar for many years. In 1950 they moved to Winnipeg, where Clarence died in 1959.

Hector Gunn was born in Green Ridge on September 26, 1892. In 1917 he went overseas with the Royal Canadian Mounted Police. He returned home in 1919 in time to take part in policing the labor strike in Winnipeg. Shortly thereafter he went to Dauphin where land was available for veterans to file on. He took up land in Bield, but found the land unsatisfactory and spent the next few years roving the country.

On March 12, 1924 he returned home and married Gertrude Brewster, daughter of Ben Brewster of Green Ridge. Their first year was spent in Edmonton, Alberta, and in 1925 they returned once again to Green Ridge and bought the Ben Brewster farm. At that time Hector already owned the George Gunn farm located on the SW 5-3-4.

They had a family of five children:

Norma, married to Don Fraser of British Columbia.

Douglas, of Green Ridge.

Donna, married to Stan Stewart of New Brunswick.

Shiela, who lives in the United States.

Clayton, of Green Ridge.

In 1951 the Gunns purchased the Jim Clader farm located on 35-2-4.

In 1959 Douglas purchased the Calder farm from Gertrude and Hector, and Clayton took over the family farm. They continued to live with Clayton until his marriage in 1968, at which time they moved to Steinbach.

On March 19, 1969 Hector died and is buried in the Green Ridge cemetery.

Clayton Gunn was born on April 7, 1938. In 1955 he went to Winnipeg where he worked at a variety of jobs. In the fall of 1959 he purchased his father's farm, thus becoming the third generation on the land. In the spring of 1960 he returned to the farm permanently.

On March 9, 1968, Clayton Gunn and Eileen Schmidt of Dominion City were married.

Douglas Gunn was born September 6, 1930. He married Lillian Delf of Treherne on November 14, 1959 and purchased part of the Hector Gunn farm.

Doug and Lillian have two sons:

Gordon, who works at St. Malo and was married in 1982 to Tammy Cesmystruk.

Harvey, who is still in high school at Dominion City and St. Jean.

Annie (Riley) Gunn

Florence Mae, Emma, Clarence and Johnny.

The John Gunn boys, l to r; back, Gordon, Donald, Clarence, Hector; front, Howard, Garnet.

John and Estella Gunn

Left: Gertrude and Hector Gunn.
Right: Clayton and Eileen Gunn.

Doug, Donna and Norma Gunn.

Sheila and Clayton Gunn

Lillian, Douglas, Harvey and Gordon Gunn.

Sylvia, Gary, Laura and Garnet Gunn.

LÉON GRÉGOIRE

Born in 1823, Léon Grégoire of St. Cuthbert, Quebec, married Julie Silveste in 1846. She died after three years of marriage. He married again in 1853, this time to Olive Savoie. Léon died in St. Cuthbert, Quebec at the age of 54 in 1877.

Mrs. Léon Grégoire, came to join her son Napoléon and her sister Mrs. Liboire Baril in St. Jean Baptiste. She left in Quebec a daughter Olive, a religious sister, and brought with: Glycerie (Mrs. Philias Auger), Héloise (Mrs. Louis Arcand), Marie (Mrs. Flavien Baril), Célima (Mrs. Emerie Robert), Napoléon, who married Verginie Vandale, Grégoire, who married Caroline Bernier, Henriette (Mrs. Joseph Champagne), Félix, who married Emma Mulaire, Elizée, who married Phoébé Granger, and Ernestine (Mrs. Georges Dauteuil). Mrs. Léon Grégoire died April 2, 1905 at the home of her son Félix.

Born in 1874 at Ash Town, Rhode Island, U.S.A., Phoébé Granger came to Manitoba at the age of four with her parents, Mr. and Mrs. Arthur Granger (born Denise Duphrene), her sister Rosalie (Mrs. Joseph Asselin) and her brother Arthur.

Elizée Grégoire, son of Mrs. Léon Grégoire arrived at St. Jean Baptiste at the age of 14 years. Elizée married Phoébé Granger on January 10, 1893. They lived in different places in St. Jean Baptiste, until they finally settled on River Lot 204 on St. Mary's Road South. Their grandson David Grégoire now owns the land.

Mr. and Mrs. Elizée Grégoire had 15 children but only seven lived. Elizée had an inexhaustible repertoire of songs. He said that he knew 100 songs by heart.

Their family was: Anna, Hermas, Laurent, Fortunat, Maurice, Alexandrine, and Léon.

Later they took in Aimé Grégoire, son of Baptiste Grégoire, and brought him up as their own.

In 1935 Elizée Grégoire, his wife, his daughter and Aimé retired in the village of St. Jean Baptiste. Mrs. Grégoire died on June 4, 1977 and Elizée on March 2, 1954.

The marriage of Hermas and Alphonsine (1899-1959), daughter of Hercule Barnabë and Marie-Claire took place at Letellier, June 6, 1923.

Hermas and Alphonsine bought their first establishment five miles east of St. Jean Baptiste. They had five children: Adéline, Berthe, Léola, Alphonse, and Célima.

Hermas rented a quarter section in wood which he broke himself for the sum of two crops; the first crop was completely hailed out but the second one was fair. In 1938, he bought five quarter sections from Bob Moore and sold one quarter to his brother Maurice and his first land to his brother Laurent. With his son Alphonse, they broke two river lots. Alphonse inherited the land from his father.

The flood of 1950 followed the burning of their house. One afternoon during the flood, Hermas wanting news from his brother Laurent, started with a row boat accompanied by Alphonse and cousin Aimé Grégoire on the Marais River. On their way back at dawn, a high wind arose, filled the boat and sank it. Thinking they were in the middle of the river where the water was deep they cried "This is it, we are finished." To their surprise the water was only up to the neck. Hermas and Aimé held the boat at arms length above the water while Alphonse emptied it with an old tabacco tin.

When Alphonsine became sick with cancer, Hermas moved to the village of St. Jean Baptiste. She died in 1959.

When Hermas was no longer able to work, he retired at the manor in St. Jean Baptiste and became friends of his co-renters. Still able to drive his car, he made himself useful by accompanying them here and there, to see the crops, spring waters, to Bingo, to see the doctor or going for coffee at Gray's or Pembina. He died on December 26, 1975.

Adéline married Marcel Fillion.

Berthe married Peter Goertzen.

Léola went to Normal School and taught school for one year at Youville School and two years at Taché School in St. Joseph.

Alphonse married Aurore Sabourin. He worked on the farm with his father until his marriage.

Célima married Georges Bruneau.

After his marriage to Thérése Grégoire of Letellier, Laurent settled on the farm of his brother Hermas.

His family included: Guy, Laurent Jr, Marcel, Florence, Cécile, Lucie. Bertrand. Madelaine. Denise. Lise. Michel. and Jaques.

His land was passed on to his son Laurent Jr. who remained a resident of the village of St. Jean Baptiste. The parishoners of St. Jean Baptiste welcomed Mr. and Mrs. Laurent Grégoire where they retired in 1965.

The marriage of Maurice Grégoire and Germaine Bérard was celebrated at St. Jean Baptiste. Maurice bought a piece of land near that of his brother Hermas.

Two children died at an early age, and only one survived:

Louis.

He left the farm to live in town, but finding

Elizeé and Phoébé (Granger) Grégoire.

236

town life boring, he bought a river lot on St. Mary's Road North, one mile from St. Jean.

In 1956 he agreed to a serious heart operation; pneumonia set in, and he died at the age of 46. Germaine died in 1967.

Alphonse was born on July 2, 1930. On July 27, 1959, he married Aurore Sabourin, born July 24, 1936, daughter of Omer Sabourin and Irene St. Vincent.

He took over part of the family farm, consisting of 500 acres. There Aurore and Alphonse became parents of six children:

Carol, lives in Winnipeg.

Raymond, works for his father on the farm.

Gilles, also works for his father on the farm.

Robert, is in high school in Dominion City.

Gerald, is also still in school.

Alain, is also in school.

Alphonse is increasing his holdings to keep his boys occupied and giving them a start in farming.

Back, Mr. and Mrs. Grégoire, Carol, Robert, Raymond, Gilles; front, Gerald and Alain.

FRANK P. GOERTZEN

Frank, son of Peter F. Goertzen, was born in the village of Alexanderpol, Southern Russia, July 28, 1889. Frank and Helene arrived in Canada in 1924 with their children: Frank Jr., Agnes, Peter, and Cornie.

Helene, was born in Canada.

John, was also born in Canada, in 1926.

In the same year, they moved to Franklin Municipality to the Lyman Ranch I.

Frank P. Goertzen was 39 when he died suddenly on March 31, 1928. He is buried in the Arnaud United Church Cemetery.

Helene Goertzen had to leave Ranch I since the eldest son, Frank, was too young to take over the farm. Agnes and Peter were sent to live with their aunt, Agatha Unger of Steinbach. Agnes stayed a year and a half, then returned to live with her mother. Moving many times, Helene finally settled at Dominion City, where she stayed for 10 years. There, Cornie, Helene and John finished their education.

In June 1933, Agnes married Bernard Waters, editor and publisher of the Dominion City Star. They had 10 children. After Bert died, Agnes moved to Winnipeg, where she married Aron Schulz and had two more boys. She moved to British Columbia after the death of her second husband.

At age 14, Peter came to live with his family.

The Goertzens moved into the W. R. Johnston farm buildings in 1941. Two years later, with the help of Cornie and John, they rented the Johnston land and started farming.

Helene, her daughter, opened a hairdressing shop in St. Claude, where she married Michael Kustra in 1948. They have five children and live in Winnipeg.

In 1948 Frank and John bought a half section of land three miles south of Arnaud where they

Hermas and Alphonsine (Barnabé) Grégoire.

Maruice Grégoire. Laurent Grégoire.

moved with their mother.

Cornie went to British Columbia and married Mary Braun and had two children.

Peter married Berthe Grégoire of St. Jean in 1949 and stayed on the Johnston farm. They have four children.

John married Norma Poole of Butte Falls, U.S.A. in 1962. They have four children and live in Dominion City.

Helene Goertzen lived with Frank, who remained a bachelor, until her death on October 21, 1976. She is buried in the Dominion City Cemetery.

Frank is retired in Winnipeg.

Roger, George, Peter, Bertha; front, Marie, Suzanne.

Helene Goertzen and Agnes

Cornie, Helen, Peter, Mrs. Geortzen, Frank Jr. and John.

Marie is the wife of Norman Beaudette. They bought the former Arthur Touchette farm at St. Jean Baptiste. They have three children: Martin, Joelene and Tina.

Suzanne married Loren Braun. They have one boy, Colin and reside in Neubergthal.

George married Evelyne Lamoureux, of St. Pierre. Their children are Brigitte and Robert.

LEON GRABOSKI

Leon and Mary Graboski came to North Dakota in 1895. Leon came from Germany and Mary from Poland. They came to SW ¼ 14-1-5 E1 in 1897.

Graboski brothers, l to r, Stanley, Jiony, John, Lawrence, Jacob, Victor, Vincent, Leonard.

Ambrose and Joe Graboski

Leon was a Rawleigh dealer for a number of years, and played the organ in church. They had 11 children. When Leon and Mary retired, Lawrence, their son, took the farm.

Lawrence and Mary had three children. Today Joey and Ambrose, their sons, live with Mary on the Graboski homestead.

H JOHN HUTCHINSON

John Hutchinson came from Malton, Ontario in 1880 to homestead the SE¼ of 16-2-4 E1.

Sarah (Hurd) Hutchinson was a sister of Wilbur Hurd of Woodmore. John was a brother of Mrs. Thos. Snead of Woodmore.

The Hutchinsons stayed a few years, went to Winnipeg for 10 years, then moved to North Battleford. Their daughter Edith married a Captain Kirby.

John and Sarah died in North Battleford and the Kirbys went to British Columbia.

Jack and Sarah Hutchinson

HARRY HANCOX

Harry Hancox came from Welford on Avon, England. Edith Hancox (nee Hopkins) came from Preston near Stratford on Avon, England. They came to Canada, September 7, 1893 and settled at Emerson.

In 1902 he bought a farm at Dominion City, Sec. 25-2-2E. His son Edward and grandson Harry, farm it in 1982.

Mr. and Mrs. Hancox had eight children, Alfred married Annie Waite; Nellie married Frank Jones; Elizabeth married Walter Wood; William (Jim) married Grace Jamison; Constance married Art Hatch; Edith remained single; Edward (Ted) married Edna Pott; Louise married Charlie Harteg.

Alfred Hancox is eldest son of Harry and Edith Hancox. Alfred was born in England and was one and a half years old when he came to Canada with his parents in Sept. 1893.

He married Annie Waite in 1952 and died in 1972.

Frank and Nell Jones married in Winnipeg in March 1918. They had five children, Florence (Mrs. H. Hendershot, Montana), Phyllis, (Mrs. Allan Barber, Winnipeg), John, Carnduff, Saskatchewan, Jeff, Evansburg, Alberta and Emily deceased at 12 years as the result of polio.

In 1922 Frank and Nell (nee Hancox) returned to Dominion City. For many years Frank drayed and cut ice for the town. He also hauled mail to Green Ridge and Woodmore by horse and sleigh.

Earl and Lavina (nee Hancox) Pickell have four girls and one boy, Sherry, Dean, Shelley and Judy. They live in Winnipeg.

Harry and Sharon (Abrams) Hancox married in 1969. They have four children, Lori Leanne, born in 1970, Patrick Neil, born in 1971, Keith Michael, born in 1976 and Holly Jolene, born in 1978.

Edith graduated from Grace Hospital in 1930 winning a Gold Medal for General Proficiency. Edith lives in Winnipeg.

Lila, the oldest daughter of William Hancox, married Fred Stone. Their children are, Larry, Bonnie-Lynne and Randy. They live in Alsask, Saskatchewan.

Ellen (Hancox) and Bob Abrams married in 1965. Their children are Lisa, Pam, Chris and Kathy.

William Hancox married Grace Jamison. They had five children. They are Glenn, Wallace, Clifford, Lorne and Ralph.

Glenn married Elaine Davies and lives at Morris. They have three children, Kathy, Kelly and Tracy.

Wallace married Myra Wynch and lives in Winnipeg. They have four children, Kenny, Doug, Gordon and Valorie.

Clifford married Trudy Arthurs and lives in Teulon. They have three children, Mark, Trevor and Lorie-Lee.

Lorne married Jessie Arthurs and lives in Thompson. They have two children, Calvin and Donna-Mae.

Ralph married Denise La Fleche and lives in St. Adolphe. They have six children, Jackie, Diane, Ronald, Robert, Richard and Loraine.

Grace Hancox passed away in 1981. William Hancox lives in Dominion City.

Constance married Art Hatch of Birch River. They had one son Harry and a daughter Gail (Mrs. John Chalmers of Stonewall).

Connie passed away in 1971.

Edward Hancox and Edna Pott married November 25, 1940. They are now farming the land homesteaded by Harry Hancox senior together with their children Harry and Sharon.

Their children are: Ellen, married Bob Abrams October 30, 1965. Dorothy married Barry Bautet May 15, 1965, Harry married Sharon Abrams, November 1, 1969, Linda married Cam Yeo, August 2, 1969 and Joan Schultz.

Harry and Edith Hancox

Left: Florence Hancox, wife of Harry Hancox and mother of Louise Hartig.
Right: Joan Wood, daughter of Lizzie Woods Hancox.

Walter and Elizabeth (Hancox) Wood

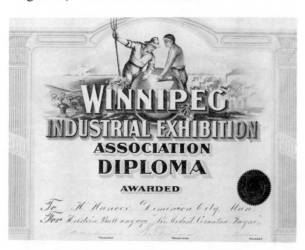

To H. Hancox, Dominion City, Manitoba
For Holstein Bull any age "Sir Modest Colantha Fayne" - 1910.

Arthur and Constance (Hancox) Hatel

240

Alfred and Annie Hancox

Left: Jeff Jones. *Right:* Mrs. Eliza Jones, mother of Frank Jones.

Wiliam Hancox, delivering milk, 1922. Son of Harry Hancox who came to Dominion City in 1904.

Left: Florence (Jones) Hendershot.
Right: Emily Jones, youngest daughter of Frank Jones; passed away at age 12 of polio.

Frank, Nellie and John Jones.

L to r; back, Paul and Cris Barnabé, Arnold and Roberta Bailey, Gordon and Joanne Kirkland; seated, Robert and Jean Pow with Tara Kirkland; front, standing, Melanie and Mandy Barnabé, Todd and Scott Kirkland, Jean Paw, daughter of Lizzie (Hancox) Woods.

Phyllis, Nellie and Florence Jones.

William and Grace Hancox, Nellie Jones, 1977.

Charlie Hartig, Louise (Hancox, daughter of Harry Hancox) Debbie, Kevin; front, Cristy.

Judy, Shelley, Jim and Sherry (Pickell) Friess, Dean, Wayne Sawatzky, Levina and Earl Pickell; front, Jean (Sawatsky) Pickell, Corey and David Friess.

Harry and Sharon Hancox with children Lori, Patrick, Keith and Holly.

Edith Hancox

Larry, Bonnie, Lynne, Fred, Lyla and Randy Stone.

Back, Lisa, Ellen, Bob; front, Pam, Chris and Kathy Abrams.

William and Grace Hancox and family. Lyla, Glenn, Wallace, Cliff, Lavina, Lorne, Ralph.

Left: Edward and Edna Hancox.
Right: Joan Schultz holding Daryl Allan.

Back, Connie holding Gail, Art Hatch; front, Harry Hancox Sr. holding grandson Harry.

Cam and Linda Yeo

Cameron, Donna and Shelly Yeo.

JOHN HUNTER

John Hunter, born March 8, 1830, in Renfrew, and Margaret Clark, born October 14, 1827 in Paisley, both in Renfrew Shire, Scotland, were married April 29, 1857. In Ontario they set up a woolen mill on the Ottawa River near Almonte. Their children were James, born 1860, Archibald, born 1863, Jessie, born c. 1865, died December 23, c. 1866, and Jessie Stewart, born 1869. After a fire destroyed their mill, they came to Franklin Municipality in 1875, to homestead the W ½ 3-2-3 E1. In 1876 they removed to SE ¼ 32-2-4 E1, land on the ridge acquired through Metis script. A tree planting claim, the SW ¼ of 32-2-4 E1 was in Margaret's name.

Margaret died in 1904, John went back to Ontario, where he married Isabella McEwen. John died 1907, Isabella 1919, both are buried in Beechwood Cemetery, Ottawa.

Jessie married Clarence Allan Taft in 1907. She died 1927.

John Hunter, 16 took homestead rights to the N½ of 32-2-4 in 1876. In 1891 he married Barbara Oatway, daughter of Richard M. and Annie (Knox) Oatway, who was born 1864. Their children were Margaret May, born 1891. She married John William Palmer in 1915. They had a family of Margaret, James H., Jane, George, twins Lily and Rose, Bert and Wilfred. She died in 1974.

Lillian Annie, 1895, married William Sutherland in 1916. Their children are Eleanor, Dorothy, Osborne, Donald, Lorraine and Betty.

Nellie Beatrice was born 1899, married John Richard Varey. She died 1972.

John Clark Alexander was born in 1902 and Jessie Barbara, born 1904, died 1919.

James Hunter died in 1945, Barbara in 1958.

Clark (John Alexander Clark, born 1902) married Sarah Jane Hopkins of Ste. Elizabeth, daughter of Thomas and Mery Esther (Gainer) Hopkins in 1934. She was born in 1905.

They had three children, Clifford Clark, 1937, James Hopkins, 1939, and Margaret Jean, 1941. Margaret married Warren Steen in 1966, and is an R.N. They have one daughter, Laura Leigh. James married Ruby Vane os Stockton in 1967. They live in Regina with four children, Scott James, Heather Dawn, Kenneth Clark and Robert Leslie.

Cliff purchased farm land in Franklin, and in 1967 married Irene Alice Munroe of Winnipeg, daughter of Pearl and Norman Munroe. They have two children, David Clark, 1971, and Sharon Pearl, 1977. He took over the home farm when his parents retired in 1967. Clark died in 1973.

Archie Clark Hunter was born in Almont, Ontario, August 25, 1863. He married Janet Lumsden in 1896, in Toronto. They had four children, Marget, 1897, Elizabeth, 1899, Annabelle, 1900, John, 1902. Janet died in 1907. Archie married Jane Pott in 1910, and had three daughters, two died in infancy, Alice was born in 1913. In 1936 they retired to Winnipeg, where he died in 1940. Jane died in 1975.

Marget married Ernie Osborn, had one daughter, Jean, who lives in Edmonton. Elizabeth married Frank Pott, had four children; Gladys, married Cecil Layng, and has seven children; Norman, died in Hong Kong; Roland, married with one daughter; Gordon married and has three children, Annabell married Werner Mader, and has three sons, Donald, Douglas, and Dale, and lives in Winnipeg. John married Elsie Milliken and had eight children. Alice lived in Winnipeg until her death in 1981.

John Hunter was born in 1902, and in 1926 bought section 31-2-4 E1, and farmed with his father until 1940. John took over section 32-2-4 on the death of his father, and lives there in 1982. He married Elsie Milliken of Mather in 1944. Their children are Eleson, born 1936, died 1962. Archie, born 1944, lives on 32-2-4 E1, married Judy Biltz in 1967. Their children Michael, born 1967, Tracey, born 1970, Jordy.

Agnes, born in 1946, lives in Vancouver. Colleen, born in 1947, married Dr. Wes Gibbings in 1970, and lives in Vancouver. Patsy Lee, born in 1949, married Lawrence Ferohoff in 1977, and lives in Winnipeg. Rodney, was born in 1951, he married Diane Rogers in 1974, has two children, Matthew, 1977, and Melissa, 1980. They live in the Queen Charlotte Islands. Kathleen was born in 1952. She married David Stewner in 1980. They have two children, Melanie, 1972, David Jr. 1982, and live in Calgary. Lee, born 1957, lives in Vancouver.

Archie Hunter, his first wife Janet (Lumsden) Hunter, baby Elizabeth, and Marget.

James and Barbara Hunter

John Hunter

John Hunter, his father Archie Hunter, step mother Jane Hunter, Marget, Elizabeth, Annabelle Hunter. Inset, Alice.

Margaret Clark Hunter

244

L to r: back, James Hunter, Jessie Hunter, Archibald Hunter; middle, Mrs. James Hunter, Mrs. John Hunter, John Hunter, Mrs. Archibald Hunter; front, Annie Hunter, Margaret Hunter (children of Mr. and Mrs. James Hunter), Marget Hunter, Elizabeth Hunter (children of Mr. and Mrs. Archibald Hunter.

Maggie, Annie, Clark, Mrs. Barbara Hunter, Nellie, Jim Hunter.

Jim and Ruby Hunter, Peggy (Hunter) Steen.

Emerson MLA Albert Driedger presenting Century Farm awards to Cliff and Irene Hunter, David and Sharon and Jean Hunter.

Clark and Jean Hunter on their anniversary, December 29, 1967.

Left: John and Elsie Hunter.
Right: Patsy-Lee and Lawrence Ferchoff.

Colleen (Hunter) Gibbing; Eleson Hunter

Tracy, Archie Hunter, Michael, Judy, Jordy.

Left: back, Melanie, Kathleen; front, David Stewner, holding David Jr.
Right: Rod, Diane Hunter, Melissa, Matthew.

Agnes Hunter   Lee Hunter

Harry and Evelyn Hopkins

HARRY HOPKINS

Harry Hopkins came to Fredensthal in 1955 to take over as agent for the Manitoba Pool Elevator.

ABRAM H. HARDER

Abram Harder came to Arnaud from Russia in 1924. He was a school teacher and lay minister in the General Conference Mennonite Church. Their children were John, Theodore, Arthur, Peter, Henry, George, Sarah and Abe. Peter married Annie Isaac in October, 1933, and they have five children. Mildred married Terry Sawatsky, Wilma married Jake Poetker, Alice married Harold Funk, Peter married Carol Anderson; and Rudie, married Sharon McCarthy.

L to r; Sharlyne, Michael, Carillee, Jake Poetker, Wilma (Harder) Poetker. Jake farms, Wilma is a music teacher, 1980.

Peter Harder, holding Mildred, Wilma, Alice, Peter, back, standing, Rudie, Mrs. Harder.

ROBERT HOWARD

Robert Howard was born in England, in 1889. His father was Alfred Howard, a landscape gardener. He had three sisters, Emma, Hilda and Laura, and one brother, Albert. He worked in the Churchill area and enlisted in 1915. In 1919 he was discharged from the army and came to Ridgeville to farm on the flats. He farmed until 1929, left Franklin for one year, and then in 1930 he married Bertha Wilkinson and moved to Emerson to work at the Liquor Commission. In 1955 he retired. The Howards had five children.

Calvin, born February, 1932, married Lauretta Mae Sauve in 1956. Their children are Trevor Dale, born September 3, 1958, Mitchell Dean, born November 21, 1960, Dori Ellen, born April 11, 1964, Owen Grant born June 13, 1965, and Jodi Lynne, born March 28, 1969.

Leslie, born July 5, 1937, worked for the Emerson Journal and now for the Edmonton Journal. He married Ella Jean Hutton in 1959. Their children are Marla Dawn, born March 18, 1962,

Andrea, born March 3, 1969, Robbie, born November 25, 1971.

Gloria was born May 10, 1944, died June 4, 1945.

Irene, was born September 22, 1946. She married Ron Schaan in 1970, moved to British Columbia.

Left: Robert Howard, 1916.
Right: Bertha and Bobby Howard, 1930.

Les Howard and family, Leslie and Ella.

Grandma Wilkinson with grandson George Lenton. c. 1920.

Andrea, Ella, Les, Marla; front, Robbie.

247

L to r; Penny Oneschuk, Beverley Reid, Irene, Ron, Lenard Oneschuk, Jerry Hughes, Leslie Howard.

L to r; back, Mr. and Mrs. Sauve, Mrs. Leakey, Bertha and Bobbie Howard; front, Calvin and Lauretta.

Trevor; Mitchell

Dori, Owen, Jodi Lynn

STUART HICKS

Stuart Hicks was CNR Station Manager at Ridgeville from 1937-1945. They had three children, Keith, Jack and Phyllis.

Keith also worked for the CNR and married Dorothy Lindsay of Ridgeville, August 23, 1946. They moved to Calgary where Keith died in 1977. Dorothy now lives in Kelowna and has one daughter, Lynne, who married Garry Barros. They have two children, Linsay and Erin.

Keith, Dorothy, Lynne Hicks, 1957.

MICHAEL HRYNENKO

Michael Hrynenko was born June 6, 1922 at Rozdol, West Ukraine. Mary Zinkiewich was born at Nolyj, Lublenc on April 29, 1920.

Michael met Mary in Cornburg, Germany where they were married on October 25, 1946. Here they resided following their marriage. Michael was employed by the Camp Police and Mary worked in the kitchen of the Camp Hospital.

On April 19, 1947, their son Roman was born.

In the spring of 1949, they boarded the ship, Atlingon, at Cornburg and emigrated to Canada.

They made their home in Dufrost where Michael worked for the C.P. Railway and Mary worked on sugar beet farms.

In 1951, they purchased the SW ¼ 22-3-5E in Rosa, and farmed. In 1968 they moved to the NW ¼ 26-3-5E where they presently live.

They had three more children: Anthony, Elsie, and Jarvis.

Anthony married Cheryle McIvor on October 14, 1972. They have one son, Michael, born October 21, 1975 and one daughter Melissa born on March 21, 1978. They live in Edmonton.

Roman married Judy Kryzanowski on May 19, 1973. they have one son David born January 11, 1978. They live in Ile Des Chenes.

Elsie married Reid Runka of Edmonton February 17, 1979. They live in Edmonton with their daughter, Erin, born March 15, 1980.

Jarvis married Cindy Ostrowsky of Rosa August 1, 1981. They live in Winnipeg.

Front, Michael and Mary; back, Anthony, Roman, Jarvis and Elsie.

Erin Runka; David Hrynenko

Michael and Mary Hrynenko

Anthony, Cheryle, Michael; Inset, Melissa Hrynenko.

Jarvis and Cindy Hrynenko

WILLIAM HASSETT

William Hassett arrived in Emerson from Mount Forest, Ontario, in 1876. He homesteaded one half mile east of the old Riordan siding, on the south side of the road. He moved to a farm two miles north of Dominion City, and then in 1911 to a farm bordering the east boundary of Dominion City, where he lived until his death. Mr. Hassett married twice, and had 11 children.

L to r; back, Vernie, Alvin, Walter; front, Nellie, Grace, Dorothy, Isabel. At 1981 gathering in Detroit.

Wm. Hassett, Walter, Nellie, Harvey, Isabel, Floyd, Grace; seated, Dorothy; Alvin (baby), Mrs. Hassett, 1912. Missing, Charlie and Teresa, and Vernie, who had not been born.

REV. HINE FAMILY

The Rev. Hine's Family
Methodist Church Minister at Dominion City 1918 to 1920.

250

ALFRED HORMANN

Alfred Hormann and his wife June moved to Franklin in August 1977.

Alfred teaches at the Roseau Valley Collegiate, and June at the Dominion City Primary School.

They first rented the J. Janzen house in Arnaud, until April 1980, when they moved into the O'Brien house in Dominion City.

Carl Theodore Arnold, June Hormann's father was born in Franklin municipality in 1920. His father, Lorenzo, was managing the Ironside farm near Arnaud.

Larry and Lillian (now Beddome) attended the Langside School. Both live in Winnipeg.

June, Alfred and Darcy Hormann.

Lorenzo and Petron (Palsson) Arnold with children Lorenzo Peter, Lillian Juanita and Baby Carl Theodore, 1920.

HENRY HENNING

Henry Henning was born in Walynia, Russia, May 8, 1863. He married Emilie Karras, and five children were born there.

In 1895 Henry left his family to come to Gretna, where he found work on the farm of Phillip Hiebert. He was joined in 1896 by his wife and children. A son was born in 1897. That same year Henry purchased the SE ¼ 34-1-3E. Eight more children were born here, three dying in infancy. Rudolf (deceased), William (deceased), Gus (deceased), Julius, Julia (Mrs. Paul Kyle), Hulda (Mrs. Albert Neuman, deceased), Matilda (Mrs. Edward Woit, deceased), Emma (Mrs. Albert Zingbiel), Helen (Mrs. Louis Kreitz, deceased), Emilie (Mrs. John Walters, deceased), and Anne (Mrs. Frank Erwin).

Julius took over this farm in 1924. Henry and Emilie moved just north of Dominion City cemetery, now owned by Matt Borodenko, where Henry died suddenly in 1925. Emilie, remained there until her death in 1935.

In 1925 Julius married Matilda Kein, Emerson, who was born 1904, daughter of Mr. and Mrs. August Kein. They farmed for 36 years, then retired to Dominion City. In 1982 they live in the Franklin Manor.

Alvin succeeded to the farm in 1961, selling it in 1974.

Madeline, married Ken French, lives in Dominion City, with five children: Sherri-lyn and Blair at home; Kim, married to Sharon Hrechka, with a son, Kelcey, lives in Dominion City; Maxine, (Mrs. Alan Wood), Winnipeg; Pat, married Lorri Van Deveire, with children, Shawn, Jeffrey and Darla Dawn, in Dominion City.

Alvin, married Dorothy Bahry, lives in Winnipeg.

Winona, married Arnold Stewart, with two children, Glenn and Marie, lives in Victoria.

Harvey, married June Kovach, with daughters Brenda and Rhonda, lives in Surrey, B.C.

Donna, married Garry Glowasky, with two children, Kelly and Lisa, residing in Birds Hill.

Winona, Glenn, Arnold and Marie Stewart, 1974.

Brenda, June, Harvey and Rhonda Henning, 1972.

Madeline and Ken French with children Maxine, Patrick, Kimberley, Sherrilyn; front, Blair.

Left: Henry and Emilie Henning.
Right: Julius and Matilda Henning.

Donna, Garry, Kelly and Lisa Glowasley.

251

Left: Alvin and Dorothy Henning.
Right: Alan and Maxine Wood.

Patrick, Lorri, Shawn, Darla and Jeff French.

Sharon, Kim and Kelcey French

WASIL HOPALUK

Wasil and Polly Hopaluk were born, raised and married in Austria. In 1903 with Peter, Metro, Nick and Mary they immigrated to Canada. They bought property on Sec. 18-1-5 E1. Here two more children, Polly and John were born. In 1926 Mrs. Hopaluk died.

Mary Sosnick is in Edmonton. Metro and Nick died in Alberta. Peter died in Manitoba in 1973. Polly (Wasny) lives in Alabama.

John married Rose Kwiatkowski. They had four daughters. John and wife Rose retired to Winnipeg in 1981. John bought land a half mile east of the 18-1-5, Pete bought the home property.

Pete married Hafia Drebit in 1908. They had 11 children. Three died as infants. Pete and Hafia also raised two foster children. Helen Harrison lives in the United States and Bob Mahara, lives in Grunthal. Pete and Hafia retired to Emerson in 1957. Hafia died in 1970, Pete in 1973.

Their children are Anne Storochuk, widowed in 1980, Mary Wishnicki and husband Pete, Mike and wife Marge, Steve (died in 1980) and wife Jean all lived in Winnipeg. Jack (deceased) and Bill and wife Rose lived in Toronto. Alec and wife Louise live in Narcess, Henry and wife Hazel farmed 18-1-5 E1 for 16 years. They have three children, Sharon, Ted and Robert. After Henry's death Hazel and children moved to Winnipeg.

Ted, Hazel, Robert; front, Sharon.

Henry and Hazel Hoplock; Ruth Hoplock.

Mr. and Mrs. Peter Hoplock

L to r; back, Peter Hoplock, Wasil Hoplock, Henry, unnamed woman, Rose (Mrs. Bill Hoplock), Anne and daughter not named, Alex (head just showing); front, Mike Hoplock, unnamed child, Mary Hoplock. 1945.

Peter Hoplock, Ruth Storchuk, Sharon Hoplock, Gwen Storochuk, Hafia Hoplock; front, Ted and Robert Hoplock, 1965.

JOSEPH HUFF

On May 24, 1890 Joseph and Justine Huff immigrated from Wolinyn, Poland with Frederick, Wilhemmina, Christina and August. They were to meet Michael Jahnke at Emerson. Instead they allowed himself to be persuaded into getting off at Dominion City by one of the settlers. He dropped them off at the farm they were later to purchase in 1934 at Dominion City.

They first settled in Fredenstal.

In 1900, they moved to Winnipeg and in 1901 became naturalized Canadian Citizens. They remained in Winnipeg until 1919. Elsie was born here. In 1917 Wilhemmina married Rudolph Bultz.

From 1919-1924 they farmed outside of Franklin and returned to the Dominion City District in 1934 purchasing land from Farris Christie.

Joseph Huff died March 7, 1937 and was buried in the Fredensthal cemetery. Elsie Huff continued to farm with her mother, Frederick and August.

August Huff married Hertha Knutt on December 3. A son, Rod, was born to them on March 11, 1944.

Frederick Huff died in January 1943 and was buried in the Dominion City cemetary.

In 1946, they purchased the old Packer place and built the home presently occupied by David Kirkpatrick.

A cousin Wiliam Fritz came from Germany in January 1952 to help on the farm.

August Huff died on April 12, 1952 and was buried in the Dominion City Cemetery.

Elsie Huff sold her farm in 1961 and in 1962 built a house in Dominion City where she presently resides with cousin, Bill Fritz.

Justine Huff died on November 11, 1963 and was buried in Fredensthal.

Hertha (Huff) Seward lives in Winnipeg, as does Rod Huff, his wife Connie a daughter of Kristin.

Standing, Frederick, Christina, August; seated, Wilhemmina, Elsie, Joseph, Justine Huff.

Rod, Connie and Krisin Huff.

WILLIAM HEMPTON

William George Hempton, born 1862, in Kingston, Ontario, was the son of Thomas Hempton. He came to Dominion City in the 1880's working for the C.P.R. spur line to Green Ridge.

He married Rebecca Harriett Acres, December 12, 1888. She was born in Hazeton, Ontario in 1868, and came to Dominion City in 1879.

They raised eight children, Albert, Wilfred, Roy, Eva, Lloyd, Katie, Kenneth and Mildred. They were all born in the old home which stood where the Bryan Nichols home now stands.

Albert died an infant, Wilfred died at the age of seven, Roy died at age 23. Eva married James French and raised 12 children, two died in infancy. Wallace, Dorothy, Jean, Bernice, Thomas, Kenneth, Norma, Vaughan, Joan and Gweneth.

Lloyd married Ruth ? in 1927 and had four children Patricia, Donna, Judy and Sandra. Ruth died and he remarried Gladys ? in 1951.

Katie married William Wenninger, and had six children, George, Eileen, Douglas, William Gladys and Carol. Katie died in 1946.

Kenneth married Jean Weir, and had two children William and Bonnie. Kenneth died in 1978.

Mildred married Anthony Anderson and had a daughter Velma, who passed away in 1975 at the age of 39 years.

William Hempton died April 26, 1912. Rebecca Hempton, July 8, 1929.

William and Rebecca Hempton

PETRO HALASIS

Petro came to Canada with his wife Anna (Kolisnyk) May 23, 1898, from the West Ukraine. They brought five children Paladia, Jawdokia, Maria, Sofia and Ilko.

They settled at Vita where members of their village and family were already living. There were two more daughters born at Vita, Wasylyna and and Warwara. They farmed there till their children grew up.

When their son married and moved to live at Carlowrie they sold their farm and went to live with him. Anna died in 1927, Petro in 1929. Both are buried in the Greek Orthodox Cemetery.

Paladia born 1883 married Nick Bachynski and had five children, John, Peter, Michael, Sylvester, Bohdan.

Jawdokia born in 1887 married Nick Leskiw lived in Brandon. They had four children, Maurice, Joe, Sam, and Peter.

Maria, 1890, married Danylo Leskiw and lived in the U.S.A.

Sofia born 1894 married Alex Kiziuk.

Illko (Alex) born 1897 married Anna Fedirchuk in 1922. They had three children. Alex is deceased and Anna lives at Carlowrie.

Wasylyna born in Canada 1899 married John Slobodzian.

Warwara, 1902, married Steve Tanchak.

Meraslow married Ann ? and lives in Winnipeg. They have no children.

Marie married Eddy Koranicki and lives in Winnipeg. They have no children.

Annette married Danny Gagneon and they live in Winnipeg. They have two children, Daniel and Monique.

Dara Leskiw and Wasylyna Slobodzean.

Alex and Anna Halasis, Meroslaw.

Danny Gangeon, Alex, Annette (Gangeon), Anna Halasis; Insets, Daniel and Monique Gangeon.

Mary Leskiw and Paladia Bachynski.

Meroslaw and Ann Halasis

DAN HARLOW

Dan Harlow was a big man, weighing close to 260 pounds. He was a self taught dentist, and his method was to put the patient on the floor, put his knees on the patients chest, and pull the tooth with a set of pliers. He was known to have made a mistake and pull the wrong one.

The Harlow Drain went across his land, and was named after him.

ARCHIBALD HAY

Archibald Hay was born in Scotland in 1858. He came to Canada in 1870, and married Margaret Spencer in 1882. In 1895 they moved to a farm near Dominion City, and 1898 to a farm at Carlowrie. They had six children. Archie Jr. married Florence Gainer, and lived in Dominion City.

Margaret died August 8, 1909. Archibald spent his last years at Duncairn, Saskatchewan, where he died December 29, 1942. He is buried at Green Ridge cemetery.

Annette Gangeon, Meroslaw Halasis, Marie Koranicki; front, Alex and Anne Halesis.

Bill, Mildred and Esther Hosick.

TOM HOSICK

Tom Hosick lived on the Bill Kyle farm, and then on 3-3-4 E1. His children were Jim, who married and lived on Section 3, Bill, Esther, and Mildred. Bill, Esther and Mildred lived on the farm where the Graydons are now. They did not marry, and were the last to use horses in the municipality. Bill Hosick is remembered for his unique system in loading a wagon of grain. He would make a stroke on the bin wall for each pail he dumped, and then draw a bar across every five strokes. It took a long time to load the wagon, but his count was accurate.

I JACOB ISAAC FAMILY

L to r; back, Mary, married John Harder, and died 1948; Annie, married Peter Harder; Peter; Jake, now Dr. J. E. Isaac; front, Mary and Jacob Isaac.

JACOB P. ISAAC

Jacob P. Isaac, his wife Mary, and their children Annie (16), Mary (14), Peter (13), and Jacob (11), arrived in Franklin Municipality in 1926, where he had a store and garage business in Arnaud. The family had come to Canada from Russia in 1924.

J MICHAEL JAHNKE

Michael Jahnke was born September 29th, 1865 in Russia. In 1891 he came to Canada.

On November 19, 1893 he married Henrietta Ratchsinski. She was born on August 7, 1875 in Russia, and came to Gretna with her parents Ludwig and Susanna Ratchsinski in 1893. Her parents lived with her until their death.

In 1893 Michael and Henrietta started farming. In 1897 they bought three quarter sections of land at Friedensthal. They lived on this farm till they died, Henrietta in 1952 and Michael in 1953.

The land is now farmed by their son Gerhard Jahnke.

There were 10 children. William (died at age four), Lydia, Emil, Henriette (died an infant), Olga (Pappel, died 1962), Herman, Emilie, Elsie (Recksiedler), Gerhard, Minnie (Gaenswein).

Emilie Jahnke was born March 3, 1885, in Russia. She and her sister Louise came to Canada in 1904. They were accompanied by their father, William Jahnke, who returned to Russia after a month's visit.

Emilie and Louise came to Winnipeg, to her sister Justine Huff. They moved to Friedensthal, where they visited her brothers Michael and Ludwig, and sister Caroline Schultz. Louise married G. Lange.

After a few months working in Winnipeg, Emilie returned to Fredensthal and lived on the farm with her brother Michael and his wife until they died. She stayed with the Jahnke family on the farm till 1965. In 1965 they moved to Emerson where she died in September 1980, at age 95.

Elsie taught school for several years in the Sewell-Rosenfeld area until she married Fred Recksiedler and moved to Morris. They had two children Betty and Larry. Betty, married Peter Rempel, and lives in St. Catherines and have three children. Larry, married Sandra Wiebe. They have three children and live in Florida.

Gerhard Jahnke grew up on the home farm and farmed in Dominion City for eight years. He married Laura Mazinke June 22, 1957. They have four children, Delaine, Allan, Dianne and Loren. Delaine married Andy Colley, has two children,

Pamela and Jennifer and lives in Winnipeg.

Minnie married Alfons Gaenswein and lives in Winnipeg.

Lydia, Emil, Herman and Emilie lived on the home farm in Friedensthal until their retirement to Emerson in 1965. Emil died in 1978.

Olga married Jake Pappel in June, 1923. They lived in this municipality for several years. They had two children, Joyce and Anita. Both are living in Winnipeg. Anita married Englehardt Steltzer.

Michael and Henrietta Jahnke

Emilie Jahnke with great nieces and great nephews, l to r; Delaine, Dianne, Loren, Allen, Chris; front, twins Monica and Beth.

Laura, Allan, Delaine, Dianne, Loren and Gerhard Jahnke; Pamela and Jennifer Calley.

Fred and Elsie Recksiedler

Alphons and Minnie Gaenswien

Michael Jahnke family c. 1920.

Jake and Alga Pappel; Joyce and Anita.

WILLIAM JACK

William Jack married Ellen Telfer in Langholm, Scotland, and had eight children. They were Robert, James, William, Edward, Violet, Ella, Mary and Margaret. They came to Canada in 1882, and to Franklin in 1884, living first on the old MacDonald place north of Ridgeville. William Sr. and Robert acquired the SW ¼ and NW ¼ of 23. William Jr. and James Telfer homesteaded the E ½ of 23. Robert signed his land to his mother in a few years, and William Jr. sold his to James, and both went to work in Winnipeg.

Violet married John McBean, Jennie became a Mrs. West of Weyburne, and Ella a Mrs. McLennon, also of Saskatchewan. Mary married William Hoag of Emerson, Maggie married James Brown, an American, and died a year later. Edward (1892-1976), married Alice Buchan (1895-1965). They had three daughters. Evelyn (William Schellenberg), Delta, British Columbia; Ruth (Harold Metcalf), Cookstown, Ontario; Audrey (Morris Grier), Woodmore.

Edward was born at the Ridgeville homestead, January 13, 1892. Alice Buchan was born in Meldrum, Scotland. She came to Canada in 1914. They lived on the Jack homestead until 1963, when they retired to Dominion City. In 1968, Edward remarried to Jessie Post.

258

Ellen (Telfer) Jack was born in Langholm, Dumphane, Scotland, in 1847. She was a midwife, and served the pioneer families of the ridge faithfully. She died in 1942, at age 95.

James farmed his entire life on the homestead. His first wife, Sarah Marshall, died in 1918. They had three children, who did not live. He married Lily (Revel) Flint, a widow, in 1925, and they had three children. They were Doreen, who married Frank Kilikowski; William, who married Lillian Grier; and Lorna, who married Lorne Lamont. Lily (Revel) Flint was born in Chesterfield, England, and came to Canada in 1923. She had a daughter, Lucy Revel, who died in 1924. Lily was born 1893, died 1977. James Jack died in 1966, was born 1878.

James, Jennie, Violet, Ella, Mary, Edward and Robert Jack.

Doug, Gordon, Lillian and Bill Jack.

Lorna, Doreen, Bill, Lillian; front, Lily Jack.

William, James, Edward (on pony), William Jack Sr., Ellen, Margaret, c. 1900.

Back, Jane Kilikowski, Linda and Steve Kral; middle, Douglas, Lily and Gordon Jack; front, Elizabeth and Bonnie Kral.

Ruth, Evelyn (seated), Audrey Jack.

Edward and Alice Jack

Audrey and Morris Grier

Back, John Runge, Rhonda (Schellenberg) Hollerin, Judy and Bruce Schellenberg, Heather (Schellenberg) Runge; middle, Ian Hollerin, Evelyn and William Schellenberg; front, Ted Schellenberg, Dr. Ken Schellenberg.

Ruth and Harold Metcalf family, Harry and Jacquelyn Hirvonen, Allen and Susan Stanbury, Brian and Patricia Patterson, Harold and Ruth Metcalf.

JACOB J. JANZEN

Jacob and Katherina Janzen, Jacob, Aganetha, Kate and Susan left the Crimea, in southern Russia and came to Canada in 1924. In spring of 1925 they moved to an abandoned farm situated on the west bank of the Roseau river by the correction line between Arnaud and Dominion City. Jacob Sr. died in March 1926 and his son Jacob worked much of this land and farmed it for many years. He had one daughter, Susan, and three sons, George, Jake and John. He is now retired and living in Arnaud. Susan married Jacob Braun, of Meadows. They have two daughters, Marilyn, and Dolores, and a son Gordon. George married Katherine Klassen and they are living in Michigan. They have three children, James, Diane and Michael. Jake is married to Margaret Penner and farms in Franklin. They have four children, Lorna, Richard, Sandra and Theodore. John is married to Margaret Bergen and lives on the home place. They have three daughters, Cheryl, Corinne and Valerie.

Jacob and Katharina Janzen

Left: Jacob and Elena Janzen, 1925.
Right: Jacob and Helen Janzen, 1979.

Dolores, Marilyn, Jacob, Susan and Gordon Baun.

Sandra, Jake, Margret, Lorna, Clarence, Richard, Ted.

260

John and Marge Janzen

Valerie, Corinne and Cheryl Janzen.

James, Kathy, Michael; front, George and Diana.

ABRAM J. JANZEN

Abram J. Janzen was born in Neukirch, Russia. He came to Altona in 1924 and in 1925 he worked for the William Forresters in Emerson. He married Agnetha Janzen from Dominion City in 1925. Later with their son John they moved to a farm near Killarney. In 1936 with their children John, William, Kathleen and Margaret they moved back to a farm four miles northwest of Dominion City. In the fall of 1937 they moved to a farm northeast of Arnaud. Agnetha died in 1937 and Abram married Maria Warkentin from Headingly. They had two sons, Henry, who died in infancy, and Albert.

In 1955 the Janzens moved to section 27-3-3, the Lyman Farm.

Maria died June 18, 1969 and Abram June 18, 1977.

John, William and Albert Janzen now operate Janzen Farms Ltd.

L to r; back, Kathleen (Janzen) Driedger, John, William, Margaret (Janzen) Janzen, Abram Janzen, Albert, Maria (Warkentin) Janzen, 1951.

Margaret (Friesen), John Luann and Greg Janzen, 1981

Dennis, William, Ella (Heinrichs) Janzen, Angela, 1979

Hedy (Penner) Janzen, Shelley, Jodine, Albert, 1979.

DAVID JOHNSTON

David Johnston and Euphemia Dumma were married, Jedburgh, Scotland, April 25, 1919. David came to Canada when he was 17, and enlisted with the Winnipeg Grenadiers during World War I. After discharge he went to Scotland, married, and came to the SW ¼ 14-2-3 E1 in Franklin Municipality with the help of the Soldier's Settlement Board. Mrs. Johnston and Mary following in 1920.

January 6, 1923, Alice Lillian was born.

The Johnstons left the SW ¼ of 14-3-2 in 1927, and moved to the SE ¼ of 23-2-4 E1.

June 13, 1928 Jean Eileen was born.

At the beginning of World War II David joined his old regiment, was sent to Hong Kong, where he died June 7, 1943.

Mary married Henry Alstadt June 25, 1943. She has one daughter, Sharon, born March 14, 1945. Sharon married John Enns, Winnipeg, and her children are Jason, Justin, Noel and Tessa.

Alice married Graham Batten on April 22, 1950. They have three children and live on the family farm, 19-2-5 E1.

Jean married Herb Zilkie May 1950, and has two children, Joan and Todd. Joan is married to Tim Connell, Lac du Bonnet, has a daughter, Kelly.

In 1951 Euphemia Johnston married H. D. Lenton, selling her land to D. A. Steinert. In 1974 the Lentons retired to Franklin Manor Home. Mr. Lenton died March 18, 1975, Mrs. Lenton March 4, 1982.

Left: Jean (Johnston) Zilkie, c. 1940.
Right: Alice (Johnston) Batten, 1945, Ottawa.

Left: Wedding of David and Euphemia (Dumma) Johnston, Scotland, 1919.
Right: Mrs. David Johnston and Mary, c. 1922.

262

WILLIAM JOHNSTON

Tom and Ruth (Brewster) Ostberg, Mary (Griffith) and Wm. Johnston; front, Richard and Marilyn Johnstone, 1950.

JOSEPH JOHNSON

Joseph Johnson, born 1819, married Hannah Lee and had six children. He was a farmer and a cattlebuyer in the County of Northumberland, in England, on a farm called Plankey Ford.

He lost his wife in 1880. In the year 1888, at the age of 69, he left two sons in England and sailed to Canada with three generations of Johnsons: his sons, John Lee Johnson, wife Margaret Hannah and six week old son Joseph Henderson; Thomas Johnson and wife; Jacob Johnson, bachelor and daughter Elizabeth Ann, who later married Albert Smith and lived in Stuartburn.

Thomas settled the NW ¼ 34-2-5 E1, Jacob, SE ¼ 34-2-5 E1, Joseph, SW ¼ 34-2-5 E1, and John Lee on NW ¼ 14-2-5 E1.

The Plankey Plains School was named after their home in England.

Joseph Johnson, died in 1907 and was interred in the Greenridge cemetery.

After his father's death Thomas sold his farm and took his family to California. A few years later Jacob left for Edson, Alberta.

John Lee Johnson died in 1913 leaving his wife and four sons, Joseph Henderson, John William, Jacob Edward Lee and Fred R.

John Henderson married Ellen Pott, farmed until 1927 on SE ¼ 34-2-5 E1, and then moved his family to Winnipeg. John William moved to Ashcroft, British Columbia. A number of years later Fred R. joined him.

Jacob Edward Lee married Mary Smith of Woodmore on December 9, 1925 and farmed on 28-2-5 E1. A few years later they purchased the W ½ of 24-2-4 E1 and continued to farm this land until Jacob's death in April, 1968. Mary lives on a small portion of this property.

Jacob and Mary had three children. Louise (Mrs. Bruce Dickson) lives in Greenridge, Elva (Mrs. William McCarthy) lives in Winnipeg and Gordon, lives at Stuartburn.

Mr. and Mrs. John Lee Johnson, Joseph (Joe) Henderson; front, Fred R., John William (Bill), Jacob Edward Lee (Jac.).

Margaret Hannah Johnson and son Joseph Henderson.

Jacob and Fred Johnson, Tom Pott.

263

Mary (Mrs. Jacob) Johnson, Louise Dickson, Gordon, Elva McCarthy.

JOSEPH JAMIESON

Joseph and Sarah Jamieson came to Dominion City around 1909.

They had three daughters, Grace (Mrs. W. H. Hancox), Gladys (Mrs. Van Camp) and Eva (Mrs. Wm. McClelland), her husband deceased and she later married Richard Van Vorst. Their sons were George, Alfred, Herb, Russel and Bill.

Joseph Jamieson, centre, with two brothers (not named). He and his wife Sarah came to Dominion City around 1907.

Left: Grace Jamieson, 1925, daughter of Joseph Jamieson.
Right: Sarah, Mrs. Joseph Jamieson on left with Mrs. Hoffer.

Left: Bill Jamieson. Harvey Hasset.
Bill was the second son of Joseph Jamieson.
Right: Alfred and Ellen Jamieson. Alfred was born in 1899, the eldest son of Joseph Jamieson. They had four children Herbert, Eldred, Allan and Grace. Moved to Vernon, B.C. in 1933.

Left: Herbert Jamieson was born in 1908 in Dominion City. He moved to Vancouver in 1935, and died in 1978 in Delta, B.C.
Right: Eva Jamieson married Bill McClelland. They moved to Vancouver in 1933.

Left: George Jamieson, son of Joseph Jamieson, and Adeline holding grandchild, not named. They have two children Doris and Ruth and live in Wawkesha, Wisconsin.
Right: Russel and Mary (Dyck) Jamieson. Russel is the son of Joseph Jamieson. They had a family of four sons and seven daughters, Gordon, Leonard, Robert and Lorne. Olive (Doyle), Joanne married Cam Baskerville, Lorraine married D. Adams, Eleanor (Gerghiety), Marlene (Field), Karen (Norris), Shirley (Ennis).

264

Left: Eva McClelland married Richard Van Vorst in 1962. They live in Richmond, B.C.
Right: Gladys Jamieson married Alton Van Camp in 1927. They had four children, Keva, Raymond, Lorne and Carl, and lived in Drayton, N.D.

LEO JAHNKE

Leo Jahnke immigrated in 1924 from Turin, Lutzyk with his father, Godlieb. They worked around the Dominion City area and in Saskatchewan. In 1936, Leo bought the NW ¼ 15-2-3.

In 1932 Leo married Rosalie Rettaler, daughter of Jacob Rettaler. They had four children Louise, Elsie, Clarence, and Anne. Leo and Rose sold the farm to Glenway Colony in 1967 and moved to Dominion City. Leo passed away in 1970.

Louise died in infancy. Elsie worked in Winnipeg and married Irvin Frank, son of William of Dominion City, in 1955. They live in Pine Falls. Anne married Jim Hill of the RCMP in 1962 and lives in Ottawa. Clarence took auto mechanics training at M.I.T. and was employed by Heibert's Garage in Dominion City for 11 years. In 1963 he married Sylvia Gunn and they lived in Clarence's parents' yard. In 1967 Clarence bought the SW ½ 6-1-5 E1. He has two children, Keith and Virginia.

Keith, Sylvia (Gunn), Clarence, Virginia Jahnke.

Rose and Leo Jahnke with children Elsie, Clarence, Anne.

K TODYR KOHUT

John Kohut was born November 9, 1916 to Peter and Salka Kohut, who lived four miles north-west of Stuartburn. On June 5, 1943 John married Mary, daughter of Alex and Lena Chuba-

Seated in front are Todyr and Maria Kohut who came to Stuartburn in 1898 from the village of Synkiw, Ukraine. In back are son Stephan and wife Dokia (all deceased) with children Lena, now Mrs. Bill Yasinski of Carlowrie, and Peter Kohut of Stuartburn. Another grandson of Todyr Kohut, Alex Sherman lives in Stuartburn. Youngest child of T. Kohuts Anna Sirman died November 1981 in Stuartburn.

ty of Rosa. After their marriage they lived with John's parents on the farm for six years. In December 1949, John, Mary and their sons, Roman, Walter, and Adam moved into their own home in Roseau River on half an acre of land purchased from Henry Pott. This was the third building in town. On December 15, 1950, they opened a general store. In one corner of the store John had a barber shop.

On February 24, 1973 John passed away. Mary and daughters, Eileen, and Elsie kept the store going until March 12, 1981, when they quit the store business. The store area has been renovated and the building remains their home in 1982.

WASYL KOHUT

Wasyl and Anna Kohut (nee Ewonchuk) came to Canada in the year 1911 from the village of Senkiw, province of Tarnopol, Western Ukraine. They had three sons: Steve, John and Sam. The family spent the first year in the River Ranch district in a small log and clay cabin on the homestead of Wasyl's sister Wasylyna and Ostafiy Korotash. In 1919 Wasyl and Anna purchased land at Rosa from Jim Carleton in 23-3-5. Five children were born here, Katherine, Mary, Pete, Dan and Anne.

Wasyl and Anna Kohut remained on their farm, until their retirement. Wasyl died in 1934 and Anna in 1955. Four of their sons, Steve, John, Pete and Dan, farmed in the Rosa area, and Pete still resides on the original farm in semi-retirement. Steve married Mary Winnicky from Caliento and they had a family of 13. Steve is now deceased. Sam made his home in Winnipeg. He married Jean Shmigovaty from Selkirk and they had three children. Both Sam and Jean are now deceased. Dan farmed at Rosa and also operated a general store. He married Christina Woytowich from Poland and they had one daughter, Madeline, who resides in Winnipeg but still owns the farm and home at Rosa. Dan died in 1969.

Katherine married Steve Stepaniuk and they farmed in the Rosa area. They had six children. William and Effie, became schoolteachers. The other two daughters of Wasyl and Anna Kohut made their homes in Winnipeg. Mary married Roman Bylo and they had four children. Anne married Fred Pismenny and they raised three children.

John, married Effie Sirkiziuk in 1925. Effie and her father, Wasyl Sirkiziuk, had immigrated to Canada in the year 1923 from the village of Dzvinyachka, province of Tarnopol, Western Ukraine. John and Effie purchased land at Rosa in 23-3-5, where they still live in retirement.

John and Effie had nine children, seven of whom reached maturity: Maurice, Jennie, Anne, Walter, Mike, Elsie and Peter. Two other children, Josie and Bill, died at an early age. They have 13 grandchildren and one great-grandchild.

Maurice, the oldest son, married Stella Mandzuik from Rosa.

Maurice and Stella had four children, of which twin daughters, June and Elaine, were born at Rosa. June is the first female doctor from Franklin municipality. Maurice and Stella and their sons, James and Shaun, live in Winnipeg, and also own a farm and home at Rosa in 22-3-5.

Anne married Paul Woytowich. They live in St. Norbert and have four children. Elsie, married Donald Wabick and has two daughters.

Walter married Jean Krochenski from Fraserwood, and they live in Winnipeg with one son.

Mike remained on the family farm and is actively engaged in mixed farming. Peter, the youngest son, joined the R.C.M.P. in 1960. He is now a Staff-Sergeant in Winnipeg.

Semeon and Titana Kohut, Wasyl and Anna Kohut and Wasylina Korotosh (Wasyl's sister).

Jim, Maurice and Shawn Kohut at Rosa Catholic Church.

Anna Kohut with her children Steve, John and Semeon.

First home of Wasyl and Anna Kohut, cd. 1915.

John and Effie Kohut; Maurice and Stella Kohut.

John and Effie Kohut on their 50th anniversary.

June and Elaine Kohut

Madeline Kohut; Peter Kohut.

ALEXANDER KIRKPATRICK

Alexander Kirkpatrick was born in County Antrim, in northern Ireland, of Scottish parents, in 1820. His wife, Nancy Anne Brown, was born in Glasgow, Scotland, in 1830. Both families emigrated to Morin Heights, Quebec, where they married in 1854. All seven children were born in Quebec.

They homesteaded the NW ¼ of 12-2-4E in Franklin Municipality. Later they acquired the NE and SW quarters of 12-2-4E in what is now Woodmore.

Alexander, Nancy Anne and their seven children are buried in Green Ridge cemetery.

Jane, born in 1855, married John Lockhead. They came to Manitoba in 1879, ahead of the rest of the family. Agnes born 1857, married Henry Young. James born 1861, married Sarah Wood, Mary born 1862, was a spinster. Daniel born 1865, married Margaret Wood, Sarah Wood's sister. William, born 1868, was a bachelor. Alexander, born 1870, married Edith Post. James, Daniel and Alexander all homesteaded or bought land in Franklin.

James Kirkpatrick and Sarah Wood were married February 16, 1897 in Montreal. They homesteaded NE ¼ 10-2-4 E1.

James and Sarah's children were Everett, born

267

January 24, 1898. He enlisted in the R.C.M.P. and left for England June 5, 1918. Everett died in a London hospital of general peritonitis the 29th of that same month, and was buried in a military cemetery at Brookwood, Surrey, England.

George born in 1900, died at five weeks of age, and is buried at Green Ridge.

Gordon born June 13, 1902, married Elizabeth Hadcock, born at Winnipeg, December 4, 1906, in Bay City, Michigan. They took over the James Kirkpatrick farm, and lived there until retirement in 1963, when it was sold to Roger Durand.

Their children were Douglas Herbert, born July 3, 1930, died at 23 days of age. Barbara Grace, married and living in Mississauga. She has three children. Brian Hadcock, married and living in Illinois, and has two girls. Carolyn Joan, married and living in Kelowna, British Columbia. She has two daughters. Willard Alexander, married, lives in Calgary, Alberta and has three children.

Enid Alva was James and Sarah's older daughter, born June 4, 1908. She married Ernest Watson and lives in Vancouver. They have two daughters, Diane Beverley, married, in Vancouver, and has two children. Linda Irene, is married, lives in Kelowna, British Columbia and has two children.

Alice Muriel was born January 10, 1914, and died October 1, 1967. She married Ernest McAteer, and had one daughter, Maureen.

Mary Kirkpatrick, born 1862, never married. She lived with her parents until her death November 28, 1907.

Daniel Kirkpatrick was born 1865, and died February 12, 1927. He started farming on the NE ¼ of 16-2-4E, and later bought the SE ¼ of 7-2-4E. This quarter was below the "Ridge", and was completely under cultivation.

In 1899 he married Margaret Wood. Their first child born 1903, died.

Walter was born on January 4, 1907 and died October 1969. Walter married Janet McLennan, and had two children.

William Kirkpatrick, the bachelor of the family, remained on the original homestead after his parents died. He died November 3, 1935.

Alexander (Jr.) was born in Lachute, Quebec on December 27, 1870 and died May 8, 1934. He was nine years old when he came to Manitoba. On October 16, 1901 Alexander married Edith Post (born January 5, 1881, died February 5, 1970) and they moved to the NW ¼ 18-2-4 E1. Alexander and Edith had eight children. They are:

Elmer Alexander, born August 28, 1902, died September 3, 1980.

Ethel Irene, born November 9, 1904, married Earle Lamont and they had three sons, Lorne, Don and Hugh.

Edna Mabel, born February 23, 1907, married Jim Dunlop on August 15, 1936. They lived in Winnipeg, Oregon and are presently living in Mesa, Arizona. Their son Ronald married Ruth Ann Russel. They are the parents of two daughters, Nicole and Michelle.

Edith Mary, born January 11, 1909, died January 22, 1982. She married Ted Forge on June 6, 1936. They lived in Winnipeg, Oregon and retired to Arizona where Ted is still living.

Evelyn Louise, born July 2, 1911, married Angus McAuley in 1943. They live in St. Vital and have one daughter, Patricia, who married Todd Billingsley. Their two children are Susan and Ian.

Herbert William was born October 17, 1912 and died December 21, 1912.

Doris Viola, born June 2, 1915, married Darcy Reynolds July 3, 1937. They lived in Arnaud, then moved to Hartney where Doris lives. Darcy died July 4, 1969. They have three sons, Douglas, who married Shirley Shann. They have three children, Lori, Darcy and Bryan. George has two sons, Lee and Trevor. John married Cindy Bertholette and their three children are Sheldon, Darren and Hope.

Verna Leola, born September 18, 1917, married William Irvine of Morris on October 28, 1939. Bill died August 26, 1967.

They have five children. Wayne married Pat Thatcher and has two sons, Bradley and Stuart. Tom, married Colleen (Bonnie) Burgess. Their two children are Michael and Pamela. Ken (twin), married Karen Damsgaard and they have two children, Kristopher and Kraig. Allan, (twin), married Valerie Rutter. Their two children are Gregory and Heather. Shirley married Rick Rempel.

Iona Ida was born June 12, 1921. Iona and her mother moved to Winnipeg in 1943 where she worked until her marriage to Bill Jones from Arnaud. The Jones lived in Winnipeg and later in Oregon. Bill died September 11, 1979. Their two children are Bob and Linda. Bob married Mary Lou Fiegert.

Elmer Alexander was born in Green Ridge on August 28, 1902 and died September 3, 1980. Elmer farmed with his father until his father's death. He married Margaret Irvine of Morris on June 15, 1940, and moved to the NE ¼ 18-2-4E.

They had four children:

David Alexander, born September 27, 1943, married Beverly Stopperan of Cresco, Iowa on August 19, 1972. They have three children and live in Dominion City. Their children are Troy David, born April 26, 1975, Gina Lynn, born

April 10, 1977, and Karla Ann, born December 5, 1978.

Sharon Margaret, born August 4, 1945, married Brian Riach of Ridgeville. They have three children, Sherri Ann, Kristin Leigh and Kent Donald. They live in St. Norbert.

Dorothy Ann, born December 14, 1947, married Neil Strachan of Carman, and has three children. They are Brady Neil, Shaelyn Margaret and Morgan Alfred.

Donald Irvine was born November 21, 1951 and died June 25, 1972. Don attended school in Greenridge and Emerson. He enjoyed various sports, particularly curling. He had a keen sense of humor and made friends easily. Don's death was the result of a car accident.

Left: Elmer and Margaret Kirkpatrick.
Right: In 1926 this coyote was shot by Elmer Kirkpatrick on Sec. 2-4e which was unbroken and covered by willows.

Agnes Kirkpatrick and William Kirkpatrick

Gordon Kirkpatrick and his 1926 Essex sedan.

Alexander and Edith (Post) Kirkpatrick

L to r; the Kirkpatrick sisters, Iona Jones, Verna Irvine, Doris Reynolds, Evelyn McAuley, Edith Forge, Edna Dunlop, Ethel Lamont, Elmer Kirkpatrick.

Gordon and Beth Kirkpatrick on their 50th wedding anniversary September 21, 1979.

Part of Gordon Kirkpatrick's flock of sheep at winter quarters, c. 1937.

269

Neil, Dorothy Brady, Shaelyn and Morgan Strachan.

Brian and Sharon Riach; Don Kirkpatrick.

Dave, Bev, Karla, Gina and Troy Kirkpatrick.

IVAN KOZAK

Ivan Kozak was born in Dziniachka, Borchchiv, Galacia, Austria. He came to Franklin Municipality in 1897, and homesteaded the NE ¼ of 9-1-5 E1. His wife, Anna, and five children, came at the same time. The children were Dymtro, Tanasko, Arteman, Stefan and Maria.

Stefan married Katherine (?) of Sifton, where they ran a general store. They had two sons, Archie and Teddy. Stefan died in Hamilton, Ontario.

Marie, born 1896, married Ivan P. Mandzuik in 1915. Her husband was a priest in the Ukrainian Greek Orthodox Church, at Rhein, Saskatchewan. Maria died 1941. She had four children, Peter, Elsie, Olga, Ann.

Tonasko Kozak married Maria Saranchuk, and had seven children. They were Annie, Paul (who drowned on the farm dugout in 1933), Anton, Mike, Martin, Walter and Olga. Tanasko homesteaded on the SW ¼ of 3-1-5 E1.

Artman Kozak married ? and had nine children. They are John, Nickola, Michael, Bill, Steven, Elizabeth, Rose, Pauline and Annie.

Dymtro married Helen Kushniryk, in 1901. Helen was born in Melnycia district, Borshchiv. They homesteaded the SW ¼ of 3-1-5 E1, and had 11 children. Three children died in infancy, Bill died in 1933 at age 21. The others were John, Paul, Peter, Mary, Nettie, Olga and Pauline. Dymtro was born October 14, 1879, died November 9, 1956. Helen died January 5, 1961.

Anton and Nettie (Kozak) Tofan were married on November 18, 1939. They farmed until their retirement. They have one daughter, Patricia, who married Dennis St. Onge on August 19, 1967. She has one daughter Cheryl.

John Kozak, married Julia Drewniak on June 8, 1930. They lived with his parents, Dymtro and Helen Kozak for 12½ years. In 1942 they bought 160 acres from Jacob Hutt NW 10-1-5.

They had seven children.

Nestor, born April 3, 1931, died April 18, 1932, of high fever.

Vladimier, married Betty Goetz. They have two children, Lori and Glenn.

Theresa and Rosie were twins. Theresa married Steve Antoniuk. They have three sons: Teddy, Wally and David. Rosie married Bill Fedorchuk, they have two children, Theresa and Kenneth. Theresa married Robert Schultz of Emerson.

Bernice is living in Toronto, teaching school.

Eleanor married Ron Hart, they have two children, Debbra and Brian.

Sylvia married Kris Fjelsted, they have two sons - Krisjan, and Cody Myles born January 16, 1983.

Peter Kozak married Verna Goetz in 1944. They lived with parents Dymtro and Helen Kozak. Peter farmed till 1965, then moved to Winnipeg and retired to Tolstoi in 1980. They had four children, Billy, Nestor, Doris and Peter Jr. Doris married Leo Sokolik of Calgary. They have two sons, Michael and Johnny.

Paul married Mary Podolsky in 1934. They farmed NE ¼ township five near Tolstoi, until they moved to Emerson in 1974.

They have three children: Ernest, Richard and Nancy.

Ernest married Ruth Fostey in 1959. They lived at the Bradley school house from 1959 to 1964, where Ernest was a school teacher. They have two children, Gwen and Sheryl. They moved to Emerson, Manitoba in 1964, where they still live.

Anton and Nellie (Kozak) Tofan

L to r; Pauline (Machnee), Olga, Nettie (Tofan), Mary (Rybuck), Helen (Kuchniryk) and Dymtro Kozak, John, Paul, Peter Kozak, 1951.

Back, Robert Schultz, Theresa Schultz, Bill Fedorchuk, Kenneth Fedorchuk, Steve Antoniuk, Teddy Antoniuk, Bernice Kozak, Wally Antoniuk, Vladimier Kozak, Ron Hart, Kris Fjelsted; middle, Rose Fedorchuk and Theresa Antoniuk (twins), Julia (Drewniak) Kozak, John Kozak, Betty Kozak, Eleanor Hart, Sylvia Fjelsted and son Krisjan on her knees; front, Lorri Kozak, David Antoniuk, Glenn Kozak, Brian Hart, Debbie Hart, 1980.

Paul Demianiw, wife Iris, holding son Steven, Gerald, wife Carol, Dianne and Donald Machnee; Karen Demianiw, Nick and Pauline Machnee, holding Matthew Machnee, Jennifer and Janice Machnee. Inset, Michael Machnee, son of Gerald and Carol.

Dennis, Patricia and Cheryl St. Onge.

Back, Billy, Peter, Nestor; middle, Peter and Verna Kozak; front, Doris Sokolik, 1973.

271

Doris, Leo, Michael and Johnny Sokolik.

Sherri and Gwen Kozak

Paul, Richard, Irene and Darren Kozak.

Steve, Dymtro, Tanasko Kozak.

Mary and Paul Kozak

Steve Kozak, wife Kay, Arteman Kozak.

Nancy (Kozak), Johnny Kyrzyk, and son Jonathan.

Ruth and Ernest Kozak

L to r; Eleanor Mary (Kozak) and John Rybuck, Maurice, Peter.

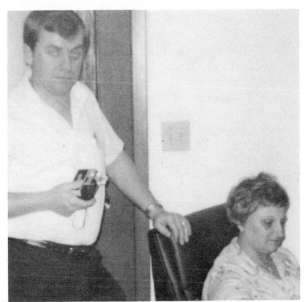

Peter and Linda Rybuck

Lucille and Maurice Rybuck; twins, Denise and Michele.

Joe and Eleona Korolash family.

KEIL AND RUFF FAMILIES

In 1903 George Henry Keil, his wife, Marie Elizabeth, brother-in-law and sister, George Adam and Suzanne Elizabeth (Keil) Ruff and daughter Mary Ruff, came to Canada from Russia. They lived in Winnipeg until 1916, when they each purchased a quarter section of the Doern property in the Overstone District, 7-1-5 E1.

The Keils had eight children.

Anne, married Jack Goetz, farmed in the area, and had a son and daughter.

Mary died as a child in 1918.

Henry, married Olga Winter, lived in Minnesota and had one son, Dennis.

Molly, married Fred Steertz, lived in Winnipeg with three daughters and one son.

Susie died in 1935.

Katherine, married Joe Fostey, lived in Winnipeg and had one daughter.

Fred, married Edith Lenton, lived in Winnipeg and had two daughters, Sharon and Linda. Fred died in 1964.

Emily, died as a child in 1918.

The Ruffs had three children. Mary, married Alex Suppes and has three daughters. Henry and Fred married and lived in Winnipeg.

Adam Ruff farmed for a year and then moved back to Winnipeg. His brother George farmed this land for several years.

In 1919 Mary Keil, 36, died. George remarried Sophie Miller (widow) with three children, Adolph, John and Della. George and Sophie had three children, Eleanor, Raymond and Isabel.

They lived on this farm until 1926 when they purchased land from A. Neuman, the NE¼ 20-1-4.

George Keil continued to live and farm on this land. He passed away in 1941.

L to r; back, Bradley (son of Dennis), Dennis (son of Henry), Gregg (son of Dennis), Henry Keil; front, Danny (son of Dennis), Muriel (wife of Dennis), Olga (wife of Henry), 1978.

273

George and Sophie Keil

Bill, Linda, William and James Palmer.

Left: Fred and Edith Keil.
Right: Sharon Elaine (Keil) Chopp.

David, Lyle and Kathryn Chopp.

274

JACOB W. KRUEGER

Jacob Krueger was born at Glenlea, to Jacob and Katharina Krueger. His wife Helen was born in the Ukraine. Her first home in Canada was in British Columbia. They were married in the Sargent Avenue Mennonite Church in Winnipeg in 1966, and have three children. They are James, Katherine and Christine. The Kruegers farm the SW ¼ of 12-1-5 E1, formerly owned by Annie Yarmie, which they purchased in 1975. Jacob also works part time at Superior Bus Manufacturing, Morris.

Helen and Jacob Krueger; children, James, Katherine and Christine, 1975.

ALEX KIZIUK

Alex Kiziuk was born in the Ukraine in 1885. He came to Canada in 1905. After working a few years he brought his father, mother, two sisters and a brother to Canada. They settled in the Caliento area. Maria married moved to British Columbia. Julia married Petruk and lives in Saskatchewan as does Kondra, a widower.

In 1913 Alex married Sofia Halasis of Vita. They farmed at Caliento for a while and then moved to Rosa. Here they rented for a few years, then finally settled at Carlowrie. He farmed here, renting land. When his children left home, he moved to Arnaud.

In his retirement he moved to St. Jean to be close to his youngest son Morris. Here Alex died, November 22, 1973 at the age of 88 years. Sofia died February 19, 1976 at the age of 81 years. They are both buried at Caliento cemetery.

They had six children, Bill, Mike, Steve, Annette, Theodore and Morris.

Bill married Ksenia Jaworiwska. They lived at Arnaud. They had one daughter Bohdana and three grandchildren, David, Robert and Katherine. Bill made his living as a carpenter and cabinet maker. Bill died November 24, 1975 at the age of 60 and is buried at Arnaud. Ksenia moved to Winnipeg and is employed there.

Mike married Mary Derewianchuk of Vita. He died March 2, 1979 at the age of 63. He is buried at the Rosa cemetery. They had three children, Elsie, Alex and Terry, also four grandchildren, Betty, Allan, Eugene and Tammy.

Steve married Lidia Shapka. He loved farming but a severe stroke put him into retirement. He lives at Arnaud and rents his land. They have four children. Margaret, married Morris Ostrowsky and has a daughter Larissa. Olga, married Werner Saxler and has two children, Peter and Lisa.

Annette married John Kraynick. They lived at Arnaud where their only son was born. After a few years they moved to Sirko where John farmed and worked at logging. Upon his death he was buried at Sirko. Annette is working in Winnipeg.

Their son Paul married Beverly Hamlin and they have three children Sherl, Lisa and a baby son.

Theodore married Doris Saranchuk. Ted and Doris have one son Jerry.

Morris married Mary Wlad. Morris worked on farms and as a combiner, and makes his home at St. Jean.

Kondra Kiziuk, Julia Petruk, Sofia Kiziuk, Alex Kiziuk, Mr. Petruk and Maurice Kiziuk.

Theodore Kiziuk

L to r; woman and child, unnamed, man, unnamed, Alex Kiziuk, holding son Mike, son Bill standing in front of Sofia Kiziuk.

Back, Peter, Morris, Werner, Olga and Liza; front Lidia (Shapka) Kiziuk, Margaret and Larissa, Steve Kiziuk.

Bill Kiziuk and Ksenia

Cheryl, Ryan and Lisa Kraynyk with Anna Kraynyk.

Paul Kraynyk and wife Beverley

Mike Kiziuk, Tammy Kiziuk and Eugene Melnychuk.

Nellie Derewianchuk, Mary Kiziuk, Elsie (Kiziuk) and Alex Melnychuk, Mike Kiziuk, Alex Derewianchuk; seated, Elsie's great-grandfather Dmytro Maximovich.

IGNACE KULCZYCKI

Ignace and Antonina Kulczycki came to Canada from Poland in 1897, with Harry, Elizabeth and Joe. They first lived in Gretna, where another son, Kweryn, was born. In 1904 they moved to the Tolstoi area, and bought a farm on 9-2-5 E1. Joe died on this farm in 1912. Another son, Walter, was born here, and he now resides in Detroit. Elizabeth, Mrs. E. Kozachenko, lives in Vita.

Kweryn was born in 1901. In 1933 he married Pauline Zulkowski, daughter of Mr. and Mrs. John Zulkowski of Vita. They took over his father's farm and lived there until retiring to Tolstoi in 1965. Their children are John and wife Rita of Coldale, Alberta, with their children

276

Marlene, Terry, and Andy.

Harry married Nellie Pawlishak, daughter of Stanley and Julia Pawlishak, in 1924. They farmed the SW ¼ of 35-1-5 E1 until their retirement to Tolstoi in 1961. They have a son, Edward and two daughters, Helen, and Victoria Ann. Helen married Clem Kalinowski, of Green Bush, North Dakota, and has four children, Greg, David, Wayne and Kathleen. Victoria married Ivan Chislett, and has two children, Heather-Lynn and Sheryl Anne. Harry Kulcheski died in 1971.

Ignace Kulczycki died in 1942, and Antonina in 1939.

The name Kulczycki is now spelled Kulcheski.

Ignace and Antonia Kulczycki

Kweryn and Pauline Kulczycki and their nine grandchildren.

Walter, John, Kweryn and Pauline Kulczycke, Carol.

Harry and Nellie Kulcheski

Eddie, Helen and Victoria Kulcheski.

LOUIS KREITZ

Louis Kreitz was born on March 15, 1877 in Volienia, Russia. His birthplace was Kiss Rovena, and Post Office was Drashna. He came to Canada by ship, in 1891, when he was 14 years old, and his nationalization papers were taken out at Emerson in 1903. He was a farm employee for many years at Gretna and Neche, North Dakota.

Caroline Jansen was born on November 1, 1888 in Warsaw, Poland. She came to Canada in 1895, when she was seven years old and her nationalization papers were taken out in 1903 at Emerson. Caroline and her sister Tenna went to the Niverville district, where they worked for and were adopted by Mr. and Mrs. Buss.

On January 11, 1906, Louis Kreitz and Caroline were married at Friedenstal. They farmed in the Dominion City district until 1917, then they moved to the Friedenstal area for 11 years. In 1927, they moved back to Dominion City until 1935 when they moved to the Old Sullivan place at Arnaud.

Louis passed away on May 15, 1945 at the age of 68 years. Caroline farmed with her sons, Louis and Walter until 1947, when she retired to Dominion City. The boys farmed for a few more years, then rented their land to the Shelly brothers.

Caroline passed away at the Emerson Municipal Hospital on January 20, 1957, at the age of 68 years. They had 12 children, four of whom died in infancy. Of the remaining children, Mildred (L. Klein) had three children and lives in Dominion City. Emma (H. Steinke) lives in Winnipeg and

has twelve children. Annie (A. Gaudry) lives in Sudbury, Ontario and has two children. Elsie (R. Ritchot) lives in Espanola, Ontario and has three children. Eileen (Art Steinke) lives in Thunder Bay, Ontario, and has three children. William lives in Kalamazoo, Michigan and has four children. Louis lives in Powell River, British Columbia, and has two children. Walter lives in Winnipeg and has two children.

MICHAEL KING

Michael King came to Wingham, Ontario in 1848 from Ireland with his father, two brothers and one sister. He married Jane Cartwright.

In 1878 he came to Franklin and purchased the SE ¼ of 18-3-4 and the N ½ of the NE ¼ of 7-3-4. He also filed homestead on the S ½ of 1-4-3 DeSalaberry Municipality.

Michael returned to Ontario in 1879. His son John F. King stayed.

In the fall of 1881 John E. returned to Wingham and in February 1882 married Margaret Kelly of Teeswater, Ontario. The couple accompanied by John's brother James returned to Manitoba. James King farmed on section 7-3-4.

John King had cleared and ploughed 17 acres by 1882.

In 1890 John's brother Owen, his sister Elizabeth and her husband Patrick Kelly arrived and purchased neighbouring land. Owen farmed part of section 7 and 8-3-4 and Patrick Kelly worked part of section 7 and 18-3-4.

The Catholic parish of St. Malo was established in 1890 and the first recorded birth was that of Margaret, daughter of Patrick and Elizabeth Kelly. The King land holding now amounted to some 1600 acres.

In 1902 James and Owen King and Patrick Kelly sold their land and moved with their families to the Calgary area.

The John E. Kings had a family of seven girls, Margaret, Mary, Winnifred, Bessie, Agnes, Irene and Kathleen and three sons Frank, Joseph and Edward.

John E. King died in May 1936 and Mrs. King died in January 1942.

Joseph P. King married Josephine Markinski April 5, 1921 and settled on the east half of the SE ¼ of 18-3-4E. He farmed with his father until 1936. After the death of his father in 1936 Joseph took over the family farm.

He had a family of eight girls. Mary Ellen of Victoria; Noreen (M. Monchamp) and Rita (Tyler), Vancouver; Patricia (A. Goodman), East Selkirk; Jean (J. Coulombe), Powerview; Florence (R. Boutet); Bernadette (F. Clement) and

Eunice (Burdyny), Toronto; and two sons John J. and William F. both of Arnaud.

The Kings retired from active farming in 1971 but remained on the farm. Joseph P. King died May 7, 1976. Josephine King then lived with her daughter Florence. She died February, 1982.

John J. King eldest son of Joseph P. King now operates the family farm. He is the fourth generation to hold title to the SE ¼ of 18-3-4.

William F. King purchased the NE ¼ of 12-3-3 in 1965 where he still resides with his wife Lorraine (Calder) and two daughters, Monica and Caroline.

John Cherwaty, operating J. P. King's Case combine, c. 1938.

The well known big Cottonwood tree located on Section 12-3-3. Diameter, 182.1 cm.; height, 25 m.; age 150 years (approx.). Bert Lang, Annie Lang, Katie Bratton, Garnet Lang and Alice Brownlow.

William F. and Lorraine (Calder) King, Monica and Caroline.

John, Patricia, Eunice, Florence, Mary Ellen, Rita, William, Bernadette, Jean, Noreen; front, Josephine and Joseph P. King.

John J. King; John E. and Margaret (Kelly) King

278

L to r; Bernie, Dave, Albert, Bill, Eva, Jake, Richard, Henry, Mary, Phillip, John, and Ann; seated, Anna and John Kehler, 1958.

JOHN KEHLER

John and Anna Kehler purchased the SW ¼ 35-2-5E from Mr. John Sawatsky in 1937. They had 12 children: Bernie, Dave, Albert, Bill, Eva (Gerbrandt), Jake, Richard, Henry, Mary (Zacharias), Phillip, John, and Ann (Bert Johnson). In 1965 they retired to Steinbach. The farm was left to Bernie and later sold to brother Dave. John Kehler died in 1969 and Mrs. Anna Kehler in 1971.

STEPHAN KOSHMAN

Mr. and Mrs. Stephan Koshman and three daughters Wasylyna (Gorman), Anna (Strimbitski) and Maria (Feniuk) left Synkiw, Ukraine in 1899, arriving in Winnipeg in June 1899. They brought with them from their homeland; dried bread, clothing, hand woven covers, pillows and vegetable seeds. After some delay, they were sent by train to Dominion City where they were met by John Kulachkowsky and Wasyl Bzovey. Both had settled in the Stuartburn district two or three years earlier. The Koshmans lived with the John Kulachkowsky family until the spring of 1900 when they bought a cancelled homestead for $30, the NE ¼ 22-2-5E. They built their home on the south half. While Stephen cleared land, his wife and oldest daughter dug seneca roots and the younger one herded a few head of cows. In 1920 they bought the former Jack Pawloski farm from Theo Wachna, NW ¼ 23-2-5E. In the spring of 1930, a spring grass fire caused the buildings to start burning. Mr. Koshman went into the burning barn to save the livestock and was burnt badly. He died a few days later on Good Friday, April 1930. Mrs. Koshman died in 1940.

Wasylyna Koshman married Sam Gorman November 11, 1900, at Stuartburn Church. Three days before the wedding, the bride and the bridesmaids walked from home to home inviting everyone to her wedding. Her wedding dress was the traditional Ukrainian costume of cross-stitched shirt, skirt and a headpiece of dried flowers and green leaf sprays. Since priests came out only a few times a year, there were 11 couples married that day.

The Gormans lived with Wasylyno's parents until 1904 when her father gave them the north half of NE ¼ 22-2-5E. In 1923, times were hard, so they sold their horses and cattle and went to the U.S.A. to look for work. After five years they moved back to Canada and bought a farm northwest of Stuartburn from Joe Nawolski.

They retired in 1957 to a home in Stuartburn. Mr. Gorman passed away a few days after moving into their newly acquired home. Mrs. Gorman died March 10, 1982 at the age of 97.

The Gormans had seven children. Kay (Wakaruk), born in 1901, died in 1930 at the age of 29. She was the mother of two. After her death Mrs. Gorman raised these children to adulthood. Anne (Coates) of Minneapolis died in 1950. Bill died in 1970; John and wife Diane and family, live in Warren, Michigan; Peter; Mary (John Tallent), lives in Nevada and Harry, who died in 1981 and had lived in Winnipeg.

PAUL KYLE

Paul Kyle came to Canada from Russia when he was 18. He worked on a farm in the Rosenfeld district where he met Julia Henning. They were married in 1903 at Friedensthal and after farming in various parts of the R.M. of Franklin settled in section 22-2-3 E1.

Julia was the daughter of Henry and Emilie Henning who came from Russia in 1896. She was one of 11 children and in September 1982 will be 97 years of age. Two sisters Anne Erwin of Casta Mesa, California, Emma Singheil of Mossbank, Saskatchewan and a brother Julius Henning who resides at Franklin Manor at Dominion City, are still living. Paul and Julia raised seven children. One son and two daughters died in infancy.

Garnet, resides in Dominion City with his wife Cecelia (Mickler).

Bertha Ladd lives in Langley Lodge, Langley, British Columbia. Edward, her husband, passed away May 1982. They had four children, Edward Jr., Ellen Farmer, Beverly Chapman and Barbara.

Anne Pearse resides in Franklin Manor at Dominion City. Stafford, her husband passed away, October, 1974. They had two children. Audrey Johnson and husband Harvey reside in Brandon, Manitoba. Stanley and wife Audrey, nee Smart, reside in Dominion City.

Lillian Loiselle and husband Toni live in Letellier. Her first husband Fred Kreitz passed away December 1968.

Helen Jackson and husband George have lived in Dominion City for six years, residing in Winnipeg prior.

Adella McClelland resides in Red Deer, Alberta. Daughter Patricia Hunter and husband Barry and two children reside in Regina. Karen also lives in Red Deer.

William Ronald Kyle married Irene Opocensky, November 1939. They farmed section 9 and 10-3-2 E1, and moved to section 7-3-3 E1 in 1951, until they retired to Dominion City in 1975. Bill died in 1982. He had three children.

William Dennis was born in December, 1941. He married Donna Faye Chase of Emerson in 1964. They have three children, Darren James, born August 25, 1970, Krisin Deanne, born May 11, 1973 and Ryan William, born November 25, 1977.

Marjorie Joan, was born October 1946. In July, 1967 she was married to James Barry Agnew of Ottawa, and lives in Toronto. They have one daughter Tracey Jane born March 1, 1973.

Deborah June was born December 1958. In 1976 she married Dennis Rodewold of Emerson. They farm the old Wm. R. Kyle place section 7-3-3E and have one daughter Janette Breanne born August 27, 1981.

Donna Faye, Wm. D. Kyle, Ryan, Darren; front, Kristin

Irene and Bill Kyle

Debbie (Kyle) and Dennis Rodewalk and Janette Breanne (Insert baby).

Snow storm, March 6, 1966. Debbie Kyle.

The Wm. R. Kyles moved from 9-3-2 E1 farmyard because of flooding. This was the 1950 flood.

Left: Marjorie (Kyle) and Barry Agnew and daughter Tracey Jane, 1982.
Right: Julia Kyle.

WASYL (WILLIAM) KOSTYNIUK

Wasyl Kostyniuk came to Canada in 1899, at the age of 17. In 1907 he married Katerine Galushka, who had come to Franklin via the United States. In 1911 Wasyl went into a general store business in Tolstoi, then to the co-op in Vita, his own store in Caliento, and back to Tolstoi in 1918 to open a grocery, lumberyard and cattle buying and shipping business. He bought the Gateway Hotel in Emerson in 1930, and sold just before prohibition in the United States, 1931. From there he and his son Nestor went to a general store in Tolstoi. In 1941 he bought the Tolstoi Creamery which he ran with Nestor until 1946, when he retired to Windsor, Ontario. He died in 1961, Mrs. Kostyniuk in 1969.

Their children were Helen, Mrs. Felix Kulick; Oriel, Mrs. Michael Nimchuk, and Nestor, married Verna Wachna, who all reside in Windsor.

Wasyl and Katerine Kostyniuk

Nestor and Verna Kostyniuk and family.

WILHELM P. KATHLER

Wilhelm and Amalia (Zietzer) Kathler with their two oldest children and Amalia's mother, Maria Zietzer, came to Canada from southern Russia. They arrived in Arnaud on March 20, 1925 and moved to the Lyman ranch. They lived on the NE¼ of 27-2-3 E1 until 1945, when they moved to the NW¼ of 14-3-2E. When this land was sold in 1949, they bought Ranch V. The Kathlers farmed 1,120 acres of land. In 1964, Mr. and Mrs. Kathler moved to Arnaud. In 1976 they took up residence in the Grunthal Menno Home. Mr. Kathler passed away on November 28, 1976 at the age of 83 years. Mrs. Kathler passed away on February 10, 1982 at the age of 85 years. They had 11 children, one of whom died in infancy.

Tena married Henry Bergen in 1958. Henry passed away in September 1981. Tena Bergen lives in Arnaud in the house which her parents built in 1963. Her children are Brenda, Warren and Keith.

Back, Bill, Mary, Walter, Rudy, Fred, Peter; front, Tena, Mr. Kathler, Johnnie, Elvin, Arthur, Mrs. Kathler, Elly.

Mary Kathler married John Sawatzky and they have four children, Shirley, Bill, Ken and David.

Peter Kathler married Elfrieda Unruh. They have four children, Robert, Richard, Monica and Marilyn.

William Kathler Jr. was born at Lyman Farms, Ranch 5, in 1925. He went to Winnipeg and married Elizabeth Penner in 1957. They have four children, Doug and wife Anne (Klassen), Kelly, Tricia and husband Paul Verwymeren and two grandsons, Christopher and Adam Verwymeren and Allyson.

Walter farmed with his Dad until 1966, after which he and his brother Art farmed in partnership. Walter and Kathy (nee Plett) with sons Russell and Leighton and daughter Shannon lived in Arnaud until November 1974, at which time they moved to the former Dave Thiessen farm.

282

Fred and Susan (nee Wiebe) work for Mennonite Central Committee in Akron, Pennsylvania. Their children are Leona, Glenn, Erwin and Brian.

Rudy and Kathy (nee Goosen) Kathler live in Kelowna and their children are Donna, Eric and Dorothy.

Johnnie and Eleanor (nee Enns) Kathler live in Arnaud. Their children are Jacqueline, Tim and Mark. They spent 10 years custom harvesting from the Texas border to Manitoba as well as farming.

Elvin and Diane Kathler and son David live in Winnipeg.

Arthur Kathler was born in Franklin, and farmed with his father until 1963. In 1963 he married Margaret Voth. They live on the NE ¼ 19-3-3 E1, and their children are Darlene, Jeffrey and Rodney.

FRIDRICH KAUTZ

Fridrich and Natalie (Schweitzer) Kautz came from Heimthal, Wolienia, Russia to Overstone in 1927. Fridrich died on January 12, 1982 at the age of 103. Natalie resides in Winnipeg.

Their children are: Gerhardt, married Sarah Hutt; Arvid, married Doris ?; Mary, married Gordon Mannes; Wilma, married Ernie Baumon; Harry; Vera, married Peter Doel; Victor, married Jay Pickop.

Gary Kautz, son of Gerhardt Kautz, his wife Addis (Dishart) Kautz, daughter Kammy.

Fridrich and Natalie (Schweitzer) Kautz; Gerhardt Kautz

Left: Arvid and Doris (Bush) Kautz.
Right: Gordon and Mary (Kautz) Mannes.

Peter and Vera (Kautz) Doel and daughter Debbie.

Richard Kautz, son of Gerhardt Kautz, and wife Linda (Falconer) Kautz, and daughters Tristien and Meagan.

Left: Ernie and Wilma (Kautz) Bauman.
Right: Harry Kautz.

Victor and Jay (Pickop) Kautz

PAUL KOROLUK

Paul Koroluk came from the Western Ukraine in 1904 at 18 years of age. To learn the English language he went to work for a farmer in North Dakota. Later he got a job with Tyndall Quarry. In 1910 he married Kalyna Maksymchuk from Stuartburn, and bought 80 acres at Rosa and started farming.

He had a family of six children, Michael, Effie, Alex, William, Olga and Margaret. Michael died at the age of 25 and William at age two.

In 1946, for health reasons he moved to Winnipeg, leaving his land to his son Alex to carry on farming. In January 1971 Paul passed away. Kalyna died in December 1975. Both are resting in Rosa church cemetery.

Paul and Kalyna Koroluk

VOLODYMIR KWASNITSKI

Volodymir and Magdalean Kwasnitski arrived in the Tolstoi area in 1903. They farmed here for the remainder of their life. They had 10 children, 32 grandchildren and 29 great-grandchildren.

Their son John and wife Teenie Kwasnitski farm and live in Tolstoi. They have six children, Delores, Patricia, Marian, Ivan, Karen and Andrea.

Daughter Annie, Mrs. P. Soloman, also lives in Franklin.

Volodymir and Magdalean Kwasnitski

JOHN KELLY

In 1878 John Kelly arrived in the Woodmore area and settled on the NE ¼ of 13-2-4 E1 near Rufus Hurd. With him came his wife Jessie (Mayne) and two small children. Four more children blessed this union. John Kelly died in 1887. His widow braved many hardships to feed her six small children.

In 1889 Jessie married Isaiah Badgley. They had two sons, John and Melville.

JOSEPH KERDA

Joseph and Marie Kerda came to the Green Ridge area from the Czech community in Kupichov, Poland in 1928 with eight year old Joseph Jr. and seven year old Bozanna, called Bessie.

In 1929, a second daughter Mary was born. Around 1932 they moved to the NW ¼ 16-2-4 E1.

In 1950 Joseph Sr. and Marie semi-retired to a small acreage in Dominion City and Joseph Jr. bought the farm.

In June 1951 Joseph Jr. married Ruth Martin of Transcona who was teaching in Green Ridge.

On the same date, Mary, married Kenneth Dushenko of Darlingford. The Dushenkos live in Morden, where Mary has been a teacher for the last 18 years.

In November 1952, Bessie married Cyril Orsag of Toronto. They have lived in California since 1962.

Joe and Ruth Kerda have six children all residing in Franklin Municipality.

Jo-Ann, born 1953, married Glen Froom of Woodmore. Their children are Audra, Jeffrey, Michele. The Frooms farm at Overstoneville.

Ronald, born in 1956, married Deborah Hunt of Winnipeg. They have two daughters, Patricia (Trish), and Tara. They farm at Overstoneville.

Judith, born 1958, married Leslie Wilkinson of Ridgeville. They have two daughters, Jodie and Lisa and live at Ridgeville. Leslie is employed at Milne Equipment, Dominion City.

Robert, born 1960, is farming with his father.

Kelly, born 1969 and Kora Lee, born in 1970 attend Roseau Valley Collegiate.

Deborah and Ronald Kerda, Patricia and Tara.

Judy and Leslie Wilkinson, Lisa and Jody.

Bessie, Joseph Jr., Mary; seated, Marie and Joseph Kerda Sr.

Glen and Jo-Ann (Kerda) Froom

Ken and Mary Dushenko, Joe and Ruth Kerda

Robert, Kelly and Kora Lee Kerda.

285

GEORGE KOWALIUK

George Kowaliuk son of Michael and Domka Kowaliuk of Arbakka, Manitoba, and Lena, daughter of Alec and Pearl Rawliuk of Gardenton, Manitoba, were married in Arbakka, on October 15, 1939. They farmed in Gardenton, 34-1-6 until 1971, when they retired to Tolstoi to the former Yarmey home. They have five children and four grandchildren.

John, married Mona Lambert of St. Malo in 1963 and has two sons, Danny and Richard. They live in Winnipeg.

Nick, married Bernice, daughter of Steve and Martha Dolynchuk of Tolstoi, on June 4, 1966. They have one daughter, Lori and live in St. Adolphe.

Elsie, married Joe Berthelette of Pine Falls on August 30, 1975. They have one son, Curtis and live in Brandon.

Wally is employed with CN and lives in Winnipeg.

Diane married Paul Kukurdza of Winnipeg and lives in Winnipeg.

Richard, John, Mona and Danny.

Walter Kowaliuk, Diane and Paul Kowaliuk.

WILLIAM KOLODZINSKI

William and Ann Kolodzinski came to Canada and Franklin in 1898. William was a teacher, played the violin, became a real estate agent, worked in a grain elevator for 14 years, and was a Justice of the Peace. His son, Walter, married Elsie Bodnarchuk.

Left: George and Lana Kowaliuk.
Right: Nick, Bernice and Lori Kowaliuk.

Elsie, Joe and Curtis Berthelette.

Back, Frank Lardal, Dennis Beyak, Paul Lukie, Walter and Elsie (Bodnarchuk) Kolodzinski, Olivia Chomichuk, Adele Lukie, Patricia Beyak, Debbie Laxdal; front, Jackie Chomichuk, Carolyn Chomichuk, Dianna Chomichuk, Curtis Beyak, Crystal Beyak and Michael Lukie.

Mr. and Mrs. William Kolozinski

NYKOLA KULYK

Nykola and Maria Kulyk and two daughters came to Canada in 1907, from Austria. They purchased 160 acres of land half a mile south of the Village of Tolstoi. They shared their house with Stephen Kulyk and his wife and four children. Eventually Stephen sold his share of the house to his brother Nykola, and moved to Alberta.

Nykola and Maria had five children, Nellie, Anna, Natalka, Felix and Lawrence. Natalka married Mike Chesko and lives on the home farm. They have two daughters, Marcella and Victoria, both in Winnipeg, and a son, Edward, a dentist, in British Columbia. Felix and his wife Helen (Kostyniak) live in Windsor, and have two children, Nestor and Mark. Lawrence lives in Los Angelos, Nellie is married and lives in Detroit, and Anna is deceased.

Nykola Kulyk was appointed a Justice of the Peace in 1915, to serve the Tolstoi area.

Nykola and Maria Kulyk, 1919.

PRONYR KORTON

Pronyr and Katherina Korton came to Canada in 1912, with four sons and two daughters.

Fred Korton was born February 17, 1890, in Kamunetz, Podolski, Yaroslawka, Russia. He worked at various places, then came to Winnipeg in 1928 where he met Lena Shpak, daughter of Jacob and Agaphia (Bzovey) Shpak, who was born at Senkiw in 1911. They were married November 11, 1930, and had one daughter, Adeline, born August 31, 1931. In 1933 Fred and Lena bought a farm at Senkiw.

Adeline married Ben Colley, and had three sons. They are Andy, Fred, and George.

Nykola and Maria Kulyk's half of the mud house, shared with brother Stephen and family. Second house built by Nykola Kulyk in background.

Andy, Fred, Adeline (Korton) and Ben Colley; front George, 1968.

Lena, Adeline and Fred Korton, 1936.

JOE KIYAN

Joe Kiyan came from the Ukraine in 1910, to farm 80 acres at Sarto, then moved to Carlowrie where Joe worked as a carpenter. Joe died in 1940, at the age of 52, Mrs. Kiyan died in 1975 at the age of 88, and both are buried in the Senkiw Greek Orthodox Cemetery.

They had five sons, Steve, died in 1980, at the age of 67 and is buried at Senkiw. John, married Annie Jackolack, and had five children, Sydney, Pat, Jerry, Valerie and Sharon. John died in 1970, at the age of 55. Jack married Mary Slobodzian. Martin died in 1981, at the age of 60. He is buried at Senkiw. Bill married Betty Stadnyk, has three children, Vernon, Randy and Judy. Bill died in 1976 at the age of 52.

JOHN KNOX

John Knox married Ellen Warren. They came from Carlton Place, Ontario, and lived on the SW ¼ of 34-2-4 E1, which they thought was the SW ¼ of 33, and had to move when the mistake was discovered.

Their children were Lena: George, who died an infant; Calvin, who remained single and brought up his sister's children on her death; Tassy, who married Andy Spence; Lily, who married Jason Timlick; and her twin Leslie; and Jessie, who married Guy Post. Lily died young and Calvin moved to Indian Head to look after her family, when they were grown, he came back to Franklin, until his death.

Front, Llewie Davison, Tassy Knox (Mrs. Andy Spence); back, Charlie and Bob Foulds.

Jessie had two sons, Warren and Garnet Post. Warren was killed when a baseball hit him during a game at school. On the death of Guy Post, she married Edward Jack. Jessie died in 1981.

L JAMES ALEXANDER LANG

James Alexander Lang was born in Glasgow, Scotland in 1841. He entered the service of the Hudson Bay Company and sailed from the Hebrides to the Northwest Territories via the Hudson Strait, landing in York Factory in 1862.

He completed five years duty at that post as tinsmith. Then he came south to Fort Garry in company with the late Isaac Cowie by way of the Nelson River, Lake Winnipeg and the Red River. He lived in Winnipeg during the Riel Rebellion at Fort Garry.

In 1868 he married Mary Spence, daughter of the late James Spence. At Fort Garry he carried on various Merchant and Contracting activities; also, during that period he played an intimate part in the Red River Settlement. For a time he was associated in businesss with his father-in-law, Mr. James Spence. The latter was the owner of Spence estate out of which the portion of Winnipeg in and around Spence Street was developed. Mr. Lang left a momento by owning and naming Langside Street.

In 1876, not wanting to raise a family in the city, he homesteaded south of Arnaud. In 1881 he bought a quarter section by the Roseau River which he added to until he owned the N ½ of Section 12, where he lived, and the S ½ of Section 13-3-3 E.

Mr. Lang lived on the farm until his death in 1927. His wife, Mary Lang, predeceased him in 1916. They had eleven children: James, Margaret, William, Samuel, George, Hattie, Bert, Annie,

Mr. and Mrs. James A. Lang

Fred, Garnet and a baby who passed away at birth. Mr. Lang gave his name to the Langside community which gradually grew about him.

After Mr. Lang's death, Fred, along with his brother Garnet, remained on the farm until they retired to Winnipeg in 1965, when they sold the farm to William King, grandson of John E. King, a pioneer neighbour.

Fred Lang passed away in March of 1966 and Garnet in November of 1976. Garnet's wife Madeline (Grey) remains in their home in Winnipeg.

WILLIAM LANGE

William Lange's great-grandfather, August Becker, was born in Lublin, Poland, in 1863, to Friedrich and Wilhemine Becker. His ancestors were Germans who had fled the baronic wars. By the time he was grown, August found himself in Wolynia, Russia, where he married Juliana Steinke, and their children Augusta, 1886, Otillie, 1888, and William, 1891, were born. August came to Canada in 1894, and to Franklin, the SW ¼ 14-1-3 E1, originally homesteaded by Robert Curran, in 1896.

August and Juliana became Canadian citizens in 1899.

Augusta married Herman Lange in 1903. Herman was the son of Wilhelm and Karoline Lange, Section 6-1-4 E1. Their first child, a daughter, died in infancy. Augusta died in 1905 after giving birth to William, December 6, 1905. William was raised by his Becker grandparents. Herman Lange remarried and moved to Saskatchewan.

Otillie married Gustave Schwark.

William Becker worked on the farm until 1917,

when he married Emma Steg, and moved to the NW ¼ of 14. William and Emma had three daughters. Anna, married Emil Schultz, Violet, married Daniel Krietz, Ruth, married August Berft. Their son Walter married Geraldine Brethauer in 1951, and took over the home quarter.

William Becker died in 1943.

August Becker died in 1933. His grandson, William Lange, married Ella Walters, daughter of Gustave and Emma Walters, in June 1933, and took over the home farm. Juliana lived with the Langes until her death in 1938. William and Ella had three children. Clarence, born 1934, married Helen Ledarney in 1964, and continued on the home place. They have one son, Dennis, born 1968. Sharon, born 1945, married John Barr, Kenora. They have one daughter, Megan. Glenn married Brenda McKay, and is a custom officer in Emerson. JoAnne lives in Winnipeg.

William and Ella Lange are retired in Emerson.

Augusta, William and Ottilice Becker.

William, Emma, Ruth, Violet and Walter c. 1930.

289

Don, Geraldine (Brethauer), Walter and James Becker.

August and Juliana (Steinke) Becker and grandson William Lange.

Clarence, Dennis and Helen (Ledarney) Lange.

Clarence, Sharon, Glenn, Jo-Ann; sitting, Ella (Walters) and William Lange.

EARLE DANIEL LAMONT

Daniel Lamont was born in 1866 at Annan, Ontario. He came west and homesteaded at Napinka, Man. On July 22, 1897 he married Jessie Telfer Thomson of Annan. They moved to Franklin in 1911 and farmed 4 miles east of Dominion City.

They had four children,

Earle Daniel, 1898.

Margaret Elizabeth, 1901.

James Thomson, 1903.

John Gordon, 1907, died 1974.

Earle Daniel Lamont married Ethel Irene Kirkpatrick of Green Ridge June 30, 1928. They farmed near Dominion City until their retirement in 1963.

They have a family of three sons,

Lorne Douglas (August 14, 1929) who lives in Dominion City.

Donald Earle (November 20, 1932) of Ottawa.

Hugh Garry (January 18, 1942) of Dominion City.

Lorne married Lorna Jack of Ridgeville. They reside in Dominion City in the home built by Daniel and Jessie Lamont on Curran St. Their children are,

Brian Douglas (July 29, 1955) of Steinbach.

Donna Mae (Scott), (July 9, 1956) of Dominion City.

Bruce Alexander (May, 29, 1959) of Dominion City.

Gregory Keith (July 15, 1961) of Jasper, Alberta.

Brian married Karla Lynn Pearsen of Hadashville. They have one son Kevin Douglas (February 6, 1981).

Donna Mae married Jim Scott of Dominion City. Their children are,

Tara Dawn (March 2, 1975).

Christopher Cannon Irving Scott (February 3, 1978). They live in Dominion City.

Donald married Lise Bouchard of Bagotville, Quebec (May 18, 1957). He was an officer in the R.C.A.F. They have three children, Linda, Robert and Susan.

Linda married Jack Irving and they reside in Moncton, New Brunswick.

Robert and Susan both live in Ottawa.

Hugh Garry married Diane Batchinsky. They reside in Dominion City. They have one daughter Shawneen Lugh (July 18, 1966). Hugh has operated a trucking business in Dominion City for over 20 years and Diane has been employed at the Canadian Imperial Bank of Commerce for sixteen years. Shawn is a student at Roseau Valley Collegiate.

Margaret married Dr. James Davidson. They

had one daughter Norma.

Norma married Dr. George Ferguson. They have three daughters, Patti, Margot and Valerie.

August Johnson was born in Sweden, 1869. He came to Rosenfeld in 1892, and worked for Canadian Pacific Railway as section man and became section foreman after 5 years. He moved to Dominion City in 1928 and continued as section foreman until retiring in 1934. He was married in 1901 and they had five daughters, Thelma Peterson, Elsie Leatherdale, Minnie Stimpson, Annie Lamont and Stella Heck.

Daniel Lamont's Hudson car, 1916.

Jessie and Daniel Lamont

First combine, Massey Harris, 1930. Jim Lamont on tractor.

Gordon, Margaret, Jessie, Danniel; sitting, Earle and James.

James married Annie (Johnson). They had two children Gayle and Darryl.

Daniel and Jessie Lamont 60th anniversary. Lorna Lamont holding Brian, Patti Ferguson, Margaret Davidson holding Donna Mae Lamont, 1957.

Jim and Margaret Davidson, Jim and Annie Lamont. Sitting, Earle and Ethel Lamont.

291

Darryl married Rosemary Godon. They have two daughters Michele Ann and Carolyn Joan.

Robert, Carl, Frank; sitting, Sherry and Gayle (Lamont) Malazdrewich.

Norma and George Ferguson; front, Valerie, Margot and Patti.

Lorna and Dennis Monax, Sid and Minnie Stimpson; front, Paul and Ryan Monax.

Standing, Jim Scott, Lorne, Bruce, Ethel and Earl Lamont, Brian and Greg; front, Lynn, Lorna, Tara Scott, Donna-Mae (Lamont) Scott holding Christopher. Inset, Kevin.

August and Mrs. Johnson, Minnie, Annie and Stella.

Elsie and Nelson Leaherdale, daughter Irene.

292

David, Beryl (now Bays) and Glen Peterson.

Minnie, Thelma, Stella and Elsie.

GEORGE LAKUSTA

George Lakusta came to Canada from Washkiwtsi, Bokobina in 1913 at 18 years old. He stayed in Montreal and worked for the Freeman Hotel for three years. Having his heart set on farming, he went to Saskatchewan and worked at Krono as a farm laborer for six years. In 1922 he came to Manitoba.

In 1923 he married Anna (Salamandyk). They went to Detroit, U.S.A., and worked there for one and a half years. Then they came back to Canada and settled on a farm at Carlowrie. They

George and Anna Lakusta; back, Maurice, Alex, Lily and Orest.

farmed till their retirement in 1963 when they moved to Vita.

George and Anne had four children, Lil, Alex, Maurice and Ernie. Alex is deceased and is buried in Steinbach.

DAN A. LENDRUM

Dan Lendrum and Isabella (Turner, daughter of Mr. and Mrs. George Turner), and their children, Jean and George, came from West Emerson in 1911 to purchase the R. Bingham farm in the Ridgeville district. Three more children, John, Murray and Marybell, were born here.

Jean married Horrace Wilkins. They had four children.

George married Joan Cancilla, and has two children,

Lynn, who is married to Mark Berege and has a son, Matthew.

Leslie, who married Tom Wiegand.

Dorothy, who married Jack Beswetherick, and have two children, Sherry and Ted.

Donald, married Joanne Holmes, and has two children, Mark and Garry.

Dennis, who married Lynnea Eliason, and has three children, Kevin, Greg and Heather.

George married Edna Lindsay, and they have three children.

Don married Peggy Charette.

David, married Alaine Desjardins.

Sandra, married Paul Barnson.

David and Sandra are twins.

John married Eleanor Lindsay, and has three children.

Catherine, married Harry Driedger in 1962. They have three children, Terry, Brad, Jeoffery.

Larry married Linda Stewart in 1970, and has two sons, Ryan and Evan.

Marlene married Terry Grier in 1971, and has three daughters, Teresa, Crystal and Deanne.

Murray is single in 1982.

Marybel married Victor Hillsden in 1946. They

Back, John, Murray, Jean, George; front, Marybel, Dan and Isabella Lendrum.

Charlie Madill and Dan Lendrum, 1959.

John and Eleanor (Lindsay) Lendrum, Larry, Cathy; front, Marlene, 1962.

Frank Larson. 1925.

Frank Larson's farm, section 31-3-3 SE c. 1958.

have three children, Ruth, married Arnold Graham in 1969, has two children, Robert and Beverly.

Murray married Jane McCaull in 1978.

Gayle.

Dan and Isabella retired to Winnipeg in 1961.

FRANK LARSON

Frank Larson was born in the south of Malma, Sweden. Upon his arrival in Canada in May, 1924, he went to work on a farm in Fielding, Saskatchewan. Due to poor crops he stayed only for three months and returned to Winnipeg. He went to work for Chris Nelson, whose farm was located near Arnaud, for three months. In 1925 he went to work for Peter Dearborn for almost 10 and a half years. In July, 1936, after an eight month visit to his homeland, he returned to Canada and stayed with John Thiessens till he purchased land on section 31-3-3 SE at $7 an acre. Forty-three acres were broken when the land was purchased but had not been cleared off. With a good friend, Eric Toews, he broke and cleared some more land leaving five and a half acres of bush and yard.

He farmed this land till 1965 when he retired. Frank Larson now resides at the Red River Valley Lodge in Morris.

294

DIEDRICH H. LOEPPKY

In 1948 Diedrich and Sarah, with their children David, Sarah and Annetta moved to a quarter section of land in the Franklin Municipality 13-2-5 E1, across the road from the Local Government district of Stuartburn. Five children, Susan, Martha, Martin, Elma and Ruth were born while living here.

Diedrich was born and raised in the Halbstadt area. He moved to Woodmore in 1938. Sarah moved to the Franklin municipality with her family the John P. Thiessen's in 1938, Diedrich and Sarah were married in 1940 on her parents farm which is next door to the farm Diedrich and Sarah have lived on for 34 years. They briefly lived near Stuartburn just after they were married.

Diedrich and Sarah still live and farm on this section of land, along with the youngest son, Martin. Martin is engaged to be married and is planning on taking the farm over from his dad.

Back, Annetta, Martin, Martha, Elma, Ruth, Annethla, Susan, David; front, Sarah Jr., Sarah Sr. Leoppky, Sheldon, Landis, Diedrich Leoppky, Elda.

David, after graduating from Winnipeg Bible College, married Elda Harder. They live in Grunthal with sons Landis and Sheldon, where David is the pastor of the Grunthal E.M.B. church.

Sarah and Susan live and work in Winnipeg.

Annetta has done mission work with Gospel Missionary Union in Eleuthera, Bahamas, for the last four years.

Martha is a librarian in Pambrun, Saskatchewan.

Elma works at the Black Forest Academy in Germany, a boarding school for missionaries' children.

Ruth graduated from Winnipeg Bible College in 1982, and works at the Christian Book Nook in Otterburne.

WILLIAM LENTON

William Lenton Sr. married Sarah Jane Vowels in Clifton, England. In 1890, William and Sarah Jane came to Canada with their five sons, William, Fred, Edward, Harry and Herbert and two daughters, Laura and Florence, and settled in Winnipeg.

When their English money was changed to Canadian currency the family of nine had 75¢ in cash to start life in the new land.

In 1893, the family came to Ridgeville and lived on the Fitzpatrick farm, 1½ miles North and 1½ miles East of the present village. William Jr. remained in Winnipeg and their daughter, Florence, died at the age of 3.

They soon moved to the former Smith farm, 1½ miles South and 4 miles East of Ridgeville and worked on a cash rent basis, until they moved to the SE¼ 19-1-5E, where they remained until 1919 when the farm and machinery were sold. At this time, William Lenton Sr. and his wife Sarah, moved to the Tom Smith house in Overstone, where they lived until William's death. Sarah then moved to Winnipeg to live with her daughter Laura.

Edward Lenton (1884-1980) moved to Winnipeg when a young man and worked as a bank messenger until his retirement. He married Jenny Gale in 1911. They had one son, Gerald, of Winnipeg.

Laura Lenton (1878-1960) married James Smith.

Herbert Lenton (1892-19) married Lila Sinclair, the daughter of a Ridgeville CNR Station Agent. They lived in Winnipeg where he worked as a barber until his death. They had two children, Lloyd and Jean, both of Winnipeg.

Harry Douglas Lenton (1887-1975) married Dora Ellen Collins on November 24, 1915. They lived in Overstone on his father's homestead until 1919, at which time the farm was sold and they moved to Ridgeville. Harry was an Imperial Oil Agent for 42 consecutive years. They had five children, Henry and Edith, born in Overstone, Thomas, Marguerita and Laura arrived after moving to Ridgeville.

Dora died November 23, 1945.

In 1951, Harry married Mrs. Euphemia (Effie) Johnston. They lived in Ridgeville until 1974 when they moved to Franklin Manor, Dominion City. He died March 19, 1975 at the age of 88. Effie died March 4, 1982, at the age of 92 years.

Henry Lenton, son of Harry, married Martha Scheibe in 1937, and lived in Ridgeville. They had one son, Wayne. Henry owned and operated his garage and was also an implement dealer. When World War II broke out, he joined the R.C.A.F. as an aerial mechanic and was stationed in Canada. He returned to Ridgeville after the war to continue his business. After a divorce he moved to Winnipeg. He married Lila Pollock and moved to Morris in 1961 where they operate the Imperial Oil Agency. They have two daughters, Heather and Tammie.

Wayne, son of Henry and Martha, married Patricia Lange of Forsyth, Montana in 1963. He has three children, Dori, Donna and Sydney.

Heather married Jacques Collette in 1978. They have one daughter Kelly and son Mitchell.

Tammie married Murray Klassen in 1980. They have one son, Justin.

William Thomas Lenton married Myrtle Louise Millar, youngest daughter of Robert Frances and Catherine Millar of Stuartburn, June 12, 1943. Their son Glen was born while Tom was overseas, during world war II. Tom worked for his father in the Imperial Oil business when he returned home in 1946, living in the former Herman Ratchinski place until 1950 when they purchased the Lenton home, in which they live in 1982.

In 1951 Cherryl Colleen was born. She is an R.N., living in Thompson.

In 1954 twins, Debbie Lee and Peggy Lou were born. Debbie is a hair dresser employed in Winnipeg at the Red River Community College, and Peggy Lou is a nurse, married to Donald Graydon. She has two children, Shawn Scott and Kimberly Dawn.

Glen married Lynne Renaud in 1981. They have one son, Carl Alan David, who is 7.

Harry and Dora Lenton in horse and buggy, courting days.

Seated at left, daughter Laura and her three children, wife Sarah at head, Harry, Herbert, Fred, Lily (Wilkinson) Lenton, Harry Clifford, Martha (Wilkinson) Clifford. William Lenton with plates in front.

Lily Victoria (Wilkinson) Lenton, holding Wallace, May, Frederick John Lenton, and Ethel, 1914. May married a man named Halliday, Ethel married Lloyd Lindsey. The Fred Lentons moved to Portage la Prairie in 1917.

William Lenton Sr. and wife Sarah Jane Vowels with three grandchildren, children of daughter, Laura. c. 1910.

Back, Bert, Harry and Edward Lenton, sons of William Lenton; middle, Effie, Lila (Sinclair), Jen. Ethel Lindsay and daughter Maureen; front, of Fred Lenton family, 1964. Jen, Mrs. Edward Lenton, was a soloist with the CBC in 1928.

Tom and Louise Lenton wedding, June 12, 1943.

Left: Tom and Louise Lenton.
Right: Donald and Peggy Lou (Lenton) Graydon, Kimberley and Shawna.

Harry Lenton auctioneer, 1947.

Back, Rita, Tom, Edith, Laura and Henry; seated, Harry and wife Dora, 1943.

Back, Debbie, Cheryl, Peggy, Don, Glen and Lynne; seated, Louise and Tom; front, Kimberley Graydon and Carl Lenton.

Lori, Sidney, Donna, Wayne Lenton; sitting, Pat Lenton, 1980.

Tammie Lenton, Heather Lenton, Mrs. Euphemia Lenton.

RUDOLPH LAUFERSWEILER

Rudolph Laufersweiler was in the blacksmith business in Ridgeville from 1910 to 1930, during which time he was the agent for Cockshutt Implements and sold gas for Imperial Oil.

In 1926 he started trucking cream to Noyes, Minnesota, Grunthal and Vita, then Palm Dairies in Winnipeg, and for a number of years to Modern Dairies in St. Boniface.

Mr. Laufersweiler died suddenly in July, 1949, Mrs. Laufersweiler in October, 1981, a daughter Louise, in 1967. They had a family of three sons

Dora (Collins) and Harry Lenton, November 24, 1915.

and three daughters, Elsie, Louise, Evelyn, Alfred, Leonard and Walter. Mrs. Laufersweiler was the former Eva Schindel of Overstone. After Mr. Laufersweiler's death, Leonard and Walter continued with the cream business until 1966, at which time they sold to Frank Nickel of Grunthal.

Alfred Laufersweiler married Rose, the youngest daughter and thirteenth child of William and Rose Wilkinson in 1934.

For a short time after their marriage, they lived in Overstone with Alf's grandfather. They then moved into a house behind the Laufersweiler store and then to a home at the south end of Ridgeville where they remained until moving to Winnipeg about 1958.

Alfred worked with his brothers, Len and Walter, driving trucks.

Rose passed away in 1966.

Alfred and Rose had four children, Marjorie, Shirley, Audrey and Reginald.

Marjorie married Teddie Ganske in 1957. They have two daughters, Debbie and Shelley.

Shirley married Vincent Lane in 1959. They have three children, Kim, Robbin and Jamie. Kim married James Wright (now divorced) and they had two children, Kristopher and Rebecca.

Audrey married Cliff Allcroft in 1960. They have two children, Roxanna and Rocky.

Reg married Yvonne Friesen, daughter of Pete and Dinah Friesen, in 1963. They have three children, Maureen, Sherry and Cora.

Len Laufersweiler and his wife the former Margaret Harvey of Gardenton, have two daughters.

Lenore, born March, 1941, lives in Winnipeg and is married to Dr. Al Loyns. They have a 15 year old son Alain.

Donna, born August, 1943, lives in Ithaca, New York and is married to Dr. Wayne Schwark. They have a son, 17 year old Dwight, and a 15 year old daughter Lisa, who is in Junior High School.

Left: Alf and Rose Laufersweiler, Debbie Ganske.
Right: Reg and Yvonne Laufersweiler.

Shirley, Audrey and Marjorie Laufersweiler.

Alfred Laufersweiler's grandchildren; back, Rocky Allcroft, Kim Lane, Debbie Ganske, Cora Laufersweiler, Robbin Lane; front, Roxanna Allcroft, Sherry Laufersweiler, Shelly Ganske, Maureen Laufersweiler, Jamie Lane.

Len and Margaret Laufersweiler

Kim (Lane) Wright, Kristopher and Rebecca.

Wayne and Donna (Laufersweiler) Schwark, Lisa, Dwight.

Al, Lenore and Alain Loyns.

Left: Elsie, Ena (Schindel) Laufersweiler, Louise Lenton, Evelyn, Rudy Laufersweiler.
Right: Vince and Shirley Lane, 1959.

Robbin and Jamie Lane

Cliff and Audrey (Laufersweiler) Allcroft, 1966; and daughter Roxanna.

Evelyn (Laufersweiler) and Murray Lochhead; top, son Douglas; centre, Eva (Schindel) Laufersweiler, mother of Evelyn.

Teddy, Debbie, Shelley and Marjorie Ganske.

JOHN LOCHHEAD

John (1885-1922) and Jane Lochhead (1855-1907) located on the Ridge in 1878. Their homestead was about a quarter mile north of the present day home of Mr. and Mrs. Joe Kerda. They later bought the farm at Section 8-2-4 E, which is presently known as the George Lochhead family farm.

Mr. Lochhead was born in St. Thérèse De Blainville, Quebec, eldest son of Robert Lochhead and Janet (Wylie) both of the parish of Galston, Scotland. He was the only member of his family to settle in Western Canada.

He married Jane Kirkpatrick, eldest daughter of Alexander Kirkpatrick and Ann Brown of Montreal.

They had six children,

Agnes Louise, 1879-1945, married Robert Seward of Ridgeville.

Robert Alexander, 1881-1915, married Annie Maud Craig.

Jessie Maude, 1883-1957, married Jim Greenley of Coulter, Man.

George David, 1886-1945, married Emily Cherneski of Ridgeville.

Ellen Gertrude, 1890-1976, married Roderick McLennan of Green Ridge.

Laura Jane, 1893-1951, married Leslie Ramsey of Green Ridge.

Robert Alexander Lochhead (1881-1915) was born here and lived in the district all his life. He married Annie Maud Craig (1882-1915). They lived on the present site of the Elmer Kirkpatrick farm home. Their house was of log and is now located at the Steinert home in the Woodmore area.

There were two sons, Murray and John. Both infants went to live with the Robert Seward family at Ridgeville after the death of their parents in 1915. The elder son, Murray, died at the age of five.

John lives in Oakville, Ontario. He married Marjorie Kerr of Peterborough, deceased. They had two children, Joanne, Mrs. Robert Packham, of Hamilton and Johny, of Burlington.

John's second marriage was to Kitty Budd of Toronto.

George David Lochhead (1886-1945) farmed in the district for many years. In 1920 he married Emily Chrneski of Ridgeville. Their first home was on Sec. 9-2-4E.

They later moved to the family farm where they remained and farmed until his death in 1945. There were seven children: Murray who lives in Calgary, Edward (1922-1978) late of Emerson, Hector (1924-1945) died overseas (with the

R.C.A.F.), Arlene (Houston), Jasper, Alberta, Robert - Winnipeg, Lorne - Calgary.

John Lochhead; George Lochhead.

Robert Alexander, Annie (Craig) Lochhead; John and Murray Lochhead.

Ellen Gertrude and Agnes Louise Lochhead.

George David and Emily (Cherneski) Lochhead

WILLIAM LINDSAY

William Lindsay (1853-) was born Enniskillen, Ireland and emigrated to Ontario in 1869. Three years later he moved to Manitoba, married Althea Empey of Ridgeville and settled on NE¼ 17-1-4 E1 where he farmed until he retired to Emerson in 1910. They had nine children, Alice, Frances married John Morrison, William, Stanley, Edith, Eva, Charley, Shaddie.

Alice May married Franklin Coates. They farmed near Dominion City. They had nine children, one died of diphtheria very young. William, Clifford, Gladys, Hazel, Ethel, Franklin, Mildred and Maxwell.

Hazel married Albert Carpenter and had two sons, Dennis and Lorne.

Ethel married John Kells and had five children, Maxine, Ardelle, Joan and Jack (twins).

Most of the family moved to eastern Canada or the United States.

William, 1886-1968, bought the home place in 1910 and farmed for three years. He then rented his land out for a year and went to Saskatchewan. In 1917 he married Alice Wilkinson, in 1945 they moved in to Ridgeville. In 1981 Alice moved to the Emerson Care home. They had five children, Lily, Laverne, Eleanor, Dorothy and Stanley.

Lily married Lorne Riach.

Eleanor married John Lendrum.

Dorothy married Keith Hicks.

Laverne served in the Air Force in World War II. In 1944 he married Pearl Jacobs of Emerson and took over the farm from his father. He retired to Morden in the 1970's. They have two sons, Robert and Aaron.

Robert married Marie Rose Proulx in 1966 and has three sons, Michel, Daniel, Patrick.

Aaron married Sharon Jackson in 1973 and has two children, Sean and Melissa.

Stanley George married Mary Froom at Green Ridge in 1955. He had a dairy business on SW 21-1-4 E till 1977 when he sold his herd and went into grain farming. They have three children Nanci, Rhonda and Shelley.

Stanley Willard (1888-1926) married Eliza Jane Parkes of Ridgeville. They farmed SE½ 17-1-4 E. They had four sons and two daughters, Lloyd, Donald, John, Elma, Edna and Allan.

Willard Lloyd (1912-1979) married Ethel Lenton of Portage la Prairie. He bought the farm S½ 28-1-4 in 1935. They have two children, Maureen and Terry.

Maureen married Marc Lemay of Letellier in 1972 and has two daughters Erin, Lori.

Donald Lyle (1913) lives in Toronto with his wife and daughters.

John Emerson (1914) married Rita Lenton of Ridgeville and has three daughters, Carol, Marilyn and Elaine.

Carol married John Andrusyk.

Elaine married Gerald Lussier.

Elma Jean (1915) married Wm. White of Winnipeg and has one daughter, Patricia.

Edna May (1917) married George Lendrum and has three children, Donald, David and Sandra (twins).

Allan (1921) married Phyllis Jerome.

Edith Lylle married John McGregor of Pratt, Manitoba. They had a family of 12, several of whom still reside in the Austin-McGregor area.

Eva Althera married Ernest Baldwin of Starbuck, and has one son, Lawrence and one daughter, Mae.

Charles Emerson, a lawyer, married Eleanor Gregg.

Shaddie Ruth married Raymond Long of Emerson. She was a very active member of the Red Cross. They have two daughters.

Lorna married John McLaughlin and has seven children.

Beverley married John Rensh and has four children.

Wm. Lindsay Sr. (with brothers and sister) John Bella and Bob.

Frank Coates, Alice Lindsay, John Morrison, Jenny Lindsay, Ernie Baldwin, Eleanor Lindsay, Ray Long and John McGregor.

Edith McGregor, Wm. Lindsay, Shaddie Long, Frances Morrison, Alice Coates, Charley Lindsay and Eva Baldwin.

William Lindsay and his family; Edith, Francis, William, Shaddie on her wedding day, William Lindsay, Alice, Charley, Evan and Stanley.

Ray and Shaddie Long; William and Alice Lindsay.

Laverne, Pearl, Aaron and Robert Lindsay.

Stanley, Dorothy, Eleanor, Laverne and Lilly Lindsay.

Terry, Ethel, Maureen and Lloyd Lindsay.

Eva, William, Edith and Charley.

Lori, Marc, Maureen and Erin Lemay.

Don, John, Allan, Elma, Edna and Lloyd Lindsay.

302

Edward, Hector and Gordon Lochhead.

ROBERT EWAR LESLIE

In the year 1913, Robert Ewar Leslie and his wife, Emma Rilla (Hall) left Hymers, Ontario where they had had a saw mill. A forest fire had burnt all the timber around them and they were unable to continue in business. They were accompanied by their youngest daughter, Olive, and son, William, his wife, Ida, and children, Clarence and Robert. They resided on the Roseau River at Green Ridge, the land on which Wilfrid Palmer now lives. Olive Leslie, youngest of their 10 children, taught school on the Indian reserve for two or three years. During the 1930's, Mr. and Mrs. Leslie left the farm to retire in Winnipeg; their son, Will, his wife, Ida, their son, Robert, went to Rosser where they operated a store. Clarence, the older son, went to Wapella, Saskatchewan, where he went banking. He later moved to Regina with his wife, Margaret, and son John. Bob Leslie married Grace Griffin of Woodmore, and after his retirement, moved to Victoria, British Columbia.

JOHANN LEHENBAUER

Johann Lehenbauer was born June 23, 1949, in Enns, Austria, the son of Johann and Maria Lehenbauer, Enns, Austria, and is married to Margaretha Barbara (Zittmayr) born November 7, 1953, daughter of Karl and Margaretha Zittmayr, St. Florian, Austria. Their children are Andrea Maria, born February 5, 1976, in Linz, Austria, and Barbara, born June 25, 1978, Winnipeg, and Matthias Johann, born April 23, 1980, Winnipeg.

The Lehenbauers came to Arnaud from Austria in 1978. They bought 1840 acres, being 26-3-3 E1, 36-3-3 E1, S½ of SW¼ of 31-3-4 E1, W½ of 30-3-4 E1, and the NE¼ of 24-3-3 E1, from Henry Sukkau. Their buildings are located on the NE¼ of 26-3-3 E1. They operate a grain farm.

Johann Sr., Maria, Andrea, Margaretha (holding Barbara) and Johann Lehenbauer Jr.

Margaretha and Karl Zittmayr

Johann, Margaretha, Barbara, Mathew and Andrea Lehenbauer.

HENRY LAWSON

Henry Lawson, 1860-1935, married Anne Catherine, nee Renwick, 1863-1959.

Their family are,

Henry R. Lawson, 1887, living in Gimli.

Marjorie Lawson, 1895-1958, married Wallace R. Baskerville, son of John D. Baskerville, 1920.

Douglas Lawson, 1901-1969.

Gordon Lawson, 1904.

Henry Lawson and his brother John came to the Rural Municipality of Franklin from Edinburgh, Scotland, in 1885. They purchased land about eight miles east of Arnaud in what was later called the Carlowrie area. In 1886, after having established a home on the farm, Henry Lawson returned to Edinburgh to marry Anne Catherine Renwick. They returned that same year, and the two brothers farmed jointly. In the first four years, three of the crops were frozen and a pure bred cattle herd was wiped out by an epidemic of black leg. Thoroughly disillusioned, they returned to Edinburgh in 1889 or 1890. Henry Lawson and his wife by this time had one son. They stayed in Edinburgh one year and decided to try Canada again. John Lawson and his wife remained in Scotland. Henry Lawson and his family came to Dominion City in 1890 or 1891 where he found employment with the Canadian Pacific Railway until he retired in 1926 as station agent. They moved to Winnipeg in 1935 and lived there until their deaths.

Henry and Anne Lawson.

The Henry Lawson family, l to r; Douglas, Henry, Anne, Marjorie, Gordon Lawson.

WILLIAM LEASK

William Leask lived on the SW ¼ of 7-3-4 E1 in 1883. His brother, R. Leask, lived on the NW ¼ of 12-3-3 E1. William Leask was accidentally shot in 1899, and the April 11, 1899 report of the Green Ridge Forresters Lodge says the order made 40 bows and 7 sashes of black crepe for the funeral. He was buried in the Green Ridge cemetery.

304

DMYTRO LENYK

Dmytro Lenyk came from the Ukraine in 1897. He brought his wife and Mary, 16, Aksentey, 14, Annie, 10, Agerpina, 5 and Alexsandra, 3 weeks. Two more children were born in Franklin Municipality, names not known. Mary married Alex Yarmey in 1900.

Mrs. Dmytro Lenyk; Pete and Margaret Hanischuk.

Wm. Hanischuk, Harry Hanischuk, Helen Hanischuk, Mary Werestuik (nee Hanischuk), Metro Hanischuk, Johnny Hanischuk, Margaret Hanischuk (mother), Annie Hanischuk (daughter-in-law), Pete Hanischuk (father), Joe Kutryk holding their Elaine, Mabel Kutryk (nee Hanischuk), Stanley Hanischuk, Donia Werestuik, adopted daughter.

WILLIAM LINKLATER

William Linklater was born in Stromness, Orkney, Scotland, March 1842. He joined the Hudson's Bay Company at age 18, and came to York Factory on a company ship in 1860. After serving his apprenticeship with the company, he ran a trap line in the James Bay area. From there he moved to Winnipeg, where he married Jemima Spence in 1868.

Jemima was the daughter of James Spence, after whom Spence Street in Winnipeg is named, and a direct descendant of one of the Lord Selkirk settlers. She was born in St. James parish, March, 1851.

In 1878 William homesteaded the E ½ 24-3-3

E1. Later he bought 240 acres on the Roseau River, section 7, which became their home. They farmed with 30 horses, on a total acreage of 1360 acres.

William and Jemima had seven children, Mary E., Mrs. Joseph Baskerville, Andrew J., William R., Edna, Mrs. C. H. Hawes, Edith M., Mrs. G. H. Ball, Ernest S., Robina A..

William died July, 1912, Jemima August, 1927. Ernest carried on the farm until he and his wife Ivy retired to White Rock. They have three daughters, Marion, Beverly and Shirley.

WILLIAM LASUTA

Left: Mary Lasuta, Miss Reimer. Mary, R.C.A.S.C., served as a truck driver for the Canadian Red Cross.
Right: Bill Lasuta, R.C.E.M.E., Chief Warrant Officer for 30 years. Served in various foreign countries.

M SAMUEL G. MAYNES

Samuel G. Maynes came to Franklin in 1892, from Granby, Quebec, by way of the United States. They farmed north east of Dominion City.
Samuel Sr. married Isabella Neill.
Their children were,
Maud, who married Robert Baskerville.
James, deceased.
Samuel Henry, married Jessie Brad.
Clifford, deceased.
William A. married Nena Deduck.
Gordon, deceased.

Left: Isabella (Neill) Maynes, Maud and Samuel George Maynes, 1900.
Right: Samuel Henry and Jessie Maynes.

Samuel Jr. and William were partners in the former Coulter Bros. Garage and Implement business in Dominion City in 1918. William died in 1955, and Samuel Jr. in 1958. Samuel G. Maynes died in 1917, and Isabella in 1930.

Clifford, Dr. Gordon and William Maynes.

One of the first Huppmobile cars in the Dominion City area owned by Samuel Maynes. Right hand drive, coil oil lamps, horn on the right hand (outside) front door.
Miss Rochford, Laura Brad, Samuel Maynes Jr. (driver) Bill Maynes, Marjorie Rochford and Jessie Brad.

PHILLIP MAYNER

Phillip Mayner married Philipena Puff. They came from Austria in 1898, and stayed in the Gretna area for a few years before moving to Overstone, where they took a homestead.

They had 10 children, Phillip, married and moved to Saskatoon, Henry married and moved to Alberta, Lizzie married and moved to Emerson, George married and moved to Snow Lake, Trissie married and moved to the United States, Millie married and moved to the United States, Margaret, Katie, Conrad and Bill.

Bill married Alvina Schnell. They farmed in the Overstone area and retired to the village of Tolstoi. Bill died in 1981. They had two children.

Shirley Mae married Barry Jeske and lives in Tuelon.

She has three children, June, Dean and Perry.

Ray married Monique Collette. They farm the Mayner farm in Overstone and have two children, Lisa and Danny.

Back, Henry, Phillip Mayner, Phillip Jr., Terrias, Philipena (Puff) Mayner, George (between parents); front, Margaret, Conrad, Lizzie.

Back, Barry and Shirley (Mayner) Jeske, Monique (Collette) and Ray Mayner; front, June Jeske, P. Mayner, Philipena (Puff) Mayner, holding Perry Jeske, Dean Jeske.

Lisa and Danny Mayner

June, Dean and Perry Jeske.

JOSEPH J. MOORE

Joseph J. Moore and his wife Martha came from Grey County, Ontario to Franklin in 1879 and homesteaded SE 14-2-4 E in Woodmore. Mr. Moore was an experienced carpenter by trade as well as farmer. He contracted the building of Green Ridge Presbyterian Church which opened in 1884 and also the first Woodmore school which opened in 1885. They had no children and later moved to Winnipeg. Mrs. Moore was buried in Green Ridge.

AARON MADILL

Aaron Madill was born in County Armagh, Ireland; the exact date is unknown but he came to Canada with his parents at the time Queen Victoria ascended the throne. He was approximately 1½ years old and they settled near Napanee, Ontario. As a young man he came to what is now known as Ridgeville, and took up a homestead on Section 4-1-4 E. This was in 1880.

In 1882 he married Maria Henrietta Osterhout who was also from Ontario, settled on Section 4-1-4 E1. They lived the rest of their lives on the homestead.

They had two sons, Charlie Aaron, born June 13, 1883 and Johnny a year and a half younger, who died at approximately 1 year old.

Charlie remained on the home farm with his parents. His mother passed away in 1922 and Mr. Madill died in 1926. He then sold the farm to Ray Empey.

On January 18, 1930 he married Vera Eleanor Dickson of Wiseton, Saskatchewan formerly of Green Ridge, daughter of James Dickson. As the depression was on, work was hard to get so they had many moves in both Manitoba and Saskatchewan.

They had two daughters, Myrtle Eloise, born in Milden, Saskatchewan August 4, 1931 and

Elizabeth Laura born at Vita, Manitoba, November 5, 1934.

Charlie's health failed, Vera got the position of telephone Operator in Wiseton and was there for 10 years, later getting work in the telephone office in Elrose, Saskatchewan till such time as the dial phones were installed. Then she got work in the Doctors office in Elrose.

Charlie passed away on August 13, 1966 and is buried at Dinsmore, Saskatchewan. Eloise married Jake Gassner, a farmer at Kindersley, and Beth married Gordon Dales, of Coleville, Saskatchewan.

On July 13, 1968, Vera was married to Roderick MacLennan, a farmer at Sovereign, Saskatchewan.

Left: Charlie Madill with one of his treasured trophies. *Right:* Charlie and Vera Madill.

WILLIAM STEWART MILLAR

Mr. and Mrs. William Stewart Millar, who homesteaded the SW¼ 16-2-6 E1 in 1881. Believed to be first European family in Stuartburn.

JOHN ALEXANDER McVICAR

John Alexander McVicar married Elizabeth, daughter of Henry and Ellen Timlick of Newbridge, on March 6, 1907. They began farming on Section 28-3-4 E but after a few years John gave this up and bought grain for Ogilvie Flour Mills from 1914-1918. He then took on the International Harvester Company and Imperial Oil agencies. In the late 1920's John returned to buying grain for the Ogilvie Flour Mills and eventually turned the International Harvester Company business over to Donald and the Imperial Oil agency over to John Jr.. John retired in 1948.

Elizabeth McVicar passed away in 1949 at the age of 64 years and Mr. McVicar in 1955 at the age of 74. They had four children, Donald, Jean, John and Marjorie.

Jean Elizabeth, married Oscar Paulin on October 21, 1933. They moved to Port Moody, British Columbia in 1957. Oscar died December 6, 1973. There were three children, Roberta, Doreen and Walter.

Roberta, born in 1936, married William Brown in 1953. They had a family of four, Allan, Kathy, Heather and Robbie (deceased).

Doreen, born in 1938, married Perry Parsons in 1956. There were four children, Perry Donald, Mary-Jean, Sandra, and Penny. Father and son were killed in an air crash, and later Doreen was killed in a car accident in October, 1972.

Walter, born in 1947, married Christine Johnson. Their family consists of Debbie, Denise and Neil.

Marjorie Ann married Lew Furse, a widower and teacher, on June 29, 1949 to become the mother of four small boys. They live in Kelowna, British Columbia. Their four boys are Glen, Donald, Robert (Bob) and Ray.

Glen Furse, born February 2, 1932, married Alma Hunt in 1958. There are four children, Donna Lea, Lynne Patricia, Karen Marjorie and Katherine Ann, and one grandson Ryan.

Donald Furse, born September 29, 1933, married Floriann Perkins. They have one son, Garry.

Robert Furse, born November 6, 1939, married Shirley Haus. They have two children, Graham and Joanna.

Ray Furse, born August 23, 1941, married Ariel Struthers. They have four children, Martin Lewis, Russell William, Shannon Dawn, and Gillian Ariel.

Donald was born November 4, 1908.

He married Viara Horn on July 31, 1935. In 1945 they moved to Dominion City to work on road maintenance. He retired in 1973. Donald died October 30, 1979.

They had three children, Carol, Earle and Leona.

Carol, born March 20, 1940, married Verna Wilkinson in 1959.

Leona, born March 8, 1948, married Brian Scobie November 18, 1967. They have two children, Corey Brian, born June 21, 1974, and Jana Leanne, born March 23, 1977.

Earl, born February 15, 1942, married Jeanine Haight in 1964. They have two sons, Mark Donald, born September 15, 1970, and Taylor Scott, born July 15, 1973. They live in Edmonton.

John Alexander McVicar was born at Green Ridge on the Henry Timlick farm in 1912, and moved into Arnaud with his parents in 1914. John married Bertha Carter from Ochre River, in 1940. Bertha was born in Dauphin in 1916. John and Bertha have two sons.

Billy Johnny McVicar, born in 1942, Cameron Cecil McVicar, born in 1947. Cameron resides in Winnipeg and is employed by Tri-Mac.

Billy married Joanne Charette in 1971. Joanne came from St. Malo and was born in 1952. On October 11, 1973 their son, Allan Jason McVicar was born. The McVicars presently reside in Arnaud, where they operate an Imperial Oil Agency.

John and Elizabeth McVicar

John and Donald McVicar

Billy, Cameron, John, grandson Allan and Bertha McVicar.

Cameron McVicar; Billy, Joanne and Allan McVicar.

Lew and Marjorie Ann Furse

Marjorie and Jean McVicar

Donald and Viara McVicar

Bob and Ray Furse
Donald and Glen Furse

Brian and Leona Scobie

Earl and Jeanine Haight

Corey and Jane Scobie

309

Mark and Tyler McVicar

Left: Donald and Viara McVicar with grandson Mark.
Right: Jean and Oscar Paulin.

Carol, Earle and Leona McVicar.

Elizabeth (holding Carol) and Donald McVicar and
Henry Timlick.

PETER McBEAN

Peter McBean was born near Inverness, Scotland, had Gaelic as his first language and English as his second. He arrived in Canada in 1852, and married Jean Coutts of Sarnia, Ontario, c. 1852. Jean was the daughter of Peter Coutts, also born in Scotland, who came to Canada in 1836. Jean was one of 13 children.

Peter McBean and Jean had nine children. Angus, Elizabeth, John, Peter, Lachlan, Annie, James, William and Albert. In 1882 the family came to Franklin, the SE¼ 9-1-4 E1. The McBeans retired to Emerson, where Peter died July 21, 1907, and Jean on March 22, 1922, at age 85.

William took over the homestead when his parents retired to Emerson. He married Nell Marshall. Their children are Maude, born 1902, and Carolyne, born 1905, Nell McBean died, and William married Jean Morrison, daughter of Mr. and Mrs. Wm. Morrison. Jean (Morrison) McBean died 1942. William in 1943. Maude married Frederick W. Armstrong in 1925. She had three children, Bill, Jack and Jean. Bill lives in Edmonton, Jack in Winnipeg, and Jean married Blair Breckon, and has four children.

Carolyne married Hugh B. Morrison in 1938, a Kaleida farmer, who died in 1957. Carolyne lives in Manitou. In 1960 she was elected one of two women members in the Manitoba legislature.

Lachlan went to live in Ontario. Peter Jr. ran a store and grain elevator at Greenway. He had three sons, Albert, Gerald and Ronald.

Annie stayed at home, and moved to Emerson when her parents retired. In 1902 she married George Gunn, and in 1903 her daughter Mary Jean Irene was born. The Gunns also had a son, Hugh John Wesley. Annie died in Norwood in 1955, at age 90 years. Her daughter Jean has a cottage in Emerson in 1982.

Albert worked for the railway at the West Emerson Junction and at Noyes, just across the American border. He died at Emerson in 1937, in his 60th year.

Angus acquired his own farm in 1880, the NW¼ 3-1-4 E1. His wife came from Sarnia, and her name was Jenny. They had three children, Bertha, Roy and Myrtle Jean. Bertha married Austin Blair of Alexander, and had three children, Keith, Roy and Murray. She died in 1945. Roy died at age 15, in 1907. Myrtle Jean became a doctor in 1925. In 1928 she married Dr. George Hoskins, dentist, Chicago. They had one daughter, Geraldine, Mrs. E. H. Spiehel, who has two children, Ronald, and Jacqueline. Myrtle Jean died 1980, her husband in 1957. They are buried in Sarnia.

James became a doctor in the United States. He died of injuries received when a street car hit his automobile while on his way to attend a car accident victim, in Detroit, March 1908. He was 40 years old, a bachelor, and is buried in Emerson.

Elizabeth married Marck Hyatt, a foreman supervising work on the Emerson Bridge in 1883. She moved to Revelstoke, and had three children, Jean, Maude and Eddie.

John went to New York, returned to Emerson to open a general store. He married Violet Jack, daughter of Mr. and Mrs. William Jack, and had 14 children. William, John, James, Angus, Alex, Arthur, Roy, Cameron, Georgina, Mrs. G. McCarthey, Doris, Mrs. D. Carruthers, Elizabeth, Mrs. D. Bell, Grace, Mrs. Robert Hayward, Edith, Mrs. Colin Boaler, Ida Jean, Mrs. Frank Atwood, Mary, Mrs. William Hoag. John and his family left Franklin Municipality early in the century.

Annie McBean; Elizabeth (McBean) Hyatt.

Jean, Eddie and Maude Hyatt.

Peter and Jane McBean

Back, William, John; middle, Jim, Angus, Peter Jr.; front, Laehlar, Albert, c. 1891.

Bertha, Ray and Myrtle Jean McBean.

311

John McBean; John Peter McBean.

Geraldine Hoskins

Grandma McBean with two granddaughters, Jean Gunn (left), Bess (McBean) Bell (right), daughter of John and Violet McBean.

Keith, Ray, Bertha (McBean) Blair and Murray.

Albert McBean; Dr. Jim McBean and Jean Gunn.

Angus and Jenny McBean

Hugh John Wesley Gunn

312

Annie (McBean) Gunn; Jean (Coutts) McBean with granddaughter Jean Gunn.

Maude and Caroline McBean

Carolyne Morrison, Jean Gunn, Dr. Myrtle Jean Hoskins and Maude Armstrong.

Hugh and Carolyne Morrison; Fred Armstrong.

William and Jean McBean; Jean Gunn, teacher for 40 years.

FEODOR MULKO

Feodor Mulko was born in Chriniky, Volyn, Ukraine, in 1912 to Andrey and Antonina Tucek. He immigrated to Canada in 1928 with his wife Sonia and brother Mefodie. In 1929 they settled on SW ¼ 29-2-3 owned by Mr. Alex Waddell. In the spring Mefodie, called Fred, bought a farm two miles south of Dominion City. Fred's wife, Teresie Kordulova, was born in Ratiskovice, Czechoslovakia, in 1913, the oldest living child of Jan and Josefa Prikaska, and came to Canada in 1927 with her mother, sister Mary and half sisters Josephine and Hedviev. Her brother George was born in Canada. Teresie lost her father in 1916, and her mother remarried.

In 1931 Fred went to Kuroki, Saskatchewan, to work for the winter, and married Teresie, his boss's daughter on October 4, 1933. They had three children, Dorothy, born 1934, George, born 1940, and John, born 1948. Dorothy married George Kucera in 1969, and lives in Chicago. George married Alice Delorme in 1962, and lives in Letellier, with four children, Sheila, David, Michelle and Melanie. John married Mabel Cowper-Smith in 1971, and lives in Edmonton with two children, Carol and Paul.

George and Dorothy Kuara; George and Alice Mulko.

Mefodie (Fred) and Teresie Mulko

David, Sheila, Melanie and Michelle Mulko.

John, Mabel, Carol and Paul Mulko.

KOST MANZIE

Mr. and Mrs. Kost Manzie, Tolstoi pioneers.

ED MURRAY

Ed, Doreen and Patrick Murray came to Dominion City in June 1955. Ed was a supervisor with Manitoba Hydro until 1965 when Dominion City amalgamated with Letellier. He now is a Business Representative with Manitoba Hydro in Morden.

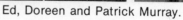

Ed, Doreen and Patrick Murray.

JOHN MANDZUIK

John and Anna Mandzuik (nee Yatskiw) immigrated to Canada in 1929 from the village of Khodachkiw Maliy, province of Tarnopol, in Western Ukraine. They were accompanied by seven children, William, Paul, Olga, Andrew, Mary, Agnes and Nick. They spent the first winter at Senkiw at the home of Michael and Mary Bereza who had immigrated earlier from the same village.

In 1932 John and Anna purchased land at Rosa in Section 15-3-5.

John died in 1959 and Anna in 1970. Paul and Nick remained on the family farm and live there in retirement. William married Barbara Furyk who also immigrated to Canada in 1929 from the same village in the Ukraine. They purchased land in Section 15-3-5 where they did mixed farming and live in retirement.

They had two children, Stella and William Jr.

Stella married Maurice Kohut from Rosa, a school teacher, and they had a family of four. They live in Winnipeg and own a farm at Rosa in Section 22-3-5.

William Jr. married Alice Ambroseychuk from Sarto and they live in Winnipeg. They have two sons, David and Nathan. They own a farm at Rosa.

Andrew Mandziuk married Anne Kohut from Carlowrie and they farmed on Section 10-3-5 until Anne's death in 1979. They had two children, Mary and John.

Mary married Roman Smook from Stuartburn and they live in Stuartburn with their two children.

John married Margaret Pohrebniuk from Rosa and they live in Winnipeg with their three daughters. They own a farm at Rosa in Section 11-3-5.

Olga, married Harry Yarema, and they farmed in the Rosa area in Section 10-3-5 until Olga's death in 1960. They had one son.

Walter, who married Irene Novak from Sarto, and they reside in Sarto with their two children. They also own some land at Rosa in Section 11 and Section 15-3-5.

Mary married Michael Mokrynski. They moved into the Rosa district in 1942 where they operated a general store. Michael died in 1979.

Their daughter Lillian married Taras Pohrebniuk from Rosa. They live in Roseau River with their two children.

Agnes, married John W. Kohut from Stuartburn and lives in Winnipeg. They have four daughters.

John and Anna Mandziuk; William and Barbara Mandziuk.

Anna and Nick Kohut surrounded by family.

ANTHONY MIHAYCHUK

Anthony Mihaychuk immigrated to Canada in 1912 from the Ukraine at 17 years of age. He spent a few years working for a wealthy farmer, earning money to buy land at Rosa. In 1922 he married Catherine Danylchuk from Carlowrie.

They had three children.

Mary married Steve Polischuk and lives in Winnipeg. They have a daughter Iris and son Jim.

Peter married Jennie Kohut from Rosa. They have two sons, Ronald and Mervin.

Ronald married Grace Yanisiw and they have a daughter, Carla, and live in Winnipeg.

Mervin married Brenda Rekrut and lives in Winnipeg.

Ronald and Mervin are active on the home farm in their spare time.

William, and his wife Kathleen, live in Winnipeg. They have three children, Patricia, Terry and Anthony.

Anthony has seven grandchildren and nine great-grandchildren. His wife, Catherine, passed away in April, 1980.

315

Anthony and Catherine Mihaychuk; back, Mary, Peter and William.

Peter and Jennie Mihaychuk; Ronald, Grace and Carla Mihaychuk.

Mervin and Brenda Mihaychuk

RODERICK ALFRED McLENNAN

Roderick Alfred McLennan (originally MacLennon) was born in Banffshire, Scotland, in 1837, and his wife's people were O'Neils from County Antrim, North Ireland. Mary Ann McLennan was born in 1845, in Canada.

Roderick came to Manitoba in 1878 and to a homestead on 20-2-4 E1.

There were six children.

Isabella, 1872-1959, married John Spence.
Clara, 1873-1892.
Roderick, 1874-1967, married Ellen Lochhead.
Sarah, 1876-1965, married Thomas Spence.
Samuel, 1877-   , never married.
Flora, 1879-1953, married Joseph Casson.
Janet, 1880-1968, married James Seward.
John, 1882-1976, never married.
William, 1884-1965, married Elnora Froom.
Mary, 1885-1976, was a nurse, never married.
Annie, 1887-1983, married Geo. Hurd.

They are all buried at Green Ridge except Janet and Samuel.

One of the Second Generation, Raderick, Jr. married Ellen Lochhead June 22, 1910.

Ellen was born and raised in the Green Ridge area. She was the daughter of John and Joan Lochhead. Roderick Jr. and Ellen made their home on the farm the north ½ of Section 5-2-4 E.

They had five children Allan, Janet, Kenneth, Aileen and Hugh.

Roderick and Ellen farmed till 1948 when Allan bought the farm. They continued to live on the farm for the next 18 years. Roderick Jr. passed away in 1967 and Ellen in 1976.

Kenneth was born 1917. He spent time in the services during the second World War, coming home in 1945 to farm the SW ¼ 7-2-4 E1 and the N ½ of the NW ¼ 3-2-4 E, where the home is located. He married Elsie Ganske in 1948, and has two daughters.

Roderick and Mary Ann MacLennan

Gail married Marcel Gobiel and lives in Winnipeg with children Robert and Jaclyn.

Darlene married Marvin Wilkinson, and lives on the Green Ridge road.

One of the Third Generation, Allan, married Irene Spence of Woodmore, the daughter of Garry and Ethel Spence. They were married March 20, 1940 and had three children, Sandra, Karen and Delores. They live on a farm at Green Ridge.

Roderick MacLennan children, l-r; back, John, William, Sarah (Spence), Janet (Seward), Roderick; front, Isabella (Spence), Ann (Hurd), Flora (Casson), Mary.

Roderick and Ellen MacLennan Jr.

Allan, Mrs. MacLennan, Hugh, Kenneth; front, Aileen and Janet.

Allan and Irene; William and Nora MacLennan.

Allan holding Delores, Sandra, Irene and Karen.

Allan, Ethel Spence and Irene MacLennan.

EPHREM MARION

Father Fillion, parish priest, was interested in getting more settlers to live in St. Jean Baptiste. He went east to recruit families. Ephrem and Elise Marion were young and enterprising so in 1879 came to live here with their first born son, Albert, born at St. Gabriel de Brandon, Quebec on December 29, 1877. Children born here were Léona, Mrs. Wilfrid Delorme, Lumina, Mrs. Sinaï Paul, Alma, Mrs. Charles Loiselle, Frederic, Eliza, Sister of the Holy Names, Laurent, Anna, Mrs. Flavien Chaput, Ulric, Eugenie, Mrs. Achille

Roy, Alphonse, Angeline, Mrs. Ludger Bruneau, Albertine, Mrs. Donat Asselin, Yvonne, Mrs. Desiré Belánger.

Ephrem had purchased 620 acres of fertile land east of the Red River. He lived on a smaller homestead near the town of St. Jean Baptiste. All the boys grew up to be farmers and married local girls. Most resided in the Red River Valley. Ephrem Marion died in 1915 at the age of 58 years and Elsie in 1925, aged 68 years.

Albert married Antoinette Dupuis in 1905. They lived in St. Elizabeth. Five children were born there — Alma, Adonaï, Edouard, Philip and Simone.

Later Albert bought a farm owned by a brother-in-law, Flavien Chaput. Yvon and Clement were born there.

In 1917, he moved to the former Walter Timlick's farm. Gérard and Rita were born there.

My parents lived on the farm until 1946, then retired to St. Malo. Albert died in 1953 at the age of 76 and Antoinette died in 1970 at the age of 85. Clement stayed on the home farm. After the high flood, the house was moved to Dufrost where Edouard and his family lived until their retirement to St. Malo in 1976.

Adonai, Edouard and Philip rented land in the Arnaud district during the 1930's, and later bought land here.

Clement was born in 1918. He took over the family farm, and has farmed from 1945 to 1979. In winter Clement lives with his brother Yvon in St. Malo and in summer in his little house on the farm. In 1979 he retired his land to Laurent Grégore of St. Jean. He comes back to live in his house every summer, and enjoys making his garden, picking wild fruit and fishing.

Albert and Antoinette Marion

Flood

Philip, Adonaï, Edouard, Clement; seated, Gerard, Sister Alma and Yvon.

WASYL MELOSKY

Wasyl and Olena Melosky came to Canada from the Western Ukraine just before the turn of the century. They and their children first went to the Dauphin area, where Jarvis Walter, the youngest, was born in 1895.

In 1933 Jarvis purchased a farm along the Roseau River, the NW ¼ of 8-3-4 E1. In 1934 he quit teaching and brought his wife May, sons Walter and Louis and daughter Roxy to Franklin. He kept bees, while Walter worked the 20 acre field. A fruit orchard was started but the severe Manitoba winters damaged buddings and graftings. In 1950 Jarvis left the farm to go back to teaching. That year Walter married Mary Antoniuk.

Jarvis had married May Luhouvy, born in Oakburn in 1904, in 1925. Her parents were Panko and Aplonnia Luhouvy, who came from the Western Ukraine. Jarvis and May retired to St. Vital in 1962, where they live in 1982.

Mary (Antoniuk) Melosky, was the daughter of Harry and Anastasia (Podworny) Antoniuk, who came to Canada in 1904. The Podworny family also came from Western Ukraine. Antoniuk died March 13, 1963 on the farm in Senkiw where they moved to in 1939, and Mrs. Antoniuk in 1981 in Vita. There were 11 children, two died in infancy, and Lena (Antoniuk) Mokry died June 10, 1980.

Mary and Walter remained on the Melosky home farm, which they purchased for $5,000 in 1956. Their children are Linda Mae Brown, Walter Louis, Audrey Marie, and Gerald Patrick. One child died in infancy. The Meloskys still live in Green Ridge.

Louis, Roxie, Walter; seated, May and Jarvis Melosky.

Harry and Anastasia Antoniuk; Louis and Mary Melosky.

Walter and Audrey Melosky

Brian, Linda and Victoria Brown.

Ron and Roxie White, Lorne, Gordon and Sandra.

Walter and Mary Melosky, Linda and Victoria Brown, Audrey and Patrick Melosky.

PETER MAKOWESKI

Mr. and Mrs. Peter Makoweski immigrated to Canada from the villge of Postilivka, W. Ukraine in 1914. They purchased a farm at Tolstoi, 1-1-5 E1. Hard times set in and in 1923 they left the farm to go to Chicago. In 1929 they returned to their farm, and continued farming, and some carpentering. They had two sons, John and Paul, two daughters, Mary Cherkos of Chicago, and Sally Scatnicks of Lancaster, Minnesota. Peter Makoweski passed away in 1947 and Anna in 1972.

Jacob and Clara Hutt were married in 1926 in Overstone, and farmed on SW 10-1-5 E1 until their retirement in 1960. Clara is the daughter of Mr. and Mrs. Otto Geiler, Jacob was the son of Mr. and Mrs. Jacob Hutt. Both were born at Tolstoi.

Jacob Hutt passed away in 1968. Clara Hutt has a residence at the Joyce and Paul Makoweski farm.

Paul took over his parent's farm 1-1-5 E. In 1955 he married Joyce Hutt, only daughter of Mr. and Mrs. Jacob Hutt.

They have two sons and one daughter.

Peter married Marcia Bice of Fergus Falls, North Dakota in 1981.

Tony is at home.

Carol married Richard Schultz, son of Mr. and Mrs. August Schultz of Emerson in 1979.

John married Teanie Drewniak, the daughter of the late Mr. and Mrs. Andruk Drewniak of Tolstoi. They farmed the NW ¼ 6-1-6 E1, and continue to live on the farm, having retired in 1980.

They have one daughter, Jean, and son-in-law Mike Yarmie, of Winnipeg.

Left: Peter and Anna Makoweski.
Right: top, Paul and Joyce Makoweski; bottom, son Tony.

John and Teanie Makoweski, Jean and Mike Yarmie.

Jacob and Clara Hutt

Mike Tymkiw, Sally Scotnicki, Delores Tymkiw. Newlyweds, Peter and Marcia Makoweski, John and Teanie Makoweski; seated, Mike and Jean Yarmie.

Peter and Marcia Makoweski; Richard and Carol Schultz.

Mike and Jean Yarmie

320

WILLIAM MORRISON

William Morrison married Mary Campbell. Their children were:

Jean married William McBean.

Annie married in Ontario to a man named Couch. They had eight children.

Maggie married Hamilton Stewart.

Minnie married Will Ross who was killed in an accident when his horse ran away. She then married his brother, Guy, who died of tuberculosis. She married a man named Code in Ontario. She had one child from her first marriage who died at the age of 17.

Eva married Salem Root of Emerson. Their children were, Myrtle, Laverne, Emilie and Dorothy.

John married Francis Lindsay, daughter of William Lindsay Sr. in 1909. They had a family of five boys, Wallace, Harold, Garnet, Clayton and Carman.

Garnet is married and has one daughter.

Clayton married Agnes Ingram and they have two sons and two daughters.

Harold was killed in 1941 in a truck accident.

Wallace and Carman have not married and live on the family farm in 1982.

William Morrison and his brother Aleck homesteaded the NW ¼ 9-1-4 E1 and the SW ¼ 9-1-4 E1 in 1879. Wm. settled on the NW ¼, and Aleck changed his mind and did not bring his family to Manitoba.

John Morrison and George Turner boys; Wallace Morrison, Stuart Turner, Harold Morrison, Russel Turner, Garnet Morrison, Vernon Turner, Carman Morrison, Ross Turner; Roy Turner in front.

Children of William and Mary (Campbell) Morrison, l to r; Maggie (Mrs. Hamilton Stewart), John Morrison, Eva (Mrs. Salem Root), Jean (Mrs. Wm. McBean). Others in the family were Annie (Mrs. Couch) and Minnie (Mrs. Code).

Wedding of Mr. and Mrs. John Morrison in 1909 at the home of her parents, Mr. and Mrs. William Lindsay Sr. who homesteaded on NE 17-1-4E. Mr. and Mrs. Morrison are in the centre row in the centre of the picture, just in front of the windows. Second and third from right hand end, back, Mr and Mrs. Salem Root (Eva Morrison). Stanley Lindsay, brother of the bride, is seated in the foreground with fingers interlocked. His wife, Jenny (Parkes) Lindsay is just over his left shoulder. To her left is Violet Stowe (Parkes); centre, first lady from right hand end, Edith (Lindsay) McGregor, second Shaddie Lindsay; bottom, first from left hand end, Mrs. Frank Coates (nee Alice Lindsay), Mrs. William Morrison, first lady from right hand end, Mrs. Robert Coates, man between the bride and groom, back, is Will McBean.

Mr. and Mrs. John Morrison and Garnet c. 1920. Morrison parents homesteaded on NW ¼ 9-1-4 E1 in 1880.

John Morrison's family; Wallace, Harold, Garnet, Clayton, Carman, 1940.

WILFRED MARSH

The Wilfred Marsh family came from England in 1964, farmed the former George Marks (Hamilton Stewart farm before that) farm, NW 10-1-4 E until 1972.

Jim, Marion, Shirley, Muriel and Wilf.

CHRISTOPHER MILLER

Christopher and Caroline (Reimer) Miller and their children Leah, William, Daniel. Mr. and Mrs. Christopher Miller homesteaded in Overstone in 1898 section 7, range 5, township 1.

JOHN R. MAYNE

John R. Mayne was born near Tweed, in Bruce County, Ontario on June 28, 1862. He came to Manitoba in 1898 and worked in the Morris and Dominion City area. In 1902 he bought a Hudson Bay quarter section of land in Woodmore, SE ¼ 26-2-4 E for $800.

A brother Frank and sister Julie Mills (Wm. McCoy) settled in Woodbay, and John Mayne and sister Jessie Ann who had married John Kelly, settled in Woodmore.

In 1904 Annie E. Park, a Canadian Irish woman whose family had come to Ontario c. 1814, visited her sister Mrs. Wilbur Hurd. The Hurds farmed across the road from the J. Mayne farm. They met and were married December 29, 1904. Following their marriage they drove with team and cutter, to Woodbay, for his bride to meet members of his family. The trip to Woodbay was 100 miles and took two days each way. They broke the journey by stopping over night at Morris. On their return their neighbours gathered at their house and had a dinner of roast goose and all the trimmings ready. They also presented the Maynes with a 12 piece set of china which is treasured in their son's home in 1982.

The Maynes had one son, Russell.

Russell Mayne is still farming the Hudson Bay quarter which his father homesteaded. He bought the NE ¼ of the same section from John Graham and farms the east half of 26-2-4.

He is married to Marguerite, youngest daughter of the late Mr. and Mrs. W. Ward. They have three sons, Donald, Robert and Ronald.

Mr. and Mrs. John R. Mayne on their 200 mile honeymoon trip to Woodbay in December, 1904.

Donald married Dorothy Froom, eldest daughter of Mr. and Mrs. Herbert Froom October 1, 1960. They own the former San Graham farm, East ½ of section 27-2-4, and operate a mixed farm. Water was a problem on his farm until a deep well was drilled. This well taps a spring which never runs dry. Donald and Dorothy have two children. Gwen graduated from grade 12 in 1981, and Allan is a student at Roseau Valley Collegiate.

Robert Earle joined the Proffessional Engineering staff of Underwood-McLellan Ltd. in 1968 and is their Director of Planning and Surveys.

While working on Surveys in Hay River, Alberta, he met Theresa Kamieniechi, a girl from Manning, Alberta. They were married on December 28, 1958, and have three children, Carol, Ann and Jonathan.

Donald and Dorothy Mayne

CYRIL McCAUGHAN

Cyril and Brenda McCaughan were married June, 1958. They had three children, Ronald, born June 1959, Cory, born June 1964 and Darcy, born September, 1967. Son Ronald passed away in September, 1959. They purchased the Esso Service Station at the corner of 59 and 201 from William and Dorthy Unrau in March, 1976 which has since been operated as Cec's Esso Service. It was destroyed by fire in April of 1980 and rebuilt and reopened in November of the same year. At that time they lived on the ¼ section SE of 59 and 201 which they purchased from Ted Ganske in 1978, then sold to Mr. and Mrs. G. Johnson in 1981.

Left: Russell and Marguerite, and Ronald Mayne. *Right:* Russell and Marguerite Mayne, Donald, Robert and Ronald.

Robert, Theresa, Ann; front, Jonathon and Carol.

Gwen and Allan Mayne

Cory, Cyril, Brenda and Darcy McCaughen.

Nykola and Nastasia Mandzie

NYKOLA MANDZIE

Nykola Mandzie came to Canada with his parents, Kost and Anna Mandzie from Western Ukraine, at the age of 17. He homesteaded on NE 34-1-5, and in 1903 he married Nastasia Boyko. They had 10 children, only four are living presently: Bill of Gardenton, Jack of Winnipeg, Metro and Mary of Tolstoi. Nykola had four sisters, Tekina Kowalchuk (deceased) who was in the Blind Institute; Mary Holowachuk (deceased) who was in International Fall, Minn., Mrs. Boychuk (deceased) lived in Sundown, Mrs. Natasia Kasian, formerly of Tolstoi, now makes her home with her daughter, Olga and Bernard in Winnipeg.

ROBERT KENNEDY MILLAR

Robert Kennedy Millar proved up his land, the SE ¼ 34-2-4 E1, in 1878. He married Agnes Burrell in 1879. Their children were Robert, who was killed in the First World War, Jack, who never married and remained on the home farm where he met a tragic death while attempting to remove a stone from a field. There were three girls, Meta, who was in a home at Grunthal for a time and is now in Minnedosa, Maggie, who married Jack Palmer and lived at Petersfield, Mary, who married a man named Mitchell. Mary had a daughter, Hazel, who married a man named Schleg, and lives in Birch River.

ROBERT CHARLES McLAREN

Robert Charles McLaren and his wife Bridget (Switzer) came to Franklin in 1881. Robert was born in Perthshire, Scotland and came to Canada in the 1830's. He had seven children, Malcolm, Robert Campbell, Peter, Duncan, Jack, Mary and Annie.

Mary married a United States marshall and moved to Minnesota.

Annie married John Johnson and died when their only child, Jean, was five years old.

Jean was raised by relatives in Ottawa, married Wesley Hurd, son of Wilbur Hurd, of Franklin.

Robert and Malcolm went to the Yukon in 1898. They married and both died in their 80's, Robert in Vancouver and Malcolm in Seattle.

Jack had a flour mill at Headingly, and married Minnie Alcock of Woodmore.

Duncan and Peter did not marry. Peter was known for his strength and died in the 1930's. Duncan died in a car accident in St. Boniface in 1926. Both are buried at Brookside.

Robert McLaren died in 1906, and Bridget in 1918. They are buried at Green Ridge.

N JOHN NEDOHIN

John Nedohin came to Canada from the Ukraine with his parents, Etnach and Anastasia in June 1896 at the age of 16 years. He had two brothers, Peter and William and two sisters Anna and Pollyanne.

They landed in Halifax. The Immigration Agency had them designated to Stuartburn, Manitoba. They settled on a homestead on the NE ½ of 31-1-5 E in the municipality of Franklin.

In 1902 John chose a bride, Mary Bially, who also immigrated to Canada with her parents c. 1896. They filed for a homestead on the NE ¼ 31-5-5 E.

By 1913 they had seven children.

In 1923, to supplement farm expenses, Dad engaged in a J.R. Watkins dealership in the southeastern area of Manitoba. Mother and the family worked the farm with Dad's help and supervision on the weekends. One weekend Dad came home suffering with one of his attacks which resulted in a ruptured appendix, with no train to Winnipeg until Tuesday. He was admitted to hospital on Wednesday, beyond help. John Nedohin passed away 27th of March 1927 leaving behind his wife Mary and 13 children, Pollyanne, Steven, Julia, Bill, Fanny, Anne, Neta, Lena, Milton, Bert, Kathleen, Elizabeth and Donald. Mother carried on farming with the family. Steve, Julia, Bill, Neta and Lena worked the land and did the heavy chores. There were five children nine years and under; Milton, Bert, Kathleen, Elizabeth and Donald. Pollyanne was finishing High School in Winnipeg, Fanny and Annie were working full time in Winnipeg. Julia and Neta worked out part time.

In the spring of 1931 Mary married John Urbanowski, a widower with two children, Joe, 11 and Annie nine years. Joe died in 1940.

Bert (Bohdan) the fourth son of John and Mary always lived in Franklin municipality. After serving four years with Canadian Armed Services, he came home and took over his mother's farm in 1945, purchasing it four years later.

In 1947 Bert married Pauline Shenderevich who was a teacher in Zelota School.

Bert and Pauline have two sons. Brian is an Agricultural Representative in Morden. He is married to Janet Gurman of Arbakka. They have two daughters Dawn and Erin.

Ken works for the Manitoba Telephone System and lives in Winnipeg. He is married to Karen Dunlop of Killarney. They have one daughter, Lindsay.

Donald purchased a farm and when Bert took over the home place, Mary went to live with him. Donald married and Mary went to live with daughter Elizabeth and Sid Penhall in Winnipeg. Mary suffered for many years with diabetes, finally had both limbs amputated and went blind and passed away September 1, 1965.

Brother Steve predeceased her in December 1951. In 1982 the John Nedohin family members number 129.

John and Mary Nedohin, 1912.

Front, Lena Runke, Mary Urbanowski, mother Annie Palamer, Julia Gaetz.
Back, Katherine Dowhan, Bert Nedohin, Neta Gunn, Donald Nedohin, Fanny Waslphen, Polly Ann Moen, Milton Nedohin, Betty Penhall, 1962.

Bert, Kenny, Brian and Pauline Nedohin.

Brian and Janet with Erin and Dawn.

Ken and Karen with Lindsay Nedohin.

BRYAN NICHOLS

Bryan and Gwen Nichols were married in Dominion City in 1962. They have two sons James and Todd born in 1964 and Dean Clark born in 1966. Both boys are receiving their education in Dominion City.

Bryan is the son of Dewith and Christine Nichols of Arnaud.

Gwen is the youngest daughter of the late Mr. and Mrs. James French.

In 1974 Bryan and Gwen purchased the

Todd, Bryan, Gwen and Dean Nichols.

Macleods Store which they operated until the fall of 1981.

Bryan is now working for the Boundry School Division as the supervisor of transportation and maintenance.

WILLIAM NEDOHIN

William Nedohin came to Canada in 1897, from Austria, where he was born in August of 1886. His parents and two brothers and two sisters came at the same time. He married on July 12, 1906, and farmed in Overstoneville until his retirement to Emerson in 1956. The Nedohins had six boys and six girls.

Mrs. Nedohin was a self taught chiropractor, and through this God given talent brought relief from suffering to many, both in Manitoba and across the International boundary into the United States. In her capacity as midwife she delivered 90 babies. She had been born in the Ukraine in 1892.

IVAN NAZAREWICH

Ivan Ivan and wife Horpina Nazarewich and two small sons Joseph and Jacob immigrated to Canada from West Ukraine in 1902. They homesteaded the SE¼ 1-2-5 E1 and after six years bought a farm on 23-1-5 E1.

Jacob, who became a school teacher died in 1936.

Horpina Nazarewich died in 1949 at age 75. Ivan died in April 1951 in Tolstoi. They are survived by sons Joseph of Tolstoi and John of Winnipeg. Two daughters Teresa Melenek of Winnipeg, and Mrs. A. Senkiw of Sarto passed away. The third daughter Tienie Kudryk is living in Watson, Saskatchewan.

Joseph continued farming. In 1919 he married Mary Slotuik of Sarto. Joe and Mary retired from farming in 1964, and are residing in Tolstoi. They have one son Boris, who married Marilyn, nee Lakomey, and have three children Tanis, Donna and Kathy.

326

Ivan and Horpina Nazarewich

Joseph and Mary Nazarewich

Kathy, Donna and Tanis Nazarewich.

MINORU NAMBA

In April, 1942, when the Second World War was in progress, Minoru and Sumi Namba were among the Japanese who were removed from the coastal waters of Canada, for security reasons. They left sunny British Columbia, green grass and spring flowers, and were brought to Manitoba, where it was still winter. They were met with snow, mud and water everywhere.

Their family of five girls and three boys were born in Franklin Municipality, and educated in Dominion City. In 1982 they are all married and away from home. They feel very much a part of the community, however, and come back to take part in local activities as often as they can.

The Nambas are retired, and enjoy life with their extended family, including 11 grandchildren and four great-grandchildren, with whom they have a close relationship.

GEORGE NICKEL

George Nickel, born 1927, married Mary Thiessen, born 1927, in 1946, and has lived all his married life in Franklin Municipality. They farmed various lands in the district, until 1952, when they bought the 12-2-5 E1 from Joseph Horbetz.

Their family are - John, born 1947, who married Mary Anne Penner in 1973, and has a dairy operation at Gardenton. They have three children, Sharon, Roxanne, and Wesley.

Sarah, born 1949, married Edward Peters in 1972. They farm, and have two boys, Darryl and Colin.

Anne, born 1951 married Menno Braun in

Front, Darryl, Colin, Michella, Timothy, Karen, Norman, Sharon and Roxanne.
Middle, Sarah, Hildie, Lena, Mary, George, Corrinne, Angela, Anne, Gary, Mary, and Wesley.
Back, Edward, Bill, Jake, Margaret, Ben, Bertha, Henry, Menno and John.

1972. They have three children, Norman, Karen and Gary.

Bill, born 1953, married Hildie Unrau in 1977. He farms and has two children, Timothy and Michella.

Henry, born 1955, married Corinne Dueck, and has a daughter Angela. They live in Steinbach.

Jake, born 1957, married Lena Unrau in 1979, and is an electrician in Steinbach.

Nettie, born in 1959, died in infancy.

Margaret, born 1960, is employed at Loewen Millwork and lives in Steinbach.

Ben, born 1962, works at Ste. Anne Co-op.

Bertha, 1966, is a student at Shevchenko School.

HOMER NISELY

Homer Nisely, born January 27, 1854, came to Canada from Illinois in 1882. He came with a man named Mann to Newbridge. He lived with Mr. Mann on the NE ¼ 15-3-4 E1, until he bought the SW ¼ 15-3-4 E and the N ½ of the NW ¼ of section 10-3-4 E1.

On December 20, 1888 he married Annie Isobel O'Hara daughter of Thomas and Isobel O'Hara of Langside. The O'Hara's lived on the N ½ 10-3-3 E.

Mr. Nisely built a log house on the SW ¼ 15-3-4 E1, replaced in 1906 with a large, modern house, in which they lived until their deaths.

They had seven children:

William Thomas, born November 23, 1889, remained on the farm until his death in 1965.

Hazel Edith, born January 30, 1891, married George Calder of Carlowrie and died in 1922.

Albert Allen, born February 10, 1893, left the farm and went west. He married Nellie Bartlett of Calgary. He passed away in 1952.

Mary Alice, born February 24, 1896, became a school teacher and married James H. Timlick of Newbridge. She died December 20, 1948.

Ralph, born December 11, 1899, died in infancy.

Mabel Esther, born July 12, 1901, lived on the farm until 1964 when she moved to Dominion City.

George Washington, born November 17, 1906, married Winnifred Hamblin October 22, 1936 and lived in the Newbridge and Greenridge districts. He died in 1971.

The Hamblin family came from England, where Albert Hamblin was born in 1851, and his wife Annie Sgevens in 1861. They married in the late 1870's, and came to Canada in 1882 with daughter Alice. Two children were born in Winnipeg where Mr. Hamblin worked for J. H.

Ashdown, Lillian in 1883, and Fred in 1885. Shortly thereafter the Hamblins moved to the NE ¼ 24-2-5 E1, in Franklin Municipality, where Thomas was born in 1889. He purchased the 24-2-4 E1 from a Mr. Black, and six more children were born here. This farm was sold to a man named Bell from Portage la Prairie in 1920. Albert died in 1908.

Alice married Frank Smith of Woodmore, and has four sons and four daughters.

Lillian married John Moore, and had four children.

Albert Fred was born in Winnipeg May 17, 1885. He married Emily Primrose Pott, eldest daughter of John E. Pott of Woodmore, born September 9, 1889, Wittington, Staffordshire, England. She and her family arrived in Franklin in 1907. Fred and Emily were married July 1, 1908.

They bought the E ½ of 13-2-4 E1, and later the N ½ of 14-2-4 E1 from Jim Gilbert. In 1920 he bought the N ½ of 15-2-4 E1 from a man named Adams, in order to take advantage of school busing. Fred also farmed section 24-2-4 E1 for many years. In 1934 they left Franklin to buy a farm in St. Jean.

Their children are: Edward, married Martha Stieben, Arnaud, 1940; Winnifred, married George Nisely of Green Ridge, 1936; Thomas, married Kathleen Knowles of Emerson, 1946; Lloyd, married Dorothy Binding, Winnipeg, 1945; Irene, married Ralph Calder, Carlowrie, 1940; Fred farmed until his death in 1969, and Emily lived with her family until 1974, when she went to live in the Red River Valley Lodge in Morris.

Thomas married Minnie Craig of Ridgeville and farmed in Woodmore until they opened a garage in Dominion City and in 1922 a hotel in Arnaud, moving to Winnipeg in 1924. They have three daughters and two sons.

Walter farmed with his father. Returning home in 1918 from service in the first World War, he sold the old home, worked for the garage in Dominion City with his brother Thomas, then moved to Winnipeg. He married Olive Brown of Winnipeg, and has three daughters.

Violet married Archie Craig, and farmed in Ridgeville. She has two daughters and two sons. Rose married Ben Ramsey of Dominion City. She ha three daughters.

Gertrude became a teacher, and married Clifford Brown of Stephensfield. She has three children, two sons and one daughter.

Ada married William Turner, a barber in Dominion City. She has one daughter. Nellie was a teacher, and married Cecil Stevenson of

Graysville. She has one son.

George Nisely and Winnifred Hamblin, eldest daughter of Fred and Emily Hamblin were married October 22, 1936.

They lived at the Nisely home at Newbridge until the fall of 1937, when they moved to the N ½ of 15-2-4 E, where George lived until his death in 1971 and Winnie lives in retirement.

They had two children, Hazel and Ian. Hazel became a school teacher and in 1961 married Aime Carriere of St. Malo. Aime is the son of Mr. and Mrs. William Carrriere (nee Florence Nault) of St. Malo.

They purchased land owned by William and Mabel Nisely, SW ¼ 15-3-4 E and N ½ NW ¼ 10-3-4 E, land now in the Nisely family for 100 years. In 1971, they purchased the SE ¼ 33-2-4 E1 and in 1974 the N ½ 15-2-4 E.

Their children are Gerald Howard born December 9, 1965, and Laurel Lynn, born March 1, 1968.

Aime is a seventh generation descendent of the hunter, trapper and voyageur Jean Baptiste Lagimodiere, the man who walked from Red River to Montreal to deliver papers to Lord Selkirk regarding the situation at the Red River settlement. He left Fort Douglas on October 7, 1815, and reached Montreal on March 10, 1816, a distance of 1800 miles. According to the map, he must have passed very close to the land we now own.

Another important figure in this family tree is Louis Riel Jr. a third generation descendent of Lagimodiere. Riel was hanged in Regina in 1885.

Goerge and Winnie farmed the N ½ 15-2-4 E, the SE ¼ of 33-2-4 E, at one time farmed the NW ¼ 14-2-4 E, the NW ¼ 30-2-4 E and for a few years SW ¼ of 15-3-4 E and N ½ of the NW ¼ of 10-3-4 E.

Homer and Annie Nisely and their children; George, Mabel, Hazel, Mary, Albert and William c. 1911.

Left: Homer and Annie Nisely.
Right: Annie MacPherson, a cousin of Annie Nisely, came from Smith Falls, Ontario, to live with her aunt Mrs. T. O'Hara in Dominion City.

Ian, Winnie and George Nisely, Hazel with husband Aime Carriere, 1962.

Standing, Fred Hamblin, Ian Nisely, Aime Carriere; sitting, Emily (Grisely) Hamblin, Winnie and George Nisely, with grandson Gerald Carriere, Hazel (Nisely) Carriere, with Laurel.

Laurel and Gerald Carriere

Standing, Lillian, Thomas, Violet, Walter; sitting, Fred, Mr. Hamblin with Ada on his knee, Mrs. Hamblin with Nellie on her knee; on the floor, Rose and Gertie.

Fred and Emily Hamblin family; George and Winnie Nisely, Hazel and Ian, Ralph and Irene, ? Calder, Lorraine and Colin, Edwarth and Martha Hamblin, Evelyn, Shirley, Beverly and Linda, Tom and Kaye Hamblin, Barbara, Patricia, Elaine and Robert, Lloyd and Dorothy Hamblin, Marian, Donald and Lorne.

MICHAEL NEUMANN

In 1885, the year that the last spike was driven at Craigellichi, Michael Neumann, age 25, married Juliana Fuerst, age 27, in the Government District of Wolhynien, Russia. Their ancestors had come from the Schleswig-Holstein area of Germany, in the late 18th century.

Their first children, August Michael, 1884, Emilie, 1886, Gottlieb, 1888, and Albert, 1890, were born near the Austrian border, at Wolhynien.

In 1891 they set out for Canada, but ran out of funds in Liverpool, England. Michael worked in a sugar factory until his sister Emilie, who lived in Lang, Saskatchewan sent money for him to travel to Canada alone. Juliana took in laundry to support herself and her children, and gave birth to a son, William, who died in infancy of measles.

329

Michael found his way to Plum Coulee where he worked for Mennonite farmers until 1893, when he sent for his family. The entire family worked for the Mennonite people around Plum Coulee, Juliana doing washing and ironing, helping with butchering animals for meat, and the children herded cows along roadways and on grassland. Two sons were born here, Heinrich in 1894, and Hermann in 1896.

In 1898 the Neumann family moved to the NW ¼ of 4-23-3 E1. Two daughters were born here, Bertha, 1899, and Agusta in 1901.

In 1899, Gottlieb age 11, in spite of repeated warnings, tied the rope of one of the horses he was watering around his arm. The horse was startled and ran into the barn, hitting the boy against the doorframe. He died instantly of a broken neck. In 1907 Heinrich died of typhoid. In 1908 Emilie died giving birth to her first child, stillborn. In 1910 Michael suffered a ruptured appendix while walking home from Dominion City. He died, age 50.

In 1917 the home farm was sold to Rudolf Doern, and Albert purchased the E ½ of 20-1-4 E1, near Ridgeville, where they farmed until 1927. That year they moved to the NW ¼ of 4-1-3 E1. In 1937 Albert bought River lots 22 to 32, and remodelled a house on lot 32. They lived here until 1947, when they retired to Emerson.

Juliana with Herman, Agusta and Bertha, moved to Morris in 1915, and then to Winnipeg.

Michael Neumann, born September 17, 1860 in Russia, died October 9, 1910 in Emerson. His wife Juliana, born 1858 in Russia, died April 8, 1939 in Melville, Saskatchewan. They are buried in Brookside Cemetery, Winnipeg.

Their children:

August Michael was born in 1884 in Russia. In 1915 he married Hulda Magner. Their children are William, born 1916 in Winnipeg, and presently living in Winnipeg. Harry, born 1917 in Winnipeg, presently lives in Kamsack, Saskatchewan. Edward, born in 1918 in Winnipeg, presently lives in Atikokan, Ontario. Freda (Moore), born 1919 in Sutherland, Saskatchewan presently lives in Winnipeg. Bertha (Henderson) born in Sutherland, Saskatchewan, presently lives in Wynard, Saskatchewan. Alma (Foreman) born in Sutherland, Saskatchewan presently lives in Kamloops, British Columbia. Leonard born in Blutcher, Saskatchewan died accidently in 1979.

August died September 22, 1954 at the Winnipeg General Hospital.

Emilee, born March 4, 1886 in Russia, died January 7, 1908 in Emerson.

Gottlieb, born February 2, 1888 in Russia, died September 3, 1899 in Emerson.

Albert, born January 16, 1890 in Russia, married Hulda Hennig on July 14, 1913. Their children were; Anton Walter, born October 29, 1914. On October 14, 1939 he married Meta Walters, born June 30, 1918, died April 7, 1977. They had one son, Ronald Larry, born March 3, 1943. On September 16, 1967 he married Audrey Marie McNabb, born November 21, 1946, on September 16, 1967. They have a son Todd Allan born September 8, 1969.

Antonia Adele (Della) born February 22, 1916, married Arthur Hartwig November 5, 1938. She passed away June 6, 1976. Martha Gertrude, born August 1, 1921, married Theodore Schwark October 26, 1940. Edna Emma, born November 14, 1924 married Thomas Fortier August 4, 1951. Albert Lawrence Clifford, born August 25, 1933, married Mary Irene Pokrant, born February 7, 1932. Their children are Gregory Clifford, born April 27, 1959 and Lawrence Edward, born January 3, 196?.

Albert died August 11, 1962 in Emerson.

William, died of measles in infancy in 1892 in Liverpool, England.

Heinrich, born May 27, 1894, in Plum Coulee, Manitoba, died December 27, 1907 in Emerson.

Herman (Harry), born October 22, 1896, in Plum Coulee, Manitoba, married Marie Wunsch in 1920. Their children were: Richard, born 1921, married Jean Cross in 1955. They now live in London, Ontario. Bernice, born 1923, married Gordon Edgar in 1945 and now lives in Delta, British Columbia. Rosemary, born 1935, married Fred Isford in 1956, they now live in Winnipeg.

Herman died October 12, 1981 in Winnipeg.

Bertha, born June 26, 1899 in Emerson, lives in Thunder Bay, Ontario. She married Bin Ursel in 1921.

Agusta (Gertie), born 1901 in Emerson, died in 1966 in Penticton, British Columbia. She married Henry Kiel in 1927.

Mata and Walter Neumann, 1974.

Albert and Hulda (Hennig) Neumann, July 14th, 1913.

L to r; Walter Neumann, Martha Schwark, Edna Fortier, Cliff Neumann and Della Hartwig.

O RICHARD M. OATWAY

Richard M. Oatway came to Canada from Barnstaple, Devonshire, England with his parents in 1841. They settled in Perth, Ontario. In 1860 he married Annie Knox of Carlton Place. They lived at Almonte for some years. They had 10 children when they came to Manitoba in 1880.

Mr. Oatway was a stone mason and plasterer by trade which stood him to good use when building his home and farm.

Three children were born at Green Ridge. The children were John, Sarah, William, Lillian, Barbara, Robert, Ellen, Bertha, Richard, Jessie, Hector, Melville, and Edward. Richard M. Oatway died in 1892 of tuberculosis.

Sarah married John D. Baskerville. Barbara married James Hunter. Ellen died in 1893 of tuberculosis. William was a medical doctor and went to Millwakee. Lillian passed away in 1892. Bertha taught school and then married Rev. John Russell. Richard Jr. was a medical doctor and had a practice at Stony Plains, Alberta. Jessie married John Thomas of Carlton Place, Ontario. Hector was a druggist and was employed by Owls Drugs of Vancouver. Melville passed away in 1907. Edward was employed by T. Eaton commpany of Edmonton. He is retired and makes his home in Edmonton. In 1894 John Oatway married Margaret Dickson. They had two children, Wilfred and Annie. John had a farm two miles north of the home place. George Olden owns the farm now. Margaret Oatway passed away in 1898. Grandma Dickson, living in Woodmore took the children. John Oatway died in 1917. Wilfred was left the farm after his father's death. Wilfred married Polly Provo in 1918. They had four children, Lillian, Margaret, Lloyd and Boyd. Wilfred sold the farm in 1924 and moved to Quill Lake, Saskatchewn where he still lives, a retired school teacher.

Annie Oatway married Robert Hay and moved to Vancouver.

L to r; Marie, Todd Allan and Ron Neumann, 1982.

L to r; Greg, Mary, Cliff and Larry Neumann, 1982.

Robert Oatway took over the farm in 1901. On November 20, 1901 Robert married Margaret McEwen who taught school at Greenridge for three years previous to her marriage. They had seven children, Roslyn, Jean, Maitland, Mavis, Ida, Beatrice and R. Douglas.

Jean taught school for 17 years. She married Henry Boles of Deloraine, and died in 1946.

Mavis is employed with the Department of Public Works of Canada at Edmonton.

Ida is employed with Manpower at Winnipeg.

Beatrice married William Lenkins in 1942 in San Jose, California.

Douglas graduated as a medical Doctor in 1942, joined the medical corps, served overseas with the Queen's Own Rifles of Toronto, took post graduating surgery at Edinborough, Scotland, and in 1952 he received a fellowship. He has a practice in Winnipeg.

Roslyn worked the home farm with his father.

In 1952 the Oatways retired to Winnipeg. Richard died in 1957, Annie in 1960. In 1955 Rosa rented the farm and left to work for the Canadian Customs at Emerson. He sold the farm in 1964. It had been in the Oatway name for 85 years.

In 1964 Roslyn married Margaret (Craig) Johnston. He retired from the customs in 1969 and makes his home in Emerson.

This farm was rented for a year or two by Mr. and Mrs. Henry Casper, then Pete Peters. It was bought by Mr. and Mrs. Stan Walters and sold to Lloyd Ramsey, who lives there during summer and winters in Texas. Ray Ramsey now farms it.

Robert and Margaret (McEwan) Oatway, 1951.

Hector, Dr. Richard and Edward Oatway.

Jean Oatway Boles; Dr. Doug Oatway.

Richard and Annie Oatway

L to r; Wilfred Oatway, Annie (Oatway) Hay and Polly (Mrs. Wilfred Oatway). Wilfred born in Green Ridge 1896, Annie 1898. Wilfred died in the 1970's. Ann lives in British Columbia. Polly lives in Wadena, 1966.

Ross and Margaret Oatway

Bill and Betty (Oatway) Linkins and Ross Oatway.

Left: Betty, Ida and Annie Oatway.
Right: Mavis, Betty and Ida Oatway.

Left: Annie Oatway and brother Wilfred.
Right: Ross Oatway, Customs Officer, Tolstoi.

Wilfred and Polly Oatway and family on their 50th anniversary.

FREDERICH OPOCENSKY

Fred and his wife Blanche (Rzepka) and three daughters, Anna, Georgina, and Marie arrived in Halifax, June 13, 1924 from Boratyn, Municipality Volyn, Poland.

In 1924 they located on River Lots 106, 108 and 110 with the aid of Manitoba Farm Loans. In 1925 they farmed this land with brother Jaroslav and his wife Marie, until October, 1931. Then Fred moved to the "Flats". Two sons, Joseph Milo and Fred Jr., were born in Canada.

Georgina was employed in the local Queens Hotel owned by J.M. Waddell where she met W.A. Taylor whom she married in 1943.

Anna married an American, Harvey Brarmer. They had two sons, Elisson and Fred. Marie, deceased May, 1981, married Olaf Larson, son of local C.P.R. Foreman and had two sons Nelson and Dayeton.

Joe, farming the home place, married Ann Hutch of Netley, who died in August, 1978. They had a son, Ron, who now farms the place with his wife Marlyn.

Joe Opocensky, Georgina Taylor, Mrs. Fred Opocensky, Anna Braemer, Fred Opocensky Jr.

Fred Jr. met Ann Vintr at the Windsor, Ontario, Customs, where they both worked. They married July, 1957. When Joe married, Fred and Blanche moved to the Graham place which they owned, and in 1966 retired to Dominion City to the home that Marie and Ollie left when they moved to Labrador.

Fred Sr. passed away January, 1968. Blanche continues to live in her retirement home.

Anna Braemer on tractor, Joe Opocensky beside car. Extremely wet fall, starting to rain August 29, and continued to mid September. Farmers waited for frost. Taken December 27, 1944.

Blanche (Rzepka) and Frederick Opocensky; children, Georgina, Marie, Anna, 1924.

Forming the straw pile; feeding sheaves into threshing machine is Fred Opocensky, observers (grandchildren) Elisson Braemer and Cheryl Taylor c. 1950.

Joe and seaman Fred Jr. Opocensky, c. 1943.

Front, Marie, Josef, Fred Jr., Georgina; back, Fred, Anna, Blanche Opocensky.

Back, Blanche Opocensky (Mrs. F.), Marie Opocensky (Mrs. J.); front, Anna (between Mother and Aunt), Marie, Irene, Georgina, Fred Opocensky, 1926.

Fred Opocensky and family, Georgina, Blanche, Marie, Fred, Anna; front, Freddie Jr. and Joseph, 1929.

Back, Joe Kostal, J. B. Opocensky, Frederick Opocensky, Joe Rzepka, his sister Blanche Opocensky, (Mrs. Fred); front, Marie, Georgina, Anna, Irene, George, Joe. Little one in front with hand on face, Fred Opocensky Jr., old Model T. Ford, c. 1929.

ERNEST CHARLES OLDEN

Ernest Charles Olden, born August 2, 1881, to George and Bertha (nee Maybe), at Milbrook Place, near Southhampton, England. In January, 1905, Ernest married Maud Lily Richards, born in 1880. In March, 1905, they came to Canada. They went to Paynton, Saskatchewan to a homestead.

On December 12, 1905, Gladys Irene was born. October 14, 1912, George Richard was born, Merton Ernest arrived October 4, 1918.

In 1921, Ernest and his family returned to England and went into market gardening at New Milton. In the fall of 1924 Ernest sold the market gardens and returned to Canada. He bought a farm from Wilfred Oatway on the Roseau River in the Green Ridge district, where the family has farmed to the present day.

Irene was married in Montreal to Sylvian Mandowsky from Switzerland. They had one son, Eric, two grandchildren, and three great-grandchildren. Following the death of her husband, Irene married Joseph Bagutti, also from Switzerland. She died in July, 1980.

George, served in the R.C.A.F. and R.A.F. during the Second World War. On his return he bought his father's farm, where he is still farming. He was married in 1974 to Gwendolyn Stewart (nee Timlick). There are two stepchildren and four grandchildren.

Ernest Olden passed away in 1961 and his wife, Maud, in 1965.

Merton, married Margaret Bernice Griffin of Woodmore in 1945. They bought the farm owned first by John F. Gunn, and later Garnet Gunn, along the Roseau River where they are still farming. Their daughter, Glennis, married Bill Philipation, and lives in Minnedosa with children Michelle and Tyler.

Ernest and Maud (Richards) Olden, 50th wedding anniversary.

Left: George and Gwen Olden on their wedding day.
Right: George, Merton and Margaret Olden.

JAROSLAV OPOCENSKY

In 1914 Jaro B. Opocensky set sail for the United States from Boratyn, Poland. One stormy night, when the ship was halfway across the Atlantic Ocean, the captain announced that war had broken out in Europe. It was the captain's decision to keep going or to turn back. The captain chose to keep going. As a result, after spending some time in Virginia with relatives, Jaro became a hardworking tailor in Cleveland, where he spent the next six years.

At a social gathering one evening Jaro met Marie Vancura, who had also immigrated to the United States from Czechoslovakia. They were married in Cleveland, on August 17, 1916.

In 1920 Jaro and Marie decided to return to Europe to settle the family estate. While there Irene was born on March 15, 1921.

The United States was limiting immigration when they decided to return and they came to Canada. They came to Franklin after a short stop in Saskatchewan in 1924. In 1925 Jaro and his brother Fred purchased river lots, 106, 108 and 110 in the Parish of St. Agathe on the Red River. George was born on October 20, 1925.

In 1931 a land swindle deprived them of this land and the brothers separated. Jaro remained on the river lot, renting the land for the next three years. In 1934 he purchased the N ½ of section 2-3-2 E1, known as the Baskerville farm, on which George still resides.

They lived on the home farm until 1951 when Jaro purchased the NW ¼ of section 24-2-2 E where he and Marie lived until Marie suffered a stroke in 1968. Marie remained an invalid until her passing in September 1978. Jaro B. resided in the Dominion City Manor until his death in August 1974.

Their daughter, Irene, born in Boratyn, Poland, married William R. Kyle on November 11, 1939. They had three children, William Dennis, Marjorie Jean, and Debbie June.

George married Faye Clementine Boutet on June 18, 1949. They have five children, Robert, Janet, Julie, Jean and Angela.

Faye died on January 16, 1972.

Robert Jordy, was born July 31, 1950. He was in grade 12 at Dominion City when he had an accident which took his life on April 17, 1968.

Janet Leigh, married Stephen C.P. Carroll, a businessman, and they have one daughter, Christine Louise, born August 12, 1981.

Julie Ann, a singer, married Agostine Masi in 1981 and lives in Toronto where she pursues her musical career.

Beverly Joan married Frank Gardener and lives in Medicine Hat. She has two lovely daughters, Jessica Lee, born September 5, 1978, and Victoria Brianne, born January 26, 1980.

Angela Marie, is in high school at the Roseau Valley Collegiate, and lives on the farm with her father.

Marie (Mancura) and Jaroslav Opocensky, 1924.

The George Opocensky daughters; Janet Leigh, Angela Marie, Julie Ann, Beverly Joan; forefront, Vicki Gardner, Joan's daughter, 1981.

Janet, Joan, Faye, Robert, George, Julie. Angela missing, 1963.

Robert Jordy Opocensky, 1967, deceased April 17, 1968; George and Faye (Boutet) Opocensky, June 18, 1949.

WILLIAM OSCAR OSTBERG

William Oscar Ostberg was born in Gottenberg, Sweden. He came to Canada by himself at 15 years of age, in 1892. Later one brother and sister came to the United States.

William's first summer in Canada was spent as a water boy on the railroad line between Kenora, called Sprague at that time, and Fort William. He ended up in Winnipeg, spent time around the livery stables, and found work on a farm in Clearsprings, north of Steinbach. There he met and in 1898 married Isabella Laing. They farmed in the district and their two children were born there, Thomas in July, 1900, and Mary in 1906. The family moved to Winnipeg in 1912 where they lived for five years.

In 1917 William brought his family to Lyman Ranch I where he was farm manager until 1920. He purchased the NW ¼ 32-2-3 E1 where they lived until 1925, when he bought the ¼ NE 31-2-3 E1. William retired in 1944, and moved to Winnipeg. William passed away in 1952, Isabella in April 1980, at the age of 102 years.

Tom Ostberg married Ruth Alice Brewster of Green Ridge in 1927, they made their home on NW 32-2-3 E where their only son Harold was born in January, 1929.

Ruth passed away in January, 1957.

Tom Ostberg retired from farming in 1957 and moved to Winipeg. In 1963 he married Jessie (Brad) Maynes. They returned to Dominion City in 1982.

Mary Ostberg graduated from grade 11 in Dominion City School in 1924. She moved to Winnipeg where she worked as a dentist's receptionist. In 1935 she married Neil Baskerville, they had one son Robert. Mary lives in Winnipeg.

Harold Ostberg married Doreen Ramsey of Green Ridge in 1952. They have four children, Vicki born September, 1956; Randall, born June 1958; Mitchell born October, 1961 and Carl born

June, 1963. Vicki married Randy Gushuliak of Emerson in 1975 and they have one son Lane, born September, 1981 and live in St. Adolphe, Randall and Carl are at home farming with their dad on the Dominion City farm originally owned by their great-grandfather, William Ostberg. Mitchell attends the University of Manitoba.

Left: Mrs. Ostberg 100th birthday in 1978.
Right: Mrs. Ostberg with quilt she made in 1974.

William and Isabella Ostberg, 1944; Tom and Ruth Ostberg, 1952.

Ostberg family, 1982, back, Randy Gushuliak and Lane, Vicki Gushuliak, Harold, Doreen, Tom, Jessie; front, Carl, Mitch and Randy Ostberg.

Isabella Ostberg, winter of 1935, with her horse Bell in front of the Ostberg farm home at 31-2-3 E1.

Five members of Ostberg family holding private pilots licenses standing by their Cessna Hawk XP, 1982; Randy Ostberg, Randy and Vicki Gushuliak, Doreen and Harold Ostberg.

JOHN OSTROWSKY

John Ostrowsky, born December 22, 1897 in Teresholwec, Podolsk, Russia came to Canada in 1914.

On December 11, 1915 he enlisted in the 144th Overseas Battalion and accompanied the unit to France where he was wounded in the left shoulder and chest. There he remained hospitalized for two years. On April 22, 1918, he was medically discharged and returned to Canada to live in Winnipeg with Mr. Mozienko.

In the 1920's, he was employed by the firm that constructed the water line to Shoal Lake.

In 1924 he married the former Lena Smook. They had one step daughter, Olga Patrick who now lives in Winnipeg. In 1927, they moved to the SE ¼ of 19-3-5 E at Carlowrie. Lena, died in 1934.

In 1936, he married Nellie Chubey of Carlowrie. They had eight children.

William married Alice Ratchinsky. They have one daughter, Cindy, who married Jarvis Hrynenko. They live at Rosa.

Peter married Nellie Kantimer. They have two daughters, Rachel and Barbie. They live at Senkiw.

Florence married Ken Nielsen of Winnipeg. They have three daughters, Karen, Cathy and Debbie, and one son, Jimmy.

Harry married Doreen Froom. They have two children, Johnny and Wanda. They live near Roseau River.

Rosie married Bill Smook of Senkiw. They have four children, Mary Ann, Nancy, Christine and Harry.

Ann, Rosie's twin sister, lives in Winnipeg.

Morris married Margaret Kiziuk. They have one daughter, Larissa, and live in Winnipeg.

338

Bobby married Rose Peech. They have four children, Robert, Darin, Shayne and Stacy. They live in Winnipeg.

In 1951, John and Nellie moved to the NW ¼ of 18-3-5 E1. John died in 1963. Nellie has remained on the farm at Carlowrie.

John and Nellie Ostrowsky

Harry and Doreen, Johnny and Wanda Ostrowsky.

Morris and Margaret (Kiziuk) Ostrowsky and Larissa.

Ann Ostrowsky, 1968.

Ken and Florence Nielson, Karen, Cathy, Debbie and Jimmy.

Rosie and Bill Smook with children Harry, Mary Ann, Christine and Nancy.

William and Alice (Ratchinsky) Ostrowsky and daughter Cindy with her husband Jarvis Hrynenko.

Peter and Nellie Ostrowsky, Rachel and Barbie Ostrowsky.

Bob and Rose; Robert, Darin, Shayne and Stacy Ostrowsky.

339

P WILLIAM HENRY PALMER

William Henry Palmer, a master butcher by trade, and his wife Christian Martyn brought their three children from the County of Somerset, England to Franklin in 1890. They homesteaded the NE ¼ of 13-2-4 E1. Shortly afterward, they moved one-half mile north to the SE ¼ of 12-2-4 E1, which they farmed until their deaths in 1916 and 1917, repectively. Both William Henry and Christian Martyn are buried in the Green Ridge cemetery.

Mary, who was eight years old when the family came to the district, returned to Devonshire, England in 1917, married Percy Evans, and did not return .

John Martyn married Margaret Miller of the Green Ridge district and moved to Petersfield, in 1920. They had four children:

Stewart, who lives in Toronto.

Glen, who continues to farm at Petersfield.

Neil, of Vancouver.

Carol, a United Church minister in Pierson.

William Henry, married Martha Cain, of Treherne in 1926 and operated the original family farm until they retired to Dominion City in 1952. They have five sons:

Martyn, of Winnipeg.

Harold, of Hamilton.

Jack, who passed away in Kenora, in 1972.

Cliff, of Edmonton.

Dale, of Westaskiwin, Alberta.

Bill passed away in 1965 and Martha in 1980. Both are buried in the Dominion City cemetery.

The farm was sold to Harry Griffin in 1952.

William Palmer, 1919; Mary Palmer.

JOHN PENNER

John and Tina Penner (nee Thiessen) were married June 27, 1954. They lived in the Grunthal-Pansy area until 1960 when they moved to Roseau River. Here they bought the NE ¼ 23-2-5E from Peter Palowski. They have two daughters and three sons:

Kathy, born in 1955, is engaged to Leonard Friesen and is to be married on August 2, 1982.

Elizabeth, born in 1956, is married to Ike Doerksen and has one daughter, Stephanie.

Edward, born in 1958, is married to Yvonne Funk and has one son, Delbert.

David, also born in 1958 is engaged to Joyce Funk, wedding to be July 24, 1982.

William, born in 1963, is working for Vita Co-op and lives at home.

They operate a dairy farm, also John drove cream truck for Vita Co-op for 10 years. They are members of the Sommerfeld Church where John in secretary.

William, Henry and Christian (Martyn) Palmer.

Kathy, David, Tina, William, John, son-in-law Ike, Elizabeth, Edward and daughter-in-law Yvonne; 25th wedding anniversary.

CORNELIUS F. PETERS

Cornelius F. Peters was born in 1904 in Southern Russia. In 1926 he came to Canada as did Maria Penner who was to become his wife in April, 1928.

For two years after marriage they worked as farm-help, first near Emerson and then in Saskatchewan. In 1930 they, with daughter Katie, moved to Green Ridge and the south west quarter of section six.

Eight years and four more children later they moved to section 8, next to Roseau River. The family increased to 12 children, six daughters and six sons.

Peter farmed the Ross Oatway place during 1959 to 1962.

In 1971 Cornelius and Maria sold the farm at Green Ridge and moved to Steinbach because illness had left Cornelius handicapped since 1964. On March 19, 1977 at the age of 72, Cornelius passed away.

Maria Peters is still living in Steinbach and keeps herself busy with knitting and crocheting for children and grandchildren, sewing MCC quilts and spinning wool at the Steinbach Village Museum and the Mennonite Pavilion at Folklorama.

Katie married Henry Paetkau and they farm in Alberta with their three children.

Corny married Betty (Ballingall), has two children and lives in Winnipeg.

Peter married Helen (Stevenson) and he lives in Winnipeg with his two children.

Marie married John Zacharias, a minister at MacGregor. They have four children.

Daniel married Judy (Saunders) and lives in Winnipeg.

Frank married Linda (Bennett), they have three children and live in Winnipeg.

The Cornelius F. Peters family.

David lives with Maria in Steinbach.

Margaret married Werner Pauls and they and their three children live at Ile des Chenes.

Henry married Irene (Michalowski) and they and their two children live in Alberta.

Helena married David Kitzan and they have three children and live in Winnipeg.

Susie lives in Moose Jaw, with her three children. Her husband, Henry Thiessen, died in 1978.

Elizabeth married Walter Harms who died in January of 1975. She lives and nurses in Altona.

JOHN PALEY

John Paley was born on June 16, 1890 in the village of Senkiw, Western Ukraine. He immigrated to Canada with his parents in 1900, accompanied by two brothers and two sisters. They first settled near the Roseau River at Senkiw. His older brother Samuel married in 1904, bought a parcel of land in Rosa and moved there in 1906. John moved in with Samuel and helped him with the buildings and the clearing of land.

Several years later John purchased part of Sec. 27-3-5 E; and married Wasylyna Bzowy of Stuartburn on February 29, 1911. She was born on January 14, 1895, in the same village as John and came to Franklin in 1897. They farmed here until 1937.

Seven children were born here:
William on June 10, 1912.
Peter on June 1, 1914.
Stephen on March 25, 1916.
Daniel on August 15, 1917.
Anne on November 10, 1919.
Maurice on April 8, 1922.
Wilma on January 25, 1924.

John farmed until 1944, when he purchased lots in Dominion City and built the Great West Motors service garage. He moved to town in 1945, and was joined by Peter and Maurice in the garage business. In 1952 John built a house on O'Brien Street, and retired.

Wasylyna died January 19, 1977, and John on February 26, 1977. Both are interred in the Ukrainian Catholic cemetery at Rosa.

William attended high school in Winnipeg, apprenticed in a Drug store for a year and went to the United States. He married Ruth Schuckmell in Chicago on December 26, 1936. They have two sons, William and Phillip. They live in Chicago.

Peter attended high school in Winnipeg. He left the farm in Dominion City in July 1937 and enlisted with the R.C.M.P. He married Caroline Pyrch on August 27, 1946 at Edmonton, Alberta. They have two children, Richard and Phyllis.

Peter took his discharge from the R.C.M.P., returned to Dominion City in 1948 and started operating Great West Motors with brother Maurice, in the garage that his father built. In April 1952 he left the business with Maurice and re-enlisted with the R.C.M.P., retiring in October 1972 after 29½ years service. Since 1974 Peter has helped Maurice with his business and now farming.

Stephen lived with his parents until his death in 1952.

Daniel left the family farm in Dominion City in 1939 and was employed in Hamilton, Ontario where he married Marjorie Howis in 1941. They have two sons, Gordon and Craig. He was divorced from Marjorie and married Adeline Smith in Chicago in 1957.

Anne left the farm in 1940 and was employed in Winnipeg for a period. She married Valmore Connor Frith on July 14, 1940 at Winnipeg. They have two sons, William and Russell.

Maurice came to the Dominion City farm with his parents, and farmed with his father. He helped build the garage in Dominion City, and he and his brother Peter operated Great West Motors in 1948. Maurice married Dorothy Irene Johnston in Dominion City on October 28, 1950. They have two children, David Maurice born on September 11, 1951 and Paula Nicole born December 8, 1953. David was married to Elizabeth Morin in Winnipeg on January 12, 1974. They have one child, Carla Irene born on June 20, 1974. Carla is living with her grandparents, Maurice and Dorothy at Dominion City. Nicole was married to Henricus Bogers, a member of the R.C.M.P., on July 12, 1975 at Dominion City. They adopted twins, Dana Maria and Dustin Mathew born May 7, 1982 at Winnipeg. They live in Roblin. Maurice purchased the W ½ Sec. 16-2-3 E in 1974 and in 1975 purchased his father's farm Sec. 11-3-2 E.

In 1979 he sold his Farm Implement business.

Wilma left the farm in 1941 and worked in Winnipeg at the C.K.Y. Radio Station, then Toronto and Montreal. She married John Michael Hayes on September 7, 1960 in London, England. They have one son, William John. John died in 1979 and Wilma lives in Toronto.

John Paley's D-4 Caterpillar tractor with farm-made brush-cutter attached.

John Paley farm buildings at Rosa; four-horse percheron team, John holding horse on right; Wasylyna with three youngest children at side of house.

Back, Wasylyna, Maurice and John Paley; front, Daniel, Stephen, Peter, William; Anne in foreground.

L to r; Phyllis, Caroline, Richard, Peter Paley, 1961.

Maurice and Dorothy Paley, Nicole and Hank Bogers, David Paley.

Carla Paley, Dustin and Dana Bogers.

Ford full of Paleys. In rear seat; Stephen, Daniel, Peter, Wasylyna; front seat, Anne, Maurice, William, John Paley, 1923.

Left: Daniel and Adeline on their 25th Wedding anniversary, 1982.
Right: Wilma, William, and John Michael Hayes, Toronto, 1969.

Ruth (Schuckmell) and William Paley, William Jr., Phillip, 1939 in Boston.

John and Wasylyna Paley, 1971.

Left: Valmore Connor Frith, Russell, William, Anne (Paley) Frith. Dressed for Centennial celebrations at Dunnville, Ontario, 1965.
Right: Constable Peter Paley, R.C.M.P. with mother, 1942.

ELIAS PANCHYSHYN

Elias and Dokia (Andrushko) Panchyshyn came to Canada from Senkiw Zalischyku, West Ukraine with two daughters, Wasylyna and Anna in 1897. They settled in Stuartburn.

Wasylyna married John Salamandyk, and when they came to live at Senkiw, they built a small house for her parents.

Elias and Dokia are now deceased.

Anna married Wasyl Salamandyk and farmed at Stuartburn. They had six children: Alex, John, Peter, Joe, Doris and Mary.

Anna and Wasyl are deceased, as is their son Peter.

Doris married Wasyl Vereha.

Mary married a man named Kantimer and lived at Senkiw for some time. They now live in Winnipeg.

ANDY PENNER

Andy and Elaine Penner (nee Hildebrandt) were married in 1966. They spent a few years in Plum Coulee and Winnipeg before purchasing the farm from Mr. and Mrs. Abe Zacharias (SE ¼ 23-2-5E) on June 27, 1969. Their main source of income was dairy and beef. They sold their farm to Mr. and Mrs. Gerry Purnell in August, 1974. Andy and Elaine had four children:

Michelle, born 1967.
Craig, born 1969 and passed away in 1971.
Michael, born 1970.
Niomie, born 1980.

They presently reside in Mariapolis and Andy is a sales representative for Sterling Implements of Pilot Mound.

JOHN PETERS

John and Elizabeth Peters (nee Penner) bought the NE ¼ 34-2-5E on September 27, 1951 from George Nickel. They moved here from Winkler and retired back to Winkler in 1979. They have nine children:

Margaret married Gary Smith.
Grace married Abe Kehler from Ridgeville.
Marion married Ike Wiebe.
Ruth married John Nickel.
Edward married Sara Nickel.
Harold married Martha Friesen.
Abe married Mathilda Reimer.
Shirley married Albert Jentes.
Dave married Helen Kornelson.

Ruth and John Nickel were married September 11, 1967 at the old Sommerfeld church in Stuartburn. They lived in Winnipeg, on a dairy farm at Tolstoi, at Niverville, and then at New Bothwell, all the while John worked in Winnipeg. On September 11, 1967 they purchased the farm on the NE ¼ 34-2-5 E1 from Ruth's father, John Peters, plus another 75 acres on the SE ¼ 34-2-5E. They operate a pig and beef farm. Their children are Darlene, born 1969; Katherine, born 1976, and Barbara, born 1982.

SIMEON PALEY

Simeon was born in the village of Senkiw, county of Zalischyky, Western Ukraine, on November 28, 1880 to Oleksa Paley and his second wife, Oksana Toffan. Oleksa's resolve to emigrate to Canada came as a result of a fire, which not only destroyed his home, but also killed his wife.

When Simeon expressed a desire to go to Canada where many of the village folk had already emigrated in 1896, Oleksa decided that the whole family would leave, including the three younger children: Wasylyna, Anne and John. When Todyr, a son of the first marriage, pleaded to be included, Oleksa agreed and the whole group arrived in Canada in the spring of 1900. They settled at Senkiw. Two years later, Simeon met Maria Maksymchuk and they were married on January 19, 1902.

Maria Maksymchuk was the daughter of Oleksa Maksymchuk and Wasylyna Olynyk. She was born in the village of Bilche-Zloty, Western Ukraine. Her family was encouraged to come to Canada by the letters they received from relatives who had emigrated in 1896. They arrived in Canada in May of 1901 and went to Stuartburn where they were met by a relative, Kost Manziy.

Simeon and Maria lived with his father and the rest of the family at Senkiw for a while, and in 1904 bought a farm at Rosa, Sec. 27-3-5. They farmed and kept a grocery store there until 1941 when they retired to Winnipeg.

Simeon passed away in Winnipeg in 1946. Maria moved to Edmonton to live with her youngest daughter, Sonia. She passed away in 1978 at the age of 95.

Simeon and Maria had four sons and two daughters. Anne is married to Isidore Goresky, a teacher, principal and school inspector. They live in Edmonton, with their five children: Adelaide (Banting), Walter, Natalie (Lupul), Donna (Perch) and Dennis.

William married Kate Bord. He left Manitoba in 1927 and moved to Alberta, and retired to Vernon, B.C. They have one daughter, Shirley (Decker).

Nicholas married Margaret Salamandyk. They farmed in the Rosa and New Bridge districts, and

Simeon and Maria Paley

Front, Sonia and Jerry Pryma, Maria Paley (age 87), Isidore and wife Anne Goresky; back, Peter, Mary, John, Anne, Nick, Margaret, William, Kate, 1969.

retired to Winnipeg in 1968.

John married Anne Zaporzan. They lived at Rosa, where he took over his father's grocery store business as well as the International Implement Agency. He passed away in 1981 at the age of 68. They had two sons, Ronald and Taras.

Peter married Mary Kolodzinski. They farmed at Rosa and New Bridge districts, and Mary taught school. Later they moved to Winnipeg, where they are retired. They have one son, Peter William, and a daughter, Maureen (Taylor).

Sonia moved to Edmonton. She married Jerry Pryma and they operate a photo studio in Edmonton. They have three children: Simon, Anna Marie (Novak) and Raymond.

SAMUEL POST

Samuel Post was born in Essex, England in 1782. In 1808 he married Mary Sprague and immigrated to Vermont, U.S. From Vermont they moved to Pennsylvania and then to Iowa. They had nine children. The eldest was Stephen born January 3, 1810 in Vermont. In 1833 Stephen married Jane Force in Sparta, Pa. and they had nine children.

The two youngest Orlin and Ellery, lived in the Woodmore district. Stephen, accompanied by his son Ellery, was sent to establish a branch of the Mormon Church in Manitoba. His wife, Jane, who joined him later was appointed Assistant President and was a prophetess. Stephen continued to hold the church together until his death in 1879. Stephen and Jane are buried at their homestead, the S.E. ¼ 31-2-5 E1.

Ellery married Elizabeth Bowen November 7, 1880. Elizabeth came to Kanasa, U.S.A. from Glasgow, Scotland, with her Mother, sisters Sarah and Susan and brother James. Her mother, a widow, married Henry Hinkle and came to Manitoba.

Ellery and Elizabeth had six children:

Effie (Mrs. E. Spencer), Saskatchewan; 11 children.

Emma (Mrs. J. Stewart); four children.

Ella (Mrs. Bob Dickson); three children.

Ezra married Edith Law; two children.

Ellery married Marjorie McInnis, Rainy River.

Edward married Willa Boyd, Winnipeg. They had two sons.

William married Cynthia Colley; three children.

Robert married Fae Kinsley, living in Winnipeg, and have two children.

Orlin, Stephen's son, was born in Attica, Penn. He married Candace Thomas on June 24, 1875. In 1888 they and their two sons came to Gardenton for four years, then to S.W. ¼ 17-2-5 E1 at Woodmore. They had seven children:

Herb (born May 24, 1876 - died Oct. 11, 1962, 86 years.) He married Susan Howard of Fort Worth, Texas. She died in 1926. On June 30, 1928 he married Carrie Perin. He ran a garage in Ridgeville.

Stephen (born February, 1878 - died February, 1954, 76 years.) Stephen lived and worked with his parents until 1898, when he filed on a homestead. In 1903, he bought the N.W. ¼ of 9-3-4 E1 and in March, 1904, moved to this land and lived there until his death.

March 10, 1908 he married Orythia M. Post, who was born at Green Ridge May 22, 1887.

Stephen died in 1954 and his wife in 1963. They are survived by one son, Elsworth F. Post, and a daughter, C. Myrtle Post, both of whom resided on the farm until December, 1976 when they moved to Dominion City, buying the house owned by Mr. Jack.

Edith (born January 5, 1881 - died February 15, 1970, 89 years.) On October 16, 1901 Edith married Alexander Kirkpatrick and moved to Green Ridge.

Ida (born February 7, 1883 - died in 1937, 54 years.) Ida married William Stewart and they lived in Ridgeville, Rainy River and in British Columbia. They had two children, Harrison (deceased) and Elaine. Elaine married Tom Brown and their two children are Donald and Marie.

Guy (born March 22, 1885 - died February 4, 1967, 82 years.) Guy married Jessie Knox. They lived in Indian Head, Saskatchewan, and came to Woodmore in 1920 and retired to Dominion City. They had two sons; Warren was killed accidentally in 1940, and Garnet, married Bernice Timlick in 1941, is living in Brandon. Jessie married Edward Jack in 1968.

Mabel (born April, 1887). She married David Timlick and lived at Newbridge. They had seven children: Wallace, Irene, Pearl, Gwen, Theodore, Grant and Russell.

LeRoy (born June 1, 1889 - died August 13, 1950, 61 years.) LeRoy married Maude Burdette and lived in Ridgeville, and later moved to Ontario. They had two children: Jimmy (Ottawa) and Marjorie. Marjorie married Ed Deremiens and they have two daughters, Janice and Aileene.

Emma, Effie, Edward, Ella, Ezra; sitting, Ellery and Elizabeth (Bowen) Post.

Guy and Jessie (Knox) Post, 1962.

Back, Darlene Post, Rod Masse, Bernice (Timlich) Post, Garnet Post, Jessie (Knox, Post) Jack, Edward Jack. The other family members on picture are Warren, Herbie, Calvin, Beverley, Barry, and Wendy.

HENRY PALMER

Henry Palmer and Elizabeth Jane Francis were married in England and had four sons and one daughter. They are: James, Henry Austin, Sarah, John and George.

They emigrated from Bedfordshire, England to Canada in 1906, all except James who remained in England, and worked on a farm in the Carey District known as the Carey Farm.

In 1907 they moved to Dominion City where Henry started an abbatoir and butcher shop, and Elizabeth did sewing.

Sarah Palmer married Arthur Boaler, the foreman from the Carey Farm on December 25, 1907. They farmed at Carey and had nine children: Nora, George, Lilian, Elsie, Henry, Colin, Alan, Lewis and Mary.

Their first child was still born and is buried in the Dominion City cemetery in the Palmer plot under the name of "Baby".

Mary Boaler married Gordon Brad in 1953. They live in Dominion City and have two sons: Dale and Calvin.

Dale Brad married Sharon Sawka in 1977. They live in Dominion City and have one son, Dustin.

Henry Austin was born in the village of Barton, Bedfordshire, England, and worked for his father as a butcher. He married Bertha Blanche Pass. Born to them was Horace Henry Austin, Bertha Blanche, William Arthur and Violet May.

In 1909 Henry and Bertha and family immigrated to Canada, arriving at Dominion City, where his parents had established a butcher business in 1907.

Austin Palmer started a butcher shop in Arnaud. During these years two sons were born and died in their infancy from pneumonia, and are buried in the Dominion City cemetery. Two more sons were born: Henness Austin and John Arnaud.

Mrs. Palmer died with typhoid fever in 1914. She is buried in the Dominion City cemetery.

Henry moved to Saskatchewan in 1915 where he took up land.

John returned to Manitoba in 1937 and when the Second World War broke out he enlisted and served overseas. He came back to Franklin after the war and married A. Eleanor S. Casson, January 7, 1947. In 1948 they bought the John R. Post farm from Richard Post, where they have made their home since. Raising their family of: John Myles Howard, Alanna Holly Faith and Jennifer Elizabeth Joyce.

Myles is renting the family farm. Holly has finished her fourth year of law in the University of Windsor. Jennifer married Robert Stefanchuk and they live in Morris.

Sarah and Arthur Boaler

Back, Henry, Colin, Alan and Lewis; front, Mary, Nora, George, Lily, Elsie Boaler, 1960.

Henry and Elizabeth Palmer; Gordon and Mary Brad.

John, Jennifer Palmer; Alanna (Palmer) and Stephan G. Wieting.

A. Eleanor (Casson) Palmer, Alanna Holly Faith and Jennifer Elizabeth Joyce.

PETER ARCHIBALD POST

Peter Archibald was born February 8, 1915 in Stuartburn to Fred and Sarah Post. He was the fourth born and the eldest son of eleven children. His mother was born in Essex, England and came to Canada in 1892. His father was born in Napanee, Ontario of Dutch extraction and came to Manitoba in 1904. In 1909 his parents married and farmed in Franklin until 1948, when they moved to Winnipeg.

Archie joined the army in June 1940. He met Hazel Johnson, and was married on September 7, 1940. He served with The Royal Winnipeg

Rifles in Canada until early 1945. For a time he was an elevator operator with Confederation Life. In 1948 he began employment with the City of Winnipeg Engineering Department where he worked for 30 years.

They had three girls and five boys.

Hazel died on July 9, 1966, at the age of 45. Archie looked after his young family alone until June, 1970, when he married Maria Anderson. He died on June 16, 1978.

D. G. PICKELL

Duncan and Juel Pickell and their children, Faye, Earle and Roy moved to Ridgeville in 1938 from Assiniboia, Saskatchewan.

Duncan ran the N. M. Paterson elevator until 1956. He and Juel went north with the Department of Transport operating power plants for weather stations. They have lived in Winnipeg since 1961.

Faye married Walter Schultz of Friedensthal. They farmed until 1971, then moved to Winnipeg. They have three daughters: Lyn, Lois and Lori.

Lyn married Douglas Casper of Dominion City, R.C.M.P. They have two children Tanya and Troy.

Lois lives in Winnipeg.

Lori married Rick Zaparaniuk of Esterhazy, Saskatchewan.

Earl married Lavina Hancox of Dominion City in 1957. Earl is employed with the Department of Transport and lives in Winnipeg. They have five children: Sherry, Dean, Jean, Shelley and Judy.

Sherry married Jim Friess of Winnipeg. They have two children, Carey and David.

Jean married Wayne Sawatzky of Dominion City and lives in Winnipeg.

Roy married Carol Froom of Dominion City in 1960. He taught school one year at Ridgeville, then joined the R.C.M.P. Roy is inspector in the R.C.M.P. in Winnipeg. They have four children: Blake, Derek, Juel and Trevor.

Duncan and Juel; Faye, Earl and Ray Pickell.

WILLIAM PEARSE

William Pearse, his wife, two daughters, Elisa and Sarah, and sons George, Peter and Herman arrived from England in 1884.

They spent their first two years in Manitoba, and then came to Franklin Municipality.

Peter Pearse married Helen Stewart Knox in Dominion City in 1896. Helen had come to Canada with her parents at age four. Peter and Helen's children were: William, Archibald, Margaret, Elsie and Florence.

Edith, died at an early age.

William was born January 1, 1898 on the NE ¼ 22-3-2 E1. He spent his entire life of 63 years, three months and 20 days in the Timlick district. He married Eva Margaret Weedmark on the 8th of October, 1934, in Dominion City, officiated by Rev. David Spear. Eva was the daughter of George and Mary Ellen (Crampton) Weedmark, and had one sister, Myrtle, and two brothers, George and Ted.

In 1938 William and Eva moved to the NE ¼ of 23-3-2 E1, land formerly owned by Peter Pearse. That same year a son was born: John William Stewart.

Archibald James was born June 29, 1902. He lived on Section 22-3-2 E1 all his life. Peter and Helen moved to Dominion City in 1928 and left him to farm. He married Laura Pott, born to George and Mary Ellen (Dawson) Pott in 1916. They had two children: Ronald and Patricia, who married Frank Gaetz of Tolstoi.

After Archibald's death in 1974, Laura moved to Dominion City.

Ronald, born May, 1941, married the daughter of Oscar and Alma Olson, Marlys Olson of Starbuck, in 1970. They live on 28-2-3 E1, which Ronald bought in 1966 and farmed with his father. They have three children: Rhonda, Beverley and Richard.

George Pearse had a son, Stafford.

Stafford married Annie Kyle, daughter of Paul Kyle. Staffor and Annie had two children:

Audrey, who married Harvey Johnson, and lives in Brandon.

Stanley, who married Audrey Smart in 1952.

Audrey's parents came to Canada from Suffolk, England, in 1918, and to Dominion City in 1947. Her father was section foreman for the Canadian Pacific Railway at Dominion City until 1957, when he retired to Winnipeg. After his death, Mrs. Smart moved to the Franklin Manor until her demise in 1979.

Stan and Audrey Pearse have three children: Sandra, married Mark Waddell and has three children, Brooks, and twin daughters Amber and Angela.

Terry, married Kim VanDeviere.

Jill, who married Bruce Borodenko.

Peter and Helen Pearse

Maggie, Eva, Archie, Helen, Florence, Peter, Ronald, Laura, Bill and Stuart Pearse.

Ronald, Mr. and Mrs. Archie Pearse, Patricia.

Ronald and Marlys; Richard, Beverley and Rhonda Pearse.

William and Florence Smart; Clifford and Anne Pearse.

Jill and Bruce Borodenko, Kim and Terry Pearse, Mark; sitting, Stanley holding Brooke, Audrey holding Angela and Sandra holding Amber.

GEORGE PARKES

Born in 1845 near Wingham, Ontario, he was one of a family of 22 children.

He married Rachel Montgomery in 1873. They homesteaded in Manitoba in 1882 on the N.W. ¼ of 30-1-4E, presently owned by Ross Collins. Then they moved and bought the S.W. ¼ 29-1-4 E1 that was delegated as school land in 1888. This land is presently owned by Bryce Chubaty.

George lived on the S.E. ¼ 29-1-4E where the school was for awhile because of lack of water. They later moved and built a home on the S.W. ¼.

They raised a family of seven sons and three daughters. George died in 1928.

His daughter Violet Ann married William H. Stowe.

William was born in Cambridgeshire, England in 1889. He came to Canada in 1910 and joined the R.C.M.P. and took his training in Regina. He joined the Emerson detachment from 1914-1917, when he and Violet married.

They raised four sons and one daughter, Avis.

He farmed the land formerly owned by George Parkes namely S.E. ¼ 29-1-4E until his death in 1952.

In 1947 Avis Stowe married Alvin Riach who was born in Ridgeville in 1927. He was the son of W. E. Riach. He took his schooling in Ridgeville, later driving fuel truck for Shell Oil and working with the lumber and gravel business.

They raised a family of two:

Carolyn, who married Ken Schwark in 1969 and lives on the Schwark farm near Emerson.

Greg, at home and presently employed by Brown and Rutherford.

Alvin worked in partnership with two older brothers until 1967. He worked one year for the municipality, then in 1968 moved to Winnipeg where he is presently employed with Primco Western.

William H. Stowe R.C.M.P. Shown patrolling the International border from Emerson east.

Earle, John, Charles; back, Avis and Cecil Stowe.

George Parkes; William and Violet (Parkes) Stowe lived on SW ¼ 29-1-4 E.

Alvin and Avis (Stowe) Riach; Greg.

Ken and Carolyne; Kerry and Corinee Schwark.

HARRY PRESTON

Harry Preston was a banker in the private bank, Mortlock, and a founder of the Dominion City Anglican Church parish.

NICK POLISCHUK

Nick and Maria Polischuk and several children came to Canada c. 1897 and settled in the area north of Stuartburn. Soon after their arrival, the children became sick and died. They moved twice before settling on the S ½ of NW ¼ 25-2-5E and SW ¼ 25-2-5E.

They have six children born in Canada:

Pauline, born in 1898, married Peter Kohut (deceased).

Peter, born in 1900 and passed away in 1922.

Paul, (deceased) born in 1905 and married Ann Chubaty.

Mary, married to John Cherwaty.

Helen, (deceased), married Paul Slusarchuk (deceased).

Sabina, (deceased) married Joe Borkewski (deceased).

Nick Polischuk passed away in 1939. Maria lived with Paul and family from 1943 until her death in 1945.

Paul and Ann Chubaty were married in November, 1934 and lived with his parents on S ½ of NW ¼ 25-2-5 E and SW ¼ 25-2-5 E. In 1947 they moved to Woodmore. They bought SE ¼ 29-2-5E from Fred Batten and a few years later bought from Fred Post the quarter across the road, NE ¼ 20-2-5E.

They had four children:

Jean, born in November, 1935, married to Steve Slobodzian and living in Winnipeg.

Walter, born in March, 1937, married to Kathy Cekanauskas and living at Woodmore.

Elsie, born in July, 1939, married to Stanley Bialkowski and living in Winnipeg.

Kathleen, born in 1944 and passed away in 1945 at eight months of age.

Paul Polischuk passed away November 24, 1964 and Ann lives in Winnipeg since 1965.

Pauline Polischuk married Peter Kohut in 1913 and lived in Emerson before buying NE ¼ 25-3-4E in 1936. They farmed here until 1950, when they retired to Vita. Then they moved to Roseau River in 1966 and lived on the same yard with their daughter and son-in-law, Ann and Andrew Mandzuik.

Peter Kohut passed away October 1967 and Pauline Kohut still resides in her home.

They had nine children:

Paul, died December 16, 1976, was married to Ann Kischuk and lived in Niagara Falls, Ontario.

Mary, married Bernie Pott and lives in Woodmore.

Ann, passed away April 11, 1979, was married to Andrew Mandzuik and lived in Roseau River.

Helen, married Alex Balazs and lives in Alymer, Ontario.

Dan, married Steffie Rybuck and lives in Niagara Falls.

John, married Joyce Bachinski and lives in Thunder Bay, Ontario.

Bill, married to Elsie Buck, lives in Winnipeg.

Mike, married to Lorraine Rodi, lives in Thunder Bay.

Olga, married Henry Anderson and lives in London, Ontario.

Walter married Kathy Cekanauskas October 10, 1959. They farmed with his parents until his father's death in 1964, when they took over the farm. They have a mixed farm with the main income in beef.

They have four children:

Betty, born in November, 1960.

Nick, born in November, 1961.

Pauline, born in December 1962.

Danny, born in July, 1964, at home and attending school.

Betty, Nick, and Pauline are all employed in Winnipeg.

Stan Bialkowski, who married Elsie Polischuk, is employed with C.A. Killeen & Sons Ltd., and Elsie is employed with Elmcrest Furniture Mfg. Ltd.

Their children are:

Patricia, is working with the Canadian Grain Commission as a secretary in the Grain Inspection Division.

Theresa, enrolled in the RIA program at the

University of Manitoba and is working full-time for the Department of Natural Resources as a receptionist in the Personnel Services Section.

Steve was employed with the City of Winnipeg, East Kildonan Water Maintenance for 27 years, and is now retired.

Steve and Jean have been foster parents for 20 years and presently have four foster children:

Tony, attends grade one at Victory School.

Keri, attends the day nursery that Jean is operating in her home.

Kitty, also attends the day nursery in Steve and Jean's home.

Allan, attending the day nursery as well.

George is employed by Manitoba Hydro.

Barbara is employed as a cosmetician at Sears.

Patty graduated from Marvel's School of Hairdressing, and is now an instructor of hairdressing.

Kathie is employed part time at Sears.

Mary is presently attending West Kildonan Collegiate, in grade 11.

John is in grade three at Victory School.

Walter and Kathy Polischuk with Pauline, Betty, Nick and Danny.

Nick and Mary Polischuk

Paul, Jean, Walter, Elsie and Ann Polischuk.

Back, George McMath, his sons David and John, John Slobodzian beside his father Steve Slobodzian. Seated on left corner is Mary Slobodzian and on opposite corner is Jean (Polischuk) Slobodzian.

Front, Foster child Tony and younger brother Keri, Barbara McMath holding youngest son Christopher, Katherine Slobodzian holding foster child Kitty, sister of Tony and Keri. Next is Patricia (Slobodzian) Valentonis holding son Stevie. Standing is foster child Allan.

Patricia, Stan, Elsie and Theresa Bialkowski.

TARAS POHREBNIUK

Michael Mohrynski came to Canada in 1914 and worked in Montreal, Quebec as a cook. Mary Mandziuk came to Canada with her parents in 1929 and worked as domestic help and waitress in Montreal. They married there on November 20, 1937 and moved to the Rosa district in 1942, purchasing a store from Tom Pott in 1944 and building a new store in 1945. Operated the general store business and gas pumps till retirement in 1973. Michael suffered a stroke in 1974 and after five years of hospitalization died at Vita Personal Care Home on February 14, 1979.

Lillian, born June 18, 1943 married Taras Pohrebniuk in 1965.

Taras was born May 18, 1941, at Rosa.

Taras and Lillian lived in Winnipeg until 1973. Taras started a backhoe contracting business and Lillian took over the running of her father's general store at Roseau River. Lillian quit the store business in December 1975.

They have two children:

Patricia Anne Marie, born March 24, 1976.

Richard Michael, born March 21, 1978.

Lillian is presently postmistress at Roseau River.

Mary continues to live in the remodelled premises where the store used to be.

Michael Kasian was born in 1870 in the Western Ukraine, and Anastasia, his wife, was born in 1876, also in the Western Ukraine. They came to Canada with their parents in 1899, and were married in Stuartburn Church in 1902. They farmed at Sarto for a couple of years and then moved to Overstoneville. In 1915 they moved to Rosa.

Michael died in 1948, and Anastasia in 1961.

They had six sons and nine daughters:

John, married Doris Mushaluk in 1943, and is residing in Vita with two children.

Bill, married Gloria Bugera in 1937, and lives in Winnipeg.

Walter, married Olga Salamandyk in 1949, lives in Winnipeg and has twin boys.

Peter, left home at an early age, is married and lives in B.C.

Joe, also left home young, is married and lives in B.C.

Mary, married Steve Ewanchuk in 1920, farmed in Rosa district. Steve passed away in 1977. Mary lives in Rosa. They have four children.

Lena, married Bill Wakaruk in 1925, and died in 1978. They had seven children.

Anne, married Andrew Pohrebniuk in 1933.

Andrew came to Canada in 1926, working at odd jobs across Western Canada and Western Manitoba. He purchased section 14-3-5 E1 and did mixed farming till retirement. Andrew died on February 21, 1981 and Anne lives at the Vita Personal Care Home.

Anne and Andrew had four children:

Nettie, born August 17, 1933, married Walter Senchuk September 25, 1954. They have one son, Allen, born April 15, 1965.

Olga, born August 11, 1935, married Ernie Hawrsyzko in 1960. They have two daughters, Linda, born February 23, 1967 and Ivy, born October 28, 1969. They live in Winnipeg.

Taras, born May 18, 1941, married to Lillian Mokrynski on May 15, 1965. They have two children, Patricia, born March 24, 1976 and Richard, born March 21, 1978. They live in Roseau River.

Margaret, born on November 11, 1943, married John Mandziuk in 1965. They have three daughters, Cindy, born April 9, 1965, Bonnie, born March 28, 1969, Kimmy, born September 2, 1970. They live in Winnipeg.

Kay, married Fred Pike in 1952, and they live in Hamilton, Ontario.

Pauline, married Art Nelson in 1948, and they reside in Hamilton, Ontario with three children.

Doris, married Maurice Idachuk in 1952, and they live in Hamilton, Ontario with five children.

Olga, married Mike Swidinsky in 1950, and they live in Winnipeg with one child.

Sonia, married Tony Drewniak in 1944, and they live in Winnipeg with three children.

Stella, married Walter Mikolayanko in 1951, and they live in Winnipeg with three children.

Andrew, married Jean Wichnenko in 1963, and they lived in the Rosa district until Andrew's death on November 24, 1978. Jean lives in the Rosa district.

Mary and Michael Mokrynski

Michael and Anastasia Kasian; Ann (Kasian) and Andrew Pohrebniuk.

MICHAEL PANISIAK

Michael Panisiak, with his wife and son, Bill, age nine, came to Canada in 1897. He bought NW ¼ of 2-2-5 E1 in 1900 for $10. They lost three children in the 1918 influenza epidemic, and their other children are: Bill, Dora, Anne, John, Metro, Nick and Peter.

Now, only Dora Bozyk of Gardenton and John Panisiak of Chicago are living.

Five of Michael's sons went to the United States.

At age 66, Michael wrote to his son, Nick, asking him to take over the farm, and Nick came home to do so in 1931. He had been working for General Motors in Lansing, Michigan.

Nick met and married Josephine Tworkowski of Winnipeg, in 1932. Nick was 32, and Josie, 17. They lived on the Panisiak farm, together with Nick and Maria Panisiak.

Nick died in 1942, and Maria spent her time between Nick and other members of the family.

Maria died on February 5, 1959, at the age of 91.

Nick and Josephine's children are:
Nancy, born in 1934.
Larry, died of scarlet fever.
Nestor, born in 1944
Joanne, born in 1948.
Sylvia, born in 1951.
Nick died on November 12, 1973.

Josie remarried after selling the farm and going to live with her daughter Nancy in Winnipeg. Her married name is Slobodian.

Left: Michael Panisiak born 1862 in Synkiw district, Zalishchyky, Galaicia, Austria.
Right: Michael Panisiak when he died in 1942.

Nick and Josie Panisiak; Nick Panisiak c. 1928.

Little Larry Panisiak when he died at 4½ months with his father Nick Panisiak behind the casket and some of the family.

Nestor, Sylvia and Joanne Panisiak.

354

Left: Back, Roman, Helen, Anne; front, Paul, Dymtro and Danny Panisiak.
Right: Nancy Panisiak (in dark jacket).

DYMTRO AND ANNA PANISIAK

Dymtro, son of Michael and Maria Panisiak, farmed on NE 10-2-5.

He had nine children:

Frank, of Winnipeg.

Steve, of the Yukon Territories.

Fred and Doris Blairmore, of Alberta.

Carie, of Winnipeg.

Alex, of Blairmore, Alberta.

Helen, of Winnipeg.

Roman and Doris, of Tolstoi.

Paul and Jean, of Blairmore, Alberta.

Danny, of Fort Simpson, Northwest Territories.

NORMAN POW

Norman W. B. and Mary Ann Pow purchased the N ½ 6-25E from Michael and Justyna Ottawa in August, 1969. At the time of purchase, the farm had been primarily used as a mixed beef and milking farm supported by some cereal grains, pasture and wild hay.

A year or so after they came, they broke more land, planted alfalfa and corn for silage, moved a barn onto the home site and established a milking herd of 40 holstein cows, running a total herd of 80 to 90 head at all times.

In June of 1972, John A. R. Pow was born.

In the fall of 1979, the Pows bought the SW ¼ 19-25 E1 on which they grow grain and corn. This was purchased from Graham and Alice Batten.

GEORGE PARK

George Park, a brother of Mrs. J. R. Mayne, and Mrs. W. Hurd, came to Woodmore from Flesherton, Ontario. He ran the livery barn at Ridgeville for a number of years; later he moved to a house on the J. R. Mayne farm where he travelled a stallion for service. He returned to Ontario in the 1930s.

George Park

STANLEY PAWLISHAK

Mr. and Mrs. Stanley Pawlishak were married in 1897 in Poland.

Stanley immigrated to Pennsylvania in 1903, and his wife, Julia, and two children, Anthony and Mary, came to Canada in 1905 where Stanley joined them.

They had tree daughters and two sons born here in Tolstoi.

Nellie, Mrs. Harry Kulcheski, of Tolstoi.

Verna, born in 1914, and died in 1947.

Helen, Mrs. H. Sharp, of Edmonton. Their eldest daughter, Mary Doyle, lives in Winnipeg.

Frank, of Tolstoi.

William, of St. Catharines, Ontario.

Frank farmed after his father retired, then moved to New Jersey where he married Janina Vishnowski in 1963. Frank and Janina have lived in Tolstoi since his retirement in 1973.

Stanley passed away in 1956. Julia Pawlishak died in 1967.

Stanley and Julia Pawlishak; Frank and Janine Pawlishak, nephew.

355

JOHN HUBERT PETERSON

John Hubert Peterson arrived with his family to be manager at the Canadian Imperial Bank of Commerce, Dominion City, in November 1967.

The family consists of wife, Olive Isabel, and their children: Lorne David, John Morley and Laura Anne.

Lorne married Ellen Margaret Jorden at Emo, Ontario in December, 1972. They have two children, Angela Marie and John Leonard. Lorne was employed by the Bank of Commerce for several years and then went to the Ontario Police Academy and on graduation worked for the Fort Frances Dept. He now lives in Winnipeg.

John lives in Dominion City and is employed by the Water Resources Branch.

Laura was married to Donald G. Baird in June, 1973, and has two children, Virginia Lorene and Joseph William. Joey died of cancer in Children's Hospital in Winnipeg at the age of three. Laura is now divorced and is employed as a licensed practical nurse in the Boissevain Hospital.

Isabel Peterson is office secretary for the Boundary School Division.

John is presently assistant manager in Altona, commuting from Dominion City.

Left: Virginia and Laura Baird.
Right: Ellen, Angela, Lorne, and John Peterson.

LEONARD HENRY PETO

Leonard Henry Peto (1861-1947) immigrated to Canada from Suffolk, England in 1883. He settled in the Springfield area and during 1885 he freighted for the Government forces in the Riel Rebellion at Battleford, Saskatchewan.

He married Emily Symes (1863-1944) at Winnipeg and moved to Emerson in 1886 settling on River Lots 56, 58 and 60 of that year.

They had nine children:

Walter Leonard (1887-1975) married Kate Aime.

Jessie Kathleen (1889-1954) married A. R. Knowles.

Morton Edward (1891-1974) married Ethel Margaret Empey.

Edgar James (1893-1969) married Myrtle Mines.

Mabel Wender (1896) married Peter Brown.

Hilda Ellen (1899) married L. H. Ashby.

Marjorie Alice (1902-1982) married Frank Hutton.

Frank Herbert (1905-1980) married Ruth Robertson.

Howard Broadhurst (1909) married Lillian Stevens.

Morton Edward (1891-1974) married Ethel Margaret Empey (1895-1973). He was born on River Lot 58 and lived there until 1945 when he moved to Emerson. Farming was his life and he also promoted the Sugar Beet Industry in Manitoba, growing beets in 1931-1934 and also as a "field man" in Manitoba 1940-1943.

They had four children, all born on River Lot 56:

Lorne Edward married Margaret Gibson.

Dorothy Ethel married Lloyd Morrow.

Marian Alice married Roy Ash.

Gladys Estelle married Douglas Murray.

Isabel, Lorne, Laura, John Jr. and John Peterson.

Laura holding Virginia, Donald Baird, holding Joseph, 1979.

Lorne Edward Peto married Margaret Peto and they had three children:

Sandra Margaret married Howard Casper.

Elaine Gail married Al Hengstler.

Allen Edward married Karen Nesbitt.

Allen Edward Peto married Karen Nesbitt and they have one daughter:

Sarah Margaret.

River Lots 56,58 and 60 have been farmed since 1886 by four generations of the Peto family: L. H. Peto — Morton Peto — Lorne Peto — and presently by Allen Peto.

Leonard and Emily Peto

Morton and Ethel Peto

Lorne and Margret; Allan and Karen, Sarah Margaret Peto.

HEINRICH POMRENKE

Heinrich Pomrenke immigrated to Canada from the Russian Ukraine around 1893. He worked in the Gretna area until 1897 at which time he came to settle in Friedensthal on the place which is still occupied by the third generation of the Pomrenke family. The land was bought from a man named Thompson.

Heinrich married Augusta Mantei before he immigrated to Canada. Of this union, nine children were born, three daughters and six sons. Of these nine only three remained in the Municipality of Franklin.

The original Pomrenke home has been in continuous ownership by the family sice 1897. When Heinrich retired his son August bought the farm. He and his wife Bertha nee Steg lived on it until 1946 when they moved to Emerson.

They had two children: Emil and Velma.

The farm is presently being operated by Emil. Velma lives in Akron, Ohio.

These are the children of Heinrich and Augusta:

Ida, married Gustav Neugebauer and moved to Dafoe, Saskatchewan. They had six children.

Gustav married Alvina Saiger. They lived in Franklin Municipality all their lives. Their four children are:

Herman, married to Florence Morkan.

William, married Sue Hiebert, who died in 1981. Their children are Arlene and Larry.

Eleanore married Sydney Head. They have four daughters, Nancy, Bonnie, Marilyn and Betty.

Howard married Alice Schwab. Their children are Elaine, Dwayne and Christine.

Ludwig (Louis) married Mathilda Hemminger. They reside in Assiniboia, Saskatchewan. They had three daughters and one son.

William married Emily Klempke and lived in Saskatchewan. Their children are Helen, Harvey and James.

August married Bertha Steg and lived on the family farm before retiring to Emerson. Their children are Emil, married to Margaret Felsch, and Velma. Emil and Margaret's children are Kathleen, Marlene and Mark.

Albert married Lydia Buss and lives in Franklin. Their children are Helen, Arthur, Gilbert, Donald and Gary.

Augusta (Gertie) married Claude Reid and lives in the United States.

Emil married Isobel. Their children are Velma, Florence and Ronald. They lived in Ontario.

Elsie married Mike O'Shea and lived in Saskatchewan. Their children are Tom and Bill.

Bill and Emily, Helen; Emil Pomrenke.

Emil, Kathleen, Mark and Margaret Pomrenke.

THOMAS POTT

Thomas and Maria Pott, and 10 children, left Stafordshire, England and arrived in Winnipeg in March, 1892. While Maria stayed in Winnipeg because the children had measles, Thomas went by train to Dominion City. He was met by his brother Frank, who came to homestead five years before. When the children were better, Mrs. Pott and children joined her husband in Roseau River, on their homestead 2-3-5 E1.

Thomas Pott Sr. retired to Dominion City in 1918. Thomas Jr. rented the land from his Dad until 1922 when Thomas Jr. bought it.

Maria Pott died on December 19, 1935 and Thomas Pott followed one month later on January 15, 1936.

Thomas and Maria had 13 children:

Elizabeth, married Thomas Mason and had two children. She passed away in 1900 at the age of 22.

Alice, married Charles Higham and had five children. She passed away at the age of 89.

Mary, married Jim Froom and had seven children. She passed away at the age of 96.

John, married Edith Post and had four children. He passed away at the age of 85.

Thomas stayed single and passed away at the age of 88.

Jane, married Archie Hunter and had two girls, plus four children that were Archie's from a previous marriage. Jane died at the age of 91.

Frank, maried Elizabeth Hunter and had one girl and three boys. He died at the age of 90.

George, married Mary Ellen Dawson in 1911 and had seven children. He passed away at age 72.

Sarah Ann, married Fred Post and had 11 children and passed away at age 77.

Edmond, married Catherine Lincoln, born in 1890, and had six children. He is retired. His son, Wilfred married Jessie Yatsko of Sundown August 17, 1951. They lived in the Sundown area farming and trucking until 1958, when they bought 27-2-5 E1. In 1970, they sold their farm to Dave and Martha Runke, built a home on the south end of Roseau River and went into trucking and construction. They sold their equipment to Wiebe's Trucking and are semi-retired.

Ida, Elsie; Albert, Gus, Gus Neugebauer; front, August and Louis Pomrenke.

Mrs. Karbach, Heinrich, August and Emil Pomrenke, Martha Mantai, Velma Pomrenke, Mrs. Pomrenke, Will Mantai, Minnie Fietz c. 1940.

Bertha, Velma and Marlene Pomrenke.

They have three children:

Ted, married to Joyce Broesky.

Bernice, married to Ray Hook.

Mavis.

Charles Horace, born in 1892, joined the army during World War I and died of wounds from battle at the age of 25.

Ann Maria, married Fred Batten, born in 1900, and had one girl and one boy. She passed away in 1974.

George lived with his uncle Frank Pott until 1928. He married Mary Ellen Dawson in 1911, who came from Derby, England in 1910. They had seven children.

Frank G., who purchased land through the Manitoba Farm Loans Board in 1936. He was single, and George and Mary Ellen moved in with him for the next seven years. He supplemented his farm income by working on the building of Highway 201 from Gilberts Hill to Stuartburn from 1938 through the war years. On October 30, 1943, he married Emily Smith, who was born on this farm when her grandfather Albert Hamblin owned it. They had one child:

Wendy, born in August, 1944, who married Bill Hildebrand of Steinbach. Bill and Wendy now live on the Frank Pott farm, and have three children:

Janice, born in 1962.

Tracy, born in 1963.

Trevor, born in 1966.

Janice married Stuart Loewen in 1981, and lives at Rosenort.

Edna, married Ted Hancox of Dominion City.

Laura, married Archie Pearse of Dominion City.

Horace, married Rose Palmer and lived in Emerson until his death in August, 1978.

Harold, married Lily Palmer and lilves in Woodmore.

Maria, married Eddie Pott and lived in Woodmore until her death in October, 1969.

Marget, married Bryce Badgley and lives in Woodmore.

Mary Ellen died in 1957.

George died in 1959.

Philip Henry, born 1895, and Ada Larson of Bergland, Ontario were married in 1926 and bought Thomas Sr.'s homestead 2-3-5 E1, in 1934, in partnership with Tom Jr. In 1936 Henry purchased the NW¼ 32-2-5 E1, and in 1947 he bought Tom Jr.'s share of the homestead. Henry and Ada farmed until retirement in 1960.

They had four children:

Charles, born in 1926, married Jean Roth and lives in British Columbia.

Janet, born in 1928, married Nels Malmas and lives in Rosser.

Joyce, born in 1935, married Marvin Schurko and lives in Roseau River.

Allan, born in 1937, married Isabel Budinsky and they have four children:

Brenda, born August, 1959, is married to Corney Dyck and have two boys, Calvin, born December 1960, Randall, born in 1962, and Sandra, born January, 1964.

FRANK POTT

Frank and Ann Pott came to Canada from Stafordshire, England in 1887 and settled on NE¼ 34-2-5E. They had no children but helped his brother Thomas Pott raise some of his children when they came to Canada. Their home was built around 1898 and the main building is still standing today. Ann was midwife and delivered many babies. Frank died in April, 1910. In 1928 Ann sold her farm and went to live with her nephew Thomas Pott Jr. until her death in 1933.

JOHN POTT

John Pott, a brother of Frank and Thomas, and his wife Emily, left Abbots Bormly, England, in 1907, to farm section 24-2-5 E1 in Franklin Municipality.

Their four sons and three daughters were: Jack, Tom, Frank and Bernie; Emily, Mrs. F. Hamblin, Elizabeth, Mrs. C. Casson; Ellen, Mrs. J. Johnson.

Their children came with them to Franklin. John soon purchased the NW¼ 13-2-4 E1 from Thomas Stewart.

John died in 1935. Bernie took over the farm, and Emily remained with him until 1937 when he married Mary Kohut. She made several moves before moving to a house in her son Tom's yard where she lived until her death.

Bernie had five children:

John, born in 1939, joined the R.C.M.P. in 1957. He married Marie Pivoras in 1960. He has a son Douglas Stuart in the force, and a daughter Leanne.

Lloyd, born in July, 1940, a teacher who drowned accidentally May 21, 1964 at Round Lake, Ontario.

Robert, born in April, 1942, married Carol Doan in 1972. They have one daughter and a son. A daughter died in infancy in 1975.

Dennis, born in July, 1943, married Lillian Horbath in 1969. They have three girls.

Doris, born in 1944, is a teacher, married to Larry Schnell in 1967, and lives in Saskatchewan. They have three sons.

Jack married Minnie Greer in 1916. They lived on the NW¼ 34-2-5 E1. They had two children, Ruby and Vernon. In 1939 Jack sold his farm and moved to Winnipeg.

Frank married Lizzie Drysdale in 1927, and rented land from George Post. They had three sons, Cliff, Bill and Albert. Frank sold his farm in 1944 and moved to Winnipeg, later to Lundar, where his sons live.

Thomas joined the army in 1916. While overseas he married Doris Treadwell of Tamworth, England. They came to Canada in 1919, and purchased the SW ¼ 13-2-4 E1 from John Palmer. They had eleven children, three dying in infancy. They were, Eddie, Raymond, Ernie, Gordon, Lorne, Margaret and Mathilda.

In 1955 W. Treadwell, Doris' father came from England to spend his last years with his daughter. In the late forties, Tom purchased the NE ¼ 11-2-4 E1 and in 1966 sold his land to Lorne, keeping two acres on the SW corner, where he and Doris live.

Eddie married Maria Pott in 1945, and farmed the NW ¼ 2-2-4 E1. They had two sons, Brian and Wayne, who are both married and living in Winnipeg. Maria died in 1969. Eddie moved to Winnipeg, selling his farm to C. Graydon. In 1978 he married Ann Rattai of Winnipeg.

Margaret married Anthony Samborski and farmed in the Roseau River area for 30 years. In 1976 they moved to Stuartburn to make their home. They have three daughters, Lorraine, Barbara, and Donna and one son Toni.

Matilda married Norman Snead and they reside in Woodmore. They have one son and he is married and lives in Steinbach.

Mavis married Walter Maslow of Lac du Bonnet. They lived on a farm until 1980, when they moved to town. They had two sons, Blaine (deceased June 21, 1971, at the age of 16 years) and Darwin.

Ernie married Eileen Burkowski of Roseau River. They have three children, Debbie, Darlene and Gary and they live in Lac du Bonnet.

Lorne, born July 27, 1940, married Margaret Cowan from Biggar, Saskatchewan, on May 7, 1966. He bought Thomas' farm, and farmed until about 1968. They had three children, Lorna May, born July 7, 1967; James Frederick, born June 29, 1969; Tammy Lee, born July 7, 1970. In 1974 Lorne moved his family back into Franklin Municipality, and works for the Manitoba Highways Department at Woodmore.

Raymond Bernard married Ina Mae Ramsey, daughter of Leslie and Laura Ramsey, on November 10, 1956. They lived in Winnipeg until 1960, when they bought the General Store at Woodmore from Clifford Ward. They have two children, Donald Allan and Carol Ann. In 1977 Raymond and Ina sold the store and built a house

at Green Ridge. Raymond is employed at Riach's Lumber in Ridgeville and drives a school bus. Ina is relief postmaster.

Gordon married Velma Roth April 2, 1960. They purchased Isabelle Lendrum's farm at Ridgeville in 1963, NW ¼ 11-1-4 E1, where they live. They have four children, Evelyn, married to Ken Kouk in 1982, is living in Winnipeg; Keith, died in infancy in 1962; Murray is in grade 11 at Roseau Valley Collegiate; Karen is 13 years old.

Thomas and Maria Pott Sr. taken in their favorite place, the flower garden, c. 1900. Both loved to work in the garden and produced fabulous results.

Children of Thomas and Maria Pott, 1946, back, Tom; second row, John, George; third row, Mary; fourth row, Jane, Sarah, Anne; front; Edmund, Frank and Henry. Missing is Alice.

Thomas Sr. and Maria Pott's first car taken on the Archie Hunter Farm, c. 1917, a Model T ford. Shown with Thomas Sr. and Moria Pott are Alice and Janet Hunter.

360

Tom, Ada and Charles Pott making ice cream. House in background was built in 1895 by Mr. Thomas Pott Sr. and lived in until 1951.

Front, George and Mary Ellen Pott with Ronald Pearse, Ken Pott, Ellen Abrams (Hancox). Standing behind is Horace Pott holding niece Wendy Hildebrand (Pott), Archie Pearse, Rose Pott (Palmer), Ted Hancox, Laura Pearse (Pott), Emily Pott (Smith), Lily Pott (Palmer), Frank Pott, Harold Pott, Marget Badgley (Pott), Moria Pott, Edna Hancox (Pott) holding Dorothy Boutet (Hancox) and Eddie Pott, 1946.

Edmond and Catherine (Lincoln) Pott, 50th Wedding Anniversary, 1970. Donald, Violet, Wilfred, Henry (Harry), Dorothy and Ellison. They farmed NE 27-2-5 E1 1920-1950 and now live in Peterborough, Ontario.

Left: Bernard and Mary (Kohut) Pott.
Right: Back, Robert, Bernard Pott; middle, Mary (Kohut) Pott, Dennis, Lloyd; front, Doris, John.

Left: Frank and Emma (Smith) Pott, 1979.
Right: Norman, Tillie, Susie and Kerry Snead.

Stuart Loewen, Bill, Tracy, Wendy (Pott); sitting, Janice Loewen, Trevor Hildebrand, 1981.

The Henry Pott family in 1979 in their beautiful treed yard along the banks of the Roseau River. Shown are Joyce (Pott) Schurko, Charles Pott, Ada (Larson) Pott, Henry Pott, Allan Pott and Janet Malmas.

Walter, Mavis, Blain and Darwin Maslow.

Margaret, Donna, and Anthony Samborski.

Wayne, Brian, Maria and Eddie Pott.

Sandra, Brenda, Joyce (Pott), Calvin, Marvin and Randall Shurko, 1979.

John and Emily Pott

Gordon and Velma Pott, Evelyn and Ken Kouk, Karen and Murray Pott.

Tom and Doris Pott, Tillie, Margaret, Mavis; Ray, Gordy and Lorne.

362

Mavis, Raymond, Doris and Thomas Pott, Ed, Mathilda, Ernest; front, Gordon and Lorne.

Ernie and Eileen; front, Darlene and Gary.

Donald, Ina, Raymond and Carol Pott.

Margaret, Tammy, Lorna, Jim and Lorne Pott.

JOHN ROYAL POST

John Royal Post came to Manitoba in 1882. He was born in Foxboro, Hastings County, Ontario, April 13, 1846 to Peter and Amelia Post. Two of his brothers, Fred and Archie, and a sister Delilah Addison, also came to Green Ridge.

John was a descendent of United Empire Loyalists and married Almira Ann McGunnion in 1871. Almira's ancestor, Francois DePew, had come to New York State in 1661. Almira was born in Madoc, Ontario in 1845 to Anna and Peter McGunnion. She and John had six children: Calista, Emma, twins, Ethel and Edith, twins, Richard and Ridley.

Edith died an infant.

Almira, her five children, and sister Permelia McGunnion arrived in Franklin in 1884. In 1885 John took up the SE¼ and half of the NE¼ 4-3-4 E1.

Calista became a teacher, married R. E. Gunn in 1894. She had three children, and moved to Vancouver in 1920.

Emma married J. M. Smith in 1904.

Richard and Ridley farmed, with Richard buying the farm on Ridley's death of pneumonia in 1901.

John Post died in 1933, and Almira in 1937.

Theo Gunn — eldest son of R. E. and Calista (Post) Gunn, left Winnipeg August, 1914 with the 34th Fort Garry Horse Regiment and was transferred to the Strathcona Horse Regiment the following spring. Leaving their horses in England, the regiment was sent to France and were in the trenches nine months before their horses were

Lance Sergt, Theo Gunn.

363

Front, J. Fred Post, Arch Post, John R. Post, (brothers); second row, Mrs. J. F. Post, Mrs. J. R. Post, Permelia McGunnion (sisters); third row, Abram McGunnion, Mrs. Ed McGunnion and Ed McGunnion.

sent over. Theo was sent to England in January, 1918 to receive a coomission in the Imperial Cavalry. Before receiving his commission an urgent call came for all soldiers to return to France. He returned to rejoin his regiment and he was instantly killed in battle near Amiens on March 30, 1918.

CORNELIUS PENNER

Corny and Anna Penner bought a farm at Carlowrie from Sam Devitt in 1971. They have five children:

Corny and Anna Penner family.

Edna, married Peter Peters in 1964, and they have four sons, Karl, Keith, Harvey and Quentin.

Harold, married Marianne Tiessen in 1971, and farms with his parents. Their children are, Adelee Joan, born 1973, Cynthia Ann, born 1976, and Doyle Nathaniel, born 1981.

Paul, works in Ontario.

Linda, also works in Ontario.

Kenneth, is at home.

R GEORGE ROBERTSON

Mr. and Mrs. Robertson and family came from Grunthal to Dominion City in August, 1956. In 1959 the family moved to Piney. While in Dominion City Mr. Robertson served as town policeman.

Back, James, Mary (Robertson) Sawatsky; front, Christina holding Wayne Sawatsky, Mrs. and Mr. Robertson.

ROY RETTALER

Roy Rudolph Rettaler lived in the Woodmore area for seven years before marrying Edna Emma Herman of Sewell, Manitoba on October 17, 1952.

September 22, 1953 Lavern Irene was born. She married Dan Manson. They have three girls, Tammie, Lisa and Theresa, and live in St. Norbert.

On August 22, Richard Roy was born. He farms with his mother.

Barbara Anne was born November 4, 1967, and also farms with her mother.

Roy Rudolph passed away on April 5, 1979.

Edna, with Rick and Barbara, have carried on farming.

Edna (Herman), Laverne, Rick, Barbara, Roy Rattaler, 1968.

Barbara Rattaler, and horse Leather, 1980.

JACK RETTALER

Jack Rettaler married Lynda Perchaliuk May 21, 1949. They lived four years in Dominion City, then moved to the Rettaler homestead, the SW ¼ 14-2-4 E1 in 1954.

Shirley (1950) married Joey Dreger. Their children are, Shelley and Stacey. They are living in Kleefeld.

Rosemary (1952) married Doug Empson. Their children are Grant and Teresa. They are living in Grunthal.

Patsy (1953) married Clyde Gregoire in 1970. They have one son, Kelly, born in 1971. They moved back to the Woodmore area in 1978 to set up a welding and mechanical shop known as Clyde's Welding and Mechanical.

Larry (1954) married Debbie Granger. They have one son, Jackie, and are living in Ridgeville.

There is a graveyard site on the southeast part of the Rettaler homestead where a mother and her three children are buried, who died from typhoid fever in the early 1900's.

Larry, Jackie, Debbie (Granger) Rettaler.

Laverne (Rattaler) Manson holding Lisa, Theresa, Dan Manson, holding Tammy.

Left: standing, Larry, Jack Sr.; sitting, Jack Jr., great-grandfather Jacob Rettaler.
Right: back, Linda (Perchaliuk) Rettaler, Shirley (Rettaler) Dreiger; front, Marie Perchaliuk, Shelley Dreiger.

Patsy (Rettaler) Kelly, Clyde Gregoire.

365

Left: Joey, Shirley (Rettaler); Shelly and Stacey Dreiger.
Right: Douglas, Rose Mary (Rettaler); Grant and Teressa Empson.

JOHN RETTALER

John and Rose Rettaler moved from Rosenfeld to Dominion City in July, 1941. In May, 1949, they moved to the NE ¼ 2-2-4 E1.

They had four children, and two more were born on the farm.

They sold in the fall of 1965 to Gordon Johnson, and bought 26 acres on NW ¼ 22-2-3 E1. They lived here for four years. In the fall of 1969 they moved to Winnipeg.

Kathy, Donald, Daniel, Rose and John Rettaler, Lorraine, Dorothy and Adell.

Patsy, Rosemary, Shirley, Linda (Perchaliuk) Rettaler, Jac A. Rettaler, Larry.

OTTO RODEWALD

Otto Rodewald was born in Volenia, Russia April 1, 1896. He was married in June, 1921 to Rosalie Ailkie who was also born in Volenia, Russia May 10, 1898. They immigrated to Canada in April, 1925 and worked on the farm for Louis Steg and Fred Remus.

In 1935 they purchased the former Matchett farm three miles east of Emerson. Here they resided till 1944 when they purchased the former Louis Lembke farm five miles north of Emerson. In 1952 they retired to Emerson.

Rosalie passed away July 20, 1955 and Otto passed away September 26, 1965.

Otto and Rosalie raised five children:

Robert was born in Germany January 6, 1923. He farmed with his father and in 1950 he purchased the former William McKray farm. On September 9, 1950 he married Verna Babrowski. They had two children:

Karen, born January 28, 1952, married Harry Winnemueller on August 28, 1972. They have two children, Jennifer, born January 30, 1974, and Michael, born December 5, 1976. They live in Winnipeg.

James, born September 2, 1953, married on July 24, 1916 and they have one daughter, Charlene, born June 5, 1980.

On November 16, 1955 Robert was killed in a tragic tractor accident.

Herbert was born on November 7, 1924 in Germany. He served in the armed forces during World War II, from 1942 to 1945.

In 1946 he purchased land in Franklin, and on September 29, 1951 he married Irene Ratchinsky and they lived on the farm formerly owned by Herb's father. In 1979 Herb and Irene moved to Emerson. Herb is still actively farming.

They raised five children:

Dennis was born April 15, 1952. He married Debbie Kyle on October 16, 1976. Dennis farms and lives on the former William Kyle farm. They have one daughter, Janette, born August 27, 1981.

Wendy was born March 8, 1954. She married Dwight Gibson September 1, 1973 and they live in Winnipeg. They have two daughters, Kyla, born March 18, 1976; Jill, born February 21, 1978.

Tom was born January 16, 1957. He is employed with Canada Customs in Calgary. He married Debbie Knutt April 9, 1977 and they have two children, Maurie and Michael.

Jeffrey was born January 11, 1959. He farms with Herb. He married Shelly Wightman September 22, 1979 and they have one son, Chad, born February 6, 1981.

Mark was born June 24, 1961. He is employed with the Bank of Commerce.

Louis was born July 10, 1926. He married Linda Striech September 26, 1952. Louis farms five miles north of Emerson, land formerly owned by Otto Rodewald.

They raised four children:

Terry was born on March 11, 1955. She married Sheldon Friesen on September 6, 1975 and now have two children. Curtis was born on February 7, 1977 and on October 19, 1979 they had a daughter, Erin. In 1975 Sheldon and Terry bought a river lot from Dennis Hrynyk and in 1977 they bought Clayton Gray's farm. At present Sheldon is the Credit Union manager in Emerson and farms.

Grant was born on April 12, 1957. On August 25, 1979 he married Valdine Christiansen. In 1977 they bought Lloyd Gray's farm. Valdine works with Customs in Emerson and Grant farms.

Pat was born on January 17, 1959. She has a son, Brent who was born on February 4, 1977. In 1981 Pat graduated from the University of Manitoba with a Bachelor of Nursing. Presently she is employed in Morris as a public health nurse, covering the R. M. of Franklin.

Bruce was born on January 13, 1965. He is attending high school in Dominion City.

Walter was born February 12, 1928. He received his doctor's degree in Science at the University of Manitoba after which he taught school in Brandon for 18 years. He then became owner and operator of three different Rodeway Inns at Brandon, Saskatoon and Dauphin. He is now a businessman still living in Brandon. Walter married Betty Schwartz August 9, 1956.

They have two daughters:

Lynda, born in 1957, a graduate pharmacist in Winnipeg.

Judy, born in 1959, lab technician in Brandon.

Hildegard, was born November 14, 1933. She married Frank Horner August 25, 1959 and lives in Winnipeg.

They have three children:

Lynn, born March 9, 1960, a chartered accountant.

William, born January 30, 1962, a student at the University of Manitoba.

Tracy, born August 23, 1965, a high school student.

Lynn, William and Tracy Horner.

Judy and Lynda Rodewald

Otto and Rosalie (Ailkie) Rodewald).

Back, Grant, Linda, Louis and Bruce Rodewald and Sheldon Friesen; middle, Valdine and Pat Rodewald and Terry Friesen; front, Brent Rodewald, Erin and Curtis Friesen.

367

Karen, Robert, Verna and Jim Rodewald

Left: Verna Rodewald, Karen (Rodewald), Jennifer and Michael Winnemueller.
Right: Jim and Charlene Rodewald.

Herb, Hildegard (Rodewald) Horner, Walter and Louis Rodewald.

Irene and Herb Rodewald, Hildegard and Frank Horner, Betty and Walter Rodewald, Linda and Louis Rodewald.

Wendy, Jeff, Dennis, Tom and Mark, sitting Irene and Herb Rodewald.

Dennis and Debbie Rodewald, Dwight and Wendy Gibson, Mark, Shelley and Jeff Rodewald; sitting, Tom and Debbie Rodewald.

Kyla and Jill Gibson; Chad Rodewald.

Janette Rodewald; Maurie and Michael Rodewald.

JOHN RIACH

John and Johanna Riach and their four oldest children, one son and three daughters, arrived in Franklin in 1879 from Bruce County, Ontario. Two more sons, John Jr. and William Ernest, were born in Manitoba. They homesteaded the SE ¼ 32-1-4 E1 and a few years later purchased the SW ¼ of the same section.

In 1906 they sold their west quarter to Andrew Parker, and the east quarter to their son Ernie, and moved to Leslieville, Alberta. They went from here to the Okanagan Valley in British Columbia where Mrs. Riach died in 1919 and Mr. Riach in 1929.

William Ernest Riach farmed the original homestead for several years. In 1915 he became manager of the Monarch Lumber Company yard in Ridgeville. That same year he married Alma Stewart and they raised a family of seven, four boys and three girls.

In 1931 he purchased the lumber yard from the Monarch Lumber Company. In 1938 he took the North Star Oil Agency. He sold the business to three of his sons in 1947 and purchased a home in Winnipeg, where he retired.

He passed away in 1962 and Alma moved back to Ridgeville. She returns to her home each summer and spends the winters in Winnipeg with her daughter, Myrtle.

Myrtle became a school teacher. In 1945 she married A. E. Lee of Gunton, where they farmed until he passed away in 1965. They had two girls, Linda and Lesley. She retired from teaching in 1977 and lives in Winnipeg.

Eleanor tried her hand at several occupations in different parts of Canada, and now lives in Calgary. She is semi-retired, and spends the summers in Calgary and the winters in Winnipeg helping care for her mother.

Mildred lives in Saskatoon with her husband William McCraig. They raised a family of five, three sons and two daughters.

Clarence became a lawyer. He married Thelma Keast of Roblin in 1956. They have three children Ronald, Signe and Russell. Clarence works for the Department of Indian Affairs and lives in Vancouver.

The other three sons, Lorne, Stewart and Alvin purchased the business in 1947, changing the name from W. E. Riach Lumber and Hardware to Riach Bros.

Lorne married Lillie Lindsay in 1945 and raised a family of five, Brian, Duaine, Gayle, Karen and Marilyn. Lillie had a stroke in 1970 and died in 1974.

Stewart married Lorraine Goetz in 1952. They had one daughter, Patricia. Stewart died in 1978.

Alvin married Avis Stowe in 1947. They had a daughter, Carolyn and a son Gregory. Alvin left the firm in 1967 and obtained a job operating a municipal backhoe. In 1968 he moved to Winnipeg and went into the trucking business.

In 1968 Riach Bros. was dissolved. Stewart bought the farming portion of the business, which he operated until 1978. Duaine, Lorne's second son, bought the lumber hardware and fuel part of the business.

Lorne became secretary-treasurer of the Boundary School Division until 1979, when he retired.

Duaine married Lynne Ramsey in 1968. They have a daughter Laura and a son Kyle.

Portrait taken by Abbott in Emerson, 1893. Standing, John Jr., Sadie, Sam, Ernie; seated, Etta, John G. and Johanna Riach, Elizabeth.

Back, Alvin; middle, Lorne, Mildred, Johanna and John Riach, Stewart, Myrtle; front, Eleanor and Clarence, 1955.

W. E. and Alma (Stewart) Riach, 1961.

Lorne, Stewart, Clarence, Alvin; front, Myrtle, Eleanor, Mildred Riach, 1970.

Back, Brian, Duaine; front, Karen, Lorne, Marilyn, Lillie, Gayle Riach, 1961.

Thelma, Russell, Ronald, Signe, Clarence Riach, 1978.

Craig and Marilyn and Claude Lemay.

Carolyn, Avis and Alvin Riach, Gregory, 1972.

Stewart, Patricia and Lorraine Riach, 1968.

Rod and Gayle, Patrick, Deryk, Heather Campbell.

Art and Karen, Brett, Kara Bremaud.

Duaine and Lynne, Laura, Kyle Riach.

Brian, Sharon Riach, Sherri, Kristin; front, Kent.

Linda, Ted and Myrtle, Lee, Lesley, 1963.

Debra, Valerie, Rick, Kim, Ian; sitting, Mildred and Bill McCaig.

JOSEPH H. RAW

Joseph H. Raw, blacksmith, came to Canada in 1902. He was born in Wisconsin, in 1878, and died 1957. He was a veteran of the First World War. Mrs. Raw was born in Orangeville, Ontario, in 1884, and died in 1963.

Garth T. Raw, one of the twin sons of Mr. and Mrs. Joseph Raw of Dominion City, was born in Dominion City in 1922. He was assistant agent at United Grain Growers Elevator in Dominion City between 1944 and 1960. Later, parts manager at Great West Motors for some 12 years.

Mrs. Raw, Garth, Joseph H. Raw, 1926; Garth, 1942.

THOMAS RAW

Thomas Raw was born in England to James and Bessie Raw in 1844. C.1850 they came to Wisconsin, United States. Tom was a teacher and a lay minister in the Methodist Church. He married Mary Jane Odgers, born in Shullsburg, LaFayette County, Winsconsin, August, 1848.

They had 10 children. They were: Joseph, John, James, George, Mathew, Priscilla Dunba, Mary Janetta Hendershott, Sarah, Estelle Isobella Heck and Alethia Murchieson.

The children were all born in the United States.

Tom and Mary Jane and most of the family came to Dominion City in 1903 and settled on a farm west of town known as the Houston farm. In 1911 James died after a long illness. Ten days later Tom took sick and died in a few hours.

In 1921 Matt and his mother built a house in Dominion City, where Mary Jane lived until her death in 1933.

Joseph had married and was living in town, as well as Estelle Heck and Alethia Murchieson, with their families. Two daughters and George were living in the United States.

In 1982 the Raw family and their spouses have died with the exception of Matt's wife, Mary, who moved to Winnipeg in 1981. Several grandchildren still live in the municipality with their families. They are Mrs. S. Ginn; Mrs. G. Sullivan; Mrs. R. Carver (daughters of John and Belle (Raw) Heck), Albert Raw, son of George Raw, Garth Raw, son of Joe Raw, and Mrs. W. Cleem, daughter of Matt Raw.

Joe Raw had a blacksmith shop in Dominion City for many years. He was a World War I veteran. Joe died in 1957 and his wife Ruth in 1962. George Raw died in 1964, and Belle Heck in 1930; Alethia Murchieson in 1927. Matt Raw died in 1973. Matt's father was a teacher, but Matt had little schooling. He was born sickly, and his parents were told by doctors that he would not grow up. He was 83 when he died, the last of the Raw family. He worked for the Highways Department until 1963, and retired after his 73rd birthday. He married Mary Weedmark and had eight children. Jeannetta Smith lives in Flin Flon, Lenore Lawrence, Jim and Glenda Richards live in Winnipeg, Wilma Cleem in Green Ridge and Sharon Evershed in Brampton. Yvonne Nasselquist lives in Creighton, Saskatchewan. There are 30 grandchildren and eight great-grandchildren.

Mary and Matt Raw with (granddaughter) Patricia and Don Fotti.

Matt Raw family: standing, Wilma (Raw) Cleem, Jim, Lenore, Jeannetta, Mary (Weedmark) Raw, Lawrence; sitting, Yvonne, Glenda, Sharon.

Joe Raw, May Heck; front, Alethia (Raw) Murchieson, Mary Jane Raw, 1918. Inset: Thomas Raw.

MICHAEL RATCHINSKY

Michael Ratchinsky (August 15, 1864) married Minnie Hartwig (July 2, 1865) in Poland in 1886. They immigrated to Canada in 1893 and settled in the Plum Coulee area for a short time. After a few years, they moved to the Ridgeville area and began farming.

Michael and Minnie had 10 children: Annie (Stark), Tillie (Stunko), Julius, Jessie (Behn), Lena (Gable), Jean (Strenke), Fred, Olga (Eritz), Herman and Henry.

Michael died January 1, 1931, and Minnie died April 24, 1927.

Henry Ratchinsky (July 22, 1906) began farming in the Ridgeville area in 1930. In 1938 he married Hilda Casper (December 11, 1917). They moved to Dominion City in 1956. Prior to his retirement in 1971 he was employed by the Province of Manitoba.

They have three children:

Clarence (October 10, 1938) married Evelyn Dreger. They live in Winnipeg. Clarence is employed by the Province of Manitoba and Evelyn by the Manitoba Public Insurance Corporation.

Alice Donna (April 5, 1940) married William Ostrowsky. They own a farm in the Roseau River area. Alice has taught school for Boundary School Division for several years. They have one daughter, Cindy Lou, who is married to Jarvis Hrynenko, and lives in Winnipeg.

Diane Jeannette (January 7, 1947) married Hugh Lamant and lives in Dominion City. They have one daughter, Shauneen Lugh.

Julius Ratchinsky, born in 1894 in the Plum Coulee area, was married to Martha Hemminger,

from Morden in 1918. They farmed in the Emerson, Dominion City and Ridgeville areas. In 1947 they retired to Dominion City and in 1958 moved to Winnipeg.

Julius passed away September 9, 1964, and Martha November 6, 1981.

They had three daughters:

Adeline, Mrs. Ralph Wendeborn, born in 1920, died in a car accident near Ottawa in 1975.

Lillian, Mrs. Gerhard Schultz, lives in Emerson.

June, Mrs. Herb Rodewald, lives in Emerson.

Henry and Hilda Ratchinsky; Clarence and Evelyn Ratchinsky.

Julius and Martha Ratchinsky

Lillian, Adeline and Irene (Ratchinsky).

REINHOLD REMUS

Reinhold Remus was two years old when he came to Canada, from Europe, in 1891 with his parents, William F. and Maria (Deutschlander) Remus.

Cindy (Ostrowsky) and Jarvis Hrynenko, Hilda (Casper) and Henry Ratchinsky, Shaun Lamont, Clarence and Evelyn (Dreger) Ratchinsky. Diane (Ratchinsky) and Hugh Lamont, Alice (Ratchinsky) and William Ostrowsky.

Reinhold married Mary Lembke and they farmed in North Dakota before purchasing their farm on the east side of the Red River in 1917. The river lots are located two and a half miles north of Emerson. Reinhold operated a blacksmith shop, known as the Manchester Repair Shop, plus cleaned seed for neighboring farmers.

They had six children:

George and Helma (Anderson) Remus of Piney.

Alma (Remus) and Ewald Bohn of Atikokan, Ontario.

Mabel (Remus) and Bill Hadden of Winnipeg.

Art and Ann (Schultz) Remus of Emerson.

Beatrice (Remus) and Arnold Schewe of Emerson.

Edna (Remus) and George Streick of Portage la Prairie.

Arthur and Ann Remus purchased their farm from the Remus family in 1950.

They had two sons: Rodnay and Barry.

Arthur currently owns the farm which is operated by his son Barry and wife Terry (Scott) of Dominion City.

Barry and Terry Remus bought the Arnold Schewe farm located one mile east of Dominion City in 1979.

Terry is the daughter of Osborne and Theresa Scott from Dominion City.

Barry and Terry have two daughters:
Colleen Marie, born March 9, 1979.
Michelle Leah, born April 27, 1981.

Arthur, Ann, Barry and Rodney Remus.

Colleen and Michelle Remus

Barry and Terry Remus

LEONARD GEORGE RAMSEY

Leonard George Ramsey came from Pointe Levis, Quebec, in 1874, and worked on the construction of the Soo-line railway from Winnipeg to the United States boundary. His family arrived on the first passenger train on the line. There were 10, his oldest son, George, remained in Quebec. They were: his wife, Matilda Ramsey, her sister Bessie Skillen, sons James, Robert, John, and daughters Charlotte, Minnie, Eleanor, Annie and Grace. They homesteaded on the SE ¼ 24-2-3 E1.

Charlotte married Edgar Froom in 1880, and farmed. The Ramsey family moved to Stuartburn, where they farmed, operated the post office and sold farm machinery.

James married Mary McKellop and operated a Massey Harris agency.

Minnie married Joe Robinson and moved to British Columbia; Eleanor married Archie Reid, a carpenter, and lived on the SW ¼ 21-2-4 E1.

John married Nina Millar of Stuartburn.

Annie married Thos Collier and farmed and kept the post office at Overstone, before moving to Graysville.

Grace married Bill Millar, son of Stuart Millar of Stuartburn, and farmed. They had one son, soon after which Bill died of typhoid fever. Grace married James Whitehead, and moved to England.

Robert married Margaret Edith Froom in 1889 and farmed the NE ¼ 17-2-4 E1 until 1918. They had eight children:

Leslie.

Mildred (Murphy), deceased.

Gladys (Baltzell, Jennings), living in Arkansas.

Benjamin, married Rose Hamblin, both deceased.

Dorothy (Baltzell), deceased.

Harold, married Edith Lowe, deceased. Harold lives in Missesauga.

Dudley, married Bud Coutts and lives in Carberry.

Muriel (Copeland) lives in Emerson.

Margaret (Froom) Ramsey died in 1949 and Robert in 1956.

Leslie married Laura Jane Lockhead in 1915, and farmed, and had a transfer business.

They had six children:

Lorne (deceased).

Lloyd.

Jean (Solnes).

Doreen (Ostberg).

Ina Mae (Pott).

Jack married Carole Young, who died in 1962. Jack then married Mildred Cretney, and lives in Edmonton.

Laura died in 1951 and Leslie in 1973.

Lorne married Ruth Bultz in 1939. He worked with his father in the transfer business until joining the R.C.A.F. in 1943. After the war he worked for George Bieber until 1948 when he started the North Star Oil business in Dominion City, which later became Shell Oil. He operated this business until turning it over to his son Ronald in 1981.

Lorne and Ruth raised a family of five:

Donald married Donna Markowsky and lives in Edmonton.

Calvin married Mary Jane Goosen and lives in Steinbach.

Valorie married Ed Thom and lives in Russell.

Ronald married Linda Fredrickson and lives in Dominion City.

Cathy nurses in Saskatoon.

Ronald and Linda and sons, Tyson and Tyler, live in Dominion City and operate the Shell Oil business.

Lloyd married Clara McLennan in 1936. He worked with his father in the transfer business until joining the R.C.A.F. in 1942. Since his discharge from the service, he has farmed.

Their four children are:

Myrna, married Ernie Mol and they live in Winnipeg.

Lynn, married Duaine Riach and they live in Ridgeville.

Raymond, married Danneale McClelland. They have a daughter, Stacey, and one son, Lloyd. Raymond took over the family farm.

Debby, married Jim Burch and they live in Winnipeg.

In April, 1918, Benjamin joined the Royal North West Mounted Police and returned to the farm in 1919. In 1922 he married Lelah Rose Hamblin, who was born October, 1896, daughter of Albert Thomas Hamblin of Woodmore.

They had three children:

Eugenie Bernice, born in March, 1923.

Elizabeth Margaret Rose, born in May, 1924.

Phyllis May, born in February, 1926.

In 1937 Ben started work with the Drainage Maintenance Board for Franklin, and in 1946 transferred to the Manitoba Highways Branch where he worked until his retirement in 1965.

He died in May, 1971, and Rose in April, 1961.

Elizabeth married Irving Wildred Scott in March, 1948. Irving was born in Baldur in 1924, son of Wilf and Mary Scott. He served in the second world war, and came to Dominion City in 1946 to buy the Dominion City Transfer Business with his uncle James Aitken.

They had three children:

Rhonda Leigh, born in December, 1948.

Richard James Irving, born in June, 1953.

Perry Dean, born in July, 1958.

In 1951 Irving sold the transfer and worked with the Province of Manitoba Highways Branch, moving to Steinbach in 1971.

While in Winnipeg Rose met and became friends with Mr. and Mrs. Richard Scambler. Around 1930, having lost all of their family, they came to live with Ben and Rose Ramsey in Franklin.

Robert, Dudley, Harold, Ben, Leslie, Margaret; front, Muriel, Dorothy, Gladys, Mildred Ramsey.

Leslie and Robert Ramsey (his 90th birthday).

Irving and Betty Scott; Irving, 1942.

Left: Ben and Bernice Ramsey.
Right: Richard and Donna Mae; Tara and Christopher Lamont.

Betty, Phyllis and Bernice Ramsey.

Bernice and Jack Baltzell; Judy, Richard, Geoffrey and (in front) Donald Bennett.

Rhonda and Wayne Guidelin; Perry Scott.

Benjamin Ramsey; Mr. and Mrs. Richard Scrambler.

Robert and Edith Ramsey

376

Leslie Robert and Laura Jane Ramsey, c. 1915.

Valorie and Ed Thom; Pat, Carla and Krista.

Back, Kelly, Donald Ramsey; front, Lisa, Mark, Donna (Markowesky) Ramsey, 1977.

Donald, Lorne and Ruth, Calvin; front, Kathy, Ronald and Valorie Ramsey.

Back, Angela Mol, Clara and Lloyd Ramsey holding Kelsey and Keith Burch, Robert Mol; front, Laura Riach, Lloyd Jr. and Stacey Ramsey and Kyle Riach.

Ronald and Linda; Tyson and Tyler Ramsey.

Lloyd Ramsey family; Myrna, Lynette, Raymond and Debbie.

Mary Jane and Calvin Ramsey, Jennifer; front, Jamie and Timothy.

Kathy Ramsey

ALBERT EDWARD RUNKE

Albert Edward Runke was born in 1912 in Rib Lake, Wisconsin, U.S.A. He came to Franklin with his father in 1925.

Albert was 13 years old when he left home and stayed with Daniel Kirkpatrick, and attended Green Ridge school until he was 14 years of age. He worked on the farm for Morten Peto for eight years.

He and Lena Nedohin of Emerson were married on November 20, 1937. In 1940 he bought 80 acres; SE ¼ 29-1-5 E1.

By 1944 they had three sons: Alvin Edolbert, John Daniel and David Eward.

They farmed until 1974, then sold their land to Toni Lazaruk, and moved to four and a half acres on the SW ¼ 1-2-5 E1.

In 1978 Albert passed away.

Alvin Adolbert has his own electrical contracting business. In 1963 he married Marie Maz and they have three children: Cheryl, Kevin and Gregory.

They live in Winnipeg.

John Daniel is a teacher. He married Sandy ? and they have four children: Lisa, Danielle, Petrina and Justin.

They live in Ladysmith, B.C.

David Edward and Martha Berg were married on August 26, 1967. After living for one year in Winnipeg and spending one year with Dave's parents, in 1970 they purchased the NE ¼ 27-2-5 E1 and the SW ¼ 27-2-5 E1 from Wilfred Pott. In 1971 they purchased the farm across the road (160 acres) NW ¼ 26-2-5 E1, the former Guenther place. In 1981 they bought 400 acres from H. Loewen.

Dave and Martha have six children:
Darrel, 1968.
Brenda, 1970.
Dwayne, 1975.
Cyndi, 1976.
Pamela, 1978.
Wesley, 1979.

Albert and Lena (Nedohin) Runke, with sons Alvin, John, David, 1953.

Back: Brenda, Darrel, Martha and Dave Runke; front, Cyndi, Pamela, Wesley and Dwayne.

DEMYON RYBUCH

Demyon Rybuch came to Senkiw from the Ukraine in 1911, and lived with Steve Rybuch until he was able to raise enough cash by working at various jobs to send for his family. During the winter he helped Steve with chores. By 1922 he was able to pay passage for his wife and two sons: John and Mike.

In 1922 he took over a farm by mortgage default from a finance company. In 1936 he gave up that same mortgage with $200 still to pay, which he could not manage. He moved to Senkiw and lived there until they both, he and his wife, passed away.

John had a small farm at Senkiw and he supplemented his income by working as a carpenter until retirement. He was well known for his carpenter skill in the Rural Municipality of Franklin, and by Winnipeg contractors. In winter he made axe handles, which he sold to Woodmore store for 25 cents each, which paid for any groceries his family of two boys, Peter and Maurice, and daughter, Eleanor, needed. He also made vanities and cedar trunks for Eaton's in Winnipeg.

STEVE RYBUCH

Steve Rybuch came to Canada in 1913. He married Dora Goyman, whose parents had also immigrated from the Ukraine about 1904.

They had 12 children: Margret, Jennie, Mildred, Stephen, Raymond, Walter, Victoria, John, Frances, Irene, Stanley and Sylvia.

Front, Mrs. and Mr. John Rybuch; back, Mr. and Mrs. Demyon Rybuch, Joe and Eleanor (Rybuch) Karlash, Matt Karlash.

S EDWARD SNOWBALL

Edward Snowball, Grace (Snowball) Brown, Mrs. Snowball, Eddie. The Snowballs lived on the NE ¼ 6-3-5 E1.

MICHAEL STADNYK

Michael Stadnyk and his wife, Kathryn, brought their family from the Ukraine in 1897.

The family members were: Wasyl, Tom, Onufrey, Peter Helen (Olena) and Anne.

They came from Repinchia, Ukraine.

Wasyl married Anna Genick, born in Bereziw Wuznie, Ukraine, in 1888, in February of 1906. Anna came to Canada with her parents, Nickolai and Dokia Genik, brothers Ivan and Michael, and sister Pearl, in 1903.

Wasyl and Anna had 12 children, three of whom died in infancy during the flu epidemic and are buried at Stuartburn South cemetery.

They are: Nick, who died in a paper mill accident in Prince Charlotte Islands in 1943, Mike, Andrew, Alex, Edward, Peter, Steve, Pearl and Mary.

In 1921 Wasyl moved his family to Dufrost, to farm and blacksmith. He sharpened plow shares, harrows, and fixed machinery for neighbors who were too poor to pay. Anna sewed and knitted clothing for her family. A philosophy which Wasyl and Anna handed down to their children was that a neighbour was deserving of help before family members who had left home. One needed one's community and one's neighbours for survival. In 1941 Wasyl lost his land to a finance company, being unable to pay off a mortgage in an amount that can be earned in three or four days in 1982.

Of the 12 Stadnyk children, only Pearl and Steve live in Franklin Municipality in 1982. They live on 35-3-4, Wasyl's former land, and are mixed farmers.

Wasyl died in 1953, and Anna in 1956. They

Wasyl and Anna Stadnyk

Herbert, Margaret (Stimpson) Smith; Harold, Mrs. and Mr. Charles Stimpson, Gladys (Mrs. L. Johnston), Sid, May (Mrs. R. McAdam).

Peter and Anna Stadnyk

Mr. and Mrs. Charles Stimpson

are buried in Senkiw cemetery.

Peter Stadnyk married Anna Farina in 1928, and continued to live with his parents, Michael and Kathryn.

He had nine children: Bill, Nick, Paul, Nestor, Sylvestor, Kathy, Luba, Mary and Elsie.

Bill is on the home farm.

Nick is in Edmonton.

Elsie, Mrs. Laurent Catellier, lives in St. Malo.

Kathy, Luba and Mary live in Winnipeg.

CHARLES STIMPSON

The Stimpson family came to Franklin from Sprague in 1920. Mr. Stimpson became town drayman and owned and operated a livery stable. Later they bought the Red and White Store from Anderson Bros. In 1941 they retired to Winnipeg.

Back, Douglas, Lincoln Johnston; front, Nancy, Gladys (Stimpson) Johnston.

380

FRED SIMPSON

Fred Simpson brought his family to Franklin Municipality c.1879. He was of United Empire Loyalist background from Brighton, Ontario.

There were five girls and three boys in the family, being: Gertie, Roy, Dolly, Harry, Maude, Irvine and Flo.

Gussie and his wife Rebecca (Post) Simpson.

Roy Simpson lost his life in the First World War.

Harry did not marry.

Irvine married Ida Scott, daughter of Robert Scott, in 1897.

There were seven children: Robert Frederick, Willet Scott, Maurice Irvine, Earle Cleve.

Robert lost his life in the first world war.

The daughters were: Vey, Meryle and Gladys.

Meryle was totally blinded at the age of five.

Irvine died c.1918.

Ida (Scott) Simpson was the first woman to hold a driver's license in Franklin, and drove the mail between Dominion City, Green Ridge and Woodmore for 20 years.

In 1982 Earle Simpson still lives in the house in which he was born.

Gertie became a Mrs. Anderson.

Dolly married Jack Knox.

Maude married Jimmy Hales.

Flo married Sol Johns.

Gussie married H. Wright.

Earle married Catherine McCormick, and their children are: Harry, Meryle, Jim, Troy, Murray, Bert and Glen.

By a previous marriage Earle had a son, Willet, and daughter Vivian.

Left, Bill Turner, barber in Dominion City, died 1964; right, Willet Simpson. Willet went to United States, married Alma Pyns of Milwaukee, died 1947 at age 45, c. 1920.

Fred and Rebecca (Post) Simpson

Back, Gertie, Roy, Dolly, Harry, Maude, Irvine; front, Flo, Fred Simpson, Rebecca (Post) Simpson, Gussie.

Irvine Simpson; Ida (Scott) Simpson, 1950, at age 80.

Maurice Simpson, behind his wife Amy, Gladys (Simpson) Anderson, Hilton Anderson, Meryle (Simpson) Lowe, Vey (Simpson) Gaynor, Ida (Scott) Simpson, Charles Gaynor, Catherine (McCormick) Simpson, Earle Simpson, 1953.

Robert Frederick Simpson; Earle and Catherine (McCormick) Simpson.

Back, Murray, Bert, Glen Simpson, Willet Simpson and Vivian (Simpson) Asham; front, Harry, Meryle, Jim and Roy Simpson.

Mary and Willet Simpson with Christopher, Scott and Laurie.

Left: Bert, David, Mary; sitting, Joey and Cathy.
Right: Meryle, Ben and Samantha Berg.

Glen and Joan, Brian; front, Cindy, Glen Jr. and Bridgette Simpson.

Roy and Sharron (Lord) Simpson; Carrie, Tracie, and Shawn.

Left: Murray and Susan (Berg) Simpson with Stephanie and Jennifer.
Right: Jim and Delores Simpson with Dean and Debbie.

ED SMITH

Edmonston Smith was born in the Shetland Islands, Scotland, in 1871. He married in 1889. He was one of seven boys born to the Reverend and Mrs. William Cromarty Smith. Ed and three brothers came to Canada in 1890, and to Franklin Municipality c.1900. The Smith brothers had a store in Arnaud, in which they carried a general line of merchandise, and a lumber yard across the street. Ed was also postmaster. His brother L. D. was a lawyer, magistrate and real estate salesman, and Tom farmed.

Ed had eight children. They are:

Harry Edmondston.

John Ingram, who died at age 17.

Guy Edmondston, deceased, a professional engineer.

Arnaud E., who became a doctor, now deceased.

Wallace E., died at age 5.

Grace Dorothy E., now deceased, who went to the United States.

Nesta Edmonston, music teacher, who will be 86 September, 1982.

William Thomas, who was 82, May 30, 1982, a professional engineer.

Tom Smith married a Miss Doucett, a school teacher at Arnaud and a commercial traveller out of Winnipeg before operating a bookstore in Saskatoon.

L. D. Smith died at the age of 56.

FRANK SMITH

Frank Smith was born in England in 1876. He came to Canada in 1899 and worked for farmers in the district. In 1901 he married Alice Hamblin of Woodmore, and for four years they farmed on the SE ¼ 24-2-5E. They then moved to the SE ¼ 24-2-4E. In 1907 he bought the E ½ 19-2-5E from original owner Thomas Nixon, who bought it in 1876.

In 1920 Mr. Smith put up a new house and barn and moved to the NE ¼ 19-2-5E.

They raised eight children: Thomas, Henry, Mary, Emma, Albert, Margaret, Garnet and Irene.

Frank passed away in 1929 and Alice in 1972.

Thomas was born in 1902. In 1925 he rented the N ½ 18-2-5 E1 from Henry Batten. In 1935 he married Fern Griffin, the daughter of James Griffin. The Griffins moved into the large frame house with Thomas in 1934, and remained there after Tom and Fern were married.

Tom and Fern had two boys: Dennis Cameron and Garry Thomas.

In 1965 Dennis and Garry bought the farm, and Tom and Fern retired to a new home on 18-2-5 E. Tom died May 13, 1971. Fern lives in the house with granddaughter, Lynne.

Garry Thomas married Lesia Janet Machula of Vita in October, 1970. They have two daughters: Rachel Anne, age 11 and DeAnne, age 5.

They purchased the former Albert Steinert residence in 1971. Garry is in partnership with his brother Dennis, together farming "Smith Brothers". They are actively engaged in both beef and grain farming.

Dennis and his wife Helen and their three children live on 18-2-5E. Their children are: Lynne, Barbara and Barry.

Lynne is the assistant secretary-treasurer for the Rural Municipality of Franklin.

Barbara is the manager of the Co-op store in Dominion City.

Barry is at home.

Henry stayed on the home farm, the E ½ 19-2-5E and married Aileen Stewart in 1944. They are engaged in mixed farming and have two daughters, Joan and Judith.

There is still wild fruit to be picked on this farm and the buildings are the same ones that Mr. Frank Smith built in 1920.

Henry owned and farmed the SE ¼ 30-2-5 E1, the former Isiah Badgley farm, for 51 years, selling to daughter Judy in 1976.

Albert grew up on the home farm on NE ¼ 19-2-5 E1. In 1936 he married Elizabeth Post and they farmed at Green Ridge. In 1939 he bought the W ½ 20-2-5 E1, the original Richard Batten homestead. Bert built a store there and operated it for about three years. They moved back to

Green Ridge for a couple of years and in 1945 they bought a farm at St. Germain.

They have one daughter, Patricia, now Mrs. Doug Vandenburge, who has three sons.

Garnet grew up on the home farm on NE ¼ 19-2-5E, working at home until he married Jessie Post in 1940 and moved to the SW ¼ 20-2-5 E1, where he farmed until 1951.

They raised five children: Frances, Gail, Bob, Gerald and Lyle.

In 1951 he sold out to William Mumford and moved to Oak Bluff.

Francis, Bob, Jessie (Post) Smith, holding Lyle, Gerald, Gail.

Betty (Post), Patricia and Albert Smith.

Mary, Frank holding Garnet, Alice holding Irene, Emma, 1921.

Joan, Henry and Aileen (Stewart) Smith, holding Judith.

Tom and Fern Smith

Dennis and Helen Smith

Gary, Lesia, Rachel and DeAnne Smith.

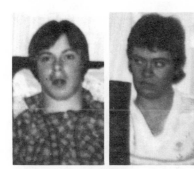

Barry, Barbara, and Lynne Smith.

HANS SCHULTZ

Hans Schultz married Agnes Spence, born 1867, at Bowesmont, North Dakota. They came to Franklin Municipality and settled on the SW¼ of 36-2-4E. Hans was fond of horses and took special pride in his driving team, "Sis" and "Bird". This team, hitched to a top buggy, took them to church every Sunday, and every 10 days they delivered cream and eggs to Roy Whitman's store in Ridgeville. Hans and Agnes had a large herd of Ayrshire milk cows, raised white leg horns, and kept bees. They had no children.

Hans and Agnes (Sperrce) Schultz

LUDWIG H. SCHULTZ

Ludwig H. Schultz was born February 6, 1878 in Tutchen, county Rovna in Russia. In 1894 he and his brother Gustave Martin Schultz immigrated to Canada. They stayed with friends at Rosenfeld and worked for farmers at Gretna for several years.

In 1897 Ludwig went to Alberta where he homesteaded for two years but had to abandon his claim, due to frost killing his crops.

In 1899 he came back to Franklin and bought the NE¼ of 2-1-3 E1.

In 1902, November 24, he married Caroline Schmidt (nee Jahnke) a widow with one son, John. John grew up in this district but spent most of his life farming in Saskatchewan. He is now living in Weyburn.

In 1903 William was born.

Henry was born in 1905, but died in infancy.

Emil was born in 1908.

Mathilda was born in 1911.

Fredrich ws born in 1914.

Gerhard in 1915. He died as a teenager.

Arthur was born in 1918.

Albert was born in 1920.

Ludwig and Caroline lived at Fredensthal until 1945 when they retired to Emerson. They lived at Emerson until 1966, moved to Winnipeg in 1967, and died in 1969.

William Schultz married Olga Berft of Emerson on November 26, 1932.

They had two children: Allister and Myrna.

Allister married Gail Gray in 1959 and had one daughter, Kimberley.

Myrna married William MacGregor of Vancouver and has one son, Tavish.

Emil Schultz married Johanna Berft of Emerson in 1939. He worked for the C.N.R. and lives in Emerson.

They had one son, Wayne, who married Sandra Pettitt. They have two children, Jennifer and Jason, and live in Winnipeg.

Mathilda Schultz married Adolf Schwark in 1934.

They had one son, Lorne, who died at the age of three.

Adolf Schwark died in 1955 and Mathilda died in 1980.

Arthur Schultz married Lilliam Steg in 1948, and lives on the NW¼ of 7-1-4E their married life.

They have one son and one daughter:

Donald, married Bonnie Lee Jones in 1974 and is an employee of the Canadian Imperial Bank of Commerce in Edmonton. They have one daughter, Nicole Dawne.

Joan, is an R.N. and is presently enrolled in the University of Alberta working for a degree in nursing.

Albert Schultz married Elfrieda Bohn in 1948 and moved to Winnipeg.

They have two children:

Carol Ann, who married Larry Domes of Winnipeg, and has two children, Jaclynn and Lindsay.

Allen, who lives in Winnipeg, and is an employee of Sears.

Ludwig and Caroline (Jahnke) Schultz

Ludwig Schultz family, 1967, John Schmidt on left.

William and Olga Schultz with Allister and Myrna.

L to r; Elfrieda (Bohn), Allan, Carol Ann, Albert Schultz.

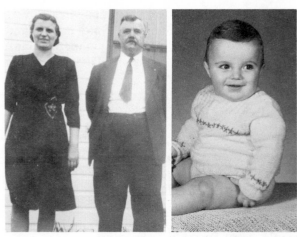

Matilda, Adolf and Lorne Schwark.

Emil, Johanna and Wayne Schultz.

Arthur and Lillian Schultz, Donald and Joan.

Joan holds a Bachelors Degree in Nursing.

Donald, Bonnie Lee (Jones) and Nicole Dawne Schultz live in Edmonton where he is a bank manager.

Fred and Thelma (Knutt) Schultz married in 1945, live on the SE of 26-1-3. They have two sons, Harold and Laurence.

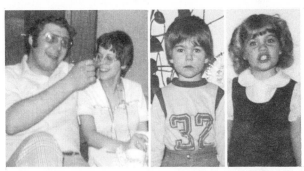

Harold, Christine (Volkert) and Ryan and Julie Schultz, live in Gimli where he is a bank manager.

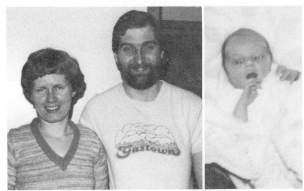

Lawrence, Elaine (Pomrenke) and Michelle Deanne Schultz live in Minnedosa where he is a bank manager.

LUDWIG SCHULTZ

Ludwig Schultz married Jalegornor Wojitt (Woitt). The Schultz family left Anelufka Volhynia Russia in 1891 by horse and wagon to a seaport in Germany. Here they sold their horses and wagon and traveled by small boat to England and then by ship to Canada, and by rail to Gretna, Manitoba. They lived here for three years.

Gustav died in 1894.

From Gretna they moved to Wetaskiwin, Alberta, where they farmed. Their crop froze three years in succession.

Friedrich, the youngest, and Emilie (Mrs. Theadore Ziebart) the oldest daughter, stayed in Wetaskiwin, while Ludwig and the rest of his family moved to Fredensthal where they farmed until they died. They are buried in Fredensthal cemetery.

Their children are:

Emilie, married Theodore Zieborth.

Bertha, married August Kein.

Rudolf, married Justyna Dreger.

Gustav, married Mary Sager.

Mathilda, married Reinhold Weiss.

Ida, married Emil Walters.

Theodore, married Adoline Buss.

Henry, married Anna Scheibe.

Theodore Schultz worked on his father's farm until the outbreak of the first world war, when he served as a Military Police at Camp Valcor, Quebec. Upon discharge he farmed the SE ¼ of 7-1-4 E1. In 1923 he married Adoline Buss, who had arrived from Poland in July of that year.

They had three children: Herbert, Ruth and Lily May.

Ted and Adoline moved to Emerson in 1948, continuing to farm until 1970. Ted died December 21, 1971, Adoline lives at the South Gate Haven in Emerson.

Ruth died June 11, 1944.

Lily married Vernon Pott and moved to Mission, British Columbia.

Herbert married Lillian Doern, and lives on the family farm.

They have two children: Dennis, and Carol, who is married to Les Szumskyj, and lives in Winnipeg.

Rudolf married Justyna Dreger in 1902. They farmed the SE ¼ of 17-1-2 E1 until 1936, when they moved to Emerson. Rudolf died in 1958, Justyna in 1974. They are buried in Fredensthal cemetery.

Their children are:

William, married Lilia Casper.

Elsie, married Gottlieb Weiss.

Elmina, married Adolph Bothe.

Gerhard, married Lillian Rotchinsky.

Johanna, married William Scheibe.

Gustav Schultz was born in 1884 and his wife, Marie Saiger of Neche, North Dakota, was born in 1892. They were married in 1909 and started farming that year. Their farm was the NE ¼ of 11-1-3 E1, located one mile south of Fredensthal.

Their children are:

Emil, married Annie Becker.

Alfred, married Iona Webster.

August, married Elsie Zeismann.

Walter, married Faye Pickell.

Ann, married Arthur Remus.

Henry Schultz, youngest son of Ludwig and Jaligornor (Woitt) was born in 1899. In 1921 he married Anna Scheibe. They farmed the NW quarter of 5-1-4 E1. Anna died in 1958 and Henry in 1961. Both are buried at Fredensthal.

Their children are:

Edmund, married Velma Steg.

Alice, married John Evans.

Melvin, married Sarah Hiebert.

Leonard, married Sandra Gnazdowsky.

Ludwig and Jalegornor Schultz

Theodore and Adeline Schultz

Herbert, Ruth and Lily Schultz.

Herb and Lillian Schultz

Les and Carol Szumskyj; Dennis Schultz.

Back, William, Elsie, Elmina, Gerhard; front, Johanna Justyna and Rudolf Schultz.

William T. and Lilly Schultzz; Darlene and Bonnie.

Gerhard and Lillian Schultz; Alan, Laura and Ryan Schultz.

Ken and Nancy Schultz, Kara and Kurt.

Elmina and Adolph Bothe, Ruth Anne and Elaine.

Back, Emil, Alfred, August, Walter; front, Marie (Saiger) Schultz, Ann, Gustav Schultz.

Emil and Anne Schultz; Leslie and Alice Schultz.

Walter and Faye Schultz, Lori and Rick Zaparaniuk, Lois Schultz, Tim Burns, Lyn and Doug Casper; front, Tanya and Troy Casper.

Stephen, Raymond and Douglas Schultz.

August Schultz family; l to r; Marilyn (married Lynden Franks (divorced), Desi Franks, Elsie (Ziesman) Schultz, Richard (married Carol Makoweski, Tolstoi), August Schultz, Timothy (married Joan Hancox, Dominion City, separated, has son Daryl), and Perry. Inset: Daryl Allan.

Robert and Theresa (Fedorchuk) Schultz, Alfred and Iona (Webster) Schultz, Lyle and Kathy (Schultz) Dunsmore.

Andrew Schultz, Richard and Carol Schultz.

390

Henry and Anna Schultz

John Schultz, Laurene (Schultz) Koswin, Velma (Steg) Schultz, Karron (Schultz) Clay, Edmund Schultz, Linda (Schultz) Bukoski, Kathleen Schultz; front, Wilma Schultz.

Melvin and Sarah (Hiebert) Schultz

Len and Sandra (Gnazdowsky) Schultz; Alice (Schultz) and John Evans.

Elizabeth and Trevor Evans; Michael Clay.

Allan, Dale, and Marilyn Schultz (Melvin).

Kevin and Jeffrey Kosowin; Kelly Bukoski.

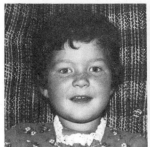

Leah Anne and Lenna Schultz (Len).

FRANK O. SHELBY

Frank O. Shelby was born January 28, 1873, at Evergreen Grove, his father's homestead in Butternut Valley, Blue Earth County, Mihnesota. May 18, 1898, Frank married Mary Jane Lewis, born October 21, 1877 at Lake Crystal, Minnesota. In 1906 Frank bought the NE ¼ of 25-3-3 E1 in Franklin, and his brother Theodore bought the NW ¼ of 25-3-3 E1. Frank and Mary Jane, with sons, David, Alvin (Bob) and Floyd arrived at Arnaud October 14, 1908. Roy had died in infancy, and was buried at Lake Crystal. They lived their first year in Bill Green's house, sharing

391

it with hired hand Alex Jones, and the winter after moved to a nearby farm. In 1909 they bought a house in Arnaud, dismantled it and rebuilt it on the NE ¼ of 25-3-3 E1. Theodore Shelby returned to Minnesota, selling his land to Frank. Three children were born on this farm, Melvin, Agnes and Isla.

Agnes died in 1932, age 19. Alvin met an accidental death in 1934, age 33. Frank and Mary Jane retired to Dominion City in 1939. Frank died February 1952. Mary Jane lived in Winnipeg until her death, July 1968. They are buried in the Dominion City Cemetery.

Dave worked on the Lyman Ranches from 1917 to 1923, then for various farmers and at several locations before going to British Columbia. He married Pat Benson in 1975, and is retired in rural British Columbia.

Melvin bought 6-4-4 E1 in 1937. He married Violet Strange in 1937. Their children are: Robert, married Eileen Alstadt, and has two children, Cindy and Kevin. Frances, married George Regier, and has two children, George, attending University of Manitoba, and Sherri, a real estage agent. Ronald, is a stationary engineer. Myrna married Lance Ian Beselaere, and has three children, Shawn, Daniel and Angela. Her husband farms at Waskada. Violet died September 7, 1974.

Floyd farmed with his dad until his retirement in 1939. He married Dorothy Strange September 29, 1939, and took over the home farm, in partnership with his brother Mike. They retired in 1982, renting the land. Floyd remained an American citizen until 1963. The Shelbys have three children. Gordon married Edithe Neveux, and lives in Winnipeg with son Jeffrey, born January 3, 1976. Glen is married to Sharon Muller, and has two children, Robin Lee, born February 5, 1975, and Derek, born March 5, 1979. Mitzi Lee travels with her American husband, Buddy Knox, who owns and operates an entertainment corporation. They have a son, Jesse Lee, born May 26, 1981. The land presently owned by Floyd Shelby, being the NE and NW ¼ of 25-3-3 E1, has had the following owners since 1883. Isaac Casson, 1883, A. and J. Gynelle held the NW ¼ until 1900, and the NE ¼ until 1904, S. Smith took the NW ¼ in 1902, and J. Parent bought same in 1903. After 1903 a land company paid taxes on the land. In 1906 Theodore and Frank Shelby bought the quarter sections from a land and investment company, Madelia, Minnesota.

Isla married Bill Hopkins, and lives in Winnipeg. She has three children. Larry, married Elsie Chubey. They have a son, Tom. Jo Anne is a teacher, and Robert works for the City of Winnipeg with Insect Control.

Bob and Dave Shelby

Agnes, Isla and Melvin (Mike); standing Floyd H. Shelby.

Frank O. and Mary Jane Shelby

Floyd and Dorothy Shelby

Edithe, Gordon and Jeffrey Shelby.

Glen and Sharon Shelby.

Robin and Derek Shelby

Buddy, Mitzi and JesseLee Knox.

WASYL SMOOK

Wasyl Smook and his wife Maria (Karlash) Smook came to Canada from Sinow, Zalischyku, West Ukraine, on April 24, 1897. They had a son Dmytro, born September 24, 1887, and a daughter Wasylyna, born 1889. Another son, Peter, was born in Canada.

They settled at Senkiw on the NW ¼ of 17-3-5 E1, later added the S ½ of 20-3-5 E1. Wasyl died at age 48, and is buried in Senkiw Orthodox Cemetery. Maria died November 18, 1954, age 77, and is buried in the same cemetery.

Dmytro married Anellia Nawolsky of Carlowrie, and farmed. They had five children. Harry, Bill, Mary, Olga and Anna.

Harry was born September 13, 1924, enlisted in the Royal Canadian Air Force, went overseas during the second world war and was lost in action over Norway February 9, 1944. Bill farmed with his father, and married Rosie Ostrowsky. They raise cattle, and have four children, Mary, Nancy, Christine and Harry, and lived on the old Smook farm at Senkiw.

Mary married Harry Andrusyk and lives in Woodmore. They raise cattle, and have one son, Roman.

Olga married Steve Kushka and lives in Ontario. They have two children, Christine and Bruno.

Anna married Tony Dumanski and lives in Ontario.

Anellia's parents, Michael and Pawlina Nawolsky came to Canada from Zalishyku, West Ukraine. They came to Carlowrie, the SW ¼ of 30-3-5 E1 with four children, Maria, Wladz, Carl and Anellia. Michael died young and is buried in the Rosa Cemetery, as is Pawlina.

Maria married Semeon Tofan, and farmed the SE ¼ of 19-3-5 E1. They had three children, Anna, Peter and Olga. They moved to Ontario, and are buried in Simcoe.

Wladz married Anna Hobbul, and farmed at Stuartburn. He had three children. Wladz is deceased, buried in Rosa Cemetery. Anna lives at Stuartburn.

Carl married Wasylyna Smook, a cousin to Dmytro Smook. They farmed the SW ¼ of 19-3-5 E1. They had three children, Adline, Eugene and Rosalia. Carl died June 11, 1974, and is buried in the Senkiw Greek Orthodox Cemetery. Wasylyna lives in Winnipeg.

Wasylyna Smook married Alex Shumovetski. They had one daughter, Olga. Alex died during the flu epidemic. Wasylyna died when Olga was a teenager, and Olga went to live with her grandmother, Maria Smook. She married Peter Patrick and lives in Winnipeg. Wasylyna and Alex are buried in the Senkiw Orthodox Cemetery.

Peter Smook married, and lives in the United States with his three children.

Carl and Wasylyna Nawolsky; Maria Tofan.

Wladz and Anna Nawolsky

Harry and William Smook before Harry enlisted; Flying officer Harry Smook.

Mary (Smook) Andrusyk, Mary (Nawolsky) Tofan and Semeon Tofan.

Back, Dmytro Smook, Anellia (Nawolsky) Smook, grandson Harry Smook, Rosie (Ostrowski) Smook, neighbor John Pupeza, Bill Smook; front, niece Olga (Shumovetsky) Patrick, granddaughters Christine, Mary Ann and Nancy Smook.

Peter and Sofia Tofan at his sister Anna's funeral.

Wasylyna Nawolsky, Bruno and Christina Kushka, Anna and Tony Dumanski; front, Anellia Smook.

Tony and Anna Dumanski, Bruno, Olga and Steve Kushka.

JAMES SEWARD II

James Seward II, 1841 to 1903, was the fifth child of James I and Hannah (Grady) of Castletown Rorke, Cork, Ireland, who came to Ontario in 1832. He married Mary Jane Bingham April 19, 1871. They came to Ridgeville in 1881, to homestead the NE¼ of 22-1-3 E1. Their children were, William Bingham, 1873 to 1907; Margaret Elizabeth, 1874 to 1901; James Thrasher, 1876 to 1961; Robert, 1878 to 1936; Mathie Louisa 1880 to 1946; George 1881 to 1958; Abram 1882 to 1957; Mary Jane 1884 to 1907; Charlotte Olive 1886 to 1915; Lydia Mae 1889 to 1977.

Olive died of typhoid in the epidemic. In 1887 the Sewards moved to the NW¼ of 29-2-4 E1.

In 1901 James Seward III farmed the Se¼ of 32-1-4 E1, later owned by Bert, then Bert's son Wilbert, and in 1982 it is the home of Wilbert's son Dennis.

James Seward II died August 1, 1903, Mary Jane May 19, 1905. Both are buried in Green Ridge cemetery, as well as Olive, Minnie, Bert, George and Abe. The last member of this generation of Sewards, Elsie (Redshaw) Seward, widow of Abe, died May, 1982.

Robert Seward purchased the NE¼ of 32-1-4 E1 from C. Harder in 1902. In 1914 he married Agnes Louise Lockhead. They had three children, Robert (still-born), Wilbert, 1916, Louise, 1919. They raised two orphaned nephews, Murray and John Lockhead, who came to them in 1915. Murray died in 1918, age 5, from rheumatic fever.

Robert was accidently killed in a gun mishap February 7, 1936. Wilbert took over the farm. Agnes died August 19, 1945.

Wilbert married Loraine Iola Spence in 1940. They had three sons, Danny Blair, born September 2, 1944, Dennis Wilbert, born March 31, 1942, Robert Dale, born August 9, 1949.

Wilbert and Loraine retired to Emerson in 1975, and Dennis took over the farm.

Danny married Lynda Szmigelsi in 1967, and lives in Thompson. They have two children, Derek Michael, born January 12, 1971, and Dana Michelle, born October 30, 1974.

Dale lives at Fairview, Alberta, and has a daughter, Candace Crystal, born February 11, 1971.

Back, Johny Lockhead, Clayton Hermiston, Garnet Craig, Evelyn Hermiston; front, Jack Hermiston, Lorne Hermiston in sailor suit, Louise Seward.

Johny Lockhead, Wib and Jimmy Seward about 1919. A few months later Johny and Wib were playing with matches in the hay loft and the big barn burned to the ground.

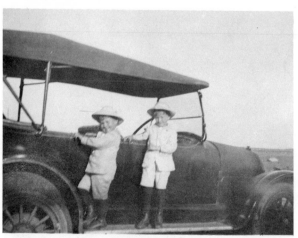

Wilbert Seward and Johny Lockhead ready for a joy ride in the "Overland" car, c. 1920.

Mae, Grandpa and Grandma Seward, Minnie, Abe, George, Bert, Ollie (in the wagon) Louise and Jim.

Bert and Agnes Seward with Wib, Louise and Johny (Lockhead).

Wilbert and Loraine Seward

Wib and Allan Seward on their pet donkey "Noodles".

Robert and Agnes Seward

Robert and Agnes Seward, Wilbert, Louise and nephew Johny Lockhead.

Jack and Mae (Seward) Hermiston, 1911.

Loraine, Dennis, Dale, Danny and Wilbert Seward.

Jack and Mae Hermiston family, Evelyn, Clayton, ɔrne and baby Jack.

Abe and Elsie Seward, 1914. They lived on what is now the Rzepka farm, and they had four children, Allan, Jim, Walter and Olive.

George and Jessie Seward married December 28, 1910. Spent most of their lifetime in Franklin municipality.

DANYLO STRUZOWSKY

Danylo and Annie Struzowsky came to Canada on May 23, 1898. They arrived at Halifax on the S.S. Pisa. Danylo was born in 1860 in Ivanie Puste district, Borshchiv, Galicia, Austria, son of Semen Struzowski and Katharina Shyman. Danylo died in Tolstoi November 17, 1918. His wife Annie ? was born in 1872, in the same place. Nellie was four years old when they arrived in Franklin Municipality. John, Mary, Mike and William were born here.

Danylo Struzowsky homesteaded the SE ¼ of 2-5-5 E1.

Nellie married Nykola Kranyk in 1912, and moved to Griffin, Saskatchewan in 1928. Nellie died in 1982, Nykola in 1964.

John, born in 1900, immigrated to Chicago in 1923, to Detroit in 1931, and died there in 1971.

Mary, born 1903, died in 1958.

Mike, born in 1905, lived in Prospect Heights, Illinois.

William, born in 1909, lives on the Struzowsky homestead.

Mike Struzowsky and wife, 1973.

John Struzowsky and wife, Detroit, 1957; William Struzowsky.

Nellie (Struzowsky) Kronyk; Annie, Mrs. Danyls Struzowsky; and daughter-in-law. Unidentified grandchildren in front, 1957.

ROBERT SCOTT

Robert Scott arrived from Almonte with his wife Lydia (Acres), Will, twins Cuthbert and Edwin, and Ida Jane, a daughter by a previous marriage. They arrived at Roseau Crossing in 1878, and farmed three and a half miles south of Dominion City. Edwin took over the farm when Robert and Lydia retired to the house in Dominion City now owned by Albert Raw.

Lydia died in 1918, at age 67, a victim of typhoid fever, and Robert in 1925, at age 83. Their son Edwin died in 1925 at age 48.

Ida married Irvine Simpson, Laura married Harvey Leonard, Emma married Harry Wellband, Myrtle married William Brisley, Lila married William Brown. Jessie, an adopted daughter, married Jim Turner, an American. Cuthbert married Minnie Farrion, Edwin married Polly Brewster, Howard married Ethel Brad, and Will Scott married Emma Pringle of Whitewater, Manitoba.

Back, Margaret, Will, Edith; center, Janet and James Scott; front, Ethel, Ray, Edna, c. 1915.

Robert and Lydia; Ida Jane Scott.

Left: Raymond Scott; Only surviving member of the James Scott family. Born May 3, 1902. retired in 1968 from Queen's Printers and lives in Winnipeg.
Right: Mrs. Annie Scott; widow of the late Wm. S. Scott and last surviving member of the Jim Hunter family of Green Ridge.

Emma, R. Cuthbert, Laura, Liela, Edwin, and Myrtle Scott. Children not identified.

Osborne and Theresa (Clupp) Scott, daughter Terry and sons, Bruce, Dale and Ronald.
Osborne, the eldest son of Will and Annie Scott married Theresa Clupp on April 11, 1946. They reside on the original family farm SW¼ 30-2-3 E1.

Cuthbert, Edwin, Howard and Will Scott.

Reg, Lorraine (Scott) Hopkins, (daughter of W. S. Scott), Gloria (Hopkins) Allen, Jim Hopkins, Shelley, 1979.

399

Left, Dale and wife (nee Gibb) with son Michael on knee Bruce and wife Bonnie (nee Kilfoyle) with children Jason and Megan, Nancy (nee Stanowski) and husband Ronald, Barrie Remus and wife Terry (nee Scott) with daughter Colleen on knee. Inset, Jennifer, daughter of Dale and Pat, Michelle daughter of Barry and Terry Remus. Fourth generation; Bruce is the eldest son of Osborne and Theresa Scott. Bruce owns part of the farm his great grandfather homesteaded in 1882, Section 30-2-3 E1.

Back, Osborne, Lorraine (Scott) Hopkins, Eleanor (Scott) Sharrott, Dorothy (Scott) Stewart, Donald, Betty (Scott) Weiss; front, Annie (Hunter) Scott, William Scott, 1959.

William S. Scott was born in 1888 on the farm his father homesteaded in 1882. Married in 1916 to Annie Hunter of Green Ridge. He farmed until 1946.

Donald Scott; Donald is the second son of Will and Annie (Hunter) Scott. He farms the NW¼ 30-2-3 E1 which his grandfather homesteaded in 1882 and which his father farmed before retiring in 1946. Donald chose to remain a bachelor.

LARS SOLNES

Lars and Ellen Solnes moved to Dominion City in the fall of 1933 to a farm five miles from town, now owned by Mike Brad.

When the family was grown, they moved into town, later to Burnaby, where they died; Ellen in 1959 and Lars in 1961.

Eddie, his wife Dorothy (French) and daughters Del and Sandra, moved to Copper Mountain, Princeton and then Burnaby. He lost his life on a construction job in 1965, leaving a young son, Darryl.

Sandra is married to Norman Harry and has three sons, Brian, Bradley and Brent.

Del married Cal Desrosiers and they have one son Darrin and Cheryl, a daughter.

Roy lives in the Caribou country. He lost his wife, Rose, in a car accident in 1958. They had no family.

Rose married James Craig, an Air Force man. They had two sons, Noel and Earl. She passed away in 1964.

Nora married Everett Brown at Copper Mountain. They have one son, David.

David married Janice MacPherson and has two sons, Douglas and Gordon.

Both Eddie and Nora were in the services during the war. Eddie in Manitoba Dragoons, and Nora in the C.W.A.C.

Ellen, Roy, Nora, Rose and Lars Solnes.

Eddie Solnes; Nora (Solnes) Brown.

J. B. SMITH

James Brown Smith and his wife Janet (nee McKay) and their family of five boys and one girl arrived in Manitoba from Lanark County, Ontario on March 24, 1881. Their children were James M., Jack, Alex, Nettie, Billy and Hugh. Katherine, Annie, Robert (who died in infancy), and Albert were born in Manitoba.

They applied for a homestead and in November 1884 were granted the patent for N ½ 30-3-3E.

About 1885 the family, discouraged with the short supply of good water, took possession of SE ¼ of 9 and ½ of NE ¼ in 3-4 E1. Mr. Smith's brother, Robert D. Smith and his brother-in-law had come from Ontario around 1883 and each took homesteads in the area nearby.

In 1886 Hugh was accidentally drowned in the Roseau River.

In 1887 James' widowed mother, Catherine, came from Eganville, Ontario, at age 71. She kept house for Robert, until she died in 1895.

In 1893 J. B. bought the Robert Ferguson SW ¼ 10 and ½ of NW ¼ of 10-3-4E. When this farm was sold to Dave Timlick in 1902, the Smith family moved to a farm at LaRiviere. James M. remained at Green Ridge to farm section 10. In 1904 he married Emma Louise Post, daughter of John R. and Almira Post. James M. and Emma had four children, Maxwell, Birdie, Kathleen and Arthur. James M. died in 1948, Emma in 1920.

In 1935 Max married Gunda Moen and they took over the Smith farm. When Max died in 1970 Gunda leased the land until it was taken over by their son, Glen, of Transcona, who leases it to Merton Olden. Gunda lives in Dominion City. Max and Gunda's children are Florence, Glen and Helen. Glen and Martha Smith have one son, Geoffrey.

Birdie was secretary to the Woods Manager of The Abitibi Paper Company in Pine Falls. Arthur joined the R.C.A.S.C. during World War II.

Art, Birdie and Kathleen live in Winnipeg.

Jack Smith became a grain buyer in Shellmouth where he met and married Susanna MacFadyen in 1901. Alex and Billy moved to Saskatchewan and Nettie married George Hoggarth at LaRiviere in 1905, later moving to Crystal City. Albert married Annie Armstrong in 1911 and settled in Crystal City. In 1911 J. B. and Janet Smith retired from farming and, along with daughters Katherine and Annie, moved to Crystal City, where James B. died in 1913, and Janet in 1936.

Glen, Martha, Gunda holding Geoffrey Smith.

James B. and Janet (McKay) Smith; Arthur W. Smith (R.C.A.S.C.).

Back, James M. Smith Emma (Post), P. Smith, Mrs. R. E. Gunn, Mrs. R. E. Post, Ethel Gunn; middle, Birdie, Kathleen, Arthur and Maxwell Smith, Hazel Gunn and R. E. Post and son Theo; front, R.E. Gunn and son Lewis, c. 1916.

James M. and Emma (Post) Smith, Maxwell and Birdie, c. 1909.

JAMES SMITH

In 1882 the Smith family, father, James Sr., and three sons, Will, James Jr. and Tom, homesteaded a section of land (12-1-4E) southeast of Ridgeville. Will later relinquished his claim in favour of his widowed aunt, Mrs. Sarah Gilchrist, who came from Ontario in 1893. In 1891 James Jr. filed a homestead on the S.E. ¼ 12-1-4E.

James Sr. and his wife, Ellen, had four children: Will, who never married; Tom, who married Minnie Thom; James Jr. who married Laura Lenton, and Ella, who married Andrew Gilchrist.

James Jr. married Laura Lenton in 1898. James Jr. was born in Barrie, Ontario on November 5, 1872. Laura was born in Bedfordshire, England in 1880 and died December 6, 1960. They had seven children:

Jean married Bob Stutter.

Sue married R. E. Davis.

James married Lexie Davidson. He died at the age of 27 or 28.

Bert married Kay Petter.

Agnes married William Bubbs.

Florence married Jack Parsons.

Gladys married Frank Stoddart.

During the North-west Rebellion, a Mounted Police post was established at the Smith farm to remain for more than 10 years. They also had a group of surveyors stay at their place.

Home of James Smith Sr. (SE ¼ 12-1-4E) which was signed over to James Smith Jr. October 2, 1891.

James and Laura (Lenton) Smith

Left: Andy Gilchrist, Jim Smith; front, Ella Gilchrist and Laura Smith.
Right: Herbert, Kay and Ronald Smith.

A group of surveyors who stayed at the Smith farm. The four women are l to r; Girlie Angus, Ella and Sarah Smith, Mrs. James Smith Sr.

L to r; James Smith Jr., Andy Gilchrist, James Smith Sr., Thomas Smith.

Bert, Glad, Sue, Jean, Kay, Flo, Flo (Lenton); front, Reg Smith.

SAMUEL V. STEWART

When Samuel Stewart, born in North Gower, Ontario, in 1858, and a veteran of 1885, came back to Canada after four years of farming in North Dakota his intention was to settle farther west. But his cattle had to spend some time in quarantine so he and his wife, formerly Matilda Jane Ellis, born in 1867 in Pakenham, Ontario, later of Winnipeg, and their five children stayed in Emerson for the winter of 1893-94. While there they were urged to file on the abandoned homestead of Joe Robbins S.W. 2-1-4E. This they did, moving there in May of 1894 with Harriet, May, William, Archie and Robert. Six more children were born on the homestead, James, Edna, John, Frances, Donald and Gordon. The last three still survive and the original homestead is still in the family.

Mathilda Stewart; Gordon Stewart - "water witcher" in the Ridgeville area.

Sargent Exham - No. 5 Company, Winnipeg Light Infantry; Private Peebles - Winnipeg Calvary Dragoon; Corporal Samuel Stewart - No. 6 Company 91st Winnipeg Light Infantry.

May and Edna Stewart

Francis and Donald Stewart

Archie, James, Bill, Bob, John, Donald and Gordon Stewart.

JOHN STEWART

The John Stewart family, from Loughbrickland, County Down, Ireland, immigrated to Canada in 1881 and settled at Emerson. They had five children, Andrew, William, Sarah, Tom and John. After four or five years in Emerson, they bought a farm in the Gardenton area on the Roseau River. At that time, the Post Office was at Stuartburn and there was no school. Mr. Stewart found a teacher and held classes in a granary. They grew wheat, oats, rye and raised cattle, pigs and chickens. In those early years, there were no game laws so for meat they shot prairie chickens, partridges, wild geese, ducks and deer.

In 1905 John Jr. bought the NW 8-2-5E in Woodmore. In 1907 he built a house and barn, and on December 25 of that year, he married Emma Post of Woodmore.

They were engaged in mixed farming and in the following years, bought the NE and then the South half of section 8. This land had been owned by an American speculator, but no one else had lived on it. There was plenty of wooded land and a creek.

John and Emma raised four children, Lloyd, Aileen, Jean and Chester.

Lloyd was in the army from 1941-45. Aileen married Henry Smith in 1944 and went to live on section 19-2-5E. In 1946, John and family moved to a farm on the Red River, southwest of Dominion City. Chester married Dorothy Scott of Dominion City in 1946.

In 1955, John passed away and in 1966 Mrs. Stewart, Lloyd and Jean sold out to Chester and moved to Winnipeg. Mrs. Stewart died on December 30, 1975.

Tom Stewart, born in County Down in 1875, was six years old when his parents came to Canada. He had his first farm in the Woodmore district in the early 1900's, later selling to John Pott. In 1908 he purchased the NE ¼ of 30-2-5 E1 and the SE ¼ of 30-2-5 E1, from his brother-in-law Cecil Stockdale. He lived here for the remainer of his life. He later added the NE ¼ of 29-2-5 E1, and became a mixed farmer.

Tom married Gertrude Jewell, daughter of Mr. and Mrs. William Jewell of Gardenton in 1908. Gertrude died in 1909, leaving one daughter, Lavina. In 1914 Tom married Olive Grier, daughter of Mathew and Sarah Grier of Woodmore. There were three children, Lyla, Hazel and Llewellyn.

Lavina married Mervin Craig of Ridgeville, and moved to Calgary. She had three children, Joyce, Shirley and Kelvin. Lavina died in January, 1982.

Lyla married Chester Leslie of Calgary, and raised two sons, Stewart of Calgary and Thomas of Madden, Alberta. Chester died September, 1967.

Hazel married Theodore Schlorff of Lac du Bonnet, where they operate a business.

Llewellyn farmed with his parents until the fall of 1946, when he moved to Winnipeg. He became a carpenter, and died in August, 1977.

Thomas passed away July 16, 1945, and Olive

on April 22, 1966.

Previous owners of the Thomas Stewart land, the NE ¼ and SE ¼ of 30-2-5 E1 were Mr. and Mrs. Bohn, Preston and Robinson, and Cecil Stackdale.

CHESTER STEWART

Chester moved with his parents to Dominion City from Woodmore in 1946. On July 2, 1946 he married Dorothy Scott. They farm section 11-2-2 E1. Floods forced them to moved their house to town in 1974.

Glenn is the eldest son of Chester and Dorothy Stewart. On July 2, 1971 he married Carmen Cadieux, daughter of Clare and the late Aimé Cadieux of Letellier. They have two sons, Chad and Troy, and live in Winnipeg.

David, twin son of Chester and Dorothy Stewart married Carol Richmond on July 14, 1979. They have one son, Sean David (eight months) and live in Winnipeg.

Don is the twin son of Chester and Dorothy Stewart. He married Ró-Jean, daughter of Jim and Margaret Anstett, October 27, 1973. They have two daughters, Jodi Dawne (two years) and Tammy Nicole (six years). After taking a diploma course in agriculture at the University of Manitoba, he returned to the farm with his father, taking over the family farm in 1980. In 1978 he built his own house in town at 192 Waddel St.

Aileen, John, Emma, Jean; front, Lloyd and Chester Stewart.

John Stewart's black horse. Jean and Chester on the way to school. Don took the children to school for about 15 years.

Back, Donovan, Glenn, David; front, Dorothy and Chester Stewart.

Glenn and Carman Stewart, Chad and Troy.

David, Carol and Sean Stewart.

Don and Ro-Jean Stewart, Jodie and Tammy.

Olive (Grier) and Thomas Stewart, 1938.

Mrs. Fogg, Olive Stewart, Mrs. Ellery Post; front, Mrs. W. Hurd, and Mrs. Thomas Batten, 1930.

ADOLPH STEG

Adolph (1863-1956) and Susanna (1865-1934) Steg were born and married in Poland. They came to Canada in 1899 with five children: Augusta, Tillie, Ludwig, Henry and Emma.

Two children died in Poland at a young age: Minnie and Reinhold.

Five children were born in Canada: Bertha, Martha, Emile, Ottelia (died as an infant) and Albert.

In 1924 they retired from farming and bought a home in E. Emerson.

Matilda Steg married Albert Boehler in 1907.

Augusta Steg married Henry Schultz in 1908.

Emma Steg married William Becker in 1917.

Bertha Steg married August Pomerenke in 1921.

Martha Steg married Charles Collins in 1923.

Ludwig (1890-1972) married Anna Schwark (1893-1949) in 1912; later married Lisa Krauter in 1952.

Ludwig farmed in the Ridgeville area from 1912 until 1920, he then bought a farm at Fredensthal, where he farmed until 1944. They retired to Emerson. There were three children: Theodor Albert, Elsie and Alma Bertha.

Theodor Steg married Edna Otto in 1938.

They farmed in the Ridgeville area since 1937 and have two children, Lloyd Albert and Mary Ann.

Mary Ann married Norman Pow in 1966.

Lloyd Albert married Delores Walters in 1965. They have two children Doreen and Barbara.

Elsie married Frank Casper in 1936.

Alma Bertha married Theodor Hartwig in 1944.

Albert married Annie Walters in 1933 and farmed in the Fredensthal area before moving to Emerson, where he was employed as school janitor until he retired.

They have one daughter, Ruth Ann, who married Emile Cherewayko.

Emile (1903-1978) married Lydia Walters in 1924.

They farmed the land where his father had settled on in 1899, moved to Emerson in 1954, but operated the farm until 1969, at which time they retired. They had four children: Velma, Arthur, Raymond and June.

Velma married Edmund Schultz.

Arthur married Thelma Wiess. They have two children, David and Barry.

David married Wendy Seaman.

Barry married Josephine Chodoccheck.

Raymond married Iris Melynchuk. Raymond is an officer with the Royal Canadian Mounted Police. They have two children, Shanon and Sean.

Shanon Steg is married to David Parker.

Sean is at home.

June married Bruce Irvin.

Henry Steg (1892-1972) married Minnie Otto in 1916. They farmed the SE¼ 13-1-3 E1 from 1916 until 1955, when they retired to Emerson. They had three children: William, Lillian and Arthur.

William married Emily Berft, of Emerson, in 1943 and has four children:

Ronnie, married Ruth Bargen, of Carman, Manitoba, and has two children: Robert and Rachel.

They presently live in Carman.

Dale, is working for the provincial government and is living in Winnipeg.

Arlene, does secretarial work and lives in Winnipeg.

Terry, works at Emerson and lives on the NW¼ of 18-1-4E.

Lillian married Arthur Schultz in 1948. They have two children:

Donald, married to Bonnie Lee Jones and has a daughter, Nicole Dawn.

Joan.

Arthur married Eleanor Schwab 1955. They have two daughters: Lori and Wendy.

Adolph and Susanna Steg

Albert and Annie Steg; Emile and Lydia Steg.

Ludwig and Anna Steg

Henry and Minnie Steg; William and Emily Steg.

Lorie, Eleanor and Arthur Steg, Wendy.

Donald, Lillian and Arthur Schultz, Joan.

Ron, Arleen and Dale. Inset, Terry.

WILFRED CHARLES STRINGER

Wilfred Charles Stringer and his wife Lillian Beatrice, purchased a homestead through the Soldiers Settlement Board in 1919, the SW ¼ 12-2-3 E1.

Charlie was a 'Jack of all trades'. One of his jobs seemed to involve frequent trips by moonlight across the border. Farming on the Flats produced very few crops, as there were no ditches at that time to drain the land. Finally they left Manitoba to seek their fortune in Alberta. Lillian was a midwife.

Charles and Lillian Stringer.

They returned to Ridgeville in 1951. Charlie worked as gravel checker and at carpenter jobs until his death on February 7, 1966 at the age of 78. Lillian moved to the Franklin Manor in Dominion City on March 11, 1972 where she presently resides. She will be 90 in 1982.

ARTHUR LEONARD STRINGER

Arthur Leonard (Sam) Stringer, veteran of the 1914-1918 war, acquired the NW ¼ 7-2-4E in 1919. The land was purchased through the Soldiers Settlement Board. Sam was from Eastbourne, England.

Sam married Beatrice Wilkinson, daughter of William and Rose Wilkinson, in St. Mary's Anglican Church at Ridgeville on November 16, 1921.

They had three children: Florence Alice, Ethel Rose and Arthur John.

They farmed for six years. Each crop was hailed, frozen or flooded out. He secured a job operating a dredge digging government ditches in Fannystelle. They gave up farming in 1927. He applied for the job of postmaster, and moved his family to Ridgeville in 1928. He was completing his final job, when fire broke out in the dredge, causing burns to three quarters of his body. He died October 28, 1928, at the age of 30.

Beatrice made application for the job of postmistress, which she obtained and held to retirement July 25, 1962. She had a new home built in 1935 at the cost of $1,300 and lived there until 1979 when she moved to Emerson into the Dufferin Courts. She will be 87 on July 17, 1982.

Beatrice remarried to John William Stringer, a brother of Sam in June, 1952. He died at the Emerson Hospital May 1, 1967.

Sam and Beatrice's eldest daughter, Florence, married Raymond C. McMurray, living in Winnipeg.

They have three daughters:

Brenda Christine, married Jon Bemister, Regina, and has two girls, Christie and Chera.

Wendy Diane married Charles Porter, living in Winnipeg. They have four children, Michaela, Stuart, Erin O., and Courtney.

Laura, single, employed as a zoo keeper at Assiniboine Park in Winnipeg.

Ethel Rose married John M. Curran, living in Dominion City.

They have one son:

Jay Franklin, living in Winnipeg.

Arthur John married Inez Thompson, living in Victoria. He spent 25 years in the navy, now cook in the Royal Jubilee Hospital.

They have three children: David, Lee Ann and Adele.

Sam Stringer's homestead, 1923; Ethel and Florence.

Raymond, Florence and Laura Stringer.

Arthur and Beatrice Stringer

Ethel, Jack and Jay Curran.

Jon and Brenda Bemister, Christie and Chera.

Arthur and Inez Stringer; front, Adele, David and Lee.

Charles and Wendy Porter, Michaela holding Courtney, Stuart and Erin O.

WASYL S. SMOOK

Wasyl S. Smook was born in 1868, Senkiew, Zalischyky, Western Ukraine. He married Anna Saracnhuk, who was born in April, 1877, of the same village. John was born in August , 1898. He came to Franklin Municipality in 1900, and homesteaded the W ½ of the NE ¼ of 8-3-5 E1, Hudson's Bay land.

They Smooks had four children: John, Mary , Lena and Stephen.

John was born in the Ukraine in 1898. He married Wasylyna Maximchuk in 1927, and they had one son, Roman. John spent most of his life in Franklin, farming, operating a garage, and other work. Roman, a teacher, married Mary Mand-

Wasyl and Anna Smook; Stephen and Mary Smook.

ziuk. John died in April 15, 1982, and Wasylyna in May 12, 1982.

Mary married William Andrusyk. They have one son, Stanley, who married Lena Drebit, who have two children, Rose and Lawrence.

Lena married Charles Nawolsky in 1927.

They have three children: Adeline, Rose and Eugene.

Charles died in 1974. Lena lives in Winnipeg.

Stephen, born in 1912, married Mary Pupeza of Rosa. They bought the SE ¼ 8-3-5 E1. They retired to 40 acres on the NE ¼ of 15-3-5 E1 in 1974.

Steve, John W., Wasyl and Anna, Mary, Lena Smook.

Wasylyna, John W. and Roman Smook, 1929.

Stephen, Wasylyna, Mary and Roman Smook.

Lena and Stephen Smook on a six foot right hand McCormack binder.

Charles and Lena, Adeline Nowalsky.

Left: Stephen and Mary Smook.
Right: Angela and Roman; front, John and Mary Smook.

MICHAEL SOKOLYK

The Sokolyk family were one of the first Ukrainian settlers in the Stuartburn area in 1896.

Micheal and Anne Smook were married in 1943.

In 1948 Mike and Anne purchased a grocery store which they operated until 1974 when a new building was opened.

Micheal was active in the Conservative party, Holy Trinity Catholic Church, D.C. Town Council and was a charter member of the D.C. Elks.

Their children:

Geraldine married Robert Fallis, they have 2 daughters, Jennifer and Kristen.

Taras married Janice Casper. They continue to operate the family store now entering its 35th year of uninterrupted business.

John W. and Wasylyna Smook; William and Mary Andrusyk.

410

Nykola and Wasylena Smook.

Taras in front of old Sokolyk store.

Simeon and Aksona Smook.

Opening of the new Sokolyk store, 1973.

Iwan and Anna Sokolyk.

Mike and Anne Sokolyk.

Michael and Anne Sokolyk, Geraldine and Robert Fallis; front, Jan and Taras Sokolyk.

Kristen and Jennifer Fallis.

JOHN SCHNELL

John Schnell immigrated to Canada from Austria in the year 1895 and settled in the Gretna area, later homesteaded at Tolstoi. He was born in 1848 and died in 1936. He married Magdolena Schoeffer, who died in 1927.

They had five sons and two daughters:

Christopher, farmed at Tolstoi all his life. He married Dora Schindel in 1902 at the Overstone Lutheran Church. Dora was the daughter of Michael Schindel, who came to Canada from Austria in 1897. Chris and Dora were of German descent.

They had six children. They were:

1) Dora Rose, married Charles Wakefield. They farmed in the Tolstoi area until Charles' death. Dorothy lives on her sister, Violet Krashy's yard.

2) Otto, married Dorothy Schwab. They farmed in Tolstoi and retired to Tolstoi.

They have three children:

Larry, married Doris Pott. They have three children, Curtis, Randy and Kelly, and live in Saskatchewan.

Ralph, works in Winnipeg and lives at home.

Debbie, works in Morris and lives in Tolstoi.

3) Fred, married Ruth Schwab. They farm in Tolstoi, and have seven children:

Ronald married Janice Walters. They have two children, Jodi and Tammy. Ronald is a mechanic and farms.

Delores, married Robert Jacobson. They have two children, Cynthia and Tracy, and farm in Arborg.

Kennith, married Judith Perry. They have four children, John, Brett, Wade, and Shane. They live in British Columbia.

Ross, married Lee Bjornson. They have two children, Carrie and Christopher.

Joan, married Ed Halonia and lives in Winnipeg.

Valarie and Theresa.

4) Alvina, married William Mayner.

5) Elsie, married William Gaetz.

6) Violet married William Krashy. They have one son Charles who completed high school and farms with his parents in Tolstoi.

Other members of the John Schnell family, who lived here and then moved were: Jacob, Maggie, Louis, John, Steve and Katharine.

Most moved to Saskatchewan.

Other members of the Michael Schindel family who lived in the district and moved were: Chris, John and Eva.

Left back, John; back row, Theresa, Judith, Ken, Ron, Janice, Robert, Leu, Delores, Ross holding Chris; children (standing), Brett, Wade, Jodi, Cindy; seated, Valerie, Ed, Joan, Ruth and Fred Schnell; children (sitting), Tracy, Shane, Tammy and Carrie.

John and Magdalena Schnell; Michael and Christine Schindel.

Charlie and Dorothy Wakefield; Fred and Ruth Schnell.

Otto and Dorothy Schnell; Curtis, Randy and Kelly Schnell.

Otto and Dorothy Schnell, Larry, Ralph and Debbie.

Violet and Bill Krashy; Charles.

SEMEON SALAMANDYK

Semeon Salamandyk came to Canada in 1897 from the Ukraine and settled on the SE ¼ 28-3-6 E1. He brought four children: Ivan (John), Wasyl (called William), Peter and Dokia.

John, born at Sinkow, West Ukraine, 1878, married Wasylyna Panchyshyn in 1898. They farmed at Stuartburn for eight years then moved to Senkiw.

They had eight children: William, Anna, Alex, Peter, Steve, Mary, Kay and Sam.

They retired to Vita. John passed away July 7, 1962 at age 84 years, and is buried at Senkiw Greek Orthodox Cemetery.

Wasylyna went to live in Winnipeg with Kay. In her last years she came to live at the Vita Personal Care Home. She died July 18, 1981, and is buried beside her husband.

In 1904 William's mother died at childbirth and William married Mary Pupeza. Mary was the daughter of Peter and Wasylyna (Toffan) Pupeza. She was born in Western Ukraine, her father died when she was little and her mother married Tanasko Wakaruh, and came to Canada in 1899. She had two brothers, Sam and Bill.

After William and Mary were married, they lived with William's father, brother Peter and sister Dora, who was only four years old. William's father, died in 1908 at the age of 57 with bronchial asthma. The family moved to 6-3-5 E1. Dora married Wasyl Smook when she was 18 and moved to Alberta. William and Peter worked together until 1924. Peter bought a farm on 21-3-4 E1. He never married, and finally moved to Toronto, where he died in 1945, age 52.

William died at Carlowrie, November 2, 1962. Mary moved to her son John's in Winnipeg, and died on January 15, 1970.

They had six children:

John married Irene Ewanchuk and farmed at Carlowrie, moving to Winnipeg in 1966. Irene died in 1969, age 59. They had two children,

413

Natalie (Patrick) and Walter.

Anne married Bill Fedirchuk. They lived in Toronto and had one son, Bill. She died in 1962.

Peter married Nettie Lazaruk. They farmed at Carlowrie, later moving to Winnipeg and then to Vancouver. They have two sons, Adam and Vincent.

Violet married Mike Sapach. They farmed at Carlowrie. Later they moved to Vancouver and now live in Winnipeg. They have three children, Louise (Gagnon), Lawrence and Patricia (Walters).

Olga married Walter Kasian. They lived at Dufrost, then moved to Winnipeg. They have twin sons, Dennis and Donald.

Peter didn't marry. He farmed at Carlowrie, then retired to Toronto. Deceased. Buried at Senkiw Greek Orthodox Cemetery.

Dokia, born March 4, 1900, married Wasyl Smook, and lives in Alberta.

John and Wasylyna had eight children:

William, married Mary Klym of Rosa. They lived in Minneapolis. They had three children, John, Gloria and Delores. William died in 1979 and is buried in Minneapolis.

Anna, married George Lakusta.

Alex, married Helen Kantimer and farmed at Senkiw, was postmaster, then moved to Winnipeg. Alex and Helen had three children, Roman, Bill and Frances. Helen passed away in 1974. Alex passed away in 1976. They are both buried in Senkiw Orthodox Cemetery.

Peter, was married to Margaret Volk. They had two children, Earl and Judy. Peter moved to Grand Forks, British Columbia. He passed away in 1973 and is buried in Grand Forks.

Steve, married Ann Goy and they farmed in the Roseau River area. They had three children, Maurice, Adam and Linda. When the children started leaving home they moved to Winnipeg. Steve passed away in 1973. Ann lives in Winnipeg.

Linda married a man named Shydlowski, both are in the entertainment field.

Mary, married Fred Zaharia and moved to Saskatchewan. Fred and Mary had six children, John, Don, Paul, Rose, Lil and Sherl. They retired to Vancouver. Mary passed away in 1981.

Kay, married Dmytro Mihaychuk, lived at Vita, then moved to Winnipeg. They had three children, John, Rosemarie and Maryann. John passed away and is buried at Senkiw Orthodox Cemetery. Kay is now married to Harry Meleshko.

Sam, married Julia Antoniuk. They farmed his father's farm. They had three children, Patricia, Elsie and Gloria. Sam lives in Stuartburn and is remarried.

John and Wasylyna (Panchyshyn) Salamandyk; back William, Sam, Kay, Anna, Steve.

Alex and Mary Salamandyk.

Three generations, William Salamandyk family; first generation, l to r; middle, Irene Salamandyk, (John's wife), William and Dora Smook of Vegreville, Alberta (sister to William), Mary and William Salamandyk, George and Anne Lakusta (a niece to William); second generation, top, Walter and Olga Kasian, Nick and Margaret Paley, Mike and Violet Sapach, John Salamandyk, Adam Salamandyk (Peter's son), Walter Salamandyk (John's son), Nettie Salamandyk (Peter's wife) and Natalie Salamandyk (John's daughter); bottom, Patricia Sapach, Donald Kasian, Dennis Kasian, Lawrence Sapach, Vincent Salamandyk (Peter's son) and Louise Sapach.

Missing from the picture is Peter Salamandyk, who was taking the picture, and Anne and Bill Fedirchuk and son Bill.

HERMAN SIPMA

Herman and Hilda Sipma boarded an aeroplane in Amsterdam on the 13th of April, 1957 to start a new life in Canada. They arrived in Dominion City on the 18th of April. Herman worked for Herman Ballast, after five months moved his family to Niverville where he worked for W. G. Leppky for two and a half years. His aim was to start something on his own and on the 13th of April, 1960, opened his own welding shop. Herman reached retirement age in 1979, but is still serving his customers. Albert, their oldest son, lives in Winnipeg with his wife, Pat, and son, Scott. Hans lives in Vancouver since 1973, and their youngest son, Rudy, died accidentally on November 4, 1972 at age 18. Albert Yzer is a son from Hilda Sipma's first marriage.

Herman and Hilda Sipma, Albert and Hans. Inset, Rudy.

Herman holding Rudy, Hilda; front, Albert (Yzer) and Hans Sipma.

Albert and Pat Yzer; Scott.

THOMAS SNEAD

Thomas Snead came from Yorkshire, England with his parents and family to Barrie, Ontario, in 1845. At the age of 16 he went to the United States to work. He returned to Ontario, and in 1893 married Ellen Hutchinson of Malton. Ellen was a seamstress.

They had a family of two sons: Frederick and Edgar.

In 1898 they came to Woodmore, and purchased the W ½ 26-2-4 E1 from Percy Carrol, and rented the SE ¼ 14-2-4 E1 from Joseph Moore.

Thomas passed away in 1921. At this time their youngest son Edgar took over the farmstead and still resides on it. Ellen Snead spent her life on the farm, except for a few years she spent visiting relations in Ontario. Falling and breaking her hip in 1952, she was hospitalized until her death in 1955.

In 1924 Edgar married Gladys Ward, the daughter of William Ward of Woodmore. Gladys was born in Cornwall, England.

Edgar and Gladys had a family of two sons: Norman and Kenneth.

Ken lives on the home place with his parents.

Norman joined the service for two years, then returned to the farm. In 1951 Norman married Matilda Pott of Woodmore and lives on the NW ¼ 26-2-4E.

Norman and Kenneth grain farm and raise beef cattle.

Norman and Matilda have a son, Kerry, who married Susan Gretschman, and lives in Steinbach.

JOHN SAMBORSKI

John Samborski came to Canada from Poland with his parents in 1898, age ?. They settled at Stuartburn. In 1908, he married Barbara Polischuk who came to Canada in 1905, age 14.

John and Barbara lived on 2-3-5 E1 and raised seven children:

Paul, married Nettie Golowaychuk (deceased), has three children, and lives in Roseau River.

Anton, married Margaret Pott, has four children and lives in Stuartburn.

Helen, married Peter Kohut, has two children and lives in Winnipeg.

Joe, married Mary Kushnir, has one child and lives in Stuartburn and Winnipeg.

Mike, married Jean Kantimere in 1954. Mike hauled lumber from various places in Ontario and Manitoba to Winnipeg for ten years, then began hauling rails and fence posts. In 1959, Jean's mother passed away at the age of 43, leaving four small children. Besides their own three children, they raised Jean's brother and sisters. Their three children are:

Jerry, married to Verna Catellier.

Sharon, at home.

Randy, who died in 1974 at age 13.

Jean works in the restaurant at the Queen's Hotel in Dominion City. They live in Roseau River.

Peter, married Mary Nault, has six children, and lives in Winnipeg.

Walter, married Helen Chubaty, has five children and lives in Edmonton.

John Samborski passed away in 1970, and Barbara Samborski in 1973.

GEORG SUPPES

Georg Suppes came to Canada from Russia in 1902, with his wife Emilie, four sons, George, Conrad, Alex and Fred, and daughter Marrila. They came to Winnipeg, and got work with the City, digging sewers by hand. In 1903 George married Elizabeth Schwartz, and they had seven children:

David, married Ann Nyhus, went to the United States and retired to Lake Bronson.

Jake, married Margaret Goetz, operated a garage and farmed at Basswood and Plumas, where he now lives.

John, married Mabel Weiss, worked for Franklin Municipality for 27 years, and is now retired in Dominion City.

Mildred, married Harvey Neilson, and lives at Hallock, Minnesota.

Elsie, died in 1942 from tuberculosis.

Fred, married Martha Hartwig. He served in the army for four years and lives in Winnipeg.

Elmer, married Myrtle Zilkie and is farming the original farm.

In 1907, Georg and George left Winnipeg and came to the Overstone district and the SE ¼ 18-1-5 E1. A couple of years later Georg bought the SW ¼ of 17-1-5 E1 and the two families separated.

Georg Suppes died January 9, 1953, at age 94, without even suffering an illness. Emilie died October 25, 1946, age 87.

George, born December 9, 1882, died December 9, 1969, age 87. Anna Elizabeth, born March 16, 1882, died February 15, 1957, age 75.

Georg and Emilie Suppes; standing, Mrs. Maynor, 1910.

Mildred, Elizabeth and George, John Suppes.

416

John and Mabel Suppes; Larry and Terry Suppes.

Left: Dave and Anne Suppes; front, Diane.
Right: David and Diane Stephens; front, Dan, Scott and Randy.

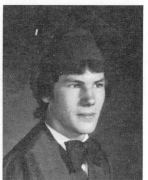

Bill and Cindy Suppes; Gary Suppes.

Jake and Margaret Suppes; Elmer and Myrtle Suppes.

Howard and Lana Omoto, Dean and Kim.

John, Elmer and Fred Suppes.

JOHN STASIUK

John Stasiuk is the son of Steve and Elisbeth Stasiuk of Caliento.

Helen Stasiuk is the daughter of Steve and Antonia Stasiuk of Poplarfield.

They were married in 1946, lived in Caliento from 1946 to 1952, then moved to St. Andrews of Winnipeg. John worked for Soo-Security Motorway for 23 years. In 1975 they moved to Tolstoi and bought Dolynchuk's General Store.

They have two daughters and two sons:

Beatrice, married Ray Miazgz from Winnipeg.

Doreen, married Mike Cheaszewski from Skylake.

Daniel, married Sharon Korloliuk from Winnipeg.

Ken, married Gail Bray of Eddystone.

They have nine grandchildren.

417

John and Helen Stasiuk; Ken and Gail Stasiuk.

David, Mike and Doreen Chaszewski; front, Peter and Michelle.

PETER SOLOMAN

Peter and Sophia Solomon came to Canada in 1897 with two children, John and Dokia. They got a homestead here on which John farmed until he died.

Peter and Sophia had seven children:

John, bachelor, now deceased.

Dokia, married M. Pashko, both deceased.

Maria, married P. Slusarchuk, both deceased.

Paraska, married J. Iotoryn, both deceased.

Fred, deceased.

Anna, married Bill Olinyk, living in Fort Francis.

Paul, married Annie Kwasnitski, farmed on the homestead. Paul died, and Peter is now farming with mother Annie.

Paul and Annie had six children:

Maurice, married Eileen Buxman. They have two children.

Peter, married Jean Drewniak. They have three children.

Martha, married Ralph Erawko. They have one son and live in Calgary.

Elsie married Bob Kennedy, and they have two children. They live in Winnipeg.

Joe, married Marlene Switzer. They have one child.

Donald, died at the age of 14.

Peter and Sophia Solomon.

JAKE SCHNELL

Jake Schnell and Irene Davison were married at Kenton on September 25, 1943. They farmed one and one half miles south of Dominion City. In 1967 they retired to Dominion City. The Schnells have three children. They are:

Sharon, who married Dale Palmer. They live in Wetaskiwin, Alberta, and have two girls and two boys.

Gayle, who married Douglas McClelland, lives in Winnipeg, and has one daughter.

Jack, who lives in Winnipeg.

Sharon, Irene (Davidson) Schnell, Jake Schnell; front, Jack, Gayle.

Jennifer Rae McClelland, baby Debra LeAnn, Angela Joy, Scott Everett, and Curtis Dale Palmer.

ALFRED SAWATSKY

Back, Sharon, Jean, Wayne, Arthur, Irene; front, Mary (Robertson) holding Ivan, Alfred Sawatsky.

HAMILTON STEWART

Hamilton Stewart, son of Elizabeth McBritnie and Hamilton Stewart Sr., was born September 9, 1861, at Kinburn, Ontario. He had a twin, Robert, and three older brothers. His mother died at his birth. Hamilton came to Franklin Municipality NW ¼ 10-1-4 E1 in the 1870's. On April 3, 1889, he married Maggie Morrison, and had eight children:

Eva, married George Turner, and farmed at Ridgeville. They had ten children, nine living in 1982.

Alma, married Ernest Riach, who had the lumber yard at Ridgeville, and they had seven children.

Hazel, a teacher, married Harvey Sutton in 1921, farmed at Roland, and had three sons.

Annie, a teacher, married Norman McLean in 1926, and farmed at Emerson. They had two children.

Maggie Mae, a teacher, married Alder Johnston in 1925, farmed near Emerson, and had one daughter, Goenadelle. Alder died in 1938, and Maggie married Harry Brick in 1942, farmed, and retired to Treherne.

William, married Jessie Sinclair and had seven children. He took over the home farm in 1922. Bill died in 1935, and his family left the farm in the 1940's.

Bessie, married Frank Turner, and farmed in Franklin Municipality until retired to Emerson. They had one daughter, Joan, who married Brian Kirkpatrick.

John, a teacher, had one son.

Hamilton and Maggie retired to Emerson when William married.

Alma, Hazel, Bessie, Hamilton Stewart, John, Maggie (Morrison) Stewart, Anne, Margaret, Eva.

John, Bessie, Bill, Margaret, Anne, Hazel, Alma, Eva, Maggie (Morrison) and Hamilton Stewart, 1925.

419

JOHN STEPHENS

Gertrude Stephens, Heather, John Stephens, John Jr., James, 1982. John Stephens purchased 10-1-4 E1 from Wilfred Marsh family in 1972.

Stephen's farm - 10-1-4 E1.

JOHN SLOBODZIAN

John was born March 3, 1893 at Chlopiwka, West Ukraine. He came to Canada in 1911 and did casual labour for a few years. He married Wasylyna Holasis, born at Vita, June 15, 1899. They farmed for 40 years.

John and Wasylyna had seven children; all moved to Winnipeg in search of employment:

Stella, married Kazmir Hrabi. They had six children. Stella is deceased.

Mary, married Jack Kiyon. They had four children.

Annie, married Edmund Wachal, had three children.

Jennie, married Mike Michelenko. They have one son.

Antonette, married Kazmir Michelenko. They have four children.

Rosie, married Ernie Bush. They have three children.

John and Wasylyna Slobidzian

Steve married Jean Polischuk.

In 1953 John and Wasylyna sold the farm and retired to Winnipeg, to live with Steve.

Wasylyna died July 19, 1954, age 55, and is buried in Winnipeg. John died June 15, 1967, age. 73.

ARNOLD SCHEWE

Arnold Schewe was born on a farm near Beausejour, son of Mr and Mrs G. Schewe.

On October 14, 1944, he married Beatrice Remus, daughter of Reinhold and Mary Remus. They lived on a farm near Beausejour for two years.

Lenore (Schewe) and Don Nicol, Jason, (born 1974) and Shawn (born 1976), 1979. Lenore, a teacher, married Don Nicol in 1968. They live in Pilot Mound.

420

Arnold and, Beatrice (Remus) Schewe, Lenore and Robert. Robert is a building contractor in Winnipeg.

In 1946 they bought a farm on the banks of the Red River, river lots 100, 102 and 104. Robert was born there.

In 1957 they moved to 21-2-3 E1. They farmed there for 22 years retiring to Emerson in 1979.

HYACINTHE SABOURIN

Hyacinthe Sabourin born at St. Augustin of Deux Montagnes, Quebec, married Eloise Charbonneau of St. Hermas, Quebec. He had immigrated to Canada from France in 1869. In 1891 he came to Manitoba with his family and settled north of St. Jean Baptiste along the Red River. His family consisted of:

Hyacinthe, deceased.
Joseph, married Marie-Louise Fillion.
Délima, married Wilfrid Vermette.
Placide, married Flore Clement.
Joseph Adonias, a priest.
Léonard, married Eugenie Baril.
Omer, married Mathilda Clement.
Rosine, married Rosario Dupuis.
Arthur, deceased.
Yvonne, died at age seven.
Ildege, married Exilda Beaudette.
Angelina, married Armand Champagne.
Marie-Anne, married Joseph Beaudette.
Jean-Baptiste and David, deceased.
Ulric, married Elizabeth Beaudette.
Besides his 16 children, they adopted two girls, Mathilde Nadon, married Paul Piloquin and Christina Bazelo, married Charles Maufflier who is still residing in St. Pierre-Jolys in 1981.

Hyacinthe was kicked in the back by his horse, on March 11, 1922, and died as a result. He was 74 years old.

Eloise lived in St. Pierre-Jolys with Adonias, until her death, October 21, 1938. She wsa 85 years old.

Ulric was born February 15, 1899. He married Elizabeth, daughter of Rodolphe (Délima Beaudette) April 21, 1919. They lived on river lot 202, where their son Luc, presently lives.

They had 11 children: Florence (Gérard Talbot) St. Léon, Cécile (Roland Provost) St. Norbert, Rose Aimée (Louis Pavlic) Verdigre, Nebraska, Théodore (Bella Desrochers), Lucie (Norbert Clement) Shilo, Amedée (Thérèse Larivière), Denise (Donat Touchette), Roland (Corinne Garant), Lorraine (Bernard Ricard) St. Norbert, Luc (Yvette Lafond) and Marc.

Ulric died in 1947, at age 47. When Luc married, he took over the family home, Elizabeth and Marc moved to a new house close by. Elizabeth had been left a widow with eight children at home. She died February 14, 1975, age 77.

Amedée was born September 5, 1926. He stayed on the farm with his father. July 15, 1950 he married Thérèse Larivière, daughter of Joseph and Emilie Larivière of St. Pierre. She is the seventh of a family of 13. Amedée established his home one and a half miles east of his father's farm, where four children were born. In 1957 he bought Joseph Vermette's farm, situated five miles east of the village of St. Jean Baptiste.

Diane, born May 29, 1951, is a teacher at the Precious Blood School in Winnipeg.

Ulric, born April 29, 1953, bought Roger Lafond's farm in 1973, and Maurice Landry's farm in 1977. He married Jacqueline, daughter of Pierre Barnabé (Isabelle Marion) November 30,

Back, Roland, Luc, Amédeé, Theodore; front, Lorraine, Rose, Denise, Mrs. Elizabeth Sabourin, Lucie, Florence and Cecile.

Amédeé and Thérése Sabourin, Ulric, Rejeanne, Dianne, Hubert, Daniel; front, Marie, Paul and Gaitanne.

1974. They have a daughter and two sons.

Réjane was born June 26, 1954, and on July 12, 1975, married Denis, son of Marcel Fillion (Adéline Grégoire).

Hubert, born November 22, 1956, married Edmée, daughter of Gérard Bilodeau (Aline Dumesnil) of Ste Agathe, May 29, 1976. In 1979 he bought his father's farm. They have two daughters and a son.

Amedée and Thérèse live in Albert Duval's house in the town of St. Jean Baptiste.

Daniel, born October 18, 1958, is an employee of Manitoba Pool Elevator in St. Jean Baptiste. July 26, 1980, he married Terry, daughter of Edouard Landry (Esther Doerksen).

Géatane, born June 30, 1965 and Marie-Paule, born March 3, 1969 are still in school.

HENRY SUKKAU

Henry Sukkau, Sr. and family, Henry Sukkau Jr. and George Sukkau families came to Franklin Municipality from the Ukraine in 1926. They farmed section 26-3-3 E1, the N ½ of 36-3-3 E1, W ½ of 30-3-4 E1, and part of the NW ¼ of 31-3-4 E1.

The three families farmed together until the George Sukkau family, with daughter Irma, moved to British Columbia in 1939. In 1941 Henry Sukkau Sr. with daughter Annie moved to British Columbia.

Four children were born to Anna and Henry Sukkau Jr. They are: Elly, Mr. C. B. Fast of Winnipeg, Walter, John and Harry.

Henry Jr. continued to farm with his sons adding the NW ½ of 36-3-3 E1. In 1957 Walter and Harry leased the land, and in 1958 Walter and his wife, Helen (Hiebert), established a new farmyard on the SW ¼ of 36-3-3 E1. They farmed until 1977, when the land was sold and they mov-

Carl and Joyce Sukkau, Rebecca.

ed to Winnipeg with their children, Joan, Patricia, and Richard.

Harry married Hilda Penner from Gnadenthal, and farmed the home farm, until 1975. In 1977 they moved to Winkler.

They have seven children:

Virginia, married Dan Thiessen, and has three boys and a girl.

Carl, married Joyce Horst from Ontario, and has a daughter.

Orlando, lives at Kane.

David, lives in Winnipeg.

Anna, married Edward Schellenberg of Roland, and has two daughters.

Ruth, lives at home.

Alisa, is in school.

CHRIS SCHWABE

Chris Schwabe was born in Jackson, Minnesota June 9, 1900, the third child of Wilhelm Schwabe. He had two brothers and three sisters. His family came to Saskatchewan in 1928, and in 1937 Chris came to Manitoba to get work at harvest time. He came to Langside, and had an offer to rent the Ernie Linklater farm.

In 1949 he married Myrtle Weedmark of Dominion City. In 1955 he bought land formerly owned by Emil Bohn, and in 1960 sold the farm to Donald Mayne and moved to Dominion City. Chris died in August, 1971.

Conrad and Amalia Schwab

CONRAD SCHWAB

Conrad and Amalia Schwab. 1911.

Conrad Schwab was born in Russia in 1880, and Amalia in 1881. They came to Canada in 1896.

The Schwabs moved to Mowbray in 1927, returning to Overstone in 1941, and farmed until 1967. They had a family of nine children and four sons, of which only Mrs. Otto Schnell and Mrs. Fred Schnell remain in Franklin Municipality.

LOUIS SOLNES

Louis Solnes emigrated from Flors, Norway, in 1922. He sailed on the Mantrose to Montreal, then by train to Winnipeg. He worked and lived with his uncle Alfred Solnes. In 1936 he rented land from Alfred Lang. He married Mabel Casper in 1944. From 1945 to 1978 they operated Solnes Cafe in Dominion City. He bought the farm he rented in 1969, and in 1975 sold the farm to his two sons, Wesley and Dwayne.

Louis and Mabel Solnes

Dwayne and Sharon Solnes

Wesley and Lonna Solnes, Dayna and Signe.

In 1971 Wesley married Lonna Weninger. They have two daughters: Dayna and Signe.

Dwayne married Sharon Yaremko in 1980.

Louis and Mabel are retired in Dominion City.

ALFRED SOLNES

Alfred Solnes was born in Flors, Norway, May 1890, one of 15 children. Hanna Englund was born in Judhult Gotryd, Sweden, September 1894, one of 12 children. They emigrated to the United States in the early 1900's, met in Chicago, and married in 1917. In 1919 they and daughter Bernice came to Arnaud, where Norman and Mildred were born. In 1930 they moved to a farm north west of Dominion City. Here Gordon and Boyd were born. This farm is now owned by Norman.

Alfred Solnes passed away January 1963. Hanna remarried in 1968, to Carl Lundquist. They spent winters in Florida, summers with Bernice.

Bernice married Dick Weninger in 1948, and lives in Dominion City. She retired in May, 1982, after 26 years with the Bank of Commerce.

She has two daughters:

Lonna, married Wes Solnes of Winnipeg in 1971, and has two children, Dayna and Signe.

Louise, married Brett Monroe of Vancouver in 1979.

Hanna, Bernice, Lonna and Dayna were each first born children.

Mildred, married Bill Bultz in 1947, and lives

Norman, Bernice, Gordon, Mildred, Boyd; front, Alfred and Hanna Solnes.

at Langside, and has four daughters. Judy married Archie Hunter in 1967.

Gordon, married Iris Ginn and lives in Vancouver with three children, Michael, Carla and Andrea.

Boyd married Rita Haycock, lives in Roblin, and has two children, Grant and Onalee.

Norman married Jean Ramsey, has two sons, Barry, who married Beth Goossen, lives in Sarnia, and has two children, Chris and Cara, and Brian married Barbara Pohl of Emerson. Brian has two sons Scott and Tori, and lives in the house built by his grandfather Alfred in Dominion City.

MELVIN SCHLORFF

Gertrude, Melvin, Mrs. Jenny Schlorff, Fred, Sandra, Raymond.

SAM STOROSCHUK

Sam and Shirley Storoschuk, Roxann.

CURT SCHEIBE

Curt Scheibe came from Dresden, Germany in 1897. He married Frances Hruda in 1900. They lived first at the Marias, and in 1919 they settled on the NW ¼ 21-1-4.

Curt died in 1950, Frances in 1943. Both are buried at Fredensthal.

Their children are:

Anna, married Henry Schultz.

Fred, 1903-1974.

Rudy, 1905-1977.

William, 1907-1980, married Johanna Schultz.

Joseph.

Martha, married Henry Lenton.

Emma, married Nelson Gilchrist.

Alma, married Harry Paulsen in 1948.

Anna, Martha, Emma, Alma; back, Fred, Rudy, Bill and Joe Scheibe.

Curt and Frances Scheibe

Bill (1907-1980) and Johanna (1911-1981) Scheibe.

Gene, Almie and Harry Paulsen, Diedre.

Larry, son of Bill Scheibe, Kellie and Jonathon Scheibe, Larry's children.

JOSEPH DAVID SULLIVAN

Joe Sullivan was born at Dublin, Ontario, and came to Dominion City in 1879. He married Alice Henriett Graydon in 1891. Alice was born in Orilla, Ontario, Joseph had a farm at Arnaud, and ran the Oglivie Elevator at Arnaud for 28 years.

Joe and Alice had four children: Frank, George, Tracy and Lenore.

Joseph passed away February, 1939, and Alice in July, 1957.

Frank moved to Saskatchewan in 1913, age 22. He married Pearl Waddell in 1923, and died May 9, 1969.

He had four children: Harry, Florence Eileen, Norah Lillian and Glen Robert.

George Henry lived on his father's farm at Arnaud until 1932, then moved to Saskatchewan. He came back to Franklin in 1944, married Myrtle May Nichols in 1945. He farmed until 1963. Myrtle died in 1959, and George married Pearl Neely in 1964. He moved to Plumas, where he died in 1966.

Tracy William married Jennie Burnell in 1923, and farmed in Arnaud from 1923 to 1929. He moved to Saskatchewan, where he died in 1953.

He had eight children: Lois Lila June, Alice Lorraine, Verna Rae, Harold Tracy, John Lyle, Donald Clare, Norma Marie and Dallis Janet.

Lenore married Arthur Taylor. She died in 1958, Arthur in 1960.

They had four children: Eloise, Larry, Dallas and Vance.

Lenore and Arthur are buried in Dominion City.

AUGUST SCHWARK

August Schwark was born February 16, 1854, married Bertha Lutz, and lived in Village of Berestowitz, Wothynia, Russia. The Lutz family came from Poland originally, the Schwarks from Germany. They left Russia in company with eight other families in April, 1891, arriving in Quebec, June 2, 1891, Winnipeg, June 5. August and Bertha, with three sons, Gustav, Adolph and Theodore, stayed with a Schellenberg family at Gretna. In 1903 they moved to Fredensthal and the NE ¼ of 7-1-4 E1, bought from Peter Coutts for $800. Coutts was the original homesteader in 1880.

In 1913 August sold his farm to his son Gustav. He died 1938, and Bertha in 1917, at age 57.

August and Bertha's children were: Gustav 1883-1953, Adolph 1888-1955, Theodore 1890-1958, Annie 1893-1949, born in Canada were

425

Emilie 1896-1948, and William 1899-1902.

Gustav married Ottilie Becker November 24, 1909. In 1913 they bought the NE¼ 7-1-4 E1 from August. In 1927 they purchased the SE¼ 7-1-4 from Theodore Schultz for $6,200, and in 1933 Ottilie inherited the SE¼ of 12¾-1-3 E1. They farmed this land until 1936, when they rented it to Ted and William. Gustav and Ottilie retired to Emerson in 1940, when Ted took over the farm.

Gustav died May 21, 1953, Ottilie December 21, 1973, age 85.

Their children were: Elsie, 1911, died an infant; Ted, March 5, 1913; William, April 25, 1915; Bertha Juliana, August 5, 1917 married Ted Walters in 1938, and live in Emerson; and Arthur Gustave, March 2, 1924.

Adolph married Matilda Weiss in 1908, divorced. In November, 1921 he married Hulda Rentz. Hulda died July, 1929. In 1934 he married Tillie Schultz. They had one son, Lorne Adolph William, who died at age three. Adolph was in the armed forces in World War I, farmed the NE¼ 5-2-3 E1 when he returned to Manitoba. In 1927 he bought the NW¼ of 7-1-4 E1, and farmed until 1938, when he retired to Dominion City. He died October, 1955, Tillie in December, 1980.

Theodore married Matilda Hartwig November 28, 1912. He farmed on 3-1-3 E1. They retired to Emerson in 1949. Theodore died in August, 1958, Matilda in January 1968, age 78. Their children are:

Anna Euphorsina, born September 10, 1913, married Alfred Wagner in 1948, lives in Emerson.

Alma, 1914-1916.

Arthur Adolf, born March 26, 1918.

Two girls died in infancy.

Annie married Louis Steg in 1912.

Emilie married William Wolskie in 1918, he died nine months later in flu epidemic of 1918. In 1920 she married John Hildebrandt of Haskett, where she and her husband farmed until retirement. Emilie died in 1948.

William died at age three years.

Ted, son of Gustav and Ottilie, married Martha Gertrude Neumann October 26, 1940. He bought the NE¼ 7-1-4, the family farm. In time they purchased the SE¼ of 7 and SE¼ 12-1-3 E1, and farmed until 1977 when they rented the land and moved to Emerson. Ted is employed with Trans Canada Pipe Lines, and had two children: Lorraine Sharon, born July 22, 1943 and Dennis Garry, born October 5, 1944.

Lorraine a home economist, died accidently on the job at Swan River in 1966, age 22.

Dennis married Margaret Agnes Geiler in 1964,

farms the SE¼ 12-1-3 E1, works for Trans Canada Pipe Lines, and lives in Ile des Chenes. He has two children: Michael William, born 1964, and Kristin Lorraine, born 1969.

William, second son of Gustav and Ottilie, married Bertha Dora Walters in 1938. He farmed the NE¼ of 25-1-3 E1 until 1966, when he moved to Minnedosa, and became supervisor for Manitoba Crop Insurance Corporation. In 1972 they moved to Winnipeg, and retired in 1977. They have one son, Wayne Stanley, born 1942. Wayne married Donna May Laufersweiler in 1963, and live in Ithaca, New York since 1972, where Wayne lectures in Veterinary Medicine and Research. They have two children: Dwight Wayne, born 1964, and Lisa Lynn, born 1967.

Arthur, third son of Gustav and Ottilie, was in the navy in 1942. On his return he joined the Customs staff at Emerson, where he worked for 18 years. He married Sofie Chernoski in 1949, and died in 1964, age 40. Arthur and Sofie had five children:

Carla, born 1951, married Keith McAllister. They have two children: Kendall and Colleen.

Vernon, born 1952, is in the navy.

Paula, born 1953, married Bob Keehn, has one child, Robert.

Dale, born 1954.

Eric, born 1959.

Arthur, son of Theodore and Matilda Schwark, married Helen Ruth Weiss, who was born January 23, 1921, Dominion City, on November 19, 1943, and farmed the NW¼ 2-1-3 W1, from the estate of Henry Hartwig Sr., his father's maternal grandfather. In 1953 they bought the SE¼ 2-1-3 E1. They farmed 34 years, until their retirement to Emerson in 1977. Their daughter Leona and husband Real Tétrault farm their land. Their children are: Kenneth Arthur, born 1947, Robert Gordon, born 1949, died 1951, Leona Ruth

Gustav and Ottilie Schwark.

426

Mathilda, born 1952, married Real Tétrault in 1971. Kenneth married Carolyn Ann Riach, born 1947, in 1969. They lived in Winnipeg, in 1974 bought the NE ¼ of 5-1-4 E1 and SW ¼ 8-1-4 E1 from Art W. Steg, and the S ½ of 3-1-3 E1 and SW ¼ of 3-1-3 E1 from Alf Wagner, formerly owned by Kenneth's grandfather Theodore Schwark. They have two children: Kerry Robert, born 1973, and Corinne Ruth Ann, born 1975.

William and Bertha Schwark

August Schwark, 1917; Adolf Schwark (son).

Dwight, Donna, Lisa and Wayne Schwark.

Theodore and Mathilda Schwark

Carla, Eric, Vernon; back, Paula and Dale Schwark.

Arthur and Sophie Schwark; Arthur 1942.

Arthur and Ruth Schwark

427

Kenneth and Carolynn Schwark, Kerry and Corinne.

Ted and Martha Schwark, Lorraine.

Dennis and Margaret Schwark, Michael and Kristin.

JULIUS SCHMIDT

Julius Schmidt arrived in the Ridgeville area from Warsaw Province in Poland on June 5, 1928. With the exception of four years, from 1938 to 1942, he lived in Franklin Municipality. Those four years were spent working in Winnipeg.

In October of 1942 he married Olga Bohn who was born in Franklin. From 1942 to 1958 the family farmed at Green Ridge.

During this time, nine children were born to them.

The fifth child, Edward, died in infancy and was buried in Green Ridge cemetery in 1949.

The eldest, Elsie is married to Bill Berg and has three children, Todd, Steven and Michael.

Florence, married to Bob Stanke, has one son, Bruce.

Clarence, who married Janice Dobka, has three children: Trevor, Karen and Krista.

Eileen is married to Clayton Gunn.

Doreen, who is married to John Wilson, has one daughter, Breccan.

Leo is married to the former Janice Baker and they have two children: Paul and Clinton.

Raymond and Albert have elected to remain single.

Olga and Julius Schmidt

Leo, Albert, Doreen, Raymond, Eileen, Florence, Clarence, Elsie, Olga, Julius Schmidt.

With the exception of Clarence, who lives in Regina, Raymond, who is in Kingston, Ontario, and Eileen in Green Ridge, the others live in Winnipeg.

Julius Schmidt went to work for the Province of Manitoba in 1957, Department of Highways. In 1958 the family moved to Dominion City. Julius retired in 1970.

LUDWIG STEINKE

Ludwig Steinke came to Canada from Volenia, Russia in 1889, and in 1892 his wife Pauline and son August, age seven, joined him. One son, Gustav, went to South America and William to the U.S.A. Daughter Pauline, Mrs Gottlieb Weiss, lived in Franklin Municipality. The family came to Manitoba c.1905.

August farmed on section 27-1-3 E1 in the Fredensthal area. In 1907 he married Emily Steinke and in 1913 moved to section 35-1-3 E1 where most of the family were born.

Ludwig died in 1917 and Emily stayed with August. They moved to 19-2-4 E1 on March 3, 1931. Pauline died in the fall of 1939 at the age of 101 years. August died in 1944, age 64. Emily, with Louis, moved to Dominion City in 1953 and lived there till her death in March 1963, age 78 years.

There were four sons and three daughters:

Gustav was born in 1909, started as shoemaker in 1935 in Ridgeville till 1938, worked at casual labour till 1941, farmed on section 22-2-4 till 1966, moved to Steinbach and is retired there. Gustav married Emilia Steinert in 1943. They have three sons: Alfred of Toronto, Walter of Maple Creek, Sask., and Ronald of Winnipeg, and a daughter Louise, of Winnipeg.

Reinhold was born in 1916 and took over the home farm, 19-2-4 E1 formerly the Bill Gunn homestead. He married Annie Craig in 1953 and lives on the farm.

Emma, born 1918, married Alfred Gruenke of Emerson in 1947. They farmed the Gruenke home place till 1976, then retired to Morris. They have one daughter, Maxine, in Winnipeg.

Frederick, born 1919, served with the Armed Forces, worked as farm help for a couple of years, and in 1948 acquired the John Storuschuck farm, 7-2-5 E1. In 1949 he married Linda Steinert. They have three sons: Robert, William and Gordon, all of Winnipeg.

Louis, born November 1922, stayed on the home farm till 1953. In 1957 he married Audrey Timlick who died in late 1958. They had a daughter Nancy, now in British Columbia. Louis remarried in 1963, and divorced. He married

again in 1967 to Dorothy St Germaine. He has lived in Winnipeg since 1957.

Ida, born in 1925, married Carl Kellberg in 1952 and lived in Milwauke and Vermillion Bay. Carl is deceased. She has two daughters: Shirley and Caroline. She later married Joe Kowal and has a son, Garry and daughter Gayle, and lives in Winnipeg.

Martha was born in 1928. She married Reinhold Ganske in 1949. They farm section 24-1-4 E1, mainly a beef operation. They have two daughters: Gloria and Sharon, of Winnipeg, and one son, Randi of Edmonton.

Back, Gus Steinke, Reinhold, Louis, Audrey, Emma and Alfred Gruenke, Fred and Linda Steinke; middle, Louise, Emily, Annie, Emilie (Steinart), Ida Kellberg; front, Ronnie Steinke, Elaine Calder (visitor), Alfred and Walter Steinke, Maxine Gruenke, Bob, Bill and Gordon Steinke.

Ludwig, August and Pauline Steinke.

Reinhold and Annie Steinke

REVEREND DAVID SPEAR

Rev. David and Mrs Margaret Spear arrived in Dominion City on Halloween night 1907 on the crack, C.P.R. train "The Flyer", the fast train to the Twin Cities, Minneapolis and St. Paul, with their family: William David, 11; Thomas Arnott, 10; Robert Wallace, 8; and Agnes Helen, 6 from Winnipeg.

They took up residence in the Presbyterian "Manse". Rev. Spear was the resident minister in Dominion City from 1907 until 1911. He held services in Arnaud, Green Ridge and Ridgeville, as well, on alternate Sundays. Full time minister's salary during 1907 to 1911 was $1,000 per year. If the congregation could not raise the $1,000 he took what they could collect, sometimes half his salary.

After 1911 and until shortly before his death, in 1948, Rev. Spear was farming on a quarter section a mile north of Dominion City.

Bill and Tom went overseas in 1914. Bill was killed in 1918. Tom came back to Dominion City in 1918 where he joined the C.P.R. He worked for the C.P.R. in various positions until he retired at age 65 in Calgary.

Wally looked after the farm for several years after Bill was killed, then joined the Bank of Ottawa in Emerson. His first wife died in 1962. He remarried and he and his wife, Anne, live in Winnipeg. Wally has one son, Robert, in California with his wife and two children, and a daughter, Helen, who married Don Nevill and has four children.

Margaret Spear's mother, Margaret Watt Ballingal, lived in Dominion City for many years. She died in 1930 at the age of 104. The Scottish Society of Winnipeg hired a plane to fly from Winnipeg to Dominion City to take Mrs Ballingal for her first and only airplane ride on her 101st birthday.

Rev. Spear died in 1948 at the age of 90 and Margaret died in 1957, at the age of 96, both in excellent health until their death. All are buried in the Dominion City cemetery.

Rev. David and Margaret Spear, c. 1915.

Rev. D. Spear, Tommy Brock, Helen (Spear) Brock, Bob Spear son of Wallace, Joan Brock, Lon, Mrs. Wallace Spear; Thanksgiving Day in 1945.

Tom (10), Wallace (7), William (12) Spear

Left: Anne and Wallace Spear, nephew of Rev. D. Spear, 1975.
Right: Rev. David Spear and Mrs. Watt Ballingal, age 101.

JOHN SHYDLOWSKY

John Shydlowsky, born on October 15, 1883, in the village of Postoliwka, in Western Ukraine, came to Canada in June of 1911 at the age of 28 and settled in the town of Tolstoi. He was a carpenter by trade for most of his life.

In 1920 he married Natalka Bednar from Caliento. Natalka came to Canada with her parents on June 16, 1909. She was four and a half years of age at that time.

After their marriage, John and Natalka lived in Tolstoi. They had six children: Alex, Steve, Mary, William, Nettie and Peter.

Alex lives in Tolstoi and had three children: Orest, Tris and Nestor.

Steve lives in Minneapolis and has two children: Nellie Ann and John.

Mary lives in Toronto and had two children: Eugene and Patricia.

William lives in Tolstoi in his parents premises. Nettie lives in Brantford, Ontario and has four sons: Donald, Dennis, Lester and Dwayne.

Peter, in Toronto, has two sons: Andrew and John.

John Shydlowsky passed away at the age of 74 on December 23, 1957. His wife Natalka passed away on June 8, 1965.

STEFAN STEPANIUK

Stefan Stepaniuk emigrated to Canada in 1928 from the village of Stoyaniv in Western Ukraine. He purchased his eight acre farm from Maxim Smook.

An artisan from Ukraine, he brought with him a variety of skills. At Rosa he worked as a carpenter, blacksmith and barber.

On November 1, 1931 he married Katie Kohut, eldest daughter of Wasyl and Anna Kohut. They had one daughter and five sons.

William, a teacher, married Elsie Evanchyshin of Malonton. They had three children: Stephen, Nancy and Glen. He is teaching in Winnipeg.

Effie, a teacher, married Louis Tataryn from Arborg. They have four children, Philip, Sandra, Sharon and Brian. They live in Winnipeg.

Peter married Sophie Melnyk from Trentham. They have three children: Michael, Andrew and Elanor, and live in Saskatoon.

John married Anneliese Lysak of Dufrost. They have three sons and one daughter: John, Beverly, Paul and Mark. John farms at Rosa, also employed by the C.N.R.

Michael married Marjorie Graydon of Green Ridge. They have four children: Tammy, Vincent, Robert and Walter. Michael farms at Rosa, and

works at the Manitoba Sugar Refinery.

Roman passed away in September 1979.

Left: Stefan and Katie (Kohut) Stepaniuk, and William.
Right: Katie Stepaniuk with son, Roman.

William and Elsie (Enanchyshin) Stepanuik, Stephen, Nancy and Glen.

Louis and Effie (Stepaniuk) Tataryn, Sharon, Philip, Sandra and Brian.

431

Peter and Sophie (Melnyk) Stepaniuk, Andrew, Michael, and Eleanor.

John and Anneliese (Lysak) Stepaniuk, John Jr., Beverly, Paul and Mark.

Michael and Marjorie (Graydon) Stepaniuk, Tammy, Robert, Vincent and Walter.

DAVID A. STEINERT

David A. Steinert, born June 1, 1889 in the village of Dreispitze, Russia, of German parents, immigrated to Kansas in 1891. He took over the farm from his father, married in 1910.

In 1913 David and Maria and baby son immigrated to Saskatchewan.

In 1917 Maria died, leaving two sons.

In 1917 David met Holdina Patzer who at age 10, in 1909, immigrated with her parents and family from Berestowitz, Province of Wolhynia, Russia to Saskatchewan January 3, 1918.

David and Holdina were married and continued to farm at Sagathun until the drought of the thirties. The government offered to help the farmers by moving them to more productive parts of the country. They had heard about the good land in the Red River Valley. Having cousins in the area, Mr. Steinert and Alex came east. They bought Hurd property, NE¼ 23-2-4 E1.

In October 1937 David and Holdina Steinert, Alexander, David, Emilie, William, Albert, Linda, Ferdinand, Mildred and August became residents of Franklin. A year later Laura was born.

Alex and David returned to the homestead in Saskatchewan in 1940.

The property of David Johnstone, Jack Varey and Gus Steinke were added, making one and one half sections. David and Holdina continued to be active on the farm.

David passed away March 3, 1975 at age 85, Holdina continued to live with her two sons until her death February 22, 1982, age 82.

Ferdinand and August continue to mix farm. Albert was drafted into the army in the second

Back, Ferdinand holding Ronald, Alma and Bill Steinert, August Steinert, Gus Steinke; middle, Albert and Janet Steinert, Linda (Steinert) Steinke, Laura Steinert, Emilie (Gus) (Steinert) Steinke; seated, Holdina (mother) and David (father) Steinert; front, grandchildren, Walter, Steinke, Gordon Steinert, Bobby Steinke, Louise Steinke, Mark Steinert, Alfred Steinke.

world war, and Bill went to Ontario in 1945.

Laura Steinert married David Volkenant, born March 5, 1945 in Mt. Clemens, Michigan, on October 1, 1977. David immigrated to Franklin Municipality in October 1967. He purchased SW ¼ 22-1-5 from Otto Rosner, and moved in on Halloween night, 1967. He has a mixed farm. In 1981 he became part owner, with his parents, of the Dale Rosner property.

L to r; back, Albert, Holdina, Laura, David, Emilie; front, Mildred, Bill, Ferdinand, August and Linda.

David and Laura Volkenant

JAMES SKENE

James and Margaret (McDonald) Skene, and five year old daughter, Margaret, arrived from Bamshire, Scotland in 1903.

Other children were: Jenny, Jessie, Katie and Bessie. They went to North Dakota, where Nellie and John were born. The family came to Franklin Municipality in 1910. Here, Dick, Violet and Chester were born. Their maternal grandfather, William McDonald was living here. Mr. McDonald died suddenly at the age of 103, of pneumonia. He had been healthy and chopping wood until several days before his death.

Jenny married Cliff Rothrock of Anaheim, U.S.A., and have four sons: Cliff Jr., Gordon, Ralph and Marshall.

Jessie married Albert Oldershaw of Winnipeg, and had two children: Ed and Margaret.

Katie married Harry Hicks.

Nellie married Robert Taylor and lives in Vancouver.

John and his wife Ruth live in Boisse, Idaho. They have two sons.

Dick and his wife Jean live in Winnipeg. They have two sons: Wayne and family of Edmonton, and Barry of Winnipeg.

Violet married Wilfred Gillespie, and had two sons: Gordon and family, and Brian of Winnipeg.

Chester was married to Norma McCloud, and they had one daughter Valerie. They lived in Dominion City where Chester was employed by the Rural Municipality of Franklin. He died October, 1969. Norma, and daughter Valerie, live in Winnipeg.

Margaret Ginn is the only one of this family to remain in Franklin and is living in the Franklin Manor in Dominion City.

James and Margaret Skene

Bessie, Jenn, Margaret, Eleanor, Kate and Violet.

Wm. "Scottie" McDonald, 1903; Wm. McDonald and Glennie Ginn, 1940.

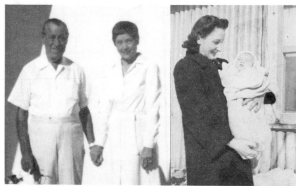

Bob and Eleanor Taylor; Jean Skene and Wayne.

bert and Jessie Oldershaw; Jack and Ruth Skene.

Katie, Dick, Marj, Violet, Eleanor.

Cliff Rothrock with Cliff Jr., Gordon, Ralph and Marshall.

Jen Rothrock with family.

Chester and Norma Skene; Dick Skene.

Valerie Skene; Katie (Skene) Hicks.

434

JOHN SPENCE

John Spence was born 1837 in the Orkney Islands, and came to Annprior, Ontario, married Jane Croskery, and came to Franklin Municipality and the NW ¼ 36-2-4 E1. There were eleven children: John, Agnes, James, Thomas, Jane, Dave, Margaret, Christopher, Andrew, Annie and Henry.

William John, 1866-1939, married Isabella McLennan, Green Ridge, and farmed on 2-3-4 E1. He had three children: Earle, 1899-1921, Hector and Claire.

Hector, born 1902, married Alfie Moen. They had three children: Regene, married Doug Hurd, Gordon, Malcolm. Hector farms the NE ¼ 35-2-4 E1. Malcolm married Vi Pott of Roseau River in 1961, farms with his father. Has two children: Belinda and Robert, and one grandson.

Claire, born 1907, married Jane Palmer, farms SE ¼ 2-3-4 E1. Lost a daughter in infancy, has son John. John married Darlene Wiebe, has two sons: Kelly and Trevor.

James, 1869 married Janet Gilchrist and lived SW ¼ 35-2-4 E1. They had ten children: Archie, Jean, John, William, Annie, Walter, Russell, Ethel, Maxwell, and Gladys.

Thomas, 1871 to 1952, married Sarah McLenna, teacher. Farmed NW ¼ 36-2-4 E1, had six children: Helena, Emma, Laura, Dorothy, Donald and Dugald.

Helena married Fred Snead, has five children: Audrey, Patricia, Jessie, Jeanette and Tom.

Emma married Jack McIntosh, has two sons.

Dorothy married Jack Horn, has five children: Anne, Nancy, John, Donald and Sally.

Donald farmed the home place until retiring to Emerson.

Dugald lives at Pine Falls.

Dave, 1876-1951, married Bessie Sullivan, had two daughters: Thelma, married Harry Ford, and Alma, married William Clayton.

Christopher, 1881, married Daisy Lydall, had three children. Lived in Saskatchewan.

Andrew, 1883, married Tassie Knox. They farmed in Saskatchewan until 1919. Tassie died in the flu epidemic, leaving daughters: Ella, Marjory and Muriel. Jane Cheales raised girls in Franklin, Andy went to Winnipeg.

Annie, 1886, worked for Victorian Order of Nurses, died single in late 30's.

Harry, 1888-1949, married Ethel Scott in 1917, in Saskatchewan. Came to Woodmore 1932, farmed SE ¼ 36-2-4 E1. Harry died in a highway accident, Ethel lives in Franklin Manor. They had eight children: Loraine, Irene, Wayne, Beverley, Keith, Ronald, Leonard and Garry.

Wayne married Susan O'Hara of Dominion City, was in the army during World War II, and had three children: Glenn, died in infancy; Carol, married Al Gerbrandt and has two children, Wendy and Wesley; and Kenneth.

Beverley married Norma Smyth and was in the army during World War II. Retired to Green Ridge and died 1981. Has three sons: Garry, with the RCMP, Terry and Cameron.

Keith joined the Armored Corps in 1945, moved to Victoria, and married Lois McLaren. He has four children: Wanda, married to Rick ?, has two children, Ricky and Spence; Douglas; Terri, married Terry Ptolmey, has son, Syney; and Warren.

Ronald took over the home farm in 1949. Married Eileen Francis 1954, in 1967 he bought a blacksmith shop in Ridgeville, ten years later Ridgeville General Store, and took over the post office. In 1980 they sold the farm. They have six children: Cindy, married Milton Braun; Lauran, married Marc Dubois; David, married JoAnne Ewanchuk in 1979, has son Joseph Ronald; Randall lives in Edmonton; Kevin and Kristi at home.

Leonard joined the Air Force as a career. In 1959 he married Lois Zass of Ridgeville, and lives in Winnipeg. Have two children: Gregory and Shelley.

Garry moved to Victoria and is an electrician.

John and Jane Spence

Dave and Bessie Spence; Andy and Tassie Spence.

Sarah, Dugald and Thomas Spence.

Cameron and Beverly Spence; Terry and Margaret Spence.

Harry and Ethel Spence

Constable Garry Spence; Warren and Keith Spence.

Back, Al and Carol Gerbrandt, not known, Ken Spence; front, Wesley Gerbrandt, Wayne and Susan Spence, Wendy Gerbrandt.

Wanda Ashmere holding Spence; Ricky.

Wayne, Beverly, Keith, Ronald, John, Barry; seated Loraine and Irene Spence.

Terri Ptolmey holding Sydney; Garry Spence.

Shelley and Greg Spence

Ron and Eileen Spence

Robert, Violet, Malcolm and Belinda Spence, 1981.
Farm NE¼ 35-2-4 E1.

Lori, Kevin, Eileen, Randy, Ron, Cindy holding Kristi,
Dave Spence.

Keith, Ethel Spence, Janet.

David and Jo-Anne Spence; Joseph Spence.

Lois, Ethel Spence, Leonard.

Randy, Kristi and Kevin Spence.

437

VALENTINE SCHOLTE

The Scholte family came to Manitoba from North Dakota in 1900 and settled on the NW ¼ 6-2-3 E1.

Mary Overturf came to Manitoba, with her parents, in 1917. She married Art Schalte in 1920, and they farmed until 1939, when they retired to Dominion City. Art was janitor of the Dominion City school for 12 years, and Mary worked in the John Baldwin drug store for eight years.

Mary and Art had a family of three boys and one girl: John Arthur, born 1922, deceased 1942; Willis, born 1925, deceased; Brian, died at birth; Lucille (Mrs. Kirk Devlin), husband Kirk deceased 1973, has one son, Dwight, born 1957.

Left to right: Alice, Valentine Scholte, Marie (Mrs. Jim Gillespie), Pearl (Mrs. P. McTaggart - husband deceased, married Walace Taylor), Mabel (Mrs. Ferg Graham), Arthur.
(Missing from picture: son, Edgar, died as result of ruptured appendix; operated on at the farm on the kitchen table by Dr. O'Brian.)

Mary and Art Scholte.

STEWART FAMILY

The 1883 map of the municipality shows the Stewart family on the flats. There were five children: John, Daniel, Neil, Hal and Bella.

Neil went to Weyburne, Saskatchewan to homestead.

Hal played hockey for Chicago.

Bella married Valentine Winkler, who became the Minister of Agriculture for Manitoba, and after whom the town of Winkler is named.

THEODORE STRANGE

Theodore Strange, 1847-1879, was born in Ipswich, England, son of Edward Harris Strange. He received his education in England and at the age of 17 went to the United States where he joined the second regiment of the New Hampshire Volunteers on November 16, 1863. He returned to England and attended Working Man's College in Ipswich, taking French and Writing, from October to March, 1867. He then sailed for Canada, arriving in Welland, Ontario, where the canal was under construction. Here he married Mary Ann Griffeth, of DeCou House, Beaver Dams. Ellen May was born here in 1872, Nita Margaret in 1876, and Theodore Sims in 1874. When the Welland Canal was finished, Theodore came to Manitoba to homestead the NE ¼ of 33-2-4 E1.

The Stranges took over a house built by a Mr. May on the St. Paul Trail about due south of the present home, where Mrs. Strange and family joined him.

George Edward Harris was born March 15, 1879. Mr. Strange died October 9, 1879, from complications caused by war wounds. Mr. A. Davison had donated land for the Green Ridge graveyard and Theodore Strange was the first grave in it.

In 1880 Mary Ann married A. Davison, keeping the original Strange homestead which became a tree claim in her name.

Andrew Davison had come from Alnmouth, Northumershire, England. He homesteaded the N ½ of 21-2-4 E1.

At age 16 Ella married a man from Ireland, Norman Macdougal. She had eight children by him before they separated, and Ella later married another Irishman, whose surname was Coote. She had three more children.

Nita went to British Columbia about 1906, where she married Will Moore.

Sims married Elizabeth Pryce from Wales, farmed at Carlowrie, and had two boys and four girls.

His son Theodore went to school at Green

Ridge, and inherited the original homestead. Clifford moved to Dominion City.

His daughter Violet married Melvin Shelby, and Dorothy married Floyd Shelby, both of Arnaud. Kathleen married Fred Lutomski and lives at Carlowrie. Francis married Bill McLelland, son of Dr. McLelland of Dominion City. On his death she married Dave Hodgson, and lives in Winnipeg.

George Strange married Annie Froom, daughter of Willis Froom, and farmed the SW ¼

The children of Norman and Ella (Strange) Mac-Dougal, 1905, l to r; back, Gladys, Don, Millie; front, Lucy, Nettie, housekeeper, (no name), Dorothy. Missing are Steve and Harry.

Clifford and Francis Strange, with daughter Karen, 1961. Clifford was born on the farm his father homesteaded in the Carlowrie area. His father was Sims Strange and his mother Elizabeth Pryce. Clifford was the second son in a family of two boys and four girls. He and Frances McClinton were married in 1946, and they farmed for ? years, living in a house across the road from his parents. Their only daughter Karen attended the University of Manitoba, and now resides in California. Clifford retired in 1976, and he and Frances live in Dominion City.

of 21, but this was not a success, so he joined the Lyman Ranch staff.

Mary ann Davison gave birth to the following children:

Llewelyn Sadie, August 13, 1884. She taught at Green Ridge, then took business education and moved to British Columbia, where she died in 1975 at age 94.

Mary Griffeths, 1883, became a nursemaid, joined the Salvation Army, and went to British Columbia where she married.

Annie Elizabeth, 1886. Married Charles Thompson of Minnedosa.

William Andrew, 1888. Farmed, developed tuberculosis, died at age 48.

Herbert Ward, 1890. Farmed, attended Agricultural College, served overseas in the first world war, and took over the farm on his father's death in 1933, with his brother William. On William's death, he and Theodore Strange carried on the farm.

Left: Mary Davison Shannon.
Right: Ella Coote (Strange, MacDougall), returned to the Davison home to care for her 90 year old mother.

Nita Strange and husband William Moore, 1912.

Left: Sims and Elizabeth Strange.
Right: Theodore Strange, who died age 33, 1879.

L to r; Rev. Carl Ridd, Dorothy (Strange) Shelby, Fred Lutomski, Kathleen Strange. Last wedding in Newbridge United Church, December 22, 1962.

Left: Bill Davison at Ninette Sanitorium in the 1920's.
Right: H. W. Davison, youngest son of Mary Anne and Andrew Davison.

Llewellian Davison, son Jack, husband Charles Digby.

Edith Thompson, granddaughter of Andrew Davison, with fall arrangement for W.I.'s 40th anniversary. Arranged on small hay bale grown on original Davison homestead.

Charles and Elizabeth (Davison) Thompson, 1941.

L to r; back, Clifford, Sims Strange, Theodore; front, Kathleen, Frances, Dorothy, Violet.

440

Left: Mary Ann Davison (Giffiths Strange) in her late 80's.
Middle: Llewelyn (Davison) Digby, who lived to be 94. 1974.
Right: Andrew Davison.

Left: Francis Strange with first husband, William McClellend, son of Dr. C. V. McClellend.
Right: Theodore Strange and Clifford Strange, 1981.

T PETER TIMCHUK

Peter Timchuk came to Canada from Austria in 1896. He married Annie Tanaschuk in 1905, and farmed the SE ¼ of 36-1-4 E1. They had ten children: Mary, John, Bill, Annie, Steve, Faye, Pauline, Teena and Michael. Peter eventually acquired seven quarters of land, which he divided among his sons.

Mary married Steve Lozowy in 1923. They have three sons: Roy, Paul and Fred.

Roy married Lena Holowaty in 1966. They have three children: Jaunita, Darsy and Mark.

Fred married Brenda Chapman in 1969. They have three children: Rebecca, Nathan and Jason.

Bill married Mary Bodz in 1934. They farmed NW ¼ 5-2-5 E1. They have three children: Ted, Margaret and Anthony.

Ted married Marily Holland in 1962 and has four children: Richard, Karen, Robert and Curtis.

Margaret married Allan Graham in 1961 and has three children: Debra, Donna and Wayne.

Anthony married Jackie Yvon in 1971 and they have two children: Randy and Charlene.

Anne married Bloom Croft in 1937.

Steve farmed in Franklin from 1937 to 1970.

Nancy married George Magoon in 1946, and has three children: Denise, Caprice and George II.

Denise married George Nannette in 1966, and they have three children: Shannon, Caprice and Stephen.

Caprice married George Sutton in 1975, and they have two children: George Jr. and Jennifer.

Pauline married Marley Gibson in 1938, and they have two children: Carole and Joan.

Carole married Trevor Gordon in 1962, and they have three children: Paula, Robert and Jamie.

Michael married Maria Dawydiuk in 1944. They live on NE ¼ 26-1-4 and also farm SE ¼ 26-1-4. They have four children: Lorne, Charlotte, Raymond and Bruce.

Lorne married JoAnne Reimer in 1970 and they have two children: Lee and Lacey.

Bruce married Linda Hermanson in 1979 and they have two children: Troy and Jessica.

Peter and Annie Timchuk

Mary, Annie, Pauline, Faye and Teena Timchuk.

441

Steve and Mary Lozowy, Paul, Fred and Roy.

Left: Bill and Mary Timchuk, (holding) Tony, Margaret and Ted.
Right: Pauline and Morley Gibson, Carole and Joan.

Bloom and Annie Croft; Steve Timchuk.

Michael and Maria Timchuk; George and Nancy Magoon.

442

ED THIESSEN

Ed Thiessen came to Canada in 1924, from Russia, with his parents Frank and Susan Thiessen. His wife, Eleanor (Isaac) arrived at the same time with her parents, Aron and Mary Isaacs.

Mr. and Mrs. Frank Thiessen retired to Winnipeg, where Frank died in 1965. Susan Thiessen lives at Sunset House, in Winnipeg, a healthy 92 years.

Aron and Mary Isaacs moved to Ontario in 1972. Aron died April, 1981, Mary lives in retirement in Winnipeg.

Ed and Eleanor farm section 35-3-3 E1, and have four children: Lois, lives in Steinbach; Mark, at home; Carol and Gwen, are in school in Dominion City.

Frank and Susan Thiessen

Front, Marty, Eleanore, Henry and Aron J. Isaac; back, Abe, Aron Jr., Menno, Walter.

Back, Mark, Ed, Lois; front, Eleanor, Gwen and Carol Thiessen.

JACOB AND JOHN THIESSEN

Jacob and John Thiessen came to the municipality in 1938, from Russia, and lived on this farm until 1953, when he went to Winnipeg, returning in 1974. Susan, his wife, was born in the municipality. They married in 1963. They have three boys and one girl: Wesley, in grade 11; Donald, grade 10; Rachel, grade 8; and Ernest, grade 5. They live on 6-3-3 E1, the former Stanley Romaniuk farm.

Jacob's brother, John and Rose Thiessen farm section 14-2-5 E1, purchased from the William P. Thiessens in 1948. The land has been registered in the names of The Crown, John Lee Johnson, Robert A. Dicksen, Theodosy Wachna, William P. Thiessen 1935. They have seven children: Darlene, Grace, Carol, Arthur, Marilyn, Lois, Debbie and Kelvin.

Darlene married David Holland, and has a daughter and son.

Grace married Ralph Gliege, has a son and daughter.

Carol is a nurse and married Ted Hartag, has one son.

Arthur married Jacqueline Kimber, has two sons.

Marilyn married Melvin Thiessen and lives in Carlowrie, and has a daughter.

Lois is a graduate of Winnipeg Bible College. Debbie from Briercrest Bible Institute. Kelvin is in school in Vita.

Jacob and Susan Thiessen, Rachel.

Ernest, Donald and Wesley Thiessen.

Ted Hartog, Kelvin Thiessen, David Holland, Lois Thiessen, John Thiessen, Arthor Thiessen, Ralph Gliege and Debbie Thiessen, Melvin Thiessen, Carol Hartog holding Clinton, Darlene Holland, Rose Thiessen, Jacqueline Thiessen holding Trevor, Grace Gliege and Lynden, Marilyn Thiessen holding Charlene Thiessen, Shelley Hartog and Darren Holland, Jeffrey Thiessen, Luanne Gliege.

ALEXANDER ANDERSON TAYLOR

Alexander Anderson Taylor was born in Craickie, ForFar, Scotland, 1860. He came to the United States in 1878, in 1885 to Manitoba. At Morris he married Mary Charrette of LaSalle in 1903. They had 12 children: Joseph, Josephine, Elizabeth, Kathleen, Louis, James, Annie, William, Sarah Agnes, Stelle, and two daughters deceased.

In 1919 they moved to the CPR section house in Dominion City where Alex continued as section foreman until retirement into the Scott house, in which son William lives.

Joseph married Christina Hoas of Meadows.

Josie married Dawson Baskerville, had 10 children.

Lizzie married Jim Dowswell, had three children.

Kay married Bob Vollett of Winnipeg.

Louis married Agatha Veitch, had two daughters: Nancy (Armstrong), and Nita (Dey) of Van, B.C.

James married Nancy Miller, a war bride.

Annie married Jim Waddell, had four children.

Bill married Georgina Opocensky, had five daughters.

Mary Jane married Bill Ball.

Stelle married Sid Varcoe, and had a son, Stormer.

Lizzie, Annie and Bill are living in 1982.

Bill's children are: Cheryl Leith, born August, Tanys, Jillayn, Ginger Lynden, Melodie Joy, 1958, died an infant.

Cheryl, a single parent, has two children, Tiffany and Ryder Taylor.

Tanys married Michael Empson from Marais and has two sons, Jaison and Brittain.

Jill married Bob Barlow from Myrtle, and has two daughters: Tanner Quinn and Jessica.

Ginger lives in Vancouver.

Bill became postmaster in 1951, retired in 1981. Georgina retired as assistant postmaster in 1981.

James, 1913 to 1977, had a daughter Catherine, born in 1942, in England; and Andrew, 1950; David, 1953 in Canada. Andrew joined the navy, and married Leslie Keelin, has two daughters: Kathleen and Jaimie. David is a chartered accountant.

Alexander and Mary Taylor

William and Georgina Taylor

Georgina and Bill Taylor; back, Jill, Ginger, Tanys and Cheryl.

Jason and Brittain Moore Empson.

Tiffany and Ryder Taylor.

WASYL TANCHUK

Wasyl Tanchuk came to Canada with his wife Maria (Andrushko) and sons: Petro, born 1880; Ivan, born 1884; and Stefan, 1893. Maria was 40 years, and Wasyl, born 1854, 43. They came from Galacia, to the SW ¼ 10-3-5 E1. They farmed here until 1919, when they moved to a 10 acre lot at Rosa, where they lived until their death.

Ivan, called John, married Anna Ferenetz, and bought the SE ¼ 25-3-5 E1. Later he bought a store at Alonsa. He had no children. They retired to Winnipeg and then to Vancouver. John died November 4, 1957, Anna October 4, 1972. Buried in Vancouver.

Petro, called Peter, had learned the latin alphabet in Galacia, and learned English quickly. He married Maria Mihaychuk, born 1883, from Bukovina. They farmed the SE ¼ 9-3-5 E1, and in 1907 took the post office into his house. He named it Rosa, for ros sa, meaning dew in Ukrainian.

In 1910 he moved to the NE ¼ 22-3-5 E1, and S ½ 27-3-5 E1, taking the post office with him. He kept a store for 27 years. They had seven children. They are: William, teacher, went to Vancouver, deceased; John, teacher, married Doris Osadchuk, had a store at Ridgeville for 36 years, and has two children; Dmytro was born in 1907, teacher, married Nastazia Machnee in 1934. In 1939 they bought a house in Tolstoi, had a garage, retired in 1972, had one son, Manuel, and two grandsons, Sydney and Michael; Helen, teacher, retired in Ottawa; Manuel, teacher, retired to British Columbia; Steve, ran his father's farm, joined RCAF, became a commercial pilot, deceased; Maurice lived on farm with his mother after father died, enlisted RCAF during war, then went to Neepawa, and to Vancouver where he is in the automobile business.

Jill, Bob, Jessica and Tanner Barlow.

Wasyl and Maria Tanchuk, Steve, Ann and John.

445

Peter and Maria Tanchuk, Helen.

John, Dan, Manuel and Helen Tanchuk.

Left: The Andrushko sisters, Dokia (Panchyshyn) and Maria (Tanchuk).
Right: Steven Tanchuk.

William, Anna and Elena Tanchuk.

JACK TURNER

Jack and Mary Turner of Moose Jaw, moved to Dominion City in 1918 to manage the hardware store for C. A. Whitman of Emerson. He had two children: Edwin and Irene. Jack managed the store until the time of his death in 1937 at which time Edwin and Mary Turner managed the store until 1943, when Edwin joined the services. The store was sold to North American Lumber.

In 1940 Edwin married Doris Davies of Otterburne. They had three children: Diana, John and Brenda. Edwin died in 1977.

Irene was married in 1939 to Bob Davies of Otterburne. They had two children: Alice and Jim, both live in Winnipeg.

Alice married Lloyd Fariest of Niverville, and has two children: Donna and Delwyn.

Mary Turner made her home with Irene until the time of her death in 1972.

Maurice and Rose Tanchuk

Jack and Mary Turner

Edwin and Doris Turner

GEORGE WILLIAM TURNER

George William Turner, born 1858, came from Moortown, Ontario. He married Jean Clarkson Ross in 1883, and they came to live along boundary at Emerson.

He bought the Peter and Angus McBean farms, 9-1-4 E1 and 3-1-4 E1. George had seven children by his first wife, and three by another, with one child dying young. His second wife was Eva Stewart Turner. Their children were: Russell Hamilton, George Stewart, Margaret Mae (Elkin), Velma Jean (Groenwald), Vernon Franklin, Clarence Calvin, killed in World War II, Ross Emerson, Roy Ernest, Joyce Irene (Newgard) and Morris Lyle.

Stewart Turner bought the farm from his father in 1947, and sold to Malcolm Cook in 1977.

Four generations of Turners: George Turner Jr., George Turner Sr., Russell Turner and his son, Jim Turner, 1919.

Left: Frank Turner, Bessie (Stewart) Turner and daughter Joan, farmed on Section 3-1-4 E1. They retired to Emerson.
Right: Calvin Turner - 1942 bomber pilot killed overseas in 1943.

Back, Margaret, Stuart, Roy; centre, Vernon, Morris, Joyce, Velma, Ross; front, Russell c. 1980.

Lois Turner, her husband Craig Lang and children Kelly and Darren, 1981.

447

Tom and Doris Trottier, Jason and Bryan.

TOM TROTTIER

Tom and Doris Trottier came to Dominion City from North Dakota in 1973. Their sons are: Jason and Bryan, born here.

ALEX TKACHYK

Alex and Frosyna Tkachyk came to Canada in 1898 with five children: Alex, Alexandra, Anna, Olenka and Jack. Homestead on NE 10-2-5E.

Alex Tkachyk was born in 1857 in Khudykivci district, Borchchiv, Galacia, Austria.

Frosyna was born in 1859, daughter of Ivan Larga and Maria Andrunyk.

Alex died December 7, 1941 in Melfort, Saskatchewan. Maria died June 22, 1920, in Tolstoi.

Two daughters, Mary and Katherina were born in Canada.

Jack married Anna Fedirchyk in 1921. They had four children: Elsie, Mary, Helen and Billy. They retired to Vita in the early 1960's.

Elsie married Peter Martiniuk, and lives in Winnipeg. They have three children: Shirley, Richard and Gordon. Gordon is married and has one son; Richard is married and has one son and one daughter; Shirley is married.

Mary married Eric Anderson, and lives in Emerson. They have a son, Eric who is married and has a son, Eric Jr.

Helen married Maurice Ottawa, and lives in Vita. They have a daughter, Theresa. Theresa is married to Allen Skrumeda and they have a son, Shawn.

Billy was killed in a car accident in November, 1957.

Alex and Frosyna Tkackyk; Billy Tkackyk.

Elsie and Peter Martiniuk, Jack and Anna Tkackyk, Helen and Maurice Ottawa.

Mary Anderson; Theresa Skrumeda.

Eric Jr., Mary and Eric Anderson.

Peter and Elsie Marteniuk, Richard, Shirley and Gordon.

HENRY TIMLICK

Henry Timlick was born in North Augusta, Ontario. He married Ellen Ferguson on July 4, 1874. In 1878 they travelled by horse and buggy to Manitoba, which took all summer. With no place to live, Henry dug two holes in the bank of the Marsh River, one for the family and one for the horses.

The Red River flooded three years out of four, and they moved to 14-3-4 E1. Henry farmed there until he retired to Winnipeg in 1922, and James took over the farm. Henry lived to be 106 years old. He died January 18, 1951. Ellen predeceased him in 1940.

The Timlicks had 10 children: Robert, who married Teresa Sullivan and had seven children; David, who married Mabel Post and had seven children; Maggie, who married Ferg Reed and had 14 children; Jason, who married Lily Knox and had six children; Lizzie, who married John McVicar and had four children; James, who married Mary Nisely, and following her death, Annie Calder; Nellie, who married James Brunton and had two girls; and Mary, Jenny, and John.

David, who was born September 16, 1879, homesteaded at St. Jean when he was 18. He received help from his uncle, David Timlick, of Domain. Later, he sold his homestead and moved to Newbridge where he bought the E ½ 9-3-4 E1. He married Mabel Post, daughter of Candace and Orlin Post of Woodmore, born April 25, 1887. She died in October of 1977. They had seven children.

Dave Timlick died in 1936. His widow remained and owned the farm until just before her death at age 92. She sold the farm to her son, Grant, who had been 30 years in the R.C.A.F. Grant decided not to farm, and retired in Vernon, B.C. with wife, Marion and daughter, Lesley Ann.

Wallace passed away in 1939.

Russell passed away at age two years in 1911.

Irene married George Anderson, and they have three children: Wendy (Bezan), George Jr., and

Margaret (Laurie). There are 10 grandchildren.

Pearl married Norman Munroe and they had three children: Irene (Hunter), Barbara (Campbell) and Sandra (Wyenberg). They have six grandchildren.

Theodore married Sigrun Johnson, and had two children: Malcolm and Karen (LeMaistre). Malcolm has a daughter.

Gwendolyn, the youngest daughter, following the death of her first husband, Andy Stewart, married George Olden, and lives at Green Ridge.

Henry and Ellen Timlick

David, Robert, Henry and Ellen Timlick, Jennie, John; front, Maggie, Jim, Elizabeth and Nellie.

Mary Timlick; Jason Timlick.

David and Mabel Timlick

David, Wesley, George, Henry Timlick, sister Mary Griffin.

Nellie and Jim Brunton, Mabel and Lillian.

Mary, Jim and Warren Timlick.

NYKOLA TOFAN

Nykola Tofan (1901-1978) arrived in Canada in 1897. He was born December 17, 1863 in Synkiw, Western Ukraine. His wife, Maria (Tanashyk) was born 1873, also in Synkiw. They had three children: Annytza, 4; Ivan, 3; and Sofia, 1.

Nykola Tofan and his family homesteaded the NE ¼ 13-1-5 in 1901. He lived here until 1953. After the death of Nykola, January 21, 1953, son Anthony farmed until 1978.

Annytza married William Saranchuk, died in 1980, at Primrose, Alberta. She is survived by three sons, one daughter and six grandchildren and seven great-grandchildren.

Ivan, single, lives in Edmonton.

Sofia, married Joe Domonski, and has two sons and four grandchildren, and three great-grandchildren.

Bill, married Millie Pachailo, in Fort Frances, Ontario, and has two sons, one daughter, 12 grandchildren and six great-grandchildren.

Peter, married Margaret Peleshok, Detroit, and has three sons, eight grandchildren, and two great-grandchildren.

Steve, married Lena Druzuik, Michigan, and has two children.

Annytza, John, William, Nykola, Sofia, Maria holding Steve; front, Peter Tofan, 1908.

Pauline, Ann and Sophie; standing, Matt, Peter, Anton, Steve, John, Mike Tofan.

Metro and Mike, twins born September 28, 1908. Metro married Alexandra Stasiuk, and has one daughter, two sons and three grandchildren. Mike is single, lived in Windsor, now in Tolstoi, and is employed by Ford of Canada.

Pauline, lives in Winnipeg.

Anton, married Nettie Kozak, lived on the home place until 1978, now retired to Tolstoi on 36-1-5. They have one daughter, Patricia, and son-in-law Dennis of Naniamo, B.C., and one granddaughter Sheryl of St. Onge.

STEVE TANCHUK

Steve Tanchuk came to Senkiw with his parents in 1897. At age 14 he was hired to do kitchen work during harvest for an English farmer, and learned English.

In 1910, age 17, he bought the SW ¼ of 28-3-5 E1 and S ½ of the NW ¼ of 28-3-5 E1 from the Hudson's Bay Company at $3 an acre.

In 1919 he married Warwara Holasis. Their daughter Maria and husband Wasyl Paley looked after the farm when they retired.

Steve died in 1964, and is buried in Senkiw Orthodox Cemetery. Warwara lived with the Paleys after Steve's death, suffered a stroke in 1979, died 1981.

Steve and Warwara had two daughters:

Anna, born January 3, 1931, worked in a bank, taught school, joined the RCAF, then married Louis Auriat, a teacher. They have two children: Damien and Nadia, and live at Embrum, Ontario.

Maria, married Wasyl Paley in 1948. They had one son, Wasyl Jr., known as Bill, who farmed and then went to Winnipeg. Maria and Wasyl lived on the Tanchuk farm, while Wasyl did construction work until c.1970, when a heart condition forced him into retirement. He died in 1975. Maria continues to live on the farm.

Wasyl, son of Hryhori and Anna (Zaparzan) Palij (Paley), was born in Senkow, Ukraine. His father was an Austrian soldier, and was mobilized during the second world war, as was Wasyl. When the war ended, Wasyl wrote to his cousin, Nick Paley of Rosa, and obtained permission to come to Canada. He came December 20, 1947.

Steve and Warwara Tanchuk

Wasyl, son Wasyl Harry Jr. and Maria Paley.

Left: St. Louis Charles Auriat as a teacher in the Navy.
Right: Anna (Auriat) Tanchuk.

451

Domain Auriat with Grandmother Warwara Tanchak; Nadia Auriat.

Sally Todoruk and Mary (Todoruk) Zahara.

PROKOP TODORUK

Prokop Todoruk came to Canada in 1907 at the age of 15. He worked for the CN and then bought the SW ¼ of 24-1-5E.

Anelia, his wife, daughter of the late J. Drewniak came to Canada at the age of 12 in 1910 from the West Ukraine.

Prokop and Anelia were married in 1914. Amelia was well known for her cooking at banquets, weddings and other occasions.

Their children are Sally Gawron, Mary Zahara, who married Mike Zahara, Annie who died in infancy in 1929. Mike, married Daphnee Ivamy of Burnaby, B.C.

Mrs. Todoruk passed away in 1955. Prokop Todoruk passed away April, 1975 at the age of 82.

They have seven grandchildren and five great-grandchildren. The grandchildren are Nester Gawron, Donna Todoruk, Donald, Gordon, Allan and Eddie Zahara and Eva Goletski (nee Zahara).

Mike Todoruk, daughter Donna, wife Daphnee.

RÉAL TETRAULT

Réal Tetrault born in 1948, was raised at Letellier and attended school at Letellier and St. Jean. When he was five and a half years old his father Marcel Tetrault was accidently killed. His mother married Paul Fortier and they reside in Letellier.

Réal worked in the Bank at St. Jean and Winnipeg for six years. In July 1971 he married Leona Schwark, daughter of Art and Ruth Schwark. Leona graduated as a Medical Labratory Technologist from the St. Boniface Hospital in 1972. Réal graduated in 1976 from the Diploma course in Agriculture and the same year they moved to Franklin Municipality and farmed with Art and Ken Schwark. In 1977 they bought the farms NW ¼ of 2-1-3 and SE ¼ of 2-1-3 from Art Schwark. They have two children - René Bryan born July 7, 1978 and Lisa Marie born January 31, 1980.

In November 1980 Réal became councillor of Ward 1 of Franklin Municipality - which is the

Prokop and Anelia Todoruk

same Ward as Leona's grandfather Reinhold Weiss was councillor of for 19 years.

This land NW ¼ of 2-1-3 was farmed by a Mr. Vickers in 1883. In 1899 Henry Hartwig Sr., great-grandfather to Leona Tetrault bought the land. The house, a barn and some other buildings were there at that time. In 1926 a new barn was built, a hip roof barn 50 x 30 - painted red. The loft floor is made of four inch fir flooring so made an excellent dance floor. The Seed Club held several dances on this loft. Local people played for the dances - Emil Steg, Ted Lange, Charlie Marks, Mr. Gonske and others. All other original buildings are still there and in use. A bin built in 1900, a car shed, a summer kitchen converted to a brooder house and is now used as a bin. An ice house was used until 1949 when electricity came in.

Henry Hartwig Sr. passed away in 1931 and the land was worked by two children, Henry Hartwig Jr. and Mathilda, Mrs. Theodore Schwark. The house was rented for two to three years and was vacant until 1942 when Art Schwark grandson to Henry Hartwig Sr. bought the land. At that time a basement was put under the house, new shingles over the old ones, new siding, and windows. It was also remodelled inside.

An addition was also added to the barn to store machinery in 1967.

Art and Ruth Schwark retired in 1977 and at that time Réal and Leona bought their two farms. They again remodelled the interior of the house but the original walls, roof, floors and floor joists remain. In 1981 a patio was added and the barn received new shingles and was painted white. In 55 years it was painted three times. Several steel bins and a grain drying facility have been added to the yard. Réal and Leona live on the N.E. ¼ of 2-1-3.

Real Tetrault, holding Rene Bryan, Leona (Schwark) Tetrault, holding Lisa Marie.

OTTO VON DRACEK

Otto Von Dracek, his wife and son Joseph, came from Poland in 1928. They bought a farm at Ridgeville, lost it, and moved to Tolstoi. They rented a house for $25 a year, and earned $28 harvesting. In 1935 he bought 80 acres. In 1946 Otto bought a larger farm, on which Joseph is living. Otto died in 1969, age 80. Anna lives in a retirement house on the farm.

Joseph married Blanche Minarz, daughter of Joseph Minarz of Darlingford. They farmed at Tolstoi until 1954, moved to Darlingford for two years, then back to Tolstoi. They have three daughters and one son: Emily Ann, Lillian Elizabeth, Carol Diane and Jerry James.

Anna and Otto Von Dracek, 1960.

Jerry, Lillian, Joseph, Emily, Carol; seated, Blanche, 1973.

Jerry, James and Iris (Poschner) Von Dracek.

Walter, Emily and Candice Harder

Shauneen and Larry Chubey; Tim, Kelly and Brett Namba.

LEON VANDEVEIRE

Leon and Vivian VanDeveire moved to Dominion City in 1960. Leon opened the Co-op store in 1961.

In 1964 the Dominion City Credit Union was founded and Leon became it's first manager. In 1964 Leon and Vivian purchased the farm of Victor Crook, where they farmed until 1978, when they moved to Dominion City. Leon is employed by Simplot Soilbuilders.

They have four daughters: Shauneen, Lorri, Kelly and Kimberly.

Shauneen married Larry Chubey, son of Jack Chubey of Overstoneville.

Lorri married Patrick French, son of Ken French of Dominion City. They have three children: Shawn, Jeffery and Darla Dawn.

Kelly married Tim Namba, son of Min Namba of Dominion City. They have one son, Brett.

Kimberly married Terry Pearse, and have one son, Stan Pearse.

THOMAS AND NOAH VAREY

Thomas and Noah Varey, brothers, came from England about 1873.

Thomas married a Daniels girl from St. Vincent, and had two sons: Mark died at Hallock, North Dakota; and Henry lived in Minneapolis.

Noah married a half sister of Thomas's wife, and farmed the W ½ of 22-3-4 E1. He built the first brick house in the area, with bricks from the Dominion City Brickyard and lime from his own farm. He was a trained bricklayer, and many chimneys, culverts and basements show his skill as a mason. There was no resident minister when he came to Franklin, and a transient man of the cloth caught him up on his own roof making the chimney. He climbed down long enough to fetch his bride and he married, and then continued with the chimney.

Noah had six children: Jack remained on the home farm, and married Nellie Hunter. He died in Winnipeg in 1980 at age 90; Alice kept house for Jack until his marriage and then lived with Art in Winnipeg; Art lived in Winnipeg; Mary married a man named Angele and lived in St.

Paul, Minnesota; Bella married a man named Brown; and Bill farmed and later moved to Winnipeg.

The Noah Varey homestead is owned by nephews of Jack, being Bill and Cal Varey, in 1982.

Mrs. Tom Varey

Leon and Vivian VanDeveire, Shauneen, Lorri, Kelly and Kim.

W GUSTAV WALTERS

Gustav Walters was born in Valenia, Poland, 1876. He immigrated to Neche, North Dakota, with his mother Henrietta Walters, four brothers and one sister. His father died in Poland. In 1902 he met Emma Kein, from Poland, born 1884. She lived at Gretna with her parents Andrew and Julianna Kein, four sisters and one brother. They were married January 6, 1903. They farmed at Fredendsthal on her parents land, and had eight children: Lydia (Mrs. Emil Steg), Theodore, Emil, Albert, Annie (Mrs. Albert Steg), Ella (Mrs. William Lange), Mae (Mrs. Walter Neuman) deceased April 7, 1977, Ruth (Mrs. Len Flagel) and Henry, died an infant.

Gustav and Emma retired to Emerson in 1946, and Albert took over the farm. Albert and his wife Hilda farmed there for 26 years, had four children: Norman, Ken, Janice (Mrs. Ron Schnell) and Allan.

In 1972 Albert and Hilda retired to Emerson and Allan took over. Allan and his wife Donna have since sold the farm and moved to Woodmore.

Theodore, farmed with Emil, but did not like it. After various jobs, including work on the assembly line in Detroit, he purchased a repair shop in Ridgeville in 1937 from Mrs. H. Francis for $100. In 1938 he married Bertha Schwark, daughter of Gustav and Ottilie Schwark. In 1960 he moved to Emerson, buying the Border Service Garage. They have three children: Evelyn, teacher, lives in Montreal; Joan, an assistant professor, is in Winnipeg; Don, operates the family garage in partnership with Maurice Dupuis. Ted and Bertha are retired in Emerson.

Emil married Ida Schultz, in 1909, went to Alberta for a while, came back to Franklin in 1912 to farm. They had eight children: Ted, married Alma Casper in 1939 and farmed until 1973 when he retired to Morris. Has one son, Larry, married Geraldine Carriere, now deceased. He has two children: Angela and Sheldon, lives in Morris.

William, single, farmed until his death in 1973, age 61.

Bertha married Wiliam Schwark in 1938. Farmed, retired to Winnipeg. Has one son, Wayne, married Donna Laufersweiler, has two children, Dwight and Lisa.

Paul married Mabel Casper in 1946, farmed, moved to Dominion City in 1965. Has one daughter, Velinda Lynn, married Karl Humeniuk. Has two children: Melissia Dawn and Michael Paul, lives in Saskatchewan.

Alma married Willis Finney in 1944, farmed until 1970. Has three children: Sandra, Mrs.

Robert Olson, who has three children: Melissa and Anna-Liesa; Joyce, married Bryan Lofberg, Texas, has two children: Brandon and Jillayne; Norma, married Judson Nelson, farms in Minnisota, has one daughter, Kerry.

Annie married Kalvin Sylvester at Hallock in 1942. Has one son, Terrance, married to Mary Jane Woinarwiez, who has two daughters: Beth and Lisa.

Stanley married Dorothy Triechel and farmed at Green Ridge, moved to Steinbach and then to the North West Territories.

Gustav and Emma Walters, Mae.

Emil, Albert, Ted, Lydia; front, Ruth, Mae, Ella, and Annie.

Paul and Mabel Walters; Karl and Velinda Humeniuk, Michael and Melissia.

455

Ted and Alma Walters, Larry. Sheldon and Angela.

THOMAS WOODS

Thomas Woods was born in Trowbridge, England in 1865. He immigrated to Wisconsin where he married Ida Agnes Hanson in 1894.

In 1896 they came to Emerson. Arthur and Dora were born here. Thomas homesteaded the NW ¼ 13-1-4 E1 in 1898.

In 1900 the family moved to the farm. Lily was born in 1900; Annie, September 9, 1902; Thomas, May 7, 1905; William Henry, November 26, 1907, died February 23, 1912 of pneumonia; Agnes, November 20, 1910.

Thomas and Ida farmed until Ida's death in 1933. In 1938 Harry and Lily (Woods) Wilkinson bought the farm. Thomas died April 13, 1950.

Arthur served in the first world war. On his return he farmed SE ¼ 19-1-5 E1. He married Gladys Butt, and had one son, Lorne. He moved to the United States where he worked for the Ford Co. in St. Paul, Minnesota, later farmed.

Lorne married Betty ? and has two children: Lorie and Susan. Lorne and Arthur are deceased.

Dora married George Millar of Stuartburn in 1926, and had one daughter, Eileen. George died in 1948. Dora married Robert Bullock, and lives in Vancouver, B.C.

Eileen married John Feechuk, and had one son, Dale.

Thomas Jr. farmed at Ridgeville and then immigrated to the United States. He married Aurelia Reder on July 2, 1931. They had six children: Beverley, Thomas, Richard and Robert (twins), Gary and Debbie.

Emil and Ida Walters; Stanley and Dorothy Walters.

Ted and Bertha Walters.

Dora, Ida (Hanson) Woods holding Tom, Lily, Thomas Woods holding Annie, Arthur.

Thomas and Ida Woods; Dora and George Miller.

Woods family with their horses in front of a log barn that is still on the farm of a grandson, Vernon Wilkinson (13-1-4E). L to r; Thomas Woods, Dora, Annie, Ida Woods, Arthur.

Thomas and Aurelia (Reder) Woods, Bob, Gary, Dick, Beverly, Thomas Jr. and Debbie, 1981.

WILLIAM HERBERT WILKINSON

William Herbert Wilkinson, 1859, was born in Burgh Lee Marsh, England. In 1885 he worked on the C.P.R. and met Rose Martha Fields who worked at Dominion City Queen's Hotel. They married July 13, 1886. William took up a homestead near Overstoneville, and lived with Rose's parents on SW ¼ 27-1-4 E1. They were post masters at the old log cabin till the post office moved into town in 1902, and took over the farm when William Fields died in 1888.

Rose and William had 14 children: Lily, married Fred Lenton; Martha, married Harry Clifford and then Herb Francis; Herbert; George, 1892-1914; Alice married William Lindsay; Beatrice, married Sam Stringer and then Jack Stringer; Tom (died age one and a half); Harry; Albert; Bertha married Bob Howard; Nelson; stillborn daughter; Rose married Alf Laufesswieler; and Clifford.

William Herbert (1891-1958) was in the army in World War I. In 1919 he bought the James Auld farm, NE ¼ 28-1-4 E1, and married Lucy Knaggs of England in 1922. They had three children: Roy, William and Nancy.

Roy Frederick married Lillian Weiss of Ridgeville in 1949. He served in the World War II army. They were in the dairy business on SE 27-1-4E. They have three sons: Marvin, Sidney and Leslie.

Marvin married Darlene McLennan in 1975. They live in Green Ridge.

Sidney farms the NE 27-1-4E.

Leslie married Judy Kerda in 1976. They live on SW 16-1-4E. They have two girls: Jodie and Lisa.

William Herbert married Eleanor Weiss of Ridgeville in 1952. He took over his father's farm in 1958 and later purchased the Fields - Wilkinson homestead. They have two children: Sherry and Allan.

Sherry married Robert Gibson in 1974 and has two sons: Michael and Steven.

Nancy Rose is an R.N. at Concordia Hospital in Winnipeg.

Harry, 1898, married Lily Woods of Ridgeville in 1928, and bought the NW ¼ 13-1-4 E1. They have retired to Dufferin Courts, Emerson. They have three sons: Elton, Vernon and Glenn.

Elton married Joan Braun of Plum Coulee in 1965, and lives in The Pas. They have three children: Michelle, Douglas and Kimberly.

Vernon married Carol McVicar of Dominion City in 1959. In 1966 they bought the home farm and are in the dairy business on NW ¼ 13-1-4E plus two other quarters which previously supported the Kraynik, Cherneski, Leach, Bredin, E. Goetz (NE ¼ 13-1-4 E1) and Buffey (SE ¼ 13-1-4 E1) families. They have two sons: Timothy and Richard.

Glenn married Betty Weiss of Dominion City in 1961 and lives in Transcona. They have one son, Mark.

James Albert (1900-1956) married Frances

457

Cherneski in 1925 (who died in 1926). October 31, 1927 he married Annie Woods of Ridgeville. They bought the Eichman home in Ridgeville and Albert did mechanical work. In 1951 they moved to the NE ¼ 22-1-4 E1, where they lived until his death. They had four children: Willis, Ardith, Delores (married George Wasson), and Garry.

Willis Neil married Jean Kubas in 1955 and they have four children: Cynthia, Conrad, Corinne and Christopher.

Ardith June married Charles Jackman in 1954 and had four children: Cory, Dean, Kimberley and Colin. She married Harvey Ducharme in 1965 and they have four children: Harvey Jr., Wesley, and twins Denise and Tanis.

Garry Thomas married Carolyn Reinisch and has twins Shier and Charmaine.

Nelson Marshall, 1904, married Evelyn Brittain of Winnipeg in 1929. He worked for the Winnipeg Parks Board, then retired to Landmark. They have two children: Joyce and Donald.

Joyce Corinne married Joe Kruk in 1957 and has three children: Shannon, Cameron and Dana.

Donald Lorne married Eileen Harding in 1952 and has four children: Gregory, married Susan Woodley in 1974 and has two children: Drew and Heather; Leslie, married Doug Kemash in 1979 and has one son, Ryan; Dean; Tracy, married Carl Bennett in 1980.

Clifford Edward, 1910, farmed the home place in 1928-1956. He then moved into town and worked on Tanchuk's Turkey farm until retirement.

Rose Wilkinson on her 88th birthday; back, Rose, Clifford, Nelson, Bertha, Martha, Albert, Herbert, Harry, Beatrice and Alice.

George Wilkinson; Nancy Wilkinson.

William and Lucy Wilkinson.

William and Rose Wilkinson

Bill and Eleanor Wilkinson, Allan and Sherry Gibson.

Darlene, Marvin, Judy, Lisa, Sidney, Roy; front, Leslie, Jody and Lillian.

Bob Gibson, Michael and Steven.

Left: Harry and Lily Wilkinson.
Right: Elton and Joan Wilkinson, Doug, Michelle and Kimberly.

Left: Vernon and Carol Wilkinson, Tim and Rick.
Right: Glen and Betty Wilkinson, Mark.

Albert Wilkinson; Charmaine and Shier Wilkinson.

Ardith, Annie Wilkinson, Delores; back, Garry and Willis.

Jean and Willis Wilkinson, Corinne, Conrad, Cynthia; front, Annie Wilkinson and Christopher.

Back, Joe Kruk, Joyce (Wilkinson) Kruk, Eileen (Harding) Wilkinson, Doug Komash, with Ryan, Leslie (Kruk) Kemash; front, Dana Kruk, Evelyn (Brittain) and Nelson Wilkinson, Cameron Kruk. Shannon Kruk.

Left: Ardith Jackman, Kimberley, Dean, Colin and Cory.
Right: Ardith and Harney Ducharme, twins Denise and Tanis, Harney Jr. and Wesley.

Joyce and Don Wilkinson

ALEX WADDELL

Alex Waddell came to Franklin Municipality from Orono, Ontario, in 1874, to homestead the NW ¼ of 20 and the NW ¼ of 21. In 1876 he married Isabelle McKercher, daughter of Duncan McKercher, who arrived in 1874.

Alex and Isabelle had three children:

Nina, born 1879, married Peter Dahlberg. She was a graduate in pharmacy from the University of Manitoba in 1914.

James, married Ann Taylor, was a civil engineer. He had five children: Shelagh, married Wally Wiebe and has three children: Tannis, Hillary and Holly; Shannon, married John Friesen and has a son, Troy; Sandra, married Gerry Kenner and has three children: James, Robin and Jonathon; Pamela, married Paul Clemens and has a daughter, Christina; Mark,

460

married Sandra Pearse and has three children: Amber, Brooke and Angela.

Lena, born 1881, married Gordon Kippen and had two children: Isabella (Mousseau), and James. She studied law and education at the University of Manitoba.

Alex and Isabelle Waddell

Lena, Nina and James Waddell.

Troy and Shannon Friesen; Ann Waddell.

James Kippon; Isabella Morrisseau.

Wally and Shelagh Wiebe, Tannis, Hilary and Holly.

Gerry and Sandra Kenner, James, Robin and Jonathon.

Paul, Pamela and Christiana Clemens.

Mark and Sandra Waddell, Amber, Brooke and Angela.

BILL WHITEWAY

Judy and Bill Whiteway, Erin and Brian. Bill is a teacher at Roseau Valley Collegiate, and came to Dominion City in 1977.

WILLIAM WALTER WEEDMARK

William Walter Weedmark came to the SW ¼ of 10-3-2 E1 in 1881, with his wife Christina (McVean) and John, three, and William, nine months. George was born in 1884, and Ada Mae in 1888. William was not a farmer, and soon moved to Dominion City, where he did odd jobs.

John went to Saskatchewan, married Nellie Green, and had three boys and one girl.

William married Susan Wallman and had four

461

boys and five girls. Like his parents, he went blind. He died in 1966, at the home of his daughter Mary Raw. Susan died in 1967, a victim of arthritis. Their nine children are: Katie, Mrs. R. Wennett, Regina; Joseph, died 1977; Mary, married M. Raw; Isobelle Wallman, died 1978; Walter; Susie Somerville Inkster, died 1974; Christina, married G. Jones, Brandon; Ralph, Ontario; Jacob, died 1980.

Ada Mae married George Raw, had two sons: Harold and Albert and a daughter Evelyn (Robson), divorced and married James Grismer.

William died in 1931, and Christina in 1931. They were both blind before their deaths.

George married Mary Ellen Crampton, born c.1889, daughter of John and Alvina (Cottrell) Crampton. George had a dairy, and raised four children: Eva, married William Pearse; Myrtle married Chris Schwabe; George remained single, died 1979; Frederick Robert married Margaret Brooks, Emerson, and had eight boys and three girls.

George and Mary Ellen live with their daughter, Myrtle Schwabe. Frederick lives in Dominion City, and Eva Pearse and son live on a farm nearby.

Back, Annie Wallman O'Hara, Mae and Jim Grismer; front, Susz and Bill, George and Ella Weedmark.

Frederick, George Jr., George Sr. and Mary Ellen Weedmark, Eva and Myrtle.

462

Back, John, Frederick Robert Jr.; front, Dale, Frederick Robert Sr., George Weedmark, Stephan and James Weedmark, four generations.

JOHN WNUK

John Wnuk came to Gretna in 1895, with wife Anna, Joey, Nellie and Julia. They were cowherders in a Mennonite village until 1902. Peter was born in 1897, Frank in 1899, died in infancy, John born in 1901.

John moved to SE ¼ of 10-1-5 E1, where Mary was born in 1904. He sold the SE ¼ and bought the NE ¼ of 10-1-5 E1 in 1913. John died in 1923, leaving the land to Peter and John.

Julia married Joseph Olsonowski in 1915, and went to the United States. Joey married Sophie Gabrey in 1912, and went to Alberta. Nellie became blind and spent her life in Tache Nursing Home, died 1981, 88 years.

Mary married Adam Gaetz in 1922, and farmed at Tolstoi. She died 1944, leaving 11 children. Peter married Mary Gaetz in 1923, Anna Wnuk lived with them for six years.

John married Mary Sagan in 1929. He and Peter farmed the home place until 1942, when they divided the land. In 1958 Pete sold to son Joey and moved to Winnipeg. John and Mary live on their farm in retirement, and have a daughter Adeline in Winnipeg.

John Wnuk family

Harvey, Anna and Alfred Wagner, Ronald.

ALFRED WAGNER

Alfred was born April 23, 1903 in Silia, Germany. He immigrated to Canada in 1928. He worked in Saskatchewan, and in 1948 he married Anna Euphorsina Schwark, daughter of Theodore and Matilda Schwark. They came to Franklin Municipality in 1949.

In 1950 they rented from Theodore Schwark and in 1961 bought the SW ¼ 3-1-3 and the S ½ of NW 3-1-3. They farmed here until their retirement. In 1974 they sold to Ken Schwark, a nephew.

Alfred and Anna have two sons: Harvey Arthur, born October 14, 1949; and Ronald Alfred, born March 13, 1951, both in Winnipeg.

BERNARD WATERS

In 1933, Bernard Waters of Dominion City married Agatha Goertzen, oldest daughter of Frank Goertzen Sr., of Dominion City.

Agnes was born June 4, 1916 in Alexandrapole, Russia, and came to Canada in 1924.

Bernard was born June 26, 1881 in Yorkshire, England and came to Canada in 1910. In 1914 he joined the Armed Forces, the 44th Battalion Company A of Winnipeg and was overseas for four years.

Agnes (Goertzen, Waters, Schultz) Hohendorff with her twelve children.

Bernard and Agnes Waters

Bernard owned and operated the "Dominion City Star" for approximately five and a half years.

Bert and Agnes had 10 children. They are: Lillian and Dorothy (twins), Elizabeth, Jean, Sally, Richard, Robert, Norman and Norma (twins) and Linda. All are living in B.C. except Dorothy who lives in St. John, New Brunswick and Betty in Aubigny.

Bert died December 23, 1952. He is buried in Dominion City cemetery.

Agnes married Aron Shultz in 1954. She had two more children: Kennith and David Aron who died July 7, 1964. Agnes moved to British Columbia

On December 16, 1971 Agnes married Emil Hohendorff. They live in Richmond, B.C.

RODNEY WIELER

Rodney and Margaret (Fehr) Wieler moved from Hudson Hope, British Columbia to the SW ¼ of 12-1-4 in 1968. Rodney as born and raised at Winkler, and was a diamond driller for nine years. Margaret grew up at Hasket. They married in 1964, and their children are: Bobbi, Josephine and Suzy.

Back, Josephine, Rodney Wieler, Bobbi; front, Marg and Suzy.

Iris and William Wachna; Elaine, Kathleen; sitting, Marcia and Teddy.

WILLIAM WACHNA

Dmytro Wachna immigrated to Canada from West Ukraine in 1897, settled in Stuartburn, where he married Anna Kohut.

William Wachna was the youngest son in a family of 13. Eight brothers and sisters died during the 1918 outbreak of diphtheria.

William bought Ridgeville Transfer from Jerry Kryml in 1950. In 1952 he purchased Woodmore Transfer from John Didychuk and extended his services from Ridgeville and district to the east border of Franklin.

On September 10, 1955 William married Iris Andrusyk, daughter of Michael Andrusyk of Senkiw. They made their home on the former Albert Wilkinson property purchased from Henry Lenton.

William and Iris have four children:

Elaine, teaches school in Winnipeg; married Edward Segstro in 1979.

Marcia, is attending University of Manitoba.

Kathleen and Teddy attend Roseau Valley Collegiate.

REINHOLD WEISS

Reinhold Weiss was born in Poland in 1885 and came to Gretna with his parents in 1894. In 1896 the family moved to Franklin Municipality. In 1895 Reinhold bought land at Emerson. He married Matilda Schultz, born in Poland in 1886, came to Canada in 1891.

They went to Alberta for 10 years, where Bill, Elsie, Mabel, Tom and Annie were born. In 1917 they came back to Franklin and in 1918 bought land from John Schmidtke. Here Walter, Airdrie, Ruth, Thelma and Clarence were born.

Reinhold Weiss died in 1968, and Matilda in 1976. Both are intered in Fredensthal Lutheran Cemetery.

William Theodore, born 1908, married Anne Kein 1935, no children.

Elsie Helena, born 1909, married Donald Beckstead in 1931, has three sons. Donald died in 1974. Gary and Betty and children: Blake, Scott, Barbara and grandson, Thomas. Garfield and Sanae and children: Mika and Donald. Dean and Diane and children: Laurie and Adam.

Neta, born 1911, married John Suppes in 1938, and has two children: Leona Elaine, born 1943, died an infant; James and Theresa.

Thomas Frederick, born 1914, married Catherine Oberholtzer in 1943, and has six children: Janet and Dale Forth and children: Douglas, Karen and Ian; Lorna and Gene Foss and children: Chantell and Chay; Elizabeth and Laurie Ball and son, Matthew; Shirley and David Maki and children: Brian Todd and Jennifer; Gary Thomas and Catherine.

Anna Bertha, born 1915, married Arthur Casper in 1938, one son, Ernie and Sandra and sons: Kevin and Curtis. Art died 1978.

Walter Theodore, born 1919, married Ruth Eby in 1941, and has two daughters: Linda and Gerald Gaetz and children: Elaine and Lana; Tilda and Larry Cumming and children: Jennifer and Jeferson.

Helene Ruth, born 1921, married Art Schwark, 1943. They had three children: Kenneth and Carolynn and children: Kerry and Corinne; Robert Gordon, 1949-1951 deceased; Leona and Real Tetrault and children: Rene and Lisa Marie.

Arthur Herbert, born 1922, married Jean Calder, 1947, and had two daughters: Beverley and Bob Thomas and son, Burke; Marlene and Barry Waltman.

Thelma Mathilda, born 1924, married Art Steg 1947, and had two sons: David and Wendy; and Barry and Josephine.

Clarence Allan, born 1931, married Betty Scott,1952, and had two daughters: Jennifer and Dan Clayton; and Jocelyn Susan. Enda, born 1918, died at seven days; Leona, born 1925, died one month and 17 days; and Florence, born 1926, died March, 1936.

Reinhold's parents were Frederick and Emilie (Steinke) Weiss, his brothers and sisters were:

Bertha, born 1880, married Thomas Guy. Their children are: Bertie, Thomas, Kathleen and Gordon.

Ottilie, died an infant.

Mathilda, born 1890, married Adolf Schwark, divorced and married Roy Klein, and had two daughters: Irene and Leona.

Theodore, born 1894, married Martha Langner in 1926, and had two girls: Helen and Betty.

Helene, born 1895, married Thomas Ross, and

has a son, Thomas.

Albert, born 1898, married Ruth Royce, 1932, and has three girls: Jean, Kathleen, and Alberta. Emil, born 1900, died 1916 with typhoid fever.

Frederick died at Emerson in 1915, Emilie in 1917. Buried at Fredensthal Cemetery.

Reinhold and Mathilda Weiss; Walter.

Back, Clarence, Walter, Arthur, Thomas, William; front, Elsie Beckstead, Meta (Mabel) Suppes, Anna Casper, Ruth Schwark, Thelma Steg, 1979.

Back, Todd Maki, Chantell Foss, Jennifer Maki; middle, Garry Weiss, Shirley Maki, Liz and Mathew Ball, Lorna Foss, Karen Forth, Janet Forth; front, Gene Foss, Chay Foss, Dave Maki, Mr. and Mrs. Thomas Weiss, Doug Forth and Dale Forth.

Clarence and Betty Weiss, Jennifer and Joycelon.

GOTTLIEB WEISS

Gottlieb Weiss married Pauline Steinke, 1886, in Russia and came to Canada in 1897. They moved to Dominion City in 1912, and had a family of seven boys and two girls.

Pauline died in 1943, Gottlieb in 1925.

Their children are:

Louie married Mary Wackernagel of Morris in 1920, and moved to SE ¼ 26-1-3E. They farmed there till 1938, then moved to SW ¼ 34-1-4. In 1968 they retired to Franklin Manor in Dominion City. Mary died in 1973, Louie in 1979. They had five children: Delma, married Ernie Buss; Lillian, married Roy Wilkinson; Eleanor, married William Wilkinson; Richard; and Alvin.

Richard married Mildred Steinert of Woodmore. They bought the home place in 1963 where they farm. They have one son, Russell. Russell married Angela Durand in 1979 and farms SE ¼ 21-1-4.

Alvin and Anne Weiss live in Alberta and have three children: David, Mary Ann and Terry.

John married Elsie Schultz and has 10 children:

Melvin married Mary Elleck and has two children: Tammy and Todd.

Betty married Glenn Wilkinson.

Evelyn married Bob McJannet and has three children: Brenda, Crystal and Kory.

Doris married Paul Taylor and has two children: Gavin and Regan.

Shirley.

Linda married John Mullier.

Lily married Gord Merry and has two children: Kiersten and Chelsey.

Lorraine married Gary Walker and has one child, Sean.

Dennis married Virginia Morken of Dominion City and has two children: Rieshan and Curtis.

Wendy lives with her mother in Emerson.

Alvin and Anna Weiss, David, Mary Ann and Terry.

Louis and Mary Weiss, Delma, Richard, Alvin, Lillian and Eleanor.

Richard and Mildred Weiss; Russ and Angela Weiss.

WILLIAM THOS. WARD

William Thos. Ward, born 1871, in Cornwall, England, came to Winnipeg by cattle boat in 1904. His wife Lily and five children joined him in 1906. William did odd jobs until 1913, when he bought part of 20-2-5 E1, from Mrs. Richard Batten. Their children were:

William, born 1893, died young.

Winnifred, born 1895, also died young.

James Reginald, born 1897, married Sara Toews, and had two children: Phylis and Rita.

Elizabeth Florence, born 1899, married Stanley Leach, and had one daughter, Mabel.

Nora Lavina, born 1902, died young.

Horace, Gladys, Marguerite, Clifford, Lily, Florence and Reginald.

466

Mabel Gladys, born 1904, married Edgar Snead, and had two children: Norman and Kenneth.

Horace Francis, born 1907, married Ellen Francis, and had four children: Derrol, Florence, Eleanor and Kelvin.

Lillian May, born 1909, married Ben Froome.

Marguerite, born 1911, married Russel Mayne, and had three children: Donald, Robert and Ronald.

Clifford, born 1913, married Frances Batten in 1940, (Frances passed away in 1967) and remarried to Edith Keil (Lenton) in 1977. They had one son, Larry.

Back, William and Lily Ward, Florence; front, Clifford, Marguerite, Lily, 1923.

25th anniversary, Cliff and Frances Ward.

Edith and Cliff Ward married June 1977; Larry.

PETER WASYLISHEN

In 1898, Peter Wasylishen, his wife Hafia, and three sons: Jacob, Gabriel and Paul arrived in Canad. They settled on the SW ¼ 33-1-5. Jacob married in 1910, moved to Alberta in 1911. An additional 100 acres was bought by Peter, SE ¼ 32-1-5 known as Gravel Pit, Overstoneville. Paul and Gabriel loaded many train cars of gravel with a shovel and wheelbarrow.

Gabriel married in 1917 and farmed the homestead. Gabriel moved to Oakbank in 1938.

Peter died in 1919, age 66, and Hafia lived to be 93.

In 1921, Paul established himself on SE ¼ 33-1-5 where he built a home and opened a store. Paul was a barber by profession. He moved to Tolstoi in 1938 and built a Pool Hall and barber shop. The Pool Hall was renovated into a coffee-shop in 1958.

Paul married Fanny Nedohin in 1941. They had two children: Tony, from Paul's first marriage; and Elizabeth, born 1943.

Tony married in 1954.

Elizabeth married Maurice Yarmie, son of Wasyl Yarmie of Tolstoi, in 1961. They have two children: Rodney and Debbie.

Y THOMAS YABLONSKI

Thomas and Rose Yablonski came to Canada from Poland in 1902, and were married in Winnipeg in 1907. They owned a house and sawmill in Winnipeg, which they traded for a quarter of land at Ridgeville, the SW ¼ of 30-1-5 E1, in 1913.

Thomas and Rose had five children: Stanley, Mary, Alice, Emily and Anne.

Stanley married Rose Wolfe of Vita in 1931. They farmed at Ridgeville and had three sons: Joe, Frank and Leonard. Stanley moved to Winnipeg and then to Vancouver.

Mary married Mike Stadnyk of Sundown, in 1928. They owned and operated the store and post office at Overstoneville until moving to Winnipeg in 1956. They have two daughters: Mrs. Betty Kiyan and Mrs. Beatrice Gawryluk.

Alice married John Lipischak of Arnaud in 1930. They farmed in the Carlowrie district, retiring to Selkirk. They had seven daughters and three sons: Mrs. Mary Payonk, Mrs. Bernice House, Mrs. Elizabeth McDairmid, Mrs. Rose Jeanson, Mrs. Frances McMurray, Mrs. Pat Sitarz, Mrs. Linda Yamniuk, and sons, Frank, Stanley and Vincent. Both Alice and John are deceased.

Emily married Albin Dziedzic of Inwood in 1937. They took the family farm until 1974, then retired to Winnipeg. They have one daughter, Mrs. Florence Kosowan, and one son, Clarence.

Anne married William Fedorak, Inwood, in 1956, moved to California, and has a son, Gregory.

Thomas Yablonski died in 1958 and Rose in 1972. They are buried in the Holy Trinity Church cemetery at Tolstoi.

Thomas and Rose Yablonski

Annie (Fedoruk) Yablonski, Thomas Yablonski, Alex Dziedzic, Rose Yablonski, Emily Dziedzic. Children - Florence Kosowan and Clarence Dziedzic.

467

Farewell dinner gathering at the Oleksa Yarmie home, before leaving Tolstoi, 1935.

OLEKSA (ALEX) YARMIE

Oleksa (Alex) Yarmie arrived in Canada in 1897, and took a homestead two miles west of the present site of Tolstoi, the William Stege farm. He kept a post office in his home, called Oleskiw. In 1900 he married Mary Lenik. Their children were: Steve, Don, Yaris, Nestor, Bill, Ann, Alexandra and Olga.

The Yarmie family left for Ontario in 1935. In 1936 Olga married John Domytrak of Tolstoi.

NYKOLA YASINSKI

Nykola Yasinski came to Rosa in 1912 from the Western Ukraine. His wife Paraska and William, five, came in 1914. In 1916 Nykola bought a farm, and continued working at Carlowrie, doing casual labour. Their son Alex was born here. In March, 1923, Nykola died, age 42. Two years later Paraska married Wasyle Pohribney, and they continued farming the Yasinski land.

Paraska Pohribney died on March 24, 1967, at age 82. Wasyle Pohribney died in November, 1977, age 86.

William married Lena Kohut from Stuartburn, daughter of Stephen Kohut, in 1932. They lived at Carlowrie, and have three children: Victor, Doreen and Dorothy.

Victor and Jean live at Carlowrie.

Twins, Doreen, and Dorothy who married Douglas Peabody, live in Winnipeg.

Alex married Lena Ewanchuk, daughter of John Ewanchuk of Rosa, in 1939. They live in Winnipeg with their two children and five granchildren.

Mr. and Mrs. Nykola Yasinski, William and Alex, 1902.

William Yasinski, wife Lena, Victor and twins Doreen and Dorothy; Alex Yasinski, his wife Lena, Nick and Audrey.

Ronald, Jarvis, Audrey, Jean and Victor Yasinski.

Douglas and Dorothy (Yasinski) Peabody, 1980.

Z ABE W. ZACHARIAS

Abe W. Zacharias married Mary Kehler in 1939. They bought the SE ¼ of 23-2-5 E1 in 1948 from Peter Penner, who moved to South America. They had a mixed farm until 1969, when they sold to Andy Penner, and moved to Altona. Their children are: Marion, Dorothy, Jackie and Danny, born 1954.

Back, Jackie, Dorothy, Marion, Danny; front, Abe W. and Mary (Kehler) Zacharias, 1964.

MIKE ZAHARA

Mary, daughter of Prokop Todoruk, married Mike, son of Jacob Zahara of Gardenton, on October 16, 1943. They lived on his farm in Gardenton until 1952, when they moved to Tolstoi to farm on 23-1-5 E1. Their children are:

Gordon, married Suzanne DeBois of St. Malo, who have two children: Beverley and Jason.

Eva, married Edward Goletski and has three children: Cindy, Charlene and Ryan.

Donald, lives in Winnipeg.

Twin sons, Allan and Eddie, are at home.

Mike and Mary (Todoruk) Zahara, 1981.

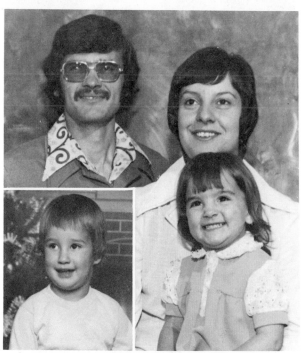
Gordon, Suzanne (DeBois) and Beverley Zahara. Inset, Jason.

Donald, Eddie and Allan.

469

SAM ZAPORZAN

Sam Zaporzan, son of Ivan and Anna Zaporzan, arrived from the Western Ukraine in 1897. Sam married Mary Boychuk at Sundown in 1924. Their children are:

Esther, married John Sabanski, Assiniboia, Saskatchewan, who has a daughter Rose Marie, married to Walter Tymkiw, Tolstoi.

Melton, married Jean Kiansky, lives in Steinbach, and has three sons: Douglas, Glenn, Dwayne, and daughter Kimberly.

Donald, married Eileen Thomson and lives in Winnipeg with sons: Timothy and Richard.

Billy, married Erna Bartel, lives in Grunthal with two children: Gayle and Murray.

Erna and Bill Zaporzan, Eileen and Donald Zaporzan, Mary (Boychuk) Zaporzan, Sam Zaporzan, Milton Zaporzan, John Sabanski, Jean Zaporzan, Esther Sabanski.

Bill Zaporzan, 1943. Picture taken by Alex Hoplock, at Tolstoi, in front of the present Val-u-food store, at that time operated by Dan and Anne Ewacha. Travelled in style in warm, heated van.

470

GUSTAVE ZASS

Gustave Zass, born in Revna, Russia, married Bertha Hemminger, who was born in Berlin. They had nine children. In 1897 they came to North Dakota, in 1898 to Gretna. In 1903 Gustave bought a quarter in section 18 from a man named Christy, for $50. In 1909 he rented the Pax farm at Ridgeville. Mrs Pax and her son Charlie lived with them from 1916 to 1918, after Mr. Pax froze to death walking home from Ridgeville.

In 1918 Gustave bought the Coates land, 15-1-4 E1. There are three of the nine Zass children living in 1982: Helen Schwartz in Michigan; Tillie, who married Jack Gilchrist; and Gus.

Gus went to the United States, then came back to farm 15-1-4 E1 from 1933 to 1973. In 1935 he married Rena Timmins, Kenora. He retired to Ridgeville in 1981. Gus and Rena have three children:

Lois, married John Spence, Winnipeg.

Myrna, married Edwin Russell, Clearwater.

John and his wife Carol, Kenora.

Their grandchildren are: Gregory and Shelly Spence, Darren, Perry and Carla ~~Maye~~ Mae Russell, Corwin and Derrick Zass.

ZILKIE FAMILY

Grandfather Zilkie immigrated to Canada c.1894, with his sons, Adolph, 14, and Julius, 16. When he had earned enough money, he sent for his wife and three other children, being: Charles, Fred and Millie.

They settled in the Overstone district on 6-1-5 E1. The Zilkies had a lime kiln, which provided lime used in many buildings in Emerson.

Adolphe Zilkie family
Back row: Annie, Rosie, Cliff, Albert, Edna, Richard.
Front row: Herb, Adolph, Myrtle, Mary (Mrs. Adolph), Ruth. Missing from picture - Sam.

Adolph's son, Albert, married Agnes Woods, daughter of Thomas and Ida Woods, in 1931. In 1929 Albert had bought a quarter on 1-1-4 E1. In 1950 he took over his father's land on 6-1-5 E1.

Agnes and Albert have five sons: Orville, Earl, Dennis, Don and Laird, known as Larry. Albert passed away October 9, 1973.

Orville married Nora Anderson in 1955. They have two sons: Dean and Kenny.

Earl married Willena Thompson in 1956. They have three sons: Robert, Lorne and Jeffrey.

Dennis married Joyce Huff in 1958. They have five children: Rose Marie, Edward, Leslie and twins, Patrick and Paul.

Rose Marie married Rocky Pascetilli, and has three children: Sheldon, Jodee and Shawn.

Don married Doreen Wood in 1957. They have three children: Sharon, Donna and Blake.

Larry married Lois Epp in 1963. They have two children: Andrea and Jason.

Orville and Nora (Anderson) Zilkie

Kenny and Dean Zilkie

Back, Edna and Jake Fast, Ruth Zilkie, Sam Zilkie, Lydia Toews, Maude (Mrs. Sam Zilkie), Cliff and Richard Zilkie, Roy Toews holding Earl, Herb Zilkie, Rosie Toews, Annie Gilchrist holding Marvin, Albert and Agnes Zilkie holding Don, Jack Gilchrist; front, Earl Zilkie, Grandpa Adolph holding Dennis Zilkie, Orville Zilkie, Grandma holding Irvine Fast, Vernette Gilchrist, 1939.

Albert and Agnes (Woods) Zilkie

Back, Lesley, Rose Marie, Edward; front, twins Patrick and Paul, Zilkie.

Jodee, Shawn, Sheldon.

Larry and Lois (Epp) Zilkie

Don, Doreen (Wood) and Sharon Zilkie.

Andrea and Jason Zilkie

Earl and Eva (Thompson) Zilkie; Dennis and Joyce (Huff) Zilkie.

Sharon, Blake, Donna.

JULIUS ZILKIE

Robert, Jeffrey, Lorne Zilkie.

Julius Zilkie family - 1917. Back, Art, Richard, Dan, Robert, Harold, Fred, John; front, Herman, Leslie, Eleanor, Mrs. Eva Zilkie, Esther.

Julius and Eva (Miller) Zilke, 1908. Herman, Bertha, Fred Zilke.

Left: Fred and Martha (Locht) Zilkie. They have three children, Marvin, Lorna and Maureen.
Right: Herman and Lean (Bredin) Zilkie, Edith and Louise.

Bert and Eleanor (Zilkie) Milner, Philip, Ted, Gerald, Richard and David.

Les and Joyce (Kort) Zilkie, Lori, Wesley and Sherilyn.

Left: Dan and Vera (Walters) Zilkie, have two children, Doug and Kattie.
Right: Art and Ann Zilkie, missing Barry Zilkie and family.

473

Richard and Ruth (Boggs) Zilkie, Ron, Bob and Gaylene (Zilkie) Paschke, Jared and Danny.

Harold and Rose (Goetz) Zilkie

Otto and Esther (Zilkie) Nash, Lorne, Dennis and Ardith.

Bob and Lil (Walters) Zilkie, with granddaughter Virginia Zilkie.

Marvin and Margo Zilke, Taunya and Todd.

John and Mina (Walters) Zilkie, Walter and Darlene Zilkie, Aaron and Adam. Missing are Ed and Marily (Zilkie) Bergman.

George and Lorna (Zilkie) Betcher, Jeffrey, Cheryl, Colleen and Mark.

474

Gib and Maureen (Zilkie) Rempel, Roland and Darren.

Back row: Doug Zilke, Bob Houston.
Middle row: Vera Zilke, Kathie (Zilke) Houston, Josh and Bev Zilke.
Front row: Mr. and Mrs. Dave Walters and Paula Zilke.

Terry and Carol Zilkie, Brian and Darrel.

Wayne and Valerie Zilke, Virginia.

MIKE ZULUK

Mike Zuluk arrived in Canada in 1908, and worked for the Canadian National Railways. He walked 10 miles to work, until he could afford a horse. His wife Anastazia, was born in the Ukraine in 1889.

They moved to Tolstoi in 1952. Mike and Anastazia had one daughter, Annie.

Annie married Alex Shydlowski, and lives in Winnipeg. Her children are:

Iris, married Tony Buchel, and has two sons: Brian and Bruce.

Orest, married Helen Syrnik.

Nestor, married Linda Salamandyk, and has two children: Elisha and Christopher.

Anastazia passed away July 3, 1981.

Railway pass

Iris Buchel, Orest, Alex and Annie (Zulak) Shydlowski, and Nestor.

Ed Baxter and Edward Kennedy.

In most areas of Franklin Municipality there were settlers who came, stayed a short while, long enough to make a little mark by which they are remembered, and then moved on. We do not know where they went or what happened to them, but their achievements furthered the lifestyle of the people living here.

George Perrin, William Hewett, Henry Arthur, Oscar and Stephen Burrett, Morris Watts and William Ross all lived here in 1881.

John May built one of the first houses in the Green Ridge area, before 1878. His house became a stopping place for pioneer families as they arrived. For at least 10 years folks would live in this house until they got one built for themselves. This house was located near the St. Paul Trail.

John Grant's name is one the 1883 map of the municipality. He had land here in 1875, and is listed as a Military Bounty Homesteader. He may be the same Grant who helped with the first survey of the land, and seems to have chosen some of the best land on the ridge. We do not know whether he proved up on the land, but it was sold soon after he acquired it.

John K. Wright lived along the Roseau near Langside on the south bank. He ferried Mrs. Isaac Casson across the Roseau when she was joining her husband near the Casson homestead east of Arnaud.

A man named Hart owned land in the early days, and was accidentally killed while killing a beast for food.

A family named Walton lived near the Jordan River, and had a lime kiln on the land now owned by John Graydon.

The hired man was an important person, especialy in the very early days of farming in Franklin Municipality. The farm required a great deal of brute labour, and many of the pioneers were young people with either no or small children. Neighbors helped each other as best they could, but during harvest, illness, or spring seeding, that was not enough, because each had his own work to do at home. Hired men were the answer. Most did not stay long, since houses were small, and living quarters cramped. Some came from wealthy families in Great Britain, and others were trying to earn enough money to begin their own homestead.

Harry Ball came from England c.1870's, and worked for John Post. He married a Linklater, and had a farm near the Roseau River. Harry took time off to go to the Boer War, and then close to Dominion City and raised bees.

Ernie Heathfield was another Englishman. He worked for the Lochhead family. A great singer, he often performed duets with Mrs. Sparks.

Jack Bland was a hired hand at the Oatway farm, and married an Oatway daughter.

Tom Mason worked for the Oatway and Casson farms. He married a girl from Woodmore. While fighting in the Philippine War, he lost a finger.

Charles Woollard came to work in Green Ridge, but left to fight in the Boer War. On his return he reported on the war to the local Foresters, of whom he was a member. After leaving Franklin he studied to be a medical doctor, and was a prominent medical head in the first world war.

Ed Baxter was a handsome Scotsman who spent several years working on the Hunter and Davidson farms. In 1960 he was working for the federal government in Ottawa.

Other hired men were John Fick, James E. Brown, A. Vince, A. White, W. Stockdale, Edward Kennedy, Frank Chalmers and Norman Macdougall. These men were in Franklin before 1900.

THE NATURALIZATION ACT.

CERTIFICATE OF NATURALIZATION.

[REV. STATS. CAN., C. 77, S. 22.]

DOMINION OF CANADA,

PROVINCE OF MANITOBA.

IN THE COUNTY COURT OF...... **Emerson**...

WHEREAS...... **Mykolaj Kulik**.. formerly of

.... **Austria**.. now of .... **Tolstoi**........
(Name of Country)

in the Province of Manitoba. **farmer**................... has complied with the several requirements

of *The Naturalization Act*, and has duly resided in Canada for the period of .... **three**..........

years. And whereas the particulars of certificate granted to the said ... **Mykolaj Kulik**.....

under the fifteenth section of the said Act has been duly announced in Court, and thereupon by order of the said Court the said certificate has been filed of record in the same pursuant to the said Act. This is therefore to certify to all whom it may concern, that under and by virtue of the said Act

.... **Mykolaj Kulik**.. has become na-

turalized as a British subject, and is within Canada, entitled to all political and other rights, powers and privileges, and subject to all obligations to which a natural-born British subject is entitled or subject within Canada, with this qualification, that he shall not, when within the limits of the foreign State of which he was a subject (or citizen) previous to the date hereof, be deemed to be a British subject unless he has ceased to be a subject (or citizen) of that State, in pursuance of the laws thereof, or in pursuance of a treaty or convention to that effect.

Given under the Seal of the said Court this .... **Nineteenth**................... day of

September................... one thousand nine hundred and .. **twelve**......

[SEAL]

Clerk